Trust Modeling and Management in Digital Environments:
From Social Concept to System Development

Zheng Yan
Nokia Research Center, Finland

INFORMATION SCIENCE REFERENCE

Hershey · New York

Director of Editorial Content:	Kristin Klinger
Director of Book Publications:	Julia Mosemann
Development Editor:	Tyler Heath
Publishing Assistant:	Sean Woznicki
Typesetter:	Jamie Snavely, Sean Woznicki
Quality Control:	Jamie Snavely
Cover Design:	Lisa Tosheff
Printed at:	Yurchak Printing Inc.

Published in the United States of America by
Information Science Reference (an imprint of IGI Global)
701 E. Chocolate Avenue
Hershey PA 17033
Tel: 717-533-8845
Fax: 717-533-8661
E-mail: cust@igi-global.com
Web site: http://www.igi-global.com/reference

Library of Congress Cataloging-in-Publication Data

Trust modeling and management in digital environments : from social concept to system development / Zheng Yan, editor.
    p. cm.

 Includes bibliographical references and index.
 Summary: "This book investigates various definitions of trust and their characteristics in distributed systems and digital computing, and details how to model and implement trust in a digital system"--Provided by publisher.

 ISBN 978-1-61520-682-7 (hardcover) -- ISBN 978-1-61520-683-4 (ebook) 1.
Trust. 2. Digital electronics. 3. Electronic systems. 4. Technological
innovations. I. Yan, Zheng, 1972-
 BF575.T7T795 2010
 005.8--dc22
                        2009045242

British Cataloguing in Publication Data
A Cataloguing in Publication record for this book is available from the British Library.

Table of Contents

Section 1
Security Enhanced Trust Management Solutions

Xuhua Ding, Singapore Management University, Singapore
Liang Gu, Peking University, China
Robert H. Deng, Singapore Management University, Singapore
Bing Xie, Peking University, China
Hong Mei, Peking University, China

Andreas U. Schmidt, CREATE-NET Research Centre, Italy
Andreas Leicher, Johann Wolfgang Goethe-Universität, Germany
Inhyok Cha, InterDigital Communications, USA

Jan-Erik Ekberg, Nokia Research Center, Finland

Section 2
Evaluation Based Trust Management Solutions

Section 3
Trust Modeling and Management Driven by Social Study

Detailed Table of Contents

Section 1
Security Enhanced Trust Management Solutions

This chapter presents a systematic study on an important trust establishment mechanism among computing platforms – remote attestation based on the root trust module specified in trusted computing technologies. A new conceptual model for remote attestation is proposed to examine and analyze existing remote attestation schemes by grouping them into two main types: *integrity attestation* and *quality attestation*. The authors further provide their discussions on the applicability of different solutions in distributed environments based on the strength and the limitations of each type of schemes.

This chapter shifts the traditional concept about trust and security from access control and policy enforcement towards decentralized methods for trust establishment among loosely connected computing platforms. The synergetic cooperation of trust and enforcement technologies is expected due to a number of practical issues. The chapter describes the methods that allow scaling between trust and enforcement according to capabilities of devices and networks, requirements of use cases, and needs of stakeholders, where trusted computing platforms play as the technical basis for trust in systems.

This chapter introduces mobile trusted module (MTM) – a root trust module for mobile devices specified by the Trusted Computing Group. A brief security analysis of the MTM components is provided followed by a number of suggestions to further extend MTM and make it more versatile.

This chapter explores the problem of malware that could ruin software execution trust. The authors present a proof-of-concept implementation of *BinAuth*, a practical, lightweight in-kernel binary authentication system for Microsoft Windows, in order to establish trust on the integrity of binary executables.

This chapter introduces the trust issues in multimedia content distribution, such as authorization, authentication, privacy, payment, ownership, illegal distribution, and forgery. It also reviews the latest research progress of the solutions, and discusses a number of open issues and promising research topics.

This chapter discusses potential roles of trust in future aviation information systems. It describes two recent abstractions of such aviation systems – an electronic distribution system connecting aircraft with ground components for exchanging updates and data of onboard software, and a radio frequency identification (RFID) system for logistics and maintenance of aircraft – which use digital certificates to establish trust in integrity and authenticity of information assets as well as in authorized components handling these assets. The unique challenges of aviation such as regulations and business models are also discussed because they could complicate the current implementation and verification.

Section 2
Evaluation Based Trust Management Solutions

Trust management is a major issue in the shared Grid environment because Grid participants are generally unknown with each other and usually belong to separate administrative domains, with little or no common trust in the security of opposite infrastructures. This chapter provides a valuable survey on proposals for enhancing trust management in Grid systems.

This chapter proposed a conceptual trust framework that models an entity's trust as a relation whose state gets updated as relevant conditions change. Based on the trustor entity's specification on trust adaptation, end-to-end trust assessment for a particular activity in collaborative environments can be derived by examining and aggregating multiple trust relationships in a bottom-up evaluation manner.

A peer-to-peer system is another digital environment that lacks trust among system entities. Thus the trust evaluation prior to and posterior to entities' interactions becomes a very important issue to overcome security challenges and help in security related decisions. This chapter presents a dynamic peer trust evaluation model, which aims to measure responding peers' recommendation trust, and hence filter out low credibility recommendations and obtain more accurate and objective trust values.

Chapter 10

This chapter describes the distinctive characteristics of ad hoc networks and presents an overview of the underlying technologies and protocols for ad hoc networks, as well as analyzes the vulnerabilities and potential attacks of these networks. The authors further discuss the utilization of trust to mitigate these attacks and vulnerabilities on the basis of ad-hoc trust management architecture with regard to autonomic trust reasoning by each node and the collaboration among nodes. Interesting applications of trust management in ad hoc networks include the utilization of trust for choosing alternative routes, and visualization of trust as a human oriented metric of the behavior and performance of ad hoc networks.

Chapter 11

This chapter proposed a context-aware trust model to facilitate secure ad hoc collaborations. This model can measure trust in a given context even though sometimes enough information is not available about a given context to calculate the trust value. In order to achieve this purpose, the authors apply a context graph to formalize the relationships between contexts. It allows extrapolating values from related contexts to approximate a trust value of an entity.

Chapter 12

This chapter proposes an evaluation framework based on the trace-simulator paradigm to conduct comparative analysis on reputation algorithms. Trace file generation emulates a variety of network configurations and pays particular attention to modeling malicious user behaviors. The chapter reports on the framework's design decisions and demonstrates this general-purpose simulator with two reputation algorithms (EigenTrust and a modified TNA-SL) under varied network conditions. As one of the first studies in the area of trust management effectiveness research, the described framework is available as open source so that researchers can evaluate the effectiveness of other reputation management techniques and/or extend its functionalities.

This chapter provides a trust management framework to conduct trust/reputation evaluation for services in mobile networks by detecting misbehavior or inaccuracy in service executions and for rating them according to user preferences. Thus, it is possible to reduce and prevent the interaction with misbehaving mobile nodes since the framework can also be responsible for determining the risk of interactions.

This chapter presents a multi-attribute trust management model that incorporates trust, transaction costs and product warranties. The new trust management system enables potential buyers to determine the risk level of a product before committing to proceed with the transaction in electronic market places.

This chapter concerns privacy and trust issues in context-aware pervasive computing. The authors discuss new challenges, opportunities and requirements, as well as existing solutions regarding privacy, trust and security in a pervasive computing environment.

This chapter discusses the relationship of trust and stability in heterogeneous distributed computing systems. In such a context, trust is interpreted as the confidence in the association of a stable network execution to the efficient distribution of multimedia products in the final user. The author studies the property of stability under various compositions of contention-resolution protocols and different packet trajectories trying to characterize this property in terms of network topologies. The results indicate that a composition of protocols leads to worst stability behaviour than having a single unstable protocol for contention-resolution.

Section 3
Trust Modeling and Management Driven by Social Study

This chapter reviews the literature of trust in sociology and psychology. By introducing the conception, theory model and measurement of trust, the author discusses trust in three important social contexts: interpersonal situation, organizational settings and Internet life and proposes a synthetic trust model with a multi-disciplinary approach as a future research direction.

This chapter introduces a project 'Anshin' to study emotional trust issue: an emotional state of one's mind in peace. The authors introduce the concept of Anshin and its research issues. Instructively, they present how to use statistical analysis methods to derive the factors of Anshin, which is identified as a key component of emotional trust.

This chapter utilises a case study of citizen identification systems to illustrate the continuum of trust-related considerations and technology adoption, ranging from theoretical underpinnings of trust, to empirical studies, through to practical design guidelines. A mixed methodological approach that combines the best from various disciplines is presented by applying it into the citizen identification systems.

This chapter reviews the concept of trust and the main factors that affect a user's trust in human-machine interaction. The author discusses the current state, challenges, problems and limitations in this area and evaluates the existing solutions for improving the user's trust appropriately, especially in an e-commerce environment.

This chapter discusses a proposal for a more realistic mobility model that captures key features of human movements in pervasive markets. The findings based on users' mobility behaviors lead to a non-traditional mobility model. It can be used to reconstruct the statistical patterns commonly observed in the literature, and facilitate the study of mobile communication and software engineering design problems under the context of pervasive computing for markets. This model could imply a trust relationship between the user and the markets that can be used for the design of a pervasive service.

Foreword

We cannot have any security without at least some sort of trust. Building a secure system, small or large, always assumes a certain trust model. Let us take an example. The GSM cellular communication system has been around for almost two decades. It contains, as an essential ingredient, a global security system that allows every user to be authenticated and every call to be secured. This can be guaranteed whether the user is near home or travelling on the other side of the world. To enable all this, a complex trust network exists between mobile operators. As part of the trust network, operators from different parts of the world have to settle roaming agreements and exchange session keys and other authentication data. It is vital for each operator to maintain a good reputation as a trustworthy roaming partner.

Continuing with our example, trust plays a major role also on the user's side. Authentication of the user depends on the assumption that user takes good care of the little smart card inside the mobile device. Furthermore, the user has to have some degree of trust to each person who can have access to the mobile device because it is fairly easy to replace the SIM card inside the device by another one (a handy feature that makes it possible to change the mobile device without a need to contact the operator). From the user's point of view, the smart card itself needs to be trusted: it has to function as it is intended to do. Of course, the user has to have a lot of trust on the operator, especially for correct billing.

The example of the GSM security system highlights several crucial aspects of trust that today everybody is exposed to. The co-existence and convergence of physical and digital worlds imply new notions of trust that people are not yet used to. One aspect is reputation on the global scale, required by (e.g., on-line shopping). Another aspect is dependence on correct behavior of technology around us (e.g., need for trusted hardware and software). Furthermore, popular social networking services have shown that we need to re-evaluate the role of trust as regards the other users of the same services.

This book sheds light on the intriguing notion of trust from all of the angles mentioned above. Dr. Zheng Yan has succeeded in collecting a comprehensive and impressive selection of chapters, each of which stems from practical issues in the modern digital world and shows the way forward in managing these issues via better understanding of trust as a key concept. Several chapters of the book are devoted to each of the following key questions in trust management:

- how to provide trustworthy technologies?
- how to evaluate and measure trust?
- how do people understand and use trust in different contexts?

Trust modeling and management are becoming more and more important areas because of increased usage of automation and people's presence in both physical and digital dimensions. There is a lot that research can do in helping us to meet the challenges ahead. Chapters in this book give overwhelming evidence on the power of research and they also serve as great stimulation for further research.

Valtteri Niemi
Nokia Fellow
Chairman of the 3GPP security working group
Nokia Research Center, Switzerland

Valtteri Niemi *received a PhD degree from the University of Turku, Finland, Mathematics Department, in 1989. After serving in various positions in the University of Turku, he was an Associate Professor in the Mathematics and Statistics Department of the University of Vaasa, Finland, during 1993-97. He joined Nokia Research Center (NRC), Helsinki in 1997 and in 1999 he was nominated as a Research Fellow. During 2004-2006, he was responsible for Nokia research in wireless security area as a Senior Research Manager. During 2007-2008, Dr. Niemi led the Trustworthy Communications and Identities team in the Internet laboratory of NRC, Helsinki. He recently moved to the new NRC laboratory in Lausanne, Switzerland, where his main focus is on privacy-enhancing technologies. He was also nominated as a Nokia Fellow in 2009. Dr. Niemi's work has been on security issues of future mobile networks and terminals, the main emphasis being on cryptological aspects. He has participated 3GPP SA3 (security) standardization group from the beginning. Starting from 2003, he has been the chairman of the group. Before 3GPP, Niemi took part in ETSI SMG 10 for GSM security work. In addition to cryptology and security, Dr. Niemi has done research on the area of formal languages. He has published more than 40 scientific articles and he is a co-author of three books.*

Preface

Trust plays a crucial role in our social life. With the rapid development of digital technology and networking technology, trust has become an important factor that influences the success of our digital life. Trust modeling and trust management play as a useful means to control and manage trust in digital systems. Transforming from a social concept of trust to a digital concept, trust modeling and management help in designing and implementing a trustworthy digital system, especially in distributed systems and for digital computing. Nowadays, trust management is emerging as a promising technology to facilitate collaboration among entities in an environment where traditional security paradigms cannot be enforced due to lack of centralized control and incomplete knowledge of the environment.

Trust is first a social phenomenon. It is a multidimensional, multidisciplinary and multifaceted concept. The concept of trust has been studied in disciplines ranging from economics to psychology, from sociology to medicine, and to information and computer science. We can find various definitions of trust in the literature although researchers in different disciplines have agreed the importance of trust in the conduct of human affairs. Overall, the different trust definitions often reflect the paradigms of the particular academic discipline of the researchers. Common to these definitions are the notions of confidence, belief, faith, hope, expectation, dependence, and reliance on the goodness, strength, reliability, integrity, ability, or characters of a person or thing. Generally, a trust relationship involves at least two parties: a trustor and a trustee. The trustor is the trusting subject who holds confidence, belief, etc. on the reliability, integrity, ability, etc. of another person or thing, which is the object of trust - the trustee. The discussion of different trust concepts and constructs does not aim at reaching consensus on a single definition of trust. Generally, researchers derived their understanding of trust that has its roots crossing multiple disciplines, as you will find in this book.

Various trust management systems have been described in the literature. Basically, there are two categories of trust management systems. One is security enhanced trust management solutions (e.g., trusted computing technology based solutions). This kind of solutions applies sound security technologies in order to ensure a computer system's trustworthiness. It deals with root trust module, security policies, credentials, integrity, privacy and trust relationships. The other is trust evaluation based solutions (e.g., reputation systems). Trust evaluation is a technical approach of representing trustworthiness for digital processing, in which the factors influencing trust will be evaluated by a continuous or discrete real number, referred to as a trust value. Generally, a trust model is applied in order to specify, evaluate and set up trust relationships amongst entities for calculating trust. The trust model could be linguistic, graphic and mathematic, corresponding to different researches conducted in different disciplines for different purposes. Embedding a trust evaluation mechanism is a necessity in order to provide trust intelligence in future computing devices or systems. In particular, reputation is a measure that is derived from direct or indirect knowledge or experiences on entities and is used to assess the level of trust an entity puts into another entity. Thus, reputation based trust management (or simply reputation system) is a specific approach to evaluate and control trust. Trust and reputation mechanisms have been proposed in various fields of distributed systems, such as ad hoc networks, peer-to-peer systems, Grid computing, pervasive computing and e-commerce. However, each kind of above solution has its own shortcomings. Generally, the first kind of solution lacks intelligence to provide autonomic trust management, while the second one needs a root trust module in order to ensure the trustworthiness of trust evaluation mechanism. From the system development point of view, both solutions should be concerned or somehow integrated with each other.

Trust is a subjective concept: different people hold different opinions on it even in the same situation. In order to represent a user and behave as his/her agent, the user's device should understand his/her trust criteria. Therefore, user-device interaction is needed in order to fulfill trust management purposes in some situations, such as e-commerce. But this could cause usability issues since it is not good to require users to make many trust related decisions, especially when they lack the information and knowledge needed to make them. Thus, usable trust management is expected with regard to useful information collection for trust evaluation, valuable trust information notification and dissemination for reputation generation. Once again, social trust study becomes essential, but with additional requirements and objectives in order to design and deploy a usable trust management solution that can be easily accepted by the users.

This book looks into how trust is transferred from a social concept to a digital one and thus helps users build up their trust in the digital system. Furthermore, we hope that understanding the current challenges, solutions and their limitations will not only inform researchers of a better design for establishing and maintaining a trustworthy digital system, but also assist in the understanding of the intricate concept of trust in a digital environment. Trust modeling and management is a subject area across multiple disciplines. From sociological and psychological study on trust, this book focuses more on studying trust in information and computer science. Our special attention will be paid to trustworthy distributed systems and trusted computing, as well as usable trust management. More importantly, we aim to reveal how to digitize trust based on social and technical understanding and how to apply digital trust to benefit social trust in reverse.

This book:

- Investigates various definitions or understandings of trust and its characteristics;
- Overviews the literature of trust modeling and management in distributed systems and digital computing;
- Studies how to model and compute trust and implement the model for establishing and managing trust in a digital system;
- Studies the psychological and sociological approaches for designing and developing a trustworthy digital system;
- Provides expert views on special areas of trust modeling and management (e.g., trust model validation), and other related issues to trust, such as security, privacy, risk, stability, context-aware modeling, multimedia content distribution, mobile computing platform, and so forth.

The prospective audience would be anyone who is interested in trust and security; academics, technical managers, sociologists, psychologists, and information security officers. The book can be used as a reference to get a general overview of trust modeling and management. IT industrial designers and architects may also refer to this book when designing and developing a trust management system.

ORGANIZATION OF THE BOOK

This book is organized into three sections, with a total of 21 chapters. The first section investigates security enhanced trust management solutions, which includes six chapters.

- **Chapter 1:** Remote Platform Attestation: The Testimony for Trust Management, by Xuhua Ding, Liang Gu, Robert H. Deng, Bing Xie, Hong Mei

This chapter presents a systematic study on an important trust establishment mechanism among computing platforms – remote attestation based on the root trust module specified in trusted computing technologies. A new conceptual model for remote attestation is proposed to examine and analyze existing remote attestation schemes by grouping them into two main types: *integrity attestation* and *quality attestation*. The authors further provide their discussions on the applicability of different solutions in distributed environments based on the strength and the limitations of each type of schemes.

- **Chapter 2:** Scaling Concepts between Trust and Enforcement, by Andreas U. Schmidt, Andreas Leicher, Inhyok Cha

This chapter shifts the traditional concept about trust and security from access control and policy enforcement towards decentralized methods for trust establishment among loosely connected computing platforms. The synergetic cooperation of trust and enforcement technologies is expected due to a number of practical issues. The chapter describes the methods that allow scaling between trust and enforcement according to capabilities of devices and networks, requirements of use cases, and needs of stakeholders, where trusted computing platforms play as the technical basis for trust in systems.

- **Chapter 3:** Mobile Trusted Computing Based on MTM, by Jan-Erik Ekberg

This chapter introduces mobile trusted module (MTM) – a root trust module for mobile devices specified by the Trusted Computing Group. A brief security analysis of the MTM components is provided followed by a number of suggestions to further extend MTM and make it more versatile.

- **Chapter 4:** Establishing Software Integrity Trust: A Survey and Lightweight Authentication System for Windows, by Yongzheng Wu, Sufatrio, Roland H.C. Yap, Rajiv Ramnath, Felix Halim

This chapter explores the problem of malware that could ruin software execution trust. The authors present a proof-of-concept implementation of *BinAuth*, a practical, lightweight in-kernel binary authentication system for Microsoft Windows, in order to establish trust on the integrity of binary executables.

- **Chapter 5:** Trust Issues and Solutions in Multimedia Content Distribution, by Shiguo Lian

This chapter introduces the trust issues in multimedia content distribution, such as authorization, authentication, privacy, payment, ownership, illegal distribution, and forgery. It also reviews the latest research progress of the solutions, and discusses a number of open issues and promising research topics.

- **Chapter 6:** Certificate-Based Trust Establishment in eEnabled Airplane Applications: Challenges and Approaches, by Mingyan Li, Krishna Sampigethaya, Radha Poovendran

This chapter discusses potential roles of trust in future aviation information systems. It describes two recent abstractions of such aviation systems – an electronic distribution system connecting aircraft with ground components for exchanging updates and data of onboard software, and a radio frequency identification (RFID) system for logistics and maintenance of aircraft – which use digital certificates to establish trust in integrity and authenticity of information assets as well as in authorized components handling these assets. The unique challenges of aviation such as regulations and business models are also discussed because they could complicate the current implementation and verification.

The second section explores trust evaluation based trust management solutions in the areas of distributed systems, such as Grid computing, peer-to peer systems, ad-hoc networks, pervasive computing systems, mobile networks, multimedia networks and e-commerce systems. It contains ten chapters. The discussions cover trust modeling, evaluation and management with special concerns on trust characteristics (e.g., dynamic, subjective, and transferable), context-awareness (e.g., purpose and time), trustee's behavior and performance, stability, privacy and risk. Particularly, the verification on the effectiveness of various trust/reputation mechanisms is an interesting research topic with regard to the performance of different trust management solutions. It is an issue of "trust's trust."

- **Chapter 7:** Trust Management for Grid Systems, by Benjamin Aziz, Alvaro Arenas, Fabio Martinelli, Paolo Mori, Marinella Petrocchi, Michael Wilson

Trust management is a major issue in the shared Grid environment because Grid participants are generally unknown with each other and usually belong to separate administrative domains, with little or no common trust in the security of opposite infrastructures. This chapter provides a valuable survey on proposals for enhancing trust management in Grid systems.

- **Chapter 8:** Formalizing and Managing Activity-Aware Trust in Collaborative Environments, by Ioanna Dionysiou, David E. Bakken

This chapter proposed a conceptual trust framework that models an entity's trust as a relation whose state gets updated as relevant conditions change. Based on the trustor entity's specification on trust adaptation, end-to-end trust assessment for a particular activity in collaborative environments can be derived by examining and aggregating multiple trust relationships in a bottom-up evaluation manner.

- **Chapter 9:** Trust Development in Peer-to-Peer Environments, by Yan Wang

A peer-to-peer system is another digital environment that lacks trust among system entities. Thus the trust evaluation prior to and posterior to entities' interactions becomes a very important issue to overcome security challenges and help in security related decisions. This chapter presents a dynamic peer trust evaluation model, which aims to measure responding peers' recommendation trust, and hence filter out low credibility recommendations and obtain more accurate and objective trust values.

- **Chapter 10:** Trust Management in Ad Hoc Networks, by Rafael Timóteo De Sousa Júnior, Ricardo Staciarini Puttini

This chapter describes the distinctive characteristics of ad hoc networks and presents an overview of the underlying technologies and protocols for ad hoc networks, as well as analyzes the vulnerabilities and potential attacks of these networks. The authors further discuss the utilization of trust to mitigate these attacks and vulnerabilities on the basis of ad-hoc trust management architecture with regard to autonomic trust reasoning by each node and the collaboration among nodes. Interesting applications of trust management in ad hoc networks include the utilization of trust for choosing alternative routes, and visualization of trust as a human oriented metric of the behavior and performance of ad hoc networks.

- **Chapter 11:** A Context-Aware Model of Trust for Facilitating Secure Ad Hoc Collaborations, by Indrajit Ray, Indrakshi Ray , Sudip Chakraborty

This chapter proposed a context-aware trust model to facilitate secure ad hoc collaborations. This model can measure trust in a given context even though sometimes enough information is not available about a given context to calculate the trust value. In order to achieve this purpose, the authors apply a context graph to formalize the relationships between contexts. It allows extrapolating values from related contexts to approximate a trust value of an entity.

- **Chapter 12:** An Evaluation Framework for Reputation Management Systems, by Andrew G. West, Sampath Kannan, Insup Lee, Oleg Sokolsky

This chapter proposes an evaluation framework based on the trace-simulator paradigm to conduct comparative analysis on reputation algorithms. Trace file generation emulates a variety of network configurations and pays particular attention to modeling malicious user behaviors. The chapter reports on the framework's design decisions and demonstrates this general-purpose simulator with two reputation algorithms (EigenTrust and a modified TNA-SL) under varied network conditions. As one of the first studies in the area of trust management effectiveness research, the described framework is available as open source so that researchers can evaluate the effectiveness of other reputation management techniques and/or extend its functionalities.

- **Chapter 13:** Observation-Based Trust Management for Services in Mobile Networks, by André Paul, Carsten Jacob, Heiko Pfeffer, Stephan Steglich

This chapter provides a trust management framework to conduct trust/reputation evaluation for services in mobile networks by detecting misbehavior or inaccuracy in service executions and for rating them according to user preferences. Thus, it is possible to reduce and prevent the interaction with misbehaving mobile nodes since the framework can also be responsible for determining the risk of interactions.

- **Chapter 14:** Risk-Based Trust Management for E-Commerce, by Soon-Keow Chong, Jemal H. Abawajy

This chapter presents a multi-attribute trust management model that incorporates trust, transaction costs and product warranties. The new trust management system enables potential buyers to determine the risk level of a product before committing to proceed with the transaction in electronic market places.

- **Chapter 15:** Privacy and Trust Issues in Context-Aware Pervasive Computing: State-of-the-Art and Future Directions, by Pierre E. Abi-Char, Abdallah M'hamed, Bachar El-Hassan, Mounir Moukhtari

This chapter concerns privacy and trust issues in context-aware pervasive computing. The authors discuss new challenges, opportunities and requirements, as well as existing solutions regarding privacy, trust and security in a pervasive computing environment.

- **Chapter 16:** Trust and Stability in Heterogeneous Multimedia Networks, by Dimitrios Koukopoulos

This chapter discusses the relationship of trust and stability in heterogeneous distributed computing systems. In such a context, trust is interpreted as the confidence in the association of a stable network execution to the efficient distribution of multimedia products in the final user. The author studies the property of stability under various compositions of contention-resolution protocols and different packet trajectories trying to characterize this property in terms of network topologies. The results indicate that a composition of protocols leads to worst stability behaviour than having a single unstable protocol for contention-resolution.

The last section consists of five chapters about social trust studies across multiple disciplines. This kind of study provides valuable guidelines for trust modeling and management in order to design and develop a trustworthy digital system.

- **Chapter 17:** The Role of Trust in Social Life, by Yan Dong

This chapter reviews the literature of trust in sociology and psychology. By introducing the conception, theory model and measurement of trust, the author discusses trust in three important social contexts: interpersonal situation, organizational settings and Internet life and proposes a synthetic trust model with a multi-disciplinary approach as a future research direction.

- **Chapter 18:** Issues on Anshin and its Factors, by Yuko Murayama, Yasuhiro Fujihara

This chapter introduces a project 'Anshin' to study emotional trust issue: an emotional state of one's mind in peace. The authors introduce the concept of Anshin and its research issues. Instructively, they present how to use statistical analysis methods to derive the factors of Anshin, which is identified as a key component of emotional trust.

- **Chapter 19:** Trust in Identification Systems: From Empirical Observations to Design Guidelines, by Piotr Cofta, Hazel Lacohée

This chapter utilises a case study of citizen identification systems to illustrate the continuum of trust-related considerations and technology adoption, ranging from theoretical underpinnings of trust, to empirical studies, through to practical design guidelines. A mixed methodological approach that combines the best from various disciplines is presented by applying it into the citizen identification systems.

- **Chapter 20:** Human-Machine Trust Interaction: a Technical Overview, by Conghui Liu

This chapter reviews the concept of trust and the main factors that affect a user's trust in human-machine interaction. The author discusses the current state, challenges, problems and limitations in this area and evaluates the existing solutions for improving the user's trust appropriately, especially in an e-commerce environment.

- **Chapter 21:** Rethinking Realistic Wireless Network Mobility: Model and Trust, by Lu Yan

This chapter discusses a proposal for a more realistic mobility model that captures key features of human movements in pervasive markets. The findings based on users' mobility behaviors lead to a non-traditional mobility model. It can be used to reconstruct the statistical patterns commonly observed in the literature, and facilitate the study of mobile communication and software engineering design problems under the context of pervasive computing for markets. This model could imply a trust relationship between the user and the markets that can be used for the design of a pervasive service.

From a social concept to system development, the book covers the entire scope of research for developing a trustworthy digital system: from traditional security enhanced technologies to computational trust based approaches; from social trust studies to digital trust researches; from hardware based designs to software development; from system framework and architecture to user interface and human-machine interaction. It provides a comprehensive study on trust management system development. Editing this book has been an enlightening and thought-provoking experience to me. I hope you enjoying reading this book. I will be happy if you find this book helpful and your interest in the field of trust modeling and management could be further aroused by reading various perspectives presented herein.

Zheng Yan
Editor
Nokia Research Center
Helsinki, Finland
May, 2009

Acknowledgment

I started my study on trust since 2002 based on a number of projects conducted at the Nokia Research Center: from hardware based trust solution to software one, from security technology enhanced solutions to computational trust modeling and management, and then to human-machine trust interaction towards usable trust management. All above form the basic scope of this book and my understanding of trust management. I would like to express my sincere gratitude to Dr. Valtteri Niemi, Nokia Fellow for writing the foreword. Some essence of this book was roused from our previous discussion on human-machine trust interaction and his inducement to figure out a usable trust management solution.

I am grateful to the Nokia Research Center for supporting my research on trust modeling and management. I would like to extend my gratitude to my superior Dr. N.Asokan, who supported me to complete this book project. Particularly, I appreciate my colleagues at the Nokia Research Center: Dr. Valtteri Niemi, Dr. Silke Holtmanns, Dr. Christian Prehofer, Jan-Erik Ekberg, Kari Kostiainen, Sampo Sovio, Philip GinzBoorg who contributed a lot to the review work. Philip also kindly commented the preface. Meanwhile, I would like to express my deep thanks to other Editorial Advisory Board members Prof. Robert H. Deng, Prof. Shengnan Han, Dr. Piotr Cofta, Dr. Gabriele Lenzini, Prof. Christian Damsgard Jensen, and Dr. Yan Zhang for their great help in the book chapters' review, which was a big work load.

This project began in May, 2008 and end in June, 2009. I was fortunate in having a quite number of excellent authors all over the world. Without their contributions to the book contents and active participation in the anonymous review process, this book would not have been possible. My sincere thanks to all of them!

I would like to thank Kristin M. Klinger, IGI Global for inviting me to develop this book; Jan Travers for handling the contract details; Tyler Heath and **Beth Ardner**, the editorial assistants whose efficient and cheerful assistance throughout the project make it an enjoyable experience.

Finally, I feel deeply indebted to my husband Peng for his endless support on both of my life and work, which has been a great source of inspiration in the completion of this book. Actually, it was him who motivated me to develop a book to summarize my perspectives on trust management. And last but not the least, my love and thanks to my son Kuan who is always the source of my happiness and my strength to overcome challenges in the life. The book is for my love: Peng and Kuan.

Zheng Yan
Helsinki, Finland
May 30th, 2009

Section 1
Security Enhanced Trust Management Solutions

Chapter 1
Remote Platform Attestation:
The Testimony for Trust Management

Xuhua Ding
Singapore Management University, Singapore

Liang Gu
Peking University, China

Robert H. Deng
Singapore Management University, Singapore

Bing Xie
Peking University, China

Hong Mei
Peking University, China

ABSTRACT

One of the key mechanisms for trust establishment among different platforms is remote attestation, which allows a platform to vouch for its trust related characteristics to a remote challenger. In this chapter, the authors propose a new conceptual model for remote attestation consisting of four basic ingredients: root of trust, attestation objective, object measurement, and attestation process. With this model, they present a systematic study on the remote attestation, including the methodologies applied for implementing the four elements and the principles for designing an attestation scheme. The authors also examine existing remote attestation schemes in the literature by grouping them into two main types: integrity attestation and quality attestation. They discuss both the strength and the limitations of each type of scheme and explain how they can be applied in trust management in distributed environment.

DOI: 10.4018/978-1-61520-682-7.ch001

INTRODUCTION

Motivation

Many applications nowadays are conducted on open computer platforms across heterogeneous domains or over the public Internet. The openness of the platforms and the open infrastructure of the Internet provide the essential flexibility to enable widespread adoptions of numerous innovative applications. However, entities involved in such distributed and open environments normally have different interests and motivations, and may not trust each other for critical operations or transactions. As such, it is important to study the means for establishing and managing trust among individual platforms, from the perspectives of the different entities involved. To further illustrate this point, consider the following two applications.

A corporate intranet is required to be accessible for its employees outside its premises, e.g. an employee on travel. This presents a threat to the corporation's information facility, due to the lack of assurance on the sanity of the client systems used by those employees. Though the users are trusted, the remote systems could be malicious, which may download confidential corporate information, modify sensitive data, or even infect other nodes in the intranet. Existing security measures based on authentication, firewall and access control are insufficient to defeat these attacks. It is desirable for the corporation to have the ability of evaluating the trustworthiness of the remote systems before admitting them into the intranet.

Another typical application requiring trust management is distributed computing which consists of a job supervisor and multiple participants. The supervisor splits a large computation job into tasks and assigns them to the participants. Each participant accomplishes the assigned task by performing certain computations and returns the results back to the supervisor. There have been a surge of interests in using this computing paradigm to solve computation intensive problems, e.g.,

the well-known SETI@Home project (Korpela, Werthimer, Anderson, Cobb, & Lebofsky, 2001; SETI@Home, 2007), the Great Internet Mersenne Prime Project (GIMPS, 2007), and the Folding@ Home project (Folding@home, 2007). The most vital requirement of such applications is that the results returned by the participants should be trustworthy in the sense that the participants' computing processes are not tampered with.

Similar issues also exist in other distributed applications, such as distributed firewalls (Ioannidis, Keromytis, Bellovin, & Smith, 2000), digital rights management, P2P applications, ad hoc trust routing, Web services and Grid Computing. The transactions among participants in these applications can be securely executed only when the participants are trustworthy. For example, DRM protected content is transferred only to devices that are able to prove its trustworthiness.

Trust management usually begins with trust evaluation followed by policy enforcement. Therefore, a reliable trust evaluation is the premise of the entire trust management framework. A prerequisite to evaluate a platform's trustworthiness is the knowledge of its trust related attributes, such as its system configurations and software, its access policies and its dynamic behavior. Remote attestation serves exactly for this purpose.

Remote Attestation

The Trusted Computing Group, or TCG (TCG, 2003), has been actively prompting trusted computing for years. The basic idea of TCG is to attach a tamper-resistant chip, called Trusted Platform Module or TPM (Trusted Computing Group, 2006), to a host platform (e.g. a personal computer or a mobile device). TPM is regarded as the root of trust and facilitates building a trusted computing environment. One of the core function proposed by TCG is *remote platform attestation,* or *remote attestation* for short. According to the TCG specifications, remote attestation is a security mechanism to remotely authenticate the states of a platform, called an attester. The TPM securely measures the attester by computing the hash digests of the platform states. Upon an attestation request from a challenger, the TPM signs the measurements and returns them as the response. The challenger establishes trust on the attester by verifying the signature with a set of known-good measurements.

The attestation functionality offered by TPM only ensures integrity of a platform's configurations. Beyond that, no other security conclusion can be drawn. Though primitive, this functionality provides a basis for building sophisticated attestation schemes to portrait more sophisticated security characteristics, as in (Chen, Landfermann, Löhr, Rohe, Sadeghi, &Stüble, 2006; Garfinkel, Pfaff, Chow, Rosenblum, & Boneh, 2003; Gu, Ding, Deng, Xie, & Mei, 2008; Gu, Ding, Deng, Zou et al., 2008; Haldar, Chandra, & Franz, 2004; Jaeger, Sailer, & Shankar, 2006; Kühn, Selhorst, & Stüble, 2007; Li, Shen, & Zuo, 2006; J. Poritz, Schunter, Herreweghen, & Waidner, 2004; Sadegh & Stüble, 2004; Sailer, Zhang, Jaeger, & Doorn, 2004; Shi, Perrig, & Doorn, 2005).

Besides TPM-based remote attestation schemes, recent years have seen interests in software-based remote attestation. Exemplary research efforts include Genuinity (Kennell & Jamieson, 2003), SWATT (Seshadri, Perrig, Doorn, & Khosla, 2004), Pioneer (Seshadri, Luk, Shi, Perrig, Doorn, & Khosla, 2005), SCUBA (Seshadri, Luk, Perrig, van Doorn, & Khosla, 2006). Without using any tamper-resistant hardware, software-based attestation features a small block of code which is trusted to behave as expected. Such an approach is applicable to cost-constrained devices where the inclusion of an embedded tamper-resistant hardware cannot be afforded.

In this chapter, we first briefly explain the background of trusted computing. Then, we propose a new conceptual model of remote attestation. With this model, we provide a systematic analysis of existing remote attestation schemes, as well as our insights into the relation between trust management and platform attestation from the application perspective.

BACKGROUND OF TRUSTED COMPUTING

The core of TCG's trusted computing framework is TPM, a tamper-resistant module embedded in a platform. A TPM chip is designed to resist all software attacks and moderate hardware attacks. It encloses a non-volatile storage, a set of platform configuration registers (PCRs) and an engine for cryptographic operations. The TCG specifications define a suit of mechanisms including memory curtaining, secure I/O, secure storage, platform measurement and remote attestation. All are based on the TPM chip and its supporting software called TCG Software Stack (TSS).

Memory Curtaining

One of the threats to the execution of security sensitive applications is the unauthorized memory access by malware residing in the same platform. The malware can spy on other processes' execution or even manipulate the data. Memory curtaining is a hardware-enforced memory isolation scheme to guarantee the intactness of the process execution. When a process is running under memory curtaining protection, no adversarial process can read from or write to its memory space and CPU states.

Secure Storage and Sealed Storage

In the TCG specification, a hierarchy of storage encryption keys can be used to protect both the confidentiality and the integrity of data stored in hard disks. The root of the key hierarchy is the storage root key (SRK) which is stored inside the TPM chip when a user takes the ownership of the TPM. SRK is used to encrypt its children storage keys which can be further used to encrypt children keys in the next level. The *sealed storage* function defined by TCG can securely bind data encryption/decryption to a platform state. To seal a data item, both the data itself and the relevant PCR values are encrypted together. The sealed data can only be decrypted by the TPM on which it was encrypted. To unseal the data item, the TPM decrypts it internally and compares the decrypted PRC values with the current ones. The data is released on the condition that both PCR values are the same. On-board Credential (ObC) (Ekberg, Asokan, Kostiainen, & Rantala, 2008), a platform of credential management, extends the sealed storage function to the application level by supporting "credential program" to run in a secure execution environment.

Platform Measurement

The TCG specifications introduce the root of trust for measurement (RTM) to reliably measure the platform states. To measure a process or application, RTM computes the hash value of the relevant software component and stores the hash in one of the TPM PCRs immediately before the program execution. Multiple rounds of measurements are stored in the same PCR by hashing the concatenation of a new measurement with the existing content of a PCR and then storing the output hash value in the register. A detailed record of all measured components is stored in the Stored Measurement Log (SML), which is maintained externally to the TPM chip. With platform measurement, a TCG-compliant platform can have either a secure booting or an authenticated booting. In both booting processes, the RTM measures every components the host is about to load, starting from BIOS, to the operating system loader and to the operating system. The secure booting is to detect malicious mutation of the platform. A component is allowed to be loaded only when its measurement is known to be trustworthy. In contrast, the RTM does not enforce such a matching policy during an authenticated booting. The platform only makes use of the measurements to convince others about the system it has booted into.

Platform Attestation

Platform attestation is the process with which the platform measurement is signed and transported to a challenger. Figure 1 shows the involved parties and the process of remote attestation in TCG's specification. First, the challenger sends the remote attestation request with a random *nonce* to the attester platform. After receiving the challenge request, the attester platform retrieves the corresponding SML, and calls TPM to sign the relevant PCR values using the *nonce* and its Attestation Identity Key (AIK). Then the attester platform collects the credentials vouching for the TPM. The signature on the PCR values and related SML records, together with the credentials, are sent back to the challenger as the attestation response. The challenger verifies the signature and compares the received platform measurement with known-good ones, which can be retrieved from its local storage or a trusted third party.

A requirement for the signatures in use is the anonymity of a TPM chip. The signatures are generated by using the AIK. A TPM chip may have multiple AIKs certified by a special certification authority called Privacy CA (P-CA). A certificate for an AIK does not reveal the TPM's identity. Instead, it only certifies that the key owner is compliant to the TCG specifications. Another approach to providing anonymity without the cost and risk of involving P-CA, is the Direct Anonymous Attestation (DAA) scheme (Brickell, Camenisch, & Chen, 2004), which has been adopted by the TPMv1.2 standard as an option. A DAA issuer presents a zero-knowledge proof on its platform credential, without exposing its private information. Nonetheless, the computation cost of both signature generation and verification in DAA are higher than standard RSA signature operations.

Figure 1. TCG Remote Attestation

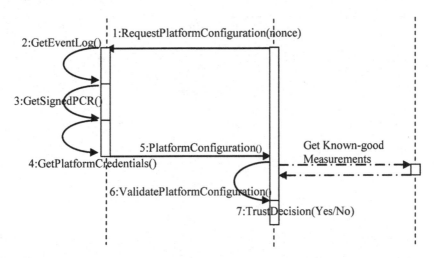

A Conceptual Model of Remote Attestation

The notion of remote attestation proposed in the TCG specifications only deals with integrity of the configurations of a platform, which does not satisfy the needs from applications where the trust establishment is based on sophisticated platform properties. In this section, we make an extension of the original notion of attestation by treating it as a generalized security primitive from the trust management perspective. By proposing an abstract architecture to model the paradigm of remote attestation, we describe the composition of remote attestation schemes and explain the function of each component.

The Conceptual Model of Remote Attestation

Remote attestation is an interactive protocol between two entities: a challenger and an attester. The challenger initiates the protocol via a remote attestation request and the attester responds with its measurement result. The measurement serves as the attester's testimonial for the challenger to make trust-related decisions on the attester's platform. Such a challenge and response exchange may be

iterated if necessary. Note that how to derive the trustworthiness of the attester from the attestation outcome varies with platforms and applications, and is beyond the scope of the chapter.

Our proposed model of remote attestation consists of the following components: *root of trust, attestation objective, object measurement,* and *attestation process.*

- The *root of trust* is a hardware or software component on the attester platform that is trusted to behave as expected. Since the actual behavior of a root of trust cannot be verified, its implementation is usually based on sound and advanced security techniques widely accepted by the public. For example, the certified TPM chip in a TCG-compliant platform is the root of trust for attestation, since the design of a TPM chip has adopted tamper-resistant techniques to counter any software attacks.

- The *attestation objective* is the security assertion the challenger attempts to derive from the execution of the remote attestation protocol. The assertion is typically on one or multiple platform properties, based on which the challenger evaluates the trustworthiness of the attester platform.

Figure 2. A conceptual model for remote attestation

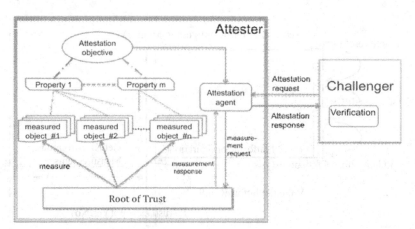

- The *object measurement* is the core function of remote attestation. It outputs the needed data to depict the attester's security attributes relevant to the attestation objective. It first determines the set of software objects in the attester platform. Then, it determines the proper method and time to measure those objects, and performs the measurement through the root of trust.
- The *attestation process* is a challenge-response protocol which describes how the attester securely presents its platform measurement to the challenger, and how the challenger verifies the measurement.

Figure 2 shows the architecture of our proposed conceptual model for remote attestation. The communication channel between the attester and the challenger is usually safeguarded using a standard security protocol, e.g. TLS/SSL. In this model, the challenger trusts the root of trust on the attester platform. Other components are potential adversaries who may attempt to cheat. The remote attestation process at the attester end is trigger by an attestation request from the challenger. In our conceptual model, we introduce an attestation agent, which is a program at the application layer dedicated to manage the attestation process. According to the attestation objective specified in

the attestation request, the agent first determines which properties of the platform and which objects are relevant to the objective. Then, it instructs the root of trust to measure each needed objects. The measurement results, together with necessary credentials and SML records, are complied by the agent to form an attestation response sent to the challenger. The challenger verifies them and determines the trustworthiness of the attester.

We use PRIMA (Jaeger, Sailer, & Shankar, 2006) as an example to illustrate the model. The root of trust in PRIMA is a TPM chip and its software. The attestation objective of PRIMA is to attest whether the attester platform satisfies the CW-Lite model (Shankar, Jaeger, & Sailer, 2006), a set of policies regarding information flow. Therefore, the measured objects in PRIMA include mandatory access control policies in use, a set of subjects that involved in information flows and a runtime mapping between a code and a subject's type. In the following, we elaborate the details of each component in the model by explaining their functionalities and design principles.

ROOT OF TRUST

The root of trust is the security bedrock in all attestation schemes, since the soundness of a measurement of the attester platform is established upon the assumption that the root of trust behaves as expected. A remote challenger has essentially no provable way to verify the root of trust. Therefore, a common principle is to keep a root of trust as small as possible and its function as simple as possible. There exist three types of root of trust: hardware-based, software-based and hybrid.

Hardware-Based Root of Trust

The hardware-based root of trust mainly refers to the TPM. The entire TPM chip and its software stack (TSS) are trusted by the challenger. Specifically, the root of trust with respect to attestation consists of the root of trust for measurement (RTM) and the root of trust for reporting (RTR). RTM consists of a core component (C-RTM) and a computing engine to run C-RTM generating hash digests of software components on the platform. RTR consists of a software engine for reporting the hash values to a remote challenger.

A challenger has to examine the presence of the TPM chip in the attester's platform and its identity. One approach is to verify a TPM's credential to ensure that the attester indeed has a certified TPM. Nonetheless, the verification is subject to the so-called cuckoo attacks, whereby a malicious attester presents a certificate of another TPM and uses malware to simulate the operations supposed done by a local TPM. It remains as an open problem how to deal with this attack.

Software-Based Root of Trust

A software-based root of trust is a specially designed program that can verify its own execution. The trustworthiness of this program relies on the root's tamper detection mechanism. Existing approaches include result checking (Blum & Kanna, 1989; Wasserman & Blum, 1997) and self-checking (Chang & Atallah, 2001; Horne, Matheson, Sheehan, & Tarjan, 2001). Wireless Sensors Attestation (Shaneck, Mahadevan, Kher,

& Kim, 2005) and Pioneer (Seshadri, Luk, Shi, Perrig, Doorn, & Khosla, 2005) are two attestation schemes with software-based root of trust. Basically, the root of trust checks certain characteristics at runtime, such as the output and time-cost for a specific task execution. Pioneer uses a verification function based on a checksum code which has the following properties: time-optimal implementation, iterative checksum code, strongly-ordered checksum function, small code size, low variance of execution time, and pseudo-random memory traversal. This verification function allows Pioneer to use a small piece of code to detect any attacks.

Attacking a hardware component usually is much more difficult than attacking a software component. Many attacks on hardware require manual intervention and physical accesses to the victim. In contrast, subverting a program is easier. Therefore, a hardware-based root of trust is more reliable but generally costs more in manufacturing, deployment and maintenance and more difficult to upgrade when flaws are found. Software-based root of trust enjoys flexibility, low cost, easy upgrade and compatibility. It could also be beneficial for legacy platforms and remote device management. It is more suitable to computing environments with resource and cost constraints. However, a software-base root usually requires strong assumptions, which limit the scope of its applications. For example, Pioneer requires that the challenger knows exactly the CPU model and memory latency and the platform does not run with symmetric multi-threading.

Hybrid Root of Trust

Secure Kernel (SK) was introduced as a hybrid software and hardware solution to build a trust chain from hardware to software. SK runs in a privileged execution mode of modern processors, for example, AMD's Secure Execution Mode (SEM) (AMD, 2003). It functions as a middle layer between the operating system and the hardware.

SK offers only a few necessary interfaces to the operating system, which makes its code compact and allows for software verification. SK runs at the core of the privilege ring and uses hardware protection mechanisms to protect itself as well as other sensitive processes and data. SK is also compatible with the CPU late-launch technology, e.g., AMD's Secure Virtual Machine (SVM) architecture (AMD, 2005) and Intel's Trusted Execution Technology (TXT) (Intel, 2006). Coupled with the Intel Virtualization technology, TXT provides a hardware support for the creation of parallel, protected environments that enable a much stronger protection for code execution and confidential information.

Trust Chain of Remote Attestation

To minimize the cost, the root of trust is usually compact, only providing a primitive function. Therefore, it is infeasible to utilize the root of trust to perform sophisticated attestation directly. A commonly used solution is to build a trustable object chain headed by the root of trust. Trust on each object in this chain, except the root of trust, is verified by its predecessor.

Usually, a trust chain is established in two steps. First, the root of trust checks the integrity of an object's binary executables. Then, the memory curtaining or a process isolation technique is employed to prevent the object's execution from being tampered with by unauthorized processes. Therefore, the integrity of executing processes is ensured.

Attestation Objective

An attestation objective is the criteria used by a challenger to evaluate the trustworthiness of an attester platform. The objective of an attestation scheme affects the selection of objects to measure. In general, there exist two attestation objectives: *integrity attestation* and *quality attestation*.

An integrity attestation scheme checks the integrity of one or multiple components of the attester, such as data integrity, program code integrity. It is achieved by object measurement, specifically the root of trust's signature on the object digests. By checking the measurement, the challenger identifies the attester's software/system version, which consequently leads to trust establishment. The most primitive scheme in this category is the TCG platform attestation (Trusted Computing Group, 2006), which verifies software integrity from BIOS up to the bootstrap loader. IMA (Sailer, Zhang et al., 2004) extends the TCG's attestation from the bootstrap loader up to the application layer. A challenger can also verify just one specific component of his interest. For examples, Copilot (Petroni, Fraser, Molina, & Arbaugh, 2004) verifies the Linux kernel loaded in the main memory of the attester platform, and BIND (Shi et al., 2005) verifies the integrity of a segment of code in execution.

A quality attestation scheme allows a challenger to establish trust on an attester by assessing the latter's traits. The attested traits may include the semantic of a program, the behavior of the system, the enforced policy model etc. For example, PRIMA (Jaeger et al., 2006) examines whether the CW-lite policy (Shankar et al., 2006) is enforced on the attester platform. A challenger can also check whether a platform offers expected properties (Chen et al., 2006; Haldar et al., 2004; Haldar & Franz, 2004; J. Poritz et al., 2004; J. A. Poritz, 2006), or whether a program is correctly executed (Gu, Ding, Deng, Xie et al., 2008). Quality attestation requires object measurement as well. Different from integrity attestation, the measurement for quality attestation is on the running states of the objects. The challenger in quality attestation is not interested in identifying the attester's software/system version. Instead, it evaluates the semantic/behavior of the objects from the measurement results. The evaluation is trait-specific. Namely the needed object measurements and the logic of assessment vary with the attested trait. We will discuss how to select the needed object to measure and how to measure in the next section.

The advantage of integrity attestation is its lower cost in comparison with quality attestation, as it only involves hashes and signatures of static objects. Integrity attestation suffers from two major downsides. First, it is platform dependent. It requires the challenger to have a priori knowledge of those known-good signatures stored in a signature database. Due to the diversity and complexity of nowadays' hardware and software, especially a vast number of OS patches, the signature database is cumbersome and difficult to manage. Secondly, the trust assurance offered by integrity attestation is limited. Integrity attestation is based the measurement of the initial state of an object, e.g. the binary code of a process, which is not equivalent to a correct execution as a malicious attester may launch a different version. Moreover, a trustworthy object could be tampered during its execution. This weakness can be slightly alleviated with the recent advance of CPU late-launch, which builds a temporarily secure environment for code execution. However, late-launch is not feasible to large applications, due to the immense system overhead.

The limitations of integrity attestation are exactly the motivation for quality attestation. Quality-based attestation is platform-independent and provides a stronger assurance for trust establishment, since it relies on the actual behavior of the attester. Nonetheless, the merit of quality-based attestation is at the cost of performance degradation due to the runtime measurement overhead. Another downside of quality-based attestation is the logic used to derive security assurance from runtime measurement which is a just snapshot of the system. There exists no universal theory or security model to infer a notion of security about an object's behavior. Although ad hoc solutions exist, e.g. PRIMA's policy checking, many existing quality attestation schemes lack of soundness

and completeness. The third disadvantage of quality-based attestation is its need for a complicated trustworthy attestation agent, which may or may not in the operating system kernel. Since the object measurement for integrity attestation is straightforward and clearly defined, a root of trust such as TPM is capable for the measurement task. For quality attestation, it is a complicate task to select the appropriate objects to measure and to measure them. It is beyond the root of trust's capability. Thus, quality attestation usually requires a sophisticated chain of trust, which surely entails more overhead and may require special hardware support.

Object Measurement

The object measurement is the core of any attestation scheme, because all trust related inferences are based on the result of object measurement. Object measurement comprises three elements: the objects to measure, measurement methods, measurement timing.

Objects to Measure

It is an indispensable step for any attestation scheme to identify a set of objects to measure. The selection of objects is based on the attestation objective. Although the exact objects to measure vary with the attestation schemes, a general principle is that an object should be measured if its states or attributes affect the trustworthiness of the attester. Those objects can be any component in a platform, including the OS loader, the OS kernel and other OS components, system libraries, application packages and configuration files. For example, the TCG platform attestation measures all the objects involved in the boot-up process, since its goal is just to demonstrate its boot-up sate. PRIMA (Jaeger et al., 2006) identifies those component related to information flow, such as subjects, objects and interfaces, because it verifies whether the CW-lite model is enforced. The execution attestation (Gu, Ding, Deng, Xie et al., 2008) verifies the correctness of a program execution and therefore measures all objects which a target program has data/control dependence to.

A key issue related to objects to measure is object granularity. The input to the measurement function can vary from a software package of megabytes to a segment of instructions of dozens of bytes. The choice of granularity is essentially a tradeoff between performance and flexibility. A coarse-grained attestation measures the objects of large size, e.g. the files, whereas a fine-grained attestation measures objects of small size, e.g. instructions. The former approach does not require detailed prior knowledge of the objects since they are measured as whole, and it needs fewer signature generations. Nonetheless, it lacks of flexibility. For any legitimate update on an object, the challenger needs a new entry in its known-good signature database, even though the update may be irrelevant to the attestation objective. In contrast, the fine-grained approach is more flexible. Irrelevant software updates do not result in database expanse. However, seeking the exact segment of an object to measure requires sufficient prior knowledge of the object, which is not always available in many scenarios.

Measurement Methods

The most widely used method of measurement is the TCG style hash-then-sign. An attested object is treated as a binary string. A hash digest of the object is computed and then signed by the root of trust. In particular, the TPM employs SHA-1 to hash the configuration information and stores the hash digest in one of the PCRs. The values in PCRs are then signed by a TPM AIK. Software-based attestation mechanisms usually employ checksums to measure an object. For example, Chang and Atallah (2001) and Horne et al. (2001) employ checksums to provide tamper resistance. However, the checksum approach is not appli-

cable on certain platforms. Wurster et al. (2005) have successfully attacked this kind of checksum mechanisms by taking advantage of the new functions of modern processors.

Measurement Timing

The measurement timing is also critical to the correct evaluation of trustworthiness, because the state of an object could vary in time, usually with the executions. It is straightforward to observe that timing has greater significance for quality attestation than integrity attestation, since that the latter measures static attributes. Quality attestation measures an object at runtime, typically when the object is accessed or executed. Note that the root of trust such as a TPM chip is passive. Therefore, a runtime measurement is triggered by system call traps. The hook for the involved system call is modified for measurement invocation.

Another issue is the gap between time-of-measurement and time-of-use. The time when an object is measured is not always the time when it is used. Due to this gap, the measurement may not correctly vouch for the claimed property. Ideally, the gap should be as little as possible. Two types of approaches have been proposed to tackle this issue. One approach is to deploy of strong security mechanisms to protect program executions, which minimizes the possibility of object state mutation during the gap. For example, Terra (Garfinkel et al., 2003) introduces ahead-of-time attestation and an optimistic attestation to attest target programs in its Trusted Virtual Machine. Assuming that a Virtual Machine protects the code execution, ahead-of-time attestation means that the attestation occurs when the code is loaded, while for the Virtual Machine, optimistic attestation attests the loading block of the VM at runtime. Another example is BIND (Shi et al., 2005) which measures the code block of the target program immediately before it is executed and assumes that the Secure Kernel can provide a secure execution environment for the target program's execution. The second approach is to minimize the gap as in IMA (Sailer, Zhang et al., 2004), which employs loading time measurement to measure the attesting target twice: before and after its execution. Obviously, the second approach has double attestation cost. However, it is applicable for scenarios where schemes for safeguarding program execution are not available.

Attestation Process

Many attestation schemes require the attester to sign its platform measurement to ensure integrity and non-repudiation. The signatures, however, may allow a challenger to identify the attester or link two attestation sessions, which could be undesirable in many privacy sensitive scenarios. Therefore, the challenge-response protocol should be designed to protect the attester's anonymity and unlinkability. The TCG specification proposes to use the Direct Anonymous Attestation (DAA) (Brickell et al., 2004), which is more expensive than standard signature schemes. An alternative is not to expose the attester's internal states so that the communication channel is not necessarily anonymous. One exemplary scheme is the property-based attestation (Chen, Landfermann, Löhr, & Rohe et al., 2006), whereby the attester does not deliver the hash digests of measured objects. Instead, it only proves that the objects in the platform provide certain properties.

The verification methods vary with the attestation objectives. For integrity-based attestation, the challenger compares the reported measurement with those known-good ones stored in a database initialized by the challenger or a trusted third party. The evaluation method for quality-based attestation schemes is usually policy-based verification.

SUMMARY: DESIGN PRINCIPLES FOR ATTESTATION SCHEMES

We summarize this section by providing the general design principles for attestation schemes. Recall that our conceptual model comprises the root of trust, the attestation objective, object measurement and the attestation process. Among these four elements, the attestation objective is application specific and the attestation process has also been standardized. Therefore, the root of trust and the object measurement are the two elements whose designs impact on effectiveness and efficiency of an attestation scheme.

The trustworthiness provided by the root of trust is the foundation of the attestation scheme. Therefore, it must be reliable in the sense that its execution and internal states should resist attacks from the hosting platform. If tamper-resistance is not affordable, an alternative is to allow the challenger to easily detect all attacks from the host on the root of trust. The root of trust is usually selected from those hardware/software components with well-known security properties.

The design of object measurement mandates a sound security analysis on the attestation objective in order to identify the appropriate objects to measure and the measurement method. On the one hand, the object set must enclose all objects whose behaviors/properties may alter the platform's behavior/properties relevant to the attestation objective. On the other hand, for the efficiency purpose, the object set should not enclose any unwanted object which has no impacts on the attestation objective. The general methodology is a top-down approach, as shown in Figure 2. Starting from the attestation objective, the scheme determines the relevant platform properties, and then the objects reflecting those properties.

The measurement methods resolves the issues about measurement timing and which component to perform the measurement. The measurement timing is chosen based on the platform properties in attestation. The general principle is that the time

Table 1. Existing remote attestation schemes

Attestation Type	Existing Schemes	Attestation objective	Root of Trust	Measurement Object
Integrity-based	Copilot (Petroni et al.., 2004)	Integrity of Linux kernel loaded in memory	TPM	loaded Linux kernel
	TCG Attestation	Configuration Integrity of Platform	TPM	objects involved in the boot-up process
	Terra (Garfinkel et al., 2003)	Authenticate applications in Trusted Virtual Machine	TVMM	all objects in trusted domain
	Pioneer (Seshadri et al., 2005)	Program code integrity	Special routine	security critical codes
	BIND (Shi et al., 2005)	Integrity of program	TPM	program code and data
	IMA (Sailer et al.., 2004)	System Integrity	TPM	all objects on platform including applications.
	Wireless Sensors Attestation (Shaneck et al.. 2005)	Memory content integrity in sensor nodes	Special routine	Memory content of sensor node
Quality-based	PRIMA (Jaeger et al., 2006)	Integrity model of remote system	TPM	Trusted objects and filtering objects
	Behavior based Attestation (Li et al., 2006)	Whether the behaviors of the system are trustworthy	TPM	All system behaviors
	Semantic remote attestation (Haldar et al., 2004)	Dynamic and arbitrary system properties	TVM with TPM	Not specified
	Property based attestation	Specified by challenger	TPM	Not specified
	Remote attestation on program execution (Gu et al.. 2008)	The correct execution of program in complex system	SK with TPM	all objects a program's attestation depends on

of measuring an object is as close to the time of the object execution as possible. This minimizes the likelihood that the object mutates after being measured. Ideally, it is the root of trust that performs the measurement, since it removes the need for intermediary objects, and therefore reduces the risk of mistakenly trusting a malicious object. However, as the root of trust only offers the basic functions, it is not feasible for the root to perform the complex measurement, especially for quality attestation. The recent advance in CPU technology provides a feasible solution to this dilemma. The new security features of CPU, e.g. late launch and memory curtaining, allow a trust chain to be built from the root of trust. The chain may consist of various agile software components capable of performing sophisticated measurements. Note that a long trust chain should be avoided, since it incurs more security risks.

Existing Remote Attestation Schemes

In this section, we discuss several landmark remote attestation schemes proposed in the literature. We classify them into two groups based on their attestation objectives. Table 1 provides a summary of them with respect to the attestation objective, root of trust and the objects to measure.

Integrity-Based Attestation

Integrity-based attestation is to evaluate and verify the integrity of the attesting target, e.g., the integrity of binary code and the configuration of a platform. In general, the hash digest of the measured object is signed as the evidence, with which the challenger can identify the object and evaluate its trustworthiness. Three types of integrity attestation are introduced below: TCG attestation, data attestation and program integrity attestation.

TCG Attestation

TCG attestation is to verify the integrity of the attester platform configuration. The measured objects include BIOS and the operating system loader. The digests of the objects are stored in the TPM's PCRs. To respond to a challenger, an attester signs the PRC values and replies with the signature together with SML.

Though simple and efficient, this approach has several drawbacks. First, it does not achieve the goal stated in TCG's definition of trust due to the aforementioned gap between the time-of-measurement and the time-of-use. A platform may load different modules after booting and TCG attestation is not able to handle possible changes after attestation. Secondly, the approach has poor scalability due to the large verification cost. Software, e.g. the operating system, is often distributed in many versions with different updates and patches. Therefore, the TCG attestation requires the maintenance of enormous number of known-good states to enumerate all possibilities. Nonetheless, this approach serves as a primitive to support other high-level remote attestation schemes.

Data Attestation

The outcome of a program execution depends not only on its binary code, but also on the input data. Therefore, it is desirable to attest the integrity of the data used by an application. Data can be classified into *structured data* and *unstructured data* (Sailer, Zhang et al., 2004). Structured data refers to those with identifiable integrity semantics, e.g. a configuration file. This type of data can be attested by using hashes as in the TCG attestation. Unstructured data refers to those without identifiable integrity semantics, such as user input. For

this type of data, the attester measures the process which creates/modifies the data. Data can also be classified into *primitive data* and *derived data* based on their origins (Shi et al., 2005). Primitive data is the external input, which can be attested using semantic check, certificates or a trusted path. Derived data is the output of a process. BIND authenticates the runtime state of the derived data by binding the data and its producer each time when it is altered or produced. Before a process uses the data, it checks not only the data origin, but also the processes bound to the data.

Program Integrity Attestation

The TCG platform attestation only measures the system bootstrap processes without covering OS modules or applications. IMA (Sailer, Zhang et al., 2004) extends it to all kernel modules, dynamically loadable libraries, and user-level executables loaded by the operating system. The measurement mechanism is implemented in the Linux kernel and uses the measurement service provided by TPM to generate the hashed record of a specific data block. The approach used by IMA is to modify the OS kernel with new hooks so that a measurement is invoked when the first line of code is loaded into a process. For example, IMA modifies file_mmap(), so that the file is measured when memory is being mapped as executable code. It also modifies load_module() to measure each loaded OS module.

In some scenarios, only the security sensitive code block is required for integrity check. BIND (Shi et al., 2005) is such an attestation scheme. It builds up its trust chain from the Secure Kernel based on TPM. The key idea of BIND is to bind the program and its output data for runtime code attestation. A code developer inserts two tags right before and after a block of security-sensitive code. At runtime, when the Secure Kernel receives an attestation request, it first verifies the authenticator on the input data to the process. If the verification fails, the kernel raises a failure signal; otherwise, the kernel hashes the target process together with its input data, and then sets up the secure execution environment for the target process. In the end, an authenticator is attached to the output of the process, which is used for future verification. Compared with IMA, BIND is not compatible with legacy systems. Nonetheless, it is a fine-grained attestation, which offers more flexibility than IMA, as discussed in the previous section.

Both IMA and BIND use TPM as the root of trust. Pioneer (Seshadri, Luk, Shi, Perrig, Doorn, & Khosla, 2005) is a software-based program integrity attestation scheme. It builds its root of trust on its specially designed routine: a verification function without any support from trusted hardware. The verification function is a small block of code which performs a pseudo-random memory traversal. Since any modification on the code leads to variance of the traversal time, the function can check its integrity by verifying the time cost. Several assumptions are needed for this approach to work. Firstly, the system clock in CPU cannot be changed. Secondly, the checksum code is executed at the highest privilege level with all interrupts being turned off. Lastly, the program has to acquire the prior knowledge of the CPU clock as well as memory latency. As there exists no formal proof for the verification function, the security offered by Pioneer is heuristic.

Quality-Based Attestation

In a quality-based attestation scheme, the attester vouches for its trustworthiness with respect to a given metric. Many existing schemes choose access policies as the metric. For example, one can attest that a process does not leak sensitive information to unauthorized processes, in compliance with an access control policy model. It is envisioned that the metric may also include software service attributes like reliability and performance, so that one can verify a service based on the Service Level Agreement.

Although quality-based attestation evaluates a platform's attributes, the collection of the needed testimonial in most schemes still make use of measurement in the hash-then-sign style, as in integrity-based attestation schemes. The main difference is on the objects to measure and the timing of measurement. It may employ other methods, such as the test suites to verify the attestation requirements used in distributed computing (Molnar, 2000). In the following, we discuss quality-based attestation from three perspectives: security property, execution correctness and policy conformance.

Security Property Attestation

Although the notion of property-based attestation (Chen et al., 2006; Kühn et al., 2007; J. Poritz et al., 2004; Sadegh & Stüble, 2004) is originally introduced to address the privacy protection problem in the standard TCG platform attestation, it fundamentally changs the attestation paradigm because the trustworthiness is not established upon identification. Property-based attestation asserts that a platform or an application does or does not possess certain expected properties. The term *security property* refers to security related characteristic requested by the challenger, such as information leakage prevention, execution states of a program, installation of a privacy preserving mechanism, and presence of a secure kernel. One such popular approach is called delegation based attestation (Chen et al., 2006; Kühn et al., 2007; J. Poritz et al., 2004; Sadegh & Stüble, 2004). The basic idea is that an offline trusted authority issues a property-certificate to the attester platform based upon its configuration. To vouch for the property, the attester proves to the challenger that it possesses the property certificate without revealing the exact details of the platform. Poritz et al. (2004) have proposed another approach by introducing an online trusted agent. On the one hand, the agent verifies the attester platform configuration; on the other hand, it proves the platform property to the challenger. This approach allows for policy negotiations at the cost of an online trusted third party. All existing property-based attestation schemes rely on integrity-based attestation which is used by a trusted party to issue certificates.

The main drawbacks of property attestation include its reliance on a trusted third party for authorization. It remains as an open problem how to attest a property without a trusted third party examining the attester platform's binary integrity. Moreover, the property certification actually does not guarantee the attester's trustworthy in real time. The state of the platform may have been changed after being certified. Therefore, the property attestation is more suitable for honest attesters for the purpose of privacy protection.

Execution Correctness Attestation

In many Internet-based applications, e.g. cloud computing, a client outsources a program's execution to a remote computing service provider. It is desirable to have an attestation scheme with which the server attests to the correctness of the computation to the client. Remote attestation on program execution (Gu, Ding, Deng, Xie et al., 2008) is designed for this need. The rationale of this scheme is that the correctness of a program's execution depends on both its binary code and all its inputs, which can originate from users through peripheral devices such as keyboard or from other processes. Therefore, to attest a program execution, the attester vouches for not only the program's code and the inputs, but also the correctness of the data if it is produced by another process. The second part implies a recursive attestation on the correctness of the data producer's execution. In the proposed scheme, the attester applies a recursive program analysis to identify all processes whose executions affect the final output of the target program. Whenever a data object is accessed or a relevant process is invoked due to the execution of the target program, its state is measured

for attestation. Therefore, all runtime information flow relevant to the target program's execution is measured by capturing the related system calls. Nonetheless, the approach used by Gu et al. (2008) is still in its infancy, since it entails significant runtime cost due to the intense measurement.

Policy Conformance Attestation

The quality of an attester platform can also be evaluated based on its conformance with a designated policy. Several schemes are designed from this perspective. Haldar et al. (Haldar et al., 2004; Haldar & Franz, 2004) have proposed a scheme to attest software behavior. The main approach is to build a trusted virtual machine, which monitors the software behavior and checks whether it satisfies certain behavior patterns. However, Haldar et al. do not clarify how to practically and dynamically identify, measure and verify a program's behavior. Moreover, the assumption on a trusted virtual machine does not hold in most applications. Another approach is based on the TCG platform attestation, such as PRIMA (Jaeger et al., 2006) and the scheme in (Li et al., 2006). In these schemes, the attester platform has a monitoring agent whose integrity is verified using the standard TCG attestation primitive. With the assistance of this trusted agent, the attester measures all policy enforcement operations, e.g. the policy used when a subject requests an access to an object. The result of measurement then is sent to the challenger, which verifies it based on the expected policy model. For example, PRIMA checks the policy for information flow and attests whether the information flow on the attester platform complies with the CW-lite model. Note that the security of these attestation schemes relies on the trustworthiness of the monitoring component in the attester platform. Although it is suggested that its integrity (an agent or a virtual machine) is checked by the TCG attestation, an adversary can still compromise it by exploiting the gap between time-of-measurement and time-of-use. Therefore, if the component is overly complex, it is difficult to ensure the security of these schemes.

Applying Attestation in Trust Management

Trust management deals with security policies, credentials, and trust relationships (Blaze, Feigenbaum, & Lacy, 1996). Many trust management systems are reputation based. The trust on a target entity is built upon the credits received from a collection of peer entities or a single trusted authority. Typically, a peer's evaluation is given according to its historical interactions with the target. Therefore, the credit is subjective and erroneous since there hardly exists unified common criteria for peer evaluations. Moreover, such a trust management system can easily be misused. A dishonest entity may gain advantage by manipulating the evaluation system. For example, one can mount Sybil attacks to maliciously elevate his own credit or degrade other's. Although using an authority to certify the trust credit provides a remedy to some of these problems, it suffers from single point of failure and poor scalability.

Remote attestation evaluates whether an attester platform holds certain trustworthy characteristics satisfying the challenger's requirement. It offers a new venue to establish trust between two entities. Through attestation, the challenger obtains a security testimony on specific attributes of the attester platform, such as integrity or enforcement of security policies. Since the attestation protocol does not involve third parties, it is immune to those attacks on peer review systems. Another benefit is that it allows much flexibility for trust management since one may choose his local trust policy independently, without being in consistency with others.

Several studies explicitly propose using remote attestation to support trust establishment, such as a kernel rootkit detector (Seshadri, Luk, Shi, Perrig, Doorn, & Khosla, 2005), remote access mechanism with attestation-based policy enforcement

(Sailer, Jaeger, Zhang, & Doorn, 2004) and secure tunnel endpoints (Goldman, Perez, & Sailer, 2006). Nonetheless, the existing attestation techniques are not matured enough to fully support all types of trust management. Integrity-based attestation is easy to implement, but it does not give sufficient indication on the correctness of a platform or a program's runtime behavior. It is not a safe practice to establish trust only based on integrity. Quality-based attestation provides much more solid ground for trust, at the price of considerable overhead due to complicated measurements. In addition, it remains an open problem how to theoretically prove the attestation objective using the measurement results. Moreover, reputation-based trust scheme cannot be completely replaced by remote attestation. The trust in many applications is relevant to subjective peer evaluation, which cannot be attested at all. Remote attestation may be applied to help those applications to defeat attacks on reputation evaluation.

Trust can also be built upon non-security attributes, such as the dependability of software, which may include availability, reliability, safety, and maintainability, according to (Avizienis, Laprie, Randell, & Landwehr, 2004). It is an interesting challenge to design attestation schemes for testifying those software attributes.

CONCLUSION

Remote attestation is an interactive protocol between a challenger and an attester, whereby the attester vouches for one or multiple attributes of its platform. We have proposed a conceptual model of remote attestation schemes which consists of four components: the root of trust, the attestation objective, the object measurement and the attestation process. Based on the root of trust, attestation schemes can be classified into hardware-based and software-based schemes. From the attestation objective perspective, remote attestation schemes can be divided into integrity-based attestation and quality-based attestation. The former is easy to implement but integrity alone is not sufficient to demonstrate trustworthiness of applications. Quality-based attestation produces a more solid ground for trust management; nonetheless, its overhead is high due to its intrusive measurements. In short, remote attestation facilitates the trust evaluation in distributed systems. It complements the existing reputation-based trust evaluation systems.

ACKNOWLEDGMENT

This research is supported by the Office of Research, Singapore Management University. This research is also partly supported by the following projects: the High-Tech Research and Development Program of China under Grant No. 2007AA010301, the National Basic Research Program of China (973) under Grant No. 2009CB320703, and National Natural Science Foundation of China under Grant No. 60803011.

REFERENCES

AMD. (2003). AMD platform for trustworthy computing. *Microsoft Win-HEC 2003*. Retrieved December 30, 2008, from http://download.microsoft.com/download/5/7/7/577a5684-8a83-43ae-9272-ff260a9c20e2/AMD_WinHEC-2003_whitepaper.doc

AMD. *(2005)*. AMD64 Virtualization Codenamed ``Pacifica'' Technology-Secure Virtual Machine Architecture Reference Manual. *AMD.*

Avizienis, A., Laprie, J.-C., Randell, B., & Landwehr, C. E. (2004). Basic Concepts and Taxonomy of Dependable and Secure Computing. *IEEE Trans. Dependable Sec. Comput.*, *1*(1), 11–33. doi:10.1109/TDSC.2004.2

Blaze, M., Feigenbaum, J., & Lacy, J. (1996). Decentralized Trust Management. In *Proceedings of the IEEE Conference on Security and Privacy,* Oakland, CA.

Blum, M., & Kanna, S. (1989). Designing programs that check their work. In *Proceedings of the twenty-first annual ACM Symposium on Theory of Computing,* Seattle, WA (pp. 86-97).

Brickell, E. F., Camenisch, J., & Chen, L. (2004). Direct anonymous attestation. In *Proceedings of the ACM Conference on Computer and Communications Security* (pp. 132-145).

Chang, H., & Atallah, M. J. (2001). Protecting Software Code by Guards. In . *Proceedings of the Digital Rights Management Workshop, 2320,* 160–175.

Chen, L., Landfermann, R., Löhr, H., Rohe, M., Sadeghi, A.-R., & Stüble, C. (2006). A Protocol for Property-based Attestation. In *Proceedings of the first ACM workshop on Scalable Trusted Computing,* Alexandria, VA, USA.

Ekberg, J.-E., Asokan, N., Kostiainen, K., & Rantala, A. (2008). Scheduling execution of credentials in constrained secure environments. In *Proceedings of the 3rd ACM workshop on Scalable trusted computing.* Folding@home. (2007). *The folding@home project.* Retrieved December 30, 2008, from http://folding.stanford.edu/

Garfinkel, T., Pfaff, B., Chow, J., Rosenblum, M., & Boneh, D. (2003). Terra A Virtual Machine-Based Platform for Trusted Computing. In *Proceedings of the SOSP '03,* Bolton Landing, NY, USA.

GIMPS. (2007). *The great internet mersenne prime search.* Retrieved December 30, 2008, from http://www.mersenne.org/prime.htm

Goldman, K., Perez, R., & Sailer, R. (2006). Linking Remote Attestation to Secure Tunnel Endpoints. In *Proceedings of the First ACM Workshop on Scalable Trusted Computing* (pp. 21-24).

Gu, L., Ding, X., Deng, R. H., Xie, B., & Mei, H. (2008). Remote Attestation on Program Execution. In *Proceedings of the STC '08: the 2008 ACM workshop on Scalable Trusted Computing*.

Gu, L., Ding, X., Deng, R. H., Zou, Y., Xie, B., Shao, W., et al. (2008). Model-Driven Remote Attestation: Attesting Remote System from the Behavioral Aspect. In *Proceedings of the International Symposium on Trusted Computing (TrustCom 08)*.

Haldar, V., Chandra, D., & Franz, M. (2004). Semantic Remote Attestation —A Virtual Machine directed approach to Trusted Computing. In *Proceedings of the Third virtual Machine Research and Technology Symposium (VM '04). USENIX.*

Haldar, V., & Franz, M. (2004). Symmetric behavior-based trust: a new paradigm for internet computing. In *Proceedings of the New Security Paradigms Workshop 2004*, Nova Scotia, Canada (pp. 79-84).

Horne, B. G., Matheson, L. R., Sheehan, C., & Tarjan, R. E. (2001). Dynamic Self-Checking Techniques for Improved Tamper Resistance. In *. Proceedings of the Digital Rights Management Workshop, 2320*, 141–159.

Intel, C. (2006). *LaGrande Technology Preliminary Architecture Specification*. Intel Corporation.

Ioannidis, S., Keromytis, A. D., Bellovin, S. M., & Smith, J. M. (2000). Implementing a Distributed Firewall. In *Proceedings of the SIGSAC: 7th ACM Conference on Computer and Communications Security*.

Jaeger, T., Sailer, R., & Shankar, U. (2006). PRIMA: policy-reduced integrity measurement architecture. In *Proceedings of the eleventh ACM symposium on Access control models and technologies*.

Kennell, R., & Jamieson, L. H. (2003). Establishing the Genuinity of Remote Computer Systems. In *Proceedings of the 12th USENIX Security Symposium*, Washington, D.C., USA.

Korpela, E., Werthimer, D., Anderson, D., Cobb, J., & Lebofsky, M. (2001). SETI@home-Massively Distributed Computing for SETI. *Computing in Science & Engineering, 3*(1), 78–83. doi:10.1109/5992.895191

Kühn, U., Selhorst, M., & Stüble, C. (2007). Realizing property-based attestation and sealing with commonly available hard- and software. In *Proceedings of the STC '07: the 2007 ACM workshop on Scalable trusted computing* (pp. 50-57).

Li, X.-Y., Shen, C.-X., & Zuo, X.-D. (2006). An Efficient Attestation for Trustworthiness of Computing Platform. In *Proceedings of the 2006 International Conference on Intelligent Information Hiding and Multimedia Signal Processing (IIH-MSP '06)*.

McCune, J. M., Parno, B. J., Perrig, A., Reiter, M. K., & Isozaki, H. (2008). Flicker: an execution infrastructure for tcb minimization. In *Proceedings of the 3rd ACM SIGOPS/EuroSys European Conference on Computer Systems 2008*.

Molnar, D. (2000). *The SETI@Home Problem*. Retrieved December 30, 2008, from http://www.acm.org/crossroads/columns/onpatrol/september2000.html

Petroni, N. L., Jr., Fraser, T., Molina, J., & Arbaugh, W. A. (2004). Copilot - a coprocessor-based kernel runtime integrity monitor. In *Proceedings of the 13th conference on USENIX Security Symposium - Volume 13*.

Poritz, J., Schunter, M., Herreweghen, E. V., & Waidner, M. (2004). *Property attestation — scalable and privacy-friendly security assessment of peer computers* (IBM Research Report RZ 3548).

Poritz, J. A. (2006). Trust[ed | in] computing, signed code and the heat death of the internet. In *Proceedings of the 2006 ACM symposium on Applied computing*, Dijon, France.

Sadegh, A.-R., & Stüble, C. (2004). Property-based attestation for computing platforms: caring about properties, not mechanisms. In *Proceedings of the 2004 workshop on New security paradigms.*

Sailer, R., Jaeger, T., Zhang, X., & Doorn, L. v. (2004). Attestation-based policy enforcement for remote access. In *Proceedings of the 11th ACM Conference on Computer and Communications Security.*

Sailer, R., Zhang, X., Jaeger, T., & Doorn, L. v. (2004). Design and Implementation of a TCG-based Integrity Measurement Architecture. In *Proceedings of the 13th USENIX Security Symposium,* San Diego, CA, USA.

Seshadri, A., Luk, M., Perrig, A., van Doorn, L., & Khosla, P. (2006). SCUBA: Secure Code Update By Attestation in Sensor Networks. In *Proceedings of the ACM Workshop on Wireless Security (WiSe 2006).*

Seshadri, A., Luk, M., Shi, E., Perrig, A., Doorn, L. v., & Khosla, P. (2005, October 23-26). Pioneer: Verifying Code Integrity and Enforcing Untampered Code Execution on Legacy Systems. In *Proceedings of the SOSP '05*, Brighton, United Kingdom.

Seshadri, A., Perrig, A., Doorn, L. v., & Khosla, P. (2004). SWATT: softWare-based attestation for embedded devices. In *Proceedings of the IEEE Symposium on Security and Privacy.* SETI@ Home. (2007). *The search for extraterrestrial intelligence project.* Retrieved December 30, 2008, from http://setiathome.berkeley.edu

Shaneck, M., Mahadevan, K., Kher, V., & Kim, Y. (2005). Remote Software-based Attestation for Wireless Sensors. In *Proceedings of the Security and privacy in ad-hoc and sensor networks (Second European workshop, ESAS 2005),* Visegrad, Hungary.

Shankar, U., Jaeger, T., & Sailer, R. (2006). Toward Automated Information-Flow Integrity Verification for Security-Critical Applications. In *Proceedings of the Network and Distributed System Security Symposium (NDSS).*

Shi, E., Perrig, A., & Doorn, L. V. (2005). BIND: A Fine-Grained Attestation Service for Secure Distributed Systems. In *Proceedings of the 2005 IEEE Symposium on Security and Privacy (S&P '05).*

TCG. (2003). *Trusted Computing Group.* Retrieved December 30, 2008, from http://www.trustedcomputinggroup.org

Trusted Computing Group. (2006). *Trusted Platform Module (TPM) Main Specification. Version 1.2, Revision 103.* Retrieved December 30, 2008, from http://www.trustedcomputinggroup.org

Wasserman, H., & Blum, M. (1997). Software Reliability via Run-Time Result-Checking. *JACM . Journal of the ACM*, 44.

Wurster, G., van Oorschot, P. C., & Somayaji, A. (2005). A Generic Attack on Checksumming-Based Software Tamper Resistance. In *Proceedings of the IEEE Symposium on Security and Privacy* (pp. 127-138).

Chapter 2
Scaling Concepts between Trust and Enforcement

Andreas U. Schmidt
CREATE-NET Research Centre, Italy

Andreas Leicher
Johann Wolfgang Goethe-Universität, Germany

Inhyok Cha
InterDigital Communications, USA

ABSTRACT

Enforcement and trust are opposite concepts in information security. This chapter reflects on the paradigm shift from traditional concepts of access control and policy enforcement toward de-centralised methods for establishing trust between loosely connected entities. By delegating parts of enforcement tasks to trusted elements dispersed in a system, the system can establish transitive trust relationships. This is the most advanced evolution of the organisational method of separation of duties within IT security. The technological basis for trust in systems – trusted computing platforms – is described on conceptual levels allowing comparison with other top-level security concepts and mapping to application domains. Important applications in modern information systems and networks are exhibited.

INTRODUCTION

One of the major elements of the success of a technology is the adoption and integration by the target group. Therefore, the target group has to put *trust*, defined as the confidence that a trustor can rely on, in the technology. The adopter can, therefore, allow certain vulnerability on his or her own part, weighing security against cost. Thus, trust is a process that needs to be understood, and it is an issue that

needs to be explored through collaboration from social and technical perspectives as proposed by Cofta (2007).

In IT-Security as an applied science, the last four decades of research have been centred on *enforcement* as a base concept. On a systemic level, enforcement is the only way to establish security properties with certainty, e.g., carry out formal security proofs, i.e., to exclude every risk. But this also rules out trust and thus has disadvantages in situations where global enforcement is not completely possible. Even if it is possible, it may not be desir-

DOI: 10.4018/978-1-61520-682-7.ch002

able universally due to cost of implementation. On the other hand, trust and its mirror concept of risk inherently include the notion of the cost, since risks are quantified using expected costs of not meeting them. The growing trend toward de-centralised open systems produces numerous situations in which enforcement, by practical necessity, has to be complemented by controlled risk, that is, trust. This chapter emphasises the contradistinction between trust and enforcement with the aim to come to a useful synthesis of both – *scalability of trust in systems*.

In the next part of this chapter, notions of trust are reviewed and integrated into a synthetic definition of trust in technical systems, i.e., the trustworthiness of a machine processing information and interacting with its surrounding, which can be effective in applications. This is contrasted with traditional notions of enforcement. Then, enforcement and trust technologies are circumscribed systematically on a high level to make the corresponding concepts comparable. Emphasis is on the means to establish trust in systems, based on trusted computing technologies, since those are relatively young. Some concrete details of the life and operational cycles of trusted systems are given. We then show some recent applications exhibiting how trust and enforcement can go hand-in-hand using de-centralisation and separation of duties as core paradigms. Furthermore, future research directions in scalable trust are described. They emerge from the evolution of communication networks and the Internet, where nodes become ever more heterogeneous and connections more short-lived, and ephemeral. Important new insights may also emerge from economics, sociology, psychology, and theories of complex systems that are self-organizing and/or evolutionary.

BACKGROUND

According to Dwyer & Cofta (2008), the socio-cognitive model of trust holds that a trustor makes a decision based on an assessment of cues of evidence about a specific situation and a trustee. A more formal definition is given by Gambretta (1988), and Jøsang, Gray & Kinateder (2003) re-cite it as follows: "trust (or, symmetrically, distrust) is a particular level of the subjective probability with which an agent will perform a particular action, both before (the trustor) can monitor such action (or independently of his capacity of ever to be able to monitor it) and in a context in which it affects (the trustor's) own action" (p. 213). Trust, as the underlying concept for each economic process needs a good understanding before it can be formalised within a specific model and applied to technology. An important requisite for trust is a risk, or having something invested, as Gambetta (1988) remarks. Castelfranchi and Falcone (1998) extend the definition of Gambretta (1988) to include the notion of *competence* along with *predictability*. In all these definitions, trust is considered as a subjective notion, that is, it is not *per se* linked to empirical observation of the trustees' behaviour. Grandison and Sloman (2000) stress the aspect of *contextuality* of trust, meaning that the expectable actions of the trustor are conditioned by the world state in which they occur. This is also emphasised in the language of information systems by Yahalom, Klein & Beth (1993).

The need to use the concept of trust only arises in a risky situation. The exact relation between trust and risk can be complex (Deutsch, 1958; Mayer, Davis & Schoorman, 1995). Trust in technical systems and trust building mechanisms between them have long been studied and are varied (Aberer & Despotovic, 2001; Blaze, Feigenbaum & Lacey, 1996). So called *trust metrics* (Toone, Gertz & Devanbu, 2003; Kamvar, Schlosser & Garcia-Molina, 2003) are only an intermediate step on the way of constructing this relationship, since they do not yield statistical statements on observable system behaviour. Steps toward a statistical, and, therefore, empirical, description of trust are reputation systems, such as TNA-SL of Jøsang, Hayward & Pope (2006), which use past measured behaviour to feed subjective logic at the trustor's part. Reputation systems provide, to some extent and in a special case, the hitherto weak connection of trust to past observation. Reputation systems, according to Resnick *et al.* (2000) "seek to establish the shadow of the future [the expectation of reciprocity or retaliation in future interactions, cf. Axelrod (1984)] to each transaction by creating an expectation that other people will look back on it" (p. 45). That observational part of building trust is also the weakest point of reputation systems. The links between observations on trustees and prediction of their behaviour may be broken by changes of trustees' identities. In fact, the best known individual attack on reputation systems uses Sybils to obtain a disproportionately large influence (Douceur, 2002). Friedman & Resnick (2001) point to the general problem of "cheapness" of pseudonyms in marketplaces and reputation systems, since with name changes dishonest players easily shed negative reputation.

As we see, there are various meanings to trust between entities, but only a few can be applied without much distortion to the relations between technical systems. In synthesis of the above, we propose to apply the following consistent **operational interpretation of trust**, or short, **operational trust**, to the relations and interactions between technical systems and between technical systems and human beings:

An entity can be trusted if it predictably and observably behaves in the expected manner for the intended purpose.

This is essentially also a synthesis of the meanings that for instance the standardisation organisations Trusted Computing Group (TCG) and the International Standardisation Organisation (ISO) attribute to trust, cf. Pearson (2002b). The operational interpretation, which is actually rooted in physicists' prevalent understanding of

quantum systems (Haag 1992; Lamb, 1969 & 2001), has three salient features:

- **Predictability** designates a priori knowledge about a system that can be used to a) assess the risk incurred in interacting with that system, and b) allow to obtain knowledge about the system during the interaction by reasoning on observations.
- **Observability** specifies the means by, and extent to which knowledge about a system can be gained in interactions. It is closely linked to predictability, in that observations, together with predictions, yield further knowledge on a system's state, properties, and, by that, its future behaviour.
- **Contextuality** designates information delineating the scope of interactions with the system in which predictions hold and observations can be made.

Formally, all three kinds of information can be expressed in terms of logical predicates and clauses. But their interpretation is essentially *statistical*. This provides the link to the interpretation of trust as effectively mitigated risk. The three properties allow, at least in principle, a mapping between the socio-economic concept of trust and technical concepts. Taken together, they allow an **assessment of the trustworthiness** of an entity, or reciprocally, the risk it poses to a trustor.

The analogy to physics may seem diagonal, but is conceptually fruitful. For instance, the relation of statistical interpretation to economic risk entails the question of an analogous interpretation of the system-apparatus interaction in measurements. It follows that the notion of contextuality, when applied to the risk incurred, needs to take into account both the cost of failure of the system to behave properly and the cost of observing that. That is, risk and trust will need to rely on a comprehensive cost-benefit analysis including the measures for establishment of trust. We conclude that if the efforts to produce and verify the evidence that can attest to the system's trustworthiness are too great, then even if it is trustworthy in terms of the bare risk incurred in operating the system, it would be impossible for an observer to actually know that. Therefore, the system cannot be trusted operationally. The reader might feel the resemblance to Heisenberg's uncertainty relation. Also, like experimental settings and apparatus' change, evaluations of operational trust are bound to change as open systems and means to monitor them evolve.

In contradistinction to the observational perspective embodied in our definition of trust, information security takes an active stance with regard to the achievement of *protection goals* (classically confidentiality, integrity and availability of data) within a global information system. It rules out threats by trying to absolutely assure specific system behaviour to a relying party, that is, by **enforcing** it. The main results of the enforcement approach are twofold. In the interaction between entities, it led to the development of specific *protocols* that systems have to follow to provably reach the desired protection goals. Prime examples are non-repudiation and fair exchange. Enforcement of security by protocols has also shown some principal roadblocks, for instance the impossibility for two parties to perform a fair exchange of an information item without a trusted third party (TTP), as proven by Pagnia, Vogt & Gärtner (2003). The second aspect is the enforcement of system behaviour by *policies*. A policy, according to Dulay, Lupu, Sloman & Damianou (2002) is a "rule governing the choices in behaviour of a managed system" (p. 14). It requires monitoring the system's dynamics and continuous matching to the rules set forth in the policies. According to application context, policies come in many variants and have given rise to many ramifications of research directions, most notably:

- *Access Control* focusing on policies for controlling access to documents and resources, in particular authorisation

constraints, contextual constraints, and delegation rules.

- *Policy-Based Management* that gives declarative definitions of rules constraining system behaviour. The main advantage is dynamisation of policies, i.e., the possibility to manage them during system operation.

- *Privacy* focuses on the handling of information relating to individual persons such as restricting the communication of, and access to, personally identifiable information based on, e.g., Data Protection regulations.

- *Enterprise Rights Management* (*ERM*) focuses on the distribution of sensitive information within and between cooperating organisations.

- *Digital Rights Management* (*DRM*) focuses on the policies applying to the distribution of copyrighted material and in particular media, or in general, digital goods (Becker, Buhse, Günnewig, & Rump, 2003; Schmidt 2008). DRM and ERM are subsumed under the term *Information Rights Management (IRM)*.

It is obvious that in application to real-world systems – which are the empirical basis of computer science, both enforcement and trust stand on feet of clay. In the lack of methods to establish operational trust in distributed systems (Blaze, Feigenbaum & Lacey, 1996) refer to trust as a systematic framework for security provided by specific network services: "It is our thesis that a coherent intellectual framework is needed for the study of security policies, security credentials, and trust relationships. We refer collectively to these components of network services as the *trust management problem*" (p. 164). Trust management systems show only limited trust in the operational sense defined above. In particular, it is difficult to obtain observations on behaviour after authorisation decisions are made by a PDP. Authorisation decisions cannot be revoked or modified, and thus, one may say that trust management systems have a monotonically increasing measure of trust[1], since with every positive decision, a system obtains more access rights. Negative decisions, on the other hand, cannot be "held against" a system in future policy decisions, since policy evaluation is independent in each case. Such an approach, with limited operational trust in the components of a distributed system, does not allow solid assessment of the risk mitigation qualities of security measures therein, let alone a quantitative one. However, it has been acknowledged that operational trust is desirable in highly distributed environments such as grid computing. Azzedin & Maheswaran (2002) start from enforcement approaches which are "conservative and implement techniques such as sandboxing, encryption, and other access control mechanisms on all elements of the Grid. However, the overhead caused by such a design may negate the advantages of Grid computing" (p. 452), and examine "a model for incorporating trust into Grid systems" (p. 452), in which the notion of behavioral trust based on observations is similar to ours. Xiong & Liu (2004) describe PeerTrust, a system to calculate trust values from feedback received from peers in online communities.

We conclude that, despite the mentioned efforts to combine trust and "conservative" security technology, there is still a conceptual and technological gap between trust and enforcement. It is mainly caused by the lack of technical means to establish operational trust in systems – while theoretical foundations on both sides, policy enforcement and computational approaches to trust, are strong. This shortcoming has become more obvious with growing heterogeneity of interconnected systems beyond client-server relationships. In such environments, and given the state-of-the-art of security technology, enforcement and operational trust cannot easily be combined, since there is no harmonised infrastructure for that. Systems lack a) ubiquitous technical means to establish operational

trust, b) overarching infrastructures for enforcement, and c) means to convey information on trustworthiness, and applicable security levels to external entities. Only these basic building blocks can enable a dynamical balancing of trust and enforcement reflecting real-world requirements, that is, *scalable trust in systems*.

Enforcement Technology

Information systems and technology for the enforcement of policies have come a long way from simple models for control of access to data (La Padula & Bell, 1973; Bell 2005) to means to implement and manage complex, and natural-language security requirements in distributed systems. This also goes beyond the well-known security paradigms in client-server relationships. The main thrust in applied research is the implementation of policies on inter-organisational data exchange using formal methods and IRM. Figure 1 shows a very simplified architecture for this.

In the generation of policies enforceable by an IRM system, three levels of formality can be distinguished: i) a **business level policy** – a human-readable representation of the policy which addresses the risks and threats related to exposing data outside the organisation; ii) a **formal high-level policy** – a representation of the agreement using a formal language, which is suitable for logical analysis and reasoning about the agreement; and iii) an **enforceable (or operational) policy** – a representation of the policy in an executable policy language, which enforces data access and usage according to the policy clauses.

A **Policy Authoring** tool is a (often graphical, to make complexity manageable for human policy authors) tool to support the drafting of the business level policy, and to transform the business level representation into the formal one. It rests fundamentally on an **ontology** for the domain that is covered by use cases and business level policies. One of the most popular ontology editors is the

Figure 1. Policy systems range from informal requirements to technical enforcement

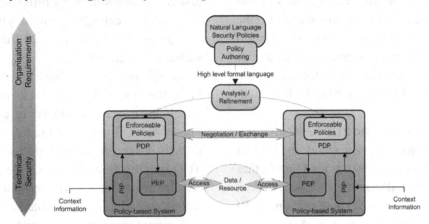

open source system Protégé (2009) of Stanford University. It supports, in particular, Web ontology languages such as OWL (2004).

There are two recent, relevant approaches for the translation of business-level policies into formal languages. The project COSoDIS (2009), proposes to write contracts directly in a formal specification language called *CL*. The modelling of natural English-based policy clauses of a contract into CL is done based on *patterns* (Gamma, Helm, Johnson & Vlissides, 1995; Workflow Patterns, 2007). Then, a translation function is defined that maps the contract into a variant of the *mu-calculus* (Emerson, 1996), after which formal reasoning can be applied by way of the NuSMV model checking tool (Cimatti *et al.*, 2002). The second approach is based on the authorisation language SecPAL of Becker, Fournet & Gordon (2007), in which a grammar of the controlled language of policy clauses is created and then translated into the formal language using parsing and compiling tools.

As policy authoring is mainly a human effort, only supported by tools for partial automation, the outcome is prone to inconsistencies and gaps. The high-level formal policies are, therefore, inspected in a process called **policy analysis** to ascertain that they satisfy the desired properties, in particular protection goals on data and resources. Such is commonly done by model checking tools work-

ing on state machines and theorem provers. This area of research is vast; we name only the Athena security protocol analysis tool of Song, Berezin & Perrig (2001) and Zhang, Ryan, & Guelev (2005) as well-known examples (not claiming representativeness or completeness). Finally, a complete set of high-level policies is translated into an enforceable language in an automated process called **refinement** (Gorrieri, Rensink & Zamboni, 2001; Bandara, Lupu, Moffett & Russo, 2004).

Operational policies are distributed to the systems which are consuming data or accessing resources. The common enforcement architecture deployed on such systems generically consists of a **Policy Decision Point (PDP)** and a **Policy Enforcement Point (PEP)**. The main reference for this model is the COPS architecture (Boyle, Cohen, Herzog, Rajan & Sastry, 2000; cf. also Law & Saxena, 2003). On a request from an application to access a resource which underlies policy control, the PDP evaluates the *policy conditions* against locally available data. As a relatively recent development, PDPs may exchange, retrieve, or negotiate policies (Ajayi, Sinnott & Stell, 2008). This may happen on a client-server or peer-to-peer basis.

The decision is passed to the PEP, along with obligations, i.e., those conditions or actions that must be fulfilled by either the users or the system after the decision (Bettini, Jajodia, Wang & Wijesekera, 2002). The PEP exerts control over the resource, for instance by performing an authorized retrieval from a protected external provider, and/or by releasing encryption secrets to the consuming application. The PEP also controls the fulfilment of obligations.

To evaluate policies, the PDP needs information about the requesting subject, i.e., the context in which the access request is made and other (internal and external) parameters that are taken into account. The **Policy Information Point (PIP)** component performs this function. A real-world example of particular importance is the location of a mobile device.

Trust Technology

A system needs certain security-relevant elements and capabilities so that it can be operationally trusted (Rand Corporation, 1970). The ideas to endow systems with trust are not new, and emerged in the context of military applications (Department of Defense, 1985). This context can be viewed as paradigmatic for operational trust – they need to securely operate in situations where any kind of external enforcement may fail and a fallback to inherently trustworthy functionality is a core requirement. Accordingly, the US Department of Defense (1985) differentiates trusted systems into systems and parts of a system of various security levels.

The building blocks of a trusted system establish its trust boundary, and sometimes provide methods to extend it, and to convey trust to an outside entity by making its behaviour and operation predictable and observable to a certain extent. The key techniques in this section comprise (hardware) *security anchors, Roots of Trust, Trusted (Sub-) systems* and *ownership, secure storage and paths*, authorisation, *authenticated and secure boot* processes, and *remote attestation*. By combination of these methods, systems can be constructed which combine characteristics of trust

and enforcement in many different ways. Thus, they enable a scaling of technology between these two poles, that is, operational trust, and local/global enforcement.

In this part of the chapter, we describe the basic functional building blocks of technology, which have been developed to establish trust into systems. The bulk of the terms used here is directly taken, or slightly abstracted, from the TCG specifications. However, we also make an attempt to provide a unified terminology for trust technology, which also takes literature background and current research into account.

Trusted Systems

A **hardware security anchor** is the key to the protection of the system behaviour. This is a part of the system which is protected against unauthorized access by hardware measures known to be secure enough for the intended purpose to effectively mitigate risks of attacks against it. It holds, in particular, the **Root of Trust (RoT)** for its secure operation. The RoT is an abstract system element which enables

a) Securing the internal system operation, and

b) Exposing properties and/or the identity (individually or as a member of a group such as make and model) of the system to external entities in a secure and authentic way.

Genuinely, a system can contain more than one RoT for distinct purposes. Some of them are introduced below. Typical examples for RoTs are asymmetric key pairs together with digital certificates of a trusted third party for them. Also, the symmetric secrets of Subscriber Identification Module (SIM) cards in cellular networks may be viewed as RoTs for the closed, trusted system embodied by the SIM card.

Secondly, functional building blocks in a system that are assumed to be trusted, i.e., to behave in a well-defined manner for the intended purpose, form the **Trusted Computing Base (TCB)** of the system. The TCB comprises such components of a system which cannot be examined for their operational trust properties when the system is deployed in the field and during operation, but only by out-of-band processes like compliance and conformance testing, and certification. This kind of certification is usually carried out by an independent evaluator, for instance on behalf of the manufacturer of a certain technical element of the TCB or the TCB as a whole, according to established security evaluation standards such as Common Criteria (2009). For such a certification to be useful, the TCB, respectively, its elements need to be endowed with information identifying them as such certified pieces of technology.

A system equipped with defined security anchor, RoTs, and TCB is called a **Trusted System (TS)**[2]. This is a slight refinement of the common notion of Trusted Platforms which, according to Pearson (2002a), is "a computing platform which has a trusted component, probably in the form of built-in hardware which it uses to create a foundation of trust for software processes", cf. Mitchell (2005). When one or more trusted systems reside within a TS, they are called Trusted Subsystems (TSS). Examples comprise virtual execution environments on a Personal Computer platform which inherit a certain trustworthiness from the hardware Trusted Platform Module (TPM, TCG 2007a) of the host. Another example is the specification of a trusted engine, together with its Trusted Computing Base, in the TCG Mobile Phone Working Group (MPWG) specifications (TCG 2008a, b). In the following, 'TS' is interchangeably used as a shorthand for 'TS or TSS' where not explicitly stated otherwise.

Below, various capabilities, processes, and architectural elements, summarised under the term **trusted resources (TRs)**, of TS are described. Two kinds of TRs must be generally distinguished: First, TRs which belong to the TCB, and second, TRs which are outside the TCB. Genuine examples

for the latter are trusted parts of the operating system, and trusted applications which build on the TCB by using its capabilities. While assertions about the trustworthiness of the TR in the TCB depend on the defined security of the TCB, the trustworthiness of the other TRs can, at most, be derived from that of the TCB. In such a case, the TCB must provide certain internal TRs that allow extension of the **trust boundary**, i.e., the totality of components of a TS that are considered trustworthy in a given context, to the TRs outside the TCB, for instance authenticated or secure boot as described below. TRs within the TCB often share the same hardware protection with the RoT, for instance, reside on the same tamper-resistant chip. TRs outside the TCB may be realised as logical units in software. Note that the trust boundaries, especially involving TRs that are outside of the TCB, may be ephemeral. They may exist for some time for certain purposes, and then may cease to exist afterwards.

A general model process to extend the trust boundary beyond the TCB is **verification**. This is itself a TR implementing the verification process. We call this process and corresponding TR a **verification entity**, or **verifier**, to distinguish it from the process of **validation** of a TS by an *external* entity, the **validator**[3]. Verification, since it is a process to include a new component in the trust boundary, can come in essentially two flavours. First, and as a simplest option, the verifier **measures** a new component at the time of its initialisation. That is, the component, its status and configuration are uniquely identified. The result of this measurement is then stored. As an extension of this, the verifier can compare the measurements with **reference values** and decide whether or not to extend the trust boundary. That is, the verifier makes and enforces a policy decision. From the operational viewpoint, verification corresponds to predictability of the TS, as it can be assumed to be in a certain, pre-defined state after the verification process is completed. Validation, on the other hand, makes this property observable and therefore trustworthy. It means that a **reporting entity** transfers the results of verification to another party. The third, intermediate step performed by the reporting entity is that of **attestation**. Attestation is a logical consequence of verification and a logical precondition for validation. It is the process of vouching for the accuracy of measurement information, such that a relying party – the validator – can use it to decide whether it trusts the remote TS. For this, the measurement information must be bound to the specific TS and then be transmitted in a way that protects its authenticity. Verification, attestation, and validation are core concepts for operational trust which are tied to the lifecycle of a TS. This is detailed below.

A TS is **owned** by an entity (a person or other technical system) who or which is authorised to access certain TRs within the trust boundary, for instance the RoT. Ownership may implicitly be realised by physical possession of the TS, respectively, the platform containing it, or explicitly, for instance, by authentication of the owner through certain credentials. In the context of the TCG TPM specifications, the provisioning of such authentication data is called **take ownership** (TCG 2007a). An owner interacting directly with a TS is called **local owner**, whereas an owner whose communication with the TS is mediated in any way, e.g., through a communication network, is called a **remote owner**. When more than one TSS is contained in a TS, each may or may not have a different owner.

Figure 2 shows the separation of computing domains of TSS according to the TCG MPWG architecture (TCG 2008b). A TSS there consists of a dedicated Mobile Trusted Module (MTM), the hardware security anchor of MPWG specifications containing the mentioned RoTs, TRs (trusted resources and services in MPWG parlance), and normal software services and components outside the trust boundary. The so called **trusted engine** in which all these reside is a secure computing environment, based on the RoTs providing, in particular, separation and controlled communication between different TSS. TSS can share TRs and even functions of MTMs with other TSS, conditioned by inter-domain validation and authorisation. Trusted engines, but also some of the MTMs, can be realised in software as long as at least one hardware MTM is present from which the RoTs of the soft ones are derived. Each TSS can be under the control of a local or remote stakeholder viz. owner. In the lifecycle of a mobile device, not all stakeholders' TSS might be present. It is, therefore, necessary to define a process by which a (remote) stakeholder initialise the creation of a new TSS and take ownership of it. A variant of such a **remote take ownership** procedure is described below.

Trusted Functional Building Blocks

Special TRs of a TS are **cryptographic capabilities** which are usually within the TCB and may include one or more of the following:

- Symmetric and asymmetric encryption
- Hash value generation and verification
- Random number generation, e.g., with physical entropy sources
- Digital signature creation and verification

A TS may provide **secure storage**, i.e., places where, and methods by which data are protected from unauthorized access. For instance, cryptographic key material may only be used by a TS' owner. A TS may have secure storage as a TR and for use by other TR within the TCB. As storage space there is commonly limited, general methods to extend secure storage have been envisaged, e.g., within the TCG standards (TCG 2007a). The secure storage within the TCB contains a **RoT for Storage (RTS)** for that, e.g., a cryptographic key. The RTS is then used to protect data outside the TCB, e.g., by encrypting them. A TS often has **authorisation** functionality incorporated to protect access to TRs. TPM authorisation is operated

Figure 2. Domain separation of trusted subsystems according to MPWG

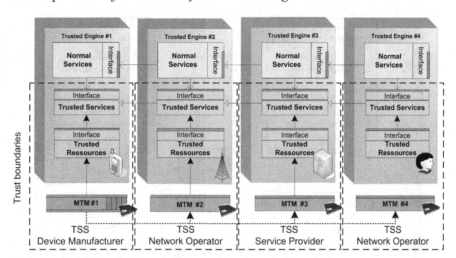

by storing 160 Bit secrets, e.g., password digests, within the hardware protected storage inside the TCB, namely the TPM chip. Similar concepts and possible application scenarios are discussed in the requirements of the Open Mobile Trusted Platform (OMTP), Advanced Trusted Environment TR1 (OMTP, 2009).

Concepts between Trust and Enforcement

With the novel technologies of Trusted Computing, architectures of networked systems can be envisaged, in which trust in nodes and terminals is scalable to a large extent. In this section, we develop a general model for interconnected TS, highlighting the main entities for trust establishment and the interactions between them.

Since trust involves the willingness to accept a certain level of risk, it is an essential ability to detect changes in the trustworthiness of a system. This requirement emerges immediately, if we take the temporal axis into account for the notion of operational trust. Due to the dynamic nature of trust relationships, such changes can lead to distrust in a system. Enforcement techniques can then be applied to behave accordingly, e.g. restrict access to the TS, or communication by the TS. Also,

enforced changes of the TS could be envisaged, to re-establish a trustworthy state of it.

With the concepts presented below, a natural bridge between operational trust and enforcement emerges. Simply put, a relying party can trust a TS, in the operational sense, if the TS can provide information and evidence that its predicted, observable behaviour in the future will be the desired one. In turn, this is quite naturally established by local enforcement of certain operational policies on the part of the TS, and true reporting of its operation. Therefore, trust can be established by providing trustworthy information about enforcement.

The following subsection outlines how trust in technical systems is established in organisational contexts. Then we introduce the most important building blocks of *local state verification*, and *external state validation* of a TS. Finally, we show how these trust establishment methods connect to enforcement methods.

Establishment of Trust

Between trust and enforcement, the main bridging concept is separation of duties (Botha, R. A. and Eloff, J. H. P., 2001). It is genuinely thought of as a method to support certain protection goals in

Figure 3. Trust between platforms is mediated by organisational and technical methods

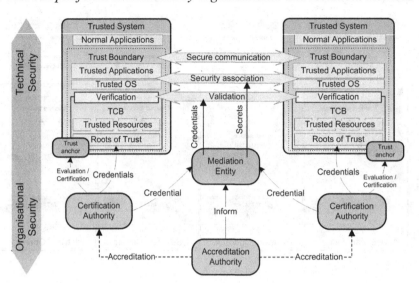

distributed systems, for instance privacy in client-server relations. A server may issue policies to a client who in turn enforces them using private local information, as described above. That is, separation of duties is normally understood as referring to duties on *enforcement*. But there is a natural relationship to trust. The relying party can delegate the enforcement to the other system only if it is operationally trustworthy. The establishment of operational trust between TS rests on the controlled exchange of information to enable observability and the pre-establishment of predictability. The latter can only be done outside of the TS.

Figure 3 shows a generic model exhibiting the role of external entities providing organisational assurance to TS. The security properties of a TS are rooted in the hardware trust anchor and the RoTs. These technical components cannot be examined while the system is deployed and operational. Therefore, they undergo a security evaluation during design and development. This is performed by an independent authority which, upon successful evaluation, issues certificates of security to the manufacturer of the security critical components. Apart from RoTs and trust anchor, this process may also comprise other TRs

in the TCB, and involve different **certification authorities**. To ensure the homogeneous quality of evaluation processes and the different certification authorities, they are in turn assessed and certified by **accreditation authorities**, which may, for instance, be private entities with state permits, or para-statal entities. The accreditation authorities can also serve to provide bridging information between certification authorities.

Certification authorities or technical entities informed by them, issue credentials to TS which are used by the TRs. These credentials are certificates in the sense that they are verifiable in their integrity and provenance. A prime example is the **Endorsement Key (EK) certificate** issued to the TPM's main RoT (the EK) by its manufacturer, as well as the *Platform Certificate* and other components' certificates. These credentials and secrets derived from them by cryptographic means, are then also used in the interaction with external entities, in particular another TS. First, validation needs authentication and in many cases also confidentiality. Furthermore, secrets and credentials with trust inherited from the TS credentials are essential for operating system and trusted applications to build security associations, that is, channels which provide authentication, confidentiality, and integrity of communication. On top of security associations, applications within the extended trust boundary can build secure communication channels with well defined operational trust properties.

Trust establishment can hardly be effective without a mediator facilitating the various interactions just sketched. One key task of a **mediation entity** is to issue fundamental statements about the trustworthiness of a TS to another TS or relying party. Most importantly, the mediator identifies the TCB (or selected elements, e.g., the trust anchor) as such, trusted and certified, component. To this end, the mediation entity needs to know the certificates issued by the certification entities, verify them when it receives it from a TS, and issue an according assurance statement to a relying party. It should be noted that validation is impossible without a mediator, if not all TS know the credentials of all other TS. Thus, mediation is, in fact, fundamental for validation. The best-known example for a mediator is the **Privacy Certification Authority (PCA)** defined in TCG standards, and described below in more detail. As we have seen, the role of a mediator between TS can extend further than protecting the TS privacy in validation processes. For instance, a mediator can also facilitate subsequent security association and secure communication, similarly to a CA in Public Key Infrastructures (PKI).

Though the model described above is generic and complete, this kind of trust provisioning infrastructure is not yet established in practice. Next, we exhibit main building blocks for trust establishment.

Verification

Verification is, in essence, a recording and controlling of state changes of a TS to the desired granularity. As such, it must be tightly bound to the operational cycle of the platform on which a TS resides, from initialisation to shutdown. There-fore, practical verification methods are mostly integrated with the boot process and operational cycle of platforms.

One general method for the internal verification of a TS is **authenticated boot**, and uses capabilities of the TCB to assess the trustworthiness of loaded or started software or hardware components at the time the TS is initialised, e.g., on power on. Authenticated boot is realised by starting certain functions of the RoT and the TCB before other parts of the TS. These parts operate as a **RoT for Measurement (RTM)**. This means that components that are started or loaded later on, are **measured**, i.e., they, and their status and configuration after start are uniquely identified, e.g., by forming cryptographic digest values over a (binary) representation of hardware component's embedded code and loaded programs. According to the specific requirements, the measurement values may be stored in secure storage. Together with data necessary to retrace the system state from them, e.g., software names and versions, they form the **Stored Measurement Log (SML)** of the TS. On PC platforms, authenticated boot may include all components from the BIOS to the Operating System (OS) loader and the OS itself. One of the first proposals for authenticated boot procedures was the AEGIS system of Arbaugh, Farber & Smith (1997).

The most important existing realisation of authenticated boot is the one specified by the TCG. The system state is measured by a reporting process, with the TPM as central authority, receiving measurement values and calculating a unique representation of the state using hash values. For this, the TPM has several protected **Platform Configuration Registers (PCRs)**. Beginning with the system initialisation at power-up, for each loaded or started component a measurement value, e.g., a hash value over the BIOS, is reported to the TPM and stored securely in the SML, using the RTM. Concurrently, the active PCR is updated by an extend procedure. This operation appends the measurement value to the

Figure 4. Secure boot by local verification

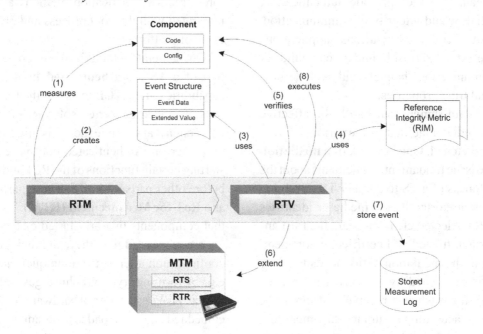

current PCR value, calculates a digest value over these data, and stores it back in the PCR. In this way, it is said that a transitive chain of trust is built containing all started and loaded components. As a single PCR stores only one value, it can only provide "footprint-like" integrity validation data. This value allows a validator to verify this chain of trust by recalculating this footprint, only in conjunction with the SML.

Secure boot is an extension of authenticated boot. It is of particular importance for devices like set-top boxes or mobile handsets that necessarily have some stand-alone and offline functional requirements. The common characteristic of devices equipped with secure boot is that they are required to operate in a trustworthy set of states when they are not able to communicate assertions on their trustworthiness to the exterior, e.g. before network access. In secure boot, the TS is equipped with a **local verifier** (a verification entity) and **local enforcer** supervising the boot process, which establishes the combination of a Policy Enforcement Point (PEP) and Policy Decision Point (PDP) to control the secure boot process. The local verifier

compares measurement values of newly loaded or started components with **Reference Integrity Measurement (RIM)** values which reside in the TCB, or are protected within the TS by a TR, e.g., they are located in protected storage space, and decide whether they are loaded, resp. started, or not. Thus, the system is ensured to boot into a defined, trustworthy state.

An embodiment of secure boot is described by the TCG MPWG (TCG 2008b). Initially, the RTM measures a software component (1) and creates a so-called **Event Structure** (2). An Event Structure contains an extend value, i.e., the actual result of a digest operation on the component's code and extend data. As indicated in Figure 4, the RTM assigns the verification task to the **RoT for Verification (RTV)**. Then the RTV uses the Event Structure (3) with the taken measurements (4) and verifies it against a set of available RIM (5). If the verification is accepted, the RTV extends the data to a dedicated PCR (6) and stores the Event Structure in the Stored Measurement Log (SML) (7). The SML contains the Event Structures for all measurements in the TPM and can be stored in any non-volatile storage, e.g., hard disk. Finally, the RTV executes the software component (8). The **RoT for Reporting (RTR)** is a dedicated secure element for a later validation. In the framework of policy enforcement, the RTM corresponds to a PIP which gathers information about the new component which lies yet outside the trust boundary. The RTV is a PDE/PEP combination. It is, therefore, responsible for evaluation of policies by matching measurements to RIMs, to allow or disallow component execution, and ultimately to make the new system state attestable by the RTR by storing it protected inside the TCB.

It is important to note a dual aspect of RIMs. On the one hand, they serve the local verification in a secure boot process. For that, they are complemented by a RIM provisioning infrastructure (TCG 2008b) that allows, for instance, updates of measured components, by provisioning of new RIMs to the TS. For an external entity to validate a TS after secure boot, it needs to compare the received event structure with stored RIMs *and* to verify the associated RIM certificates. Thus, RIMs and RIM certificates play an important role not only in verification, but also in validation.

Freshness of the attestation information is a key issue for validation (Guttman, et al. 2008). This necessitates extending the verification process from boot to operation time of the TS, which is a technically hard task in complex open systems. Such *run-time attestation*[4] was first incorporated in IBM's Integrity measurement Architecture (IMA, see Sailer, Zhang, Jaeger & van Doorn, L 2004). BIND (Shi, Perrig, van Doorn, 2005) is a method for fine-grained attestation of system memory that addresses only specific, definable pieces of code.

Validation

The mentioned separation of duties is also present on the process of validating a TS. Namely, based on the result of verification, the trustworthiness of the system may be assessed and, accordingly, policy decisions can be made in the validation. The separation of tasks in this process between TS and validator leads to three variant categories of validation. The validation therefore relies on the chain of trust built from the RoT of the TS. With integrity measurement and reporting, this trust boundary is then extended. Since the RoTs are immutable parts of every TS, the validation reveals compromised parts of the TS. Depending on the validation method, appropriate actions can be taken in such a case. Before we introduce and compare the different methods for validation, we discuss one common base concept needed for any kind of validation. **Validation** means the ability to technically assess the state of a system for all security-relevant properties.

Means to validate a system in its operational phase are different from pre-deployment testing and certification, or formal security proofs on a design. They lead into the realm of trusted systems and trusted computing. We can distinguish three main variants. We name **autonomous validation** the model of closed systems, like smart cards, which arrive at a secure state merely by local means, and do not communicate state information to the exterior. As the other extreme, **remote validation** is an abstraction of what the TCG has specified as *remote attestation*. Basically an (open, meaning mostly unrestricted in operational state changes) system only reports state information in a secure way in this second option. A broad spectrum of other variants lies in between the range marked by these extremes. We call this spectrum (not a single method) **semi-autonomous validation (SAV)**. One concrete example for a SAV, at least on the level of technical specifications, namely, what the TCG's MPWG has specified as *secure boot*, which was described in detail above. Let us now try to get a stronger grip on the three notions, and discuss their pros and cons.

Validation Identities

A validation process of a TS must be supported by a **validation identity** which is exhibited to the validator. The validation identity must come directly or indirectly from a RoT, namely the RTR. As was noted before, validation is not possible without a mediator. This **validation identity provider** has the task to assert that the holder of the validation identity is a TS. Provisioning of a validation identity is an extension of identity provisioning in identity management (IdM) systems. The provider has to perform checks on credentials of the TS, including some or all TRs in the TCB, to assess if the TS is in a trustworthy state for validation. Furthermore, the provisioning of validation identities must be performed in a secure process, e.g., a security protocol on a dedicated secure channel. In case of remote validation, the validation identity may coincide with a global identity of the TS.

Validation using unique *persistent* validation identities is critical with regard to security. Validation may occur frequently and indiscriminately to many validators for varied purposes. Though the validation identities used may each not be easily associated to a user identity, they generally allow a tracing of the TS' behaviour. Using the same validation identity for a group or all TS is not an option to resolve this for security reasons. Such a group identity would be a single point of attack/failure, that is, if one TS of the group is compromised, then all others cannot perform validation any more. The other option is to use *ephemeral* validation identities generated, for instance, once in each boot cycle, with determined frequency, or generated by the RTR for each validation.

Autonomous Validation

Autonomous validation is a procedure whereby the validation of the TS does not depend upon external entities, and verification is assumed to have occurred before the TS will allow further communication attempts with the exterior or other operation. Thus, the verification process is assumed to be absolutely secure in this case, as no direct evidence of the verification is provided to the outside world. The outside world makes the assumption that, due to the way in which TS are specified and implemented, a TS which fails verification will be prevented by its TCB, e.g., from, attaching itself to a network, or obtaining an authenticated connection to a remote entity. Autonomous validation lays all enforcement duties on the TS.

The system model of autonomous validation is very simple. It is the model of a closed, immutable system, in essence the blueprint of smart cards. The TS verifies itself using the TCB, and the result is a binary value "success" or "failure". Validation is then an implicit process by which the TS allows certain interaction with the exterior, such as network attachment. A typical example is the release of an authentication secret, e.g., a cryptographic key, by a smart card.

Autonomous validation may be realised in such a way that verification is reactive to certain conditions, e.g., by not allowing certain functions, or by closing the device down and going to re-boot, depending on failure policy. This avoids network connections and, therefore, seems advantageous from an efficiency viewpoint. But such a feature is also a vector for denial-of-service (DoS) attacks. The device must not attach to the network in a compromised state and, thus, has little chance to revert to a secure state. Compromised devices could only be recovered by an in-field replacement which is to be considered costly due to the distributed nature of application scenarios. An important example, machine-to-machine communication, is discussed below in the application section. Remote management is also difficult, specifically there may be a loss of security in software download and installation since it potentially delivers values (software, secrets) to rogue devices. Thus, autonomous validation is prone to entailing out-of-band maintenance. For instance, failure of the update of software of a TR may lead to a state in which network connection is impossible. A lot of risk and potential cost of operation rest with the owner of such a TS.

Security resting only on devices has been broken in the past and is more likely to be broken as, for instance, mobile devices become open computing platforms. Autonomous validation delivers little information for advanced security requirements. If we consider systems which stay connected to a network for long periods of time, we encounter the problem of a partially compromised system which stays connected to the network after the compromise. Autonomous validation provides no means to detect such breaches, e.g., on the part of the network operator. The compromise will only be detected upon restart and re-validation of the device. Policies could enforce regular restarting of the device. In the case of a compromised device, then, autonomous validation will fail and put the device into a state without network connectivity. Depending on the use case, the consequences might range from annoying servicing tasks, e.g., in-field replacement, up to application critical issues, e.g. failure of a monitoring or surveillance system. A controlled, regular labelling of rogue devices is therefore impossible for practical applications, meaning that an exploit might proliferate without being noticed and cause significant damage to other stakeholders, such as network operators, before it can be contained.

But also the validators bear additional burden since they have to keep track of the state of every autonomously validating TS. That is, if its state changes for instance by an externally forced update, this is only signaled through the next re-validation, which has no further informational content. It is the validators duty to update his database with the new TS state. If multiple validators can force updates on a TS, this may become complicated.

Finally, with autonomous validation, the freshness of the verification data is not by itself guaranteed. For this security property to be ful-filled, autonomous validation would have to take place automatically on every system state change, strictly speaking. As autonomous validation happens infrequently in practice, e.g., during network attachment, the TS' state may change significantly during operation of the TS, in a manner unobservable by the validator. Thus, an attacker may use this gap, for instance, to introduce malicious software. Autonomous validation is extremely prone to this kind of timing attack.

Remote Validation

In **remote validation,** the validator directly assesses the validity of the TS based on the evidence for the verification he receives. The verification is only passive in this case, and the full SML must be conveyed to the validator. The model case for this is verification by authenticated boot and following validation. All policy decisions rest with the validator.

The main existing realisation of validation is one of remote validation. In a **remote attestation**, a TCG trusted platform exhibits SML and PCR, signed by an **Attestation Identity Key (AIK)** to the validator. The AIKs are ephemeral asymmetric key pairs, certified by a **Privacy Certification Authority (PCA)** which acts as validation identity provider. More details on this process are found in (Leicher, Kuntze & Schmidt, 2009). The pseudonymity provided in remote attestation may not be sufficient in all cases. The TCG has additionally defined **Direct Anonymous Attestation (DAA)** (Brickell, Camenisch, Chen, 2004; Camenisch, 2004), which is based on zero-knowledge proofs (Chaum, 1985).

In comparison with autonomous validation, remote validation allows the validator to request a re-validation, and the intervals of integrity reporting and verification are not necessarily bound to boot cycles of the device. Furthermore, a compromised device, which is detected during the re-validation, could be put in a quarantined network since the device will still have network connectivity. As both remote and autonomous validations are extremes of a spectrum of options which is subsumed in semi-autonomous validation below, also remote validation has some disadvantages. Remote validation, as represented by remote attestation, poses practical problems with respect to scalability and complexity, as it lays the full computational load for validation on (central) access points to networks or services. In particular, the validation of an SML can be very costly for platforms like personal computers with a large number of soft- and hardware components in numerous versions and configurations. This also requires an enormous database of RIMs, together with an infrastructure, to enable stakeholders to define the desired target configurations of TS. The same arguments make **remote management** of TS, i.e., the controlled and validated change of configuration, impractical with remote validation. Furthermore, run-time verifications are desirable with remote validation, as otherwise only the state after boot is exhibited to the validator. The SML can be "withered" at time of validation, for instance, if a component is re-loaded after an update at run-time. Thus, run-time verification becomes meaningless if it is not directly followed by validation, which would necessitate very frequent remote validations. Finally, remote validation of complex open TS' compromises privacy, in spite of usage of a PCA, since the revealed SML might be almost unique to a TS. A similar, economic argument is the possibility of discrimination by remote attestation. There is a threat that only recent versions of software of major vendors enter into RIM databases, which would force users of other programs to switch to these, or loose service access. Some of the disadvantages might be alleviated by refined forms of remote attestation, such as semantic (Haldar, Chandra & Franz, 2004) or property-based attestation (Sadeghi & Stüble, 2004; Chen, *et al.*, 2006), aiming at exhibiting the characteristics of components rather than a concrete implementa-

tion. These options, however, need more research before they may become practicable.

Semi-Autonomous Validation

Semi-autonomous validation is another procedure whereby the TS' validity is assessed during verification within itself without depending on external entities, and policy decisions are made during verification. But in this case, the result of the local verification and required evidence are signaled to the validator, who can make decisions based on the content of the validation messages from the TS. The signalling from TS to validator must be protected to provide authentication, integrity, and confidentiality if desired. A model case for semi-autonomous validation is secure boot, followed by a signalling of the event structure and indication of RIMs to the validator. As opposed to remote validation, the TS is not required to send the full SML to the validator. Furthermore, it is possible to request a re-validation. By symmetrically distributing verification and enforcement tasks between TS and validator, semi-autonomous validation addresses security and practical problems encountered in remote and autonomous validation.

Specifically, in secure boot, the TS makes decisions at load time of components, while the validator can enforce decisions on the interactions permitted to the TS upon validation, based on the state evidence provided. This design allows, for instance, putting a device into a quarantined network first, which allows it to signal the outcome of the internal validation to the validator. The validator then allows or rejects access to the main network. By scheduling a regular re-validation, or by prescribing events upon whose occurrence re-validation can be initiated, compromised devices can be detected and can be contained in the quarantine network, e.g., to provide remote updates. This is a major advantage over autonomous validation in which the devices are not be able to connect to any network. As semi-autonomous validation sends much less data than a remote validation process, the re-validation intervals can be scheduled at a higher frequency, allowing for faster detection of compromised devices.

Semi-autonomous validation may be a promising avenue to a remedy for the disadvantages of the other two validation options. It can potentially transport the validation information more efficiently in the form of indicators of the RIMs used in verification. This can also be used to protect privacy, for instance, when such an indication designates a group of components with the same functionality and trustworthiness (such as versions). This would be similar to semantic and property-based attestation, and it is conceivable that semi-autonomous validation may be combined with the mentioned advanced forms of remote validation. The interplay of enforcement in verification during validation on the part of the validator, also opens options for remote management of a TS.

On the path to technical realisation of such opportunities, the Trusted Network Connect (TNC) working group of the TCG has introduced the concept of **remediation** (TCG 2008c), to obtain "support for the isolation and remediation of ARs [Access Requestors] which do not succeed in obtaining network access permission due to failures in integrity verification." (p. 24). This allows, in principle, "to bring the AR up to date in all integrity-related information, as defined by the current policy for authorization. Examples include OS patches, AV [Antivirus] updates, firmware upgrades, etc." (p. 25). Concrete concepts for realisation of remote management will have to rely on an infrastructure for the efficient representation and communication of RIM information. TCG MPWG has started to define such services for mobile TS (TCG 2008b), in particular to ingest RIMs for verification. The Infrastructure Working Group of the TCG is establishing a generic architecture and data structures verification and validation (TCG 2006). More research and development is needed

to devise efficient and effective semi-autonomous validation on this path.

It is important to emphasise the role played by RIM certificates in semi-autonomous validation. RIM certificates are provided by a certification authority which has assessed, directly or by delegation, the corresponding TR. Certification methods and bodies can be diverse and lead to different levels of operational trustworthiness. This leads to further flexibility for a semi-autonomous validator who gets more fine-grained information on the TS.

Semi-autonomous validation is also the only practical validation option for systems which are resource limited so that a) they lack the security qualities of a closed system needed to achieve autonomous validation, or b) lack the memory and/ or communication capabilities to perform the extensive reporting needed for remote validation.

Shaneck, Mahadevan, Kher & Kim (2005) give a specific example of semi-autonomous validation in the context of Wireless Sensor Networks, in which both limitations hold for the sensor nodes. Their proposal is to send memory probing code to the sensors that calculate a digest value of the static memory content (code and parameters) which should lead to a predictable result which is returned to the base station for validation. An attacker could obviously try to circumvent this "attestation" by using saved, original memory contents to produce the correct outcome. As long as this attack is performed on the sensor itself it will, however, inevitably lead to delays which can be enhanced by randomisation, self-modifying probing routines, and obfuscation methods. Thus, if a significant delay in the sensor's answer occurs above a certain threshold, the sensor is invalidated.

Validation and Enforcement

Validation and local verification are the central conceptual link between trusting a device and enforcing policies on its behaviour. This is, because based on the results of validation, various policy decisions can be made, and verification, in turn, can incorporate enforcement during secure boot. It is instructive, though it does not add technical content, to map the concepts of validation, in the three variants described above, to the basic architecture of enforcement systems.

Figure 5 shows a simplified picture. A common trait of all variants is that the TS needs a PIP as minimal resource to support the validity decision by the validator. The PIP has to perform the measurement of the TS' state for this and to securely record the results using the RTM. Since validation is always performed for a purpose, there is, in all cases of practical relevance, a PEP present at the part of the validator. Based on the attested information, it can enforce decisions such as granting network access. The richness of the latter information varies significantly between the validation variants.

In remote validation, the TS has no other means to build trust with the validator than to transmit the full SML to the validator, plus information binding it to the TS state and protecting its authenticity (e.g. PCR values signed by the RTR).

The validator's PIP has to contain a database of possible allowed TS states including reference measurement values. Based on the attestation and the state reference information, the PDP at the validator re-traces the SML (e.g. re-calculates the digest values). The PEP obtains a graded result from this process, stating up to which position in the SML the TS was in a good state. On this information, the PEP acts, for instance, by (dis-) allowing network access.

Autonomous validation is the other extreme. All functionality for measurement, verification, and enforcement during secure boot and runtime are localised in the TS' PIP, PDP, and PEP, respectively. No explicit attestation statement is made to the validator who has to rely on the implicit signal that can be inferred, e.g., from an authentication attempt. The validator's PEP can enforce only policies based on the static information contained in this signal, e.g., system type or identity. Since validation information is not present, no validation-specific PIP and PDP are used at the validator (however, a non-validation PIP and PDP can be constructed in this case based on TS identities, and connection history – in ef-

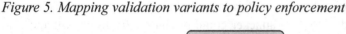

Figure 5. Mapping validation variants to policy enforcement

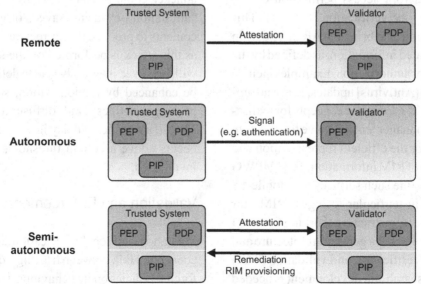

fect a traditional authentication, authorization and accounting [AAA] system, see de Laat *et al*, 2000).

Semi-autonomous validation allows for equally capable policy systems on both sides. The key to this is a codification of attestation data. It need not be transferred as a complex SML including measurement values of all components. It is replaced by a concise event log containing essentially references to RIMs, respectively, associated certificates (the precise content may depend on implementation requirements). This abstraction is made possible by the PDP in the TS which, at the time of verification, e.g., during secure boot, makes the association of component to target RIM. For that, it relies on an internal, protected, RIM database, whose management adds to the functional role of the PIP (beyond measurement). Attestation to codified RIMs allows interaction with the validator in validation. The PDP of the validator can use its own RIM database (provisioned by its PDP) to compare the attested TS state with fine granularity to a desired state. The PEP communicates the outcome to the TS and can thus initiate i) provisioning of new RIMs to the TS, ii) unload of undesired components, iii) load of new, desired components, and by that finally iv) updates of components. These processes are captured by the term remediation. To show the success of the remediation, the TS needs to revalidate only using the newly adjoined part of the event log. From the viewpoint of policy systems, RIMs add an essential piece to enable general policies for validation: A codified *ontology* on which conditions can be evaluated and decisions be taken.

A concrete example for how trust and enforcement can be combined via semi-autonomous validation was recently given by Zahng, Seifert & Aciicmez (2009). They describe a variant of a secure boot process tailored for resource restricted TS like mobile phones. It consists in the secure boot of essential components establishing a trust boundary, which particularly contains functional-

ity to enforce certain security policies on the TS' components. They control the communication between components of the system of different *integrity levels*, e.g., such inside and such outside the trust boundary. This ensures – by enforcement of a small set of policies by TRs – a partitioning of the system into a *trusted environment* (cf. the application section below) and its surrounding. Essentially, semi-autonomous validation in this case is a restriction of the secure boot to essential parts of the TS, which, in turn, comprise enforcement elements to ensure trustworthy operation of the system. The technical problem tackled in this example is the large computational overhead incurred by a verification of the whole system at boot, or at run-time (Muthukumaran, Sawani, Schiffman, Jung & Jaeger, 2008).

Remote Take Ownership

To enable applications that rely on trusted systems it is essential to cope with the management of the TS. The lifecycle of a TS begins with a conformance and compliance testing of its trust anchor and TCB. As they form the fundament for all applications contained in any of the TSS, this certification process has to be done in a standardised way. In deployment and during application, there must always be at least one TSS present for the device to be usable. In some scenarios, the deployment process is separated from the application of a TS leading to different stakeholders, who desire to own different TSS of a TS. In particular, these are the manufacturer, the provider of the device which embodies the TS, service providers, and finally device owners, respectively, users In these multi-stakeholder scenarios, there should be a way to obtain new TSS and assign them to an owner by a well-defined, trustworthy process. We give a simple example for a possible **remote take ownership (RTO)** procedure adapted from (Schmidt, Kuntze & Kasper, 2008) using the facilities of the TCG MPWG specifications. This process is rather generic, does not depend on the physical presence

Figure 6. Installation and initialisation of a TSS on behalf of a remote owner

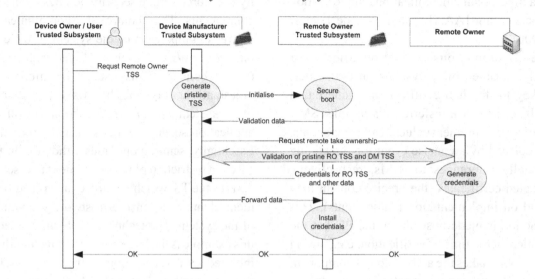

of the remote owner and can, for instance, be executed over-the-air. The involved TSS' are those of User (U), Device Manufacturer (DM), Remote Owner (RO), the latter of which is initially not present. Figure 6 shows the process.

U requests the RTO for an RO TSS from the DM TSS, for instance, by selecting a service provider. The DM TSS is equipped with a TR which allows the **pristine boot** of another TSS, i.e., the installation and initialisation, including secure boot into a pristine, unowned, but otherwise functional state. The pristine RO TSS can thus perform local verification and report corresponding validation data to RO DM. RO DM then issues an RTO request to RO and after RO acknowledges it, a validation of DM TSS and the pristine RO TSS is performed by the RO. If the RO has convinced himself of the trustworthiness of both TSS', he generates unique credentials to individualise the RO TSS. Along with other data, such as security policies and other secrets, the credentials are signed by the RO and sent to the pristine RO TSS via the DM TSS. RO TSS updates its RoTs with the new credentials received and installs the other data. It should be noted that the indirect communication between RO and RO TSS is carried out over a secure channel, which

was established previously either with the RTO request to the RO, or in validation. This means that even the DM TSS has no access to the secrets transferred to the RO TSS. The secure channel is based on the credentials, e.g., asymmetric key pairs, of the RoTs of the pristine RO TSS which are generated in pristine boot. In the last step, the status message toward the RO is also an indication that the RO TSS has passed local verification, i.e., this message constitutes semi-autonomous validation. In (Schmidt, Kuntze & Kasper, 2008) we also showed how a TSS can be migrated between devices while maintaining ownership.

Applications

One of the first applications of trust technologies was a mapping to policy enforcing systems, in particular in IRM and DRM systems, to endow the consuming client with technical security measures (Sailer, Jaeger, Zhang & van Doorn, 2004; Sandhu, Zhang, Ranganathan & Covington, 2006). TCG technology also applies to the communication with a client consuming data as we have demonstrated in (Kuntze & Schmidt 2007a) and (Schmidt & Kuntze 2009). Trust technology also applies to contextual information used by PIPs in enforcement. A good example is the location of a mobile device for which we have described a system architecture and protocols in (Schmidt, Kuntze & Abendroth 2008). A key idea bridging enforcement and trust is, in all these cases, to endow the PIP with verification information and validation tasks.

Here we outline three different applications demonstrating the synergies between operational trust and security. They demonstrate the use of trust technology in the relationships of a) users and systems, b) information systems and data, and c) autonomous systems and communication networks. The variety of applications shows that it is possible to map trust concepts to large-scale applications. Furthermore it is shown, how the combination of enforcement and trust establishment, complemented by a separation of duties between multiple entities, can lead to a variety of trustworthy solutions. The examples show that the concepts of trust and enforcement can be flexibly combined in three main application areas of current information security research: User level security, service architectures, and communication network security. By the variation in architectures in these application fields – from single user/multi-service, to multiple co-operating services in workflows, to large scale deployments of autonomous devices – we hope to sow the scalability of the concepts we have introduced.

Trust in Identity Management Systems

Identity Management (IdM) systems are following a centralised paradigm, in the sense that a party requesting access to a service has to recur to a trusted third party to obtain credentials, e.g., digital tickets. The trusted third party and the service providers, to this end, build a trust relationship mostly by out-of-band methods, for instance, contractual relationships. The lack of operational trust in the user's system leads to various vulnerabilities of IdM systems.

As a platform-neutral security infrastructure, TC offers ways to establish trust between entities that are otherwise separated by technical boundaries, e.g., different access technologies and access control structures. A very elementary use of TC in this vein is, to provide credentials for authentication to a TS protected by a hardware TPM. As a main security feature, this binds credentials to a specific TS. We have first presented this concept in (Kuntze, Mähler, Schmidt, 2006). Latze, Ultes-Nitsche and Baumgartner (2007) have proposed an application of this to authentication in wireless networks via EAP-TLS (Aboba and Simon, 1999), and shown a proof-of-concept in (Latze and Ultes-Nitsche, 2008).

Not surprisingly, some concepts of TC are rather similar to IdM and *federation*. For instance, ideas to exploit a TS for single-sign-on (SSO), simply by including the Authentication Service Provider in the TS to establish a standalone SSO system was put forward by Pashalidis & Mitchell (2003). We have explored the relationship between IdM and TC in various directions in (Kuntze & Schmidt 2007b; Fichtinger, Herrmann, Kuntze & Schmidt, 2008). As one important example, let us here consider Ticket Systems along the lines of (Leicher, Kuntze & Schmidt, 2009). In a ticket-based authentication and authorisation protocol like Kerberos (Steiner, Neuman & Schiller, 1988; Neumann, Yu, Hartman & Raeburn, 2005) software tokens are used to prove the identity of a single entity. Based on these tokens, access to certain systems is restricted to entities producing appropriate tokens. Additionally, data embodied in the token can also be used to implement an authorisation control, enabling a token based access control scheme beside the mere authentication. These tokens are an electronic analogue to physical tickets.

The Kerberos concept relies on two main servers, **Authentication Server (AS)** and **Ticket Granting Server (TGS)**, which both issue the tickets. Each ticket contains two parts: one part is encrypted for the next target server and thus cannot be decrypted by the client. This part contains a session key that will be used by the next communication step. The session key is encrypted for the client in the second part of the ticket. If the client can decrypt this part, he obtains the session key to request the next ticket. There are four main steps:

1. Request and receive the **Ticket Granting Ticket (TGT)** from the AS, store it for future use. Decrypt the session key to encrypt the authentication data for the **Service Ticket (ST)** request.
2. Send the TGT, together with the encrypted authenticator to the TGS.
3. Receive the ST from the TGS. Decrypt the new session key to encrypt the authentication data for the service request.
4. Send the ST, with the encrypted authenticator to the service provider.

The main goal of the *Trusted Kerberos protocol* is to show how TC can be used to enhance a Kerberos. The design has two targets: enhance the security by providing means to bind the tickets closely to the user's TS via the TPM, and secondly, protect the privacy of the user accessing a service. A proof-of-concept of trusted Kerberos ticket system has been realised based on the ethemba TC emulation framework (Brett & Leicher 2009).

With respect to security in particular, a duplicate of the ticket cannot be created and used on another system. In addition, there is no client secret shared between the Kerberos AS and the client. This is one weak spot in the standard protocol, as it allows eavesdroppers on the network to collect TGTs and try to decrypt them offline using brute force and dictionary attacks. Mostly, this password is chosen by the user, thus the chance of finding weak passwords if there are lots of clients in a Kerberos realm makes it easier for attackers. The impact of such an attack can become quite heavy. As the TGT represents the user's identity in the

Kerberos realm, the attacker will gain access to all services the legitimate user has. By using one-time passwords that are cryptographically strong and can only be decrypted using the target TPM, the offline attack on captured tickets becomes impracticable. The passwords can be generated on the server side, thus the system does not have to rely on the computational power of the TS. As a second point adding to the security on the server side, there is validation of the user's system included. When the user wants to acquire an ST to access a service, he is challenged by the TGS to remotely attest system conformity. This process relies on the IMA concept (Sailer, Zhang, Jaeger & van Doorn, L 2004). As a result, only clients in a certified system state will be able to access the service. Figure 7 shows the trusted Kerberos protocol. The TGT is augmented by a **TCTicket** containing the claimed identity of the TGT and service request, and which is signed by the TPM.

Privacy is protected by separation of duties between the TGS and the AS. In the presented concept, a user has to register with one AS, revealing his complete identity to the AS. Then, the user can register multiple partial identities, referred to as claimed identities. The user claims to be in possession of the identity and the AS can certify this by providing a certificate. The AS is the only instance being able to map the claimed identities to the real identity. To further enhance the privacy, no communication shall reveal information to parties other than the current communications partner. During TGT requests, communication between the client and the AS, the client's real identity information is protected as it is encrypted using the AS public key. The response from the AS is encrypted using the public EK of the TPM. When the client uses a TGT to request a ST from the TGS, the communication is encrypted by the session key from the TGT. The TGT can only be decrypted by the TGS, revealing the session key and allowing the TGS to decrypt the data provided by the client. The response is

Figure 7. Trusted extension of the Kerberos protocol

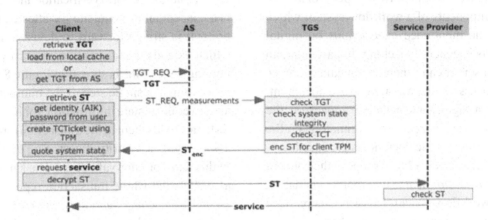

cryptographically bound to the TPM by encrypting the session key with a one-time key bound to the **Certified Signing Key (CSK)** (Kuntze & Schmidt, 2007b) from the TCTicket and secured by the TPM. Only the user in possession of the TPM and the credentials for the key usage in the TPM can decrypt the ST and, thus, use it to access a service. In the concrete embodiment, AIKs are used as one-time credentials in the TGTs, and the AS plays the role of a privacy CA. Thus the TGT request/receive process is realised as a variant of AIK certification.

Even the request to the service provider reveals no information concerning the user's identity to someone else. Only the targeted service provider will be able to decrypt the given partial identity. Due to the separation of duties, the service provider will not gain information about the real identity of the user. As he is associated to a TGS that issued the ST, a provider can contact the TGS operator in the case of misbehaving users. The TGS can then forward the message to the corresponding AS for this identity. As the AS has a mapping of the claimed, partial identities and the real identities, the user can be made liable. In addition, the service provider is not required to keep a database of existing users. So, he can register and associate with a TGS (via legal contracts), enabling multi-service single-sign-on experience for users

wanting to access multiple services. The trust relationship, established by external contracts, between the Kerberos AS/TGS servers and the service providers can be extended to the user's platform relying on both, the authentication and verification of the system's integrity. This provides a promising approach to scalable identity management solutions with a secure extension of the trust domain including the user's system.

Trust for Transactions in Workflows

There are various instances in intra- and inter-organisational workflows in which digital documents have to be changed in significant ways. At the ingestion, for instance in a (semi-) electronic postmaster system, incoming documents are scanned or transformed into a uniform data format for internal processing. In the administrative process, documents are edited, extended and other documents are spawned from them, before they are stored in an internal data warehouse for short-term use and/or an (external or internal) archiving serviced for long-term preservation. Before conveying documents to an external party, they are still, in many cases, printed for final authorisation. All these processes are increasingly supported by workflow systems. The components of such systems are organised according to the enforcement paradigm of IRM. Operational trust in the components of a workflow system which perform the mentioned *transactions* on digital documents is generally lacking. In particular, an outside observer can generally not gain evidence on the processing that was applied to a document. This has a significant negative impact on the auditing of such systems and, ultimately, on the probative force of the documents produced.

Schmidt & Loebl (2005) propose the concept of a *transformation seal* to incorporate validation data of a workflow system. This was later realised for systems performing transformations on documents (Schmidt, Kreutzer & Accorsi, 2007). The seal yields to forensic inspection many details of the process. This information has probative value due to its binding to the new document via the seal's signature. This is sufficient in many cases, e.g., when the workflow system is secured by organisational measures or physically. However, in general distributed processing, this may not be the case and the question of the trustworthiness of the workflow system becomes urgent. This problem emerges in three main application fields: First, if the workflow system is open and weakly secured; second, if the transactions are performed in a distributed fashion; and third, if the party performing the transaction has an own, specific interest in the result of it and has the system under their control. There are three requirements on *attested transactions*, i.e., seals obtaining secure, auditable information on the system on which the process is performed:

A. **Binding to the technical system and validation**. The system *and its current state* during the transaction must be uniquely identified.
B. **Binding to the transformation process**. The mentioned information must be *bound* to the particular transaction.
C. **Binding to the target.** The mentioned information must be *bound* to the new document after the transaction.

A TS able to perform verification and validation is a conceptual prerequisite for attested transactions. It is straightforward to devise a structure which extends transformation seals to yield the bindings A-C. This is shown in Figure 8. During processing in a single step of the transaction, the system collects state information, for instance the SML, and adds them to the transaction report. The TS also adds a security digest, e.g., PCR values to this data for later validation. The single steps, as well as the whole transaction report are then secured by *machine signatures*, e.g., based on AIKs as described in (Kuntze and Schmidt 2007a). The outermost of these signatures establishes the binding to the converted contents. The seal is completed by a signature of the responsible party.

The method presented above is certainly more generally applicable. It has been extended to BEPL-controlled workflows to produce what we call trusted process slips by Kuntze, Schmidt, Rudolph & Velikova (2008).

Home NodeBs and Machine-to-Machine Communication

The major industrial standardisation group for mobile communications, 3GPP, currently studies two advanced applications for their specification Releases 8 and 9, which pose specific security requirements. The latter are considered in the security working group (3GPP SA3 2009a). Both applications have in common that devices are

i)   no longer considered as closed, immutable environments for the storage and handling of sensitive data, as mobile handsets have been traditionally viewed, and
ii) under the control of a stakeholder different from the mobile network operator (MNO), and are in general connected to the core network over an insecure link

The first intended application regards general machine-to-machine (M2M) communication.

Figure 8. Information structure of a seal for attested transactions on digital documents

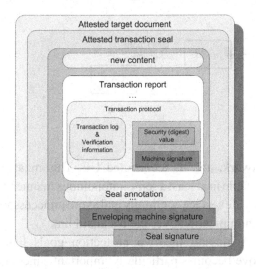

Some of the current and envisaged examples for M2M Equipment (M2ME) are, among others, vending and ticketing machines, smart metering, machine and facility maintenance, healthcare and fleet management. ity management (Kuntze and Schmidt, 2006a & 2006b). If M2ME are connected to the MNO's Core Network (CN) via a mobile network, MNOs will be enabled to offer value-added services to M2ME owners, beginning with over-the-air (OTA) management. M2ME are under the control of a stakeholder different from the MNO, and who has certain security requirements which may be different from the MNO's.

The second application regards the so-called **Home (enhanced) nodeBs**, short **H(e)NBs**[5], better known as *femtocells*. These are small, portable access points to 3G networks which are placed at the far edge of the access network, e.g., on the premises or in the homes of stakeholders called Hosting Party (HP). The Hosting Party becomes a mediator for mobile communication and services in a small, designated geographic area. H(e)NB's can provide mobile services in small, typically in-building areas that hitherto were inaccessible due to bad radio conditions. H(e)NB's can be unified access points for both broadband Internet and mobile networks. MNOs thus view H(e)NB as a very interesting new market they want to control.

In H(e)NB usage scenarios three stakeholders, Users – HP – MNO, are related by Service Level and usage agreements. The H(e)NB stores sensitive data such as the Hosting Party's authentication data, the list of User Equipment (UE) which is allowed to connect to the H(e)NB, stored as an Access Control List (ACL, called Closed Subscriber Group in 3GPP standards before Release 8), and credentials used for authentication of the H(e)NB itself. Some of this data can be private to HP and/or Users. Also, the location of the H(e)NB needs to be secure controlled to protect the mobile network from interference and prevent illegitimate extension of services.

The general security architecture between an H(e)NB, UE, and operator core network is shown in Figure 9. The key entities in this architecture are the H(e)NB, the Security Gateway (SeGW), and the OAM. The Security Gateway (SeGW) provides an access point for the H(e)NB into the operator's core network and protects the network from unauthorized connection attempts and other types of attacks from unauthorized or masqueraded H(e)NBs. The OAM lies at the backhaul of the CN and remotely manages the H(e)NB, in particular, regarding software downloads and updates, setting of radio and other parameters, etc. The threats and security requirements for H(e)NB and M2ME are studied in (3GPP SA3 2008, 2009b), respectively.

We consider the security of the H(e)NB as those are formulated more concretely at the time of this writing. Threats for the H(e)NB can be grouped into six top-level groups.

1. Compromise of Credentials,
2. Physical attacks,
3. Configuration attacks,
4. Protocol attacks on the device.
5. Attacks on the core network.
6. User Data and identity privacy attacks

Figure 9. Generic H(e)NB communication scenario

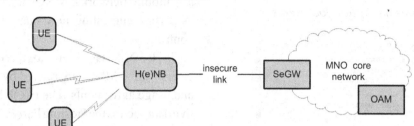

Security for H(e)NB/M2M application scenarios have two main contextual aspects: a) insecure connectivity to the core network, and b) demand for high configurability and flexibility of the equipment especially during deployment. Both aspects must be taken into account early on, to enable a broad range of use cases with optimal cost-efficiency. We view fulfilling b) under the condition of a) as the main obstacle to be overcome for the take-off of the M2M market.

Security, for the H(e)NB or the M2M applications, amounts to satisfying two concrete protection goals:

- Ensure that the device reaches and operate locally in a secure state without network connectivity.
- Enable the CN to obtain assurance of the state of the device, and to assess its security properties, and hence, trustworthy operation.

The core functional requirements which are new for both H(e)NB and M2ME compared to traditional mobile phones mainly involve authentication of the different stakeholders, and separation of functions and data between them, i.e., domain separation. In particular, the authenticity of the HP or M2ME proprietor shall be made independent of device authentication to the network. Furthermore, secret data of the HP must be protected from access by another party, even the MNO. The device also has to perform security-sensitive tasks and enforce security policies towards both the access

network, and the connected UE. This must be possible in at least a semi-autonomous manner, to provide service continuity and avoid unnecessary communication over the backhaul link.

Achieving the two protection goals listed above becomes particularly important, since the state of M2ME or the H(e)NB is to be changed in a controlled way, either by OAM or local management. In both the cases for the H(e)NB and the M2ME, both the network operator and the device owner have a clear mutual interest to have independent abilities to validate the device's state in such a case. The device needs to securely download and install software updates, data, and applications. The security requirements and also advanced OTA or remote management, require particular security features on the devices. This has led to the inception of a concept called Trusted Environment (TRE), which is nothing but the TS of our parlance. Minimal requirements on such an environment already use a lot of concepts of TS, in particular verification, secure boot, validation, and remote ownership.

Separating the authentication roles while concurrently minimising changes to the core network by reusing standard 3G authentication protocols such as EAP-AKA (Arkko et al, 2006) becomes an important practical consideration. The approaches discussed so far at the 3GPP standardisation group envisage separate authentication bearers for the device owner/subscriber and the hosting party (HP). They could be embodied in a so-called HP Module (HPM) for the hosting party, and in managed identities (MIDs) for the device owner/

subscriber. Various security concerns have been raised against usage of removable smart cards such as the UICC for authentication of the devices (both M2ME and H(e)NB). This is related to the fact that these devices will be largely left in the field without direct human intervention or protection. Thus, maintenance operations that require physical exchange of smart cards, e.g., for updates or operator change, is to be avoided, as it would be very costly for a large fleet of geographically dispersed devices. Another option cautiously considered recently is the download of authentication credentials to a secure environment in the device. We have previously described a scheme using genuine TC technology allowing for this option (Schmidt, Kuntze & Kasper 2008), called a virtual SIM. As of yet, MNOs fear the potential ease of churn, and smart card vendors fear a loss of continuous revenues by such advanced technology.

A TRE needs to interact with other parts of the system. Some of these interfaces would need to be secured too. Interestingly, TRE interfaces provide a general model for how the TCB of a TS communicates with the rest of the platform. Basically, all TRE interfaces are initialised in the secure start-up process of the TRE, and are thus assumed to operate correctly. Two broad categories of TRE interfaces can be considered:

1. Unprotected interfaces. These interfaces let the TRE with general resources of the device which are not assumed to be secured against tampering and/or eavesdropping. Even unprotected interfaces may also benefit from other security measures such as data encryption, or making the interface available only after the TRE checks the code of its counter-part resource across the interface, for example, during a secure boot.

2. Protected interfaces: These interfaces provide either protection of the integrity and/or confidentiality of the data carried across them, using either security protocols or

secure hardware. If security protocols are used, they may also provide authentication, and message authentication and/or confidentiality.

Unprotected interfaces may be chosen when the communicating entity does not provide protection of the communicated data. Protected interfaces may be chosen when there is a need to provide protection of data integrity and/or confidentiality. Various implementation choices will be available, since the capabilities of the TRE may vary. Appendix B of 3GPP SA3 (2009b) describes one proposal for a TRE within an H(e)NB and what other resources it might connect to.

FUTURE RESEARCH DIRECTIONS

The most important applications of trusted systems lie in loosely connected, heterogeneous nodes communicating via convergent communication networks. Within the European Union's seventh research Framework Programme, major efforts are made to meet the challenges of such networks, which are known under the summary term "Future Internet" (FI), (European Commission 2008). FI is characterised by distributed storage and processing of data. Network nodes are not only used for data transmission, and terminals are not only used for applications. Nodes become hosts for data and application services while terminals participate in an ad hoc, more or less controlled manner, in data transmission through the network. This is a kind of convergence that transcends every layer of the network and it goes hand-in-hand with the convergence between mobile communication networks and the core Internet.

FI security deals with a system where core capabilities, as well as application overlay networks, operate in a distributed way and – by themselves – with little functional guarantees, for instance, with regard to Quality of Services. Thus, the main challenge to guarantee security and resilience of the network in this environment is to establish a uniform foundation for trust in nodes and terminals, as well as security of communication between them. A trust foundation must establish RoTs for connected devices relying on hardware security to reach the necessary assurance level and make security scalable. This calls for a broad-scale application of the methods described in this chapter. In a *Future Trusted Internet*, we envisage three main areas of protection:

1. **Protection of nodes and devices against misconfiguration and malware**. As most attacks to the Internet infrastructure and services are launched from within – by collections of rogue nodes such as bot-nets – a node or terminal in the Future Internet should be able to bring itself into a trustworthy state and perform validation.

2. **Protection of user credentials and Privacy-friendly ID-management**. As more and more user data is processed on distant nodes not under local user control, user data, as well as his access and even personal credentials, travel over the network and require appropriate protection. The network design needs to enable the control of personalised data in a way that implements a thorough 'need to know' principle.

3. **Trust in processing and probative value of processes and communication**. FI evolves from an information transmission to an information processing facility, and bears a great deal of critical business processes. Service oriented architectures' users, for instance, heed little care about where and how their precious data are processed. They naturally assume that it is protected. New requirements stem from the necessity, nowadays implemented by global treaties, EU, and national jurisdiction almost globally, to make every operation in a business process auditable and to keep detailed, and true, records. Therefore, the FI must provide ubiquitous support for

non-repudiation not only of communication, but also of distributed data processing.

To realise the vision of the protection areas, there are main research challenges to be tackled:

1. Find methods to leverage the hitherto scattered and unconnected, hardware-based security building blocks into an overarching **trust architecture** to protect connected TS. This comprises new, high-performance, methods for application separation, perhaps beyond virtualisation. Furthermore, security primitives need to be developed that enable fundamental operations on, and communication with TS.

2. A uniform **credential management architecture** leveraging hardware trust must be envisioned. Trusted means to control operations with user credentials, such as enrolment and migration between devices, shall ensure users' privacy and seamless access to network services. Also needed are novel, secure, **multi-modal, seamless user authentication** methods, and methods to validate a TS *to the user*.

3. New and uniform methods for the provisioning of security to higher application levels must be deployed throughout the FI. This enables applications to validate the state of the host system, and in turn, the host systems to provide scaled security to each application. This security comprises, in particular, new **means to bind trust-related information to data** that is stored or communicated to other nodes. Those methods need to be independent of data formats and representations.

As we see, the main thrust of research, coming from the impact of scalable trust concepts, is an applied one. In the real-world scenarios which are the empirical basis of computer science, appropriate security concepts cannot be designed without taking the value of information into account. This is the most important ancillary condition determining scalable trust concepts for various purposes. Such applied research must be accompanied by, and integrated with, a broad interdisciplinary approach that emphasises the user perspective. Thus, realisation of trust to make future information networks such as online communities (Boyd & Ellison, 2007) needs input from sociological, economic (Kollock, 1999), psychological, and legal disciplines.

CONCLUSION

Beyond perceived antagonism between the two notions, the present chapter has provided 'blueprints' for the synergetic co-operation of trust and enforcement technologies. This synergy rests on three pillars. On the one hand, de-centralised, autonomous enforcement is only possible when a remote agent is sufficiently trustworthy. On the other hand, reaching a determined, trustworthy state locally necessitates trusted components of enforcement technology inside the agents. Finally, trust must be communicated and mediated between entities by methods of validation, which can extend to interactively changing trust relations, by way of, for instance, state remediation.

Taken together, the methods described allow for what we called scaling between trust and enforcement. That is, according to capabilities of devices and of networks, requirements of use cases, and needs of stakeholders, trust and enforcement can be deployed to a distributed system in a great variety of ways. The spectrum is broad. On one side, it ranges from monolithic systems in the spirit of smart cards, where all trust is put in the pre-defined functioning, which is locally, but invisibly, enforced. On the other side lie dynamically changing open computing platforms, in which validation of their state of trustworthiness is

a precondition to entrust (sic) them with valuable data. Trust in distributed enforcement components is, again, key to the secure processing of data in future networked environments.

The interplay between Trusted Computing technology and policy enforcement methods exhibited in many examples above, has the potential to pave the way for a safer, and yet more open and flexible, networked environment. Ultimately trust and enforcement together may mean freedom for users, in all sectors, commercial, governmental, and private.

ACKNOWLEDGMENT

The authors thank George Ballas, Bradley Blaine, Alan Carleton, Prabhakar Chitrapu, Robert DiFazio, Megan Groff, Brian Kiernan, Shigou Lian, Ilaria Matteuci, Yogendra Shah, and Davide Vernizzi for valuable suggestions, comments, and meticulous proofreading. We also thank the editor of this book and the anonymous referees for their constructive critique.

REFERENCES

Aberer, K., & Despotovic, Z. (2001). Managing Trust in a Peer-to-Peer Information System. In H. Paques, L. Liu, & D. Grossman (Eds.), *Proc. Of the 10th ACM Intl. Conf. on Information and Knowledge Management* (pp. 310-317). New York: ACM.

Aboba, B., & Simon, D. (1999). PPP EAP TLS Authentication Protocol. *IETF Network Working Group. RFC 2716.* Retrieved March 10, 2009, from http://www.ietf.org/rfc/rfc2716.txt

Ajayi, O., Sinnott, R., & Stell, A. (2008). Dynamic trust negotiation for flexible e-health collaborations. In D. S. Katz, C. Lee, T. Kosar, S. Jha, & O. Rana (Eds.), *Proc. of the 15th ACM Mardi Gras conference: From lightweight mash-ups to lambda grids: Understanding the spectrum of distributed computing requirements, applications, tools, infrastructures, interoperability, and the incremental adoption of key capabilities* (pp. 1-7). New York: ACM.

Anderson, R. (2008). *Security Engineering - A Guide to Building Dependable Distributed Systems*. Indianapolis, IN: Wiley.

Arbaugh, W. A., Farber, D. J., & Smith, J. M. (1997). A secure and reliable bootstrap architecture. In *Proc. of the 1997 IEEE Symposium on Security and Privacy* (pp. 65-71). Washington, DC: IEEE.

Arkko, J., & Haverinen, H. (2006). Extensible Authentication Protocol Method for 3rd Generation Authentication and Key Agreement (EAP-AKA). *IETF Network Working Group. RFC 4187*. Retrieved January 21, 2009, from http://www.ietf.org/rfc/rfc4187.txt

Axelrod, R. (1984). *The Evolution of Cooperation*. New York: Basic Books.

Azzedin, F., & Maheswaran, M. (2002). Towards Trust-Aware Resource Management in Grid Computing Systems. In *Proc. of the 2nd IEEE/ACM International Symposium on Cluster Computing and the Grid* (pp. 452-457). Washington, DC: IEEE.

Bandara, A. K., Lupu, E., Moffett, J. D., & Russo, A. (2004). A goal-based approach to policy refinement. In *Proceedings of the Intl. Workshop on Policies for Distributed Systems and Networks* (pp. 229-239). Washington, DC: IEEE.

Becker, E., Buhse, W., Günnewig, D., & Rump, N. (Eds.). (2003). *Digital Rights Management –Technological, Economic, Legal and Political Aspects*. New York: Springer-Verlag.

Becker, M. Y., Fournet, C., & Gordon, A. D. (2007). Design and Semantics of a Decentralized Authorization Language. In *Proceedings of the 20th IEEE Computer Security Foundations Symposium (CSF)* (pp. 3-15). Washington, DC: IEEE.

Bell, D. E. (2005). Looking Back at the Bell-La Padula Model. In *Proceedings of the 21st Annual Computer Security Applications Conference* (pp. 337-351). Washington, DC: IEEE.

Bettini, C., Jajodia, S., Wang, X. S., & Wijesekera, D. (2002). Provisions and obligations in policy management and security applications. In *Proc. of the 28th intl. Conf. on Very Large Data Bases* (pp. 502-513). Hong Kong, China: VLDB Endowment.

Blaze, M., Feigenbaum, J., & Lacey, J. (1996). Decentralized Trust Management. In *Proc. of the 1996 IEEE Symposium on Security and Privacy* (pp. 164-173).

Botha, R. A., & Eloff, J. H. P. (2001). Separation of duties for access control enforcement in workflow environments. *IBM Systems Journal, 40*, 666–682.

Boyd, D. M., & Ellison, N. B. (2007). Social network sites: Definition, history, and scholarship. *Journal of Computer-Mediated Communication, 13*(1), 11.

Boyle, J., Cohen, R., Herzog, S., Rajan, R., & Sastry, A. (2000). The COPS (Common Open Policy Service) Protocol. *IETF Network Working Group. RFC 2748*. Retrieved February 13, 2009, from http://www.ietf.org/rfc/rfc2748.txt

Brett, A., & Leicher, A. (2009). *Ethemba Trusted Host Environment Mainly Based on Attestation.* Retrieved January 29, 2009, from http://www.ethemba.info/cms/

Brickell, E., Camenisch, J., & Chen, L. (2004). Direct anonymous attestation. In B. Pfitzmann & P. Liu (Eds.), *Proc. of the 11ᵗʰ ACM Conf. on Computer and Communications Security* (pp. 132-145). New York: ACM.

Camenisch, J. (2004). Better Privacy for Trusted Computing Platforms. In *Proc. of the 9ᵗʰ European Symposium On Research in Computer Security (ESORICS 2004)* (pp. 73-88). Berlin, Germany: Springer-Verlag.

Castelfranchi, C., & Falcone, R. (1998). Principles of Trust for MAS: Cognitive Anatomy, Social Importance and Quantification. In Y. Demazeau (Ed.), *Proc. of the 3ʳᵈ Intl. Conf. on Multi-Agent Systems (ICMAS'98)* (pp. 72-79). Washington, DC: IEEE.

Chaum, D. (1985). Security without Identification: Transaction Systems to make Big Brother Obsolete. *Communications of the ACM, 28*(10), 1030–1044. doi:10.1145/4372.4373

Chen, L., Landfermann, R., Löhr, H., Rohe, M., Sadeghi, A.-R., Stüble, Ch., & Görtz, H. (2006). A protocol for property-based attestation. In *Proceedings of the first ACM workshop on Scalable trusted computing (STC '06)* (pp. 7-16). New York: ACM.

Cimatti, A., Clarke, E., Giunchiglia, E., Giunchiglia, F., Pistore, M., Roveri, M., et al. (2002). NuSMV Version 2: An OpenSource Tool for Symbolic Model Checking. In K. Brinksma & L. Guldstrand (Eds.), *Proc. of the 14ᵗʰ Intl. Conf. on Computer-Aided Verification (CAV 2002)* (pp. 359-364). Berlin, Germany: Springer-Verlag.

Cofta, P. (2007). *Trust, Complexity and Control: Confidence in a Convergent World.* Indianapolis, IN: Wiley.

Common Criteria. (2009). *Official CC/CEM versions - The Common Criteria Portal.* Retrieved February 4, 2009, from http://www.commoncriteriaportal.org/thecc.html

COSoDIS. (2009). *Contract-Oriented Software Development for Internet Services.* Retrieved January 28, 2009, from http://www.ifi.uio.no/cosodis/

de Laat, C., Gross, G., Gommans, L., Vollbrecht, J., & Spence, D. (2000). Generic AAA Architecture. *IETF Network Working Group. RFC 2903.* Retrieved February 20, 2009, from http://tools.ietf.org/html/rfc2903

Department of Defense. (1985, December 26). *Department of Defense Trusted Computer System Evaluation Criteria* (DoD 5200.28-STD).

Deutsch, M. (1958). Trust and suspicion. *The Journal of Conflict Resolution, 2,* 265–279. doi:10.1177/002200275800200401

Douceur, J. R. (2002). The sybil attack. In P. Druschel, F. Kaashoek, & A. Rowstron (Eds.), *Proc. of the First International Workshop on Peer-to-Peer Systems (IPTPS 2002)* (pp. 251-260). Berlin, Germany: Springer-Verlag.

Dulay, N., Lupu, E., Sloman, M., & Damianou, N. (2002). A Policy Deployment Model for the Ponder Language. In G. Pavlou, N. Anerousis, & A. Liotta (Eds.), *Proc. of the IEEE/IFIP Intl. Symposium on Integrated Network Management (IM'2001)* (pp. 529-543). Washington, DC: IEEE.

Dwyer, N., & Cofta, P. (2008). Understanding the grounds to trust: Game as a cultural probe. In *Proceedings of the First International Workshop on Web 2.0 Trust*, Trondheim, Norway.

Emerson, E. A. (1996). Model Checking and the Mu-calculus. In N. Immerman & P. G. Kolaitis (Eds.), *Descriptive Complexity and Finite Models* (pp. 185-214). Providence. RI: American Mathematical Society.

European Commission. (2008). *The Future of the Internet. A Compendium of European Projects on ICT Research Supported by the EU 7th Framework Programme for RTD*. Retrieved January 12, 2009, from http://ec.europa.eu/enterprise/newsroom/cf/document.cfm?doc_id=772

Fichtinger, B., Herrmann, E., Kuntze, N., & Schmidt, A. U. (2008). Trusted Infrastructures for Identities. In R. Grimm & B. Hass (Eds.), *Proc. of the 5th Intl. Workshop for Technical, Economic and Legal Aspects of Business Models for Virtual Goods*. Hauppauge, NY: Nova Publishers.

Friedman, E. J., & Resnick, P. (2001). The social cost of cheap pseudonyms. *Journal of Economics & Management Strategy, 10*, 173–199. doi:10.1162/105864001300122476

Gambetta, D. (1988). Can We Trust Trust? In D. Gambetta (Ed.), *Trust: Making and Breaking Cooperative Relations* (pp. 213-237). Oxford, UK: Basil Blackwell.

Gamma, E., Helm, R., Johnson, R., & Vlissides, J. (1995). *Design Patterns: Elements of Reusable Object-Oriented Software*. Reading, MA: Addison Wesley.

Gorrieri, R., Rensink, A., & Zamboni, M. A. (2001). Action refinement. In J.A. Bergstra, P. Di-Saia, A. Ponse, & S.A. Smolka (Eds.), *Handbook of Process Algebra* (pp. 1047-1147). Amsterdam: Elsevier.

3GPP SA3. (2008). *3rd Generation Partnership Project; Technical Specification Group Service and System Aspects; Feasibility Study on Remote Management of USIM Application on M2M Equipment; (Release 8), TR 33.812 v1.1.0 (S3-081211)*. Retrieved January 12, 2009, from ftp://ftp.3gpp.org/TSG_SA/WG3_Security/TSGS3_53_Kyoto/Docs/S3-081211.zip

3GPP SA3. (2009a). *Web Site of 3GPP SA3: Security*. Retrieved January 19, 2009, from http://www.3gpp.org/SA3/

3GPP SA3. (2009b). *3rd Generation Partnership Project; Technical Specification Group Service and System Aspects; Security of H(e) NB; (Release 8), TR 33.820 V8.0.0 (S3-090482)*. Retrieved March 30, 2009, from ftp://ftp.3gpp.org/TSG_SA/WG3_Security/ADHOCs/TSGS3_AD-HOC_Mar09_Sophia/Docs/S3-090482.zip

Grandison, T., & Sloman, M. (2000). A Survey of Trust in Internet Applications. *IEEE Communications Surveys and Tutorials, 3*(4), 2–16. doi:10.1109/COMST.2000.5340804

Guttman, J., Herzog, A., Millen, J., Monk, L., Ramsdell, J., Sheehy, J., et al. (2008). *Attestation: Evidence and Trust* (MITRE Technical Report, MTR080072). Bedford, MA: MITRE Corporation. Retrieved January 27, 2009, from http://www.mitre-corp.org/work/tech_papers/tech_papers_07/07_0186/07_0186.pdf

Haag, R. (1992). *Local Quantum Physics*. Berlin, Germany: Springer-Verlag.

Haldar, V., Chandra, D., & Franz, M. (2004). Semantic remote attestation: A virtual machine directed approach to trusted computing. In *Proceedings of the USENIX Virtual Machine Research and Technology Symposium (VM '04)* (pp. 29-41). Berkley, CA: USENIX.

Jøsang, A., Gray, E., & Kinateder, M. (2003). Analysing Topologies of Transitive Trust. In T. Dimitrakos & F. Martinelli (Eds.), *Proc. of the 1ˢᵗ Intl. Workshop of Formal Aspects of Security and Trust (FAST)*. Pisa, Italy: CNR.

Jøsang, A., Hayward, R., & Pope, S. (2006). Trust network analysis with subjective logic. In *Proc. of the 29th Australasian Computer Science Conference (ACSC '06)* (pp. 85-94).

Kamvar, S. D., Schlosser, M. T., & Garcia-Molina, H. (2003). The Eigentrust Algorithm for Reputation Management in P2P Networks. In *Proc. of the 12ᵗʰ Intl. Conf. on World Wide Web (WWW '03)* (pp. 640-651). New York: ACM.

Kuntze, N., Mähler, D., & Schmidt, A. U. (2006). Employing Trusted Computing for the forward pricing of pseudonyms in reputation systems. In K. Ng, A. Badii, & P. Bellini (Eds.), *Proc. of the 2ⁿᵈ Intl. Conf. on automated production of cross media content for multi-channel distribution (AXMEDIS). Workshops Tutorials Applications and Industrial Sessions* (pp. 145-149). Florence, Italy: Firenze University Press.

Kuntze, N., & Schmidt, A. U. (2006a). Transitive trust in mobile scenarios. In G. Müller (Ed.), *Proc. of the Intl. Conf. Emerging Trends in Information and Communication Security (ETRICS 2006)* (pp. 73-85). Berlin, Germany: Springer-Verlag.

Kuntze, N., & Schmidt, A. U. (2006b). Trusted Computing in Mobile Action. In H. S. Venter, J. H. P. Eloff, L. Labuschagne, & M. M. Eloff (Eds.), *Proc. of the ISSA 2006 From Insight to Foresight Conference*. Johannesburg, South Africa: Information Security South Africa (ISSA).

Kuntze, N., & Schmidt, A. U. (2007a). Trustworthy content push. In *Proc. of the Wireless Communications and Networking Conference WCNC 2007* (pp. 2909-2912). Washington, DC: IEEE.

Kuntze, N., & Schmidt, A. U. (2007b) Trusted Ticket Systems and Applications. In H. Venter, M. Eloff, L. Labuschagne, J. Eloff, & R. von Solms (Eds.), *New Approaches for Security, Privacy and Trust in Complex Systems* (pp. 49-60). New York: Springer-Verlag.

Kuntze, N., Schmidt, A. U., Rudolph, C., & Velikova, Z. (2008). Trust in Business Processes. In *Proc. of the 9ᵗʰ Intl. Conf. for Young Computer Scientists, 2008. ICYCS 2008.* (pp. 1992-1997). Washington, DC: IEEE.

La Padula, L. J., & Bell, D. E. (1973). *Secure Computer Systems: A Mathematical Model* (Technical Report MTR–2547, Vol. I & II). Bedford, MA: MITRE Corporation. Retrieved January 26, 2009, from http://www.albany.edu/acc/courses/ia/classics/belllapadula1.pdf

Lamb, W. E. (1969). An Operational Interpretation of Nonrelativistic Quantum Mechanics. *Physics Today, 22*, 23–28. doi:10.1063/1.3035523

Lamb, W. E. (2001). Super Classical Quantum Mechanics: The best interpretation of nonrelativistic quantum mechanics. *American Journal of Physics, 69*, 413–422. doi:10.1119/1.1349542

Latze, C., & Ultes Nitsche, U. (2008). A proof-of-concept implementation of EAP-TLS with TPM support. In H. S. Venter, J. H. P. Eloff, L. Labuschagne, & M. M. Eloff (Eds.), *Proc. of the Information Security South Africa (ISSA) Innovative Minds Conference*. Johannesburg, South Africa: ISSA.

Law, K. L. E., & Saxena, A. (2003). Scalable design of a policy-based management system and its performance. *IEEE Communications Magazine, 41*(6), 72–79. doi:10.1109/MCOM.2003.1204750

Leicher, A., Kuntze, N., & Schmidt, A. U. (2009). Implementation of a Trusted Ticket System. In *Proceedings of the IFIP sec2009*. Boston, MA: Springer-Verlag.

Mayer, R. C., Davis, J. H., & Schoorman, D. F. (1995). An Integrative Model of Organizational Trust. *Academy of Management Review, 20*(3), 709–734. doi:10.2307/258792

Mitchell, C. J. (Ed.). (2005). *Trusted Computing*. London, UK: IET.

Muthukumaran, D., Sawani, A., Schiffman, J., Jung, B. M., & Jaeger, T. (2008). Measuring integrity on mobile phone systems. In *Proc. of the 13ᵗʰ ACM Symposium on Access Control Models and Technologies*. New York: ACM.

Neumann, C., Yu, T., Hartman, S., & Raeburn, K. (2005). The Kerberos Network Authentication Service (V5). *IETF Network Working Group. RFC 4120*. Retrieved January 27, 2009, from http://www.ietf.org/rfc/rfc4120.txt

NSA. (1998). National Security Agency. *NSA Glossary of Terms Used in Security and Intrusion Detection*. Retrieved October 23, 2008, from http://www.sans.org/newlook/resources/glossary.html

OMTP. (2009). *Open Mobile Terminal Platform. Advanced Trusted Environment, OMTP TR1 v1.03.*

OWL. (2004). *Web Ontology Language Overview* (W3C Recommendation 10 February 2004). Retrieved January 28, 2009, from http://www.w3.org/TR/owl-features/

Pagnia, H., Vogt, H., & Gärtner, F. C. (2003). Fair Exchange. *The Computer Journal, 46*(1), 55–75. doi:10.1093/comjnl/46.1.55

Pashalidis, A., & Mitchell, C. J. (2003). Single sign-on using trusted platforms. In *Proc. of the 6th Intl. Conf. Information Security (ISC 2003)* (pp. 54-68). Berlin, Germany: Springer-Verlag.

Pearson, S. (2002a). *Trusted Computing Platforms, the Next Security Solution.* (Tech. Rep. HPL-2002-221). Trusted E-Services Laboratory. HP Laboratories Bristol. Retrieved January 23, 2009, from http://www.hpl.hp.com/techreports/2002/HPL-2002-221.pdf

Pearson, S. (2002b). *How Can You Trust the Computer in Front of You?* (Tech. Rep. HPL-2002-221). Trusted E-Services Laboratory. HP Laboratories Bristol. Retrieved January 23, 2009, from http://www.hpl.hp.com/techreports/2002/HPL-2002-222.pdf

Protégé. (2009). *The Protégé Ontology Editor and Knowledge Acquisition System*. Retrieved January 28, 2009, from http://protege.stanford.edu/

Rand Corporation. (1970). *Security Controls for Computer Systems. Report of Defense Science Board Task Force on Computer Security.* Retrieved December 23, 2007, from http://seclab.cs.ucdavis.edu/projects/history/papers/ware70.pdf

Resnick, P., Kuwabara, K., Zeckhauser, R., & Friedman, E. (2000). Reputation systems. *Communications of the ACM, 43*(12), 45–48. doi:10.1145/355112.355122

Sadeghi, A.-R., & Stüble, Ch. (2004). Property-based attestation for computing platforms: caring about properties, not mechanisms. In C. F. Hampelmann & V. Raskin (Eds.), *Proceedings of the 2004 workshop on new security paradigms NSPW '04* (pp. 67-77). New York: ACM.

Sailer, R., Jaeger, T., Zhang, X., & van Doorn, L. (2004). Attestation-based policy enforcement for remote access. In B. Pfitzmann & P. Liu (Eds.), *Proc. of the 11th ACM Conf. on Computer and Communications Security* (pp. 308-317). New York: ACM.

Sailer, R., Zhang, X., Jaeger, T., & van Doorn, L. (2004). Design and implementation of a TCG-based integrity measurement architecture. In *Proceedings of the 13th USENIX Security Symposium* (pp. 223-238). Berkley, CA: USENIX.

Sandhu, R., Zhang, X., Ranganathan, K., & Covington, M. J. (2006). Client-side access control enforcement using trusted computing and PEI models. *Journ. High Speed Networks, 15*, 229–245.

Schmidt, A. U. (2008). On the Superdistribution of Digital Goods. In *Proc. of the 3rd Intl. Conf. on Communications and Networking in China (CHINACOM'08)* (pp. 1236-1243). Washington, DC: IEEE.

Schmidt, A. U., Kreutzer, M., & Accorsi, R. (Eds.). (2007). *Long-Term and Dynamical Aspects of Information Security: Emerging Trends in Information and Communication Security*. Hauppauge, NY: Nova.

Schmidt, A. U., & Kuntze, N. (2009). Trust in the Value-Creation Chain of Multimedia Goods. In S. Lian & Y. Zhang (Eds.), *Handbook of Research on Secure Multimedia Distribution* (pp. 405-426). Hershey, PA: IGI Global.

Schmidt, A. U., Kuntze, N., & Abendroth, J. (2008). Trust for Location-based Authorisation. In *Proc. of the Wireless Communications and Networking Conf. (WCNC 2008)* (pp. 3169-3174). Washington, DC: IEEE.

Schmidt, A. U., Kuntze, N., & Kasper, M. (2008). Subscriber Authentication in Cellular Networks with Trusted Virtual SIMs. In *Proceedings of the 10th International Conference on Advanced Communication Technology (ICACT2008)* (pp. 903-908). Washington, DC: IEEE.

Schmidt, A. U., & Loebl, Z. (2005). Legal Security for Transformations of Signed Documents: Fundamental Concepts. In D. Chadwick & Z. Gansen (Eds.), *Proceedings of the Second European PKI Workshop: Research and Applications, EuroPKI 2005* (pp. 255-270). Berlin, Germany: Springer-Verlag.

Shaneck, M., Mahadevan, K., Kher, B., & Kim, Y. (2005). Remote Software-Based Attestation for Wireless Sensors. In R. Molva, G. Tsudik, & D. Westhoff (Eds.), *Security and Privacy in Ad-hoc and Sensor Networks* (pp. 27-41). Berlin, Germany: Springer-Verlag.

Shi, E., Perrig, A., & Van Doorn, L. (2005). BIND: a fine-grained attestation service for secure distributed systems. In *Proc. of the 2005 IEEE Symposium on Security and Privacy* (pp. 154-168). Washington, DC: IEEE.

Song, D., Berezin, S., & Perrig, A. (2001). Athena: A novel approach to efficient automatic security protocol analysis. *JCS, 9*(1,2), 47-74.

Steiner, J. G., Neuman, C., & Schiller, J. I. (1988) Kerberos: An Authentication Service for Open Network Systems. In R. Isaacs & Y. Zhou (Eds.), *Proc. of the 2008 USENIX Annual Technical Conference* (pp. 191-102). Berkley, CA: USENIX.

TCG. (2006). *TCG Infrastructure Working Group. Architecture Part II - Integrity Management. Specification Version 1.0 Revision 1.0.*

TCG. (2007a). *TPM Specification Version 1.2 Revision 103.*

TCG. (2008a). *Mobile Trusted Module Specification Version 1.0. Revision 6.*

TCG. (2008b). *TCG Mobile Reference Architecture Specification Version 1.0. Revision 5.*

TCG. (2008c). *TNC Architecture for Interoperability. Specification Version 1.3. Revision 6.*

Toone, B., Gertz, M., & Devanbu, P. (2003). Trust Mediation for Distributed Information Systems. In D. Gritzalis, S. De Capitani di Vimercati, P. Samarati, & S. K. Katsikas (Eds.), *Security and Privacy in the Age of Uncertainty, Proc. of the IFIP TC11 18th Intl. Conf. on Information Security (SEC2003)* (pp. 1-12). Dordrecht, The Netherlands: Kluwer.

Ultes-Nitsche, U., Latze, C., & Baumgartner, F. (2007) Strong Mutual Authentication in a User-Friendly Way in EAP-TLS. In *Proc. of the 15th Intl. Conf. on Software, Telecommunications and Computer Networks (SoftCOM 2007)*. Washington, DC: IEEE.

Workflow Patterns. (2007). *Workflow Patterns initiative home page*. Retrieved January 28, 2009, from http://www.workflowpatterns.com/

Xiong, L., & Liu, L. (2004). PeerTrust: supporting reputation-based trust for peer-to-peer electronic communities. *IEEE Transactions on Knowledge and Data Engineering, 16*(7), 843–857. doi:10.1109/TKDE.2004.1318566

Yahalom, R., Klein, B., & Beth, T. (1993). Trust Relationships in Secure Systems – A Distributed Authentication Perspective. In *Proc. of the 1993 IEEE Symposium on Security and Privacy* (pp. 150-164). Washington, DC: IEEE.

Zhang, N., Ryan, M., & Guelev, D. P. (2005). Evaluating access control policies through model checking. In J. Zhou, J. Lopez, R. H. Deng, & F. Bao (Eds.), *Proc. 8th Intl. Conf. on Information Security (ISC 2005)* (pp. 446-460). Berlin, Germany: Springer-Verlag.

Zhang, X., Seifert, J.-P., & Aciicmez, O. (2009). Building Efficient Integrity Measurement and Attestation for Mobile Phone Platforms. In A. U. Schmidt & S. Lian (Eds.), *Proc. of the 1ˢᵗ International ICST Conference on Security and Privacy in Mobile Information and Communication Systems (MobiSec 2009)*. Berlin, Germany: Springer.

ENDNOTES

[1] Thanks to the volume editor who put this more lucidly than I was able to.

[2] A word on nomenclature. In the present chapter, we introduce a unified wording centered on operational trust. According to this aim we deviate from the often used and often confounded notions of "trusted system" and "trustworthy system." The National Security Agency (NSA, 1998) defines a *trusted* system or component as one "whose failure can break the security policy", and a *trustworthy* system or component as one "that will not fail." The former notion is most closely related to our definition of a TS in the operational sense, more precisely a TS endowed with a particular enforcement task in a certain operational context. The notion of trustworthy system makes little sense, operationally, and relates to the TCB,

at best. For more discussion see Anderson (2008, Chapter 1).

[3] This again deviates from the literature, where mostly verifier is a receiver of some information which can be computationally matched to yield a binary answer to a question related to the security of a system. In particular in semi-autonomous validation, which we argue is the practically most important case, this function is internalized in the TS. This justifies the introduction of the term validator to denote the external entity which ultimately assesses the operational trust in a TS based on the verifier's information. "Attestation" in turn is, as we explain, the process of securely (protecting data authenticity) communicating with the validator. Remote Attestation is just one embodiment thereof.

[4] We do not claim to give a proper definition of run-time attestation here, since we think this term is not yet sufficiently stable and clearly defined. In particular, specifics of a dedicated RoT for run-time measurements and reporting, and how to concretely ensure freshness of validation data, are open questions.

[5] This somewhat clumsy terminology of 3GPP refers to "nodeB", which designates a mobile network's base stations in 3G, e.g., UMTS networks, and to the Long Term Evolution Project (LTE) of 3GPP. According to LTE conventions, entities beyond Release 9 are to be differentiated from their earlier counterparts by an (e) for "enhanced". In the case of nodeBs, the enhancements consist in additional functions taken over by the base station beyond providing radio access to terminals. For instance, Home (e)nodeBs may function as Internet modems and wireless access points.

[6] The Trusted Platform Module (TPM), as specified by the TCG, although often per-

ceived as enforcement module, is a passive security chip which is enabled by its owner and user. The TPM provides a secure RoT in a non-removable piece of hardware which is tightly bound to the system platform. It further provides a secure storage for secrets and keys. Enforcement technologies, e.g. certificate verification, which were intended to be used for DRM scenarios were explicitly removed by the TCG from the TPM specification.

Chapter 3
Mobile Trusted Computing Based on MTM

Jan-Erik Ekberg
Nokia Research Center, Finland

ABSTRACT

Trusted computing (TC) denotes a set of security-related hardware and software mechanisms that make a computing device work in a consistent manner, even in the presence of external attacks. For personal computers, TC typically is interpreted to be a software architecture designed around the trusted platform module (TPM), a hardware chip residing on the motherboard and implemented according to the specifications of the Trusted Computing Group (Trusted Computing Group, 2008A). In embedded devices, the state-of-the art in terms of hardware security and operating systems is significantly different from what is present on personal computers. So to stimulate the take-up of TCG technology on handsets as well, the recently approved mobile trusted module (MTM) specification (Trusted Computing Group, 2008B) defines new interfaces and adaptation options that match the requirements of the handset business ecosystem, as well as the hardware in use in the embedded domain. This chapter provides an overview of a few hardware security architectures (in handsets) to introduce the reader to the problem domain. The main focus of the text is in introducing the MTM specification – by first presenting its main functional concepts, and then by adapting it to one of the hardware architectures first described, essentially presenting a plausible practical deployment. The author also presents a brief security analysis of the MTM component, and a few novel ideas regarding how the (mobile) trusted module can be extended, and be made more versatile.

INTRODUCTION

In recent years, mobile phones have left the era of being closed embedded communication devices, increasingly turning into "hand-held multimedia computers". In addition to providing reliable, basic communication services (voice calls, SMS), contemporary handsets often provide the integrated services of music players, digital cameras, GPS

DOI: 10.4018/978-1-61520-682-7.ch003

navigators and gaming devices. The possibility to download and execute 3rd-party applications on the mobile platform makes handsets remarkably similar to personal computers in terms of openness and configurability.

A little-recognized fact is that this service convergence has stimulated device manufacturers to include advanced hardware- and operating system security features in their devices – this has been needed to balance user expectation and the strict regulatory requirements on the reliability of communication devices against virus and mal-ware threats that follow from introducing device openness.

Thus, there are hundreds of millions of deployed handset devices in the world today that are e.g. capable of protecting keys, assuring code integrity or making digital signatures using hardware-based features. Although these features today primarily are used to provide the necessary assurance that the handset in all possible scenarios will handle incoming and outgoing calls in an uninterruptible and reliable way, the mechanisms can as well in parallel be used for the benefit of 3rd party applications. As this happens, the role of trust modeling and trust management will play the crucial role of linking the security mechanisms to user perception and/or activity.

The traditional driver for platform security on handsets is the regulatory environment. Devices that participate in radio communication typically undergo testing to determine that the device keeps within the bandwidth allocated for the communication and that the transmission power does not exceed what is deemed safe for the user. For licensed bands also the conformance to protocol is a regulated activity. In practice this implies that both hardware and software are tested, and the approved license also includes the expectation that no (application) software installed at a later time can modify the tested and approved device features. This situation clearly motivates the need for software integrity as well as some degree of

isolation or integrity guarantees for configuration data that affects the communication.

Another important driver for handset security features is the business ecosystem in which phones often are sold. Communication service providers (operators) may sell below cost / subsidize end-user devices as a part of a long-term communication contract, where the assumption is that the monetary loss at the time of device sale is recaptured as communication revenue. In this setup the operator clearly requires some technical assurance that the device actually is used for communication, using the service provided by the operator in question. Constraints and enforcements related to this so called *SIM Lock* need to be properly rooted in hardware-assisted platform security services, since the breaking of the device lock feature by definition is a lucrative business opportunity. Digital rights management (DRM) for music and video is by nature a very similar security service.

Unfortunately the state of the art in handset trust mechanisms is that they are widely deployed, but manufacturer- or even product-specific. This is not acceptable for 3rd-party solution providers. Given a consistent, cross-platform secure trust infrastructure for handsets, at least the following services could bring clear benefits to users:

- Payment- and banking services is a specific field that has high security requirements, both in terms of protecting / isolating secrets (or value), and in terms of trusted interfacing. Payment services also resonate well with the mobility and the personal aspect of a handset.
- Authentication and access control of all sorts, whether to get access to web pages, company networks, one's car or one's apartment could be made both more convenient and more secure, if credential handling in the device is founded on a well-established trust infrastructure.

- More traditional user applications like mail clients, calendars, etc. can benefit from application-specific (or shared) secure storage - to address data privacy or to store secrets e.g. related to software licenses or session control.

This chapter introduces the first industry-wide attempt to define a common base for mobile trusted computing – the Mobile Trusted Module (MTM) specification. We start by briefly investigating the hardware landscape related to security mechanisms on handsets. We then introduce a few concepts from the TPM specification for personal computers, since many functionalities of TPM are directly used in its mobile counterpart, the MTM. Then we describe the MTM, with a specific focus on new features that the standard introduces with respect to TPM. As the MTM is intended to be deployable on contemporary security architectures, a real adaptation of MTM and especially its secure boot functionality is presented in the context of a Texas Instruments' M-Shield-enabled processor. Next we motivate the security of the MTM component in terms of the defined trust roots. The discussion of the MTM specification is rounded off by presenting both the in-device and external security ecosystems envisioned for the management of device trust, both with respect to applications and towards external entities. In the last section, the author lists a few shortcomings of the current MTM and proposes one improvement option, as well as a outlines a path forward for providing even greater flexibility (in scope of on-device trusted execution) in terms of hosting and executing credentials and other security-related services on the mobile handset.

LEGACY PLATFORM SECURITY SOLUTIONS

To understand the reasoning for the MTM architecture and to be able to map the concept of trust roots (introduced later) to the platform, one must understand how hardware platform security is achieved in contemporary embedded devices. The following three subsections outline three, increasingly powerful handset security architectures. Physically, these features are part of / embedded on the "main CPU" of the device.

Secure Boot

The basic approach to providing a degree of hardware-based platform security in embedded devices is to include a secure boot service on the ASIC itself. A general-purpose embedded processor typically will start executing from an internal boot ROM code which in turn loads and executes the "actual" boot-loader or system from external memory or storage. Assume that the same ASIC includes cryptographic accelerator hardware of some sort or enough boot ROM to include the code of some cryptographic signature – an asymmetric signature or even a keyed hash. In this setting it is trivial to include a (public) signature verification key in the boot ROM, and to require the first piece of externally loaded code (the boot-loader) to be signed by a matching signature generation key. If some asymmetric algorithm is used, no secret information needs to be stored on-chip, but we can still get the assurance that only (initial) code that is signed by a trusted entity is executed with this chip. This very basic security solution can be used to ascertain integrity of the executed code – the most crucial property e.g. for providing integrity and thus fulfilling regulatory requirements. It also provides a binding between hardware and software – making it infeasible to for a third party to reprogram the (possibly quite general-purpose) device for some unintended use case. The absence of device re-programmability is evidently very relevant for the device-lock security service.

Secure boot is by itself a very powerful enabler. However, by itself it is rarely enough, since for many security services confidentiality is needed, and this requires that a secret key is present on the device.

Secure Boot with Embedded Key

With only secure boot, the devices have no way to support data confidentiality without external help (like the user entering a passphrase). Encryption always requires the presence of a secret. For contemporary embedded ASICs, the addition of typical persistent secure storage (like Flash technology) would come at significant cost – the used number of silicon layers and the operating voltage would have to be adjusted. However, E-fuses - originally devised by IBM – provides a technology by which a limited number of "fuses" can be included within the ASIC, and selectively "burned" e.g. during manufacturing or later. By coding one bit / E-fuse, an ASIC can e.g. be labeled with a unique device identity. As the fuse programming can be done by software running on the chip, a first-boot-logic can also be made to randomly select and store a unique persistent key for itself, assuming that the ASIC includes a random number generator (RNG). Such a key is strictly local, if it is not released to the outside word. The key can thereafter be retrieved at every boot, and e.g. a local secure storage function can rely on this key for its purposes. Assuming that secure boot is deployed, we can make the argument that as only signed coded will ever be able to read the key from the E-fuses inside the ASIC, the key will not be revealed to an attacker since a correctly behaving code would not do such a thing.

The last argument makes this solution vulnerable. Clearly the logic where no part of the software leaks the key, or can be stimulated to do so by a run-time attack (like a buffer-overflow attack) only holds for small devices with very limited code-size. We must acknowledge the fact contemporary "embedded" handset OSs like Symbian or Linux are so big that coding errors always can be misused by e.g. viruses, to reveal a device key protected in this manner. There is also the additional problem

that large software is typically run from external memory (memory on a different ASIC / chip than the processor), and the protection of the memory bus (between the CPU and the memory) needs to be guaranteed for the argument presented in this section to hold.

Dedicated Platform Security Architecture in Hardware

The key leakage issue highlights the need for hardware-enforced isolation between different parts of a software system. Microprocessor cores have since the 80s included different security domains, typically in connection with (virtual) memory management. As a rule, the operating system along with event handlers runs in so called privileged mode, in which essentially all of the memory is accessible. Normal processes / programs, on the other hand are executed in user mode, where only memory relevant to that specific program and its data is accessible. Thus programs cannot interfere with each others' memory nor access the memory of the OS. The setup primarily protects against misbehaving programs corrupting the system, but clearly also serves as an isolation mechanism. Processor security architectures like Texas Instruments' M-shield (Srage & Azema, 2005 ; Sundaresan, 2003), and ARM TrustZone (ARM, 2008) on a high abstraction add a) a new, even higher privilege level to the ASIC operation and b) an entry gateway through which the operating system can call software functions executing inside this highly privileged mode. Both architectures can be configured so that only properly authenticated software can become such privileged functions, and that only such privileged functions ever can access e.g. a device secret burned in E-fuses. This kind of architecture combined with secure boot and secrets on the ASIC allows the integration of a software system where the cryptographic parts of the security critical services (say DRM) are run as signed, highly privileged functions (with access to device secrets), while we have a (recursive) secure boot providing integrity at least to the level of the OS, which in turn can isolate 3rd-party processes by the normal privileged/user mode separation. In this setup, even if an OS flaw would be found, only the integrity of the OS is potentially compromised, whereas device secrets still are hidden behind a functional interface consisting of a much smaller codebase – one that may be implemented and validated extra carefully to minimize the risk of it containing accidental vulnerabilities. Furthermore, this small code-base can be fit to run on on-processor memory, eliminating the risk of memory-bus attacks.

For the purposes of MTM, we can assume that the handset implementing an MTM in software will have hardware security that architecturally is close to the setup given in this subsection.

Security Threats

The discussion up to here does not explicitly mention security threats originating from the attacker gaining low-level physical access to the device, the chip, or communication channels e.g. between the chip and external memory. These are not irrelevant concerns, though. Many publicized attacks against existing security hardware use some degree of hardware tampering (Sparks, 2007; Samyde, Skorobogatov, Anderson & Quisquater, 2002). Also, side-channel attacks by means of timing or power analysis have been used to determine deployed keys even in smart cards, and could possibly be mass-deployed e.g. as viruses. The problem domain where environmental effects are used as a part of a security attack is, however, a science of its own, and an arms race of sorts. Smart card manufacturers have a long history in designing tamper-proof designs, and security breaches where a smart card is the root of a security problem are rare. The same goes for hardware-assisted security in larger ICs – e.g. the fact that the ARM-based Atmel 91SO100 System-On-a-Chip (SoC) microcontroller has been granted a Common Criteria EAL4+ certification (Sep-08)

for is design clearly indicates that there is in the industry a mindset and intent to also secure larger ASICs against hardware tampering.

Security Processors

Smart cards by themselves are not here considered as a platform security solution. The reasoning behind this is that smart cards typically are removable security engines, primarily used to authenticate users rather than the device. This does not preclude that smart cards or equivalent ICs could not be permanently affixed to embedded device hardware. In that case, any security service run on the smart card would also be directly bound to the device. However, without additional logic to bind smart card operations e.g. to the booting of the main ASIC, the smart card is easily bypassed at least for local security services, such as secure booting or the binding of keys to software state. One aspect of the TPM technology considered next, is to provide such a binding between a separate security chip and the main CPU.

THE TRUSTED PLATFORM MODULE (TPM)

The technology standardized by the Trusted Computing Group is a platform security architecture of special importance, since it is the first multi-vendor and multi-integrator platform security solution supported by many vendors. The Trusted Platform Module (TPM) (Trusted Computing Group, 2008A) is a hardware element that serves as the fundament for the architecture that further consists of specification work in e.g. the domain of embedded devices, trusted network access and server security. Even though TPMs are primarily geared towards the PC/Laptop market, the principles of TPM also permeate the mobile version, the Mobile Trusted Module (MTM) (Trusted Computing Group, 2008B; Trusted Computing Group, 2008C).

The TPM can be viewed as a separate security element soldered to the motherboard of the device, and in current deployments this is an accurate description – in most cases the TPM is its own ASIC with a direct connection to the main CPU. The TPM specification also specifies an API – the Trusted Software Stack (TSS) – for applications and system software to make use of TPM services. At a high level, the TPM provides e.g. asymmetric key generation and use, remote attestation and secure storage as services, all optionally bound to the current software state of the device (e.g. key usage can be constrained to be possible only in a given software state). In contrast with the embedded platform solutions listed above, the TPM module by design does not provide secure boot. Instead, it supports a mechanism denoted *trusted boot*, which can be summarized by that the TPM ASIC does not prohibit or stop the boot-up of the device, even if the booted software is wrong or infected. However, the system setup provides a guarantee – the so called *root of trust for Measurement* (RTM) - that the initial platform state including the first software to be booted is accurately measured into a set of registers in the TPM module. Possible further measurements sent to the TPM are only aggregated onto the first measurement, which cannot be replaced. Thus the TPM will contain state information that accurately represents the launch sequence, whatever it is. A "correct" launch sequence will at every step measure the next software to be executed, and augment TPM registers with this information (this is called *extending* in TPM terminology). As the measurements uniquely identify the launched code at least up to the point where it is known that the measurements up to this point represents well-behaving programs (in the TPM sense), an external or internal comparison between a well-known state and the current state can be carried out. The comparison result is the further used, among other things to a) conditionally provide or deny usage of keys residing on the TPM chip, b) conditionally provide access to

non-volatile storage on the TPM and to c) attest (by a signature) to the state for device- external validation. So even if a TPM-enabled device cannot bind the hardware and software together unconditionally, secrets like keys can be bound to well-known hardware-software combinations, and only when the device reaches that state can those keys be used.

For building the trust in the device boot-up, the measurement of the first launched software is crucial also when using the TPM. If this measurement is not accurate then neither is the first software, and thus all further measurements done by that very software cannot be trusted. As the TPM is external to the main processing unit, the TPM concept includes the RTM functional component that needs to be trusted to measure the initial software accurately. In PCs, this functionality has typically been included as an un-modifiable part of the BIOS.

TPM-compliant chips have for years been included in especially business laptops, and although they have not been in wide-spread application use, they can e.g. beneficially be used as the key store for disk encryption software.

MOBILE USE-CASES FOR A TRUSTED MODULE

The Mobile Working Group in TCG maintains a use-case list (Trusted Computing Group, 2009) – security services that are of specific interest to the handset market. The list includes *platform integrity* and *secure software download* – features of the utmost importance for (radio) devices that have to pass regulatory approval before being deployed. The *SIM lock,* i.e. the enforced binding between the network operator and the handset, is a security service that is instrumental to the business model of subsidized phones. *DRM* (digital rights management), *ticketing* and *mobile payment* are services that seem attractive enough for a portable device, but also have the property that the integrity of any such credential cannot be left to the whim of the device user, since his / her interests may well be in conflict with the service provider's.

The mentioned use-cases are not easily supported by TPM mechanisms, mostly because of their discretionary nature. Also, it is a hard sell to introduce a new (TPM) chip to already crowded and highly integrated handset hardware architectures, especially as many deployed handsets already includes legacy HW-based security. These reasons, in addition to the well known fact that having a common architecture often gives benefit to the whole industry in terms of increased efficiency as well as compatibility, motivated the work towards the Mobile Trusted Module, a lightweight "TPM variant", that also includes a few new capabilities, not seen on TPMs to date.

MTM: THE MOBILE TRUSTED MODULE

The Mobile Trusted Module (MTM v.1.0) is a security element specification (Trusted Computing Group, 2008B; Ekberg & Kylänpää, 2007) for specific use in mobile and embedded devices. Its origin lies in the TPM v. 1.2, but the mobile specification significantly differs from its peer specification on a few significant issues:

1. The concept of secure boot is introduced. Many embedded devices and handsets in particular are subject to regulatory approval. That in turn motivates the need for enforced integrity protection of software in fielded devices, and secure boot, i.e., a boot sequence not only measured, but also aborted on any non-approved state transition, is a vital building block for this security service.

2. The specification explicitly supports implementation of the MTM as a software functionality (with necessary hardware security support for isolation etc.) rather than as a physical implementation in hardware. This makes it possible for device manufacturers to add the MTM as an add-on to already deployed, proprietary security solutions.

3. A reference architecture takes into account the support of several parallel MTM instances in the same device. Some may be discretionary (MTM exposed to user applications) whereas e.g. the Device Manufacturer's MTM by definition enforces security policy (mandatory access control). The use for parallel MTMs will become evident in a later section.

4. The MTM specification minimizes the implementation footprint (whether implemented in hardware or software) by defining only a minimal set of the TPM functionality as mandatory in the scope of MTM.

MTM defines two interleaving profiles depending on the entity that holds ownership of the functionality – the Mobile Remote Owner Trusted Module (MRTM) and the Mobile Local Owner Trusted Module (MLTM) (see fig. 1). Intended to be used either by the device manufacturer or a carrier operator, the MTRM defines the necessary security architecture and interfaces to implement a securely booting, integrity-protected device. In addition, the MRTM key usage primitives can also be used as an API for application interfacing, e.g. to provide applications with a remote attestation service, or local encrypted storage. The MLTM is geared towards applications and to be managed by the user. Thus MLTM gives the using entity the right to take ownership of the module, e.g. to define authorization and authentication tokens for the MLTM functionality. The MLTM profile also provides a more comprehensive support for privacy-enabled attestation and a wider range of key management primitives. The architecture in principle also permits a device to run multiple MTMs of different profiles in parallel – if e.g. every application is provided with its own MLTM, bound to or rooted in a device MRTM, the system can better isolate state and therefore interaction

Figure 1. Trust relationships in the MTM architecture

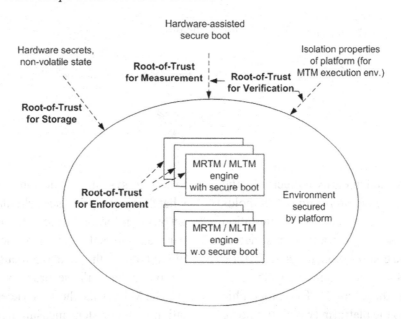

problems between applications. This is a problem otherwise inherent in the TPM architecture.

MTM Secure Boot

As the MTM standard is hardware-agnostic, it is flexible enough to accommodate several different architectures for guaranteeing the integrity of the MTM in the scope of secure boot, and also to support a variety of mechanisms for providing root secrets and immutable data storage. It is completely possible to map the MTM functionality to e.g. the ARM TrustZone processor architecture (Winter, 2008), and this is clearly one of the intents of the specification – to achieve fast deployment by making the standard deployable on contemporary embedded security architectures rather than requiring new hardware to be introduced to handsets and other embedded devices. Next we will look at the boot process as defined by the MTM specification.

During device boot-up, the MTM-enabled system will pass through two discrete standards-defined states - the *reset* and the *root-of-trust initialization*. The reset state simply describes the

fact that no software is running on the device prior to MTM setup. The initialization phase in which the software MTM is set up is defined by a set of roots of trust (RoTs), each of which describes a necessary security precondition to be satisfied in order for the MTM security to be assured. The trust roots are implemented in the context of the secure platform that is underlying the MTM. The *root of trust for Enforcement* (RTE) states that there is some logic that decides on and / or acts on the verification data related to secure boot, e.g. halts on an error. Inherited from the TPM specification, the *root of trust for Measurement* (RTM), makes the initial measurement of the system for inclusion into the MTM. Also, as the MTM is run on top of some other security infrastructure, the MTM logic (code) and the security of its future execution environment need to be validated prior to its execution. This functionality constitutes the *root of trust for Verification* (RTV), an "engine" that makes the needed security assertions (in a platform-specific way). Some form of device secret typically is needed to establish the *root of trust for Storage* (RTS) – since the MTM is no longer a physical entity its persistent state must

Figure 2. The principle of a RIM certificate

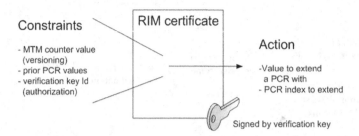

be confidentiality- and integrity protected by the platform. A *root of trust for Reporting* (RTR) holds the secrets to sign measurements for attestation purposes. As the set of the roots of trust define the security of the end solution, the specification imposes minimal security requirements for each of them, say e.g. the strength of cryptographic binding of RTS to the platform (which should be at least equivalent to a 160-bit SHA-1).

In a basic TPM, only the RTM is relevant for measurement. This is because the TPM is defined as a physical entity (an ASIC), so the integrity of data and isolation of code and secrets are implicitly handled by the physical context. For MTM, if a given secure environment cannot fulfill all five trust roots, that environment is not capable of implementing MTM.

At a high level of abstraction the MTM runs in one of three states during the boot phase. The device boots into the initialization state described above, governed by the (non MTM) security of the platform. On successful initialization (by means of RTV) the operation moves to a success state where it stays as long as the system state updates match an a-priori known state. On failing to reach such a state the MTM is moved to a failed state by the RTE, whereby it becomes in-operational, and stays that way until a device reboot. Additionally, when the MTM is in this state, the device may forcefully re-boot, lock up, disable some hardware interfaces or take any other approach necessary to preserve device security and integrity.

Most of the new commands, data and concepts introduced in MTM (with respect to TPM) relate to how the system can know in a validated manner what the right a-priori state should be, and how to act on this information correctly. There are several parallel, optional versions of the data structures involved – in this text we focus on the default setup to achieve the secure boot-up.

The MTM (like the TPM) keeps the representation of the system measurements in so called Platform Configuration Registers (PCRs). In MTM some of these registers can be defined to require validation prior to update – this selection is defined by the *verifiedPCRs* bit vector. If a register requires validation, the only way to update it is by means of a certificate, a so called reference integrity metric (RIM) certificate (fig. 2). The digital certificate contains the reference measurement (the end result that the measurer should come to if the state is correct), the value to be updated to the PCR which need not be the measurement itself, the expected current state of a set of the PCRs, and a few other constraints. It is typically signed by the RSA private key of the authority that concluded that the measurement in question was the right one. The MTM logic provides a function, *MTM_verifyRIMcertificateAndExtend,* that executes the abovementioned validations as well as the signature verification against a pre-loaded key. On successful validation, the PCR mentioned in the RIM certificate is updated with the given value.

The MTM state contains a specific trust root – *the root verification authority information* (RVAI) – that is the root of a public key hierarchy of so called verification keys. These are the keys by

Figure 3. Verification key hierarchy illustrated

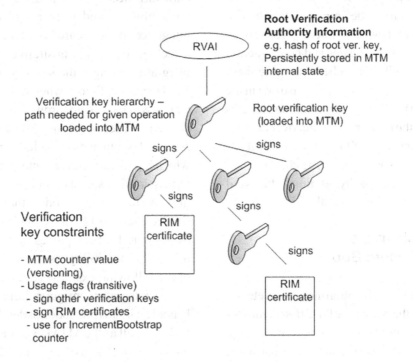

which the digital signatures in the RIM certificates are validated in the MTM (fig. 3). The keys are in turn signed in a tree hierarchy, i.e. to load the root key of the hierarchy it can be validated internally against RVAI, but to load the next key it will be validated by the fact that the to-be loaded key structure includes a signature by its parent key – a key that is assumed to be currently present in the MTM. In other words, to get the verification key for a specific RIM certificate into the MTM, first the root verification key is loaded, and then every key in sequence down the tree until the leaf "RIM certificate validating key" is reached, which in turn validates the signature on the RIM certificate that is used to update the PCR state.

This slightly complex setup of the validation process has many advantages. As the keys and accepted state updates are coded as signed "certificates", they can be stored outside the MTM, even in persistent storage with no security properties. Also, several alternative acceptable states are easily encoded as a set of RIM certificates, and the

measuring entity can after measurement decide which (if any) of the available RIM certificates match the state setup of the existing state and the measured next piece of code or data, and submit right the measurement and certificate to the MTM for evaluation. Also, the possible separation between the measurement and the value updated to the PCR, combined with secure boot, makes it possible for later components to validate PCR contents against well-known "label values" that may stay unchanged across software versions, rather than against code measurements that clearly are version dependent.

For explicit version control management, the MTM specification requires the implementation of two main secure counters. The first, the *bootstrap* counter is mainly intended for binding verification keys to the version of the firmware – either to the self-measured trust roots or the MTM code itself. This counter is incremented with an MTM-specific command – MTM_incrementBootstrapCounter, authorized by a signature with a verification key denoted for this purpose. In addition, the MTM specification requires the implementation of a RIMProtect counter, which is intended for version control of the RIM certificates and consequently the PCR updates allowed to be done using them (the counter binding is a specified constraint in the RIM certificate). The counter minimum lengths (32 updates for the bootstrap counter over the lifetime of the device, and 4096 for the RIMProtect) are such that they in principle can be implemented directly in hardware (e.g. by burning E-fuses), if no other state control is available.

MTM Example in the Context of Secure Boot

To make the MTM specification more concrete, we here exemplify the use case of multi-stakeholder boot, mentioned in (Trusted Computing Group, 2008B) in a context where the underlying hardware security architecture is either ARM TrustZone or Texas Instruments M-shield. This means a setup including a main processor with a secure execution mode, secure boot based on signatures, some on-chip RAM for the execution of secure code (in this case MTM logic), and a device secret that will be used as the fundament for RTS.

A handset, like any embedded device, is a collection of hardware components and software integrated into one. One or a few general-purpose computing cores run the software and take care of initializing secondary hardware blocks for e.g. communication and user interaction, possibly uploading software to those as well. The hardware (cores) typically come from many 3rd party sources, and software – from boot-loaders, system software, and hardware drivers all the way to applications also represent a variety of sources. In fact, in manufacturing the term integrator is often used to denote the company that puts all of the pieces together and make a working device out of them.

For platform security, traditionally the integrator has to take a central role. Software and hardware needs to be audited against security vulnerabilities and further signed or otherwise integrated in the secure boot process. From both a technical and administrative perspective the integrator manages the security. Any update for a device in the field – whether hardware or software – will have to go through the integrator to be cleared in a security sense (to get the signature). An ideal setup would include mechanisms by which the manufacturer / integrator can indicate its trust in other stakeholders, thereby distributing the overall security model, thereby decreasing time-to-market of both the device proper. as well as possible further updates or fixes. The MTM brings this possibility, as we will see in the light of the following example (fig. 4).

The integrator configures the handset to securely boot an intial (pre-)bootloader that implements RTV, as well as the MTM executable (as data). If the integrity of this code is modified, the device will not boot at all. The main operation of the code is to load the MTM code (and any static state) into secure memory on the ASIC (the MTM code itself is properly signed with a legacy signature to be uploadable). Second, it will TPM_Extend or MTM_VerifyRIMCertAndExtend the measurement of itself including the MTM code to a system PCR inside the MTM. Additionally, the dynamic state of the MTM must be retrieved from persistent storage, it is assumed to be encrypted with a platform key, thus only decryptable by the MTM code in the secure processing mode. This retrieval can be done at this instance (if the bootloader has enough capabilities to access the needed non-volatile storage) or later. If it is brought in later, such operations that are conditioned on parameters in the dynamic state must be refused until the state is available.

As a last measure the pre-bootloader will load a secondary bootloader, and related RIM certificates as well as verification keys. After loading, a measurement over the bootloader will be carried out, and if the measurement matches any of the RIM certificates, the bootloader will

Figure 4. MTM secure boot example

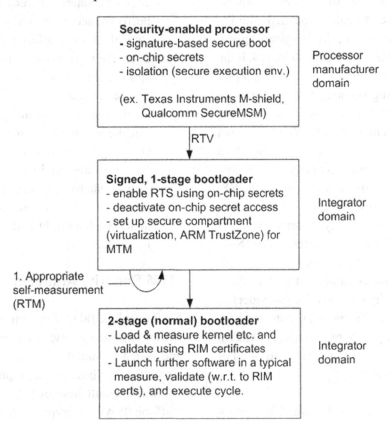

load any needed verification keys (in order) for the RIM certificate in question, and subsequently issue an *MTM_VerifyRIMCertAndExtend* with the calculated measurement. If there was no match between measurement and RIM certificate, or if the MTM command failed to execute (due to a mismatched constraint) the overall boot-up is aborted. If the command concludes successfully, the actual bootloader is launched, and from this point forward every software component that launches another component will perform the same validation step before invoking the second component, in a very similar manner in which trusted boot operates in TPM – first measure, then launch – now only adding "abort, if an error is found".

Consider the use case of multi-stakeholder boot-up, we can now elaborate on the key management of this system. Clearly, the integrator X

together with the ASIC manufacturer will handle the legacy secure boot, i.e. the launching of the MTM proper is still the responsibility of the integrator. For verification, the MTM in its persistent state will contain an RVAI that identifies a base key of the integrator. Presumably the integrator *X* will also assign other sub-keys to itself, e.g. one with the right to update the bootstrap counter, in case a flaw is found in the very initial firmware or in the MTM code itself. However, let's further imagine that we have four contracting companies *A*, *B*, *C* and *D* – *A* does the secondary bootloader, *B* provides the operating system, *C* the firmware for a DSP (uploaded by the OS) and *D* the OS driver to the functionality provided by *C*. Now *X* decides to trust the security processes of *A*, *B*, *C* and *D*, and produces four verification key certificates for the public keys of the respective companies. Additionally *X* lays out a policy, identifying a set of PCRs as well as a set of "reference values" for them. Say the certificate associated with the bootloader of A may be required to insert a given value (through a RIM certificate) in PCR 8, if the bootloader is a production version, and another value if it is a debug version. *A* can engineer its own certificates for its own code while it is being developed, and OS manufacturer *B* can construct its RIM certificates to account for the given values in PCR8. Further, say that *C* is instructed to update PCR 9 - of course it also has to consider PCR8-values in its RIM certificates, since it must make sure that the measuring entity is correct, which it can assume if PCR8 has the correct value. Now *D* can constrain its RIM certificate to PCR8 & PCR9, since it requires validity of both of these entities, whereby any other service (provider) *E*, relying only on the OS can satisfy its need for underlying integrity only by referring to known values of PCR8. It is easy to see that this kind of structure can be used to

1) Diversify the trust mechanism. The signing entity has the responsibility of only launching signed RIM certificates for code that works correctly - and also measures further code correctly if it is not a leaf of the trust chain.

2) Speed up development. Any trusted company (A/B/C/D) may sign (debug versions) also "on behalf" of the other involved parties, for code that originates from those parties, or dummy in-house interfaces that are only needed for development. The signature uniquely identifies the signing party, i.e. if such code is not labeled as a debug version and leaks, the origin can be traced back. Deployed RIM certificates would of course constrain themselves only to production PCR updates, i.e. making debug versions useless in the field.

3) Speed up patching. Any part of the secure boot can be upgraded independently. More serious vulnerabilities can be addressed by counter updates, whereby the patched code need to be accompanied by new RIM certificates also for non-affected and non-corrected code. The renewed signatures consume little space and are easy to construct e.g. by the device integrator.

4) Achieve stakeholder independence in time: The measurements themselves are not constraining the PCR update, i.e. the agreed update values need not be the same as the actual code hash, making it possible to version all pieces of the secure boot independently without tight collaboration between involved parties.

MTM Security Analysis

For the deployed algorithms, the level of data integrity and confidentiality, instantiated in signatures and sealed / bound data are directly related to the strength of the base cryptographic primitives. In MTM, by default these are SHA-1 for hashing and 2048-bit RSA for encryption / decryption. It is well known that the collision properties of SHA-1 are insufficient, and that work on standardizing a new hash algorithm (National Institute of Standards and Technology, 2009) is underway. RSA 2048 is still considered strong enough for digital signatures. The system state representation as stored in the MTM is represented as a SHA-1 hash chain, and thus only as strong as the primitive. A successful attack against the state representation could be used by an attacker to unseal / unbind data when the system is in a state where that operation otherwise would not be allowed.

A complete security analysis of the MTM will always depend on the hardware it is deployed on. For a traditional TPM isolation and platform binding are hardware features of the discrete chip. For an MTM, we can reason about the security of the MTM component on an abstract level, using the roots of trust.

***Isolation** from the rest of the computing device:* The Root-Of-Trust for Storage provides the MTM with a confidential, integrity-protected, persistent and stateful storage for any data the MTM needs to store for its own purposes. RTS will not provide access to this data for any other component. The Root-Of-Trust for Verification will provide the necessary assertions to guarantee the run-time isolation of the MTM code, as well as the attestation of the MTM code image itself. By virtue of RTS and RTV, the execution environment of MTM is isolated, and the MTM code that executes in it unmodified (with respect to some reference). Integrity is a consequence of isolation.

Platform binding: The presence of MTM secrets in the RTS indirectly proves the platform binding. However, the TPM and MTM specifications acknowledge that the configuration of a computing platform (both in terms of hardware and software) may change over time. The Root-Of-Trust for Measurement manages this aspect – it will, typically in an early boot phase, reliably inject into a TPM/MTM a first measurement that represents the current system state. Further actions (like the possibility to unseal some data bound to the MTM) can be made conditional to this measurement, effectively providing platform binding for the data. The MTM specification also explicitly defines the minimum cryptographic level of platform binding for RTV and RTS.

Secure boot is a new feature introduced by MTM. We can assume isolation and platform binding for the MTM module itself, but further we require

Integrity of information related to secure boot validation: The MTM does not as part of its own state maintain information regarding system states that are acceptable during the boot phase. Internally MTM only maintains a list of PCR registers that cannot be updated by any other means than invoking a command authenticated by a RIM certificate. We assume that all executed components during boot are measured before execution. As in normal TPM we then can assume that any measurement done by the measuring component is reliable, since

it by definition already has been measured and validated. The resulting measurement is matched against a suitable RIM certificate by the validating component, and we can trust that this comparison is done reliably. When given to the MTM, it can validate – based on cryptographic signatures validated by verification keys loaded into MTM - that the information in the RIM certificate is unmodified (integrity of reference measurement). The RIM certificate also contains necessary preconditions (e.g. PCR values) that the MTM matches against its current internal state, and thus integrity of system state is achieved – a RIM certificate can only be deployed in a state where it is defined to be deployable. The RIM certificate also defines a PCR update, i.e. the deployment of a RIM certificate causes a predefined change in the internal state of the MTM, matching the corresponding system state transition that the measurement precedes. As an end result we achieve overall integrity of the measuring action, both in terms of data and in terms of state representation (MTM internal state corresponds to a given system state).

Consistent enforcement: The MTM can tell a querying component when the secure boot has reached an unknown state, whereby an action (typically shutdown) needs to be taken. This feature is completely outsourced to the root of trust for Enforcement (RTE), i.e. it is assumed that the secure platform, i.e. the securely booting platform, can assert at all times that MTM replies related to secure boot can be acted on consistently without error.

MTM Ecosystem Trust Management

Related to the collaboration between trust stake-holders, the reference architecture of MTMv1 also specifies structures to support key management, and indicates some uses of verification key extension fields to e.g. add use-case dependent constraints or to indicate the location of a certificate revocation service in a reliable manner.

For lifecycle management of verification keys, the reference architecture introduces validity lists (i.e. white lists) – as a concept the opposite of certificate revocation lists. A validity list is issued by the entity controlling the RVAI on the devices (e.g. the device manufacturer), and it will in the list indicate all verification keys that are valid in a time interval specified as UTC time in the validity list. The task to produce and maintain validity lists are indicated as a parameter in each verification key structure. Thus the root validation entity may decide to keep the right with itself, or to delegate this task to another stakeholder. The device-internal validation of the RIM validity list is not part of the specification, but should be included in the engine to get an assurance of the validity of the delegation chain whenever a verification key is loaded into the MTM, The verification of the validity list also assumes the presence of a secure clock, which is not addressed nor required in the baseline specification. The reference architecture also introduces RIM certificate validity lists, architecturally similar to the validity lists for verification keys, but used by individual stakeholders to manage RIM certificates signed by them. These lists can be advantageously used for version control within the scope of a single stakeholder, in contrast to the versioning provided by internal counters, the updates of which requires all stakeholders to redo their respective certificates.

Transitive and Logically Parallel MTMs

In contrast to a TPM, where the hardware binding more or less defines the chip to be one single trust entity, the virtual nature of an MTM makes its applicability more or less boundless. The secure boot in MTM, and the presence of the RTV/RTE, implies that the system can be assured to enter a trusted state during boot. Thus, this fact can be advantageously used to enable transitive trust domains by means of a multitude of MTMs, possibly either situated at different levels in the system stack, or all managed and operated within the same environment as the baseline MTM, but dedicated to serve different entities at various software levels. Especially in the latter case, the security level of the sub-MTM, provided by the environment, as defined by RTV/RTE, is equivalent to the level of the base MTM. As long as the system relies on secure boot, there is not necessarily a need for the MTM user to validate all parts of the transitive trust chain, since it can be assumed, that on any failure in that chain, the device would have reacted in accordance with the platform policy, and made the MTMs inaccessible. Thus, the main challenge is to assign and maintain the mapping between the MTM users and their respective (possibly quite dynamic) MTM engines in an authenticated fashion. The authenticated sessions for MTM communication between the application and the MTM logic (so called OIAP / OSAP sessions) may help to establish this relation, but at large the problem needs to be solved separately by the target architecture.

Considering the two flavors of MTM - the remotely owned MRTM for system services that are remotely managed, and the user-owned MLTM for the user's own data, and combining this with the possibility of running many parallel MTM engines on a platform, the overall trust architecture constructed using these building blocks can be made be very versatile. With MTM, the whole architecture is based on well-defined trust roots which in turn (according to specification) are based on hardware mechanisms. When it comes to the functions inherited from the TPM v.1.2 specification, a well-defined API to the security mechanisms exists, and is already widely adopted on PC laptops. The MTM specification bridges the technology barrier and brings these services also into the mobile domain.

MTM Extensions and Other Architectural Developments

As the MTMv1 has only recently been specified, its actual deployment is still lacking. When devices adhering to the specification reach the market, we will see which use cases will be the dominant drivers for the features introduced by MTM. One clear omission with the current specifications is the lack of a defined driver API for the new commands – this easily makes application interfacing manufacturer-specific – leading to portability problems. Additionally the specification falls short in providing support for some evident use cases – one example is outlined in the following:

Stakeholder Separation in MTM

The observant reader may have noticed, that the secure boot example outlined above did not address the issue of possible mutual distrust between stakeholders participating in the construction of the device software. This is because the basic MTM-compliant verification key credentials, given to the stakeholders by the integrator, are (with the exception of a few less significant configuration options) equally powerful. In context of the earlier example, the companies A, B, C and D can all sign system components irrespectively of the domain of the respective stakeholder. For establishing e.g. liability, this is of little concern, since the signatures can still be tracked to the respective stakeholder. However, if we assume that the stakeholders are of different trustworthiness (as companies, towards the integrator), then the situation becomes troublesome, since the integrator might plausibly want to constrain the signing rights for stakeholders with less perceived reliability to only include the rights that the stakeholder actually needs. In other words, the current specification for releasing RIM certificate signing rights does not fulfill the principle of least privilege.

The dilemma is easily remedied, when the problem has been pointed out. Just like the RIM certificates can be constrained to PCR values in certain PCR registers, a verification key structure can be augmented to include a constraining field – that includes a set of PCR registers that RIM certificates, signed by this verification key are allowed modify. The check for this property can be trivially implemented by a bit-vector lookup at the time the RIM certificate is used. This extra feature would make the multi-stakeholder secure boot use-case conceptually more powerful, and likely match the reality of the use case better.

More General-Purpose Trusted Execution Environments

The security services as described in this chapter, and provided e.g. by the MTM and TPM standards are well suited to provide security in the context of a variety of well defined needs and use cases – like secure key storage, remote attestation or secure boot. However, on an abstract level, a credential typically consists of both a secret and logic that uses the secret for its processing. Sometimes the logic is also confidential. To achieve further protection for the credential logic a well isolated trusted execution environment (TrEE), accessible by 3rd parties, can provide a context in which security-critical algorithms can be executed in total isolation from the rest of the applications and operating system. Banking credentials, One-time password algorithms (OTP), DRM engines or micro-payment token-handling code are good examples of such logic.

Implementation options for trusted execution environments include OS virtualization mechanisms, dedicated hardware and the (on-chip) processor security architectures described in the first section. In terms of protection these variations primarily differ in the domain of hardware- and side-channel attacks, e.g. how well the isolation holds up against an attacker performing memory-bus sniffing attacks, memory retention attacks, chip replacement attacks etc.

Vulnerabilities aside, the main issue for executing of 3rd-party logic on a deployed platform is how the key management is handled with respect to the isolation. The dilemma is as follows: If the platform owner / integrator sets up the isolation between the 3rd-party credentials or their data based on an auditing and certification process, this entity (the issuer) easily becomes a bottleneck in terms of deployment speed and cost. On the other hand, if the execution environment is left completely open (as a sandbox of sorts), then the environment itself must not just provide the complete isolation of code and data of one credential with respect to other credentials from other unknown parties, but also a) the security of the provisioning process must be arranged for, b) a way for the 3rd-party to ascertain its trust in the sandboxing mechanism must be provided, and c) a mechanism by which a 3rd party can attest to the fact that the credential actually has been executed within such a sandbox must be directly or indirectly handled. In other words, even if the issuer does not actively participate in the credential generation and installation, the role of an issuer as a trust root cannot be eliminated.

The JavaCard technology (Chen, 2000) is a well-established example of the first type of execution environment. Well-defined specification and publicly available development tools makes it easy for anybody to write JavaCard applications. However, in order to install the application onto a deployed card, the application needs to be signed by the card issuer. As a security issue this is tied to a so called pre-verification step of the code, where some security properties of the deployed code are validated prior to uploading the logic to the JavaCard. Code that does not satisfy the pre-verification step may not adhere to the required isolation policy.

One example of an architecture that provides 3rd-party credential execution without tight issuer control is the "On-Board Credentials" (ObC)

architecture research project carried out at Nokia Research Center (Ekberg, Asokan, Kostiainen & Rantala, 2008A). Implemented on TI M-shield, a major intent of the architecture is to provide an secure and isolated credentials execution environment on mobile phones that can be used by 3rd parties without any approval process involving the device manufacturer or any assigned other trusted party. In (Ekberg, Asokan, Kostiainen & Rantala, 2008B; Kostiainen, Ekberg, Asokan & Rantala, 2009) further information is provided regarding how the provisioning and attestation properties has been solved for ObC.

Towards Application-Level Access

The handset ecosystem of today is evolving towards software openness. The legacy in the field brings along a platform security infrastructure that varies between products and manufacturers, but typically is hardware-enforced. In many cases, also the mobile operating systems like Symbian (Heath, 2006), Android (Google, 2009) and Apple iPhone (Miller, Honoroff & Mason, 2007) include mandatory access control features. Thus the outset in the mobile domain is very different from the PC environment where complete openness traditionally includes both the hardware and the OS. As the MTM specification is an industry collaboration in the mobile domain to harmonize the security services of the handsets at the intersection between the hardware and software, it also makes it possible to make these security services available to the application layer on the device in a vendor-independent manner. The TPM/MTM interfaces enable device-specific sealing, remote attestation, and the means to invoke signatures / decryption services using platform keys or newly generated keys. These functions alone can be used for a large variety of application use-cases in the security domain.

CONCLUSION

The Mobile Trusted Module is a security technology that likely will be available in handsets across the globe in a not too-distant future. The description of legacy platform security architectures provided an overview of what kind of enforcement and confidentiality / isolation services a handset of today typically includes on the chip(set) level, and these services will often serve as the foundation (trust roots) of a handset MTM implementation. We have further discussed various rationales for the MTM being what it is - e.g. the main shortcomings of TPM for mobile use-cases that has led to the introduction of secure boot and its supporting mechanisms in MTM. The TPM technology (for PCs) was shortly presented, since most fundamental TPM mechanisms are also present on the MTM. The MTM sections mainly intended to teach MTM technology, but also specifically highlight the secure boot mechanism, since this is in the core of the MTM technology as well as its use cases. The discussion on adapting the MTM into the operating system by means of MTM hierarchies, and also the section regarding how MTM credentials are managed, constitute "future research" in the sense that the MTM reference architecture presents these mechanisms, but there is neither an exact specification nor supporting academic research to validate, exemplify or build on these concepts. The last section tried to provide the insight that also the MTM specification as it stands today may still benefit from additional academic inspection, and that there also in parallel exists research that in the handset domain either aspires to break the boundaries of MTM or to provide alternative solutions.

REFERENCES

ARM. (2008). *ARM 1176 JZFS Technical reference manual*. Retrieved April 27, 2009, from http://infocenter.arm.com/help/topic/com.arm.doc.ddi0301g/DDI0301G_arm1176jzfs_r0p7_trm.pdf

Chen, Z. (2000). *Java Card Technology for Smart Cards: Architecture and Programmer's Guide*. Reading, MA: Addison-Wesley Longman Publishing Co., Inc.

Ekberg, J.-E. Asokan, N., Kostiainen, K., & Rantala, A. (2008A). *On-Board Credentials Platform Design and Implementation* (Nokia Research Center Technical Report NRC-TR-2008-01). Retrieved April 27, 2009, from http://research.nokia.com/files/NRCTR2008001.pdf

Ekberg, J.-E., Asokan, N., Kostiainen, K., & Rantala, A. (2008B). Scheduling execution of credentials in constrained secure environments. In *Proceedings of the 3rd ACM Workshop on Scalable Trusted Computing*.

Ekberg, J.-E., & Kylänpää, M. (2007). *Mobile Trusted Module (MTM) - an introduction* (Nokia Research Center, Technical report NRC-2007-015). Retrieved April 27, 2009, from http://research.nokia.com/

Gehrmann, C., & Ståhl, P. (2006). *Mobile Platform security* (Ericsson review no 02). Retrieved April 27, 2009, from http://www.ericsson.com/ericsson/corpinfo/publications/review/2006_02/03.shtml

Google. (2009). *Security and Permissions in Android*. Retrieved April 27, 2009, from http://code.google.com/android/devel/security.html

Heath, C. (2006). *Symbian OS Platform Security: Software Development Using the Symbian OS Security Architecture*. Hoboken, NJ: John Wiley & Sons Inc.

Kostiainen, K., Ekberg, J.-E., Asokan, N., & Rantala, A. (2009). On-board Credentials with Open Provisioning. In *Proceedings of ASIACCS'09, ACM Symposium on Information, Computer & Communication Security.*

Miller, C., Honoroff, J., & Mason, J. (2007). *Security evaluation of Apple's IPhone.* Retrieved April 27, 2009, from http://content.securityevaluators.com/iphone/exploitingiphone.pdf

National Institute of Standards and Technology. (2009). *Tentative Timeline of the Development of New Hash Functions.* Retrieved April 27, 2009, from http://csrc.nist.gov/groups/ST/hash/timeline.html

Quisquater, J.-J., & Samyde, D. (2002). Side channel cryptanalysis. In *Proceedings of the SECI'02, Securité des Communications sur Internet.*

Samyde, D., Skorobogatov, S., Anderson, R., & Quisquater, J.-J. (2002). On a new way to read data from memory. In *Proceedings of the First International IEEE Security in Storage Workshop.*

Sparks, E. (2007). *A Security Assessment of Trusted Platform Modules* (Dartmouth College, Computer Science Technical Report TR2007-597). Retrieved April 27, 2009, from http://www.ists.dartmouth.edu/library/341.pdf

Srage, J., & Azema, J. (2005). *M-Shield mobile security technology* [white paper]. Texas Instruments. Retrieved April 27, 2009, from http://focus.ti.com/pdfs/wtbu/ti_mshield_whitepaper.pdf

Sundaresan, H. (2003). *OMAP platform security features, July 2003* [white paper]. Texas Instruments. Retrieved April 27, 2009, from http://focus.ti.com/pdfs/vf/wireless/platformsecuritywp.pdf

Symbian. (2007). *Symbian Signed Whitepaper.* Retrieved April 27, 2009, from https://www.symbiansigned.com/Symbian_Signed_White_Paper.pdf

Trusted Computing Group. (2008A). *TPM Specification, version 1.2 Revision 103.* Retrieved April 27, 2009, from https://www.trustedcomputinggroup.org/specs/TPM/

Trusted Computing Group. (2008B). *Mobile Trusted Module Specification, Version 1.0 Revision 1.* Retrieved April 27, 2009, from https://www.trustedcomputinggroup.org/specs/mobilephone

Trusted Computing Group. (2008C). *Mobile Trusted Module Reference Architecture, Version 1.0.* Retrieved April 27, 2009, from https://www.trustedcomputinggroup.org/specs/mobilephone

Trusted Computing Group. (2009). *Mobile Phone Work Group Selected Use Case Analysis, v 1.0.* Retrieved April 27, 2009, from https://www.trustedcomputinggroup.org/specs/mobilephone

Winter, J. (2008): Trusted computing building blocks for embedded Linux-based ARM TrustZone platforms. In *Proceedings of the 3rd ACM Workshop on Scalable Trusted Computing.*

KEY TERMS AND DEFINITIONS

ASIC: Application-Specific Integrated Circuit

CPU: Central Processing Unit

IC: Integrated Circuit

DRM: Digital Rights Management

HW: Hardware

MLTM: Mobile Local-owner Trusted Module

MRTM: Mobile Remote-owner Trusted Module

MTM: Mobile Trusted Module

ObC: On-Board Credentials

OIAP: Object Independent Authorization Protocol

OSAP: Object Specific Authorization Protocol

OS: Operating system
OTP: One-time password
PCR: Platform Configuration Register
RAM: Random-access memory
RIM: Reference Integrity Metric
ROM: Read-Only Memory
RNG: Random Number Generator
RTE: Root of trust for enforcement
RTM: Root of trust for measurement
RTR: Root of trust for reporting
RTS: Root of trust for storage
RTV: Root of trust for verification
SW: Software
SoC: System-on-Chip
TPM: Trusted Platform Module
TrEE: Trusted Execution Environment

Chapter 4

Establishing Software Integrity Trust:
A Survey and Lightweight Authentication System for Windows

Yongzheng Wu
National University of Singapore, Singapore

Sufatrio
National University of Singapore, Singapore

Roland H.C. Yap
National University of Singapore, Singapore

Rajiv Ramnath
National University of Singapore, Singapore

Felix Halim
National University of Singapore, Singapore

ABSTRACT

Malware causes damage by stealing confidential data or making other software unusable. Ensuring software trustworthiness is difficult because malware may disguise itself to appear benign or trusted. This chapter explores the problem of making software more trustworthy through the use of binary integrity mechanisms. The authors review the problem of devising an effective binary integrity protection, and discuss how it complements other operating system security measures. They analyze design factors for binary integrity and compare existing systems. The authors then present a prototype which exemplifies a mandatory binary integrity mechanism and its integration within an operating system. Their system, BinAuth, demonstrates a practical, lightweight in-kernel binary authentication system for Microsoft Windows. A system like BinAuth shows that mandatory authentication is practical on complex

DOI: 10.4018/978-1-61520-682-7.ch004

commodity operating system like Windows. To deal with various constraints in the user's environments, BinAuth uses a flexible scheme which does not mandate public key infrastructure (PKI) although it can take advantage of it. The authors also combine the authentication with a simple software-ID scheme which is useful for software management and vulnerability assessment.

INTRODUCTION

Malware is a critical security threat today. A report by F-Secure (F-Secure, 2007) indicates that the amount of malware grew by 100% during 2007, and that there was as much malware produced in 2007 as in the previous 20 years altogether. A recent report from Organisation for Economic Co-operation and Development (OECD) (OECD, 2008) highlights a worrying trend that malware has now evolved from occasional exploits to a global multi-million dollar criminal industry, and is threatening the Internet economy.

Many of the system security attacks stem from the fact that distrusted code is executed on the system. A modern operating system has numerous built-in security measures designed to ensure a secure execution environment. The security measures are aimed at preventing illegal operations on a system, including illegitimate addition or modification of executable code on the file system. Due to various software vulnerabilities, such as buffer overflow (Cowan, Wagle, Calton, Beattie & Walpole, 2000) or format string vulnerability (Scut, 2001), a program however can be susceptible to local or remote attack. An attacker who succeeds in hijacking the execution of a process can perform subsequent operations under the context of the victim process. If the victim process happens to be in an elevated privilege when the attack occurs, for example root privilege due to SUID root feature in Unix/Linux, then the attacker gains unrestricted root access on the system.

Once an attacker succeeds in compromising a system, the next step is usually to install/modify executable code on the victim's file system. This could be done for several reasons: install a backdoor, plant spyware, or as a step for subsequent privilege-escalation attacks. A mechanism to deal with illegal addition or modification of executables on a system is thus a useful additional line of defense. Such a mechanism can also help prevent social engineering attacks which attempt to trick a user to install a software package that illegitimately replaces important system libraries. In more stringent environments, the protection mechanism can operate on controlled host systems to limit users to only run an approved set of executable files.

This chapter reviews the problem of establishing trust on the integrity of binary executables prior to their execution. We view file integrity mechanism as an important component for achieving a high level of software trustworthiness given the prevalence of malware and system attacks. In the rest of the chapter, we refer to any executable code stored in the file system as a *binary*. The goal of a software integrity protection system is to ensure that an executed binary only comes from trusted software providers/vendors, and that it is executed in the correct context. Later, we show that this can be efficiently achieved on complex operating systems such as Microsoft Windows[1].

A binary authentication system can provide the following authentication guarantees:

(i) *Binary-content authentication*: only binaries with previously known and trusted contents are allowed for execution; and

(ii) *Binary-location authentication*: a binary's pathname must match its purported content.

Binary-content authentication ensures that a binary has not been tampered with. For example, cmd.exe is not a trojan. Binary-location authentication ensures that we are executing an executable which we want. For instance, suppose that the contents of a file-system format and shell binaries are both authenticated. However, if an attacker swaps their pathnames, then running a shell would cause the file system to be formatted.

Most work on binary integrity authentication is done on Unix/Linux (Apvrille, Gordon, Hallyn, Pourzandi & Roy, 2004; Beattie, Black, Cowan, Pu & Yang, 2000; Doorn, Ballintijn & Arbaugh, 2001; Williams, 2002). Some of the proposed systems however only provide one from the two authentication guarantees. They also differ in several important ways according to their characteristics. This chapter develops a framework to compare authentication systems based on a number of key design factors. We then compare various existing authentication systems, and highlight their strength and weaknesses. Additionally, we discuss choices for design factors and their effectiveness in protecting a host system. In this chapter, special attention is paid to Microsoft Windows platform. This is motivated by the fact that the problem of malware is more acute in Windows. There are also many more types of executable code which come with different file types, e.g. executables (.EXE), dynamic linked libraries (.DLL), ActiveX controls, control panel applets, and drivers. This chapter focuses on mandatory binary authentication of all forms of executables in Windows prior to their execution.

Most operating systems can prevent the execution of code on the stack due to buffer overflow attack by employing hardware-based data execution protection, e.g. No eXecute (NX) protection. Combining security measures such as stack protection with binary authentication makes the attacker's task more difficult. We argue here that mandatory binary authentication is a practical and important feature required to establish trust on good software execution. Together with other security measures, it can provide stronger safeguard against the malware threat on popular commercial operating system. Binary authentication is also beneficial because it is even more important for the operating system to be protected against malicious kernel drivers, i.e. attacks which attempt to load malware into the kernel. In this chapter, we show how an effective authentication system can be achieved on complex commodity operating systems like Windows with low overheads by presenting a proof-of-concept implementation of *BinAuth*, a practical, lightweight, in-kernel binary authentication system for Windows.

A binary authentication needs to be flexible to operate under different scenarios. Our prototype finger-prints binaries using the HMAC construction (Krawczyk, Bellare & Canetti, 1997) which is more lightweight than necessitating the use of digital signatures and PKI. The authentication scheme also has other benefits. As software evolves, one needs to deal with the maintenance of the software over time. Nowadays, the number of discovered vulnerabilities grows rapidly (CMU's CERT, 2009). This means that binaries on a system (even if they are authenticated) may be vulnerable, which leads to the problem of vulnerability management and patching. We propose a simple software-ID system which leverages on the binary authentication infrastructure and existing trusted infrastructures, such as Domain Name System (DNS) and Certificate Authorities (Vishik, Johnson & Hoffman, 2007), to handle this problem.

Besides our comparison framework, a main contribution of our work is that it provides an infrastructure for in-kernel mandatory enforcement of trusted binary execution for Windows. This is significant since many of the problems of security on Windows stems from inability to distinguish between trusted and distrusted software. Our scheme provides mandatory authentication for the full range of binaries under Windows, and goes beyond code authentication mechanism in Windows XP and Vista. It also protects driver loading which gives increased kernel protection. Moreover, it provides mandatory driver authentication which 32-bit Windows does not, and can be integrated with more flexible policies which 64-bit Windows does not support. We also analyze the security of our system. Our benchmarking shows that the overhead of comprehensive binary authentication can be quite low, around 2%, with a caching strategy.

The remainder of this chapter is organized as follows. We first provide some background information on binary authentication within the context of operating system security. Then, we give a framework for comparing binary authentication systems, and survey various existing systems using the framework. We then shift our focus on analyzing important issues related to binary authentication which arise specifically on Windows. Subsequently, we then describe the design and implementation of BinAuth together with software-ID scheme. Next, we benchmark BinAuth using both system and application benchmarks. Finally, we discuss future research directions and conclude this chapter.

BACKGROUND

We give some background on binary authentication problem by: (i) explaining where it fits in connection with other operating system security measures; (ii) defining the authentication goals; and (iii) elaborating its security assumptions. Throughout this chapter, we define "Administrator" to be the trusted privileged user, such as system administrator in Windows or superuser in Unix.

Binary Authentication and Operating System Security

A modern operating system comes with built-in security features to ensure a secure operation environment. Among others, *access control* mecha-

nism (Pfleeger & Pfleeger, 2006) ascertains that an authenticated user can only perform a set of approved operations on computing resources that he/she is entitled to. *Process isolation* (Pfleeger & Pfleeger, 2006) separates and protects each process from other processes. In addition to standard mechanisms, a number of more advanced measures have been proposed and implemented to enhance security. Hardware-assisted (e.g. *NX bit*) executable space protection mechanism makes memory regions for data to be non-executable. *Address Space Layout Randomization (ASLR)* randomly arranges the positions of key areas in a process' address space to make it harder for an attacker to predict target addresses (Shacham, Page, Pfaff, Goh, Modadugu & Boneh, 2004).

When executed, a binary on a system performs various operations on resources such as files, registry and network. The execution of a malicious binary clearly can jeopardize a system if it runs with Administrator privilege. As such, the security of a system also means that the binaries must be trusted. Secure binary hosting, i.e. ensuring that a binary is not illegally modified or added into the file system, is a necessary component for establishing software trust. Other components of establishing software trust include: secure software distribution which typically requires binaries to be digitally signed for tamper protection, and timely vulnerability and patch management to ensure that a binary is vulnerability-free prior to its execution.

Although the concept of binary integrity authentication is not new, it is not commonly incorporated as a standard in-kernel mechanism in popular commercial off-the-shelf operating system, such as Windows or Unix/Linux. There exist tools for monitoring binary integrity such as *Tripwire* (Kim & Spafford, 1993) which is one of the first to deal with file integrity protection. However, Tripwire is a user-mode application program. It checks file integrity off-line, and does not provide any mandatory form of integrity checking. Several others kernel modifications were proposed, although mostly in Unix/Linux platforms. Partly motivated by the emergence of mobile code (e.g. Java applets), some operating systems extend the concept of signed code to standard binary types, and check the validity of the binary's signature particularly if it is downloaded from untrusted zone like the Internet. Windows has Authenticode (Grimes, n.d.) technology. Windows Vista User Account Control (UAC) adds binary signature checks in some special cases. The next section surveys and compares a number of existing authentication systems including Authenticode and UAC, and highlights their differences from an ideal scheme.

There have been efforts within the operating system community to realize Trusted Operating System (TOS). TOS refers to an operating system that provides sufficient support for multilevel security and evidence of correctness to meet a particular set of government requirements. One of the most common set of criteria for trusted operating system design is the Common Criteria (CCRA, 1999) which updates the Trusted Computer System Evaluation Criteria (TCSEC) also known as the Orange Book (U.S. Department of Defense, 1985). Several efforts which enhance standard operating systems towards TOS include: SELinux (Loscocco & Smalley, 2001b), Trusted Solaris which implements Solaris Trusted Extensions (Faden, 2006), and Trusted BSD (Watson, 2001). These operating systems, however, do not normally integrate full binary integrity authentication into their Trusted Computing Base (TCB). For example, SELinux, which does not claim to be a full TOS, provides mandatory access control features needed for a TOS. By an appropriate set of policies, it can protect the integrity of the kernel and other critical system files by controlling the write operations on them (Loscocco & Smalley, 2001b). SELinux, however, does not incorporate a hash or digital-signature based binary authentication in its access control infrastructure. Furthermore, specifying SELinux policies is known to be not an easy task (Archer, Leonard & Pradella, 2003).

In addition to TOS, there is the Trusted Computing initiative by the Trusted Computing Group (TCG) (http://www.trustedcomputinggroup.org). The Trusted Platform Module (TPM), promoted by the TCG, is a certified hardware in which all the basic trusted operations and the cryptographic functions are securely handled. It thus constitutes the "root of trust" aimed to provide an uninterrupted "chain of trust" which starts at system startup up to application executions. TPM can be employed, among others, to facilitate: whole-disk encryption (e.g. BitLocker) and secure startup. Currently, though, most computers shipped with TPM are disabled by default. We remark that TPM indeed does provide a higher assurance level of system security. An authentication system like BinAuth can take advantage of TPM by having TPM securely store keys and authentication data, and facilitate a secure startup service until the operating system kernel (e.g. BinAuth) takes control to protect subsequent operation of the application programs.

Binary Authentication Goals

The idea of binary authentication is not new. A number of systems, both research projects and commercial tools, do exist. However, they differ in important ways. To establish an analysis framework for binary authentication, we first define the *security goals* of binary authentication as follows:

A binary authentication system aims to ensure that a binary file B is allowed to execute only if:

- **(G1) Trusted-origin**: it comes from a source trusted by the Administrator, or the Administrator deemed it trusted at time T_B in the past;

- **(G2) Unmodified-content**: its file content is unchanged since it is released by its trusted source, or since time T_B; and

- **(G3) Vulnerability-free** *(optional)*: it is not included in the most recent disclosed list of vulnerable executables. Should the local security policy necessitate this goal, it may be determined by consulting a vulnerability management system."

Since binaries are kept in files and that they are identified by their pathnames on the local file system, goal *G2* can be further refined into the following guarantees:

- **(A1) Binary-Content Authentication**: the *content* of a binary file is unmodified from the time it is known and trusted;
- **(A2) Binary-Location Authentication**: the pathname (*location*) of a binary file must match its content.

Security Assumptions and Scope of Discussion

Software-based binary authentication systems, including BinAuth, usually make the following assumptions:

- **Trusted host's kernel**: Since the authentication systems run on top of the kernel, and thus depend on the kernel to achieve their security objectives, they need to assume that the host's kernel is uncompromised. Following a host (but not kernel) breach, an authentication system is still expected to remain trusted and function properly to prevent the execution of illegal binaries. As such, an authentication system should allow for the possibility of malware exploitation of a buffer overflow to hijack a privileged (root-level) process, but not the ability to alter kernel code (Wurster & van Oorschot, 2007). There exist storage-based authentication systems which still can function despite a kernel breach, such as one by Pennington et al. (2003). These systems usually require additional hardware and software independent from the host.

- **Trusted authentication information**: The systems also assume the security (integrity, confidentiality, and availability) of all keys used for authentication as well as any database and configuration files which are stored on the host's file system.
- **Trusted Administrator account:** Since Administrator in most operating systems virtually has unblocked access to all the files, registries, and possibly to kernel settings, we also need to assume the security of the Administrator account.

Some issues which we do not discuss are:

- We do not deal with mechanisms to protect binaries from changes or deletion. As such, we are not concerned with Denial of Service (DoS) attacks where the attacker deletes or makes changes on existing binary files. To deal with DoS in this case, we need to strengthen the operating system to prevent illegal hijacking attack, for example by means of NX-bit protection, and ASLR (Cowan, Wagle, Calton, Beattie & Walpole, 2000). Binary authentication system serves its purpose by preventing the execution of illegal binary in a compromised system, which is a better option than simply allowing the binary to run in an unprotected system.
- Basic authentication is performed on static binary files when they begin execution. We do not cover the issue of ensuring the integrity of a (running) process.
- To simplify the discussion on analyzing various authentication systems, we only consider executable files, although authentication could be extended to deal with other (non-binary) types of files as well.
- In addition to protecting file content, some authentication systems also protect file attributes. Tripwire running on Unix, for example, can detect changes to file permission

mode, ownership, modification times, and *inode* information. While acknowledging the importance of protecting binary's meta-data, we will not further discuss this issue. We remark that from a mechanism viewpoint, protecting the attributes can be easily achieved either by recording these values, or incorporating them when producing the signature/hash.

A SURVEY OF EXISTING AUTHENTICATION SYSTEMS

System Design Options

We now give a classification of the features in binary authentication systems.

1. **Location of the authentication/verifier module:**
   - *In-kernel module*: The integrity verifier module is implemented as part of the kernel, and thus runs in the kernel space.
   - *User-mode application*: Here, the module runs as an application in the user space.
2. **Authentication time:**
   - *Pre-execution*: The binary file is verified *just right before* it is loaded for execution. This does not necessarily imply that the authentication is done by in-kernel module as wrappers can be placed on various entry points of program execution, e.g. command shell and GUI-based shell.
   - *User-specified time*: The authentication timing is set independent from the time where a binary is invoked. It can be directly triggered by the user, or based on user-specified time which is put as a scheduled job. A system like this usually verifies all protected binaries within one verification session. Hence, it takes a "snapshot of the binaries representing a system state.
   - *Installation-time*: The verification is performed only at install time.
3. **Enforced mandatory authentication for *all* invoked binaries?**
   - *Yes*: All binaries must be verified before being executed.
   - *No*: Only certain classes of binaries are subject to verification. For example, only binaries which are run with Administrator privilege are checked. Another example is that only those with embedded digital signatures are checked. The rest are then allowed to run without authentication.
   - *Configurable*: Here, a system's level of enforcement is configurable. The Administrator is responsible to select one from a set of preset options to apply at a time. He/she, for instance, can apply either one of: all binaries must be authenticated, all binaries with Administrator privilege are authenticated, or no authentication is performed.

We note that for *mandatory* integrity enforcement on *all* binaries, an in-kernel pre-execution mechanism is the most robust option.

4. **Implementation platform:**
   - *Microsoft Windows*
   - *Unix/Linux*

We note that an authentication system implemented in one operating system could be ported to another operating system. In practice, however, such porting is rather difficult due to the differences in the security model and mechanisms in the underlying operating system.

5. **Authentication services provided**:
   - *Binary-Content Authentication*: as defined in (A1).
   - *Binary-Location Authentication*: as defined in (A2).
6. **Placement of the integrity information (signature/hash)**:
   - *Embedded into the executable*: In this method, the signature or hash value is embedded into the executable file. Putting the information in the file seems to result in a cleaner model of authentication system. However, as we will see there are a potential attacks on such a system.
   - *(Secure) centralized database*: The information from all protected binaries is stored in a database. If all binaries are to be mandatorily authenticated prior to execution, then the database serves as a "whitelist" of accepted applications. This contrasts with the "blacklist" approach taken for example by anti-virus software. The other advantage of using a centralized database is that the authentication system can also monitor non-binary files. The system can check the integrity of non-binary files either periodically, or continuously for all potential modification operations.
7. **Who produces the signature/hash of the binaries**:
   - *Authentication system*: Here, all the hashes/signatures come solely from the authentication system. The Administrator assumes that a binary file is good at some point in time, and then invokes the authentication system to produce a signature/hash as a reference for future executions.
   - *Developer*: All Binaries are assumed to come signed by the software

developer, which are then used during the authentication.
   - *Both*: It is possible that the Administrator produces the signatures/hashes on some of binaries. It is also possible that the Administrator reproduces the signatures/hashes based on the existing developer's signature for security or performance reasons as in our BinAuth system.
8. **Authentication mechanisms used**:
   - *Hash (private-key)*: binary integrity is checked using a private-key based hash function.
   - *Digital signature (with PKI)*: the checking is done by using digital signature and PKI.
9. **Authentication Caching is used**?
   - *Yes/No*: Whether a caching technique is employed by an in-kernel authentication system to keep track of previously authenticated binary files. This technique is employed to reduce the overheads of always checking the binary files every time they are executed. It is particularly useful on some frequently executed binaries, especially if their file sizes are large. Files which are stored externally, e.g. files on NFS, cannot be cached (Apvrille, Gordon, Hallyn, Pourzandi & Roy, 2004). One drawback of caching technique is that the authentication system now needs to monitor if a binary in the cache list is modified, which would then invalidate that cache entry.
   - *Not-Applicable*: the caching technique is not applicable in a user-mode application system, or a system by Wurster & van Oorschot (2007) which checks the integrity during binary installation.

10. **Reduced Reliance on PKI?**
    ◦ *Yes/No*: Whether there is any mechanism employed to reduce the reliance on PKI in the case where digital signatures are used.
    ◦ *Not-Applicable*: This is not applicable if only private-key based hash is used.

11. **Support for update of previously-authenticated binary?**
    ◦ *Yes/No*: Whether there is any mechanism to support secure update of a previously authenticated binary file.

Comparison

We now survey and compare various existing authentication systems. We pick a representative system/scheme for each category. We also highlight how well each authentication scheme meets the authentication goals *G1-G3*, and contrast the systems with BinAuth. Figure 1 summarizes the surveyed systems.

The concept of binary authentication, i.e. checking the integrity of stored binary programs, is not new. **Tripwire** (Kim & Spafford, 1993) is one of the first to do file integrity protection. In addition to file's content, Tripwire also monitors file's attributes. Tripwire for Unix monitors changes to file permissions, file ownership, modification times, and other significant changes to inodes as selected by the system administrator on a per-file/directory basis. Tripwire is however limited as it is a user-mode application program, and checks file integrity off-line. It does not provide any mandatory form of integrity checking, and there are many known attacks such as: file modification in between authentication times, and attacks on system daemons (e.g. cron and sendmail) and system files that it depends on (Arnold, 2001; Slaviero, Kroon & Olivier, 2005).

There are a number of in-kernel binary authentication implementations. These are mainly for Unix or Linux, such as DigSig (Apvrille,

Gordon, Hallyn, Pourzandi & Roy, 2004), Trojan-proof (Williams, 2002) and SignedExec (Doorn, Ballintijn, & Arbaugh, 2001), which modify the Unix kernel to verify the executable's digital signature before program execution. **DigSig** and **SignedExec** embed signatures within the binary itself by making use of the elf format. For efficiency, DigSig employs a caching mechanism to avoid checking binaries which have been verified already. In this chapter, we address the detailed implementation issues on Windows, which are much more complex than in Unix. It appears that DigSig provides binary-content authentication, but not binary-location authentication. The problem is that a system like DigSig stores the digital signature embedded into the binary. Hence, one signed binary replacing another signed binary would go undetected by the authentication system. One solution to this problem is that the authentication system must include the pathname in addition to the binary content when producing the digital signature. Even with this technique, the signature-embedding system still suffers from a possible attack when the attacker replaces a signed binary with an older, perhaps vulnerable, signed binary of the same pathname. DigSig has a technique called signature revocation in order to blacklist a signed binary. However, it requires a separate centralized configuration file which can grow over time, and itself requires maintenance.

Cryptomark (Beattie, Black, Cowan, Pu & Yang, 2000) is another in-kernel authentication system on Linux, and is similar to DigSig in a number of ways. The special feature of Cryptomark is that it can be configured to require valid certificates in *all* or *some* binary files. The most secure configuration is to require a certificate in every binary. A common, more permissive, configuration is to require signatures on all binaries that will run as root, whether they are suid root or simply inherit root context from their parent.

There are some mechanisms in Windows which relate to binary authentication. **Authenticode** (Grimes, n.d.) is Microsoft infrastructure for

Figure 1. Comparison of binary authentication systems

Authentication System	Verifier Module Location	Time of Authentication	Enforced Mandatory Authentication?	Platform	Authentication Provided		Placement of Integrity Information	Signature/Hash Producer	Crypto Mechanisms Used	Caching Used?	PKI Reliance Reduction?	Binary Update Support?
					Binary Content	Binary Location						
Tripwire	Application-level	User-specified	No	Unix/Linux, Windows	Yes	Yes	Centralized	Auth. System	Hash	No	-N/A-	No
DigSig	In-kernel	Pre-execution	No	Linux	Yes	No	Embedded	Auth. System	Digital Signature	Yes	No	No
Trojanproof	In-kernel	Pre-execution	Yes	Linux	Yes	Yes	Centralized	Auth. System	Hash	No	-N/A-	No
SignedExec	In-kernel	Pre-execution	Yes	Linux	Yes	No	Embedded	Auth. System	Digital Signature	Yes	No	No
CryptoMark	In-kernel	Pre-execution	Configurable	Linux	Yes	No	Embedded	Auth. System	Digital Signature	No	No	No
Emu System	In-kernel	Pre-execution	Yes	Windows	Yes	Yes	Centralized	Auth. System	Digital Signature	No	-N/A-	
BinAuth	**In-kernel**	**Pre-execution**	**Yes**	**Windows**	**Yes**	**Yes**	**Centralized**	**Auth. System, Developer**	**Hash, Digital Signature**	**Yes**	**Yes**	**Yes**
Signtool	Application-level	User-specified	No	Windows	Yes	No	Embedded	Auth. System	Digital Signature	No	No	No
Sigcheck	Application-level	User-specified	No	Windows	Yes	No	Embedded	Auth. System	Digital Signature	No	No	No
Vista UAC Signed Executables	In-kernel	Privileged-elevation	No	Windows	Yes	No	Embedded	Developer	Digital Signature	No	Yes	No
Wurster-Oorschot System	In-kernel	Installation time	No	Unix/Linux	Yes	No	Embedded	Developer	Digital Signature	-N/A-	Yes	Yes (weak)

digitally signing binaries. In Windows versions prior to Vista, such XP with SP2, Authenticode is used as follows:

- During ActiveX installation: Internet Explorer uses Authenticode to examine the ActiveX plugin, and shows a prompt which contains the publisher's information including the result of the signature check.
- A user downloads a file using Internet Explorer: If this file is executed using the Windows Explorer shell, a prompt is displayed giving the information of the publisher's information. Internet Explorer uses an NTFS feature called Alternate Data Streams to embed the untrusted Internet zone information into the file. The Windows Explorer shell detects the zone information and displays the prompt. This mechanism is not mandatory and relies on the use of zone-aware programs, as well as the browser and GUI shell cooperating with each other.

Since Authenticode runs in user space, it can be bypassed in a number of ways, e.g. from the command shell. It is also limited to files downloaded using Internet Explorer. Only the EXE binary is examined by Authenticode, but DLLs are ignored. One possible attack is then to put malware into a DLL and then execute it, e.g. with rundll32.exe. Furthermore, Authenticode relies heavily on digital certificates. Checking Certificate Revocation Lists (CRL) may add extra delay including timeouts due to the need to contact the Certificate Authority (CA). In some cases, this causes significant slowdown.

Windows Vista improves on signed checking since **User Account Control (UAC)** can be configured for mandatory checking of signed executables. However, this is quite limited since the UAC mechanism only kicks in when a process requests privileged elevation, and for certain operations on protected resources. Vista does not seem to prevent the loading of unsigned DLLs and other non EXE binaries. The 32-bit versions of Windows (including Vista 32-bit) do not check whether drivers are signed. However, the 64 bit versions (XP, Server 2003 and Vista 64-bit) require all drivers to be signed (this may be too strict and restrict hardware choices). Similar to DigSig, existing Windows mechanisms do not authenticate the binary location. Moreover, always requiring PKI infrastructure and certificate processing, we believe, poses various challenges for a general purpose mechanism.

The closest work on binary authentication in Windows is the **Emu system** (Schmid, Hill, Ghosh & Bloch, 2001). It intercepts process creation by intercepting the NtCreateProcess() system call. It is unclear, however, whether they are able authenticate all binary code since trapping at NtCreateProcess() is not sufficient to deal with DLLs. No performance benchmarks are given, so it is unclear if their system is efficient.

There is also a binary protection system which makes use of digital signatures to protect unauthorized modification of binaries already on the system during the *installation* of binary files (Wurster & van Oorschot, 2007). The system does not restrict the software which can be installed on a system, but it denies software which modifies already-installed binaries. Hence, the system does nothing to prevent malware from being installed on the system, but restricts the files that the malware can modify. Wurster & van Oorschot (2007) assume that initially the host contains a set of "trusted" OS and applications binaries, including those from security tools such as anti-virus and IDS software. By protecting the existing binaries, the trusted software is thus expected to keep functioning properly, and detect the possibly installed malware. The system purposely does not rely on PKI since no certificate or entity name is used. Rather, a public-key for verifying the binary's signature is embedded inside the signed binary. In contrast to authentication systems surveyed above, this system allows the injection of malicious binaries, whose subsequent execution might bypass the security tools in place.

One particular feature of the system in (Wurster & van Oorschot, 2007) is that it aims to allow software updates in a controlled manner. A binary on file system can only be replaced by another binary of the same name which contains a digital signature verifiable using the same public key

used in the existing binary. As a result, there is a potential attack of downgrading the binary. BinAuth, in contrast, makes use of software-ID scheme to ensure controlled software upgrading. Finally, one important problem faced by the system which has no trusted entity (e.g. CA) is key revocation. Wurster & van Oorschot (2007) propose pro-actively installing a new version of a file which does not allow future versions signed with the previous key (i.e. which excludes the old verification public key(s) from those embedded in the new version) as to limit the damage of compromised keys.

Lastly, there are **storage-based authentication systems** which still can function despite kernel breach. Pennington et al. (2003) proposes storage-based Intrusion Detection System to watch storage activity for suspicious behavior. It detect four categories of activities: modification to important system files and binaries; non-append modifications such as scrubbing system log files and reversing of inode times; content changes to critical files (e.g. illegal shells in /etc/passwd), and specific file names or content. The special feature of storage-based IDS is that it still can function even after the host is compromised, e.g. after the attacker subverted the host's software system. This is possible because the storage devices run different software on separate hardware. Hence, server-embedded security functionality is independent from, and cannot be disabled by any software running on the client systems (including the OS kernel). It is however assumed that the storage device and the IDS admin console are both uncompromised. Such an approach, however, is only applicable of files which are stored on external file servers or intelligent storage devices.

AUTHENTICATION ISSUES IN MICROSOFT WINDOWS

Windows is perhaps the most commonly exploited commercial operating system. In part, this is due to its sheer complexity, which leads to a high number of security flaws. By Microsoft Windows, we mean the various versions of Windows NT, although in this chapter particular attention is given on Windows XP. We discuss below the complexities and special problems of Windows which make it more difficult to implement binary authentication than in other operating systems such as Unix.

Windows NT (Server 2000, XP, Server 2003, Vista) is a microkernel-like operating system (Russinovich & Solomon, 2005). Programs are usually written for the Win32 API, but these are decomposed into microkernel operations. Windows is closed source —only the Win32 API is documented and not the microkernel API. Our prototype makes use of both the documented and undocumented kernel infrastructure. Thus, it is not possible to make any guarantees on the completeness of the security mechanisms (which still would be a challenge even if Windows was open source). Some of the specific issues in Windows which we deal with include:

- **Proliferation of binary types**: It is not sufficient to ensure the integrity of EXE files. In Windows, binaries can have any file name extension, or even no extension. Some of the most common extensions include EXE (regular executables), DLL (dynamic linked libraries), OCX (ActiveX controls), SYS (drivers) and CPL (control panel applets). Unlike Unix, binaries cannot be distinguished by an execution flag. Thus, without reading its contents, it is not possible to distinguish a binary from any other file type.

- **Complex process execution**: A process is created using CreateProcess() which is a Win32 library function. Unlike in Unix, this is not a system call since Windows is microkernel-like. It is instead broken up at the native API into: NtCreateFile(), NtCreateSection(), NtMapViewOfSection(), NtCreateProcess(), NtCreateThread(). Due to this architecture, NtCreateProcess() performs only a small part of what is needed to run a process. Thus, it is more complex to incorporate mandatory authentication in Windows.

- **DLL loading**: To load a DLL, a process usually uses the Win32 API LoadLibrary(). However, this is broken up in a similar way to process execution above.

- **Execute permissions**: Many code signing systems, particularly those on Linux (Apvrille, Gordon, Hallyn, Pourzandi & Roy, 2004; Doorn, Ballintijn, & Arbaugh, 2001), implement binary loading by examining the execute permission bit in the access mode of file open system-call. The same idea, however, does not work in Windows. Windows programs often set their file modes in a more permissive manner. Simply denying a file opening operation with execute mode set when its authentication fails, will cause many programs to fail which would otherwise work correctly on Windows. Instead, we need to properly intercept the right API(s) and take into account the intended operation semantics to respect Windows behavior.

Compared to other open platforms, Windows potentially also makes the issue of locating vulnerable software components more complicated. A great deal of binaries created by Microsoft contain an internal file version, which is stored as the file's meta-data. The Windows update process however does not indicate to the user which files are modified. Moreover, the meta-data of the modified file might still be kept the same. Thus, it is difficult to keep track of files changes in Windows. More precisely, one cannot ensure whether a version of a program P_i is vulnerable to an attack A. It is rather difficult for a typical Administrator who examines vulnerability information from public advisories to trace through the system and pinpoint the exact affected components. Our software naming scheme, described below, associates binaries with their version and simplifies software vulnerability management.

BINAUTH AND SOFTWARE-ID

We want a lightweight binary authentication scheme which can work under many settings without too much reliance on other infrastructure. Additionally, it should allow for better management of binaries, and incur low overhead.

Software-ID Scheme

We complement the use of binary authentication with a software-ID scheme to simplify binary management issues. The idea is that we associate a unique string called Software-ID to a particular binary of a software product. Software-ID should come either from the software developer, or alternatively be assigned by the Administrator. The key to ensuring unique Software-ID, even among different software developers, lies in the standardized format of the ID. We define Software-ID, for instance, as follows:

```
Software_ID::= <Opcode_tag || Vendor_ID
|| Product_ID || Module_ID ||
Version_ID>
```

Here, || denotes string concatenation. Opcode_tag distinguishes different naming convention, e.g. Software_ID or Custom_ID which is defined below. While a Module_ID suffices to deal with software versioning, a separate Version_ID field is useful to easily track different versions (or patched versions) of the same program. This field becomes handy when we deal with the issue of automated update of the protected binaries.

Ideally, we want to be able to uniquely assign Vendor_IDs to producers of software which can make the Software_ID unique. This problem in practice might not be as difficult as it sounds since it is similar to domain name registration or the assignment of Medium Access Control (MAC) addresses by network card manufacturers. One can leverage on existing trust infrastructures (Vishik, Johnson & Hoffman, 2007) to do this. For example, the responsibility for unique and well known vendor name can be assigned to a Certificate Authority (CA), which then allows us to define Vendor_ID as <CA_ID || Vendor_name>. Alternatively, one might be able to use the domain name of the software developer as a proxy for the Vendor_ID. The emerging trend of Extended Validation Certificate (CA/Browser Forum, 2007) within the software producer community is particularly supportive for this.

A Software_ID gives a one-to-one mapping between the binary and its ID string. This feature is useful for dealing with vulnerability management problems (Sufatrio, Yap and Zhong, 2005). Suppose a new vulnerability is found on a particular version of a piece of software. This means that certain binaries which correspond to that software version may be vulnerable. At present, however, there is no simple and standard way of automatically determining the affected binaries. Once we have Software_IDs associated with binaries, one can easily check the Software_ID against vulnerability alerts. The advisory may already contain the affected Software_ID. Automatic scanners can then be used to tie-in this checking with the dissemination of vulnerability alerts to automatically monitor, manage, or patch the software in an operating system. General management of patches in an operating system can also be done in much the same way.

In addition, a software-id scheme also allows for secure binary update. When a binary needs to be updated, the Administrator allows the replacement of a protected binary only if the new binary is of the same file name, correctly signed by the same developer, and the Software-ID has the same <Opcode_tag || Vendor_ID || Product_ID || Module_ID> prefix, with a Version_ID that is greater than the existing one.

In the case where no Software_ID comes with a software product, one can alternatively derive one. It can be constructed, for instance, using the following (coarse-grained) naming:

```
Custom_ID::= <Opcode_tag || hash(Vendor_
URL + Product_name +
File_name + salt)|| Version_ID>.
```

The salt expands the name space to reduce the risk of a hash function collision.

BinAuth Architecture

In the following discussion, we assume that binaries already come tagged with a Software_ID. During the binary authentication set-up, preferably done immediately after the targeted binary installation, we generate the Message Authentication Code (MAC) values for each binary. In the case where binaries are digitally signed by its developer, then we verify the signature and then generate the MAC for each binary. Thus, only one public-key operation needs to be done. We choose to use a keyed hash, the HMAC algorithm (Krawczyk, Bellare, & Canetti, 1997), so there is a secret key for the Administrator. This is mainly to increase the security of the stored hashes. To authenticate binary integrity for any future execution of the code, only the generated HMAC value needs to be checked. In what follows, we mostly write MAC which already covers the choice of HMAC.

One way of storing the generated MAC is by embedding it into the binary. However, doing so may interfere with file format of the signed binaries, and may also have other complications. We instead use an authentication repository file which stores all the MAC values of authenticated binaries with their pathnames. During the boot-up process, the kernel creates its own in-memory data structures for binary authentication from this file.

We ensure that the repository file is protected from further modification except under the control of the authentication system to add/remove binaries.[2] We can also customize binary authentication on a per *user* basis rather than system-wide, thus producing a white-list of binaries approved for execution for each user. In the case when the initial binary does not have a digital signature, then the Administrator can choose to approve the binary and generate a MAC for it.

There are two main components of the system: the **SignatureToMac** and **Verifier**. The Signature-ToMac maintains the authentication repository, *Digest_file*. The Verifier is a kernel driver which makes use of *Digest_file* and decides whether an execution is to be allowed.

SignatureToMac

Once a piece of software is installed on the system, Figure 2 shows how SignatureToMac processes the installed binaries:

1. It checks the validity of the binary's digital signature and corresponding certificate. If the signature or certificate is invalid, then report failure.
2. It consults the Administrator whether the software is to be trusted or not (this is similar to the Vista UAC dialog but only happens once). Other policies (possibly mandatory) can also be implemented.
3. It generates the MAC of the binary (including its Software_ID string) using a secret key, *Hashing_key*, to produce *software_digest*. The *Hashing_key* is only accessible by the authentication system, e.g. obtained on boot.
4. It adds an entry for the binary as a tuple <*path_name, software_digest*> into the *Digest_file* repository and informs the Verifier. The repository is protected against modification. Note that because the entries are signed, the repository can be read for

Figure 2. SignatureToMac: deriving the MAC

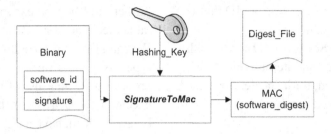

other uses, e.g. version control and vulnerability management.

Verifier

The Verifier performs mandatory binary authentication —it denies the execution of any kind of Windows binary which fails to match the MAC and pathname. There are two general approaches for the checking. One is *cached* MAC, which avoids generating the MAC for previously authenticated binaries. The other is *uncached* MAC, which always checks the MAC. As we will see, they have various tradeoffs. The cached MAC implementation needs to ensure that binaries are unmodified. Hence, the Verifier monitors the usage of previously authenticated files on the cache, and removes them from the cache if it can be potentially modified.

The core data structure of the Verifier component can be viewed as a table of tuples in the form *<Kernel_path, FileID, MAC, Authenticated_bit>* representing the allowed binaries. It is indexed on *Kernel_path +FileID* for fast lookup. The fields are as follows:

- The *Kernel_path* is Windows kernel (internal) pathname representation of a file. In Window's user space, a file can have multiple absolute pathnames due to: (i) 8.3 file naming format, e.g. "C:\Program Files\" and "C:\progra~1\" are the same; (ii) symbolic links (reparse points is similar); (iii)

hard links; (iv) volume mount points; or (v) the SUBST and APPEND DOS commands. The *Kernel_path* is a unique representation for all the possible pathnames. When the system loads *<path_name, software_digest>* from *Digest_file* during the startup, *path_name* is converted into a *Kernel_path* since all subsequent checks by Verifier in the kernel use the latter.

- The *FileID* is a pair *<device_name, NTFS_object_ID>*. The *device_name* is a Windows internal name to identify a disk or partition volume. For instance, the device name HarddiskVolume1 usually refers to C:\. The *NTFS_object_ID* is a 128-bit length number uniquely identifying a file in the file system volume (this is not the same as Unix inode numbers). The Verifier uses the *FileID* to identify the same file given more than one hard link. This prevents an attacker from creating a hard link for modifying a binary without invalidating the binary cache. The *FileID* values will be queried from the system and filled into the table during system boot. Our use of *FileID* in BinAuth poses no potential conflict with other applications using it due to the semantics of NTFS. If FAT file system is used instead of NTFS, we employ pathname to identify the binary.

- The *MAC* is same as a *software_digest* entry in *Digest_file*. Our prototype implements the HMAC-MD5 (Krawczyk,

Figure 3. Verifier: the in-kernel authentication process

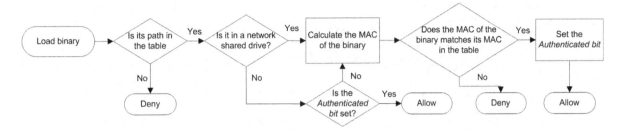

Bellare, & Canetti, 1997), HMAC-SHA-1 and HMAC-SHA-256 (Eastlake & Hansen, 2006) hash algorithms.[3]

- The *Authenticated_bit* remembers whether the binary has been previously authenticated. It is initially set to false, and set to true after successful authentication.

Figure 3 shows the authentication steps taken by the Verifier (with caching technique used) when a binary is invoked for execution:

1. It checks if the binary's *Kernel_path* exists in Verifier's table. If not, then deny the execution and optionally log the event. A notification is accordingly sent to the user.
2. If the file is on a network shared drive or removable media (e.g. floppy), go to step 4.
3. If the *Authenticated_bit* is set, then go to step 7.
4. It performs MAC algorithm operation on the binary.
5. If the resulting MAC value does not match with the *MAC* stored in the table, execution is denied.
6. It sets the *Authenticated_bit* of the binary.
7. It passes the control to the kernel to continue the execution.

To control binary execution, we intercept the system call for virtual memory section creation NtCreateSection() (Nebbett, 2000). This system

call is employed to create a section object which represents a shared memory region including the region of binaries. During the loading of any types of binaries, this system call will be invoked. Intercepting it therefore assures completeness. This mechanism is better than other options such as:

- Intercepting file opening (NtCreateFile() and NtOpenFile()): As discussed earlier, authenticating each opened file with execute access mode can cause some correct programs to fail if the files do not pass authentication. In addition, it introduces unnecessary overheads. Moreover, there are also technical difficulties to distinguish between process creation and regular file IO operations, which is not always easy given Windows microkernel nature.
- Intercepting process creation (NtCreateProcess()): This method is not effective for our purpose. Firstly, we cannot use it to control DLL loading. Secondly, it is more difficult to get the pathname of the binary because process creation is broken down into microkernel operations.

In Windows, it turns out that all code invocations from any kind of binary need to have a memory section to execute. As such, it suffices for us to intercept NtCreateSection().

In caching mode, the Verifier needs to ensure that previously authenticated binaries are not modified. The uncached Verifier, however, will

Figure 4. Pseudo code of file modification monitor.

```
procedure UponModification (FilePath)
    if (FS is NTFS)
        FileID := GetFileID(FilePath) # FileID can be NULL
        if (FilePath is in the table)
            Entry := LookupTableByPath(FilePath)
            if (FileID == NULL)
                # this can happen when the file is deleted and created again.
                # generate a new FileID and update the table
                Entry.FileID := CreateFileID(FilePath)
            else if ( FileID != Entry.FileID in the table)
                # this can happen when the drive is unmounted,
                # id changed off-line and re-mounted
                Entry.FileID := FileID
            end if
            Entry.Authenticated := false
        else if ((FileID != NULL) AND (FileID is in the table))
            Entry := LookupTableByID(FileID)
            Entry.Authenticated := false
        end if
    else if ((FS is FAT) AND (FilePath is in table))
        Entry := LookupTableByPath(FilePath)
        Entry.Authenticated := false
    end if
end procedure
```

not need to perform file monitoring. A binary with pathname P is considered modified, if any of the following occurs:

- P is created: Hence, we monitor NtCreateFile() and NtOpenFile().
- P is opened with write access mode: The previous two system calls are also intercepted for this purpose.[4]
- Another file is renamed to P: We monitor the file renaming (NtSetInformationFile (*FileRenameInformation*)).
- A drive containing P is mounted: We monitor drive mounting with IRP_MJ_VOLUME-_MOUNT.

Note that we do not need to monitor file deletion since we only care about executing correct files but not missing files. The details of file modification monitoring are given in Figure 4. Upon modification of P, we reset the *Authenticated_bit* of binary P in the table, and also update the *FileID* if it is changed.

Security Analysis

The security of binary authentication also relies on the strength of the chosen hash functions (MD5, SHA-1, SHA-256) as well as the HMAC algorithm. Thus, we assume that any change in a binary can be detected through a changed MAC value.

When authenticating binaries with digital signature, subsequent invocations only need MAC verification to ensure the authenticity of the binary. In other words, MAC authentication "preserves" the previously established properties of binary integrity derived from the digital signature. A subtlety arises when the certificate expires or is revoked at some point in time after SignatureToMac. We view that the question of whether one should keep trusting the binary for execution depends on one's level of trust on certificate expiration/revocation. If the certificate expiration or revocation means that the public key must no longer be used, but the fact that *previously established* goodness binary properties still hold, then we can keep trusting the binary for execution (as long as we still believe the issuer).

One additional issue with regard to the use of MAC instead of the developer's digital signature is the potential delay of certificate revocation information, which may happen in practice. In SignatureToMac, BinAuth ensures the validity of the developer's certificate using the available revocation infrastructure. However, it may be the case that the certificate is already revoked by that time, but the revocation notification fails to be received in time. To overcome this, we can stipulate BinAuth to monitor the developer's certificate status of a binary that has just completed SignatureToMac until the delay possibility diminishes. BinAuth can thus maintain a list of certificates to be revalidated, which are then checked periodically in the background.

We now discuss some possible attempted system attacks on the authentication system. The analysis is done by examining possible attack vectors introduced by BinAuth. The list below, however, does not claim to catalogue all possible ways that an attacker might attempt to mount an attack on the system. All the listed attack vectors below except the last two attempt to target the caching system. More precisely, the attacker attempts to modify an already authenticated binary without causing the *Authenticated_bit* to be set to false. The possible attacks are:

- **Manipulating symbolic links**: The attacker can attempt to use the pathname S which is a symbolic link of an authenticated P to indirectly modify P. However, the modified file will not be executed successfully, because the Windows kernel resolves a symbolic S to the real pathname P. As a result, the *Authenticated_bit* of P will be set to false. When P' is executed, its MAC will be recalculated and then fails authentication.
- **Manipulating hard links**: The attacker can create a hard link H on an already authenticated file P and then modify the file using path H. This attack will not succeed because we use *FileID* to identify files. H has the same *FileID* as P, thus the *Authenticated_bit* will be set to false. Note that this attack will not succeed in FAT file system either, even though we cannot use *FileID* there. This is because hard links as well as soft links are not supported in FAT.
- **Manipulating FileID**: Recall that *FileID* consists of *device_name* and *NTFS_object_ID*. The latter is optional and thus can be removed. The attacker can attempt to remove the *NTFS_object_ID*, and then performs the previous attack. We handle this attack by denying *NTFS_object_ID* removal on authenticated files. This is implemented by monitoring the file system control event FSCTL_DELETE_OBJECT_ID.
- **Time-Of-Check-To-Time-Of-Use (TOCTTOU)**: TOCTTOU refers to a race condition bug in an access control system where the resource is modified between the time of resource checking and the time of resource usage. In a binary authentication context, the binary may be modified after the time it is authenticated and before the time it is executed. However, we observed that all binaries are exclusive-write-locked when opened. This means binaries cannot be modified from the time it is opened to the time it is closed. File authenticated happens after it is opened and before it is executed. As a result, binaries cannot be modified with a TOCTTOU attack. When the binary is in a network shared volume, i.e. SMB share, and the write-lock is not properly implemented in the SMB server, an attacker would be able to modify the binary after authentication. We have observed that both Windows and Samba implement write-locking properly. Thus the attack is only possible when the SMB

server is compromised. One way to prevent this is to disallow binary loading from a SMB share.

- **Driver loading**: The binary authentication system authenticates all binaries including kernel driver. This means all drivers are authenticated thus driver attacks such as kernel rootkits and malware drivers can be prevented.

- **Offline attack**: Offline attack means a modification of the file system when Windows is not in control. For example, the attacker can boot another OS, or remove the disk drive for modification on another system. Such an attack will require physical access to the machine. An offline attack can corrupt data or change programs/files and affect the general functioning and we cannot prevent that. What we can do is to ensure the integrity of executed binaries given our earlier assumption on the security of operating system kernel and authentication information. Since the Hashing_key is not stored in the machine, it is not available to the attacker. The attacker can still change the digest file and the binaries, however, MACs of modified binaries cannot be correctly produced. Thus, modified binaries cannot be executed when the system goes online.

BINAUTH OVERHEADS

We briefly discuss the impact of BinAuth on system performance. The two factors which impact the overall system performance are: (i) Verifier checking upon binary loading (execution); and (ii) file modification monitoring. These factors affect the user's waiting time for process execution and file operations. We use both micro and macro benchmarks to determine the worst case and average performance overheads. To see the difference with digital signature based authentication system,

we also compare the performances of BinAuth against the Microsoft official Authenticode utility called Sign Tool (Microsoft Developer Network, 2008), and another Sysinternals (now acquired by Microsoft) Authenticode utility Sigcheck (Russinovich, 2009). Note that two tools are user-mode programs. They are here to illustrate the difference between non-mandatory strategies with Authenticode and our in-kernel mandatory authentication.

More details and benchmark results can be found in (Halim, Ramnath, Sufatrio, Wu, & Yap, 2008). To summarize, BinAuth with authentication caching gives about 2% overhead, while both Sign Tool and Sigcheck have overhead of about 50% on average and 50000% in the worst case. We also note that the uncached version of Bin-Auth can be several thousand times slower than the cached version in the worst case. This means that the caching technique is effective.

FUTURE RESEARCH DIRECTIONS

Given that a mandatory binary authentication system like BinAuth is feasible to use in practice, future work would be to address various practical management, administrative and deployment issues. Proposed future research directions include:

- **Automated MAC generation of binaries:** BinAuth requires installed binaries to be processed by SignatureToMAC before their first execution. However, in some cases, binaries need to be executed *immediately* following their creation. For example, some installation programs download or unpack binaries to a temporary directory and subsequently execute them. Another example is that, in the case of Integrated Development Environment (IDE), when a programmer clicks the "run" button, the IDE builds a binary and immediately executes it. In these cases, the execution of the binaries will be prevented. One solution to this issue is by allowing automated SignatureToMAC procedure on binaries satisfying (configurable) user's set of policies. A policy might also make use of trust information on several involved parties, such as: software vendors, CERT, vulnerability management software, and already trusted programs. For example, we can specify that "if a binary comes from a certain trusted software vendor, and has no known vulnerability based on the latest CERT repository, then we allow the finger-printing and execution of the binary". This is in contrast to the current scheme which exclusively depends on the Administrator to approve a binary.

- **Authenticating non-binary files**: In order to make sure that the whole system is se-cure, sometimes both the binaries and non-binaries have to be authenticated. It is thus possible to extend authentication, in some cases, to non-binaries.
- **Denial-of-service attack:** Presently, BinAuth does not deal with deletion or modification of a protected binary. However, this also means that a malware attack on a breached system can make soft-ware unavailable by modifying or deleting a binary. Future work can be done to deal with such denial-of-service attack. We re-mark though that we need to strengthen the operating system in the first place as to prevent illegal hijacking attack. Future work can extend BinAuth to also securely log any deletion or modification on the protected binaries for auditing purpose. BinAuth thus needs to also implement file access monitoring and logging features, similar to those found in a continuous mon-itoring system like WinResMon (Ramnath, Sufatrio, Yap & Yongzheng, 2006). In typi-cal current systems, however, an attacker who gains Administrator privilege can

practically remove all of his/her tracks on the system. Some tamper-resistance stor-age or TPM might therefore need to be uti-lized for this purpose.

CONCLUSION

We surveyed various binary authentication systems within the context of operating system security. For Windows, BinAuth meets most of the require-ments to ensure that only software from trusted binaries can be loaded for execution. This can also be combined with a simple software-ID scheme to simplify binary version management and allow for automated vulnerability alert processing. Our system is lightweight, and integrates well with PKI and other trust mechanisms without having to heavily rely on them. By means of our proof-of-concept implementation of BinAuth, we show how a mandatory in-kernel authentication system can provide increased trust on good software execution, while incurs acceptable performance overheads even on a complex popular operating system. In summary, this chapter illustrates the design of a practical software authentication mechanism, which is a crucial enabler for achiev-ing trustworthy systems.

ACKNOWLEDGMENT

The authors would like to acknowledge the support of project SELFMAN (contract number: 034084) and Temasek Laboratories.

REFERENCES

Apvrille, A., Gordon, D., Hallyn, S., Pourzandi, M., & Roy, V. (2004). *DigSig: Run-time authenti-cation of binaries at kernel level*. Paper presented at the 18th USENIX Large Installation System Administration Conference, LISA'04, Atlanta, USA.

Archer, M., Leonard, E., & Pradella, M. (2003). *Analyzing security-enhanced Linux policy specifications*. Paper presented at IEEE 4th International Workshop on Policies for Distributed Systems and Networks, POLICY 2003.

Arnold, E. (2001). *The trouble with Tripwire*. Retrieved April 25, 2009, from http://www.security focus.com/infocus/1398

Beattie, S., Black, A., Cowan, C., Pu, C., & Yang, L. (2000). *CryptoMark: locking the stable door ahead of the trojan horse* [white paper]. WireX Communications Inc.

CA/Browser Forum. (2007). *Guidelines for the Issuance and Management of Extended Validation Certificates* (Technical Report). Retrieved April 25, 2009, from http://cabforum.org/ EV_Certificate_Guidelines.pdf

CCRA. (1999). *Common criteria for information technology security evaluation version 2.1* (Technical Report). Retrieved April 25, 2009, from http://www.commoncriteriaportal.org/thecc.html

CMU's CERT. (2009). *CERT Statistics*. Retrieved April 25, 2009, from http://www.cert.org/stats/

Cowan, C., Wagle, F., Calton, P., Beattie, S., & Walpole, J. (2000). *Buffer overflows: attacks and defenses for the vulnerability of the decade*. Paper presented at DARPA Information Survivability Conference and Exposition, DISCEX '00.

Doorn, L., Ballintijn, G., & Arbaugh, W. (2001). *Signed Executables for Linux* (Technical Report CS-TR-4256). University of Maryland.

Eastlake, D., & Hansen, T. (2006). *US Secure Hash Algorithms (SHA and HMAC-SHA)* (RFC 4634). Retrieved April 25, 2009, from http://www.ietf.org/rfc/rfc4634.txt

F-Secure. (2007). *F-Secure reports amount of malware grew by 100% during 2007*. Retrieved April 25, 2009, from http://www.f-secure.com/en_EMEA/about-us/pressroom/news/2007/fs_news_20071204_1_eng.html

Faden, G. (2006). *Solaris Trusted Extensions: An architectural overview*. Sun Microsystems. Retrieved April 25, 2009, from http://www.opensolaris.org/os/community/security/projects/tx/ TrustedExtensions-Arch.pdf

Grimes, R. (n.d.). *Authenticode*. Microsoft Technet. Retrieved April 25, 2009, from http://technet.microsoft.com/en-us/library/cc750035.aspx

Halim, F., & Ramnath, R. Sufatrio, Wu, Y., & Yap, R.H.C. (2008). *A lightweight binary authentication system for windows*. Paper presented at Joint iTrust and PST Conferences on Privacy, Trust Management and Security, IFIPTM.

Kim, G., & Spafford, E. (1993). *The design and implementation of Tripwire: A file system integrity checker*. Paper presented at ACM Conference on Computer and Communications Security.

Krawczyk, H., Bellare, M., & Canetti, R. (1997). *HMAC: keyed-hashing for message authentication* (RFC 2104). Retrieved April 25, 2009, from http://www.ietf.org/rfc/rfc2104.txt

Loscocco, P., & Smalley, S. (2001a). *Integrating flexible support for security policies into the Linux operating system*. Paper presented at the 2001 USENIX Annual Technical Conference (FREENIX '01).

Loscocco, P., & Smalley, S. (2001b). *Meeting critical security objectives with Security-Enhanced Linux*, Paper presented at the 2001 Ottawa Linux Symposium.

Microsoft Developer Network. (2008). *SignTool*. Retrieved April 25, 2009, from http://msdn.microsoft.com/en-us/library/aa387764.aspx

Nebbett, G. (2000). *Windows NT/2000 native API reference*. Sam Publishing.

Organisation for Economic Co-operation and Development [OECD]. (2008). *Malicious software (malware): A security threat to Internet economy, Ministerial Background Report, DISTI/ICCP/ Reg(2007)5/Final*. Retrieved April 25, 2009, from http://www.oecd.org/dataoecd/53/34/40724457. pdf

Pennington, A., Strunk, J., Griffin, J., Soules, C., Goodson, G., & Ganger, G. (2003). *Storage-based intrusion detection: watching storage activity for suspicious behavior*. Paper presented at 12th USENIX Security Symposium.

Pfleeger, C. P., & Pfleeger, S. L. (2006). *Security in computing* (4th ed.). Upper Saddle River, NJ: Prentice Hall.

Ramnath, R. Sufatrio, Yap, R.H.C., & Yongzheng, W. (2006). *WinResMon: A Tool for Discovering Software Dependencies, Configuration and Requirements in Microsoft Windows*. Paper presented at 20th Large Installation System Administration Conference, LISA'06.

Russinovich, M. E. (2009). *Sigcheck v1.6*. Retrieved April 25, 2009, from http://technet. microsoft.com/en-us/sysinternals/bb897441.aspx

Russinovich, M. E., & Solomon, D. A. (2005). *Microsoft Windows internals: Microsoft Windows Server 2003, Windows XP, and Windows 2000* (4th ed.). Redmond, WA: Microsoft Press.

Schmid, M., Hill, F., Ghosh, A., & Bloch, J. (2001). *Preventing the execution of unauthorized Win32 applications*. Paper presented at DARPA Information Survivability Conf. & Exposition II.

Scut. (2001). *Exploiting format string vulnerabilities*. Team teso. Retrieved April 25, 2009, from http://julianor.tripod.com/bc/formatstring-1.2.pdf

Shacham, H., Page, M., Pfaff, B., Goh, E. J., Modadugu, N., & Boneh, D. (2004). *On the effectiveness of address-space randomization*. Paper presented at the 11th ACM Conference on Computer and Communications Security.

Slaviero, M., Kroon, J., & Olivier, M. (2005). *Attacking signed binaries*. Paper presented at 5th Annual Information Security South Africa Conference.

Sufatrio, Y. R.H.C., & Zhong, L. (2004). *A machine-oriented integrated vulnerability database for automated vulnerability detection and processing*. Paper presented at 18th Large Installation System Administration Conference, LISA'04.

U.S. Department of Defense. (1985). *Department of Defense Trusted Computer System Evaluation Criteria*. Retrieved April 25, 2009, from http:// nsi.org/Library/Compsec/orangebo.txt

Vishik, C., Johnson, S., & Hoffman, D. (2007). *Infrastructure for trusted environment: In search of a solution*. Paper presented at ISSE/SECURE 2007 Securing Electronic Business Processes, Vieweg.

Wang, X., & Yu, H. (2005). *How to break MD5 and other hash functions*. Paper presented at 24th Annual International Conference on the Theory and Applications of Cryptographic Techniques.

Watson, R. (2001). *TrustedBSD: Adding trusted operating system features to FreeBSD*, Paper presented at 2001 USENIX Annual Technical Conference.

Williams, M. (2002). *Anti-trojan and trojan detection with in-kernel digital signature testing of executables*. Retrieved April 25, 2009, from http:// www.netxsecure.net/downloads/sigexec.pdf

Wurster, G., & van Oorschot, P. C. (2007). *Self-signed executables: restricting replacement of program binaries by malware*. Paper presented at 2nd USENIX workshop on Hot topics in security.

ENDNOTES

[1] Microsoft Windows, Windows NT, Windows XP, Windows Vista are trademarks of Microsoft Corporation. All other trademarks are the property of their respective owners.

[2] Further security can be achieved by integrating binary authentication with a TPM infrastructure. We do not do so in the prototype as that is somewhat orthogonal.

[3] Due to recent concerns due to shown weaknesses and attacks against MD5 (Wang & Yu, 2005), we also have stronger hash functions, namely SHA-1 and the stronger SHA-256.

[4] An alternative way is to monitor the file (block) writing operation (NtWriteFile()). It is however less efficient because file block-write operations take place more frequently than file opening operations as one opened file for modification might be subject to multiple block writings. Furthermore, it cannot capture file-memory mapping.

Chapter 5
Trust Issues and Solutions in Multimedia Content Distribution

Shiguo Lian
France Telecom R&D (Orange Labs) Beijing, China

ABSTRACT

Multimedia content distribution is a key technique for multimedia services, which transmits multimedia content from a sender to certain receiver(s). With the popularity of multimedia services, the trust issues in content distribution becomes urgent, including the authorized access, privacy protection, trusted payment, piracy surveillance, and so forth. This chapter introduces the trust issues in multimedia content distribution (e.g., authorization, authentication, privacy, payment, ownership, illegal distribution, forgery, etc.), reviews the latest research progress of the solutions, and presents some open issues and promising research topics. It is expected to provide valuable information to researchers or engineers in this field.

INTRODUCTION

Trust (Trust, 2009) is a complicated term which has different explanations in different fields, including social science, law, digital information, finance, etc. For example, in social science, trust (Misztal, 1996) is a relationship of reliance. A trusted party is presumed to seek to fulfill policies, ethical codes, law and their previous promises. Trust does not need to involve belief in the good character, vices, or morals of the other party. Persons engaged in a criminal activity usually trust each other to some extent. Also, trust does not need to include an action that you and the other party are mutually engaged in. Trust is a prediction of reliance on an action, based on what a party knows about the other party. In sociology, the degree to which one party trusts another is a measure of belief in the honesty, benevolence and competence of the other party.

In common law legal systems, trust is an arrangement whereby property is managed by one person for the benefit of another (Hudson, 2003). A trust is created by a settlor, who entrusts some or all of his or her property to people of his choice,

DOI: 10.4018/978-1-61520-682-7.ch005

i.e., the trustees. The trustees hold legal title to the trust property, but they are obliged to hold the property for the benefit of one or more individuals or organizations, usually specified by the settlor, who hold equitable title. The trustees owe a fiduciary duty to the beneficiaries, who are the beneficial owners of the trust property. The trust is governed by the terms of the trust document, which is usually written and occasionally set out in deed form. The trustee is obliged to administer the trust in accordance with both the terms of the trust document and the governing law.

With the wide applications of digital information, trust in digital information is becoming an important topic (Kelton, et al., 2008). And, many discussions of trust in this environment focus on issues like security or technical reliability. Specially, in security engineering, a trusted system is a system that is relied upon to a specified extent to enforce a specified security policy (Taipale, 2005). As such, a trusted system is one whose failure may break a specified security policy. It is often defined from four aspects, i.e., classified information, trusted computing, policy analysis and information theory. In classified information, trusted systems are used for the processing, storage and retrieval of sensitive or classified information. In trusted computing, trust is used by the Trusted Computing Group (TCG, 2009) mainly in the sense of authorization that defines whether a user is authorized to do something. In policy analysis, trusted systems in the context of national or homeland security, law enforcement, or social control policy are systems in which some conditional prediction about the behavior of people or objects within the system has been determined prior to authorizing access to system resources. In information theory, a trusted system is based on the definition of 'Trust is that which is essential to a communication channel but cannot be transferred from a source to a destination using that channel' (Gerck, 1998). This chapter will focus on the trust in security engineering.

Multimedia content distribution (e.g., digital TV, mobile TV, IPTV, online music, etc.) is a kind of digital information system (Lian & Zhang, 2009), which becomes more and more popular with the rapid development of network technology and multimedia technology. Thus, the trust in multimedia content distribution is urgent, especially the security aspects. Generally, a multimedia distribution system, composed of the sender (and device), receiver (and device), transmission channel, storage device, etc., distributes the multimedia content from the sender(s) to receiver(s) through various communication manners. Multimedia content's properties, such as large volumes, worthy commerce value, real time interaction, etc., make multimedia distribution systems different from traditional information systems. Till now, some means to confirm the trust in multimedia distribution have been proposed (Lian, 2009). However, few works has been done to show the progress of trust issues and solutions in this field. This chapter aims to review the latest research results in trust issues and solutions for multimedia distribution, and provide valuable information to researchers or engineers.

The rest of the chapter is organized as follows. Section 2 reviews related work. A number of trust issues in multimedia content distribution are discussed in Section 3. In Section 4, solutions to ensure trust are introduced in detail. Furthermore, we propose some open issues and hot topics in Section 5. Finally, conclusions are drawn in the last section.

RELATED WORK

In digital information systems, the following trust issues have been deeply studied, including trusted computing, web of trust, and trust in electronic commerce. Considering that multimedia distribution often needs the hardware based devices, web access or electronic transactions, the trust issues and solutions in these topics may provide valuable information for trusted multimedia distribution. In the following content, these topics will be reviewed.

Trusted Computing

Trusted Computing (TC) is a technology promoted by the Trusted Computing Group (TCG, 2009). The term has a specialized meaning. With Trusted Computing, the computer will consistently behave in specific ways, and those behaviors will be enforced by hardware and software. Enforcing this trusted behavior is achieved by loading the hardware with a unique ID and unique master key. And, Trusted Computing is extremely controversial as the hardware is not merely secured for the owner, and it is secured against the owner as well.

Chip manufacturers, hardware manufacturers and operating system providers all plan to include Trusted Computing into coming generations of products (Dell, 2006). The U.S. Army requires that every new small PC it purchases must come with a Trusted Platform Module (TPM) (Lemos, 2006). According to the International Data Corporation, by 2010 essentially all portable PCs and the vast majority of desktops will include a TPM chip (Evers, 2005).

Trusted computing encompasses five key technical components, of which all are required for a fully trusted system. They are defined in TCG specifications, and are briefly introduced as follows.

Endorsement key: The endorsement key is a 2048-bit RSA public and private key pair (Andersen, 2008), which is created randomly on the chip at manufacture time and cannot be changed. The private key never leaves the chip, while the public key is used for attestation and for encryption of sensitive data sent to the chip (Safford, et al., 2003).

Secure input and output: Secure input and output refers to a protected path between the computer user and the software with which they believe they are interacting. In current computer systems, there are many ways for malicious software to intercept data as it travels between a user and a software process, e.g., keyboard loggers and screen-scrapers. Secure input and output reflects a protected and verified channel, using checksums stored in the Trusted Platform Module to verify that the software drivers used to do the input and output has not been tampered with.

Memory curtaining: Memory curtaining extends common memory protection techniques to provide full isolation of sensitive areas of memory, e.g., memories for cryptographic keys. Even the operating system does not have full access to curtained memory, so the information would be secure from an intruder who takes control of the OS, because of the use of separate protected execution environments.

Sealed storage: Sealed storage protects private information by binding it to platform configuration information, including the software and hardware being used. This means that the data can be read only by the same combination of software and hardware.

Remote attestation: Remote attestation allows changes to the user's computer to be detected by authorized parties. For examples, software companies can avoid users tampering with their software to circumvent technological protection measures. It works by having the hardware generate a certificate stating what software is currently running. The computer can then present this certificate to a remote party to show that its software has not been tampered with.

Possible applications of Trusted Computing includes digital rights management, identity theft protection, preventing cheating in online games, protection from viruses and spyware, protection of biometric authentication data, verification of remote computation for grid computing, and so on. However, there are some criticisms of Trusted Computing. Some experts claim that trust in the underlying companies is not deserved and that the technology puts too much power and control into the hands of those who design systems and software. They also believe that it may cause consumers to lose anonymity in their online interactions. Some other security experts think that it will provide computer manufacturers and software authors with increased control to impose restrictions on what users are able to do with their computers (Schneier, 2002).

Web of Trust

In cryptography, web of trust is a concept used in Pretty Good Privacy (PGP) (Zimmermann, 1995), GNU Privacy Guard (GnuPG) (Nguyen, 2004), and other OpenPGP-compatible systems to establish the authenticity of the binding between a public key and a user. As with computer networks, there are many independent webs of trust, and any user (through his identity certificate) can be a part of, and a link between, multiple webs. The web of trust concept was first put forth by PGP creator, Phil Zimmermann, in 1992 in the manual for PGP version 2.0 (Zimmermann, 1995): "As time goes on, you will accumulate keys from other people that you may want to designate as trusted introducers. Everyone else will each choose their own trusted introducers. And everyone will gradually accumulate and distribute with their key a collection of certifying signatures from other people, with the expectation that anyone receiving it will trust at least one or two of the signatures. This will cause the emergence of a decentralized fault-tolerant web of confidence for all public keys."

All OpenPGP-compliant implementations include a certificate vetting scheme to assist with this (Callas, et al., 2007). OpenPGP identity certificates can be digitally signed by other users who, by that act, endorse the association of that public key with the person or entity listed in the certificate. This is commonly done at key signing parties. OpenPGP-compliant implementations also include a vote counting scheme which can be used to determine which public key - owner

association a user will trust while using PGP. For instance, if three partially trusted endorsers have vouched for a certificate, or if one fully trusted endorser has done so, the association between owner and public key in that certificate will be trusted to be correct. The parameters are user-adjustable and can be completely bypassed if desired.

There are also problems with web of trust. Users, whether individuals or organizations, who lose track of a private key can no longer decrypt messages sent to them produced using the matching public key found in an OpenPGP certificate (Rahman, 1997). A difficulty with PGP/OpenPGP type systems is that every web of trust without a central controller depends on other users for trust. Those with new certificates will not likely be readily trusted by other users' systems, until they find enough endorsements for the new certificate.

Trust in Electronic Commerce

Lack of consumer trust in e-commerce merchants, e-commerce technology (Mahmood, 2008), and the legal infrastructures poses a major challenge to the large-scale uptake of business to consumer e-commerce. Most traditional cues for assessing trust in the physical world are not available online. Some works have been done to devise alternative methods for assessing, communicating and establishing trust in this environment.

It is commonly accepted that people will only trust and embrace e-commerce if they perceive that sufficient security is in place, and considerable effort is therefore being put into the development and deployment of security services (Andersen, 2008; Kini & Choobineh, 1998). Important requirements for e-commerce security are the need to protect sensitive information that is stored on computers before and after an e-commerce transaction, to verify the identity of the other party in the transaction, to ensure that no one can intercept the information being exchanged during the transaction, and in general to prevent

Figure 1. General architecture of multimedia distribution

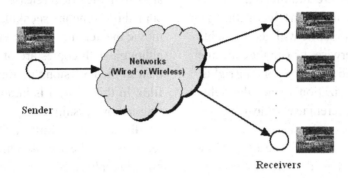

disruption of services and applications. To resist the data interception or eavesdropping over Internet, cryptographic communication security can be correctly used (Dutton, 2000). System security can be addressed by installing firewalls and intrusion detection systems, by monitoring security alerts and prompt implementation of security patches. The issues of authenticating the identity of remote transaction partners and non-repudiation of transactions can theoretically be solved by public-key cryptography (Microsoft, 2001). Human factors and user interface issues pose a major challenge to information security (Lemos, 2000; Whitten & Tygar, 1999). Although PGP is regarded as having a good user interface by general standards (Zimmermann, 1995), it is still not effective for most computer users (Whitten & Tygar, 1999), and increased emphasis on human factors in security is required.

A payment intermediary is often the only party in an e-commerce transaction that is able to verify the merchant's identity and location (Pichler, 2000). It claims that credit card companies are in an influential position because of this. Payment intermediaries can also help new merchants overcome the problem of establishing initial trust. Escrow services are one form of payment intermediary currently used in B2C, C2C, and B2B e-commerce (Escrow, 2009). They hold payments from the buyer until the buyer has received and accepted the goods, at which point payment is made to the seller. Additionally,

insurance companies are also emerging to provide insurance for e-commerce transactions. For example, Gerling offers insurance and provides a 'trusted shop' seal to participating e-commerce sites (Gerling, 2009).

Trust Issues in Multimedia Content Distribution

Multimedia services such as mobile TV, Internet TV, Online Music, and Content Sharing in Social Networks, become more and more popular in human being's life. Among them, multimedia distribution acts as the key technique, which transmits the content from one user to others, as shown in Figure 1. Generally, there are two kinds of multimedia content to be transmitted, i.e., real-time content and stored content. The former one denotes the generated content without delayed storage, such as live TV or telephone call. The latter one denotes the content stored in the database, such as the video clips for video-on-demand, music segments, web data, etc. It is similar with e-commerce in some extent, e.g., the payment, and user authentication and authorization. Differently, multimedia content distribution covers more content transmission manners and multimedia consuming properties. In security engineering, there are some trust issues in multimedia content distribution, listed as follows.

User authentication and authorization: User authentication and authorization are two important issues in secure multimedia content distribution. User authentication tells whether the user is the one itself. If so, he will get the rights assigned to him. Otherwise, he cannot consume the content according to the corresponding rights. Differently, user authorization assigns the rights to a user. Generally, different users may have different rights to operate on the same content. For example, some users can watch the film, while some others can not. Thus, the former one (user authentication) is used to avoid imposture, while the latter one (user authorization) aims to divide users into different levels.

Payment for multimedia content: Payment is an important issue for non-free multimedia services. For example, in pay-TV service, the TV program is accessed after it is paid for. Generally, the payment is managed by the Central Authorizer who is trusted by both the service providers and consumers.

Confidentiality of multimedia content: In some applications, multimedia content should not be accessed by unauthorized users. Eavesdropping is the act of surreptitiously listening to a private conversation, which is commonly thought to be unethical. Eavesdropping can be done over telephone lines, email, instant messaging, and other methods of communication considered private. To resist this kind of attack, the content's confidentiality should be protected, e.g., by encryption techniques. Thus, only the user has the key can recover the content.

Release of clear content: It means that the clear media content is non-intentionally released by the user or his devices. It may happen when the device is not secure enough or the user is not care enough. For example, the device is easily broken. To resist this issue, the secure memory or storage is required.

Ownership: Sometimes, multimedia content may be illegally reproduced, and then redistributed. For example, promotional screener DVDs distributed by movie studios are a common source of unauthorized copying when movies are still in theatrical release. Movies are also still copied by someone sneaking a camcorder into a movie theater and secretly taping the projection, although such copies are often of lesser quality than copied versions of the officially released film. In this case, it is important to identify the original ownership.

Illegal redistribution: The authorized user redistributes the accessed multimedia content to other unauthorized users, e.g., the illegal sharing of recorded music over the Internet. Generally, the illegal actions are done by authorized users. To resist it, the means able to identify the illegal distributor are expected.

Forgery: Forgery is the process of making, adapting, or imitating objects, with the intent to deceive. A forgery is essentially concerned with a produced or altered object (multimedia content, user information, etc.). For example, the face in a photo is changed into another one, the sensitive military object in a satellite image is wiped, or the image edited by the computer is presented in a photo competition. To provide the forensics for forgery, the forgery detection methods are required.

Illegal content: It is bothering if the public multimedia distribution channel is filled with illegal contents related to, e.g., sexy, violence or terrorism, etc. Whether the content is distributed intentionally or not, it'll be better to provide the content filtering component that detect and prevent these illegal contents automatically.

SOLUTIONS FOR TRUSTED MULTIMEDIA CONTENT DISTRIBUTION

Authorization, Authentication and Secure Payment

Authorization and authentication are the basic issues of trusted multimedia distribution. There exist some solutions for them, among which,

Figure 2. Typical interactions in secure content distribution

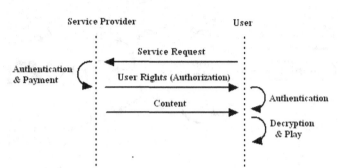

authentication protocols and trusted computing are two typical ones. The authentication protocols realize the service request, user authentication and key exchange (DVB-CPCM, 2007; ISMACryp 1.1, 2004; Tsai & Chang, 2006; GSM-03.20, 1997). They are constructed on the public-key cipher, hash function and digital signature. For example, the mutual authentication is often used (GSM-03.20, 1997), which authenticates both the service provider and the user. Trusted computing, as mentioned in Section 2.1, provides a trusted implementation, which stores the identification information or key pairs in a hardware-based manner, and exchanges the information through secure input and output.

Payment is often realized by trusted payment intermediary. Similarly with e-commerce, in multimedia distribution, the payment intermediary is often the only party in the transaction that is able to verify the identity and location of the service provider or user. Generally, it is widely accepted that credit card companies or mobile operators act as the intermediary. Thus, the payment method for media distribution is similar with the one for e-commerce mentioned in Section 2.3. The only difference is that media content has various payment models (Lian, 2008a):

- **Free model:** The media content is viewed without payment.
- **Once-pay model:** The media content is paid once for repeated views.
- **Multiple-pay model:** The media content is paid once for per view. Multiple views need multiple payments.

Till now, various secure distribution schemes have been proposed, which are all constructed on authorization, authentication and secure payment techniques. Figure 2 shows the general steps of secure content distribution. Generally, the service provider authenticates the user's request, gives the authorization and content to the user, and the user authenticates, decrypts and plays the received content. For this issue, Digital Rights Management (DRM) and Conditional Access (CA) are two typical solutions.

The role of DRM (2009) in content distribution is to enable business models whereby the consumption and use of content is controlled. As such, DRM extends beyond the physical delivery of content into managing the content lifecycle. When a user buys content, he may agree to certain constraints, e.g., by choosing between a free preview version or a full version at cost, or he may agree to pay a monthly fee. DRM allows this choice to be translated into permissions and constraints, which are then enforced when the user accesses the content.

In the context of broadcasting, DVB-H content protection & and copy management (DVB CPCM, 2007) specifies the content protection and copy management of commercial digital content delivered to consumer products. CPCM is designed in protecting all types of content, including au-

Figure 3. Secure content distribution based on media encryption

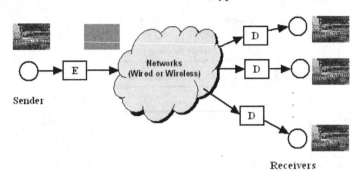

dio, video and associated applications and data. However, CPCM only defines the mechanism for designing a secure system, and it does not describe the detailed functionalities like encryption, authentication, authorization and tracking.

For mobile communications, Open Mobile Alliance DRM (OMA DRM 2.0, 2006) specifies the digital rights management. It defines the format and the protection mechanism for content and the rights objects, and also the security model for management of encryption keys. Before the content is delivered over networks, it is securely packaged to protect it from unauthorized usage. The content issuer transmits DRM content and a rights issuer produces a rights object with the encryption keys. Additionally, OMA DRM defines the super distribution mechanism, which is able to redistribute the DRM content from one terminal to other terminals.

Different from DRM, CA only provides the solution from the sender to receiver, without considering of the use cases after receiving. For example, Conditional Access (CA) systems (Jiang, et al., 2004; Park, et al., 2006; Pescador, et al., 2006) for home TV can provide secure TV program distribution from the broadcaster to TV sets. Several techniques have been standardized, e.g. ISMACryp (ISMACryp 1.1, 2004; ISMACryp 2.0, 2007), SRTP (RFC 3711, 2004) and IPSec (RFC 2401, 1998). ISMACryp defines the encryption and authentication for MPEG-4 (Li, 2001) data streams in the application layer. The ISMACryp

specification does not mandate a cipher but AES in Counter Mode (Andersen, 2008). ISMACryp is different from traditional secure protocols (SRTP and IPsec). ISMACryp encrypts MPEG-4 access units (that are in the RTP payload), SRTP encrypts the whole RTP payload in the transport layer, and IPSec encrypts packets in the network level. The secure transmission in higher layer can achieve higher security. For instance, ISMACryp is capable of achieving end-to-end security while IPSec can only realize peer-to-peer security. Generally, in content transmission, there are middle peers between the sender and the receiver. Thus, peer-to-peer security denotes the information is kept secure between two peers, while end-to-end security denotes the information is kept secure from the sender to the receiver.

Encryption for Confidentiality Protection

Multimedia encryption is the key technique to protect the content confidentiality, which transforms multimedia content into an unintelligible form. As shown in Fig. 3, the media content is often encrypted at sender side and decrypted at receiver side. Due to multimedia content's properties (e.g., high redundancy, large volumes, real time interactions, and compression) multimedia encryption algorithms often have some specific requirements, i.e., security, efficiency, compression ratio, format compliance and supporting direct operations (Lian, 2008b).

To meet these requirements, partial encryption is proposed, which encrypts only parts of multimedia content, while leaving the other parts unchanged. According to the type of multimedia content, the existing partial encryption algorithms can be classified into audio encryption, image encryption and video encryption.

Audio encryption: Audio data are often encoded before being transmitted in order to save transmission bandwidth. Thus, audio encryption is often applied to the encoded data. For example, only the parameters of Fast Fourier Transformation (FFT) during speech encoding process are encrypted (Sridharan, et al., 1991). In decryption, the decrypted parameters are used to recover the speech content. For example, in MP3 music, only the sensitive parameters of MP3 stream are encrypted, e.g., the bit allocation information (Gang, et al., 2001), which improves the efficiency by reducing the encrypted data volumes.

Image encryption: A straightforward partial encryption algorithm for images is bit-plane encryption (Podesser, et al., 2002). That is, in an image, only several significant bit-planes are encrypted, while the other bit-planes are left unchanged. By reducing the encrypted bit-planes, the encryption efficiency can be improved, while the security against replacement attacks cannot be confirmed. For compressed images, the algorithms based on DCT and wavelet codecs attract more researchers, such as JPEG or JPEG2000. The algorithm proposed in (Pfarrhofer & Uhl, 2005) encrypts only some significant bit-planes of DCT coefficients, which obtains high perception security and encryption efficiency. Another algorithm encrypts different number of significant bit-planes of wavelet coefficients in different frequency bands (Lian, et al., 2004a), which obtains high security in human perception and keeps secure against replacement attacks.

Video encryption: Since video data are of larger volumes compared with image or audio data, video data are often greatly compressed in order to reduce the bandwidth. Generally, the compressed video stream is composed of such parts as format information, frame information, texture information and motion information. Thus, partial video encryption is classified into several types, i.e., format information encryption, frame encryption, texture encryption, and both motion vector and texture encryption. Since format information helps the decoder to recover the multimedia data, encrypting the format information will make the decoder out of work (Agi & Gong, 1996). In such video codec as MPEG1/2/4, the frame is often classified into three types, i.e., I-frame, P-frame and B-frame. I-frame is often encoded directly with DCT transformation, while P/B-frame is often encoded by referencing to adjacent I/P-frame. Thus, I-frame is the referenced frame of P/B-frame. Intuitively, encrypting only I-frame will make P/B-frame unintelligible. However, experiments show that this is not secure enough. As an improved method, SECMPEG algorithm encrypts all the macroblocks encoded with DCT transformation in I/P/B-frame (Tang, 1996). The coefficients in DCT or wavelet transformation determine the intelligibility of the multimedia data. Encrypting the coefficients can protect the confidentiality of the texture information (Shi & Bhargava, 1998; Ahn, et al., 2004). To keep secure, it is necessary to encrypt both DCT/wavelet coefficient and motion vector. Considering that these two kinds of information occupy many percents in the whole video stream, they should be encrypted partially or selectively. Generally, two kinds of partial encryption method are often used, e.g., coefficient permutation and sign encryption (Zeng & Lei, 2003; Lian, et al., 2006a). These partial encryption algorithms are often of low cost, and keep the file format unchanged.

Lightweight Schemes for Secure Preview

Generally, multimedia content is produced by great efforts, and thus, its commercial value provides the reward to the producers. On the other hand,

Figure 4. An example of perceptual video encryption

(a)   (b)

the content's quality degradation will reduce the content's commercial value. To provide the content preview service without releasing the commercial value is a challenging topic. In this case, the user can preview the content freely before he/she decides to pay for it. Fortunately, two solutions have been reported, i.e., perceptual encryption (PE), and removable visible watermarking (VW).

Perceptual Encryption

Perceptual encryption is an encryption algorithm that degrades the quality of media content according to security or quality requirements. Its typical application is secure media content preview. That is, the media content is degraded by perceptual encryption. Thus, although the media content is of low quality, the customer can still understand it. If he is interested in it, he will pay for a high-quality copy. Generally, perceptual encryption is

realized by encrypting some sensitive parameters. Thus, it is a kind of partial encryption. There are two core issues in perceptual encryption. The first is how to partition media data into different parts composed of different parameters, and the second one is how to select the sensitive parameters according to security or quality requirements. There are some means that can accomplish these issues (Torrubia & Mora, 2002; Lian, et al., 2004b; Lian, et al., 2004c; Lian, et al., 2007; Li, et al., 2007). They select n (n>0) number of sensitive parameters, order them from the least significant one to the most significant one, and encrypt only the first r (r<n) ones. Thus, the encrypted content is still intelligible, while its quality is much lower than the original one. One example based on DCT coefficient encryption is shown in Figure 4. Here, the video frame is partitioned into 8*8-sized blocks, and for each block, we set n=64 and r=10. (a) is the original video frame,

Figure 5. Secure content preview based on perceptual encryption

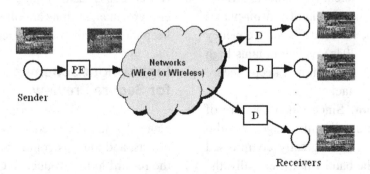

Figure 6. Secure content preview based on removable visible watermarking

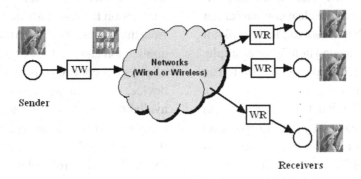

(b) is the one encrypted by perceptual encryption. Thus, without the decryption key, only the content (b) with low-quality can be previewed. Based on perceptual encryption, the secure content preview scheme can be constructed, as shown in Figure 5. Here, the media content is encrypted by perceptual encryption at the sender side, and decrypted by the authorized user at the receiver side.

Removable Visible Watermarking

In removable visible watermarking, the visible watermark is embedded in the media content at the sender side, and removed from the content at the receiver side, as shown in Fig. 6. The watermark embedding and removing operations are controlled by the key. Thus, only the authorized user with the correct key can recover the high-quality media content. Fig. 7(a), (b) and (c) show the image with visible watermarks, the one with its watermarks removed by incorrect keys, and the one with its wa-

termarks removed by the correct keys, respectively. Most of existing visible watermarking algorithms work in spatial domain (Chen, 2000), Discrete Cosine Transform (DCT) domain (Kankanhalli, et al., 1999; Nakajima, et al., 2003), or Discrete Wavelet Transform (DWT) domain (Lee, et al., 2007; Hu, et al., 2006). Compared with perceptual encryption, removable visible watermarking's security needs to be investigated.

TRUSTED HARDWARE RESISTING THE RELEASE OF CLEAR CONTENT

To resist the release of clear content, some means have been proposed, e.g., Trusted Platform Module (TPM, 2008), High-bandwidth Digital Content Protection (HDCP, 2008), and Certified Output Protection Protocol (COPP, 2006).

In trusted computing, the media content can be stored or processed in Trusted Platform Module

Figure 7. The example of removable visible watermarking ((a)-the image with visible watermarks, (b)-the image with its watermarks removed by a wrong key, and (c)-the image with its watermarks removed)

whose properties make the clear content unavailable for users. Of course, the clear content cannot be redistributed neither. However, it can still not solve the problem of "analog hole". For example, the film may be captured by a camera, or the music is recorded by a recorder.

High-bandwidth Digital Content Protection (HDCP, 2008) is developed by Intel Corporation to control digital audio and video content as it travels across Digital Visual Interface (DVI) or High-Definition Multimedia Interface (HDMI) connections. HDCP's main target is to prevent transmission of non-encrypted high definition content. Generally, three methods are adopted to meet the goal. Firstly, the authentication process disallows non-licensed devices to receive HD content. Secondly, the encryption of the actual data sent over DVI or HDMI interface prevents eavesdropping of information. It also prevents man-in-the-middle attacks. Thirdly, key revocation procedures ensure that devices manufactured by any vendors who violate the license agreement could be relatively easily blocked from receiving HD data. HD DVD, Blu-ray Disc and DVD players (with HDMI or DVI connector) use HDCP to establish an encrypted digital connection. If the display device or in the case of using a PC to decrypt and play back HD-DVD or Blu-ray media, the graphics card (hardware, drivers and playback software) does not support HDCP, then a connection cannot be established. As a result, a black picture and/or error message will likely be displayed instead of the video content.

Certified Output Protection Protocol (COPP, 2006) is a device driver technology used to enable High-bandwidth Digital Content Protection (HDCP) during the transmission of digital video between applications and high-definition displays. COPP is a Microsoft security technology for video systems that require a logo certification. For security drivers are authenticated and protected from tampering to prevent unauthorized high-quality recording from the video outputs. COPP control signals are also encrypted. Certified

Output Protection Protocol (COPP) enables an application to protect a video stream as it travels from the graphics adapter to the display device. An application can use COPP to discover what kind of physical connector is attached to the display device, and what types of output protection are available. Protection mechanisms include HDCP, Copy Generation Management System - Analog (CGMS-A) and Analog Copy Protection (ACP). COPP defines a protocol that is used to establish a secure communications channel with the graphics driver. It uses Message Authentication Codes (MACs) to verify the integrity of the COPP commands that are passed between the application and the display driver. COPP does not define anything about the digital rights policies that might apply to digital media content. Also, COPP itself does not implement any output protection systems. The COPP protocol simply provides a way to set and query protection levels on the graphics adapter, using the protection systems provided by the adapter.

Watermarking Techniques for Ownership Identification

Watermarking technique is used to protect multimedia content's ownership (Cox, et al., 2002), which embeds the ownership information (e.g., the producer's name or ID) into multimedia content by modifying the content slightly. Later, the ownership information can be extracted and used for authentication. Generally, invisible watermarking that embeds the ownership information imperceptibly is often used for ownership protection. Additionally, the watermarking algorithm should survive such operations including general signal processing operations (filtering, noising, A/D, D/A, re-sampling, recompression, etc.) and intentional attacks (rotation, scaling, shifting, transformation, tampering, etc.).

During the past decades, many watermarking algorithms have been reported. According to the carrier media type, they can be classified into image watermarking, video watermarking, audio watermarking, text watermarking and software watermarking. Among them, image watermarking embeds information in images based on images' redundancy and the perceptual property of human's eyes (Wu, et al., 2000). Video watermarking makes use of temporal information besides spatial information compared with image watermarking (Bounkong, et al., 2004; Bodo, et al., 2003). Audio watermarking adopts audio redundancy and human psychoacoustic model to hide information (Gruhl, et al., 1996). Text watermarking hides information by slightly adjusting such textures as vertical distance, horizontal distance or font (Maxemchuk & Low, 1998). This kind of watermarking is only suitable for texts but not for other data. Software watermarking is used to protect software copyright and it is often classified into two categories, i.e., static watermarking and dynamic watermarking (Collberg & Thomborson, 1999). Static watermarking embeds certain sentences in the source code, but does not change the software's functionality. Dynamic watermarking designs some dynamic information in the software, such as dynamic data structure or dynamic implementation tracking.

According to the embedding method, watermarking algorithms can be classified into three categories, i.e., replacement-based watermarking, modulation-based watermarking and encoding-based watermarking. Replacement-based watermarking replaces some parts of the cover work with watermarking. For example, the LSB method replaces the least significant bits with the transmitted message directly (Schyndel, et al., 1994). This kind of embedding method obtains high capacity, but it is seldom robust to attacks. Modulation-based watermarking modulates the cover work with the message (Cox, et al., 2002), and can realize either blind detection or non-blind detection. It is often robust to some attacks. Compared with the above two methods, encoding-based watermarking hides information by encoding some parts of the cover work. For example, Patchwork method encodes

watermarking into the relation between block pairs (Bender, et al., 1996), the authentication watermarking encodes watermarking into the relation between pixels (Ye, et al., 2004). There are also some other algorithms such as histogram-based algorithm (Coltue & Bolon, 1999) and salient-point algorithm (Rongen, et al., 1999). Although they are robust to some attacks, these encoding-based watermarking methods should be carefully designed based on the cover work's properties, and the capacity is often limited.

According to the embedding domain, watermarking can be embedded in either temporal domain, spatial domain or frequency domain. Taking video watermarking for example, the watermark can be embedded in the frame-pixels, the motion vectors or the DCT coefficients, which obtains different performances. Spatial domain watermarking embeds information in pixels directly, such as the LSB method (Schyndel, et al., 1994) and the perceptual model based methods (Podilchuk & Zeng, 1998; Swanson, et al., 1998). Generally, these methods are often not robust to signal processing or attack, although they are efficient in computing. Frequency domain Watermarking is embedded in transformation domain, such as DCT transformation (Ye, et al., 2004), wavelet transformation (Tsai, et al., 2000), etc. Compared with the watermarking in spatial domain, the one in frequency domain obtains some extra properties in robustness and imperceptibility. Temporal domain Watermarking is embedded in temporal information. For example, in audios, echo property is used to hide information, which is named echo hiding (Gruhl, et al., 1996). In videos, the temporal sequence is partitioned into static component and motive component, with information embedded into motive component (Joumaa & Davoine, 2005). Considering that human's eyes are more sensitive to static component than to motive one, embedding in motive component can often obtain higher robustness. However, error accumulation or floating makes the watermarked videos blurred in some extent, which should be improved by error compensation.

Figure 8. Secure content distribution based on robust watermarking

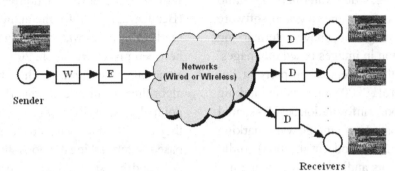

In secure content distribution, the watermark information is embedded in media content before encryption, as shown in Figure 8. And Figure 9 shows an example of video watermarking based on spread spectrum embedding (Cox, et al., 2002). Here, there are slight differences (10-times enlarged) between original media copy and the decrypted media copy.

Digital Fingerprinting for Traitor Tracing

Multimedia content distribution often faces such a problem, i.e., a customer may redistribute the received content to other unauthorized customers. The customer who redistributes the content is called the traitor. This typical problem often causes great profit-losses of content provider or service provider. As a potential solution, digital fingerprinting is recently reported and studied (Wu, et al., 2004). It embeds different information, such as Customer ID, into multimedia content,

produces a unique copy, and sends the copy to the corresponding customer. If a copy is spread to unauthorized customers, the unique information in the copy can be detected and used to trace the illegal redistributor.

The most serious threat to watermarking-based fingerprinting is collusion attack that fabricates a new copy by combining their unique copies in order to avoid the tracing. Attackers intend to remove the embedded fingerprinting by making use of the slight differences between different copies. Since the past decade, finding new solutions resisting collusion attacks has been attracting more and more researchers. The existing fingerprinting algorithms can be classified into three categories, i.e., orthogonal fingerprint, coded fingerprint and warping-based fingerprint.

In orthogonal fingerprinting (Herrigel, et al., 1998), the unique information (also named fingerprint) to be embedded is the vector independent from each other. The fingerprint can be a pseudorandom sequence, and different fingerprint

Figure 9. Examples of video watermarking ((a) original video at sender side, (b) decrypted video at receiver side, (c) 10 times of difference between (a) and (b))

corresponds to different pseudorandom sequence. The orthogonal fingerprint can resist most of the proposed collusion attacks, which benefits from the orthogonal property of the fingerprints. For example, the algorithm produces orthogonal fingerprinting for each customer (Herrigel, et al., 1998), the fingerprinting is then modulated by the cover video, and correlation detection is used to determine the ownership or colluders from the copies. For each copy, correlation detection obtains a big correlation value that determines the customer who receives the copy. For the colluded copy (e.g., averaging between N copies) the correlation value becomes R/N, which is smaller than the original correlation value R. Thus, if the correlation value R/N is still no smaller than the threshold T, the fingerprint can still be detected, otherwise, it cannot. In fact, the correlation value decreases with the rise of colluders. That is because the fingerprint is cross-affected by each other. In order to improve the detection efficiency, some detection methods are proposed, such as recursive detection (Wang, et al., 2004).

Fingerprinting can be carefully designed in codeword form, named coded fingerprinting, which can detect the colluders partially or completely. Till now, two kinds of encoding methods are often referenced, i.e., the Boneh-Shaw scheme (Boneh & Shaw, 1998) and the combinatorial design based code (Kim & Suh, 2004). Boneh-Shaw scheme is based on the Marking Assumption, i.e., only the different bits are changed by colluders, while the same bits cannot be changed. By designing the primitive binary code, at least one colluder can be captured out of up to c colluders. Differently, in combinatorial design based code, the fingerprint acts as a combinatorial codeword. The combinatorial codes have the following property: each group of colluders' fingerprint produces unique codeword that determines all the colluders in the group. The codeword is constructed based on combinatorial theory, such as AND-ACC (anti-collusion codes) or BIBD (Kim & Suh, 2004). Compared with orthogonal fingerprint-

ing, the coded fingerprinting is not only limited to additive embedding, and its correct detection rate does not depend on the number of colluders, while it is not robust against Linear Combination Collusion Attacks (LCCA).

In desynchronized fingerprinting (Mao & Mihcak, 2005; Liu, et al., 2006; Liu, et al., 2007), the multimedia content (e.g., image or video) is desynchronized imperceptibly with some geometric operations in order to make each copy different from others. This kind of fingerprinting aims to make collusion impractical under the condition of imperceptibility. That is, to de-synchronize the carrier. Thus, the colluded copy is perceptible (generates perceptual artifacts). These de-synchronization operations include random temporal sampling (video frame interpolation, temporal re-sampling, etc.), random spatial sampling (RST operations, random bending, luminance filtering or parameter smoothing) or random warping. In collusion attacks, the colluded copy is degraded so greatly that it cannot be used in high definitional applications. According to this case, warping-based fingerprinting makes collusion attacks unpractical, and thus is secure against collusion attacks. However, in this scheme, the compression ratio is often changed because of the pre-warping operations. Additionally, it is a challenge to support large number of customers by warping the content imperceptibly.

In secure media content distribution, the fingerprinting information is often embedded at the receiver side. To avoid the release of clear content from the gap between decryption and fingerprint embedding, two solutions are reported, i.e., trusted platform module (TPM) and joint fingerprint embedding and decryption (JFD). As shown in Figure 10(a), in TPM based scheme, the decryption and fingerprint embedding operations are both implemented in TPM, which avoids the content release. Differently, in JFD scheme shown in Figure 10(b), the decryption and fingerprint embedding operations are implemented simultaneously in one step (Anderson & Manifavas, 1997; Kundur & Karthik,

Figure 10. Secure content distribution based on digital fingerprinting ((a) TPM based scheme, (b) JFD scheme)

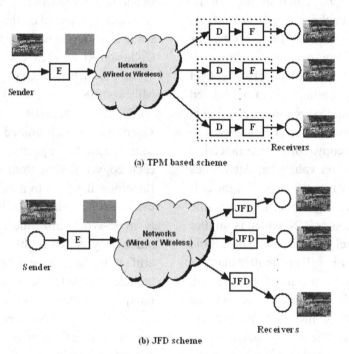

(a) TPM based scheme

(b) JFD scheme

Figure 11. Examples of video fingerprinting ((a) Decrypted video copy at the 1ˢᵗ receiver's side, (b) Decrypted video copy at the 2ⁿᵈ receiver's side, (c) 10 times of difference between (a) and (b))

(a)   (b)   (c)

2004; Lian, et al., 2006b; Lian & Wang, 2008). Figure 11 shows the example of video fingerprinting (Lian & Wang, 2008). Here, there are slight differences (10-times enlarged) between two copies decrypted by different receivers.

Multimedia Forensics for Forgery Detection

Multimedia forensics aims to tell whether the multimedia content is authentic without forgery operations (e.g., tampering and imitation). Figure 12 shows two examples for image forgery. Figure 12(a) is the picture generated by combining two pictures together. In 2006, it got the Top 10 Photos prize held by CCTV (Chinese Central Television Station). Readers worried about its authenticity because of several apparent reasons. Firstly, the antelopes should not escape in line when the train comes. Secondly, the stone at the bottom-right corner should not be same with the one in another published photo. Later, the picture's author told

Figure 12. Examples of image forgeries ((a) is the forged antelope picture, from http://www.ce.cn/culture/ today/200802/19/t20080219_14559809.shtml, (b) and (c) are the original and tampered images, from http://cs.uccs.edu/~cs525/studentproj/projS2006/sasummer/doc/CS525ProjSummersWahl.doc)

that the picture is really a forgery one. Figure 12(b) is tampered by removing the truck and replacing the original region by copying the trees, which produces the image (c). Without the original image, it is difficult to tell by eye whether the operated image is authentic or not.

In multimedia forensics, as shown in Figure 13, the intrinsic features are extracted from the operated multimedia content, then, the features' properties are analyzed and compared with a common threshold (e.g., predetermined by natural statistics), and the comparison result tells whether the content is forged or not. The extracted intrinsic features have apparent difference between the natural one and the forged one, and the difference can be distinguished by the threshold. The core technique in this scheme is to extract the distinguishable features. Generally, it depends on the model of the forgery operation, and different features will be extracted for different forgery operations.

Now, there are some forgery detection methods based on special features, i.e., correlation feature, double compression feature, light feature,

Figure 13. General architecture of forgery detection

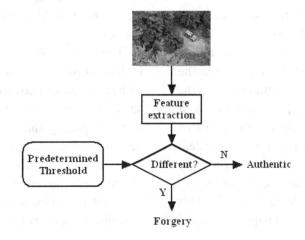

and media statistical feature, and some methods with special functionalities, e.g., duplication detection.

Correlation based detection: Some correlations between adjacent temporal or spatial sample pixels are often introduced during multimedia content generation or content operations. From the multimedia content, these correlations can be detected and used to identify forgeries, e.g., resample (Popescu & Farid, 2005a) and color filter array interpolation (Popescu & Farid, 2005b). These forgery detection methods can detect either the image's authentic or the image regions' authentic. However, they work with the assumption that the images are firstly interpolated during image generation and then modified during image forgery. Thus, they are not robust against re-interpolation attacks.

Double compression detection: In multimedia content forgery, the edition software often stores the content in compression formats, e.g. JPEG or MPEG2. Thus, the forged multimedia content may be recompressed. Intuitively, recompression introduces different distortions compared with once compression, which can be used to detect whether the multimedia content is recompressed (Wang & Farid, 2006). Thus, if an image is recompressed, the probability of forgery is increased. The method's disadvantage is the vulnerability to attacks. For example, if the modified JPEG image is cropped before being saved in JPEG format, the periodicity of distortion is difficult to be detected.

Light property based detection: In practice, the captured picture conforms to certain light direction. Suppose there is only a point light corresponding to the picture's scene, then the estimated light directions for all the objects in the picture should intersect to a point. Differently, if one object in the picture is tampered, the estimated light direction of the object will be inconsistent with other objects' light directions. Thus, by detecting the light directions, the image forgery can be detected (Johnson & Farid, 2005). This method can detect either the image's authentic

or the image objects' authentic. Its computational complexity and robustness depend on the adopted light direction estimation methods.

Feature-based detection: With respect to the different generation processes of a natural image and the forged image, there are some specific image features, which can exhibit the difference such as the high-order statistical feature, the sharpness/blurriness, and feature fusion and classifier fusion. These features can be used to detect forgeries (Sankur, et al., 2006). This method can detect whether a media region is forged or not. The challenge is how to design the optimal strategy for selecting the features or classifiers.

Duplication detection: In multimedia forgery, duplication is one of the often used tampering operations. Till now, there are various duplication detection methods, i.e., direct detection and segmentation based detection. Direct detection means to detect the duplicated regions directly without any information about the regions, e.g., DCT domain sorting (Fridrich, et al., 2003). Segmentation based detection means to detect the duplicated objects after segmentation (Farid, 2006). These methods can detect an image object's authentic, including the object deletion, healing or duplication.

Open Issues and Promising Research Topics

Based on the above discussion, we further propose some open issues and promising research topics about multimedia content distribution in this section.

Trust in distributed networks: Media distribution in distributed environments, such as p2p, ad hoc or sensor network, brings some trust issues. For example, the cost for user authentication increases greatly, and the tracing of media content becomes more difficult. Thus, the new methods are expected to model the trust in this case, and to manage the arising security issues.

Trust in network or service convergence: Ubiquitous multimedia services are becoming more and more popular, and they often converge several networks or services together. The challenge includes not only the exchange of network protocols, the bit-rate adaptation of multimedia content and the compliance of user terminals but also the trust architecture covering all the involved networks. Interoperable DRM is not the only issue, some potential application scenarios need to be investigated.

Trust of content sharing in social networks: Nowadays, content sharing social networks enrich human being's life. Some typical networks include Blog, Video Blog, P2P sharing platforms, etc., where users can upload or post multimedia content freely. However, it is noted that, more and more unhealthy contents arise in these networks, e.g., the content related to legality, sex, privacy, piracy or terror. To detect, distinguish or prevent these contents' distribution is a new topic. Some content analysis and classification techniques need to be used together with existing security solutions.

Privacy-preserving data processing: Privacy-preserving data mining addresses the necessary to protect privacy in data retrieval. However, it is now also urgent in other fields, such as multi-party interaction, remote diagnosis, content distribution, etc. Thus, the new protocols or operations need to be investigated, which aims at the new applications. The new technique, named signal processing in encryption domain, attempts to give a general solution by adopting homomorphic encryption and signal processing operations. It is still at the beginning.

Intelligent surveillance: Surveillance is now widely used in public security. With the increase of distributed surveillance cameras and collected data volumes, intelligent surveillance becomes more and more urgent, as it processes the multimedia data automatically to extract usable information. The typical intelligent processing techniques include object tracking, activity analysis, crime detection, face extraction, etc. Generally, various basic techniques are required, such as video segmentation, semantic analysis, machine learning, etc.

CONCLUSION

In this chapter, we introduced the trust issues in multimedia content distribution, investigated the existing solutions to confirm the trust, and presented some open issues and promising research topics. Trust is a multi-factory concept. Herein, we mainly focused on its security aspect in our discussion, which includes authorization, authentication, payment, ownership, illegal distribution, forgery, etc. However, we believe privacy protection and reputation systems' support could further enhance the existing trust solutions for multimedia content distribution. These could be our future work efforts.

ACKNOWLEDGMENT

The author thanks Dr. Zheng Yan for the invitation to contribute this chapter.

REFERENCES

Agi, I., & Gong, L. (1996). An empirical study of MPEG video transmissions. In *Proceedings of the Internet Society Symposium on Network and Distributed System Security*, San Diego, CA (pp. 137-144).

Ahn, J., Shim, H., Jeon, B., & Choi, I. (2004). Digital Video Scrambling Method Using Intra Prediction Mode. In *Proceedings of the 2004 Pacific-Rim Conference on Multimedia (PCM2004)* (LNCS 3333, pp. 386-393). Berlin, Germany: Springer.

Andersen, R. (2008). *Security Engineering* (2nd ed.). Hoboken, NJ: Wiley Science Publisher.

Anderson, R., & Manifavas, C. (1997). Chameleon - a new kind of stream cipher. In *Fast Software Encryption* (LNCS 1267, pp. 107-113). Berlin, Germany: Srpinger-Verlag.

Bender, W., Gruhl, D., Morimoto, N., & Lu, A. (1996). Techniques for data hiding. *IBM Systems Journal, 35*(3-4), 313–316.

Bodo, Y., Laurent, N., & Dugelay, J. (2003). Watermarking video, hierarchical embedding in motion vectors. In *Proceedings of IEEE International Conference on Image Processing*, Spain (Vol. 2, pp. 739-742).

Boneh, D., & Shaw, J. (1998). Collusion-secure fingerprinting for digital data. *IEEE Transactions on Information Theory, 44*(5), 1897–1905. doi:10.1109/18.705568

Bounkong, S., Toch, B., Saad, D., & Lowe, D. (2004). ICA for watermarking digital images . *Journal of Machine Learning Research, 4*(7-8), 1471–1498. doi:10.1162/jmlr.2003.4.7-8.1471

Callas, J., Donnerhacke, L., Finney, H., Shaw, D., & Thayer, R. (2007). *OpenPGP Message Format* (RFC 4880). Retrieved from http://tools.ietf.org/html/rfc4880

Chen, P.-M. (2000). A visible watermarking mechanism using a statistic approach. In *Proceedings of 5th International Conference on Signal Processing (WCCC-ICSP 2000)* (Vol. 2, pp. 910-913).

Collberg, C. S., & Thomborson, C. (1999). Software watermarking: models and dynamic embeddings. In *Proceeding of ACM SIGPLAN-SIGACT Symposium on Principles of Programming Languages (POPL99)*, San Antonio, TX (pp. 311-324).

Coltue, D., & Bolon, P. (1999). Watermarking by histogram specification. In *Proceeding of SPIE Electronic Imaging'99, Security and Watermarking of Multimedia Contents*, San Jose (pp. 252-263).

COPP. (2006). *Using Certified Output Protection Protocol*. Retrieved February 28, 2009, from http://msdn2.microsoft.com/en-us/library/Aa468617.aspx

Cox, I. J., Miller, M. L., & Bloom, J. A. (2002). *Digital Watermarking*. San Francisco: Morgan-Kaufmann.

Dell. (2006). Enhancing IT Security with Trusted Computing Group standards. *Dell Power Solutions*. Retrieved from http://www.dell.com/downloads/global/vectors/2007_tcgs.pdf

DRM. (2009). *Digital Rights Management*. Retrieved February 28, 2009, from http://en.wikipedia.org/wiki/Digital_rights_management

Dutton, P. (2000). Trust Issues in E-Commerce. In *Proceedings of the 6th Australasian Women in Computing Workshop*, Griffith University (pp. 15-26).

DVB-CPCM. (2007). *Digital Video Broadcasting Content Protection & Copy Management (DVB-CPCM)* (DVB Document A094 Rev. 1).

Escrow. (2009). Retrieved from http://www.escrow.com/

Evers, J. (2005). Microsoft's leaner approach to Vista security. *CNET News*. Retrieved from http://m.news.com/Microsofts+leaner+approach+to+Vista+security/2163-7355_3-5843808.html

Farid, H. (2006). Exposing digital forgeries in scientific images. In *Proceeding of ACM MM&Sec'06*, Geneva, Switzerland (pp. 29–36).

Fridrich, J., Soukal, D., & Lukas, J. (2003). Detection of copy-move forgery in digital images. In *Proceedings of 2003 Digital Forensic Research Workshop (2003)*, Cleveland, OH, USA. Retrieved from http://www.ws.binghamton.edu/fridrich/Research/copymove.pdf

Gang, L., Akansu, A. N., Ramkumar, M., & Xie, X. (2001). Online Music Protection and MP3 Compression. In *Proceedings Of International Symposium on Intelligent Multimedia, Video and Speech Processing* (pp. 13-16).

Gerck, E. (1998). Trust Points. In J. Feghhi, J. Feghhi, & P. Williams (Eds.), *Digital Certificates: Applied Internet Security* (pp. 194-195). Reading, MA: Addison-Wesley.

Gerling. (2009). Retrieved from http://www.gerling.de/

Gruhl, D., Lu, A., & Bender, W. (1996). Echo Hiding. In *Pre-Proceedings: Information Hiding*, Cambridge, UK (pp. 295-316).

GSM-03.20. (1997). *European Telecommunications Standards Institute, "GSM Technical Specification GSM 03.20 (ETS 300 534): "Digital cellular telecommunication system (Phase 2): Security related network functions"*.

HDCP. (2008). *High-bandwidth Digital Content Protection System Version 2.0*. Retrieved from http://www.digital-cp.com/

Herrigel, A., Oruanaidh, J., Petersen, H., Pereira, S., & Pun, T. (1998). Secure copyright protection techniques for digital images. In *Proceedings of the Second Information Hiding Workshop (IHW)* (LNCS 1525, pp. 169-190). Berlin, Germany: Springer-Verlag.

Hu, Y., Kwong, S., & Huang, J. (2006). An Algorithm for Removable Visible Watermarking. *IEEE Transactions on Circuits and Systems for Video Technology, 16*(1), 129–133. doi:10.1109/TCSVT.2006.884011

Hudson, A. (2003). *Equity and Trusts* (3rd ed.). London: Cavendish Publishing.

ISMACryp 1.1. (2004). *ISMA Encryption & Authentication Specification 1.1*. Retrieved from http://www.isma.tv/

ISMACryp 2.0. (2007). *ISMA Encryption & Authentication Specification 2.0*. Retrieved from http://www.isma.tv/

Jiang, T., Zheng, S., & Liu, B. (2004). Key distribution based on hierarchical access control for Conditional Access System in DTV broadcast. *IEEE Transactions on Consumer Electronics, 50*(1), 225–230. doi:10.1109/TCE.2004.1277866

Johnson, M. K., & Farid, H. (2005). Exposing digital forgeries by detecting inconsistencies in lighting. In *Proc. of the ACM Multimedia Security Workshop* (pp. 1-10).

Joumaa, H., & Davoine, F. (2005). An ICA based algorithm for video watermarking. In *Proc. of the 2005 International Conference on Acoustics, Speech, and Signal Processing (ICASSP 2005)* (Vol. 2, pp. 805-808).

Kankanhalli, M. S. Rajmohan, & Ramakrishnan, K.R. (1999). Adaptive visible watermarking of images. In *Proceedings of 1999 IEEE International Conference on Multimedia Computing and Systems* (pp. 568-573).

Kelton, K., Fleischmann, K. R., & Wallace, W. A. (2008). Trust in Digital Information. *Journal of the American Society for Information Science and Technology, 59*(3), 363–374. doi:10.1002/asi.20722

Kim, W., & Suh, Y. (2004). Short N-secure fingerprinting code for image. In *Proceeding of 2004 International Conference on Image Processing* (pp. 2167-2170).

Kini, A., & Choobineh, J. (1998). Trust in Electronic Commerce: Definition and Theoretical Considerations. In *Proceedings of Thirty-First Annual Hawaii International Conference on System Sciences (HICSS)* (Vol. 4, pp. 51).

Kundur, D., & Karthik, K. (2004). Video fingerprinting and encryption principles for digital rights management. *Proceedings of the IEEE*, *92*(6), 918–932. doi:10.1109/JPROC.2004.827356

Lee, S., Yoo, C. D., & Kalker, T. (2007). Reversible Image Watermarking Based on Integer-to-Integer Wavelet Transform. *IEEE Transactions on Information Forensics and Security*, *2*(3), 321–330. doi:10.1109/TIFS.2007.905146

Lemos, R. (2000). Mitnick teaches 'social engineering'. *ZDNet News*. Retrieved from http://zdnet.com.com/2100-11-522261.html?legacy=zdnn

Lemos, R. (2006). U.S. Army requires trusted computing. *Security Focus*. Retrieved from http://www.securityfocus.com/brief/265

Li, S., Chen, G., Cheung, A., Bhargava, B., & Lo, K.-T. (2007). On the design of perceptual MPEG-Video encryption algorithms. *IEEE Transactions on Circuits and Systems for Video Technology*, *17*(2), 214–223. doi:10.1109/TCSVT.2006.888840

Li, W. (2001). Overview of fine granularity scalability in MPEG-4 video standard. *IEEE Transactions on Circuits and Systems for Video Technology*, *11*(3), 301–317. doi:10.1109/76.911157

Lian, S. (2008a). Digital Rights Management for the Home TV Based on Scalable Video Coding. *IEEE Transactions on Consumer Electronics*, *54*(3), 1287–1293. doi:10.1109/TCE.2008.4637619

Lian, S. (2008b). *Multimedia Content Encryption: Techniques and Applications*. Boca Raton, FL: Auerbach Publications, Taylor & Francis.

Lian, S. (2009). *Multimedia communication security: recent advances*. Hauppauge, NY: Nova Science Publishers.

Lian, S., & Liu, Z. (2008). Secure Media Content Distribution Based on the Improved Set-Top Box in IPTV. *IEEE Transactions on Consumer Electronics*, *54*(2), 560–566. doi:10.1109/TCE.2008.4560130

Lian, S., Liu, Z., Ren, Z., & Wang, H. (2006a). Secure advanced video coding based on selective encryption algorithms. *IEEE Transactions on Consumer Electronics*, *52*(2), 621–629. doi:10.1109/TCE.2006.1649688

Lian, S., Liu, Z., Ren, Z., & Wang, H. (2006b). Secure Distribution Scheme for Compressed Data Streams. In *Proceeding of 2006 IEEE Conference on Image Processing (ICIP 2006)* (pp. 1953-1956).

Lian, S., Liu, Z., Ren, Z., & Wang, Z. (2007). Multimedia data encryption in block based codecs. *International Journal of Computers and Applications*, *29*(1), 18–24. doi:10.2316/Journal.202.2007.1.202-1780

Lian, S., Sun, J., & Wang, Z. (2004b). Perceptual cryptography on SPIHT compressed images or videos. In *Proceedings of the IEEE International Conference on Multimedia and Expro (I) (ICME2004)* (Vol. 3, pp. 2195-2198).

Lian, S., Sun, J., Zhang, D., & Wang, Z. (2004a). A selective image encryption scheme based on JPEG2000 Codec. In *Proceedings of the 2004 Pacific-Rim Conference on Multimedia (PCM2004)* (LNCS 3332, pp. 65-72). Berlin, Germany: Springer.

Lian, S., Wang, X., Sun, J., & Wang, Z. (2004c). Perceptual cryptography on wavelet transform encoded videos. In *Proceedings of the 2004 International Symposium on Intelligent Multimedia, Video and Speech Processing (ISIMP'2004)* (pp. 57-60).

Lian, S., & Wang, Z. (2008). Collusion-traceable Secure Multimedia Distribution Based on Controllable Modulation. *IEEE Transactions on Circuits and Systems for Video Technology, 18*(10), 1462–1467. doi:10.1109/TCSVT.2008.2002829

Lian, S., & Zhang, Y. (2009). *Handbook of Research on Secure Multimedia Distribution*. Hershey, PA: Information Science Reference.

Liu, Z., Lian, S., Gautier, J., Wang, R., et al. (2007). Secure video multicast based on desynchronized fingerprint and partial encryption. In *Proceeding of 2007 International Workshop on Digital Watermarking (IWDW2007)* (LNCS 5041, pp. 335-349).

Liu, Z., Lian, S., Wang, R., & Ren, Z. (2006). Desynchronization in compression process for collusion resilient video fingerprint. In *Proceedings of the IWDW2006* (LNCS 4283, pp. 308-322). Berlin, Germany: Springer.

Mahmood, O. (2008). Modelling trust recognition and evaluation in an electronic environment. *International Journal of Networking and Virtual Organizations, 5*(3/4), 349–368. doi:10.1504/IJNVO.2008.018827

Mao, Y., & Mihcak, M. K. (2005). Collusion-resistant international de-synchronization for digital video fingerprinting. In . *Proceedings of the IEEE Conference on Image Processing, 1*, 237–240.

Maxemchuk, N. F., & Low, S. H. (1998). Performance comparison of two text marking methods. *IEEE Journal on Selected Areas in Communications, 16*(4), 561–572. doi:10.1109/49.668978

Microsoft. (2001). *Microsoft Security Bulletin MS01-017 (March 22, 2001): Erroneous VeriSign-Issued Digital Certificates Pose Spoofing Hazard.* Retrieved from http://www.microsoft.com/technet/security/bulletin/MS01-017.asp

Misztal, B. (1996). *Trust in Modern Societies: The Search for the Bases of Social Order*, Polity Press, ISBN 0-7456-1634-8.

Nakajima, Y., Yoneyama, A., & Hatori, Y. (2003). A Fast Logo Insertion Algorithm for MPEG Compressed Video. In *Proceeding of IEEE International Conference on Consumer Electronics (ICCE 2003)* (pp. 38-39).

Nguyen, P. Q. (2004). Can We Trust Cryptographic Software? Cryptographic Flaws in GNU Privacy Guard v1.2.3. In *Proceedings of the Advances in cryptology - EUROCRYPT 2004* (LNCS 3027, pp. 555-570). Berlin, Germany: Springer.

OMA DRM 2.0. (2006). *Open Mobile Alliance, Digital Rights Management 2.0.*

Park, S., Jeong, J., & Kwon, T. (2006). Contents Distribution System Based on MPEG-4 ISMACryp in IP Set-top Box Environments. *IEEE Transactions on Consumer Electronics, 52*(2), 660–668. doi:10.1109/TCE.2006.1649694

Pescador, F., Sanz, C., Garrido, M. J., Santos, C., & Antoniello, R. (2006). A DSP Based IP Set-Top Box for Home Entertainment. *IEEE Transactions on Consumer Electronics, 52*(1), 254–262. doi:10.1109/TCE.2006.1605055

Pfarrhofer, R., & Uhl, A. (2005). Selective image encryption using JBIG. In *Proceeding of 2005 IFIP Conference on Communications and Multimedia Security* (pp. 98-107).

Pichler, R. (2000). *Trust and Reliance - Enforcement and Compliance: Enhancing Consumer Confidence in the Electronic Marketplace*. Stanford Law School. Retrieved from http://www.oecd.org/dsti/sti/it/secur/act/online trust/Consumer Confidence.pdf

Podesser, M., Schmidt, H. P., & Uhl, A. (2002). Selective bitplane encryption for secure transmission of image data in mobile environments. In *Proceedings of the 5th IEEE Nordic Signal Processing Symposium (NORSIG 2002)*, Tromso-Trondheim, Norway.

Podilchuk, C. I., & Zeng, W. (1998). Image-adaptive watermarking using visual models. *IEEE Journal on Selected Areas in Communications, 16*(4), 525–539. doi:10.1109/49.668975

Popescu, A. C., & Farid, H. (2005a). Exposing digital forgeries by detecting traces of re-sampling. *IEEE Transactions on Signal Processing, 53*(2), 758–767. doi:10.1109/TSP.2004.839932

Popescu, A. C., & Farid, H. (2005b). Exposing digital forgeries in color filter array interpolated images. *IEEE Transactions on Signal Processing, 53*(10), 3948–3959. doi:10.1109/TSP.2005.855406

Rahman, A. A. (1997). The PGP trust model. *The Journal of Electronic Commerce*. Retrieved from http://www.wim.uni-koeln.de/uploads/media/The_PGP_Trust_Model.pdf

RFC 2401. (1998). *Security Architecture for the Internet Protocol (IPSec)*. Retrieved from http://www.ietf.org/rfc/rfc2401.txt

RFC 3711. (2004). *Secure Real-time Transport Protocol (SRTP) Security profile for Real-time Transport Protocol. IETF Request for Comments document*. Retrieved from http://tools.ietf.org/html/rfc3711

Rongen, P. M., Macs, M. B., & Overveld, C. (1999). Digital image watermarking by salient point modification, In *Proc. of the SPIE Electronic Imaging'99, Security and Watermarking of Multimedia Content*, San Jose (Vol. 3657, pp. 273-282).

Safford, D., Kravitz, J., & Doorn, L. V. (2003). Take Control of TCPA. *Linux Journal*. Retrieved from http://www.linuxjournal.com/article/6633

Sankur, B., Bayram, S., Avcibas, I., & Memon, N. (2006). Image manipulation detection. *Journal of Electronic Imaging, 15*(4), 041102. doi:10.1117/1.2401138

Schneier, B. (2002). Palladium and the TCPA. *Crypto-Gram Newsletter*. Retrieved from http://www.schneier.com/crypto-gram-0208.html

Schyndel, R. G., Tirkel, A. Z., & Osborne, C. F. (1994). A digital watermark. In *Proc. of the IEEE Int. Conf. on Image Processing*, Austin, TX (Vol. 2, pp. 86-90).

Shi, C., & Bhargava, B. (1998). A fast MPEG video encryption algorithm. In *Proceedings of the 6th ACM International Multimedia Conference*, Bristol, UK (pp. 81-88).

Sridharan, S., Dawson, E., & Goldburg, B. (1991). Fast Fourier transform based speech encryption system. *IEEE Proceedings of Communications . Speech and Vision, 138*(3), 215–223.

Swanson, M. D., Zhu, B., Tewfik, A. H., & Boney, L. (1998). Robust audio watermarking using perceptual masking. *Signal Processing, 66*(3), 337–355. doi:10.1016/S0165-1684(98)00014-0

Taipale, K. A. (2005). The Trusted Systems Problem: Security Envelopes, Statistical Threat Analysis, and the Presumption of Innocence, Homeland Security - Trends and Controversies. *IEEE Intelligent Systems, 20*(5), 80–83.

Tang, L. (1996). Methods for encrypting and decrypting MPEG video data efficiently. In *Proceedings of the Fourth ACM International Multimedia Conference (ACM Multimedia'96)*, Boston, MA (pp. 219-230).

TCG. (2009). *Trusted Computing Group: FAQs*. Retrieved from https://www.trustedcomputinggroup.org/faq/

Torrubia, A., & Mora, F. (2002). Perceptual cryptography on MPEG Layer III bitstreams. *IEEE Transactions on Consumer Electronics*, *48*(4), 1046–1050. doi:10.1109/TCE.2003.1196437

TPM. (2008). *Trusted Platform Module (TPM) Specifications*. Retrieved from https://www.trustedcomputinggroup.org/specs/TPM/

Trust. (2009). Retrieved from http://en.wikipedia.org/wiki/Trust

Tsai, M. J., Yu, K. Y., & Chen, Y. Z. (2000). Joint wavelet and spatial transformation for digital watermarking. *IEEE Transactions on Consumer Electronics*, *46*(1), 241–245.

Tsai, Y.-R., & Chang, C.-J. (2006). SIM-based subscriber authentication mechanism for wireless local area networks. *Computer Communications*, *29*, 1744–1753. doi:10.1016/j.comcom.2005.09.016

Wang, W., & Farid, H. (2006). Exposing digital forgeries in video by detecting double MPEG compression, *Proceedings of the 9th workshop on Multimedia & security (MM&Sec '06)*, September 26–27, 2006, Geneva, Switzerland, pp. 35-42.

Wang, Z. J., Wu, M., Trappe, W., & Liu, K. J. R. (2004). Group-oriented fingerprinting for multimedia forensics. *EURASIP Journal on Applied Signal Processing*, (4): 2153–2173. doi:10.1155/S1110865704312151

Whitten, A., & Tygar, J. (1999). Why Johnny Can't Encrypt: A Usability Evaluation of PGP 5.0. In *Proceedings of the 8th USENIX Security Symposium*.

Wu, M., Tang, E., & Liu, B. (2000). Data hiding in digital binary images, In *Proc. of the IEEE Int'l Conf. on Multimedia and Expo*, New York, NY (pp. 393-396).

Wu, M., Trappe, W., Wang, Z. J., & Liu, R. (2004). Collusion-resistant fingerprinting for multimedia. *IEEE Signal Processing Magazine*, *21*(2), 15–27. doi:10.1109/MSP.2004.1276103

Ye, D., Mao, Y., Dai, Y., & Wang, Z. (2004). A multi-feature based invertible authentication watermarking for JPEG Images. In *Proceedings of the 3rd International Workshop on Digital Watermarking (IWDW2004)*, Seoul, Korea (pp. 152-162).

Zeng, W., & Lei, S. (2003). Efficient frequency domain selective scrambling of digital video. *IEEE Transactions on Multimedia*, *5*(1), 118–129. doi:10.1109/TMM.2003.808817

Zimmermann, P. (1995). *PGP Source Code and Internals*. Cambridge, MA: MIT Press.

Chapter 6
Certificate–Based Trust Establishment in eEnabled Airplane Applications:
Challenges and Approaches

Mingyan Li
Boeing Research & Technology, USA

Krishna Sampigethaya
Boeing Research & Technology, USA

Radha Poovendran
University of Washington, USA

ABSTRACT

This chapter describes potential roles of trust in future aviation information systems. The next-generation air transportation systems are envisioned to be a highly networked environment with aircraft digitally linked with ground systems and wireless technologies allowing real-time continuous sensing, collection and distribution of aircraft information assets. The resulting enhancements promise to revolutionize manufacturing, operation and maintenance of commercial airplanes. Safe and dependable aircraft operation as well as public well-being in these complex system-of-systems with multiple stakeholders, demands that the distributed information assets can be trusted to be correct and that the level of trustworthiness in systems can be established. This chapter considers two recent abstractions of such aviation systems – an electronic distribution system connecting aircraft with ground components for exchanging updates and data of onboard software, and a radio frequency identification (RFID) system for logistics and maintenance of aircraft – which use digital certificates to establish trust in integrity and authenticity of information assets as well as in authorized components handling these assets. The chapter presents unique challenges of aviation, such as regulations and business models, which can complicate implementation of certificate-based trust and further warrant trustworthiness proofs.

DOI: 10.4018/978-1-61520-682-7.ch006

INTRODUCTION

The emergence of the fully network-capable, also referred to as "eEnabled" airplane is a significant leap in the commercial aviation industry, introducing a wide range of applications which use computer networks and wireless links to perform automated seamless exchange of information assets between aircraft and ground systems. Some major examples for aircraft information assets include field-loadable software updates from onboard equipment manufacturers, aircraft health status data from onboard sensors, logistics and maintenance history data from onboard systems and parts (Bird, Christensen, Lutz, & Scandura, 2005). Furthermore, emerging wireless technologies, such as Radio Frequency Identification (RFID), offer unprecedented improvements for aircraft operation and maintenance by providing ways to automate data sensing, storage, update and retrieval.

Together, the advances brought by eEnabled airplanes promise to enhance the safety, efficiency and reliability of the next-generation air transportation systems. Some recent real-world examples include the electronic delivery of aircraft software and data which replaces the cumbersome and often expensive management and physical transfer of floppy disks, CDs, and signed documents via bonded postal services (Spenser, 2005); maintenance of onboard hardware using low-cost passive RFID tags and readers which replaces the inefficient and error-prone barcode scanners (Porad, 2005).

Along with the beneficial opportunities, an eEnabled airplane imposes new challenges on the realization of the network applications as it changes the assumptions and shifts the paradigm our existing solutions are based on. For example, physical delivery of airplane software and data via FedEx assumes trustworthiness of the trans-port Sneakernet. Such an assumption is violated in electronic airplane software distribution, as computer networks such as Internet have well-known vulnerabilities which must be mitigated for secure airplane operation and airline business (FAA1, 2007; FAA2, 2007). In another example, today's RFID systems are typically designed for a specific application, deployed and managed by a single party. On the other hand, future onboard RFID systems of eEnabled airplanes are envisioned to dynamically connect with different ground systems and to serve multiple purposes such as logistics, maintenance, and physical access control. At the same time, safety-criticality of onboard aircraft information mandates protection of the integrity and authenticity of information flow in aviation RFID systems.

eEnabled airplane applications generally span multiple business domains. For instance, airplane software distribution involves multiple onboard equipment and airframe manufacturers who supply software and updates for aircraft, the airlines which maintain software configurations of its fleet, and the network-capable airplane which receives software and generates configuration reports. A fundamental challenge in building secure solutions for such cross-domain distributed network applications is to establish trust among different business parties that may not have pre-established business relationships and trust.

This chapter considers electronic airplane software distribution and airplane multi-purpose RFID systems as two examples, to illustrate challenges and approaches for security solutions and certificate-based trust establishment among entities for eEnabled airplane applications. The next section gives a concise background on eEnabled airplanes and their security, followed by two sections that present the challenges and approaches to securing airplane software distribution and RFID systems for eEnabled airplanes.

BACKGROUND

Network-Enabled (eEnabled) Airplanes

Current air transportation infrastructures and aircraft avionics are becoming outdated, lacking the capacity to continue meeting the growing demands of aviation. With scope for enhancements in the delivery, availability, usage and management of information assets, eEnabled airplanes promise to improve flight safety, schedule predictability, maintenance and operational efficiencies, and passenger convenience, for enhancing future air transportation.

The eEnabled aircraft is envisioned to possess advanced sensing, computing, storage facilities, and commercial standards based networking capability that enables in-aircraft communications as well as wireless communications between aircraft and off-board systems in the shared airspace, airports, air traffic control, and airline infrastructures (Wargo & Dhas, 2003). Latest developments in commercial aviation support the realization of future eEnabled airplanes. For example, next-generation aircraft will have a version of the commercial Ethernet based architecture for the in-aircraft network (Aeronautical Radio Inc. or ARINC 664, 2009; ARINC 811, 2005), an onboard Global Positioning System sensor and terrestrial broadcast data link, e.g., 1090 MHz Extended Squitter, for performing highly accurate navigation and surveillance (Radio Technical Committee for Aeronautics Special Committee or RTCA SC 186), RFID tags on onboard parts for storing maintenance data (Porad, 2005), and an electronic distribution system for exchanging some software and data such as the electronic "flight bag" with the ground systems connected via 802.11 links at the airport (Bird, Christensen, Lutz, & Scandura, 2005).

With unprecedented features, eEnabled airplanes are expected to facilitate beneficial applications in the next-generation air transporta-

tion systems. One example, the airpalnes utilize networks to perform electronic distribution of field-loadable software and data. Field-loadable software is the onboard equipment software and databases which are designed and developed by the equipment manufacturers in accordance with well-established guidelines in RTCA/DO-178B (RTCA, 1992). Other eEnabled airplane application examples include smart sensors based aircraft health management which performs real-time and continuous diagnosis of aircraft's condition, instead of today's reactive fixed-interval maintenance of aircraft (Seidenman & Spanovich, 2007), and broadcast data link based air traffic management that improves airspace capacity and operational efficiency of traffic control (Schreckenbach, Schnell, Scalise, & Platt, 2007) by providing enhanced information sharing and situational awareness.

As intelligent nodes in an envisioned global heterogeneous network, eEnabled airplanes also open new business opportunities in providing aircraft support and services that utilize digital networking technology, such as digital delivery of aircraft data to customers, application of onboard RFID systems to enhance airline and airport logistics (Melski, Thoroe, Caus, & Schumann, 2007). Moreover, use of commercial solutions and wireless technologies can reduce airplane manufacturing and operational costs, e.g., by lowering equipment and maintenance overhead cost as well as system weight (Wargo & Dhas, 2003; Bai, Atiquzzaman, & Lilja, 2004).

Major Security Issues of eEnabled Airplanes

However, eEnabled airplanes raise new regulatory and security concerns that must be addressed. Unlike the eEnabled model, legacy aircraft were mostly isolated from off-board systems, employing aeronautical-specific protocols and technologies to communicate with ground systems. The overall design of legacy aircraft systems was highly regulated to be safe. Regulatory agencies around the world, including the Federal Aviation Administration or FAA in the United States and the European Aviation Safety Agency or EASA in Europe, are aware that guidance and regulations for certification and continued airworthiness of legacy aircraft, e.g., RTCA/DO-178B, are not adequate to address new system architectures and emerging threats to the security and availability of onboard systems and information assets of the eEnabled airplane (FAA1, 2007; FAA2, 2007; FAA3, 2008). With the use of vulnerable commercial and wireless solutions, the onboard systems of the eEnabled airplane are susceptible to unauthorized access, unanticipated interference and disruption. Consequently, today, new regulatory conditions are very carefully implemented to ensure safe and profitable operation of eEnabled aircraft. For instance, it is required that potential risks to the electronic delivery of some field-loadable software to aircraft be identified and adequately mitigated (FAA2, 2007). Also, current approval of onboard RFID is for passive-only tags and is read only when the aircraft is on the ground, in order to prevent unknown interferences with the operation of other onboard systems (FAA3, 2008).

For today's modern aviation environment, any cyber threat analysis must assume that international terrorists as well as criminals pursuing economic damage are capable of employing advanced technologies for information attacks. In this context, an adversary is assumed to be capable of passive eavesdropping of communications, active manipulation of assets, impersonation, and insider attacks. The objective of the adversary is to degrade airplane airworthiness – as in the case of international terrorists – and/or to induce unnecessary passenger safety concerns and impede airline business – as would be expected of hackers or international crime organizations. For example, an adversary could attempt to corrupt loadable software that is intended for the flight-control computer with intention of lowering safety margins. On the other hand, the adversary may intend to introduce unwarranted expenses by corrupting an RFID reading to incur false detection of asset corruption, so that flight is cancelled.

This chapter considers the scope of adversarial attacks to be limited to be only over data networks. Physical access to the aircraft is assumed to be sufficiently protected with specific physical, logical, and organizational inhibitors, checks, and control. For example, upload of field-loadable software is only performed at specified times such as when the airplane is in maintenance mode, and by authorized personnel using authorized equipment. Moreover, certain checks are in place to enable detection of corrupted software, e.g., cyclic redundancy code check and compatibility check of software at the destination hardware and software environments. It can be assumed that due to software and hardware redundancies, e.g., several code instances executing in parallel on different system platforms on the airplane, most unintentional or unsophisticated corruptions in safety-critical software are detectable after upload into the destination hardware. In other words, to effectively cripple a safety-critical function in the airplane, overwhelming adversarial effort is needed since the representation of software must be modified at several positions. This significantly increases the effort needed from the adversary.

Emerging Standards and Research on eEnabled Airplanes

Several standards are actively investigating and mitigating any impact of new onboard wireless devices on the aircraft operation. RTCA Special Committee SC 202 is considering the interference from transmitting personal electronic devices brought onboard by passengers, e.g., cellular devices, active RFID tags, embedded medical sensors, and making recommendations for their use in RTCA/DO-294B (RTCA, 2008). Further, SAE standard AS5678 (SAE, 2008) is developing a standard for the secure and reliable use of passive RFID tags on board.

A growing body of research work has just begun to address potential concerns with future eEnabled aircraft models to better inform emerging standards and regulations. Some of the major research includes evaluations of different security mechanisms that can strengthen aircraft network architectures (Wargo & Dhas, 2003; Bird, Christensen, Lutz, & Scandura, 2005; Olive, Oishi, & Arentz, 2006). Further, security frameworks for the eEnabled aircraft (Sampigethaya, Poovendran, & Bushnell, 2008) and for distribution of loadable software and data between aircraft and software suppliers in the presence of threats to airworthiness and airline business are being established (Robinson, Li, Lintelman, Sampigethaya, Poovendran, von Oheimb, Busser, & Cuellar, 2007). A symmetric key based solution approach has been proposed for protecting the air traffic data on broadcast links between aircraft and ground systems (Samuelson, Valovage, & Hall, 2006). However, this approach requires pre-established trust between the aircraft and ground systems, in the form of establishing pre-shared secret keys. For public-key based secrure distribution of loadable software, the requirement for a high level of trustworthiness and a cost-effective and time-efficient formal method based evaluation is being explored (Maidl, von Oheimb, Hartmann, & Robinson, 2008). Furthermore, secure integration of emerging wireless technologies in the e-enabled aircraft are also being considered, such as use of onboard wireless sensors for aircraft health management (Bai, Atiquzzaman, & Lilja, 2004; Sampigethaya, Li, Poovendran, Bushnell, & Robinson, 2007), RFID tags for multi-purpose aircraft applications (Falk, Kohlmayer, Koepf, & Li, 2008). The anticipated impact of the use of security solutions on the commercial aviation information systems and processes are also being identified in the aforementioned works.

Though the research addressing secure RFID systems for eEnabled airplanes is still in its inception, the security and privacy of RFID systems has attracted extensive research interests and efforts. An excellent survey was presented on the state-of-the-art solutions to RFID security and privacy (Jules, 2006; Riebak, Crispo, & Tanenbaum, 2006). A more up-to-date bibliography on security and privacy in RFID systems is available online (Avoine, 2007). There is a lack of literature on key management for RFID systems, with most of research papers devoting to tag-level privacy-preserving authentication protocols (Jules, 2008). For system-level solutions, a prototype of an end-to-end system solution for RFID security, called Authentication Processing Framework, was reported (Ayoade, Takizawa, & Nakao, 2005). However, the framework suffers from RFID tag cloning attacks. Kaya, Savas, Levi and Ercertin (2008) proposed a public-key based infrastructure for multi-context/domain RFID applications. One novel idea is that both location and time are taken into account when authenticating and authorizing the RFID readers. The multi-context RFID infrastructure implicitly assumes that the backend server keeps an exact copy of RFID tag data and hence is suitable for static data scenarios such as RFID passport. In case that there are high dynamics in RFID data, such as the tracking status embedded in RFID tags, and frequent synchronizations between tags and the backend server are infeasible, a solution is for the readers to bring back a copy of encrypted tag data for the server to decrypt. However, such a solution is vulnerable to false RFID data injection due to a lack of authenticity and integrity protection of RFID data in the multi-context RFID infrastructure. To overcome these limitations, a tag-reader mutual authentication based multi-domain RFID architecture was proposed (Li, Poovendran, Falk, Koef, Braun, Sampigethaya, Robinson, Lintelman, & Seuschek 2008). Because of the high level assurance achieved on the integrity and authenticity of the RFID data, the mutual authentication based solution is more suitable for eEnabled airplane applications that require high confidence in information assurance properties.

Figure 1. Distribution of assets during the lifecycle of an airplane in the Airplane Assets Distribution System (AADS)

Aircraft Assets Distribution System (AADS)

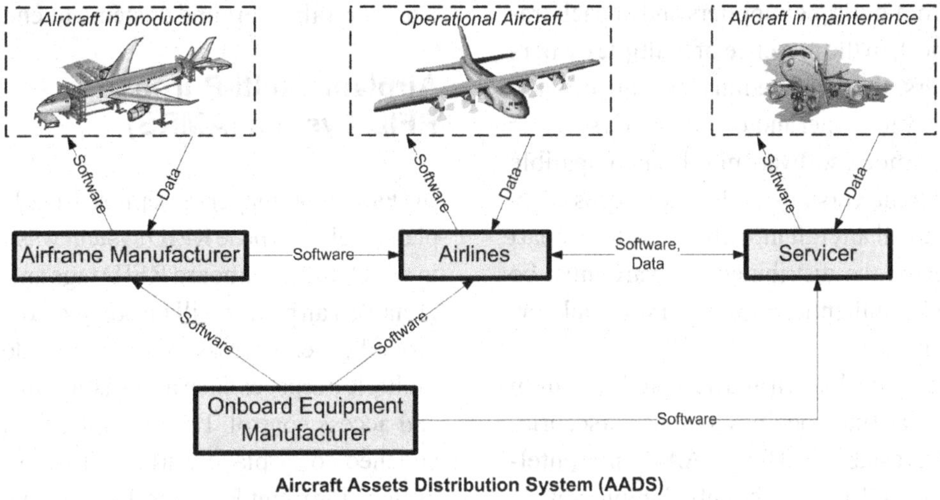

To illustrate the security and trust challenges and approaches in eEnabled airplane applications, two representative applications are introduced below, Airplane Asset Distribution System (AADS) and Airplane Multi-Domain RFID System (AMDS).

Airplane Asset Distribution System (AADS)

A generic system for the secure electronic distribution of airplane loadable software and data, called Airplane Asset Distribution System or AADS, is proposed in (Lintelman, Robinson, Li, von Oheimb, Sampigethaya, & Poovendran, 2006). Figure 1 illustrates the entities of a generic Airplane Asset Distribution System (AADS) and the distribution of assets among them. As shown, the onboard equipment and airframe manufacturers participate as multiple software suppliers. They develop field-loadable software for aircraft in accordance with RTCA/DO-178B. Airplanes may receive this software during production by airframe manufacturer, operation by airlines, or maintenance by servicers. Throughout lifecycle of eEnabled airplanes, the operating airlines

receive updates from software suppliers and may pass it on to contracted servicers, as well as receive onboard generated data from their aircraft fleet, such as software configuration reports including a list of successfully uploaded software.

The RTCA/DO-178B standard defines five safety assurance levels for loadable software and data based on the impact of their failure on flight safety, i.e., Level A—E, with decreasing safety criticality and associated certification effort. For instance, flight control computer software is a Level A software while cabin light system software is a Level E software. Furthermore, the upcoming revision of this standard is expected to specify formal methods based verification of software behavior. At the aircraft, sufficient physical, logical and organizational measures are in place to assure that received software is correctly and timely uploaded to the intended equipment. Criticality of field-loadable software and the huge investment made in the safety assurance of software design and development at the suppliers, mandates that the transport of software over networks from suppliers to the aircraft is performed so that software integrity is protected.

AADS presents some unique requirements for the eEnabled airplane. An airplane carries software from multiple suppliers and at each traversed airport, in the presence of multiple owners and servicers, the airplane must accept software distributed by its owner and/or authorized servicer only. Furthermore, software may be incompatible across different versions and is not necessarily applicable to all aircraft models. Therefore, apart from integrity, the distributed software must be ensured to be authentic, correct version and correct destination.

Using the well-known and accepted Common Criteria standard methodology as a basis, a security framework is established for the AADS in (Lintelman, Robinson, Li, von Oheimb, Sampigethaya, & Poovendran, 2006) to classify threats as well as specify security requirements and mitigation mechanisms that address the threats. Additionally, guidance is also provided to determine the level of trustworthiness needed for components handling safety-critical assets and business-critical assets. Safety-critical assets include software that is adjudged to be RTCA/DO-178B Level A-C, which impact aircraft airworthiness. Business-critical assets include software at RTCA/DO-178B Level D-E that do not impact airworthiness, but their corruption may potentially result in minor disruptions which are visible to passengers, e.g., cabin light flickering. In (Common Criteria, 2007), seven Evaluation Assurance Levels (EALs) are defined, i.e., EAL 1-7, with increasing evaluation effort, cost and time. For system components protecting the integrity and authenticity of safety-critical assets and business-critical assets, a trustworthiness level roughly equivalent to that achievable by at least EAL 5 and at most EAL 4 is recommended, respectively.

Digital signature has emerged as a well-accepted solution approach for protecting aircraft information assets in systems such as AADS. In practice, ARINC 827 (2008) is developing a format for electronic delivery of signed aircraft loadable software over networks. As described in the next section, signatures can also protect integrity and authenticity of RFID tag data during their transit from aircraft to ground systems to end-users.

Airplane Multi-Purpose RFID System (AMRS)

In (Falk, Kohlmayer, Koepf, & Li, 2008), an airplane multi-purpose RFID system was envisioned in which future onboard RFID tags and readers of eEnabled airplanes will be connected to different ground systems across administrative domains, for multiple purposes such as logistics, maintenance, and access control. For example, the RFID tags attached to airplane parts will be accessed by airlines for flight logistics, by third-party service providers for maintenance, and/or by airplane manufacturer for functions such as parts ordering. Figure 2 illustrates the example architecture for such an AMRS. An AMRS consists of onboard RFID tags, readers, Onboard RFID Processing System (ORPS) responsible for RFID data preprocessing, such as data filtering and aggregation, and data delivery to other onboard destinations, and Ground RFID Processing System (GRPS), which is a counterpart of the ORPS, responsible for data filtering and distribution to corresponding target processing systems on the ground.

Digital signature capable RFID tags provide a solution to ensure high confidence on tags data integrity during their transmission from aircraft to ground systems further onto end-users. However, the associated certificate management of the public-key based solutions for establishing and maintaining certificate-based trust across administrative domains can present significant challenges. In the following, some of the major constraints of the eEnabled airplanes that test the effective and efficient use of digital signatures are given below.

Figure 2. An architecture for Airplane Multi-Purpose RFID System (AMRS)

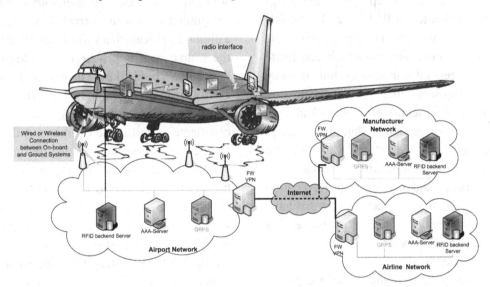

Major Constraints on Secure eEnabled Airplane Solutions

Digital signatures and certificates are widely used for Internet applications. E-commerce and financial institutions are aware of the returns from investing heavily in such security solutions for their online data transactions. However, the use of such security solutions for eEnabled airplane applications is new to the aviation industry. Several unprecedented problems arise that must be addressed, such as from the following often opposing constraints of onboard and off-board environments. (*i*) An airplane can traverse multiple airports with different wireless standards for their networks or with no network facility at all, and at each airport there may be multiple communicating off-board systems. Therefore eEnabled airplanes must seamlessly connect to the different types of networks and systems at traversed airports, but also be able to operate in the absence of online connectivity at any traversed airports. This constraint imposes the need for scalable as well as offline mechanisms for verifying digital signatures. (*ii*) As a business objective, the impact of security requirements and

applications on the airlines must be reduced, e.g., balancing added operational costs with expected returns from the security investment. This can be a major challenge to the type of evaluation approach used for establishing trustworthiness level for the system. (*iii*) Changes to the onboard system configurations, e.g., due to addition of security mechanisms, with potential impact on airplane operation, warrants reconsideration and/or modifications to aircraft regulations and guidance. The introduction of digital certificates and cryptographic keys in onboard systems clearly affects airplane operator guidance.

Before presenting specific challenges in securing the AADS and the AMRS, we will introduce terminologies used with Public Key Infrastructure (PKI) for non-security-specialist readers. PKI is the infrastructure to support digital signatures and certificate management.

Public Key Infrastructure (PKI)

Whenever a large group of entities must communicate securely based on public key cryptography without necessarily knowing or trusting each other directly, a Public Key Infrastructure (PKI) may be used to contain the cost of deploying and managing digital certificates. A PKI typically consists of a Registration Authority (RA) that verifies the identities of entities, authorizes their certificate requests, and generates unique asymmetric key pairs (unless the users' certificate requests already contain public keys); and a Certification Authority (CA) that issues corresponding digital certificates for the requesting entities. Optionally, a Certificate Repository may be present, which stores and distributes certificates and/or a Certificate Revocation List (CRL) identifying the certificates that have been declared invalid. Each entity possessing the authentic public key of a CA can verify the certificates issued by that CA.

As an alternative of using a PKI, the public key of an entity can be distributed directly to all potential signature verifiers, so long as the key's integrity is protected by physical or other means. This is often done using the format of a self-signed certificate as a container for the public key and the corresponding owner identity. Certificates of this type are referred to as trusted certificates in the following sections. Such certificates cannot be verified. In order to remain trusted, they must be stored with write access control or other means of integrity protection.

PKI based solutions form the foundation for secure Airplane Asset Distribution System (AADS) and secure Airplane Multi-Domain RFID System (AMRS), which will be elaborated in next two sections.

Secure AADS: Challenges and Approaches

In the airplane asset distribution system (AADS), the authenticity and integrity of distributed software and data for network-enabled airplanes must be ensured. A standard solution approach is to employ public key cryptography such as digital signatures (Bird, Christensen, Lutz, & Scandura, 2005). When digital signature based solution is adopted, the asset source signs each distributed asset with a private key, and appends a digital certificate that validates the link between the source and its private key while providing the source's public key. The destination uses the certificate to verify the signature on the asset, and therefore must be able to verify, or at least trust the certificate. If certificate validation and signature verification are successful, the destination will *trust* received asset to be un-tampered during transport and delivered by authenticate source. Pre-determined agreement and/or infrastructure such as PKI are needed in order to support such certificate based trust on airplane assets across multiple AADS entities. Ensuring such trust on airplane assets will not only comply with FAA requirements (FAA2, 2007) but also benefit airlines and passengers by providing a high level of assurance on safe airplane operations.

Due to high assurance requirements imposed by the safety-criticality of aircraft, and traditional lack of Information Technology (IT) infrastructure in the aviation industry, the realization of operable and affordable AADS presents unprecedented challenges on airplane manufacturing, operational, and maintenance processes. The challenges in realizing and operating the AADS are reviewed below.

Challenges in Realizing Secure AADS

Trust establishment in AADS. Conventional trust on airplane assets distributed via physical delivery vanishes once the assets are delivered through digital networks, such as in AADS, due to well known inherent vulnerabilities of Internet. In AADS, the trust on the airplane assets has been electronically coded into digital signature and associated certificates, and is non-variable in the sense that the trust is absolute if digital signature is validated and accepted otherwise no trust and the assets will be discarded. As an AADS is used to distribute both safety-critical and non-safety critical airplane assets, one unique challenge facing

AADS trust establishment is the trustworthiness level, i.e., the assurance level, has to be established to address regulatory requirements.

Assurance requirements of AADS. It is shown in (Robinson, Li, Lintelman, Sampigethaya, Poovendran, & von Oheimb, 2007) that to adequately meet security threats to safety-critical assets, such as RTCA/DO-178B (RTCA, 1992) Level A software parts, AADS must be assured at a Common Criteria Evaluation Assurance Level (EAL) of at least 4, that is methodically designed, tested, and reviewed. To the degree that reliance upon certificate integrity supports assurance of airplane software part integrity, the creation, issuance, distribution, and verification of certificates must also be assured at a minimum of EAL 4.

Entity-to-entity and end-to-end integrity protection in AADS. The integrity of software and data can be protected using either of two schemes, entity-to-entity protection or end-to-end protection. In an *entity-to-entity* protection arrangement, the airline verifies signed software from suppliers, re-signs and distributes to airplane. This contrasts with an *end-to-end* arrangement in which supplier-signed software is verified by the airplane. Entity-to-entity integrity protection requires the airplane to trust certificates of airlines only. On the other hand, end-to-end integrity requires the airplane to possess trusted or verifiable certificates of all the suppliers.

Number of certificates managed by airlines. The registered entities that require certificates include the suppliers, the manufacturer, the network-enabled airplane fleet and the airline servicers or personnel signing and verifying the airplane assets. Therefore, the expected number of certificates depends on the scale of the airline operation, including the fleet size and number of users/servicers. It is desirable to keep the number of certificates low. As will be seen later, the number of certificates can be a major concern when using the *whitelist* solution for end-to-end integrity protection.

Certificate requirements of AADS. In order to support digital signatures in AADS, the airline may choose to adopt the common X.509 format. In order to assist verifying that the airplane assets are signed by authorized entities, certificates issued to authorized entities can have an exclusive usage type to distinguish them from certificates issued by the same authority for purposes and applications other than AADS. For example, the X.509 v3 standard certificates allow certain attributes to distinguish their service for AADS. Further, the airlines must choose a strong signature algorithm. In July 2007, e.g., RSA 2048 bit with SHA-256 is considered to be robust against cryptanalytic attacks, but advances in cryptanalysis and computing power may change this soon. The lifetime of signatures, in particular those used in certificates, is another issue that must be addressed by the airlines.

Signing and verifying assets. The airlines, as well as the airplanes, must be capable of verifying signatures and certificates on received assets, and be capable of signing assets before distributing them.

Registration of signing entities at airlines. The suppliers, airplanes and airlines servicers and/or personnel signing the assets must be identified by the airline before certificates are issued for them. Further, role assignments may be more detailed to specify which entity is entitled to sign which type of asset, e.g., the safety-critical, RTCA/DO-178B level A software parts.

Key and certificate distribution to airplanes. The distribution of keys and trusted certificates to requesting entities, especially to airplanes, is challenging. This distribution must be protected either by secure online or out-of-band mechanisms. A good approach is to enable onboard generation of the airplane private key and to ensure authentic distribution of the corresponding certificate request to the airline CA, or authentic distribution of the airplane's self-signed certificate to all off-board components which require it for authenticity verification of status reports. Similarly, the integrity and authenticity of trusted certificates (either airline certificates or the CA root certificate) must be protected during distribution to the onboard repository.

Key and certificate storage onboard airplanes. The security of the AADS depends on the integrity and authenticity of trusted certificates and the confidentiality of private keys. Further, an airplane may interface with multiple networks, and its Line Replaceable Units (LRUs) – some of which store keys – may be replaced as needed over its lifecycle. Such unique constraints require careful consideration to protect the airplane's private key.

Revoking certificates onboard airplanes. In the case that a ground system's private key becomes compromised, each certificate of that ground system must be revoked in order to prevent any misuse of signatures. Consequently, before verifying a signature, the certificate status must be validated by the airplane. Similar arguments hold for the compromise of an airplane key, upon which the airplane certificate must be revoked. Note that expired certificates are considered invalid, and therefore need not be listed in the CRL.

Fallback mechanism at the airlines. The airline must be capable of using a fallback system, e.g., transfer of software parts on CDs, in the event of failure or unavailability of any AADS component.

Recording and auditing at the airlines. All security-related events throughout the AADS must be logged, and event logs protected against tampering. Further, for traceability, the reason for certificate revocation must be recorded and outdated certificates must be archived for a period of time.

Figure 3 illustrates a possible allocation of the above operational requirements imposed on the airlines by the AADS. The Certificate Authority (CA) may be an offline third party vendor from which certificates are purchased, or an online entity external or internal to airlines. To minimize overhead, these requirements may be integrated into the typical infrastructure (departments) and processes existing at many airlines. The airlines may have different approaches to handle certificates. Based on the approach, there can be a whitelist and a structured solution. We present these solutions below.

Approaches in AADS Certificate Management

Whitelist Solution: Preloading Trusted Certificates

In this approach, no central authority certifies all public keys. Instead, trusted collections of public keys are contained in certificates. The certificates may be self-signed, or signed by a local certificate

Figure 3. An assignment of new operational requirements across typical departments at airlines

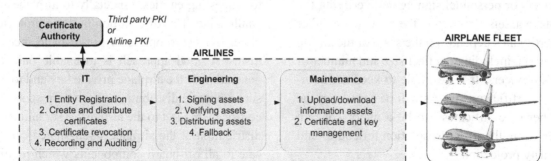

authority, or obtained from any third party. The validity of the certificates themselves cannot be verified by the airplane. Therefore the airplane must preload them via a trusted out-of-band mechanism. The same holds for the airplane certificate used to downlink data to ground systems. Further, all certificate stores must be updated periodically in order to maintain the status of certificates and to implement revocation.

Advantages. The main advantage of this solution is that it does not need additional infrastructure but can be improvised rather easily. Having a limited number of certificates to check and trust, and a limited number of corresponding private keys, reduces the probability of having a compromised key or an invalid certificate, under the assumption that a private key is not shared among multiple entities. The need to distribute only a limited number of certificates is good from a security point of view.

Drawbacks. The solution does not scale for end-to-end integrity protection, since in this case the airplane requires certificates of all suppliers apart from the airlines and manufacturer to be preloaded. Further, each airline must be able to obtain certificates from all its suppliers via an authentic channel. As the scale of the airline increases, certificate management is presented with more challenges due to increased dynamics in the ground infrastructure and increased fleet size.

Structured Solutions: Use of PKI

A better, long-term solution is to make use of a full PKI. The airline can assign the role of CA and/or RA either to a trusted third party, e.g., a commercial vendor or a Federal agency, or can implement its own PKI and itself function as CA and RA. The choice is governed by several factors, including deployment and operational costs, resource considerations, number of certificates, and trust established with third party vendors.

Advantages. A structured PKI solution offers long-term practical benefits in terms of scalabil-

ity and flexibility. Only the CA self-signed root certificate (marked grey) needs to be distributed authentically. Moreover, the availability of online certificate status checking or certificate revocation lists (discussed below) for certificate status verification by airplane enables a more secure approach than assuming correct status for all preloaded trusted certificates.

Drawbacks. The structured solution is relatively more expensive than the whitelist solution, incurring costs in set up and maintenance of PKI and its functionalities. Additionally, since the PKI is a crucial security mechanism of the AADS, it also must be evaluated (at the same assurance level), which means a significant extension of the scope of the AADS evaluation. So the resulting stringent technical and non-technical requirements on the PKI implementation may increase the costs.

Certificate Revocation

To cope with changes in business relationships or airline internal authorization rights, and for the case of compromise of a private key, certificate revocation has to be established. Commonly used solutions to obtain the revocation status of certificates are:

Online Certificate Status Protocol (OCSP)
If online connectivity is established, the airplane can check the validity status of a certificate by sending a status request to the corresponding CA, containing a cryptographic fingerprint of the certificate. The CA checks whether the certificate was revoked, and replies to the requester a signed status report. For retrieving the revocation status of X.509 certificates, the standardized protocol OCSP (IETF, 1999) can be used.

Advantages. This method allows real-time checking of certificate status. Only the certificate of the status server is required to be distributed authentically. Different CAs can be used in parallel, but then several status server certificates have to be distributed, of course.

Sub-CAs can be used even without distributing further certificates because they are certified by the root CA.

Drawbacks. Direct online connectivity to the CA or a status server is required whenever a certificate is used; that means connecting the airplane to the airline's company network, and maybe even to the Internet if supplier certificates have to be checked, too, and therefore making potential security vulnerabilities accessible much more often. If the connection cannot be established, the use of certificates is delayed or blocked. Much higher CPU performance and bandwidth of certificate repository servers are required, and not all CAs support this method.

Certificate Revocation Lists (CRL)

The CA creates lists of (serial numbers of) revoked certificates (CRLs) with a short validity time (e.g., a day or a week), and signs these lists. The CA creates a new CRL every time a certificate is revoked or at latest short before the last CRL becomes invalid. A requester can download the latest valid version of the CRL from a server and can use the CRL offline to check the validity status of a certificate. The CRL can be used at the requester as long as it is valid, however when connectivity is given, the requester can look for an up-to-date CRL every time when checking a certificate status.

Advantages. No direct connection to the CA or a status server is required. The CA has to compile and to offer for download just one list for all users, instead of checking the status of many certificates,

so the performance requirements for the CA or CRL server are much lower. This solution is most commonly used.

Drawbacks. The information about the certificate's status is not as "fresh" as in the case of the online status retrieval, though the difference is marginal in practice.

Table 1 summarizes the benefits and drawbacks of the presented solutions to providing trustworthy certificates to the airlines.

Multiple Certificate Authorities (CA) Based Solution

Suppliers, manufacturers, airlines, and servicers may already have different PKI solutions with their own local CAs within their companies. Therefore, it is impractical to assume that they will all agree to use the same PKI provider. In the following, we provide solutions to connect their own CAs to form a common trust network.

Local CAs can be connected via the following four approaches.

Common root CA: The (root) public key of each CA is signed by a new CA. This solution is the logically most simple and straight-forward solution. Yet it has the disadvantage that the root certificate changes which is installed as trust anchor in many entities and devices. This can cause a lot of organizational effort. Furthermore, the local CAs delegate the control to another instance.

Cross certification: Each CA certifies the (root) key of all other CAs which it trusts. This solution avoids the disadvantages of changing

Table 1. Comparison of whitelist and structured solution

	Whitelist Solution	Structured Solution with online protocol	Structured Solution with CRL
Benefit	Short-term	Long-term	Long-term
Scalability	Low	High	High
Certificate validity check	None (only manual revocation possible)	Real-time (online connection required)	Not real-time (offline possible, but up-to-date CRL required)

root certificates and giving away control, but may cause a lot of effort if there are many CAs which need to be brought together.

Bridge CA: Each CA certifies the public keys of the bridge CA, and gets its public key certified by the bridge CA in return. Each CA has to certify only one other CA (namely the bridge CA), and to be certified by this, which reduces the effort strongly compared to cross certification. It may be seen as a hybrid solution that combines common root CA and cross certification solutions.

Trusted lists: The entities maintain lists of trustworthy CAs, so they have several root CAs. This solution is similar to the whitelist solution discussion in section 4, but on a higher hierarchy level.

A combination of different connection methods is possible, for example, some CAs may agree to be connected using a common root CA, whereas the connection to other CAs is established via cross certification or a bridge CA.

Secure AMRS: Challenges and Approaches

In the airplane multi-purpose RFID system (AMRS), the integrity and authenticity of data stored in RFID tags have to be protected. The approach using permanent lock of RFID data (i.e., write-once) is not suitable, as AMRS needs to support writing tags multiple times, for example, in the case of writing parts maintenance log to the tags. Digital signature emerges as a promising solution to protect the integrity and authenticity of the tag data not only stored on board, but also during the transit to different ground systems. Similar to the AADS, public key based digital signature solutions in a cross-domain application require the participating entities to have pre-agreed policies and/or infrastructure to manage, verify or at least trust the certificates. In the following, the challenges in realizing secure AMRS are reviewed, and the unique challenges confronting AMRS

when compared to realization of the AADS are emphasized.

Challenges in Realizing Secure AMRS

Cross-domain trust management. As in AADS, the value of trust on information and data exchanged in AMRS is binary, i.e., trusted if the certificate is accepted and the signature is validated otherwise non-trustworthy. The trust is digitally embedded into digital signature and associated certificates. Therefore, the trust management issue becomes a certificate management issue. As an airplane travels worldwide, the onboard RFID system in AMRS will be dynamically connected with different administrative domains, such as airlines, airport, third party servicer, airplane manufacturer, and in some cases connected with multiple security domains across organization boundaries simultaneously. Credentials (such as certificates) are needed for establishing a secure connection between onboard RFID system and different infrastructures. An agreement on the cross-domain certificate management policy needs to be established, so all the involved stakeholders can verify the trustworthiness of information flow in AMRS.

Resource constraints in RFID tags. RFID tags have limited computation power, transmission range, and constrained storage. For read and especially write access, ideally, tags should have a means of verifying the identities and the permission rights of the accessing readers. However, the cryptographic computation in verifying a reader's credential demands significant power and can be prohibitive in low-cost tags. Meanwhile, RFID tags cannot be assumed to be constantly connected to the network. One approach is to store the trusted credentials locally. However, the storage limitation restricts the number of trusted certificates that can be stored in a tag locally. For the access control to the different portion of the data, it is desired that RFID tags have hardware built-in compartments that are intended for different data owners and reviewers. However, the technology of hardware compartments is challenging on low-cost RFID tags.

Tags' online access to backend server. As tags' online access to the backend server may not always be feasible, it impacts the capability of RFID tags and readers to verify the up-to-date certificate status and to obtain and enforce the latest access policy. In case of the intermittent network access to backend servers, one approach is for tags and readers to download the latest access control list/matrix and validate the status of certificates whenever there is a connection to a backend server.

Synchronization between onboard RFID tags and back-end database. To comply with FAA regulations, onboard tag data must be synchronized with the backend database of the data owner, for example, airlines. Synchronization with back-end servers also provides a fallback mechanism of onboard RFID data. To synchronize with the backend database, a tag will transmit its data to the backend system at the next connection after the data is updated, i.e., when the data is read by a reader and the reader reports back to the backend system. Tags' limited on-line access to backend systems and incurred communication overhead due to synchronization, must be taken into consideration to determine the frequency of synchronization.

Regulatory restrictions on hardware selection. The International Air Transport Association (IATA) member airlines approved the use of Ultra-High Frequency (UHF) tags and readers as RFID baggage tag system onboard and the FAA mandated the use of passive RFID on board in 2005. Compared to passive High Frequency (HF) tags, passive UHF tags have the advantage of longer reading range and affordability. However, current UHF tag technology is not suitable for item-level identification, and cannot provide adequate location accuracy for location-based net-

work applications, such as localization of missing emergency equipments (such as life jacket under each passenger seat). In addition, backscatter, the power collection technology used in UHF, does not generate as much power as HF tags that adopt inductive coupling, and hence limits the possibility of UHF performing cryptographic computation.

Change of ownership of tagged airplane parts. Unlike airplanes, airplane parts are sold from one airline to another more frequently. Along with the change of ownership of a tagged airplane part, the data stored in the tag attached to the part has to be verified and then re-signed by the new owner. Depending on the frequency of part transfers between airlines, the verification and re-signing can incur a cumbersome overhead on the purchasing airlines. Specifications must be made on where and how to locate the trusted certificates by the new airlines, and if and how long a window is allowed to accept information signed by both the new and the old owners.

Furthermore, AMRS has similar challenges as AADS in assurance establishment and certificate management, such as integrity protected key and certificate delivery, certificate renewal and revocation, and the number of certificates managed by involving entities. In the following, the approaches of certificate management for the AMRS with resource-constrained RFID tags are considered.

Approaches in Certificate Management in AMRS

The certificate management is widely known as a challenging issue for public key based applications, the resource constraints in RFID tags and intermittent access to backend server further complicate the problem.

Whitelist with Bloom Filter

In the whitelist approach, a list of trusted certificates are reloaded into tags via an out-of-band, integrity and authenticity protected mechanism. Due to limited storage resources, a tag or a sensor may contain only a limited number of certificates. To increase the number of certificates held in a tag, a Bloom filter was used to efficiently represent the current valid public keys (Ren, Lou & Young, 2007). Instead of storing a complete copy for each certificate, a Bloom filter provides a space-efficient probabilistic data structure to represent an element and to test if an element is in a set with a small probability of false positive.

In Bloom filter based public key validation, all the current valid public keys are mapped to a bit array of m bits by applying independent hash functions and setting the bits at the position indicated by hash results to 1. The m-bit Bloom filter is preloaded to each participating RFID tags. When a signed message arrives, the verifier will first check if the public key is contained in the list of valid public keys represented by the preloaded Bloom Filter. Upon the update of the status of a public key, a new Bloom filter is recomputed by the CA and only a compact representation of the changed bits is broadcast. The Bloom filter based approach improves the storage efficiency at the expense of its possibility of false positive, and false positive increases with the number of readers in the system.

Hash Chain Based Certificate Revocation

In the hash chain based certificate validation (Micali, 2002), a hash value is computed for every validity period, such as every day, week, or month. For illustration, assume that weekly validation is provided. For a certificate that is expected to be valid for a year after issued, a hash chain (X0, X1, ..., X51) is computed where $Xn = H(Xn-1) = H^n(X0)$ and H denotes the hash function, and the hash chain anchor X51 is loaded to tags or sensors. In the third week, if a reader needs to authenticate itself to a tag, the reader attaches its certificate with its digital signature and also provides the validation token, X48, obtained from the CA. To check if the certificate is valid, the tag applies the hash function H to the token X48 three times, i.e., H(H(H(X48))), and compares the result with the hash chain anchor X51. If there is a match, it demonstrates the validity of the certificate. Otherwise, the tag will discard the message and discontinue further communication with the reader.

Compared to the CRL approach, the hash chain based certificate validation significantly reduces the communication overhead for certificate validation, from the CRL size to hash size (for example, 160-bit), and only requires loose time synchronization between the verifier and the CA.

Server-Based Authentication

In the server-based authentication approach (Li, Fung, Sampigethaya, Robinson, Poovendran, Falk, & Koepf, 2008), the mutual authentication between tag and reader is realized through the server. As illustrated in Figure 4(a), the RFID reader first authenticates itself to the server. After successful authentication and validation of the reader's access right, the server will issue a session key to the reader. Then, the tag mutually authenticates with the server: the reader facilitates the process by forwarding the challenges-response exchange between the tag and the server. Please note that the reader has no incentive to disrupt this communication if the reader wants to read/write the tag. Finally, following upon the successful mutual authentication between the tag and the server, the server will issue the same session key to the tag to enable the secure communication between the tag and the reader.

The server-based approach removes the necessity of storing readers' certificates and verifying the status of readers' certificates at tags. A tag only needs to store the certificate(s) of authentication server(s). The drawback of this approach is the online tag-server connection requirement, which can be a challenge in practice. Therefore, a

Figure 4. Server-based authentication protocols (a) online based (b) offline based (T, R and S stand for tag, reader, and server.)

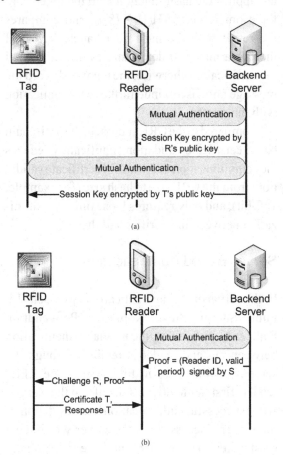

modified version of the server-based approach was presented, called offline server-based approach, to loose the online requirement by leveraging time synchronization between the tag and the server.

In the Offline Server-Based Authentication depicted in Figure 4(b), the reader and the server conduct mutual authentication first. In the responding to the challenges from the server, the reader will also send a request for a proof of the valid status of its certificate. The server will issue such a proof that is a signed copy of the reader identity, and the validation period. The reader initiates the authentication with the tag by providing the proof to the tag as well as sending a challenge to the tag. Based on the current time/date, the tag verifies the

server signed message to confirm the validity of the reader. If successful, then the tag will respond to the readers' challenge to authenticate itself to the reader. The offline server based approach requires tags to be able to acquire current time/date.

Comparisons of Resource-Efficient Certificate Management

Table 2 compares all the aforementioned approaches that address the complexity of certificate management at resource-constrained RFID tags.

As presented in Table 2, the whitelist approach with bloom filter is the most communication efficient approach, and its drawback is the potential false positive in certificate status check. The hash chain based solution has the advantage of low storage at tags; however, it requires loose synchronization with the server in terms of date (or time). As the date/time of certificate status check determines the number of hashing computations to be performed, the computation cost at tags runs from low to moderate, depending on when to check the certificate status. Certificate management at tags is significantly simplified when using either online or offline server based approach, as the tags only need to verify or trust the certificates of the server. The proof used in the offline version of sever-based approach is similar to the token used in hash-based solution. However, these two approaches differ in that hash based approach requires the hash anchor to be pre-loaded at tags while no such a requirement exists for the offline server-based approach. It follows that the server-based approach accommodates the dynamics of readers more easily.

FUTURE RESEARCH DIRECTIONS

There are multiple future research directions that worth pursuing. One problem that is of practical importance and theoretical interest is

Table 2. Comparison of certificate management Approaches for Resource-Constrained RFID systems. (mod. stands for moderate, comm. for communications)

Tag requirement	Whitelist with Bloom Filter	Hash Chain based	Server based online	Server based offline
Comm. overhead	Low	Mod.	Mod.	Mod.
Storage Requirement	Mod.	Low	Low	Low
Computation for certificate validity check	Mod.	Low ~ Mod.	Mod.	Mod.
Online Connectivity required	No	No	Yes	No
Loose Synchronization rquired	No	Yes	No	Yes

cost-efficient, easily operable certificate management for network-cable airplane applications. The motivation of this problem is the cost reduction and simple management for airlines to operate AADS and future AMRS. There is a wide spread spectrum of technical readiness levels for airlines worldwide to embrace eEnabled airplane applications, from zero IT department to a very sophisticate IT department with well established PKI. For the airlines that do not run a local CA, the option is to purchase certificates from trusted vendors. Minimizing the number of certificates required for various eEnabled airplane applications is an open research problem. Distributed certificate management and policy based certificate management worth further investigation.

End-to-end security of middle to large scale, distributed systems, such as AADS or AMRS, is difficult to achieve and verify. Meanwhile, the safety criticality of airplane assets and onboard systems requires high security assurance of asset delivery and onboard integrated systems. Leveraging the common criteria methodology and formal methods, a future research direction is to develop a framework for evaluation and assurance of end-to-end security. Benefits of this research direction include security architecture design and secure assessment for upcoming eEnabled applications, and build foundations for cost-effective certification.

Compared to AADS, a salient challenge facing AMRS is the resource constraints at end devices.

Vast research is expected to be undertaken to provide secure, resource efficient solutions. For example, trade-offs between asymmetric-key and symmetric-key based secure solutions for ARMS need to be evaluated, in terms of performance, computation, storage and communication requirements on end devices, infrastructure requirement and management overhead, technical difficulty in maintenance. Furthermore, design and verification of secure protocols using formal approach such as a machine-assisted model checker is an open research topic. Establishment, update, enforcement, and verification of access control policy in resource-constrained sensor and RFID tags is a challenging yet interesting research topic.

CONCLUSION

eEnabled airplane applications bring challenges as well opportunities. In this chapter, two eEnabled airplane applications, AADS and ARMS, are introduced and the challenges in providing information integrity and authenticity in AADS and ARMS are illustrated. In particular, certificate management is identified as the most formidable challenge in trustworthy operation of AADS and ARMS.

Various approaches to certificate management, including those suited for resource-constrained scenarios such as ARMS, are presented and the advantages and pitfalls of the approaches are compared. Successful use of digital signatures to protect information integrity depends not only on the underlying technical solutions and implementation but also business cooperation (such as an agreed certificate management policy) across stakeholders.

ACKNOWLEDGMENT

We thank Richard Robinson and Scott Lintelman from Boeing Research and Technology, David von Oheimb, Rainer Falk, Jens-Uwe Bußer and Andreas Koepf from Siemens Corporate Technology, Munich, for various discussions we had with them on these topics.

REFERENCES

Adams, C., & Lloyd, S. (2003). *Understanding PKI: concepts, standards, and deployment considerations* (2ⁿᵈ ed.). Reading, MA: Addison-Wesley Press.

Aeronautical Radio Inc. (2002). *ARINC Report 665: Loadable software standards, August.*

Aeronautical Radio Inc. (2005). *ARINC Report 811: Commercial aircraft information security concepts of operation and process framework, December.*

Aeronautical Radio Inc. (2008). *ARINC Report 827: Electronic distribution of software by crate (EDS crate), June.*

Aeronautical Radio Inc. (2009). *ARINC Report 664, Part 2: Aircraft Data Network, Part 2 - Ethernet Physical and Data Link Layer Specification, January.*

Alomair, B., Lazos, L., & Poovendran, R. (2007). Passive attacks on a class of authentication protocols for RFID. In *Proceedings of the International Conference on Information Security and Cryptology* (pp. 102-115). Berlin, Germany: Springer.

Avoine, G. (2007). *Bibliography on Security and Privacy in RFID systems*. Retrieved April 2, 2009, from http://lasecwww.epfl.ch/~gavoine/download/bib/bibliography-rfid.pdf

Ayoade, J., Takizawa, O., & Nakao, K. (2005, April). *A prototype System of the RFID Authentication Processing Framework*. Paper presented at the International Workshop in Wireless Security Technologies, London, UK.

Bai, H., Atiquzzaman, M., & Lilja, D. (2004). Wireless sensor network for aircraft health monitoring. In *Proceedings of 1ˢᵗ International Conference on Broadband Networks (BROADNETS)* (pp. 748-750). Washington, DC: IEEE Press.

Bird, G., Christensen, G., Lutz, D., & Scandura, P. (2005, November). *Use of integrated vehicle health management in the field of commercial aviation*. Paper presented in NASA ISHEM Forum, Napa, CA.

Braun, M., Hess, E., & Meyer, B. (2008). Using elliptic curves on RFID tags. *International Journal of Computer Science and Network Security, 8*(2), 1–9.

Common Criteria. (2007). *Common criteria (CC) for information technology security evaluation, Rev 3.1*. Retrieved April 2, 2009, from http://www.commoncriteriaportal.org/

Diffie, W., & Hellman, W. E. (1976). New directions in cryptography. *IEEE Transactions on Information Theory, IT-22,* 644–654. doi:10.1109/TIT.1976.1055638

FAA1. (2007). 14 CFR Part 25, Special Conditions: Boeing model 787-8 airplane; systems and data networks security isolation or protection from unauthorized passenger domain systems access (Docket No. NM364 Special Conditions No. 250701SC). *Federal Register, 72*(71). Retrieved April 2, 2009, from http://edocket.access.gpo. gov/2007/pdf/E7-7065.pdf

FAA2. (2007). 14 CFR Part 25, Special Conditions: Boeing model 787-8 airplane; systems and data networks security protection of airplane systems and data networks from unauthorized external access (Docket No. NM365 Special Conditions No. 250702SC). *Federal Register, 72*(72). Retrieved April 2, 2009, from http://edocket.access.gpo. gov/2007/pdf/07-1838.pdf

FAA3. (2008). *FAA policy for passive-only RFID devices*. Retrieved April 2, 2009, from http:// rgl.faa.gov/Regulatory and Guidance Library/ rgPolicy.nsf/0/495367dd1bd773e186257154 00718e2e Garfinkel, S., & Rosenberg, B. (2005). *RFID Applications, Security, and Privacy*. Reading, MA: Addison-Wesley.

Falk, R., Kohlmayer, F., Koepf, A., & Li, M. (2008). High-assured Avionics multi-domain processing system. In *Proceedings of the IEEE RFID conference* (pp. 43-50). Las Vegas, NV: IEEE Press.

Gaubatz, G., Kaps, J. P., Ozturk, E., & Sunar, B. (2005). State of the art in ultra-low power public key cryptography for wireless sensor networks. In *Proceedings of the 3rd International IEEE Pervasive computing and Communications Worskshops (PerCom)* (pp. 146-150). Washington, DC: IEEE Press.

IETF. (1999). *IETF Draft 2560: X.509 Internet public key infrastructure online certificate status protocol – OCSP*. Retrieved April 2, 2009, from http://tools.ietf.org/html/rfc2560

SAE International. (2008). *SAE standard AS5678 - Passive RFID tags intended for aircraft use*.

Jules, A. (2006). RFID security and privacy, a research survey. *IEEE Journal on Selected Areas in Communications, 24*(2), 381–395. doi:10.1109/ JSAC.2005.861395

Jules, A. (2008). *Four aspirations for RFID security research*. Paper presented at the ACM Conference on Wireless Network Security, Alexandria, VA. Retrieved April 2, 2009, from http://sconce. ics.uci.edu/wisec08-rfid-panel/RFID-Juels.pdf

Kaya, S. V., Savas, E., Levi, A., & Ercertin, O. (2009). Public key cryptography based privacy preserving multi-context RFID infrastructure. *Ad Hoc Networks, 7*(1), 136–152. doi:10.1016/j. adhoc.2007.12.004

Kim, D. S., Shin, T. H., & Park, J. S. (2007). A security framework in RFID multi-domain system. In *Proceedings of the 2nd International Conference on Availability, Reliability and Security, 2007 (ARES 2007)* (pp. 1227-1234). Washington, DC: IEEE Press.

Konidala, D. M., & Kim, K. (2006, January). *Mobile RFID Security Issues*. Paper presented at the Symposium on Cryptography and Information Security (SCIS), Hiroshima, Japan.

Li, M., Fung, C., Sampigethaya, K., Robinson, R., Poovendran, R., Falk, R., & Koepf, A. (2008). Public-key based authentication for secure integration of RFID and sensor data. In *Proceedings of the 1st ACM workshop on heterogonous sensor and actor networks* (pp. 61-66). New York: ACM Press.

Li, M., Poovendran, R., Falk, R., Koef, A., Braun, M., Sampigethaya, K., et al. (2008, September). *Multi-domain RFID access control using asymmetric key based tag-reader mutual authentication*. Paper presented at the 26th Congress of the International Council of the Aeronautical Sciences (ICAS), Anchorage, AK.

Lintelman, S., Li Robinson, R., von Oheimb, M., & Sampigethaya, D. K., & Poovendran, R. (2006, October). *Security Assurance for IT Infrastructure Supporting Airplane Production, Maintenance, and Operation.* Paper presented at the National Workshop on Aviation Software Systems, Alexandria, VA. Retrieved April 2, 2009, from http://chess.eecs.berkeley.edu/hcssas/papers/Lintelman-HCSS-Boeing-Position_092906_2.pdf

Melski, A., Thoroe, L., Caus, T., & Schumann, M. (2007). Beyond EPC - insights from multiple RFID case studies on the storage of additional data on tags. In *Proceedings of International Conference on Wireless Algorithms, Systems and Applications* (pp. 281-286). Chicago, IL: IEEE Press.

Micali, S. (2002). NOVOMODO - Scalable certificate validation and simplified PKI management, In *Proceedings of 1st Annual PKI Research Workshop* (pp. 15-25). Retrieved April 2, 2009, from http://www.cs.dartmouth.edu/~pki02/Micali/paper.pdf

Olive, M., Oishi, R., & Arentz, S. (2006). Commercial aircraft information security – an overview of ARINC report 811. In *Proceedings of 25th IEEE/AIAA Digital Avionics Systems Conference* (pp. 1-12). Portland, OR: IEEE Press.

Porad, K. (2005). RFID in commercial aviation. *Aircraft technology engineering & maintenance, 75,* 92-99.

Radio Technical Commission for Aeronautics (RTCA). (1992). *DO-178B: Software considerations in airborne systems and equipment certification.*

Radio Technical Commission for Aeronautics (RTCA). (2008). *DO-294B: Civil operators' training guidelines for integrated night vision imaging system equipment, December.*

Ren, K., Lou, W., & Zhang, Y. (2007). Multi-user broadcast authentication in wireless sensor networks. In *Proceedings of IEEE Conference on Sensor and Ad Hoc Communications and Networks* (pp. 223-232). San Diego, CA: IEEE Press.

Riebak, M. R., Crispo, B., & Tanenbaum, A. S. (2006). Is your Cat Infected with a Computer Virus. In *Proceedings of 4th Annual IEEE International Conference on Pervasive Computing and Communications* (*IEEE PerCom*) (pp. 170-179). Washington, DC: IEEE Press.

Robinson, R., Li, M., Lintelman, S., Sampigethaya, K., Poovendran, R., & von Oheimb, D. (2007). Challenges for IT Infrastructure Supporting Secure Network-Enabled Commercial Airplane Operations. In *Proceedings of the AIAA Infotech@ Aerospace Conference.*

Robinson, R., Li, M., Lintelman, S., Sampigethaya, K., Poovendran, R., von Oheimb, D., et al. (2007). Electronic distribution of airplane software and the impact of information security on airplane safety. In *Proceedings of 26th International Conference on Computer Safety, Reliability and Security (SAFECOMP)* (pp. 28-39). Nuremberg, Germany: Springer Press.

Robinson, R., Li, M., Lintelman, S., Sampigethaya, K., Poovendran, R., von Oheimb, D., & Bußer, J.-U. (2007, September). *Impact of public key enabled application on the operation and maintenance of commercial airplanes.* Paper presented at the AIAA ATIO Conference, Belfast, Northern Ireland.

Sampigethaya, K., Li, M., Poovendran, R., Robinson, R., Bushnell, L., & Lintelman, S. (2007). Secure wireless collection and distribution of commercial airplane health data. In *Proceedings of 26th IEEE/AIAA Digital Avionics Systems Conference* (pp. 4.E.6-1-4.E.6-8). Washington, DC: IEEE Press.

Sampigethaya, K., Poovendran, R., & Bushnell, L. (2008). Secure operation, control and maintenance of future e-enabled airplanes. *Proceedings of the IEEE*, *96*(12), 1992–2007. doi:10.1109/ JPROC.2008.2006123

Samuelson, K., Valovage, E., & Hall, D. (2006). Enhanced ADS-B research. In *Proceedings of IEEE Aerospace Conference* (IEEEAC paper #1282). Washington, DC: IEEE Press.

Schreckenbach, F., Schnell, M., Scalise, S., & Platt, P. (2007). NEWSKY -Networking the sky for aeronautical communications. In *Proceedings of the 1st International CEAS European Air and Space Conference. Council of the European Aerospace Societies*.

Seidenman, P., & Spanovich, D. J. (2007). Predicting the future: eEnabled maintenance. *Overhaul and Maintenance*, *23*(9), 32–36.

Spenser, J. (2005). Technology Pollination. *Boeing Frontiers*. Retrieved April 2, 2009, from http:// www.boeing.com/news/frontiers/archive/2005/ december/ts_sf10.html

Wander, A., Gura, N., Eberle, H., Gupta, V., & Shantz, S. (2005). Energy analysis of public-key cryptography on small wireless devices. In *Proceedings of 3rd International IEEE Pervasive computing and Communications Worskshops (PerCom)* (pp. 324-328). Washington, DC: IEEE Press.

Wargo, C., & Dhas, C. (2003). Security considerations for the eEnabled aircraft. In *Proceedings of IEEE Aerospace Conference* (pp. 4_1533- 4_1550). Washington, DC: IEEE Press.

Section 2
Evaluation Based Trust Management Solutions

Chapter 7
Trust Management
for Grid Systems

Benjamin Aziz
STFC Rutherford Appleton Laboratory, UK

Alvaro Arenas
STFC Rutherford Appleton Laboratory, UK

Fabio Martinelli
Istituto di Informatica e Telematica (IIT), CNR, Italy

Paolo Mori
Istituto di Informatica e Telematica (IIT), CNR, Italy

Marinella Petrocchi
Istituto di Informatica e Telematica (IIT), CNR, Italy

Michael Wilson
STFC Rutherford Appleton Laboratory, UK

ABSTRACT

Grid computing is a paradigm for distributed computation on shared resources. It uses a large-scale, highly decentralized infrastructure, in which a huge number of participants share heterogeneous resources for a given purpose. Each participant both provides their own resources and exploits others' resources, combining them to solve their own problems. Trust management is a major issue in the shared Grid environment because Grid participants are usually unknown to each other and usually belong to separate administrative domains, with little or no common trust in the security of opposite infrastructures. The standard security support provided by the most common Grid middleware may be regarded as one means through which such common trust may be established. However, such security solutions are insufficient to exhaustively address all the trust requirements of Grid environments. In this chapter, the authors survey proposals for enhancing trust management in Grid systems.

DOI: 10.4018/978-1-61520-682-7.ch007

INTRODUCTION

Innovations in information technology and business models are creating new security issues which require designs beyond those of traditional security solutions. In particular, the problem of guaranteeing that only authorized users have access to sensitive resources and data has been traditionally solved by adopting access control techniques. In these techniques the decision process is based on the identity or the role of the user. Since, in distributed environments with no central authority, the resource owner and the user that accesses the resource are often unknown to each other, traditional access control techniques cannot be applied. Consider an example in which a research institute adopts the policy of granting the right to execute applications on the computational resources shared by the institute, to professors of accredited universities. Although one authority may assert that the requestor's identity is Alice Black, if this identity is unknown to the research institute, this does not help in making a decision whether she is entitled to use the resources or not. The crucial information needed in such scenario is the set of rights and qualifications of the requestor asserted by recognized authorities (i.e., the university she attends) together with trust information about the authorities themselves (is that university accredited for the research institute?). Trust management (Blaze et al., 1996), was born to implement distributed access control in decentralized systems, where access control decisions are based on statements called credentials made by multiple principals.

Grid is a distributed computing environment where each participant shares a set of his resources with others (Foster et al, 2001). This environment may group participants into virtual organizations. A virtual organization is a set of individuals and/or institutions (e.g. companies, universities, research centres, industries and so on) who share their resources. A Grid user exploits this environment by searching among the available resources for a set

that can be exploited to solve his problem. These resources are heterogeneous in that they could be computational, storage, software repositories and so on. The Open Grid Forum community has developed a standard to share resources on the Grid called the Open Grid Service Architecture (OGSA) (Foster et al, 2006), which defines the concept of Grid services and it is based on the Web Service Resource Framework (WSRF) (Banks, 2006). The Globus Toolkit 4 (Foster, 2005), is the reference implementation of the OGSA standard, and in this paper we refer to this implementation as the Grid environment (although the model developed applies to any possible implementation). Security is a very important issue for the Grid, because the participants are probably unknown to each other, and they belong to distinct administrative domains that adopt different security mechanisms and apply distinct security policies. Moreover, some participants can join or leave the virtual organisation during its lifecycle.

This chapter shows how trust management techniques can be successfully applied to support and enhance Grid security mechanisms. We will describe models, architectures, and implementations of trust management systems for the Grid, especially tailored for virtual organizations deployment. We review the existing models and the proposed architectures, as well as some prominent implementations for existing Grid toolkits (e.g., Globus). Both researchers and practitioners may benefit from this survey, which provides the state of the art at a glance and hints for future research and development.

The structure of the chapter is as follows. The next section gives an overview of the paradigm of virtual organizations, commonly used to model resource sharing in Grid systems. The third section gives an overview of some popular Grid security models and architectures as a means for establishing trust. In the following section, we discuss a couple of trust models and architectures; one for enhancing a role-based and trust management language with weights and the other for utility-based reputation management in Grids. Finally, we conclude the chapter with a discussion on possible future trends for Grid trust management.

VIRTUAL ORGANIZATIONS IN GRID COMPUTING

Overview

Grid computing is a term often used to describe the amalgamation of several existing technologies such as cluster computing, Peer-to-Peer (P2P) computing and Web services technologies. In order to understand the behavior of such a heterogeneous blend of technologies, Grid systems are often modeled based on the paradigm of Virtual Organizations (VOs). In fact, the definition that Foster, Kesselman and Tuecke (2001) gave to the Grid in their article, *The Anatomy of the Grid*, is that Grid computing is concerned with *"coordinated resources sharing and problem solving in dynamic, multi-institutional virtual organizations"* (p. 2).

VOs are given attention by researchers within a wide range of fields, from social anthropology and organizational theory to computer science. Nevertheless, there has not been an agreed-upon definition of the concept, so the topic has been characterized by the amount of contributions, many of them are related to functional aspects, such as the role of IT in VOs, legal issues, social-economical aspects, etc. One such definition used in other projects (Wesner et al., 2006) is that *"a VO can be seen as a temporary or permanent coalition of geographically dispersed individuals, groups, organizational units or entire organizations that pool resources, capabilities and information in order to achieve common goals"*.

The parties that form a VO are typically part of a larger enterprise network or what is known as a *virtual breeding environment* within which the selection of partners is made in a phenomenon known as *network activation* in VO modeling

theory (Camarihna-Matos & Afsarmanesh, 2003). The entities in the universe of such networks share some broad characteristics, e.g. belonging to the same economy or market sector, and their participation in the network indicates disposition to work together in a future market opportunity.

From the above definitions, it is clear that Grid computing supports the concept of VOs. In the beginning of Grid technology, Grid VOs generally consisted of supercomputing facilities with the aim of enhancing the computing power in order to perform very complex calculations in scientific environments. In the course of time, this situation has evolved, being possible today to connect different equipment in real time, according to the necessities of the applications and the resources available. Besides, it is possible to reallocate and to replace resources, to accommodate changes in requirements or to adapt to new opportunities in the business environment. This renders the nature of Grid VOs quite dynamic. This "dynamic nature" implies that the entire set-up of a VO may change in response to the market place. In this sense, VOs of this type are temporary as to their ability to react quickly as regards the membership, the structure, the objectives, etc. Its vague/fluid boundaries and opportunism, as well as equity of partners and shared leadership mainly characterize a dynamic virtual organization.

Virtual Breeding Environments

The concept of a Virtual Breeding Environment (VBE) was introduced by Camarihna-Matos & Afsarmanesh (2003) to model and support the rapid formation of virtual organizations, where a VBE may be regarded as an association of organizations adhering to common operating principles and infrastructure and who have as their main objective the participation in potential VOs for the achievement of certain goals. Hence, we adopt the view that all VOs are formed within the scope of a more general VBE, as shown in Figure 1.

Figure 1. The concept of a VBE

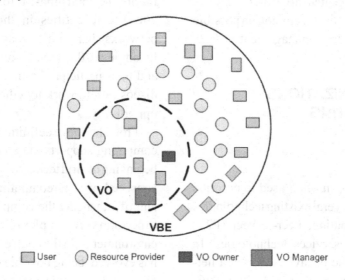

Organizations preregister to a VBE via a VO Manager service and this registration includes the details of resources and services they are willing to share in future VOs formed from the VBE as well as the list of potential users that belong to these organizations. A user willing to create a new VO assumes the role of the VO Owner, who with assistance of the VO Manager and other VO services (such as resource brokering services) is responsible for populating the VO with resources and users.

The VBE can be seen as a market place where resource providers compete to participate in VOs and users already in VOs compete for using resources. Reputation information about the resources and the organizations providing those resources could help guide VO Owners during their resource selection process. Similarly, reputation information of users registered with the VBE can be maintained, which would help VO resources providers in applying tight security measures for accessing their resources. Later, we discuss the definition of one such reputation model and its implementation that could maintain VBE-wide reputation values for both resources and their users.

VO Topologies

A VO, once it is formed out of a VBE, has a certain topology that may impact the trust and security issues within the VO. Such VO topologies have been discussed in literature (Burn et al., 1999; Katzy et al., 2000). For instance, Burn et al. (1999) define six types of VOs, ranging from organizations providing services in the web (such as web shops or newspapers on the web), which do not control any user of the service, to dynamic networks of entities collaborating to meet market opportunities. Some of the types of such VOs do not comply with our VO definition within the domain of Grid computing. Therefore, we focus here on three topologies for our VOs that were introduced initially by Katzy et al. (2000) based on network topologies.

Supply-Chain VOs

A supply chain in general may be defined as a coordinated system of organizations, people, processes and resources that moves information or services from one end called the producer (or supplier) to another end called the consumer (or customer). In our case, a supply chain consists

Figure 2. The Supply-chain VO Topology

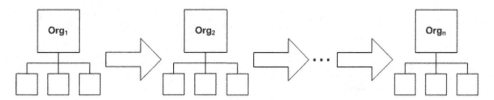

of several organizations that are collaborating to achieve the goal of supplying the consumer with the end product, as shown in Figure 2.

VOs, which adopt a supply chain topology, often use supply chain management and efficient consumer response to improve inter-organizational co-ordination and control. Integration of information flow and material flow creates transparency in the entire value chain and reduces waste and doubles effort in the virtual enterprise.

Apart from the usual security issues related to supply chains, such as the authentication of participants, maintaining the integrity of the moving product and its desirable properties, ensuring the security of the product while in transit and auditing at each stage, Kang et al. (2001) identify some security issues related to inter-organizational workflows, which may be regarded as the generic form of the VO supply chain topology. These include separation of workflow-level security requirements from organization-level security, fine-grained and context-based access control and supporting dynamic constraints in order maintain desirable properties such as the separation of duties. The Usage CONtrol (UCON) model proposed by Park and Sandhu (2004) provides a means for solving the last two issues, since access is granted based on continuous monitoring of the behavior of the entity requesting the access to some object and dynamic context-based constraints form a part of this model.

Hub-and-Spoke VOs

In the hub-and-spoke topology (also known as the star topology), partners interact with one central hub or strategic centre, as shown in Figure 3. This type of VOs corresponds to a coordinated network of interconnected members, where each member provides key functionalities, and distinguished member plays the role of a leading actor (star), coordinating the whole operation of the VO.

Despite the decline in popularity of hub-and-spoke topologies in networks, they are still considered to be a good solution in VOs for large scale enterprise application integration problems. For example, having a central management unit facilitates the control of VO membership, even though this centralized management may become a performance bottleneck and a point of failure. Traditional Grid security solutions, as those advocated in GSI (Nagaratnam et al., 2002), have been focused on this type of topology.

Peer-to-Peer VOs

Pee-to-Peer topologies are characterized by the lack of hierarchy where any peer may interact directly with any other peer, as shown in Figure 4. The management of such VOs is usually based on self-organization.

Wallach highlights a few security concerns in peer-to-peer systems. These include Secure routing, which ensures that when messages sent by non-faulty peers arrive at their non-faulty destinations without any compromises to their secrecy and/or integrity, Secure storage, where a node maintains the integrity of the data it stores and the data cannot harm the node (e.g. because the data contains a virus or a worm), distributed auditing, which is useful in resource usage monitoring and control and that could be related to other issues

Figure 3. The Hub-and-Spoke VO Topology

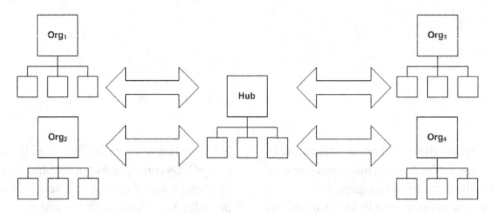

Figure 4. The Peer-to-Peer VO Topology

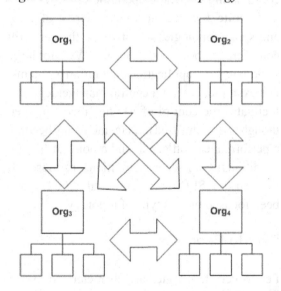

outside of security, as in load-balancing, and finally, trust and reputation, which are important factors in the security of Peer-to-Peer systems, in particular in identifying peers and evaluating their past behavior. Such an issue arises due to the lack of hierarchy in the topology.

Trust-Based VO Lifecycle

The establishment of a VO from a VBE involves issues of trust and reputation in the sense that entities in a VBE have to communicate match-

make and negotiate with other, possibly unknown, entities in the same VBE. Similarly, trust and reputation are needed during the operation of a VO during which entities belonging to trust domains that have particular reputation values related to their behavior history in the VO and the VBE attempt to access resources belonging to entities from other different trust domains. Once a VO is dissolved, the reputation that its entities have accumulated during its lifetime will be used to reflect their general VBE reputation. In general, a *VO lifecycle* demonstrates clearly the need for some notion of trust, either based on credentials or metrics or both. Finally, new organizations, resources, services and users joining a VO will have to demonstrate that they are trustworthy entities and that they will obey the VO policy during their membership.

The definition of a VO lifecycle that we adopt here is similar to that proposed by Strader et al. (1998) and adopted subsequently in several projects such as ECOLEAD (http://www.ve-forum. org/default.asp?P=284), TrustCoM (http://www. eu-trustcom.com/) and VOMAP (http://www.uni-nova.pt/~vomap/). According to this model, a VO lifecycle consists of the Identification, Formation, Operation and Evolution, and Dissolution phases, as shown in Figure 5.

We discuss these phases more in detail next.

Figure 5. The VO Lifecycle Phases

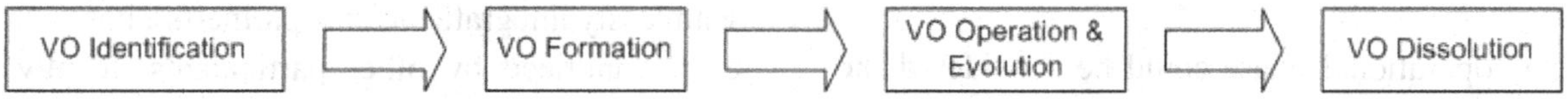

```
┌──────────────────┐      ┌──────────────┐      ┌──────────────────┐      ┌──────────────────┐
│ VO Identification│ ──▷  │ VO Formation │ ──▷  │  VO Operation &  │ ──▷  │  VO Dissolution  │
│                  │      │              │      │     Evolution    │      │                  │
└──────────────────┘      └──────────────┘      └──────────────────┘      └──────────────────┘
```

VO Identification

The identification phase addresses setting up the VO. This includes the selection of potential business partners from the network of enterprises by using search engines or looking up registries. Generally, relevant identification information contains service descriptions, security grades, trust and reputation ratings, etc. Depending on the resource types, the search process may consist of a simple matching (e.g., in the case of computational resources, processor type, available memory and respective data may be considered search parameters with clear cut matches) or of a more complex process, which involves adaptive, context-sensitive parameters. For example, the availability of a simulation program may be restricted to specific user groups or only for certain data types, like less confidential data, etc. The process may also involve metadata such as security policies or Service Level Agreement (SLA) templates with ranges of possible values and/or dependencies between them, such as bandwidth depending on the applied encryption algorithm. The identification phase ends with a list of candidates that potentially could perform the roles needed for the current VO.

VO Formation

After this initial step from the potentially large list of candidates, the most suitable ones are selected and to become VO members, depending on additional aspects that may further reduce the set of candidates. Such additional aspects cover negotiation of actual Quality of Service (QoS) parameters, availability of the service, "willingness"

of the candidate to participate, etc. It should be noted that though an exhaustive list of candidates may have been gathered during the identification phase, this does not necessarily mean that a VO can be realized. For example, consider the case where a service provider may not be able to keep the promised SLA at a specific date due to other obligations.

In principle, the intended formation may fail due to at least two reasons: (a) no provider (or not enough providers) is able to fulfill all given requirements regarding to SLA, security, etc. or (b) providers are not (fully) available at the specified time. In order to circumvent these problems, either the requirements may be reduced ("choose the best available") or the actual formation may be delayed to be re-launched at a more suitable time. Obviously there may be the case where a general restructuring of the requirements leads to a repetition of the identification phase.

At the end of the (successful) formation phase the initial set of candidates will have been reduced to a set of VO members. In order to allow these members to perform accordingly their anticipated role in the VO, they need to be configured appropriately. During the formation phase, a central component called the VO Manager distributes the VO level configuration information, such as policies, SLAs, etc. to all identified members. These VO level policies need to be mapped to local policies. This might include changes in the security settings (e.g. open access through a firewall for certain IP addresses, create users on machines on the fly, etc.) to allow secure communication, or simply translation of XML documents expressing SLAs or Obligations to a product specific format used internally.

VO Operation

The operational phase could be considered the main lifecycle phase of a VO. During this phase the identified services and resources contribute to the actual execution of the VO task(s) by executing pre-defined business processes (e.g. a workflow of simulation processes and pre- and post processing steps). A lot of additional issues related to management and supervision are involved in this phase in order to ensure smooth operation of the actual task(s). Such issues cover carrying out financial arrangements (accounting, metering), recording of and reacting to participants' performance, updating and changing roles and therefore access rights of participants according to the current status of the executed workflow, etc. In certain environments persistent information of all operations performed may be required to allow for later examination, e.g. to identify fault-sources.

Throughout the operation of the VO, service performance will be monitored. This will be used as evidence when constructing the reputation of the service providers. Any violation, e.g. an unauthorized access detected by the access control systems, and security threats, e.g. an event detected by an intrusion detection system, need to be notified to other members in order to take appropriate actions. Unusual behaviors may lead to both a trust reassessment and a contract adaptation. VO members will also need to enforce security at their local site. For example, providing access to services and adapting to changes and violations.

The evolution of the VO structure may be considered as part of the operational phase. This evolution is necessary since participants may fail all together or behave inappropriately and it becomes necessary to dynamically replace the misbehaving participants. This involves identifying new, alternative business partner(s) and service(s), as well as re-negotiating terms and providing configuration information as during identification, respectively formation phases. One of the main challenges involved with evolution is

to re-configure an existing VO structure so as to seamlessly integrate the new partner(s), possibly even unnoticed by other participants. Ideally, one would like the new service to take over the replaced partners' task at the point of its leaving without interruption and without having to reset the state of operation. There may be other reasons for participants joining or leaving the VO, mostly related to the overall business process, which might require specific services only for a limited period of time - since it is not sensible to provide an unused, yet particularly configured service to the VO for its whole lifetime, the partner may request to enter or leave the VO when not needed.

VO Dissolution

During the dissolution phase, the VO structure is dissolved and final operations are performed to annul all contractual binding of the partners. This involves the billing process for used services and an assessment of the respective participants' (or more specifically their resources) performances, like amount of SLA violations and the like. The latter may be of particular interest for further interactions respectively for other potential customers. Additionally it is required to revoke all security tokens, access rights, etc. in order to avoid that a participant may (mis)use its particular privileges. Generally the inverse actions of the formation phase have to be performed during the dissolution phase. Partial termination operations may be performed during evolution steps of the operation phase.

GRID SECURITY

Overview

Security techniques have traditionally been the main method by which trust is established in a Grid environment. The classical argument being that the more secure the system the more trustworthy it is. In this sense, the different security mechanisms utilized and shared by a number of organizations help establishing a trust domain around those organizations. An important step in the design of the security support for a given system is the definition of a threat model. A threat model is generally used to describe a given threat and the harm it could do a system if it has this vulnerability. The starting point to integrate a proper security support in the architecture of a complex system, such as the Grid, is the evaluation of a given threat model with respect to its benefits and costs.

In the literature, some threats models have been proposed, which are specific for the Grid system. Also, there exist numerous models, architectures, and implementations for enhancing the security of the Grid. In this section, after recalling three threats model, we provide an overview of the three most popular security architectures, namely the security model of the Open Grid Services Architecture (OGSA), the Grid Security Infrastructure (GSI) implementation of OGSA and the security architecture adopted by the Enabling Grids for E-sciencE (EGEE) project.

Threat Models for Grid

A threat model describes the potential for violation of a system, due to vulnerability that can be exploited to perform an attack on the system itself. Some specific threat models for the Grid environment have been proposed in the literature, see for example, (Naqvi & Riguidel, 2005), (Demchenko et al., 2005), and (Jiancheng et al, 2007).

As highlighted in (Naqvi & Riguidel, 2005), the main threats to a Grid environment are connected to its security requirements. Hence, they propose a model that identifies threats to: integrity of the physical infrastructure; confidentiality of the stored data; availability of the Grid resources; access control (i.e., authentication and authorization mechanisms).

Instead, (Demchenko et al., 2005) defines a different taxonomy that groups threats (and hence attacks) depending on their origin and the vulnerability they exploit. The authors identify the following attacks on a Grid system:

- The user credential attack, in which the user's credentials are compromised, e.g., a credential theft.
- The wire intelligence attack that can happen if service level communication is not protected enough against eavesdropping and interception;
- The malefactor initiated attacks. They are attacks executed by malicious users trying to harm the Grid services by traditional or web service specific attacks, e.g., by submitting forged XML requests, or by implementing denial of service attacks;
- The site management attack, caused by erroneous or improper configuration of the Grid security services and their management;
- The end service attack, which exploits known vulnerabilities of the specific services provided.

Starting from this classification, they propose a multilayer security framework that organizes a Grid node in security layers, or zones. For each of these zones proper security protections should be defined. However, a detailed description of the full approach is not given.

Finally, (Jiancheng et al, 2007) propose a third taxonomy, which is similar to the previous one, based on the actors that we can identify in a Grid system. In particular, they define threats to

- Users, in terms of credential theft and compromises.
- Mediators, involving attacks to the communications between the user and the service provider

- Service providers, where malicious users exploit forged service requests to hang up the service engine.
- Resource providers, including attacks on the physical and software shared resources (e.g., exploiting configuration vulnerabilities, or performing an illegitimate use of the resource.

There are similarities between the last two models, because the four classes defined by the third model can be mapped on the first four classes of the second one. In the next sections, we discuss some security models and architectures that have been developed to mitigate such threats on Grid systems.

OGSA Security

To address the Grid specific security requirements of OGSA, the OGSA Security Group proposed an architecture leveraging as much as possible from the Web Services Security specifications (Nagaratnam et al., 2002). The components of the architecture are shown in Figure 6.

As we mentioned previously, secure operation in a Grid environment requires that applications and services be able to support a variety of security functionalities, such as authentication, authorization, credential conversion, auditing and delegation. These functionalities are based on mechanisms that may evolve over time as new devices are developed or policies change. As suggested in (Siebenlist et al., 2003), Grid applications must avoid embedding security mechanisms statically.

Exposing security functionalities as services (i.e., with a Web Services Description Language (WSDL) (Christensen et al. 2001) definition) achieves a level of abstraction that helps provide an integrated, secure Grid environment. An OGSA infrastructure may use a set of primitive security functions in the form of services themselves.

Nagaratnam et al. (2003) suggest the following security services:

Authentication Service

An authentication service is concerned with verifying proof of an asserted identity. One example is the evaluation of a User ID and password combination, in which a service requestor supplies the appropriate password for an asserted user ID. Another example involves a service requestor authenticating through a Kerberos mechanism, and a ticket being passed to the service provider's hosting environment, which determines the authenticity of the ticket before the service is instantiated.

Identity Mapping Service

The identity mapping service provides the capability of transforming an identity that exists in one identity domain into an identity within another identity domain. The identity mapping service is not concerned with the authentication of the service requestor; rather it is strictly a policy driven name mapping service

Authorization Service

The authorization service is concerned with resolving a policy based access control decision. The authorization service consumes as input a credential that embodies the identity of an authenticated service requestor and for the resource that the service requestor requests, resolves based on policy, whether or not the service requestor is authorized to access the resource. It is expected that the hosting environment for OGSA compliant services will provide access control functions, and it is appropriate to further expose an abstract authorization service depending on the granularity of the access control policy that is being enforced.

Figure 6. The OGSA Security Architecture (Adapted from Nagaratnam et al. (2002), p. 13)

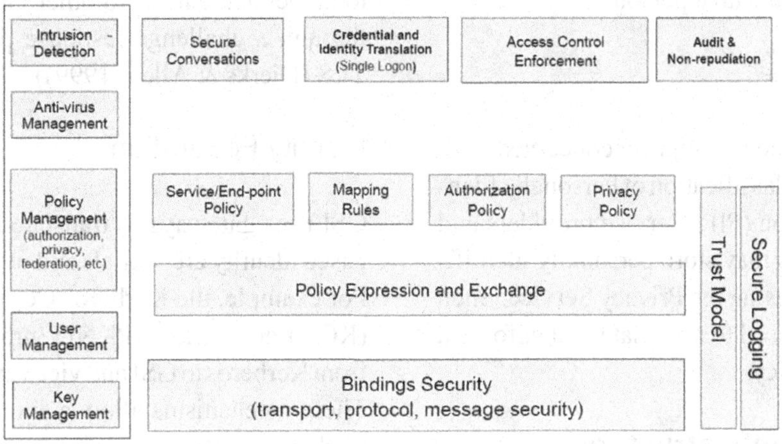

VO Policy Service

The VO policy service is concerned with the management of policies. The aggregation of the policies contained within and managed by the policy service comprises a VO's policy set. The policy service may be thought of as another primitive service, which is used by the authorization, audit, identity mapping and other services as needed.

Credential Conversion Service

The credential conversion service provides credential conversion between one type of credential to another type or form of credential. This may include such tasks as reconciling group membership, privileges, attributes and assertions associated with entities (service requestors and service providers). For example, the credential conversion service may convert a Kerberos credential to a form that is required by the authorization service. The policy driven credential conversion service facilitates the interoperability of differing credential types, which may be consumed by services. It is expected that the credential conversion service would use the identity mapping service. WS-Trust

(http://docs.oasis-open.org/ws-sx/ws-trust/v1.3/ws-trust.html) defines such a service.

Audit Service

The audit service similarly to the identity mapping and authorization services is policy driven. The audit service is responsible for producing records, which track security relevant events. The resulting audit records may be reduced and examined as to determine if the desired security policy is being enforced. Auditing and subsequently reduction tooling are used by the security administrators within a VO to determine the VO's adherence to the stated access control and authentication policies.

Profile Service

The profile service is concerned with managing service requestor's preferences and data which may not be directly consumed by the authorization service. This may be service requestor specific personalization data, which for example can be used to tailor or customize the service requestor's experience (if incorporated into an application which interfaces with end-users.) It is expected that primarily this data will be used by applications that interface with a person.

Privacy Service

The privacy service is primarily concerned with the policy driven classification of Personally Identifiable Information (PII). Service providers and service requestors may store personally identifiable information using the Privacy Service. Such a service can be used to articulate and enforce a VO's privacy policy.

Grid Security Infrastructure

The Grid Security Infrastructure (GSI) is a specific implementation of an OGSA-based Grid security architecture that has been packaged as part of the Globus Toolkit starting from version 2, GT2, up until the most recent version, i.e. GT4 (Globus Security Team, 2005; Welch et al. 2003). The GSI model in GT4 is shown in Figure 7 and is composed of the following security services.

Authentication

GSI defines a credential format based on X.509 identity certification, (Housley et al., 1999). An X.509 certificate, in conjunction with an associated private key, forms a unique credential set that a Grid entity (requestor or service provider) uses to authenticate itself to other Grid entities (e.g., through a challenge-response protocol such as TLS (Dierks & Allen, 1999)).

Identity Federation

GSI uses gateways to translate between X.509-based identity credentials and other mechanisms. For example, the Kerberos Certificate Authority (KCA) and SSLK5/PKNIT provide translation from Kerberos to GSI and vice versa, respectively. These mechanisms allow a site with an existing Kerberos infrastructure to convert credentials between Kerberos and GSI as needed.

Dynamic Entities and Delegation

GSI introduces X.509 proxy certificates, an extension to X.509 identity certificates that allows a user to assign dynamically a new X.509 identity to an entity and then delegate some subset of their rights to that identity.

Message-Level Security

Globus Toolkit Version 3 (GT3) and the subsequent version use the Web Services Security specifications (http://www.oasis-open.org/committees/tc_home.php?wg_abbrev=wss) to allow security messages and secured messages to be transported,

Figure 7. The GSI Security Architecture (Adapted from Globus Security Team (2005), p. 2)

	Message-level Security w/X.509 Credentials	Message-level Security w/Usernames and Passwords	Transport-level Security w/X.509 Credentials
Authorization	SAML and grid-mapfile	grid-mapfile	SAML and grid-mapfile
Delegation	X.509 Proxy Certificates/ WS-Trust		X.509 Proxy Certificates/ WS-Trust
Authentication	X.509 End Entity Certificates	Username/ Password	X.509 End Entity Certificates
Message Protection	WS-Security WS-SecureConversation	WS-Security	TLS
Message format	SOAP	SOAP	SOAP

understood and manipulated by standard Web services tools and software.

In relation to stateful and secured communication, GSI supports the establishment of a security context that authenticates two parties to each other and allows for the exchange of secured messages between the two parties. GT4 achieves security context establishment by implementing preliminary versions of WS-Security Conversation and WS-Trust specifications. Once the security context is established, GIS implements message protection using the Web Services standards for secured messages XML-Signature and XML-Encryption.

To allow for communication without the initial establishment of a security context, GT4 offers the ability to sign messages independent of any established security context, by using XML-Signature specification.

Trust Domains

The requirement for overlaid trust domains to establish VOs is satisfied by using both proxy certificates and security services such as CAS. GSI has an implicit policy that any two entities bearing proxy certificates issued by the same user will inherently trust each other. This policy allows users to create trust domains dynamically by issuing proxy certificates to any services that they want to interoperate.

EGEE Security Architecture

The EGEE (http://www.eu-egee.org/) security architecture (EGEE, 2004), shown in Figure 8 below, provides a number of security services including logging and auditing, authentication, authorization, delegation, data key management, sandboxing and site proxy, which can enhance the security of Grid access through EGEE's Grid middleware called gLite (http://glite.web.cern.ch/glite/). The architecture is modular (modules can be plugged in and out of the architecture), agnostic (modules can evolve) and adherent to standards. In the following sections, we give an overview of the different security services of the architecture, although not all are yet implemented by EGEE.

Logging and Auditing

The logging and auditing service is used to log information about time of security incidents, evidence of these incidents, produce incident reports and conduct security audits. Auditing on

Figure 8. The EGEE Security Architectures (Adapted from EGEE (2004), p. 11)

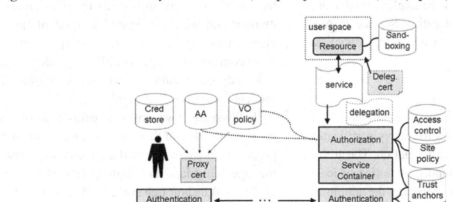

the other hand is not yet implemented, although the architecture defines it as a service that can be built based on the logging service.

Authentication

Authentication in EGEE's security architecture is based on trusted third parties called Certification Authorities, which issue X-509v3 public-key certificates to express identity assertions. Authentication is achieved by verifying the distinguished name of the subject of the certificate. The service also facilitates single sign-on by allowing proxy certificates to be defined based on identity certificates. Revocation of certificates is done via periodic distribution of revocation lists.

Authorization

The model of authorization in EGEE's security architecture is based on the push model, where the authorization service issues credentials to the Grid users, who present these credentials to the resources they wish to access. The architecture caters for two kinds of authorization services: attribute authorities and policy assertion services. Attribute authorities are implemented by the VO Membership Service (VOMS) (Alfieri et al., 2003) issuing X-509 certificates containing user role and group membership information. On the other hand, policy assertion services are implemented using the Community Authorization Service (CAS) (Pearlman et al., 2003) PERMIS (Chadwick & Otenko, 2002).

Delegation

The architecture provides for proxy certificates as a means for expressing delegation. The architecture still does not support the notion of least privilege, where an entity delegates the minimum set of rights required for achieving a task.

Data Key Management

The main aim behind the data key management service is to solve the problem of plaintext storage using the M-of-N storage technique. A full description of the problem is given in (EGEE, 2004).

Sandboxing

Sandboxing in the EGEE security architecture is achieved via tradition virtualization techniques, where services are sun within well-isolated virtual machines, which provide users with complete operating systems.

TRUST AND REPUTATION IN GRIDS

Overview

The security models and architectures of the previous section help raise the trust level of any domain, however, as we mentioned in the section on VOs, VOs have a dynamic nature where new services and resources may need to be setup quickly and VO membership evolves frequently over time. In such VOs, security infrastructures adopted by existing members may need to be integrated and made interoperable with each others' and new members' infrastructures often in an automatic manner and within a limited amount of time. Hence, adopting trust models based on past behavior becomes necessary in fulfilling such demands of high dynamic nature, where the security-based models themselves are unable to fulfill.

In this section, we turn our attention to a couple of trust models and their architectures. The first proposes an extension to the Role-based Trust-management Mark-up Language (RTML) (Li et al., 2002; Winsborough et al., 2003) with weights denoting the trust that systems place on their users. These weights are used to make decisions about whether access can be granted or not for accessing system operations. The second model proposes a reputation management system for Grids based on utility functions, which express the satisfaction users get from their interactions with Grid resources.

Trust is a general concept with numerous definitions depending on the context in which it is used. In computer science, one of the most popular definitions was put forward by Grandison and Sloman (2000), who define trust as "... *the firm belief in the competence of an entity to act dependably, securely and reliably within a specific context.*" (p. 3). This definition encapsulates desired general properties of computing systems such as dependability, security and reliability while maintaining that these are only measurable within the specific context in which the system functions. For example, a system for establishing Web security will not be trusted in the context of the reliability of aerodynamics systems.

In Grid computing, as we mentioned earlier, trust has historically been focused on the strengthening of the security of Grid systems through adopting various flavors of authentication and authorization models. However, more recently, other architectures incorporating trust directly have been proposed and implemented based on measurable models (Dimitrakos, 2001; Lin et al., 2004, Hermoso et al., 2006; Vijayakumar and Wahida Banu, 2008).

Dimitrakos (2001) proposes a definition of trust within the context of service-oriented architectures, which also underline Grid computing. According to this definition, trust of a service requestor, A, to a service provider, B, in relation to some service, X, can be defined as follows: "*Trust of a party A in a party B for a service X is the measurable belief of A in B behaving dependably for a specified period within a specified context in relation to X...*" Interestingly, the model distinguishes between the notions of distrust and the lack of trust as follows: "*Distrust of a party A to a party B for a service X is A's measurable belief in that B behaves non-dependably for a*

specified period within a specified context in relation to service X." Compared to the lack of trust, in this sense, distrust becomes a useful measure to revoke previously agreed trust, obstruct the propagation of trust, ignore recommendations and communicate a party's trust value and whether this has reached the level of a blacklist for a class of potential business transactions.

Lin et al. (2004) develop a trust management architecture for trust enhanced Grid security, providing mechanisms for trust evaluation, recommendation, and update for trust decisions. The proposed formal trust model is capable of capturing the range of trust relationships that exist in a Grid computing system. Examples of such relationships are: *Execution Trust* that is the trust in the resource provider that will allocate the resources for the execution of the job request, and *Code Trust* that is the trust towards VO users that will not submit malicious job requests or malicious applications.

Hermoso et al. (2006) define a model of trust in VOs, which are a common abstraction of Grid computing as discussed in the previous section. The model is built on the notions of confidence and reputation of an agent within a role-based organization, which are measurable by values within the range [0,1]. The reputation of an agent is measured according to how well the agent performed in some role in the past. This will impact the confidence other agent's have in this particular agent.

Finally, Vijayakumar and Wahida Banu (2008) propose a model of trust for resource selection in computational Grids. The model is based on assigning reputation weights to the different security capabilities that resources utilize and that reflect the degree of trust one can place upon these resources. For example, such capabilities include intrusion detection system capabilities, anti-virus capabilities, firewall capabilities, authentication mechanisms, secured file storage capabilities, interoperability and secured job execution. The values reflect how well these capabilities protect desirable Grid security properties such as confidentiality, availability and non-repudiation.

Other views of trust in Grid computing such as that of *trustless Grid computing* have also been proposed by Chang et al. (2002). The proposed model adopts the principle that trust (of a service being dependable, secure etc.) can only be attained through the use of rigorous mathematical proof. In this view, trust is not measurable; it is provable. The approach followed by Chang et al. (2002) is to use the *proof-carrying code* framework as first defined by Necula (1997), in order to assure the trustor of the validity of the claims made by the trustee. Proof-carrying code can be obtained as output from a special type of compilers known as certifying compilers. One big limitation of proof-carrying code-based approaches is that they are yet to be shown to be applicable in practice to large-scale systems such as Grids.

Another concept closely related to trust is reputation. Jøsang et al. (2007) define reputation as *"what is generally said or believed about a person or a thing"* (p. 622). Reputation is seen as one measurable means by which trust can be built, since one entity can trust (distrust) another based on good (bad) past experience and observations as well as collected referral information about its past behavior (Abdul-Rahman & Hailes, 2000). In recent years, the concept of reputation has shown itself to be useful in many areas of research in computer science particularly in the context of distributed and collaborative systems, such as Peer-to-peer and Grid computing, Web services and social networks, where trust and security issues are strongly manifested. Interested readers may refer to the thorough survey of the state-of-the-art literature on reputation definitions, models and systems provided by Silaghi et al. (2007). Despite the fact that Globus offers a Monitoring and Directory Service (MDS) (Fitzgerald et al., 1997), the service lacks metric information, such as reputation, about resources that would reflect the quality of those resources. This poses a severe limitation on users of these resources especially during the formation and operational phases of the VO lifecycle. As a result, enhancing Globus with a reputation service would greatly benefit VOs in a similar manner that other distributed systems have benefitted.

Up to date, there has been only few reputation solutions proposed for Grid computing despite their clear advantage in enhancing the dependability of Grid systems through improving their resource allocation and scheduling operations. The GridEigenTrust model proposed by von Laszewski et al. (2005) exploits the beneficial properties of EigenTrust (Kamvar et al., 2003), extending the model to allow its usage in grids. A trust management system is integrated as part of the QoS management framework proposing to probabilistically pre-select the resources based on their likelihood to deliver the requested capability and capacity. The global trust for an organization with regard to another organization will be built from the direct trust that can be acquired from transactions between members of the two organizations and by considering trust information acquired from third party sources. The same trust aggregation scheme can be employed at the level of organization members, each of whom stores trust values for its transaction partners.

Another system is PathTrust (Kerschbaum et al., 2006), which is a reputation system proposed for member selection in the formation phase of a VO. To enter the VO formation process, a member must register with an enterprise network infrastructure by presenting some credentials. Besides user management, the enterprise network is provided with a centralized reputation service. At the dissolution of the VO, each member leaves feedback ratings to the reputation server for other members with whom they experienced transactions. The system requires each transaction to be rated by the participants.

Role-Based Trust Management with Weights

The Role-based Trust Management framework RTML (Li et al., 2002; Winsborough et al., 2003) provides policy language, semantics, deduction engine, and concrete tools to manage access control and authorization in large-scale and decentralized system. RTML combines the strength of Role-Based Access Control (RBAC) and Trust-Management (TM). RBAC was developed to manage access control in a single organization in which the control of role membership and role permissions is relatively centralized in a few users. RTML takes from RBAC the notion of role to assign permissions to users. TM is an approach to distributed access control and authorization in which access control decision are taken on the base of policy statements made by multiple principals, e.g., Grid sites. From TM, RTML takes the principles of managing distributed authority through the use of credentials, as well as some notation denoting relationships between those authorities.

The Model

The main concept in RTML is the notion of *roles*: each principal has its own name space for defining roles, and each role is compounded by the principal name and a *role term*. For example, if A is a principal and r is a role term, then $A.r$ denotes the role r defined by principal A. Only A has the authority to issue policy statements defining the members of the role $A.r$. Roles may be parameterized, e.g., a basic credential of the form $A.r(p) \leftarrow D$ means that A assigns to D the role term r with parameter p.

In the following credential, organization IIT assigns the role of IIT researcher to Alice, whose distinguished name adopted on the Grid is "CN=Alice, OU=IIT, O=CNR, L=Pisa, C=IT".

IIT.researcher('CN=Alice, OU=IIT, O=CNR, L=Pisa, C=IT') ← Alice

In (Martinelli & Petrocchi, 2007) a basic set of RTML credentials has been enriched with trust, in order to express not only the fact that an authority assigns to someone a certain role, but also that a principal trusts someone for performing some functionality *f*, or for giving a recommendation regarding a third party able to perform that functionality. This follows the interpretation of trust encoded in the transitive trust model of (Jøsang et al., 2003; Jøsang et al., 2006), according to which trust is always linked to a purpose. The most natural situation is when one trusts another for performing a certain function/task. It is often common that principals ask other principals for suggesting/recommending a third party able to performing that function or task.

The following language enriches RTML with trust, by also specifying a trust weight *v*, i.e., a quantification of the confidence one places in the positive outcome.

Simple member. $A.r(p,v) \leftarrow D$. The role $A.r(p)$ has weight v.

Simple containment. $A.r(p,v) \leftarrow_{v2} A_1.r_1(p_1,v_1)$.

According to A, all members of role $A_1.r_1(p_1,v_1)$ with weight v_1 are members of role $A.r(p,v)$ with weight $v = v_1 \otimes v_2$. v_2 is a constant filtering A_1's authority with A's authority.

Linking containment. $A.r(p) \leftarrow A.r_1(p_1).r_2(p_2)$.

If B has role $A_1.r_1(p_1)$ with weight v_1 and D has role $B.r_2(p_2)$ with weight v_2, then D has role $A.r(p)$ with weight $v = v_1 \otimes v_2$. This works as a sort of role-based delegation.

Intersection. $A.r(p) \leftarrow A_1.r_1(p_1) \cap A_2.r_2(p_2)$.

This statement defines that if D has both roles $A_1.r_1(p_1)$ with weight v_1 and $A_2.r_2(p_2)$ with weight v_2, then D has role $A.r(p)$ with weight $v = v_1 \otimes v_2$.

Weights are not explicitly expressed in the linking and the intersection containment statements. Operators $\otimes$ and $\oplus$ combine the trust measures in the composed credentials expressed by the simple, the linking, and the intersection containment. For the sake of readability, weights are not explicitly expressed in the linking and the intersection containment statements. Generally speaking, $\otimes$ combines opinions along a path, i.e., A's opinion for B is combined with B's opinion for C into one indirect opinion that A should have for C, based on what B thinks about C. $\oplus$ combines opinions across paths, i.e., A's indirect opinion for X through path path1 is combined with A's indirect opinion for X through path path2 into one aggregate opinion that reconciles both. To work properly, these operators must form an algebraic structure called a c-semiring, (Theodorakopoulos & Baras, 2004).

Extending the Globus Architecture with RTML

Security management in the Grid environment is complicated by the need to establish secure relationships between the VO members, among which no direct trust relationships may exist a priori, because during the VO formation phase, no trust relationships are required among the parties that are joining the organization. The VO members share their computational resources for allowing the execution of unknown applications on behalf of other, possibly unknown, VO members. If an adequate security support is not adopted, the applications submitted by remote VO members during the VO operation phase could perform dangerous and even malicious actions on these resources. Hence, among the functionality of Grid security support, the authorization is a fundamental one.

In the following, we illustrate an architectural proposal for the enhancement of the security infrastructure of Globus (Foster, 2005) through the integration of the RTML framework. The proposed solution takes into account the level of trust that the VO member collected in her previous interactions with some Grid resources.

The standard authorization system provided by the Globus Toolkit is static, because the identity of each authorized user is statically mapped on a local account that is exploited to execute remote jobs on behalf of the user. Hence, given a Grid resource R, only users that have been previously registered on R can access the services provided by R. This feature is a limitation in an open and distributed environment such the Grid one.

Figure 9. Interactions between Globus and the RTML Authorization Service (Adapted from Colombo et al. (2007a), p. 451)

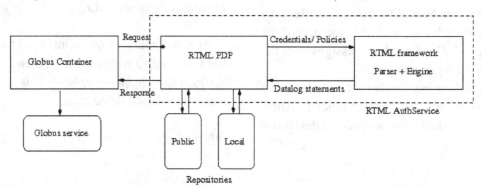

Work in (Colombo et al., 2007a) proposes an authorization system based on RTML that determines the rights of a VO member on a Grid resource exclusively according to the attributes of the user. The system considers the complex trust relationships that the user collected in the past by exploiting services on other Grid resources/ sites. These relationships are expressed in form of credentials, issued by the sites. From the Grid resource point of view, the credentials owned by a VO member determine attributes exploitable by the user on the resource. Each attribute corresponds to a set of privileges, and it is enforced through local accounts with the corresponding set of rights. The set of credentials is dynamic, because new credentials could be added by other Grid sites and some of the existing ones could be expired.

The proposed architecture is shown in Figure 9. When a VO member submits a request, the Globus container interacts with RTMLAuthzService (the authorization system based on RTML) through the Security Assertion Markup Language (SAML) (Madsen & Maler 2005) authorization Callout mechanism, to determine the rights of the user to perform the requested action on the requested service. The user request contains information about the user, the requested service and the repositories of the user's credentials. Within RTMLAuthzService, the RTML Policy Decision Point is the component in charge of determining which rights the user holds on the requested service, according to her credentials and the access policy for that service.

In the current implementation, the RTML PDP downloads the user credentials from a public repository, and the access policy from a local repository. Both the user credentials and the access policy are translated into RT statements by the RTML parser. In its turn, the RTML Engine transforms each RT statement into Datalog statements, and returns them to the RTML PDP. A policy defines which attributes are required to execute

the requested service and the PDP evaluates the Datalog statements through a Prolog engine to know which of these attributes could be granted to the user. The RTML PDP may compute more than one attribute for the user. In this case, if the user specifies the attribute he wants to exploit for the authorization process, the job will be executed with the privileges granted by that attribute. Otherwise, the RTML PDP chooses the attribute that grants the bigger set of rights to the user.

Credentials and Access Policies as RTML Statements

We present sets of user credentials that could be evaluated with respect to an access policy by the RTML authorization service in real job requests.

Trust Management example. The Center of Electronic Computation (CCE) offers a computational service to university students which are carrying out a stage at ABC Company. To access the service, a user need to supply a credential issued by the ABC Company, asserting the stage, and a credential issued by the university, granting him the role of student. Also, a credential chain is required to verify that this university is admitted by CCE. Each student with right credentials can access the computational services, even if her identity has not been registered by CCE.

Let us suppose that Alice, which is a student of University of Pisa and a collaborator at the ABC Company, wants to access the CCE computational service. She supplies the following credentials:

1) *UniPI.Student (university='University of Pisa', department='CS', id='1999s131', firstname='alice', lastname='black') ← Alice*

2) *ABC.Collaborator (role='stage', firstname='alice', lastname='black') ← Alice*

3) *MIUR.University (name='University of Pisa') ← UniPI*

The Access Policy stored by CCE is the following:

a) *CCE.University (name=?) ← MIUR*
b) *CCE.Student (university=ref_{uni}, department=?, id=?, firstname=?, lastname=?) ← CCE.University (name= ref_{uni})*
c) *CCE.ABCGuest ← ABC.Collaborator (role=?, firstname=ref_{first}, lastname=ref_{last}) ∩ CCE.Student (university=?, department=?, id=?, firstname=ref_{first}, lastname=ref_{last})*
d) *CCE.Guest ← CCE.Student (university=?, department=?, id=?, firstname=?, lastname=?)*

Symbol '?' denotes a parameter whose value is not specified.

In the first and second credentials, principals *UniPI* and *ABC* assign to Alice the attributes of, resp., *student* and *collaborator*, with the specified parameters. The owner of the third credential is *UniPI* and not Alice. This statement could be used to infer information about Alice's attributes. Indeed, rule *a)* of the access policy states that CCE considers as universities the principals that are considered Universities by MIUR, the Italian Ministry for University and Research.

The credentials and the access policy are retrieved by the RTML PDP from the repositories, and passed to the RTML Engine. The RTML Engine transforms them in a set of Datalog statements. Then, the RTML PDP reads from a configuration file that either attribute *ABCGuest* or *Guest* is required for the service requested by Alice, and invokes the Prolog Engine that evaluates the Datalog statements to verify whether Alice holds one of these roles.

Reputation Management example. Work in (Colombo et al., 2007b) exploits RTML to perform a fine grained control of the applications executed on Grid sites on behalf of remote VO members. With respect to the previous approach, this framework allows for determining not whether a certain user can execute an application on a Grid site, but it determines the allowed actions that the application can perform during its execution. Moreover, this work extends the attribute-based trust management framework for the evaluation of the user's credentials with a reputation management. Reputation of the VO member is calculated collecting past experiences encountered by Grid services with respect to that user. The more the user is well-behaved with a service, the more the service will positively recommend experiences with that user. The system architecture is shown in Figure 10. With respect to the previous approach, the RTML PDP is invoked at the level of the Globus Resource and Allocation and Management Service (GRAM), i.e., the service that allows the execution of applications on behalf of remote users. In particular, in (Colombo et al., 2007b), a behavioral PDP monitors the actions executed by the application, and invokes the RTML PDP when the security policy requires the evaluation of an attribute of the user, such as the reputation. For the sake of simplicity, here we simply show reputation predicates used to trigger the RTML PDP when the application tries to open the given file. An example of policy rule is

[RepMaxOf(Unipi.files(user),0.8)].open(filename)

This means that the action *open(filename)* can be executed by the application only if the RTML PDP evaluates the predicate *RepMaxOf(Unipi.files(user),0.8)* to true, i.e., if the user is trusted to operate on files with at least weight 0.8.

Reputation credentials are expressed as RTML statements with weights. GRID services emit two kinds of credentials. The first kind expresses trust towards a functionality, e.g., towards good behaviors, *A.f(v) ← D*, i.e., *A* trusts *D* for performing functionality f with degree v. The others are credentials of recommendation, denoted as *A.rf(v) ← D*. They express the fact that *A* trusts

Figure 10. Interactions between Globus, GRAM, and the RTML Authorization Service (Adapted from Colombo et al. (2007b), p. 1506)

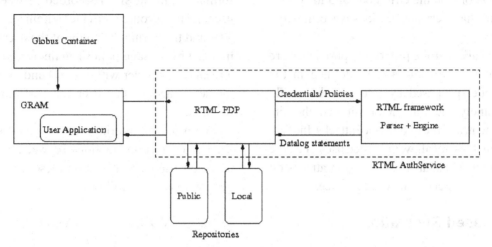

D as a recommender able to suggest someone for performing *f*. Functionalities can be instantiated in several ways, e.g., *A.files(p,v) ← D.* means that *A* trusts *D* with degree *v* for operating on a *file*.

As a simple example, imagine that Robert submits a request for executing an application on a Grid node that falls in the administrative domain of the University of Pisa UniPI. In particular, the application needs to operate on a file. UniPI considers as good recommenders the Institute for Informatics and Telematics and the University of Genoa. In order to evaluate the enforceability of the request, the RTML PDP will process the following credentials:

1) *UniGE.files('CN=Bob, 0.7)' ← Robert*
2) *IIT.files('CN=Bob, 0.8)' ← Robert*
3) *UniPI.rfiles('CN=UnivGenoa,1)' ← UniGE*
4) *UniPI.rfiles('CN=InstInfTel,1)' ← IIT*

The first two credentials say, respectively, that UniGe gives to Robert the attribute *files* (i.e., faculty of operating on files) with reputation 0.7 and that IIT gives to Robert the same attribute with reputation 0.8. The third credential says that UniPi accepts recommendations for the attribute

files from UniGe. The fourth credential says that UniPi accepts recommendations for the attribute *files* also from IIT.

Credentials are evaluated with respect to a policy of this kind:

UniPI.files(username)' ← UniPI
.rfiles(recname).files(username)

The last statement expresses trust-based delegation. UniPI trusts a set of recommenders for choosing a third party trusted for the attribute *files*. This means that, indirectly, UniPI trusts that third party for the attribute *files*.

Combining the first and third credential with the policy, result is that UniPI trusts Robert for operating on a file with weight $0.7 \otimes 1$ (0.7 when $\otimes$ is the product operator), by means of UniGE's recommendation. Similarly, combining the second and fourth credential, UniPI trusts Robert for operating on a file with weight 0.8, by means of IIT's recommendation. The latter satisfies the previous reputation predicate.

The two previous approaches have been also merged to obtain a single framework that works both at coarse and fine grain level. Hence, RTML authorization service is used both to decide whether a VO member has the right to execute his applications on the Grid node and to control the actions that these applications perform while running.

We remark that the proposed approaches are useful to fight possible attacks defined in the threat model proposed by (Demchenko et al., 2005), namely, the Malefactor Initiated, the Site Management, and the End Service attacks. Indeed, the system does not allow untrusted users, i.e., the ones that most probably will perform attacks on the resource, to access the Grid Services.

Utility-Based Reputation

Recently, utility functions have been used as the model basis for measuring reputation in Grid-based systems (Arenas et al., 2008). Utility functions are a means by which preferences can be expressed in a quantitative manner. In general, a utility function, $f: C \rightarrow R$, maps each consumed entity, C, to a real number R representing the satisfaction of the consumer from consuming that entity. Such utility functions can be used to capture the satisfaction of Grid users and resources based on their interactions with each other. For example, let's first define the following functions, where *VOId* is the set of VO identities, *User* is the set of all users, *Res* is the set of all resources and *Org* is the set of organizations:

usersVO: VOId $\rightarrow \wp$(User)

resVO: VOId $\times$ Org $\rightarrow \wp$(Res)

where *usersVO* expresses the set of users that a VO has and *resVO* the set of resources that an organization provides for a VO. Furthermore, let's assume that

sla: VOUser$\times$Res$\times$VOId $\rightarrow$ R

policy: VOUser$\times$Res$\times$VOId$\rightarrow \wp$(Action)

represents the expected quality of a resource (as formalized by an SLA) accorded between a VO user and the resource provider within a particular VO, and the normal behavior of the user (as formalized by a usage policy) again accorded with a resource provider within a VO and expressing the set of actions that user can perform on the resource.

A trusted monitoring service could then be used to capture interactions between resources and their users and based on these interactions, generate events as follows:

$$Event_{QoS} = VOUser \times Res \times VOId \times R$$

$$Event_{Usage} = Res \times VOUser \times VOId \times Action$$

where $Event_{QoS}$ reports the real qualitative value, R, generated by consuming a resource by its user within a VO and $Event_{Usage}$ reports a prohibited action performed by a user on a resource within a VO.

Based on the above functions and events, one could then define a couple of utility functions expressing the satisfaction of users and resources as follows:

$$\forall (u, r, id, v) \in Event_{QoS} : utility_{QoS}(u, r, id, v)$$
$$= \begin{cases} 1 & if \ v \geq sla(u, r, id) \\ v \ / \ SLA(U, r, id) & if \ v < sla(u, r, id) \end{cases}$$

$$\forall (r, u, vo, a) \in Event_{Usage} : utility_{Usage}(r, u, vo, a)$$
$$= \begin{cases} 1 & if \ a \in policy(u, r, vo) \\ penalty(u, r, vo, a) & if \ (a \notin policy \ u, r, vo) \end{cases}$$

where $utility_{QoS}$ expresses the QoS satisfaction of users from consuming a resource and $utility_{Usage}$ expresses the satisfaction of a resource from its interaction with a user. The *penalty: VOUser $\times$ Res $\times$ VOId $\times$ Action $\rightarrow$ [0,1)* function computes the penalty each prohibited action by the user incurs, which is a value between 0 and less than 1.

The model of Arenas et al. (2008), discussed in the next section, uses these utility functions to define a set of reputation functions for both the VO users and the VO resources, such that the reputation values are parameterized by the scope within which they occur.

A Reputation Management System for Grids

Based on the above model of utility-based reputation, a reputation management was proposed in (Arenas et al., 2008) and was implemented as a Globus service within the EU FP6 project GridTrust (www.gridtrust.eu). Figure 11 illustrates simplified system interfaces with other typical VO management services that may be running in any VO. These include a VO Manager (VOM) for managing issues such as VO membership and VO policies, a Reputation-aware Resource Broker (RRB) and a Resource Usage Control and Monitoring service (RUCM).

The Reputation Management (RM) system accepts requests from the VOM for setting-up and terminating VOs through the following interfaces it offers to the VOM:

setVO(VO ID, Resource ID List, User ID List)

endVO(VO ID)

where *VO ID* is the identity of the VO being set-up or terminated, *Resource ID List* is the list of resources of the VO, and *User ID List* is the list of users in the VO. The RRB service is used during the setting-up of new VOs by the VOM. During this phase, the RRB may request from the RM service the reputation of a resource in a particular VO or in the general VBE before proposing it to the VOM. This is achieved through the following RM interface:

Resource ID, Reputation Value: getResourceRep(Resource ID, VO ID)

where the returned values include the ID for the resource whose reputation is being requested and the value of that reputation. In case the *VO ID* is assigned a *NULL* value, the returned reputation will be the resource's reputation in the general VBE.

The RUCM service is a service that monitors requests and replies sent to and from a resource in

Figure 11. A Reputation Management System for VOs (Adapted from Arenas et al. (2008), p. 5)

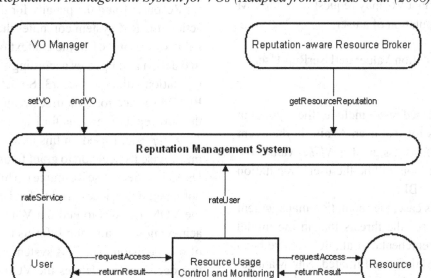

its interaction with a VO user. The RUCM service can detect any undesirable behavior by the user in its usage of the resource being protected by that instance of the RUCM service. This is represented as *prohibited actions* such as the excessive storage of data on resources beyond the user's quota and the attempt to read or write unauthorized data. Such prohibited actions are reported through the following RM interface:

reportUser(Resource ID, User ID, VO ID, Action)

The invocation of this interface will cause with RM system to update the *User_rep_eic*, *User_rep_ei*, *User_rep_e* and *User_rep* discussed earlier in the section on the utility-based reputation model. The RM system can also accept ratings by VO users of QoS levels they have experienced in their interactions with VO resources. This is done through the following interface:

rateResource(User ID, Resource ID, VO ID, QoS Value)

which will cause the system to update the reputation values for resource, i.e. *Res_rep_eic*, *Res_rep_ei*, *Res_rep_e* and *Res_rep*. Finally, any of the entities in a VO may request from the RM service the reputation of a user:

User ID, Reputation Value: getUserRep(User ID, VO ID)

where the returned result includes the reputation and ID values for that user. Again, in the event that the *VO ID* is assigned a *NULL* value, the returned reputation will be the user's reputation in the general VBE.

Also in this case, the reputation management system addresses the threats that in the model defined by (Demchenko et al., 2005) have been classified as Malefactor Initiated, Site Management and End Service attacks. Indeed, this support

prevents the Grid services to be used by VO users with a low reputation.

Usage Scenario

In this section, we demonstrate the applicability of the utility-based reputation management system of the previous section through an example of a usage scenario as depicted in Figure 12. In this scenario, we assume that the RRB starts by querying the RM system for the reputation of a couple of resources, Resource1 and Resource2, as part of the process conducted by the VOM of joining these resources to a new VO. If their reputation is satisfactory, the VOM signals to the RM system the setting up of the new VO and informs the latter of the two resources. It also informs the RM of the set of users who will be using the resources, which in this case we assume to be three, User1, User2 and User3. Once this setting-up of the VO is acknowledged by the RM system, the VO becomes operational and the users can avail of the resources offered.

During the operational phase of the VO, at some stage the RCUM service running locally at Resource1 captures a prohibited action performed by User3. It reports this action directly to the RM system. Based on the utility function for Resource1 and the penalty for the prohibited action, the RM system computes the satisfaction value of Resource1 in the context of the prohibited action and updates accordingly the different reputation values for User3. Sometime later the RCUM service for Resource1 requests to obtain the new reputation value for User3, for example, *User_rep_eic*. Based on this new value, RCUM may revise its decision to grant future accesses to User3 in order to use Resource1. This may or may not change the access rights for User3. Finally, the VOM decides to end the VO (as a result of achieving its goals) and informs the RM system of this decision. The RM system acknowledges this decision and deletes the VO entry from its database.

Figure 12. A Usage Scenario of the Reputation Management System (Adapted from Arenas et al. (2008), p. 6)

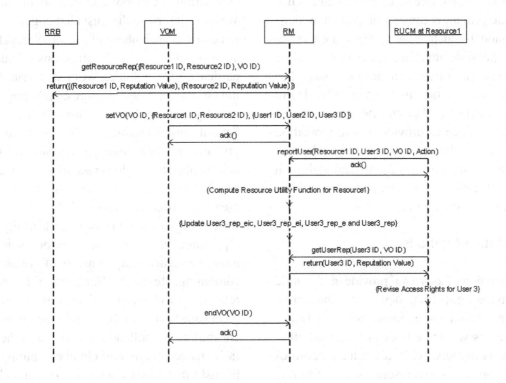

FUTURE RESEARCH DIRECTIONS

There are several areas of research that Grid trust management can be directed towards. The following sections outline some of these areas.

Comparison of Different Approaches

The different models and architectures we discussed in this chapter offer a variety of solutions to the problem of trust management in Grid systems. A comparison of the benefits and drawbacks of these solutions as well as the cost of adopting them would be one future area of research that could benefit the Grid community. There are several factors on which such a comparison could be based, which include usability entry level, cost of solution and its expressivity and maturity.

New Grid-Related Paradigms

Due to the vast technological advances in computing systems and the necessity of adapting to dynamic business demands, new distributed computing paradigms have started emerging that require Grid computing to redefine and position itself in relation to these. Of the most popular of such current paradigms is Cloud computing (Boss et al., 2007; Jones, 2008). Cloud computing, stemming from virtualization techniques as well as utility and Grid computing, poses new trust and security management challenges due to the attractive simplicity of the model underlying it. A future research direction would be to investigate how the experience obtained from current trust management solutions could be applied to Cloud computing.

Threat Models for Trust Management

Another area for future research related to Grid trust management is constructing threat models. Threat models, such as threat trees, are used to uncover possible attacking routes that could be used by malicious users to attack the system. For example, one such famous threat in P2P and Grid systems is called *collusion*, where a number of resources collude to provide a fake reputation value for some other resource. Sabotage tolerance techniques (Sarmenta, 2002) can deal with such model of threats; however, other threats could be investigated in the future.

Quantitative Methods

Quantitative methods can provide a dynamic aspect to the definition of new trust management models and architectures, in which trust and reputation values would be traded-off against other quantitative aspects such as usage fees or costs of running applications on resources. For example, in such a cost-sensitive reputation model, the general welfare of users and resources in a VO can be measured not only based on the reputation of resources and users, but also with respect to the cost of using resources and the wealth of users. Highly reputable resources could be offered by their providers for usage in VOs for a high fee. Less wealthy users could then be eliminated from buying computational power on such highly reputable resources.

CONCLUSION

In the collaborative distributed computing environment of grids the management of trust is essential in order to allow the sharing of resources in a way that meets the security requirements of all those involved. In this chapter, we have presented an overview of some of the current models, metrics, architectures and implementations for trust management in Grid computing. The structure of a Virtual Organization (VO) has been used as an abstraction of collaborative activity on the Grid. We have described the trust challenges that need to be met at each phase of the VO lifecycle, and analyzed the security implications of adopting particular VO topologies. We then described existing Grid security architectures, including OGSA security, and implementations such as the Grid Security Infrastructure and the European EGEE grid security architecture. Trust management needs to be applied to whichever security architecture is adopted. Two alternative methods of trust management have been considered in detail: role-based trust management with weights, and utility-based reputation. There is no consensus on a solution to meet the security requirements of collaborative computing. Research efforts are still needed to relate trust mechanisms with security requirements on the one hand, and the organizational and legal constraints on collaboration on the other. The fashionable paradigm of cloud computing limits the risks that arise from sharing resources in grid computing, but it also has security requirements which will require trust management for collaborative work. Trust management is integral not only in these areas, but it will also be an essential part of further research into threat analyses for Grids, the analysis of coordinated attacks in Grids, and quantitative approaches to security in open systems such as Grids.

ACKNOWLEDGMENT

This work is partially funded under the IST program of the EU Commission by the project GRIDTrust, Trust and Security for Next Generation Grids, contract No. 033827, http://www.gridtrust.eu.

REFERENCES

Abdul-Rahman, A., & Hailes, S. (2000). Supporting Trust in Virtual Communities. In *Proceedings of the Thirty-third Hawaii International Conference on System Sciences – Volume 6* (pp. 6007). Washington, DC: IEEE Computer Society.

Alfieri, R., Cecchini, R., Ciaschini, V., dell'Agnello, L., Frohner, Á., Gianoli, A., et al. (2003). VOMS, an Authorization System for Virtual Organizations. In *Proceedings of the Grid Computing, First European Across Grids Conference* (LNCS 2970, pp. 33-40). Berlin, Germany: Springer.

Arenas, A., Aziz, B., & Silaghi, G. C. (2008). Reputation Management in Grid-based Virtual Organisations. In *Proceedings of the Third International Conference on Security and Cryptography (SECRYPT 2008)*. INSTICC.

Banks, T. (2006). *Web Services Resource Framework (WSRF) – Primer v1.2. OASIS Committee Draft 02 - 23 May 2006*. Retrieved March 30, 2009, from http://docs.oasis-open.org/wsrf/wsrf-primer-1.2-primer-cd-02.pdf

Blaze, M., Feigenbaum, J., & Lacy, J. (1996). Decentralized Trust Management. In *Proceedings of the 17th Symposium on Security and Privacy* (pp. 164-173). Washington, DC: IEEE Computer Society.

Boss, G., Malladi, P., Quan, D., Legregni, L., & Hall, H. (2007). *Cloud Computing* (IBM HiPODS Report). Armonk, NY: IBM.

Burn, M., Marshall, P., & Wild, M. (1999). Managing Changes in the Virtual Organisation. In *Proceedings of the Seventh European Conference on Information Systems* (pp. 40-54).

Camarihna-Matos, L. M., & Afsarmanesh, H. (2003). Elements of a VE Infrastructure. *Journal of Computers in Industry*, *51*(2), 139–163. doi:10.1016/S0166-3615(03)00033-2

Chadwick, D. W., & Otenko, A. (2002). The PERMIS X.509 role based privilege management infrastructure. In *Proceedings of the Seventh ACM Symposium on Access Control Models and Technologies (SACMAT 2002)* (pp. 135-140). New York: ACM Press.

Chang, B. E., Crary, K., DeLap, M., Harper, R., Liszka, J., Murphy, T., & Pfenning, F. (2002). Trustless Grid Computing in ConCert. In *Proceedings of the Third International Workshop on Grid Computing* (LNCS 2536, pp. 112-125). Berlin, Germany: Springer.

Christensen, E., Curbera, F., Meredith, G., & Weerawarana, S. (2001). *Web Services Description Language (WSDL) 1.1*. Retrieved March 30, 2009, from http://www.w3.org/TR/wsdl

Colombo, M., Martinelli, F., Mori, P., Petrocchi, M., & Vaccarelli, A. (2007b). Fine Grained Access Control with Trust and Reputation Management for Globus. In *Proceedings of the OTM International Conferences* (LNCS 4804, pp. 1050-1515). Berin, Germany: Springer.

Colombo, M., Martinelli, F., Mori, P., & Vaccarelli, A. (2007a). Extending the Globus Architecture with Role-based Trust Management. In *Proceedings of the 11th International conference on Computer Aided Systems Theory (Eurocast'07)* (LNCS 4739, pp. 448-456). Berlin, Germany: Springer.

Demchenko, Y., Gommans, L., de Laat, C., & Oudenaarde, B. (2005). Web services and Grid Security Vulnerabilities and Threat Analysis and Model. In *Proc. of the 6th IEEE/ACM Intl. Workshop on Grid Computing* (pp. 262-267). Washington, DC: IEEE.

Dierks, T., & Allen, C. (1999). *RFC 2246 - The TLS Protocol (version 1.0)*.

Dimitrakos, T. (2001). System Models, e-Risk and e-Trust. In *Proceedings of the First IFIP Conference on E-Commerce, E-Business, E-Government: Towards The E-Society: E-Commerce, E-Business, and E-Government (I3E 2001)* (pp. 45-58). Amsterdam: Kluwer.

EGEE. (2004). The Global Security Architecture: For Web and Legacy Services. In *EU Deliverable DJRA3.1*.

Fitzgerald, S., Foster, I., Kesselman, C., von Laszewski, G., Smith, W., & Tuecke, S. (1997). A Directory Service for Configuring High-Performance Distributed Computations. In *Proceedings of the Sixth IEEE Symposium on High-Performance Distributed Computing (HPDC 1997)* (pp. 365-375). Washington, DC: IEEE Computer Society.

Foster, I. (2005). Globus Toolkit version 4: Software for Service Oriented Systems. In *Proceedings of the IFIP International Conference on Network and Parallel Computing* (LNCS 3779, pp. 2-13). Berlin, Germany: Springer.

Foster, I., & Kesselman, C. (2003). *The Grid: Blue Print for a New Computing Infrastructure.* San Francisco, CA: Morgan Kaufmann Publishers.

Foster, I., Kesselman, C., & Tuecke, S. (2001). The Anatomy of the Grid: Enabling Scalable Virtual Organizations. *The International Journal of Supercomputer Applications, 15*(3), 1–4.

Foster, I., Kishimoto, H., Savva, A., Berry, D., Djaoui, A., Grimshaw, A., et al. (2006). *The Open Grid Service Architecture (OGSA), Version 1.5. Open Grid Forum Document Series: GFD-I.080.* Retrieved March 30, 2009, from http://www.ogf.org/documents/GFD.80.pdf

Globus Security Team. (2005). *Globus Toolkit Version 4 Grid Security Infrastructure: A Standards Perspective.*

Grandison, T., & Sloman, M. (2000). A Survey of Trust in Internet Applications. *IEEE Communications Surveys and Tutorials, 3*(4), 2–16. doi:10.1109/COMST.2000.5340804

Hermoso, R., Billhardt, H., & Ossowski, S. (2006). Integrating Trust in Virtual Organisations. In *Proceedings of the AAMAS06 Workshop on Coordination, Organization, Institutions and Norms in Agent Systems (COIN 2006)* (LNCS 4386, pp. 19-31). Berlin, Germany: Springer.

Housley, R., Ford, W., Polk, W., & Solo, D. (1999). *RFC 2459 – Internet X.509 Public Key Infrastructure Certificate.*

Jiancheng, N., Zhishu, L., Zhonghe, G., & Jirong, S. (2007). Threat Analysis and Prevention for Grid and Web Service Security. In *Proceedings of the Software Engineering, Artificial Intelligence, Networking, and Parallel/Distributed Computing (SNPD 2007)* (pp. 526-531).

Jones, B. (2008). *Comparative Study: Grids and Clouds, Evolution or Revolution?* (EGEE Document number 925013). EGEE.

Jøsang, A., Ismail, R., & Boyd, C. (2007). A Survey of Trust and Reputation Systems for Online Service Provision. *Decision Support Systems, 43*(2), 618–644. doi:10.1016/j.dss.2005.05.019

Kamvar, S. D., Schlosser, M. T., & Garcia-Molina, H. (2003). The Eigentrust Algorithm for Reputation Management in P2P Networks. In *Proceedings of the Twelfth International Conference on World Wide Web (WWW '03)* (pp. 640-651). New York: ACM Press.

Kang, M. H., Park, J. S., & Froscher, J. N. (2001). Access Control Mechanisms for Inter-organisational Workflow. In *Proceedings of the Sixth ACM Symposium on Access Control Models and Technologies* (pp. 66-74). New York: ACM Press.

Katzy, B. R., Zhang, C., & Löh, H. (2000). Reference Models for Virtual Organizations. In L. Camarinha-Matos, H. Afsarmanesh, C. Zhang, V. Stich, I. Karvonen, B. Katzy, & A. Pawlak (Eds.), *Virtual Organizations: Systems and Practices* (pp. 45-58). Berlin, Germany: Springer.

Kerschbaum, F., Haller, J., Karabulut, Y., & Robinson, P. (2006). Pathtrust: A Trust-based Reputation Service for Virtual Organization Formation. In Proceedings of the *Fourth International Conference on Trust Management (iTrust2006)* (LNCS 3986, pp. 193-205). Berlin, Germany: Springer.

Li, N., Mitchell, J. C., & Winsborough, W. H. (2002). Design of a Role-based Trust Management Framework. In *Proceedings of the Symposium on Security and Privacy* (pp. 114-130). Washington, DC: IEEE Computer Society.

Lin, C., Varadharajan, V., Wang, Y., & Pruthi, V. (2004). Enhancing Grid Security with Trust Management. In *Proceedings of the IEEE Intl. Conference on Services Computing* (pp. 303-310).

Madsen, P., & Maler, E. (2005). *SAML V2.0 Executive Overview* (OASIS SSTC Committee Draft).

Martinelli, F., & Petrocchi, M. (2007). On relating and integrating two trust management frameworks. In *Proceedings of the Second International Workshop on Views on Designing Complex Architecturs (VODCA'06)* (pp. 191-205). ENTCS 168.

Nagaratnam, N., Janson, P., Dayka, J., Nadalin, A., Siebenlist, F., Welch, V., et al. (2002). *Security Architecture for Open Grid Services*. Retrieved November 11, 2008, from http://www.cs.virginia.edu/~humphrey/ogsa-sec-wg/OGSA-SecArch-v1-07192002.pdf

Navqi, S., & Riguidel, M. (2005). Threat Model for Grid Security Services. In *Proceedings of the Advances in Grid Computing (EGC 2005)* (LNCS 3470, pp. 1048-1055). Berlin, Germany: Springer.

Necula, G. C. (1997). Proof-Carrying Code. In *Proceedings of the Twenty-fourth ACM SIGPLAN-SIGACT Symposium on Principles of Programming Languages (POPL 1997)* (pp. 106-119). New York: ACM Press.

Park, J., & Sandhu, R. (2004). The UCON Usage Control Model. *ACM Transactions on Information and System Security*, 7(1), 128–174. doi:10.1145/984334.984339

Pearlman, L., Welch, V., Foster, I., Kesselman, C., & Tuecke., S. (2002). A Community Authorization Service for Group Collaboration. In *Proceedings of the Third International Workshop on Policies for Distributed Systems and Networks (POLICY 2002)* (pp. 50-59). Washington, DC: IEEE Computer Society.

Sarmenta, L. F. G. (2002). Sabotage-tolerance mechanisms for volunteer computing systems. *Future Generation Computer Systems*, 18(4), 561–572. doi:10.1016/S0167-739X(01)00077-2

Siebenlist, F., Nagaratnam, N., Welch, V., & Neuman, C. (2003). Security for Virtual Organizations: Federating Trust and Policy Domains. In I. Foster & C. Kesselman (Eds.), *The Grid: Blue Print for a New Computing Infrastructure*. San Francisco, CA: Morgan Kaufmann Publishers.

Silaghi, G. C., Arenas, A., & Silva, L. (2007). *Reputation-based Trust Management Systems and their Applicability to Grids* (Technical Report TR-0064). Institutes on Knowledge and Data Management and System Architecture, CoreGrid – Network of Excellence.

Strader, T. J., Lin, F., & Shaw, M. J. (1998). Information Structure for Electronic Virtual Organization Management. *Decision Support Systems*, 23, 75–94. doi:10.1016/S0167-9236(98)00037-2

Vijayakumar, V., & Wahida Banu, R. S. D. (2008). Security for Resource Selection in Grid Computing Based On Trust and Reputation Responsiveness. *International Journal of Computer Science and Network Security, 8*(11), 107–115.

von Laszewski, G., Alunkal, B. E., & Veljkovic, I. (2005). Towards Reputable Grids. *Scalable Computing: Practice and Experience, 6*(3), 95–106.

Welch, V., Siebenlist, F., Foster, I., Bresnahan, J., Czajkowski, K., Gawor, J., et al. (2003). Security for Grid Services. In *Proceedings of the Twelfth IEEE International Symposium on High Performance Distributed Computing* (pp. 48-57). Washington, DC: IEEE Computer Society Press.

Wesner, S., Shubert, L., & Dimitrakos, Th. (2006). Dynamic Virtual Organizations in Engineering. In R. Dienstbier (Ed.), *Proceedings of the Computational Science and High Performance Computing II: The 2nd Russian-German Advanced Research Workshop* (pp. 289-302). Berlin, Germany: Springer.

Winsborough, W. H., & Mitchell, J. C. (2003). Distributed Credential Chain Discovery in Trust Management. *Journal of Computer Security, 11*(1), 36–86.

Chapter 8
Formalizing and Managing Activity–Aware Trust in Collaborative Environments

Ioanna Dionysiou
University of Nicosia, Cyprus

David E. Bakken
Washington State University, USA

ABSTRACT

Trust is an abstraction of individual beliefs that an entity has for specific situations and interactions. An entity's beliefs are not static but they change as time progresses and new information is processed into knowledge. Trust must evolve in a consistent manner so that it still abstracts the entity's beliefs accurately. In this way, an entity continuously makes informed decisions based on its current beliefs. This chapter presents and discusses a conceptual trust framework that models an entity's trust as a relation whose state gets updated as relevant conditions that affect trust change. The model allows entities to reason about the specification and adaptation of trust that is placed in an entity. An intuitive and practical approach is proposed to manage end-to-end trust assessment for a particular activity, where multiple trust relationships are examined in a bottom-up evaluation manner to derive the overall trust for the activity.

INTRODUCTION

Distributed computing has evolved greatly in the last decade or so. Interactions between entities used to be mainly client-server or remote access. Recent years have seen a great increase in the kind and number of entities interacting, the patterns in which they interact, and the kinds of distributed services supporting these interactions. This ubiq-

uitous use of distributed applications provides increased convenience, safety, and enjoyment for society. However, such applications and their users are vulnerable with respect to both the diversity of the principals providing these services and the interactions between them.

Consider the North American electric power grid, for instance, with nearly 3500 utility organizations (Force, 2004). These individually owned utility systems have been connected together to form interconnected power grids, which must be operated

DOI: 10.4018/978-1-61520-682-7.ch008

in a coordinated manner. There are many points of interactions among a variety of participants and a local change can have immediate impact everywhere. In order to detect disturbances that could escalate into cascading outages and take corrective actions, real-time information about the grid dynamics must be obtained to enhance the wide-area system observability, efficiency, and reliability. Unfortunately, as of today, power utilities are reluctant to disclose information in order to protect themselves financially and legally. Sharing of data might jeopardize their business due to their inability to quantify the risk regarding interactions with other grid participants. For example, unrestricted access to a utility's data that are market-sensitive indicators could give a competitor an unfair advantage in adjusting its own contracts and prices. Similarly, a utility could distribute inaccurate data to mislead the other market participants. The *"no sharing"* policy could be relaxed under normal operating conditions if the risk of sharing were systematically contained by giving the participants the means to assess how trustworthy or not their potential and current collaborators are (Dionysiou et al., 2007).

Trust is a multifaceted concept, encompassing even more than message integrity, source authentication and reliance on other entities. While trust evaluation is an integral part of decision-making in collaborative models, there is no single correct way to determine the right level of trust, or which aspects to include. Decisions about how to weigh each facet lie with the evaluator and can differ substantially from situation to situation. This chapter presents and discusses a conceptual flexible trust framework that models an entity's trust as a relation whose state gets updated as relevant conditions that affect trust change. The model allows entities to reason about the specification and adaptation of trust that is placed in an entity and the trust assessment of data that comes through nontrivial chains of processing. This chapter will discuss the motivation behind the new trust model, its design and its theoretical

applicability in real-world scenarios; to be more specific the discussion will evolve around the following topics:

- An analysis of the emerging need to address the dynamic and composable features of trust in open environments, especially in interactions which span multiple entities residing in different administrative domains
- A set of requirements that must be met by any trust management system (TMS) in order to provide dynamic and composable trust in collaborative environments
- A trust model that implements the above requirements to establish and manage trust relationships that correspond to a particular interaction, including:
  ○ A notation for specifying trust relationships that are tied not only to a narrow context but to a broader activity
  ○ An intuitive and practical approach that manages end-to-end trust assessment for a particular activity, where multiple trust relationships are systematically synthesized in a bottom-up evaluation manner
  ○ Extending the traditional concept of trust conditions into more expressive expectations that accommodate trust monitoring, where the expectation semantics incorporate not only expected values for particular trust requirements but also covering, aggregating, and triggering parameters that manipulate observed values.

The remainder of the chapter is organized as follows. Section 2 discusses related work on trust modeling and trust management. Section 3 demonstrates the need for trust expressiveness in collaborative applications. Section 4 discusses trust among collaborators for a specific activity and a set of requirements to manage these trust relationships. Section 5 presents a conceptual trust model that addresses those requirements, with an emphasis on the trust ontology involved in deriving end-to-end trust assessments. The trust model applicability in a real-life situation is demonstrated in Section 6. Open research problems and future directions are discussed in Section 7 and Section 8 concludes.

BACKGROUND

In recent years, researchers have investigated various definitions of trust, modeling trust and its management (Vacca, 2004; Herzberg et al., 2000; TCG, 2004; Blaze et al., 1996; Chu et al., 1997; Blaze et al., 1998; Yan & Holtmanns, 2007; Grandison, 2007). Perhaps, one of the most popular and widely known trust models is the Pretty Good Privacy (PGP) trust model that focuses solely on authentication (Zimmermann, 1995). PGP creates an informal web of trust that is used for authentication purposes. The intention was to be a cryptographic tool for the masses, which bypasses the traditional hierarchical trust architecture by adopting the *web of trust* approach. There is a plethora of other trust models that describe more general trust factors. For example, the Marsh logic-based framework (Marsh, 1994) uses formal representation to capture the semantics of the social paradigms of trust. Josang's subjective logic (Josang, 1997; Josang et al., 2006) is another formal model that uses beliefs as the basis for trust. Agent-based models, such as Rahman and Hailes distributed trust model (Abdul-Rahman & Hailes, 2000) have recommendations as their central trust factor.

Contemporary trust management solutions also exist. PolicyMaker (Blaze et al., 1996), a trust management system developed at AT&T Research Laboratories, integrates the specifcation of policy with the binding of public keys to the actions that are trusted to perform. PolicyMaker combines authentication and authorization into a single system by using certifcates to authorize their legitimate owner to perform specifc actions. KeyNote (Blaze et al., 1998), the successor to PolicyMaker, was developed to improve on the weaknesses of PolicyMaker. It is based on the same design paradigms of assertions and queries with a couple of slight modifcations. REFEREE (Chu et al., 1997) is a trust management system for reaching access decisions that are related to Web documents. REFEREE provides resource access trust and service provision trust. It uses PICS labels in the same theoretical framework as PolicyMaker to interpret trust policies. It allows both policies and credentials to return answers (which is a tri-value) and statement lists. A statement list is a collection of assertions, which is the justifcation for the answer. A solution to the management of more general trust relationships is proposed by SULTAN (Grandison, 2001). SULTAN, a trust management model that uses a logic-oriented language to specify trust, is designed to facilitate the management of trust relationships using a collection of specifcation, analysis, and management tools.

A survey of contemporary trust management systems compiled by Grandison and Sloman (Grandison & Sloman, 2000) discusses the limitations of the contemporary trust management system as they mostly address access control issues rather than the more general analysis of trust. In addition, current trust models (Grandison, 2007), still focus primarily on trust establishment and reasoning while trust monitoring receives little attention. What is needed is a comprehensive trust model that will incorporate those constructs that will allow modeling of trust in a way that trust establishment, reasoning, and monitoring are all supported. As of today, there is no model or system that addresses explicitly in its semantics activity-aware trust reasoning and monitoring.

Furthermore, regardless of model or management system, there are a number of open problems dealing with the general concept of trust (Presti et al., 2003). One of the fundamental issues is the definition of the mathematical properties of trust as it is not clear what kind of properties trust has. For example, is trust a deductive or inductive property of systems? Analyzing behavior and intentions as well as assessing recommendations and feedback are also nontrivial trust issues. Initial trust formation is also an open research issue (Ryotov et al., 2007).

Trust Issues in Critical Infrastructures

The protection of critical infrastructures is an essential element of ensuring a nation's security (PCII, 2006). In order to do that, private, public, and national entities must collaborate in a way that sensitive information is shared without compromising it. This collaborative environment is very difficult to establish and operate because its participants do not have the necessary knowledge and tools to assess the quality of the received data and the risk of compromising that data.

Trust management is a service that, when used properly, has the potential to enable the entities that operate within critical infrastructures to share confidential, proprietary, and business sensitive information with reliable partners. In order to illustrate trust challenges related to the dissemination of data, two power grid application suites are considered (Figure 1). The application domain setting involves *M* utility organizations that generate data and *N* end users that receive computation results on that data. Both applications span a number of regional utility districts with different administrative policies and ownership. The *Phasor Measurement Unit (PMU) Aggregation* application involves the dissemination and aggregation of PMU data, and the *Alert Correlation* application provides (probabilistic and imperfect) early warning of an impending power crisis.

The first application suite deals with a type of real-time electric power data, which is PMU data. PMUs are instruments that take measure-

ments of voltages and currents and time-stamp these measurements with high precision. These measurements are collected and aggregated at a central place in order to derive system state estimations. These estimations are disseminated to interested end users U_j, including entities that monitor or control the grid.

A collaborative environment like the above gives rise to new challenges involving the data quality of the aggregated state estimation. Suppose that the aggregated function $f(d_1, d_2, \cdots, d_M)$ takes as inputs PMU data d_i from utility *Utility*$_i$ and outputs state estimations. An accurate state of the power grid is based on the quality of the received d_i. Accidental or malicious faults observed at *Utility*$_i$'s sensors may affect its ability to generate correct data d_i. Assume that a faulty sensor at *Utility*$_2$ produces inconsistent PMU measurements. Including these d_2 readings in f gives an inaccurate view of the current state of the power grid. Users $U_1, \cdots, U_i$ are not able to detect the source of the inaccurate readings since they only receive the aggregated result. However, suppose that users U_2, U_3, and *PMU Aggregation* entities establish a *network of trust* that allows them to exchange evidence with each other regarding the behavioral trends of the utilities. Inconsistencies could be reported by U_2, U_3. These two users, unlike the other users that do not participate in the exchange of information, will be informed about the potential faulty operation of the sensor and could act accordingly.

However, a data provider that produces correct data does not necessarily imply that the received data is also correct. An unreliable data communication medium may also tamper with the transferred data, which will result in producing inaccurate state estimations. In order to manage the risk of producing inaccurate state estimations, the entity that performs PMU aggregation must make trust assessments of all interacting entities that collaboratively execute the task of generating and delivering PMU data. *Composable* trust mechanisms must be in place to assess in a sys-

Figure 1. Power grid applications

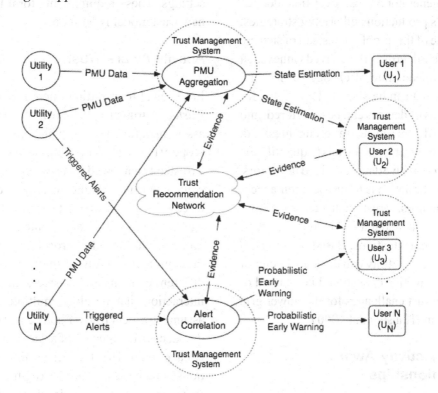

tematic manner the trust placed in a data that is derived through a chain of entities.

The second application family involves better sharing of current information beyond the scope of a single electric utility in order to help increase robustness of the power grid. Today there are two fundamental challenges in sharing more operational information between electric utilities. Better communication for the power grid can provide mechanisms to help alleviate these two problems that are explained shortly. However, these mechanisms must be controllable by trust management systems or the greater communications and sharing flexibility can make the problems worse, not better.

The first challenge is that when problems start happening in one part of the power grid, many alerts can fire in a short period of time, and utilities can get buried in the (largely redundant) barrage of such alerts. Alert correlation allows for transformations of a series of lower-level alerts into

higher-level alerts which have a much lower false alarm rate and much richer semantics, and are thus a much more useful indicator of potential problems. Such transformations should be based on taxonomies of power grid devices, and be policy-programmable, since different configurations of a given device will have different thresholds for operational reasons. However, alert correlation must be complemented by similar data quality assessment techniques as the one described in the earlier example since incorrect data may suggest a catastrophic situation that does not occur. For example, $Utility_2$'s faulty sensor incorrectly triggers alerts about device failures. In this case, user U_N will be flooded with faulty alarms whereas user U_2 will be more cautious because it has already been made aware about $Utility_2$ problems with faulty sensors.

The second challenge is that many data are market sensitive, meaning if a competitor has the reading of some key data (for example, the output of a utility's generators) it can over time deduce the company's production and pricing strategies. As an example of this problem, instead of sharing market sensitive data directly, derived values such as the instantaneous rate of change (or moving averages thereof) can be shared. Thresholds for particular kinds of devices can be monitored, and alerts generated if they exceed a certain threshold. Since there are currently no means to quantify the risk of sharing sensitive data or derived indicators, the next best alternative is to restrict their access to non-competitors. Trust management allows utilities to reason about the behavior of their peers for different situations. Based on observed behavioral trends, a utility can decide whether or not access to sensitive data should be granted or denied. More trust challenges for the power grid can be found in (Hauser et al., 2007).

Managing Activity-Aware Trust Relationships

Creating a universally acceptable set of rules and mechanisms to specify and manage trust is a difficult process because of the variety in trust interpretations. Researchers have defined trust concepts for many perspectives, with the result that trust definitions overlap or contradict each other (Presti et al., 2003). Nevertheless, trust is an abstraction of individual beliefs that an entity has for specific situations and interactions. An entity's beliefs are not static but they change as time progresses and new information is processed into knowledge. Trust must evolve in a consistent manner so that it still abstracts the entity's beliefs accurately. In this way, an entity continuously makes informed decisions based on its current beliefs.

This section focuses on the specification of activity-aware trust in a collaborative environment. It proceeds with revisiting the four activities of trust management by listing a set of requirements that a system must address in order to be able to capture the trust needs in dynamic collaborative

settings. These requirements form the basis the new trust model is built on.

Activity-Aware Trust

In a typical trust setting, there is a *trustor* and a *trustee*. A trustor is the entity that makes a trust assessment for an entity, which is the trustee. The scope of the trust relationship between a trustor and a trustee is narrowed to a specific action called a *context*. A trust relationship may be one-to-many to cover a group of trustees, which are trusted similarly within the same context (Grandison & Sloman, 2000). Such approach cannot encompass the complexity of trust in an *activity* that involves different contexts and trustees. An activity is an interaction that involves multiple trustees that assume different roles (Figure 2); in other words, the successful outcome of an activity requires the collaboration of trustees performing specific functions, which are not necessarily the same.

Consider Figure 3. In this setting, a data stream for data d is established between entity P and entity C. It could appear that entity C may assess the risk of using data d by making a trust assessment regarding entity P's ability to produce reliable data d. However, this is not sufficient. The presence of intermediate entities S_1 and S_2 that forward this data to C affect the quality of received data d. As a result, trustor C has to make trust assessments for all interacting trustees that collaboratively execute the task and combine them in order to derive an end-to-end trust assessment about the data stream. Thus, if C were to make a trust assessment concerning the *activity of the information flow between P and itself*, then the following relationships had to be examined:

- relationship $\tau(C, P, ...)$[1] between C and P regarding P's ability to *produce* data d
- relationship $\tau(C, S_1, ...)$ between C and S_1 regarding S_1's ability to *forward* data d
- relationship $\tau(C, S_2, ...)$ between C and S_2 regarding S_2's ability to *forward* data d

Figure 2. Context-aware activity

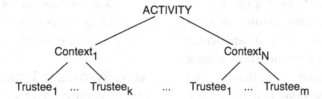

Activity-aware trust is based on the composition property of trust. All three trust relationships have to be composed to derive the end-to-end trust evaluation for data stream d. The complexity of trust composition is apparent in parameterized trust relationships, where multiple trust attributes must be synthesized in a systematic manner. Activity-aware trust also exhibits its dynamic feature. If the information flow path that delivers data d were to be replaced with another one, then C had to make new trust assessments involving the newly introduced entities that are involved in the data delivery.

Activity-Aware Trust Management System Objectives

According to (Dionysiou, 2006), there is one comprehensive conceptual framework that covers the semantics of end-to-end trust for activities in which multiple entities collaborate towards a common goal. In order to manage trust in activity-oriented collaborative environments, a trust management system (TMS) framework must be architected to meet the characteristics of these interactions: dynamic trust that deals with the evolving relationships between participants and composable trust that handles the collaboration of multiple participants for joint operations. Therefore, an activity-oriented TMS should address the following objectives:

- **Dynamic trust**: The TMS must allow changes to trust relationships during the operational lifetime of the system in such a way that they reflect the actual interactions between participants. The interactions within collaborative settings are dynamic for a number of reasons. First, new alliances between participants are formed

Figure 3. Trust relationships in an activity

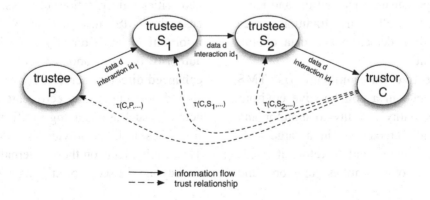

or existing ones are dissolved, and second, the dynamics of existing operational agreements change due to diverse policies, change of leadership, and experience. The underlying trust relationships among the participants should reflect the dynamic nature of the interactions that span these different administration domains. In order to support dynamic trust, the trust assessment for a given entity must be revised and updated based on experience and other information (from both itself and others) that becomes available only after the initial relationship is specified.

- **Composable Trust:** Activity-aware trust is based on the collaboration between multiple entities that cooperate to carry out the task of disseminating information from its source to its intended destination. Obtaining a comprehensive assessment of trust for such interactions requires a trustor to reason about trust not only for the information destination and source, but also for the intermediary entities that act as forwarding servers. In order to support composable trust, a number of pairwise relationships must be identified and synthesized in a systematic way that allows an entity to assess trust for end-to-end interactions.
- **Broad Trust Scope:** The TMS must cover a broad trust scope including the traditional trust usages such as access trust and identity trust as well as non-traditional ones such as fault detection and data quality assessment.
- **Collaborative Environment:** The TMS must operate in a collaborative environment. An entity's ability to monitor and manage all interactions in a large-scale system is limited and therefore it needs to rely on other entities' opinions and

experience. Users must be able to choose their collaborators and update their lists of collaborators according to their needs and the specific situation.

Activity-Aware Trust Management System Requirements

A general trust management system must support four activities as outlined in (Grandison & Sloman, 2000). The first activity is the *Trust Evidence Collection*, which is the process of collecting evidence required to make a trust decision. The second activity, *Trust Analysis*, is the process of examining trust relationships to identify implicit relationships. *Trust Evaluation* is the third activity that evaluates evidence in the context of trust relationships. Finally, *Trust Monitoring* is the activity that is responsible for updating trust relationship based on evidence.

Building a trust management service for activity-aware trust applications requires defining those issues that are necessary for extending a general trust management system to support dynamic and composable trust assessments of all entities that handle the information, not just the creator or consumer of the data. In order to architect such a TMS, a set of requirements -- categorized in groups that represent a TMS activity -- is recommended to be fulfilled by the TMS (Dionysiou, 2006) as shown below. Note that the TMS interacts with other external components such as certificate authorities and reputation networks. In the former case, the TMS must have access to certificate information, either directly from the certificate authority or from another service such as an enhanced directory service. However, the TMS should not support any certificate management activities such as managing certificate revocation lists. These tasks are provided by external entities. The requirements on these external components are beyond the scope of this chapter.

R1 EVIDENCE COLLECTION AND DISTRIBUTION

R1.1 Heterogeneous Forms of Evidence

The TMS must support multiple types of evidence, including recommendations, credentials, low-level instrumentation data, etc. Diversity in evidence types allows for a broader assessment of trust because knowledge is obtained from multiple sources.

For example, role-based access control decisions could rely on both external recommendations and profile information for a user. Not only the user's credentials could be verified prior to role assignment, but also reputation information could be utilized to assess the risk of the user abusing the privileges of the assigned role.

R1.2 Selective Collection and Distribution of Evidence

The collection and dissemination of evidence is not mandatory. An entity must be able to specify the source and frequency of received evidence. Similarly, an entity must also be able to restrict dissemination of its own evidence to selected users.

For example, a user should be able to prevent disclosure of sensitive information to business parties that are considered to be competitors.

R1.3 Dynamic Management of Evidence Streams

The evidence streams (both incoming and outgoing) should not be assumed to be static, but they are changing according to the user's policies.

For example, a recommender that acquires a reputation for favoritism or a competitor may not be reliable sources of recommendations and thus the use of the evidence stream originated at those recommenders should be used cautiously.

R2 TRUST ANALYSIS

R2.1 Time-Aware Trust Relationships

The TMS must model time as a fundamental quantity that allows reasoning about it during the specification and analysis of trust relationships.

For example, the trust assessment of a communication path that is composed of three servers can only be derived if the intersection of the valid intervals of the three trust relationships is not empty.

R2.2 Composable Trust Constructs

The TMS must provide the necessary constructs that will allow reasoning about end-to-end trust assessments for a specific activity.

Systems based on the publish-subscribe paradigm rely on intermediary entities to forward information from its source to the intended target. A trustor must derive trust assessments for all entities that actively participate in a particular data stream. For example, a secure communication link does not provide guarantees about the quality of the data from an unreliable publisher.

R3 TRUST EVALUATION

R3.1 Evidence Aggregation

The TMS must provide a wide range of mechanisms to aggregate evidence of the same or different type. The TMS must support a range of typical voting algorithms but also deal with incorrect and missing inputs to the aggregation.

For example, the feedback from recommenders is weighted based on the trust relationship between the receiver of the feedback and the recommender. All recommendations are combined by an aggregation scheme into a single output. Trustors should be allowed to choose the aggregation scheme that conforms to their policies. A weighted average aggregation scheme may be suitable for one trustor whereas a majority scheme is more appropriate for another trustor.

R3.2 Evidence-to-Expectation Mapping Functions

Expectation is defined as a requirement and its allowed values that a trustor has for a particular interaction with a trustee; these values are constrained by equality and inequality operators. The observed value for an expectation is not necessarily derived directly from a single type of evidence. The TMS must allow a user to express functions that map evidence to expectations. These functions specify the inputs to aggregation methods and may vary depending on the trusting attitude of the trustor (see R4.2 below).

For example, a trustor may choose to specify the behavior expectation as a function of reputation and reliability. Behavior is not collected directly from evidence streams, but on the contrary, recommendations and reliability measurements are manipulated to derive behavioral values. Aggregated results may be used to evaluate more than one expectation; for example, recommendations affect a trustee's reputation and at the same time they are also used to extract behavioral trends for the particular trustee.

R3.3 Expectation Satisfaction

Expectation satisfaction occurs when the trustee's observed value for a requirement falls into the range of allowed values for that particular requirement. The TMS must provide a wide range of techniques that target expectation satisfaction. The reasoning behind this requirement is similar to the one explained for the R3.1 Evidence Aggregation requirement.

R4 TRUST MONITORING

R4.1 Trust Re-Evaluation

TMS must take into consideration the dynamic nature of the network and the dynamic behavior of the network participants whenever a trust assessment is made. There are a number of situations where the dynamic nature of the network and its participants is observed. For example, new participants join the network and existing ones depart from it. Participant's performance and properties change. Legal contracts may force collaborators to become competitors. Trust relationships should reflect these social, organizational, performance and network changes.

R4.2 Trusting Attitude Support

The TMS must provide for different operational modes. Policies will have different inputs and rules depending on which mode they are in. These modes are similar to the US homeland security alert codes or intrusion detection modes. For example, during the 'red' alert mode, only a set of predefined trust relationships is active depending on the severity of the situation.

Trust Ontology Model

A new trust model is discussed now that is designed to incorporate the requirements mentioned above. The novelty of the model is its ability to integrate trust reasoning and monitoring into a single model. Trust monitoring constructs are incorporated as *expectation evaluation criteria*. The model extends the traditional concept of trust conditions into more expressive expectations, which include not only expected values for particular properties but also covering, aggregating, and triggering mechanisms that manipulate the observed value. In addition, and unlike other approaches, the model derives end-to-end trust assessments without using transitive indirect trust explicitly in the derivations.

The semantics of indirect trust are captured as one-grained recommendations that are considered to be an evidence type; the weight of this evidence on the overall trust assessment is treated like any other evidence type, which is based on the trustor-recommender existing trust relationship.

Trust Relation

The theory of sets and relations is used to represent trust between trustors and trustees (Dionysiou, 2006; Dionysiou et al., 2007). The *trust between trustors and trustees* is viewed as a relation τ, with associated attributes, properties, and operations. The notation $\tau(\gamma,\delta,c,\lambda,\iota,\varepsilon,id,s)$ represents a trust relationship between two entities and it is interpreted as "*trustor γ, based on γ's trusting attitude, believes that the extent to which trustee δ will act as expected for context c during time interval ι is λ, and this belief is subject to the satisfaction of expectation set ε. This relationship is valid for a specific interaction id and its status is indicated by s.*" The entire space of the trust ontology is illustrated in Figure 4. Due to space limitations, only a subset of the trust formalism is presented. More details can be found in (Dionysiou, 2006).

Trust Relation Attributes

The attributes of the trust relation τ are trustor γ, trustee δ, context c, levels λ, time interval ι, expectation set ε, interaction identifier id, and status s.

Trustors and Trustees

The first two attributes γ, δ of the trust relation τ represent the trustor and trustee respectively. These are entities with unique identifiers.

Context

The scope of the trust relationship is narrowed to a specific function called context. Without loss of generality, context c is portrayed as an action performed on data. In this case, action could be *producing*, *forwarding*, and *consuming* data. Data is classified based on its type, which includes *sensitive* data, *public* data, *recommendation* data, etc. Given that A is the set of actions performed on data and DT the set of data types, then context $c=(A,D)$ with $D \subset DT$.

Definition 1: Context. Context c is an ordered pair *(action, datatypes)*, with *action* $\in A$ and *datatypes* $\in DT$.

C denotes the set of all contexts and it is defined as a subset of the Cartesian product $A \times DT$. Set C may be organized in a number of *partially ordered sets* (posets), one for each action, under the relation of set inclusion $\subseteq$ on *DataTypes*. For a given action, contexts may be *dominated/dominant*, *intersecting* or *unrelated*, whereas for different actions the contexts are called *different* contexts.

Two contexts c_1 and c_2 may be related under $\subseteq$ (by definition). In this case, context c_1 is a superset of c_2 and as a result it is labeled as dominant context. Similarly, c_2 is the dominated context. As an example, consider contexts *(provide, {normal, alert})* and *(provide, {normal})* with the former being the dominant context and the latter being the dominated one.

Definition 2: Dominant/Dominated Contexts. Context c_1 dominates context c_2 if and only if $c_2 \subset c_1$ in the same poset. In this case c_1 is the dominant context and c_2 is the dominated context.

Contexts c_1 and c_2 may not be related in a poset under the $\subseteq$ relation. Take as an example the contexts *(provide, {normal, alert})*, *(provide, {alert, recommendation})*. The intersection of their respective datatypes sets outputs the singleton set *{alert}*. From this fact, it can be deduced that such contexts may be related under a secondary relation of intersection $\cap$ within the poset.

Figure 4. Trust ontology

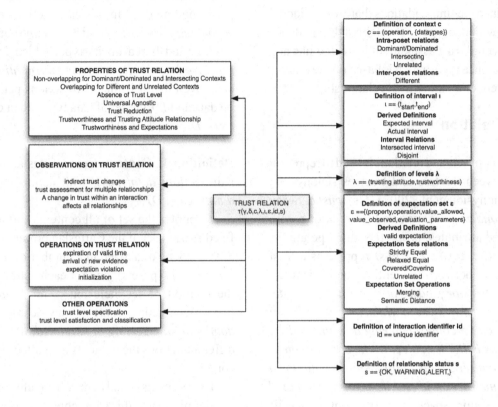

Definition 3: Intersecting Contexts.

Context c_1 intersects with context c_2 if and only if $c_1 \subset c_2$ and $c_2 \subset c_1$ do not hold in the same poset but $c_1 \cap c_2 = \emptyset$.

Finally, there is the case where contexts are simply unrelated in a poset. Any two singleton contexts fall into this category.

Definition 4: Unrelated Contexts.

Context c_1 and context c_2 are unrelated if and only if they are not related via Dominant/Dominated relation or Intersecting relation.

Contexts for different actions labeled as different. Contexts *(provide,{normal, alert})* and *(consume, {normal})* are examples of different contexts.

Definition 5: Different Contexts.

Different contexts refer to contexts c_1 and c_2 from different posets.

Trust Levels

Trust is subjective because a trustor's requirements are not met by all trustees at the same degree or a trustor's expectations for trustees vary. There are various notations to denote how much an entity is worthy of trust. Trust values (Abdul-Rahman & Hailes, 1997), degrees (Abdul-Rahman & Hailes, 2000) and levels (Grandison & Sloman, 2000) are all used by the trustor to categorize trustees based on their perceived trustworthiness.

The model adopts the term *trust level*. Trust levels are closely related to two important concepts: *trustfulness* of the trustor and *trustworthiness* of the trustee (Buskens, 2002). Trustfulness is defined as the extent to which the trustor is willing to take the risk of trust being abused by the trustee. On the other hand, trustworthiness is the extent to which the trustee honors trust, if trust is placed. The trustfulness of the trustor varies and it depends on the trustor's willingness to trust. In our model, the trustfulness of the trustor is a synonym for *trusting attitude*.

Definition 6: Level. Trust level is a label supported by a trust classification system to express trustworthiness extent and trustfulness extent.

Trust Attribute λ is an ordered pair of two levels $(\lambda_{ta}, \lambda_t)$.

Definition 7: Trust Levels. Trust levels λ is an ordered pair $(\lambda_{ta}, \lambda_t)$ with $\lambda_{ta} \in \Lambda_{ta}$, $\lambda_t \in \Lambda_t$, and its coordinates represent trusting attitude and trustworthiness extent respectively. Λ_{ta} is the set of values for trusting attitude whereas Λ_t is the set of values for trustworthiness extent. Sets Λ_{ta} and Λ_t could be equal sets.

Time Interval

A trust relation consists of trust relationships that are valid for a particular period of time. The temporal database interpretation of time is chosen for modeling time. In temporal databases, time domain T is considered to be an ordered sequence of points t_i in some application-dependent granularity (Elmasri & Navathe, 2000). The granularity of time does not affect the logic of the trust relation if it is consistent throughout the model.

Definition 8: Interval. An interval ι is an ordered pair of time points (t_s, t_e) with the first point appearing before the second point in the timeline. The set of all intervals I is the Cartesian product $T \times T$, with ι representing an element from I.

As it was mentioned earlier, the trust relation is dynamic and changes over time. *Transaction time* is the time point when the current state of the relation changes.

Definition 9: Transaction Time. A transaction time t is a time point at which the state of the trust relation changes.

There are two types of intervals: *expected interval* and *actual interval*. The expected interval indicates the anchored time duration in which a trust relationship is predicted to be valid. The actual interval is the one that the trust relationship was observed to be valid in the real world. The latter is not part of the relation, but it's recorded as past *experience* upon termination of the trust relationship.

Definition 10: Expected Interval. An expected interval is the interval that a particular trust relationship is expected to be valid in the real world.

Definition 11: Actual Interval. An actual interval is the interval that a particular trust relationship was observed to be valid in the real world.

According to Allen's algebra (Allen, 1983), there are 13 possible relationships between intervals ι_1 and ι_2. In addition to these interval relationships, the model must also account for the intersected time interval ι_s between intervals related with the equal ($=$), during (d), overlaps (o), starts (s) and finishes (f) relationships.

Definition 12: Intersected Intervals. Intervals $\iota_1 = (t_{s1}, t_{e1})$ and $\iota_2 = (t_{s2}, t_{e2})$ are intersected if and only if $\iota_1 = \iota_2 \vee \iota_1 d \iota_2 \vee \iota_1 s \iota_2 \vee \iota_1 f \iota_2 \vee \iota_1 o \iota_2$. The intersected interval ι_s is obtained as follows:

1. If $\iota_1 = \iota_2 \vee \iota_1 d \iota_2 \vee \iota_1 s \iota_2 \vee \iota_1 f \iota_2$, then $\iota_s = (t_{s1}, t_{e1})$
2. If $\iota_1 o \iota_2$, then $\iota_s = (t_{s1}, t_{e2})$

Expectation Set

The model extends the traditional concept of trust conditions into more expressive expectations. Expectations include not only expected values for particular trust requirements but also covering, aggregating, and triggering parameters that manipulate observed values. An expectation is defined as a requirement and its allowed values that a trustor has for a particular interaction with a trustee. An expectation is a tuple (π, o, v_o, v_a, ev), where π is a trust requirement, o is a standard relational operator, v_o is the observed or actual value for the requirement, v_a is the allowed value for that requirement and ev represents the evaluation criteria for the specific requirement. The observed value v_o is the aggregated value of multiple observations (also called evidence) over time. ev contains the aggregation algorithm that is used to derive the actual value.

The first expectation attribute is the trust requirement π. Trust requirements are grouped in behavioral (β), security (σ), and QoS (φ) categories. Trust requirement $\pi \in \Pi$, with $\Pi = \Pi_\beta \cup \Pi_\sigma \cup \Pi_\varphi$.

The second expectation attribute is the equality or inequality operator o. Operator o takes values from the set O that consists of the relational operators =, <, <=, >, >= and ≠.

The third and fourth attributes are the observed and allowed values respectively. Value $v \in V$, with set V consisting of values that are assigned to requirements. Set V is defined as $\cup V_i$, with V_i be the set of values that requirement π_i takes. Without loss of generality, assume that every V_i is totally ordered by <= and all operators $o \in O$ are defined for all $v \in V$.

Finally, the fifth attribute ev represents the evaluation parameters for the particular requirement. At time t, a requirement can only have one actual value, which is the result of aggregating many observed values. An element ev is a tuple *(covering, triggering, aggregation)* that describes the covering method, triggering rule, and aggregation scheme for π respectively. The covering attribute provides the conditions under which an expectation is considered valid and the remaining two characterize the *when* and *how* the observed value is updated.

Two of the covering techniques supported by the model are *strict* and *relaxed*, where in the former case the observed value satisfies the al-lowed value under operation o and in the latter case a deviation d is allowed. The expectation semantics dictate that an expectation is valid if and only if the relationship between observed value v_o and allowed value v_a under operation o and covering method is also valid. Otherwise, a violation occurs. Table 1 illustrates examples of valid expectations and violations.

Property 1: Valid Expectation. Expectation (π, o, v_o, v_a, ev) is valid if and only if $v_o\ o\ (v_a + d)$ for $o \in \{=, <, <=\}$ *and* $v_o\ o\ (v_a - d)$ *for* $o \in \{>, >=\}$ is true under the ordering of the values of set V. Value d is set to 0 for strict covering and set to the permissible deviation for relaxed covering technique.

Incoming evidence must be evaluated in the context of existing trust relationships. When triggering conditions are activated, the evidence is aggregated. Aggregation algorithms can be triggered either at predefined intervals or when a number of instances arrive at the evaluator.

Aggregating evidence can be seen as a voting mechanism where instances of evidence types are combined by a voting scheme into a single output. The aggregated result is an observed value for an expectation. The model uses aggregation of values without explicitly using transitive indirect trust in the derivations. The semantics of indirect trust are captured as one-grained recommendations disseminated as evidence and like any other evidence type its significance on the aggregated result is based on the trustor-recommender trust relationship.

There is a spectrum of aggregation algorithms that could target the aggregation of evidence from multiple instances of a single evidence type and evidence from different evidence types. The aggregation algorithms that could be supported include *average, weighted average, majority, m-out-of-n, plurality,* and any *user-defined* aggregation. These user-defined mechanisms can be provided by a virtual machine with a programmable language.

Table 1. Valid expectations and violations

o	v_o	v_a	Covering	Valid or Violation
=	3	5	Strict	Violation
=	5	3	d=2	Valid
<=	6	5	Strict	Violation
>=	6	5	d=4	valid

Consider v_{all}^j to be the aggregated evidence value for entity j, v_j^i to be evidence value by external source i for entity j, and τ_i to be the trust relationship between the evaluating trustor k and external entity i. The aggregation algorithms that trustor k can use are shown in Table 2. It is important to note that an observed value is not necessarily derived from a single evidence type. A user could specify functions that map evidence types to expectation values.

An expectation set ε describes all the requirements that a trustor has for a trustee.

Definition 13: Expectation Set. Expectation set ε is a subset of the Cartesian product $\Pi \times O \times V \times V \times EV$. Each member of the expectation set is an expectation as defined above. There is a unique tuple $(\pi, o, v_o, v_a, ev) \in \varepsilon$ that corresponds to any given π.

By itself an expectation set is not interesting unless operations are performed on its elements. However, prior to defining these operations we must first define the primitive comparison relationships between its elements. The relationships between expectation tuples determine the relationships between expectation sets. These binary relationships include the standard equality (=) and less than or equal (<=) relationships as well as the redefinition of not equal $\neq$. In addition, a new relationship called *relaxed equal* is defined. Based on the binary relationships, expectation sets when compared fall in one of the four categories: *strictly-equal, relaxed-equal, covered/covering and unrelated* (Dionysiou, 2006).

Starting with the relationships between expectation tuples, the equality relationship is presented first. Two expectation tuples are equal if their respective trust properties π_1, π_2, observed values v_{o1}, v_{o2}, allowed values v_{a1}, v_{a2}, and covering methods $covering_1$, $covering_2$ are the same. The triggering and aggregation methods do not need to be the same since they don't affect the semantics of the expectation tuples. Those attributes merely affect the when and how the observed value changes.

Definition 14: Equal Expectations (=). Expectation $(\pi_1, o_1, v_{o1}, v_{a1}, ev_1)$ is equal with expectation $(\pi_2, o_2, v_{o2}, v_{a2}, ev_2)$ if and only if $\pi_1 = \pi_2 \wedge o_1 = o_2 \wedge v_{o1} = v_{o2} \wedge v_{a1} = v_{a2} \wedge covering_1 \in ev_1 = covering_2 \in ev_2$.

The relaxed equal relationship is a new relationship that relates two expectations that refer to the same property mapped to different values.

Definition 15: Relaxed Equal Expectations ($\approx$). An expectation $(\pi_1, o_1, v_{o1}, v_{a1}, ev_1)$ is relaxed equal with another expectation $(\pi_2, o_2, v_{o2}, v_{a2}, ev_2)$ if and only if $(\pi_1 = \pi_2 \wedge o_1 = o_2 \wedge v_{o1} \neq v_{o2} \wedge v_{a1} \neq v_{a2} \wedge covering_1 = covering_2)$ or $(\pi_1 = \pi_2 \wedge o_1 = o_2 \wedge v_{o1} \neq v_{o2} \wedge v_{a1} = v_{a2} \wedge covering_1 = covering_2)$.

Definition 16: Strictly Equal Expectation Sets. Expectation set ε_1 is strictly equal to expectation set ε_2 if and only if ε_1 is an improper set of ε_2, under the equality definition.

Two expectation sets are strictly equal if they contain the same elements. Expectation sets $\varepsilon_1 = \{(cooperation, =, 1, 1, ev), (reliability, >, 0.98, 0.97,$

Table 2. Aggregation algorithms for single evidence type

Average	$v_{all}^{j} = \dfrac{1}{n}\displaystyle\sum_{i=1}^{n} v_i^{j}$ where n is the number of external sources
Weighted Average	$v_{all}^{j} = \dfrac{1}{n}\displaystyle\sum_{i=1}^{n} f(\tau_i, v_i^{j})$ where f is a function
Majority	v_{all}^{j} is the value that more than $n/2$ external sources agree on (allow for a delta deviation)
m-out-of-n	v_{all}^{j} is the value that at least m out of n external sources agree on
Plurality	v_{all}^{j} is the value that most external sources agree on
User-defined	Any customized aggregation method such as median value, etc.

ev2)} and $\varepsilon_2=\{(cooperation, =, 1, 1, ev), (reliability, >, 0.98, 0.97, ev2)\}$ are strictly equal.

Definition 17: Relaxed Equal Expectation Sets.
Expectation set ε_1 is relaxed-equal to expectation set ε_2 if and only if for all tuples $i=(\pi_1, o_1, v_{o1}, v_{a1}, ev_1) \in \varepsilon_1$ there is tuple $j=(\pi_2, o_2, v_{o2}, v_{a2}, ev_2) \in \varepsilon_2$ such as $|\varepsilon_1| = |\varepsilon_2|$ and $(i \approx j$ or $i = j)$.

The relaxed equal comparison is a generalization of the strictly equal comparison between two expectation sets. Consider expectation sets $\varepsilon_1=\{(cooperation, >, 3, 1, ev), (reliability, >, 0.98, 0.97, ev2)\}$ and $\varepsilon_2=\{(cooperation, >, 2, 1, ev), (reliability, >, 0.98, 0.97, ev2)\}$. These two sets don't have the same elements, but they both contain values for the same properties: cooperation and reliability. These two sets are called relaxed equal.

In order to address the issue of trust composition, one must provide systematic ways to synthesize a set of expectation sets to derive a new expectation set. *Merging* is an operation that accomplishes the expectation set synthesis by applying a function f_π on the values of a property. The function f_π essentially aggregates the observed and allowed values into single values respectively; average, maximum, minimum, weighted average are all candidate functions f_π.

Operation 1: Merging of Expectation Sets. Consider expectation sets ε_1 and ε_2. The merging of the two expectation sets results in a new expectation set ε_{merge} that is constructed as follows:

1. Initialize $\varepsilon_{merge} = \varnothing$
2. If $\varepsilon_1 = \varepsilon_2$, then $\varepsilon_{merge} \leftarrow \varepsilon_{merge} \cup \varepsilon_1$
3. if $\varepsilon_1 \approx \varepsilon_2$, then $\forall\ i:(\pi_1, o_1, v_{o1}, v_{a1}, ev_1) \in \varepsilon_1$, $j:(\pi_2, o_2, v_{o2}, v_{a2}, ev_2) \in \varepsilon_2$ such that $i \approx j$ then $\varepsilon_{merge} \leftarrow \varepsilon_{merge} \cup \{((\pi_1, o_1, f_\pi(v_{o1}, v_{o2}), f_\pi(v_{a1}, v_{a2}), ev_1))\}$
4. If *not* ($\varepsilon_1 = \varepsilon_2$ or $\varepsilon_1 \approx \varepsilon_2$) then $\varepsilon_{merge} \leftarrow \varepsilon_1 \cup \varepsilon_2$

Interaction id

Another trust relation attribute is the interaction identifier *id*. There is a unique identifier for each activity, the interaction *id*. There are at least two trust relationships for any activity.

Status

The last attribute is the status of a trust relationship. Status $s \in S$ where $S=\{OK, WARNING, ALERT\}$.

Trust Relation Properties and Operations

The next step in formalizing trust is the definition of its properties. The standard properties of any *n-ary* relation (reflexive, irreflexive, symmetric, antisymmetric, transitive, and equivalence) do not hold due to non-absolute characteristics of trust relationships. Thus, new properties must be investigated.

One of the characteristics of trust relation τ is its dynamic nature, meaning that $\tau(\gamma,\delta,c,\lambda,\iota,\varepsilon,id,s)$ which is valid in time t_1 may become invalid in t_2, with $t_2 > t_1$, and vice versa. Another characteristic of trust is its composable nature, meaning that existing trust relationships can be aggregated to derive an end-to-end trust assessment for a particular activity at time t. Based on these two characteristics, operations are categorized in two groups: the ones that affect and change the current state of the trust relation and the ones that use the existing state of the trust relation to make trust assessments.

Operations Changing Trust Relation State

Trust relation τ is affected by time, arrival of new evidence, and violations of expectations, to just name a few. There are other events that change the trust relation state such as the change of trusting attitude level, but these are not described here.

Operation 2: Expiration of Valid Time. A trust relationship $\tau(\gamma,\delta,c,\lambda,\iota,\varepsilon,id,s)$ does not hold in relation τ if its valid interval time expires. Thus, a trust relationship $\tau(\gamma,\delta,c,\lambda,\iota,\varepsilon,id,s)$ is not valid in τ if the current time $t > t_e$, $t_e \in \iota$.

Operation 3: Arrival of New Evidence. Suppose that new evidence is available for a particular trustee. The new value will be applied to the appropriate trust requirement according to the trustee

evaluation information for the trust requirement. Suppose that new evidence arrives at trustor γ for trustee δ. The new evidence includes the trust requirement π_r and the recommended value v_r. All trust relationships $\tau(\gamma,\delta,c,\lambda_1,\iota_1,\varepsilon_1,id_1,s_1)$ are updated to reflect the application of the new evidence on v.

Operation 4: Expectation Violation. Whenever new evidence arrives, the observed value may change according to the aggregation scheme for the specific requirement. An update in the observed value may lead to expectation violation. In this case, the respective trust relationship's status is set to *ALERT*. The relationship does not necessarily become false in τ; according to policies it might be the case that a trustor wants to monitor the relationship before terminating it. However, all other trust relationships that are associated with the alerted relationship's interaction identifier have their status set to *WARNING*. In the case that an expectation $(\pi,o,v_o,v_a,ev) \in \varepsilon$ is not valid in $\tau(\gamma,\delta,c,\lambda,\iota,\varepsilon,id,s)$, the respective relationship's status s becomes *ALERT* and all tuples associated with the same interaction identifier *id* have their status set to *WARNING*. However, a relationship's status is restored whenever the violation gets corrected during the monitoring interval. In this case, *OK* replaces the *ALERT*, and all *WARNING* are replaced with *OK*. Note that if there are multiple violations for a specific interaction, then *WARNING*(s) remain as they are until all *ALERT*(s) become *OK*.

Operations Using Trust Relation State

In order to derive end-to-end trust assessment for an activity the current state of the trust relation will be consulted to extract the trust relationships for the particular activity. This set of relationships will be divided into groups based on the context attribute. Trust relationships will be then synthesized within a context and the derived trust relationships will be combined to give the final end-to-end trust assessment. Thus, trust composition takes place within a context and across contexts.

Operation 5 Intra-Context Composition. This is the aggregated trust assessment for context c in interaction id_1. In particular, consider relationships $(\gamma_1, \delta_1, c_1, \lambda_1, \iota_1, \varepsilon_1, id_1, s_1)$ and $(\gamma_1, \delta_2, c_1, \lambda_1, \iota_2, \varepsilon_2, id_1, s_1)$ in τ. Trustor γ_1 may synthesize the two tuples to derive an aggregated trust assessment for context c during interval ι_i (the intersection of ι_1 and ι_2) by applying expectation set operations on the expectation sets ε_1 and ε_2 to derive the aggregated expectation set ε_i. Expectation set ε_i has to be checked against the various trust level specifications in order to assign the trustworthiness level λ_i for the new tuple $(\gamma_1, \delta_{1,2}, c_1, \lambda_i, \iota_i, \varepsilon_i, id_1, s_1)$.

Operation 6 Inter-Context Composition. This is the trust assessment for interaction id_1 across contexts. Suppose there are aggregated trust assessments for contexts c_1 and c_2, which are the only contexts belonging to interaction id_1; these are tuples $(\gamma_1, \delta_1, c_1, \lambda_1, \iota_1, \varepsilon_1, id_1, s_1)$ and $(\gamma_1, \delta_2, c_2, \lambda_1, \iota_2, \varepsilon_2, id_1, s_1)$. Trustor γ_1 may compose the two tuples to derive an end-to-end trust assessment for interaction id_1 during interval ι_i (the intersection of ι_1 and ι_2) by applying expectation set operations on the expectation sets ε_1 and ε_2 to derive the aggregated expectation set ε_i. Expectation set ε_i has to be checked against the various level specifications in order to assign the trustworthiness level λ for the new tuple $(\gamma_1, \delta_{1,2}, c_{1,2}, \lambda_i, \iota_i, \varepsilon_i, id_1, s_1)$.

The two operations are demonstrated with an illustrative example. Assume that Figure 5 is a graph for trust relation τ of the network depicted in Figure 3. A node represents either a trustor or a trustee. Nodes are connected by directed edges that start at a trustor node and end at a trustee node. Each edge carries the tuple that describes the relationships between the two connecting nodes. An edge may carry multiple tuples. Suppose that trustor C would like to derive the end-to-end trust assessment regarding the information flow

for data d. Then, the following trust relationships must be considered:

- relationship between C and P regarding P's ability to *produce* data d $\tau(\gamma_C, \delta_P, c_2, \lambda_P, \iota_3, \varepsilon_3, id_1, s_{OK})$
- relationship between C and S_1 regarding S_1's ability to *forward* data d $\tau(\gamma_C, \delta_{S1}, c_1, \lambda_P, \iota_1, \varepsilon_P, id_1, s_{OK})$
- relationship between C and S_2 regarding S_2's ability to *forward* data d $\tau(\gamma_C, \delta_{S2}, c_1, \lambda_P, \iota_2, \varepsilon_2, id_1, s_{OK})$

First, the trust aggregation for the same context c_1 will take place for trustees S_1 and S_2. The result will be $\tau(\gamma_C, \delta_{S1,S2}, c_1, \lambda_1, \iota_k, \varepsilon_k, id_1, s_{OK})$ with $i_k=(1,10)$ and $\varepsilon_k=\{(authentication, =, certificate, c\ ertificate, ev1), (reliability, >=, average(0.95, 0.97),\ average(0.95, 0.95), ev2)\}$. Then, the end-to-end trust assessment will take place between the new trust relationship $\tau(\gamma_C, \delta_{S1,S2}, c_1, \lambda_1, \iota_k, \varepsilon_k, id_1, s_{OK})$ and $\tau(\gamma_C, \delta_P, c_2, \lambda_1, \iota_3, \varepsilon_3, id_1, s_{OK})$. In this case, $\tau(\gamma_C, \delta_{P,S1,S2}, c_{1,2}, \lambda_1, \iota_m, \varepsilon_m, id_1, s_{OK})$, with $i_m=(1,8)$ and $\varepsilon_m=\{(authen\ tication, =, certificate, certificate, ev1), (reliability, a\ verage(0.90, 0.96), average(0.80, 0.95), ev2)\}$.

Trust Model Applicability

The power grid application scenario (Figure 1) described in a previous section is revisited to illustrate the functionality of the trust model. A trust model is integrated with the *PMU Aggregation* entity that manages trust relationships for all the entities that generate PMU data used in its state estimation calculations. The trust model also maintains trust assessments for recommenders that disseminate feedback through the trust recommendation network.

The activity that is monitored is '*Collect PMU Data for State Estimation Calculations*' and it consists of two tasks (Figure 6): '*Generate PMU Data*' and '*Deliver PMU Data*'. Starting with the '*Generate PMU Data*' task, there are two entities that provide PMU data to the aggregation entity.

Figure 5. Trust Relation Graph

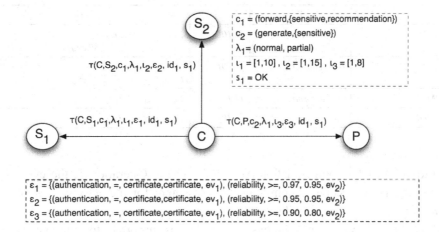

In this case the trustor is *the PMU Aggregation* entity and the trustees are *Utility₁* and *Utility₂*. There are also two entities that are associated with the '*Deliver PMU Data*' task: the communication channel *channel₁* that connects *PMU Aggregation* with *Utility₁* and the communication channel *channel₂* that connects *PMU Aggregation* with *Utility₂*.

Now that the trustees have been identified, the *PMU Aggregation* entity (γ) configures initial trust relationships for all four trustees (Table 3). Without loss of generality, all four relationships are valid for the same time interval and are categorized at the same trust level.

Relationships for '*Generate PMU Data*' context c_1

$\tau(\gamma, \delta_1, c_1, \lambda_1, \iota_1, \varepsilon_1, id_1, s_{OK})$ where δ_1 is Utility₁

$\tau(\gamma, \delta_2, c_1, \lambda_1, \iota_1, \varepsilon_2, id_1, s_{OK})$ where δ_2 is Utility₂

Relationships for '*Deliver PMU Data*' context c_2

$\tau(\gamma, \delta_3, c_2, \lambda_1, \iota_1, \varepsilon_3, id_1, s_{OK})$ where δ_3 is channel₁

$\tau(\gamma, \delta_4, c_2, \lambda_1, \iota_1, \varepsilon_4, id_1, s_{OK})$ where δ_4 is channel₂

Suppose that the evaluation criteria ev_2 is *(strict, on-arrival, average)*. The recommendations from user U_2 and U_3 are aggregated using the *average* function to derive the observed value for the *reliability* requirement. Needless to say, instead of the *average* function, the trustor could examine the trust relationships that it currently has with the recommenders and choose another aggregation

Figure 6. Contexts in PMU collection activity

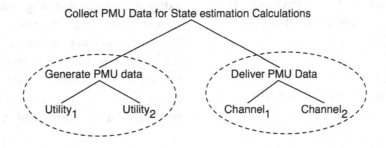

Table 3. Trust relationships in tabular representation for activity id_1

	c	λ	ι	ε	s
δ_1	*(generate,{PMU})*	*(norm,norm)*	*[1,10]*	*{(auth,=,cert,cert,ev$_1$),* *(reliability,>,0.90,0.89,ev$_2$)}*	*OK*
δ_2	*(generate,{PMU})*	*(norm,norm)*	*[1,10]*	*{(auth,=,cert,cert,ev$_3$),* *(reliability,>,0.96,0.89,ev$_4$)}*	*OK*
δ_3	*(deliver,{PMU})*	*(norm,norm)*	*[1,10]*	*{(connect,=,VPN,VPN,ev$_5$)}*	*OK*
δ_4	*(deliver,{PMU})*	*(norm,norm)*	*[1,10]*	*{(connect,=,VPN,PN,ev$_6$)}*	*OK*

scheme on how to weigh each recommendation. At transaction time t, the trustor receives recommendations *(δ_1,reliability,0.90)* and *(δ_2,reliability,0.98)* from U_2 and U_3 respectively. In this case, the trust relationship $\tau(\gamma, \delta_1, c_1, \lambda_1, \iota_1, \varepsilon_1, id_1, s_{OK})$ will be updated to reflect the new observed value for *reliability*. Thus, the expectation set ε_1 will be updated to *{(auth,=,cert,cert,ev$_1$), (reliability,>,0.94,0.89,ev$_2$)}*. Note that the status of the relationship is still *OK* since there is no expectation violation after the update of the observed value.

The trustor wants to collectively examine trust for the entire activity. In this case, the aggregation will take place in two steps (intra-context aggregation can take place in parallel) as shown in Table 4:

Aggregation for '*Generate PMU Data*' context c_1

Using Operation 1, the expectation sets are merged and the new trust relationship is $\tau(\gamma, \delta_{1,2}, c_1, \lambda_1, \iota_1, \varepsilon_5, id_1, s_{OK})$

Aggregation for '*Deliver PMU Data*' context c_2

Using Operation 1, the expectation sets are merged and the new trust relationship is $\tau(\gamma, \delta_{3,4}, c_2, \lambda_1, \iota_1, \varepsilon_6, id_1, s_{OK})$

End-to-end Aggregation for '*Collect PMU Data for State Estimation Calculations*' activity id_1

Using Operation 1, the end-to-end trust assessment for the activity is $\tau(\gamma, \delta_{1,2,3,4}, c_{1,2}, \lambda_1, \iota_1, \varepsilon_7, id_1, s_{OK})$

It is important to note that the trust relationships on Table 4 must to be re-evaluated in a bottom up manner. Therefore, every time a trust relationship within a context changes, then the aggregated intra-context trust relationship has to be re-evaluated as well as the inter-context trust relationship.

CHALLENGES AND FUTURE DIRECTIONS

Designing a trust model that incorporates all trust management activities is nontrivial due to the complexity of such a model. This chapter presented a trust model that supports trust reasoning and monitoring in a single model. However, there are still open research issues that need to be addressed in future research works. This trust model is just the starting point.

The trust model must be configurable to dictate its functionality. Low-level policies must be devised to support various operations such as external evidence mapping to an internal model format, initial trust formation, trust violation handling, evidence aggregation, trust evaluation triggering, trust relationship lifecycle, trust relationship invalidation, just to name a few. An ongoing work (Dionysiou, 2008) is currently investigating the design and implementation of

Table 4. Trust relationships composition in tabular representation for activity id$_1$

	c	λ	ι	ε	s
δ$_{1,2}$	*(generate, {PMU})*	*(norm,norm)*	*[1,10]*	*{(auth,=,cert,cert,ev), (reliability,>,0.95,0.89,ev)}*	*OK*
δ$_{3,4}$	*(deliver, {PMU})*	*(norm,norm)*	*[1,10]*	*{(connect,=,VPN,VPN,ev)}*	*OK*
δ$_{1,2,3,4,}$	*(generate+deliver,{PMU})*	*(norm,norm)*	*[1,10]*	*{(auth,=,cert,cert,ev), (reliability,>,0.95,0.89,ev), (connect,=,VPN,VPN,ev)}*	*OK*

a configurable trust management system based on the trust model presented here.

The trust model must be implemented to validate the conceptual framework. The correct architectural choices must allow a stand-alone implementation to be easily integrated and reused by a variety of systems. It is envisioned that the trust model will provide a service that will be an add-on component to complement current systems in decision-making.

In addition, it will be beneficial to explore the implications of this model in automated trust negotiations, such as the ones provided by TrustBuilder (Winslett et al., 2002), and how it leverages the capabilities of such negotiations; this is an area that is gaining increased popularity. A configurable trust model could be used to collect evidence about future collaborators, before the trust negotiation system starts its negotiation of trust. If evidence is available prior to negotiations, then credential and access control policies could be adapted according to what is already known about the negotiating party.

It will also be beneficial to investigate trust in grid computing environments. A computational grid is a collection of distributed, possibly heterogeneous resources that can be used as an ensemble to execute computational-intense applications (Foster et al., 2001). Grid applications include earth observation, climate modeling and biology applications. Grid computing enables the creation of a network among virtual communities, whose resources can be shared by its members. Thus, there are also security and trust implications that need to be addressed in this collaborative setting.

CONCLUSION

This chapter addressed the trust issues in open collaborative environments and identified a set of requirements, which must be met by trust management systems in order to support such applications. New trust paradigms were suggested in a new trust model and its associated formalisms that are devised to support the implementation of these requirements. The novelty of the new model is its ability to specify and reason about trust dynamically and when composed beyond pair wise relationships. These capabilities are expected and observed during the collaboration of a group of interacting entities. The trust relation semantics support constructs that explicitly allow trust monitoring.

The trust model is an initial attempt to combine trust reasoning and monitoring in a single framework. The aim of this chapter is to let the reader appreciate the complexity in devising trust semantics that are general enough to support and manage parameterized trust relationships. The model could serve as a basis for more expressive frameworks or could be extended to provide additional functionality.

REFERENCES

Abdul-Rahman, A., & Hailes, S. (1997, September). A distributed trust model. In *Proceedings of the ACM New Security Paradigms Workshop* (pp. 48-60).

Abdul-Rahman, A., & Hailes, S. (2000, January). Supporting trust in virtual communities. In *Proceedings of the 33th Hawaii International Conference on System Sciences (HICSS)* (pp. 1769-1777).

Allen, J. F. (1983). Maintaining knowledge about temporal intervals. *Communications of the ACM, 26*(11), 832–843. doi:10.1145/182.358434

Blaze, M., Feigenbaum, J., & Keromytis, A. D. (1998, April). Keynote: Trust management for public key infrastructures. In *Proceedings of the 6th International Workshop on Security Protocols.*

Blaze, M., Feigenbaum, J., & Lacy, J. (1996). Decentralized trust management. In *SP '96: Proceedings of the 1996 IEEE Symposium on Security and Privacy* (pp. 164). Washington, DC: IEEE Computer Society.

Buskens, V. (2002). *Social Networks and Trust, Theory and Decision Library, Series C, Game Theory, Mathematical Programming, and Operations Research.* London: Kluwer Academic Publishers.

Chu, Y.H., Feigenbaum, J., LaMacchia, B., Resnick, P., & Strauss, M. (1997). Referee: trust management for web applications. Computer Networks. *ISDN Systems, 29*(8-13), 953-964.

Dionysiou, I. (2006). *Dynamic and Composable Trust for Indirect Interactions.* Unpublished doctoral dissertation, Department of Electrical Engineering and Computer Science, Washington State University, Pullman.

Dionysiou, I. (2008). *Hestia++ Conceptual Framework* (Technical Report). University of Nicosia, Nicosia.

Dionysiou, I., Bakken, D., Hauser, D., & Frincke, D. (2008, July). Formalizing end-to-end context-aware trust relation ships in collaborative activities. In *Proceedings of the International Conference on Security and Cryptography (SECRYPT 2008), Special Session on Trust,* Porto, Portugal (pp. 546-553).

Dionysiou, I., Frincke, D., Bakken, D., & Hauser, C. (2007, October). An approach to trust management challenges for critical infrastructures. In *Proceedings of the 2ⁿᵈ International Workshop on Critical Information Infrastructures Security (CRITIS07),* Malaga, Spain (LNCS 5141, pp. 173-184). Berlin, Germany: Springer.

Elmasri, R., & Navathe, S. (2000). *Fundamentals of Database Systems.* Reading, MA: Addison-Wesley Longman, Inc.

Foster, I., Kesselman, C., & Tuecke, S. (2001). The Anatomy of the Grid: Enabling Scalable Virtual Organizations. *International J. Supercomputer Applications, 15*(3).

Grandison, T. (2001). *Trust specification and analysis for internet applications.* Unpublished doctoral dissertation, Imperial College of Science Technology and Medicine, Department of Computing, London.

Grandison, T. (2007). Conceptions of trust: Definition, constructs and models. In R. Song (Ed.), *Trust in E-Services: Technologies, Practices and Challenges* (pp. 1-28). Hershey, PA: Idea Group Inc.

Grandison, T., & Sloman, M. (2000). A survey of trust in internet applications. *IEEE Communications Surveys and Tutorials, 3*(4), 2–16. doi:10.1109/COMST.2000.5340804

Hauser, C. H., Bakken, D., Dionysiou, I., Gjermun-drod, H., Irava, V., Helkey, J., & Bose, A. (2007). Security, trust and qos in next-generation control and communication for large power systems. *International Journal of Critical Infrastructures*, *4*(1/2), 3–16. doi:10.1504/IJCIS.2008.016088

Herzberg, A., Mass, Y., Michaeli, J., Ravid, Y., & Naor, D. (2000). Access control meets public key infrastructure, or: Assigning roles to strangers. In *SP '00: Proceedings of the 2000 IEEE Symposium on Security and Privacy* (pp. 2). Washington, DC: IEEE Computer Society.

Josang, A. (1997, July). Prospectives of modeling trust in information security. In *Proceedings of the 2nd Australasian Conference on Information Security and Privacy*, Sydney, Australia.

Josang, A., Gray, E., & Kinateder, M. (2006). Simplification and analysis of transitive trust networks. *Web Intelligence and Agent Systems*, *4*(2), 139–161.

Marsh, S. (1994). *Formalizing Trust as a Computational Concept*. Unpublished doctoral dissertation, Department of Computer Science, University of Sterling.

Presti, S. L., Cusack, M., Booth, C., Allsopp, D., Kirton, M., Exon, N., et al. (2003). *Trust issues in pervasive environments* (Technical report wp2-01). University of Southampton and QinetiQ.

Protected critical infrastructure information (PCII) program. (2006). Retrieved January 19, 2009, from http://www.dhs.gov

Ryotov, T., Neuman, C., Zhou, L., & Foukia, N. (2007). Initial trust formation in virtual organizations. *International Journal of Internet Technology and Secured Transactions*, *1*, 81–94. doi:10.1504/IJITST.2007.014835

Trusted Computing Group TCG. (2004). *TCG Specification Architecture Overview*. Retrieved January 19, 2009, from https://www.trustedcomputinggroup.org

U.S. Canada Power System Outage Task Force. (2004). *Final report on the August 14, 2003 Blackout in the United States and Canada: Causes and Recommendations, March 2004*. Retrieved January 19, 2009, from https://reports.energy.gov/BlackoutFinal-Web.pdf

Vacca, J. (2004). *Public Key Infrastructure: Building Trusted Applications and Web Services*. London: Auerbach Publications.

Winslett, M., Yu, T., Seamons, K. E., Hess, A., Jacobson, J., & Jarvis, R. (2002). The Trust-builder architecture for trust negotiation. *IEEE Internet Computing*, *6*(6), 30–37. doi:10.1109/MIC.2002.1067734

Yan, Z., & Holtmanns, S. (2007). Trust modeling and management: from social trust to digital trust. In R. Subramanian (Ed.), *Computer Security, Privacy and Politics: Current Issues, Challenges and Solutions* (pp. 1-28). Hershey, PA: IGI Global.

Zimmermann, P. (1995). *The official PGP User's Guide*. Cambridge, MA: MIT Press.

ENDNOTE

[1]   For simplicity reasons, we omit for now the remaining trust attributes.

Chapter 9
Trust Development in Peer-to-Peer Environments

Yan Wang
Macquarie University, Australia

ABSTRACT

In peer-to-peer (P2P) service-oriented environments, a peer may need to interact with unknown peers for the services or products provided. Thus the trust evaluation prior to and posterior to interactions becomes a very important issue, which may be based on other peers' recommendations/evaluations. This chapter presents a dynamic peer trust evaluation model, which aims to measure responding peers' recommendation trust, and hence filter out low credibility recommendations and obtain more accurate and objective trust values. In our model, prior to any interaction with an unknown peer (target peer), the mean trust value results from the evaluations (recommendations) given by responding peers. Posterior to interactions with the target peer, the trust values are aggregated from both responding peers' recommendations and the requesting peer's experience. On aggregating trust values, the weight to the requesting peer's evaluation becomes bigger and bigger. Meanwhile, during this process, the credibility (recommendation trust) of each responding peer's recommendation can be measured round by round. This helps filter out low credibility peers and improve the trust evaluation accuracy.

INTRODUCTION

Peer-to-Peer (P2P) network is an infrastructure where each peer can play the role of a client and a service provider at the same time. P2P technique has been widely used in the field of information-sharing systems. For example, Gnutella and Napster are the most well-known systems for sharing music or movie files. Meanwhile, P2P e-commerce systems (Anancha 2003; eBay.com; P2PBazaar.com) let P2P networks go beyond the scope of information sharing systems like Napster and GNutella.

However, as most P2P systems lack the central management, the dynamic status of each peer causes trust evaluation a very complex issue. For example, in the information-sharing systems, it may

DOI: 10.4018/978-1-61520-682-7.ch009

consume several hours and some monetary cost of Internet access to download a large file (e.g. a video file). The provided file may be incomplete leading to a low quality of the service. In e-commerce environments, trust is also a critical issue (Resnick 2000). Before interacting with an unknown seller, it is rational for a buyer to doubt the trustworthiness of the seller, which results from the quality of previous transactions. Therefore, trust evaluations are useful and can make a new transaction securer.

Traditionally in security area, the common mechanism that has been used to identify the interacting entity is based on identity-based certificates. A registered peer should apply for a certificate from a Certificate Authority (CA) that can be used for authenticating the peer itself to other peers. Authentication has been used to form the basis of "trust" in deciding whether to carry out a transaction or not. However it is clear that such an approach is very limited as certificates do not necessarily convey much about the level of trust that one peer is willing to place on the other.

An alternative technique is to take into account of previous history of interactions with the target peer (Kamvar et al, 2003; Marti & Garcia-Molina 2004; Xiong & Liu 04). For example, each peer (e.g., a buyer) can rate the seller after each transaction. The rating is used to reflect the quality of the transaction delivered. Assuming that a lot of peers maintain this kind of local ratings, when an end-peer (referred to as a requesting peer) is going to have an interaction with a serving peer (referred to as a target peer), it can send a request to other peers. Once receiving the request, the peer (referred to as a responding peer) with a transaction with the target peer can respond to the request with its ratings. Thus, by collecting feedbacks from responding peers about their previous interactions, the end-peer may analyze and determine the trust value of the target peer being investigated.

The above method is the typical process for trust evaluation. However, in such a method,

another issue arises. Each responding peer may be trustworthy or not from the point view of the requesting peer. In general, it is very difficult for a requesting peer to measure the trustworthiness of a responding peer if the requesting peer has no knowledge about each responding peer. But this is also a critical issue to the responding peer. On one hand, good recommendation trust of responding peer can lead to objective trust result. On the other hand, as the requesting peer may need to know the trust level of other target peers. Knowledge of recommendation trust of other peers can avoid obtaining misleading feedback in later trust evaluations. Namely, measuring the recommendation trust of a responding peer is a critical and challenging issue in the field, which is also the focus of this work.

In this chapter, we present a peer trust evaluation model which is based on other peers' recommendations and the requesting peer's experience. In our method, prior to any interaction, the trust value of an unknown peer (target peer) can be determined by investigating its interaction history with other peers. Following this, if the evaluation result is good enough (i.e. better than a given threshold), the requesting peer can interact with the unknown peer, which becomes familiar with it hereafter. With more and more interactions, it is possible for the requesting peer to update its trust evaluation of the target peer based on the quality of the services the target peer provided. Meanwhile, other peers' evaluations on the target peer can also be collected to measure their credibility (recommendation trust) so as to filter out noise in recommendations and obtain more accurate aggregated trust values. To achieve this goal, we present a method for measuring the recommendation trust of responding peers, which is based on recommendation history and recommendation deviations from the main stream. In addition, a set of experiments has been conducted to study the properties of the proposed models. As we illustrated in the comparison section, our work improves some existing studies (e.g. Kamvar et al, 2003; Marti et al 2004; Yu et al 2004) by providing a mechanism for recommendation trust measurement and taking it into account of the trust evaluation of target peers.

This chapter is organized as follows. Section "Related Work" reviews some existing studies. Section "Trust Evaluation" presents our approach for credibility calculation and peer trust evaluation. Experimental results are illustrated in section "Experiments". In section "Comparison", we analyze several related models and compare our model with them. Finally section "Conclusions" concludes our work.

RELATED WORK

The computation of trust started to draw attention over 10 years ago. The work by S. March (Marsh 1994) is widely considered as one of the earliest studies on trust formalization. Another early work is presented by Berth et al (Berth et al, 1994), which presents the notions of direct trust, recommendation trust and derived trust.

In general, there are numerous notions of trust that satisfy different properties, which can be established differently (Xiong & Liu 2002; Marsh 1994). In terms of computer security, trust can be considered as a fundamental concept. A system is trustworthy if there is sufficient credible evidence leading to the belief that the system will meet a set of given requirements. In this context, trust can be viewed as a measure of trustworthiness, relying on the evidence provided (Bibshop 2003). For instance, in traditional client/server systems, a client should pass the authentication verification by the server before obtaining any privilege for accessing the data in the server. A more complex mechanism is proposed by Yu et al (Yu et al 2001) as the process of trust negotiation, where the two parties need to open the respective authentication policy to each other and exchange their required certificates (i.e. credentials in the work by Yu et al 2001). The outcome of credential exchange depends on if each party accepts the authentication policy of the other side and if they have sufficient evidence and credentials to meet the requirement of the other party. These models are generally based on existing standards, such as X.509 or PGP, and provide various extensions. They are valuable for initial trust establishment between two unknown peers.

But these methods only take into account the authentication and authority of a peer that may ask a certain level access privilege or intend to have a specific interaction. The outcome after authentication is simply 'Yes' or 'No' where 'Yes' means the authentication is successful and 'No' means unsuccessful. No previous interaction history is evaluated. In terms of evaluation, this is a non-calculative trust (Nooteboom 2002).

On the other hand, trust can be defined in terms of trust belief and trust behavior (Knight & Chervany 1996). Trust belief between two parties is the extent to which a party believes that the other party is trustworthy in a certain situation. Trustworthy means one is willing and able to act in the other party's interests. Trust behavior between two parties is the extent to which a party depends on the other in a given situation with a feeling of relative security, even though negative consequences are possible. If a trust belief means "party A believes that party B is trustworthy", then it will lead to a trust behavior as "A trusts B" (Xiong & Liu 2002).

Trust is also the probability by which party A expects that another party B performs a given action if the trust value is in the range of [0,1] (Jøsang et al 2007).

In the literature, there are some proposed trust models that focus on P2P environments.

Damiani et al (Damiani et al 2002) proposed *XRep*: a reputation-based approach for evaluating the reputation of peers through distributed polling algorithm before downloading any information. The approach adopts a binary rating system and it is based on Gnutella query broadcasting method using the *TTL* (*Time To Live*) limit.

EigenTrust (Kamvar et al 2003) collects *local trust values* of all peers to calculate the *global trust value* of a given peer. Additionally, *Eigen-Trust* adopts a binary rating function, interpreted as one (positive or satisfactory), zero or negative one (unsatisfactory or complaint).

Marti and Garcia-Molina (Marti & Garcia-Molina 2004) proposed a voting reputation system that collects responses from other peers on a given peer. The final reputation value is calculated by combining the values returned by responding peers and the requesting peer's experience with the given peer. However, each responded evaluation is local. Once it is sent to a requesting peer, the evaluation becomes a recommendation from the point view of the requesting peer. Therefore, in this work, it is not clear about how to trust these recommendations and how to measure the reputation or trust of the responding peers. The works in *XRep* and *EigenTrust* didn't explicitly distinguish transaction reputation and recommendation reputation. Peers with good service quality (i.e. good transaction reputation) are considered to have trustworthy recommendations. This may cause severe bias for reputation evaluation as a peer with good transaction reputation may have a bad recommendation reputation especially when recommending competitors.

Wang et al proposed several trust metrics (Wang & Varadharajan 2004a) for the trust evaluation in a decentralized environments (e.g. P2P networks) where a trust value is a probabilistic value in the range of [0, 1]. Prior to the interaction with an unknown peer P_x, the end peer collects other peers' trust evaluations on P_x. A method has been proposed for trust modification after a series of interactions with P_x. A good trust value results from the accumulation of constant good behaviors. Wang and Varadharajan (Wang & Varadharajan 2004b) also proposed that the temporal dimension should be taken into account in trust evaluations wherein fresh interactions are weighted more than old ones.

Yu et al (Yu et al 2004) extended their previous studies in 2002 (Yu & Singh 2002) and 2003

(Yu & Singh 2003), and proposed a method of exponential average taking into account of a series of interactions of the requesting peer. It is similar to the work by Wang et al (Wang & Varadharajan 2004b)). However the weight of an older interaction should not be greater than a fresher one. Meanwhile all weights should be normalized. These principles were not strictly followed in the work by Yu et al (Yu et al 2004). Yu and Singh (Yu & Singh 2003) presented a method for detecting malicious peers that is based on the requesting peer's experience. We argue that each peer's individual trust evaluation on a target peer is fully dependant on the experience, the quality of service and the honesty of the evaluating peer. The evaluations may vary from time to time and from peer to peer. However, a malicious peer's evaluation is incorrect most of the time, which may be a positive exaggeration or a negative exaggeration in a certain round. Therefore, the process to identify a liar requires a series of interactions that occur in different rounds or periods.

In the literature, the majority of earlier works on trust evaluation adopted binary rating models, such as *PeerTrust* (Xiong & Liu 2002; Xiong & Liu 2004) and *XRep* (Damiani et al 2002). These models considered the P2P network for information sharing only. As mentioned in by Yu et al (Yu et al 2004), binary ratings work pretty well for file sharing systems where a file is either the definitive correct version or a wrong version. But they cannot accurately model richer services such as web services or e-commerce applications, where a Boolean value may not adequately represent a peer's experience of the quality of service (QoS) with other peers, such as the quality of products a peer sends and the expected delivery time (Yu et al 2004). Therefore the majority of later works (Yu & Singh 2003; Wang & Varadharajan 2004a; Wang & Varadharajan 2004b; Wang et al 2007) adopted the numeral rating system where the trust values are in a range (e.g. [0, 1]).

As pointed by Mui et al (Mui et al 2002), trust is a subjective expectation that an agent has about another's future behavior based on the history of their encounters. In Peer-to-Peer environments, this is especially prominent because in order to evaluate the trust of a target peer, the requesting peer has to reply on its own experience and other peers' experience. Therefore, the following issues should be investigated in Peer-to-Peer trust evaluation.

1. How to obtain the objective trust level of a peer?
2. How to identify malicious responding peers?
3. How to identify noise in responded recommendations?
4. How to measure the recommendation trust of responding peers?
5. How to aggregate the requesting peer's experience with other peers' experience?

In this chapter we present a dynamic process for peer trust evaluation and amendment. In our model we take into account of the credibility (recommendation trust) of each responding peer, which is derived from the deviations of its recommendations, and is amended through a series of interactions by the requesting peer. Hence this model provides more precision to trust evaluation, which results from evaluations from both the requesting peer and responding peers. In the following context, we will use 'credibility' to represent the measurement of recommendation trust.

TRUST EVALUATION

Local Rating

Each peer P_A, if it has an interaction with peer P_B in round k at time period t_k, can give a local trust evaluation $T_{A \to B}{}^{(k)}$ for the interaction occurred. The value is calculated taking into account of the quality of the service provided by P_B. The quality

of the service comes from several aspects (e.g. price, warranty, delivery, etc.) represented by a set of attributes:

$$x = \{x_1, x_2, \ldots, x_n\}$$

1. For each attribute x_i, calculate its firing level F_i as:

$$F_i = K_i(x_i)$$

where K_i is the grading function of attributes, which converts the attribute values into the corresponding firing levels. These levels can be represented as linguistic values, such as "very good", "good", "moderate", "poor" or "very poor" for 5 categories.

2. Calculate the scores R_i of each attribute as:

$$R_i = S_i(F_i)$$

where S_i is the score function that maps the attribute score in 5 intervals, i.e. $\{0, 0.25, 0.5, 0.75, 1\}$.

3. An evaluation value can be obtained by calculating the overall direct trust value $T_{A \to B}$ of attribute set x as follows:

$$T_{A \to B} = \sum w_{xi} \cdot R_i \qquad (1)$$

where the relative importance assigned to each attribute is modeled as a weight w_{xi}, $\sum w_{xi} = 1$. All weights are given by the end-peer.

Aggregated Rating

If a peer P_r has no interaction history with a peer P_x, which is referred to as a *target peer*, P_r can inquire other peers about the latest trust level of P_x. Suppose the trust values from a set of responding peers $RP = \{P_1, P_2, \ldots, P_m\}$ are

$$T_{1 \to x}, T_{2 \to x}, \dots, T_{m \to x}$$

The mean trust value can be simply calculated as

$$T_x = \frac{1}{m} \sum_{i=1}^{m} T_{i \to x} \qquad (2)$$

If P_r has a number of interactions with P_x during period $[t_{start}, t_{end}] = \{t_1, t_2, \dots, t_l\}$ where $t_k < t_{k+1}$ ($1 \le k < l$), it can evaluate P_x's trust value as follows:

$$T_{r \to x} = \sum_{k=1}^{l} w^{(k)} \cdot T_{r \to x}^{(k)} \qquad (3)$$

where

$$0 \le w^{(k)} < w^{(k+1)} < 1, 1 \le k < l\text{-}1;$$
$$\sum_{k=1}^{l} w^{(k)} = 1.$$

In equation (3), recent interactions are weighted more. This is a temporal evaluation method where fresher interactions are more important than old ones. But it takes into account of P_r's experience only.

Additionally, the requesting peer P_r can inquire the trust values of P_s given by other peers so as to aggregate these values with its own experiences.

Definition 1: For the interaction in round k at time period t_k, the *aggregated trust value* by P_r can be calculated as follows:

$$\tilde{T}_{r \to x}^{(k)} = w_r^{(k)} \cdot T_{r \to x}^{(k)} + \left(1 - w_r^{(k)}\right) \cdot \bar{T}_x^{(k)} \qquad (4)$$

where

$$\bar{T}_x^{(k)} = \frac{1}{m} \sum_{i=1}^{m} T_{i \to x}^{(k)}$$

$w_r^{(k)}$ is the weight to P_r's experience in round k and $w_r^{(k-1)} < w_r^{(k)}$ ($t_{k-1} < t_k$).

Equation (4) takes into account of both P_r's experience and other peers' experience with P_x leading to a more objective trust evaluation. Moreover, with more and more interactions with P_x, P_r is more 'confident' with its own experience. This is reflected by w_r, which may be very low in the beginning (e.g. 0.1 or 0.3) but it becomes greater and greater in later rounds.

Here the aggregated trust value is not the global trust value as in *EigenTrust* (Kamvar et al 2003) which is costly and not realistic to obtain in P2P environments. In particular, $\tilde{T}$ is more subject to P_r's evaluation in later rounds. So it is still a local value but it is more objective than $\bar{T}$ from P_r's perspective.

To control the changes of w_r, we adopt a function using two parameters: α and β.

Definition 2: Given parameters α ($0.5 < \alpha < 1$) and β ($\beta \in \{1, 2, 3, \dots\}$), *the weight to P_r's evaluation in round k* can be calculated as follows:

$$w_r^{(k)} = 1 - \alpha^{k^{\frac{1}{\beta}}}, 0.5 < \alpha < 1 \text{ and } \beta \in \{1, 2, 3, \dots\} \qquad (5)$$

In equation (5), α is the initial weight for $\bar{T}_x^{(1)}$ (see equation (4)) while the weight $w_r^{(1)}$ (i.e. $k=1$) is $1 - \alpha$. Typically, $w_r^{(1)}$, the weight of $T_{r \to x}^{(1)}$, is less than 0.5 (e.g. 0.1 or 0.3) as it weights the first interaction between P_r and P_x during $[t_{start}, t_{end}]$. So the mean of trust values from other peers should be weighted more (e.g. 0.9 or 0.7). k corresponds to the *kth round* in time period t_k. Given the same α and β, the larger k, the larger $w_r^{(k)}$. This means that with more and more interactions, trust values of P_x given by P_r should be weighted more. Other peers' evaluations become less and less important. Given the same α, the increment

Figure 1. $w_r^{(k)} = 1 - \alpha^{k^{\frac{1}{\beta}}}$ *($\alpha = 0.7$)*

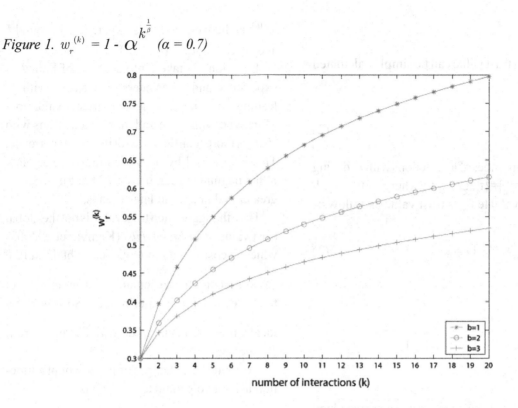

number of interactions (k)

of $w_r^{(k)}$ is subject to β. The larger β, the more slowly the $w_r^{(k)}$ increases.

The above features are depicted in Figure 1 where $\alpha = 0.7$, $k \in \{1, 2, ..., 20\}$ and β is set to be 1, 2 and 3 respectively. It illustrates that a larger β leads to a slower changing of $w_r^{(k)}$.

In addition, the valuation of β is dependant on applications. For certain applications, 20 may mean a high quantity of interactions. In this case, $\beta = 1$ is suitable. For other applications, where 100 or 300 means high quantity of interactions, $\beta = 2$ or $\beta = 3$ is more suitable.

Formulae (1)-(4) will be revisited in later sections when the credibility of each responding peer is evaluated and taken into account in the final trust calculation.

Recommendation and Noise

In the initial round evaluation (k=0), typically the requesting peer P_r can send requests to his 'friend'

peers to collect their evaluations on an unknown peer P_x. These friend peers are those peers with whom P_r has good interaction history. However, the limitation is that it is highly dependant on P_r's friend peers, i.e. the number of friend peers, and their interaction history with P_x. Furthermore, this method takes the interaction trust as the recommendation trust. Namely, recommendations from peers with trustworthy quality of services are considered to be trustworthy. Nevertheless, in the real world, interaction trust and recommendation trust are different. A good peer providing good quality of service may denigrate other peers especially when those peers provide the same kind of services, i.e. they are sellers selling the same product. Meanwhile, if P_r is a new peer, it may not have many friend peers to inquire with.

Alternatively, P_r can send requests to its neighbors and to other peers via its neighbors collecting their trust evaluations on P_x. Inevitably this method leads to noise in trust evaluation as the credibility of each responding peer is not known.

As we introduced in section "Aggregated Rating", with more and more interactions with peer P_x, which is unknown to P_r in the beginning, the requesting peer is more and more confident of its evaluations on P_x. However, equation (4) doesn't take into account of the credibility of responding peers' recommendations or filter out any possible noise in returned recommendations.

With more and more interactions with peer P_x, on one hand, P_r has more and more interaction trust values on P_x, which are *direct* interaction trust evaluations. By aggregating its direct evaluations with other peer' evaluations (*indirect evaluations*), the new aggregated evaluation becomes more and more objective from P_r's perspective. On the other hand, based on the objective aggregated trust values, it is possible for P_r to identify a responding peer with noise whose evaluations deviate from the "main stream" peers, or to identify a peer whose evaluations are close to the "main stream" peers. Thus the credibility of a responding peer can be estimated based on a series of interactions by P_r and the evaluations of other responding peers in different rounds. These credibility values of responding peers are very important references when P_r wants to know the trust values of other unknown peers. Meanwhile, with updated credibility values, the trust evaluation on P_x becomes more accurate and objective.

In our work, we classify four types of evaluations as follows:

1. **Honest evaluation:** the evaluating peer is honest and its evaluation reflects the quality of service;
2. **Positive exaggeration:** the peer's evaluation is always better than the true value by a certain extent;
3. **Negative exaggeration:** the peer's evaluation is always worse than the true value by a certain extent;
4. **Random exaggeration:** the peer's evaluation is a positive exaggeration or a negative exaggeration randomly. The mean of all

evaluations may be close to the true value. But any individual value in a certain round may have a significant deviation.

The above classification is different from the one used by Yu and Singh (Yu & Singh 2003) which replaces the 4th class with a 'complementary' class where the given value is always the complement of the true value. Namely, if the true value is 0.65, the complementary value is 1 - 0.65 = 0.35. Likewise, if the true value is 0.35, the complementary value is 1 - 0.35 = 0.65. That is not realistic in applications and it actually belongs to the above classes 2-4.

In this chapter, we don't explicitly identify 'malicious peers'. Any evaluation from a malicious peer may be an exaggeration that belongs to one of classes 2 to 4. In our model, we calculate the evaluation deviation and any evaluation deviation is identified as noise. If a peer's evaluation includes noise *in many rounds*, it leads to a low credibility. As a result this peer may be filtered out when aggregating trust values. The aim of our model is to find objective trust values, which are more accurate with less noise.

Credibility Evaluation

The evaluation deviation of a responding peer can be used to measure its credibility. If its evaluation is far away from the "main stream" peers, its credibility value will become low though it may not a malicious peer or a liar. Otherwise, the peer should obtain a high credibility value.

Some principles for credibility computation are as follows:

- **Principle 1:** The new credibility results from the deviation of the current round and the peer's previous credibility values (credibility history).
- **Principle 2:** A new credibility can be estimated first based on the deviation in the current round. A larger difference of the

existing credibility value and the newly estimated credibility value should cause more change in the credibility evaluation. In contrast, a smaller difference will have a less impact.

- **Principle 3:** Incremental number of ratings taken into account in an evaluation reduces the level of modification applied on the credibility evaluation until a certain level of confidence is achieved. Then the modification applied becomes constant.

In our method, if it is the first time to get the trust evaluation reply from a responding peer P_i, an initial value is assigned for its credibility (e.g. $c_i^{(0)} = 0.5$).

Definition 3: In the *kth* round, if the true trust value of a peer is $tt^{(k)}$ and the trust value given by peer P_i is $T_{i \to x}^{(k)}$, the *deviation* is

$$d_i^{(k)} = | T_{i \to x}^{(k)} - tt^{(k)} | \qquad (6)$$

In equation (6), *tt* is a kind of global trust value incorporating the trust evaluations of all peers. Therefore logically *tt* exists but it is impractical to obtain it due to the nature of P2P networks. In subsequent calculations, it can be replaced with the aggregated trust value or the trust value given by the requesting peer.

With d_i, we can estimate credibility c_i which should be in reverse proportion to d_i. Here we simply assume calculate credibility c_i is *approximately*

$$c_i^{(k)} = 1 - d_i^{(k)^{\frac{1}{s}}} \qquad (7)$$

where *s* is a *strictness factor* which is used to control the curve. Figure 2 depicts the relationship between d_i and c_i. For example, if d_i =0.25, then c_i =0.75, 0.5, 0.37 when *s* = 1, 2, 3 respectively. The higher the *s*, the stricter the evaluation. However,

according to principle 1, equation (7) cannot reflect any credibility history.

In the following definition, we take $1 - d_i^{(k)^{\frac{1}{s}}}$ as the *new estimated credibility* and define a new equation for credibility evaluation, which takes into account of credibility history.

Definition 4: Given the credibility $c_i^{(k-1)}$ for peer P_i in last round *k-1*, the deviation $d_i^{(k)}$ in the current round *k*, *the new credibility* $c_i^{(k)}$ can be calculated as follows:

$$c_i^{(k)} = c_i^{(k-1)} + \theta_i^{(k)} \cdot (1 - d_i^{(k)^{\frac{1}{s}}} - c_i^{(k-1)}) \qquad (8)$$

where $\theta_i^{(k)}$ is an *impact factor* in [0,0.4621], and

$$\theta_i^{(k)} = \frac{e^{|1 - d_i^{(k)^{\frac{1}{s}}} - c_i^{(k-1)}| - 1}}{e + 1} \qquad (9)$$

In equation (8), the new credibility $c_i^{(k)}$ results from the previous credibility $c_i^{(k-1)}$ and the current deviation $d_i^{(k)}$ (principle 1). The change may be an increment or a decrement, which results from $\theta_i^{(k)}$ and $(1 - d_i^{(k)^{\frac{1}{s}}} - c_i^{(k-1)})$ where $\theta_i^{(k)} \geq 0$. This means that if $1 - d_i^{(k)^{\frac{1}{s}}} > c_i^{(k-1)}$, it is an increment. Otherwise, it is a decrement. However, the quantity of the change is also controlled by $\theta_i^{(k)}$, which has the following properties.

Property 1: If $1 - d_i^{(k)^{\frac{1}{s}}} = c_i^{(k-1)}$, then $\theta_i^{(k)} = \theta_{min} = 0$;

This property means that if $1 - d_i^{(k)^{\frac{1}{s}}} = c_i^{(k-1)}$, there is no change with $c_i^{(k-1)}$ and $c_i^{(k)}$.

Property 2: If $1 - d_i^{(k)^{\frac{1}{s}}} \neq c_i^{(k-1)}$, then $\theta_i^{(k)} > 0$;

Figure 2. Relationship between d_i and c_i

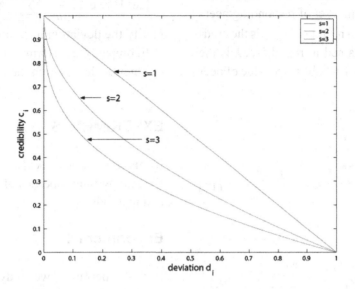

This property means that if $1 - d_i^{(k)^{\frac{1}{s}}}$ and $c_i^{(k-1)}$ are different, there will be an increment or a decrement for the credibility modification.

Property 3: The larger $|1 - d_i^{(k)^{\frac{1}{s}}} - c_i^{(k-1)}|$, the larger $\theta_i^{(k)}$. Likewise, the smaller $1 - d_i^{(k)^{\frac{1}{s}}} - c_i^{(k-1)}$, the smaller $\theta_i^{(k)}$ (principle 2);

Property 4: When $|1 - d_i^{(k)^{\frac{1}{s}}} - c_i^{(k-1)}| = 1$, $\theta_{\max}$ ≈ 0.4621.

Properties 1 to 4 outline the relationship between $|1 - d_i^{(k)^{\frac{1}{s}}} - c_i^{(k-1)}|$ and $\theta_i^{(k)}$. More properties are studied in our experiment presented in the experiment section.

With c_i, we can calculate more accurate trust values.

Definition 5: Suppose peer P_r has collected trust evaluations on peer P_x from a set of responding peers $RP = \{P_1, P_2, ..., P_m\}$ in round k. $c_i^{(k-1)}$ is the credibility of peer P_i obtained in round $k-1$. Then the trust value of peer P_x in round k is:

$$\bar{T}_x^{(k)} = \frac{1}{m} \sum_{i=1}^{m} (c_i^{(k-1)} \cdot T_{i \to x}^{(k)}) \qquad (10)$$

Herein the definition of $\bar{T}_x^{(k)}$ in Definition 1 has been amended with the credibility of each responding peer to be taken into account, where $c_i^{(k-1)} \cdot T_{i \to x}^{(k)}$ is the derived trust as defined by Berth et al (Berth et al 1994).

Thus according to equations (4) and (10), the *aggregated trust values* can be obtained as follows.

$$\bar{T}_{r \to x}^{(k)} = w_r^{(k)} \cdot T_{r \to x}^{(k)} + (1 - w_r^{(k)}) \cdot \frac{1}{m} \cdot \sum_{i=1}^{m} (c_i^{(k-1)} \cdot T_{i \to x}^{(k)}) \qquad (11)$$

According to the above method, after a series of interactions and recommendations, the credibility of each responding peer can be calculated. At a certain round, the requesting peer can apply a threshold to filter out responding peers with low credibility values. Hence these peers are blacklisted.

Suppose peer P_r has collected the trust evaluations on peer P_x from a set of responding peers $RP=\{P_1, P_2, ..., P_m\}$ in round k. $c_i^{(k-1)}$ is the credibility of peer P_i obtained in round k-1. λ is the credibility threshold. Then the trust value of peer P_x in round k is:

$$\bar{T}_{r \to x}^{(k)} = w_r^{(k)} \cdot T_{r \to x}^{(k)}$$
$$+(1 - w_r^{(k)}) \cdot \frac{1}{m'} \cdot \sum_{i=1}^{m'}(c_i^{(k-1)} \cdot T_{i \to x}^{(k)}) \quad (12)$$

where

1. $RP'=\{P_1, P_2, ..., P_{m'}\} \subseteq RP$
2. $P_i \in RP' = \{P_i| c_i^{(k-1)} \geq \lambda, \lambda \in [0,1], |RP'|=m'$
3. blacklist $BL = \{P_j| c_i^{(k-1)} < \lambda\}$

However, equation (12) can be improved further.

Definition 6: With a set of trustworthy responding peers in $RP'=\{P_1, P_2, ..., P_{m'}\}$, their recommended trust values $\{T_{r \to x}^{(k)}\}$ and credibility values $\{c_i^{(k-1)}\}$, *the aggregated trust value of peer P_x in round k is:*

$$\tilde{T}_{r \to x}^{(k)} = w_r^{(k)} \cdot T_{r \to x}^{(k)}$$
$$+(1 - w_r^{(k)}) \cdot \frac{1}{m'} \cdot \sum_{i=1}^{m'}(c_i^{(k-1)} \cdot T_{i \to x}^{(k)}) \quad (13)$$

where

$$w_i^{(k-1)} = \frac{c_i^{(k-1)}}{\sum_{i=1}^{m'} c_i^{(k-1)}} \quad (14)$$

Here, we modify equation (12) by replacing $c_i^{(k-1)}$ with $w_i^{(k-1)}$. As $c_i^{(k-1)} \leq 1$ (e.g. 0.8, 0.9), $\frac{1}{m'} \cdot \sum_{i=1}^{m'}(c_i^{(k-1)} \cdot T_{i \to x}^{(k)})$ leads to a lower trust

value. However $\frac{1}{m'} \cdot \sum_{i=1}^{m'}(c_i^{(k-1)} \cdot T_{i \to x}^{(k)})$ can rectify the deviation in some circumstances. We will compare the performance difference in our experiments illustrated in the experiment section.

EXPERIMENTS

In this section, we present the experimental results illustrating the properties of proposed equations and methods.

Experiment 1

In this experiment, we study more properties of equations (8) and (9). The strictness factor s is set to 1 in Figures 3 and 4, and 2 in Figures 5 and 6.

In Figure 3, the deviation d_i is set to 0.2 while the initial credibility $c_i^{(0)}$ is set to 0.2, 0.8 and 1.0 respectively. From the result, we can observe that when $c_i^{(0)}=0.8$, c_i is constant and $c_i=0.8=1-0.2=1-d_i$. If $c_i^{(0)}$ is set to a low value of 0.2, c_i can be increased round by round. The value reaches approximately $1-d_i$. So is the case where $c_i^{(0)}=1$ and c_i is decreased. From this experiment, it is easy to see that

$$\lim_{k \to \infty} c_i^{(k)} = 1 - d_i^{\frac{1}{s}} \quad (15)$$

In Figure 4, the deviation is set to $d_i=0.7$ while the initial credibility $c_i^{(0)}$ is set to 0.3, 0.5 and 1.0 respectively.

It is easy to see that an accurate $c_i^{(0)}$ (e.g. 0.3) leads to subsequent accurate credibility values though an inaccurate $c_i^{(0)}$ can be amended by increments or decrements. In any case, equation (15) holds.

Figures 5 and 6 plot two cases where $s=2$ and one of three initial credibility values in each case is set to $1 - d_i^{\frac{1}{2}}$. The curve change trends are exactly the same as Figures 3 and 4. As $1-0.2^{\frac{1}{2}}=0.5528$

Figure 3. Experiment 1 (d_i=0.2, s=1)

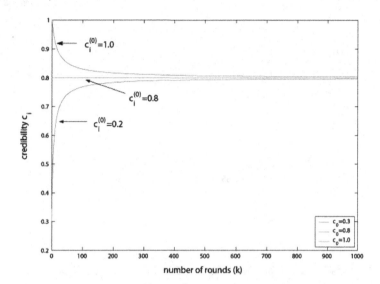

Figure 4. Experiment 1 (d_i=0.7, s=1)

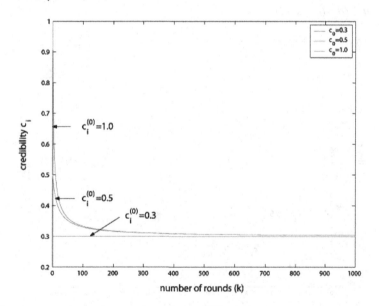

and $1 - 0.7^{\frac{1}{2}} = 0.1633$, equation (15) holds.

This property satisfies principle 3.

Experiment 2

In this experiment, we study the trust evaluation on target peer P_x, whose true trust value *tt* is assumed to be 0.65, by collecting the evaluations from a set of peers where 30% or 50% peers give negatively exaggerated evaluations. The trust value given by the requesting peer is also 0.65. We choose a trust value as 0.65 because it is the case where positive exaggeration, negative exaggeration and random exaggeration are all possible.

Figure 5. Experiment 1 ($d_i=0.2$, $s=2$)

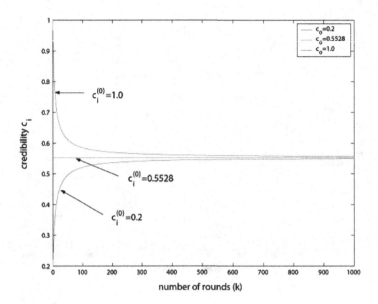

Figure 6. Experiment 1 ($d_i=0.7$, $s=2$)

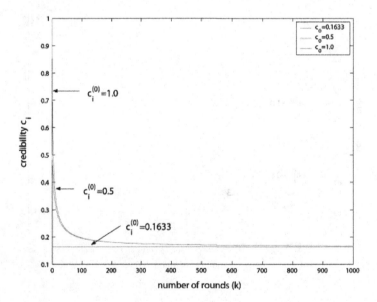

In this experiment, we set $s=2$, $\alpha=0.7$, $\beta=2$ (see Figure 7). We consider only class 1 (honest) and class 3 (negative exaggeration) peers as this is an extremely malicious environment. If all peers in classes 2, 3 and 4 are considered, their deviations may counter-balance each other.

In this experiment we compare five evaluation strategies.

- **Strategy 1:** The final trust value obtained in each round is the mean of all evaluations (see equation (2)).

Figure 7. w_r in Experiment 2 ($\alpha = 0.7$, $\beta = 2$)

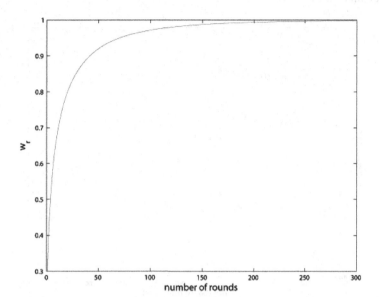

- **Strategy 2:** This strategy amends strategy 1. The credibility of each responding peer is taken into account in the trust evaluation even if the peer's credibility is very low (see equation (10)).

- **Strategy 3:** This strategy applies the weight w_r of the responding peer P_r via equation (11).

- **Strategy 4:** This strategy improves strategy 3 by ignoring low credibility peers, where the threshold is set to λ=0.6 from the *50th* round onwards. Like strategy 3, this strategy also applies weight w_r of the responding peer P_r via equation (11). Strategy 4 was originally proposed as the best strategy in our previous work (Yan & Varadharajan 2005).

- **Strategy 5:** This strategy improves strategy 3 by ignoring low credibility peers, where the threshold is set to λ=0.6 from the *50th* round onwards. Meanwhile, $c_i^{(k-1)}$ is replaced by $w_i^{(k-1)}$ (see equation (13)).

In this experiment, there are 3 classes among negatively exaggerating peers. Their mean de-viations are 0.1, 0.2 and 0.3 respectively. Their credibility values are plotted in Figure 8 where the initial credibility $c_i^{(0)}$ is set to 0.5. According to equation (8), a larger deviation leads to a low credibility, and a lower deviation leads to a higher credibility. In contrast, the deviation of an honest peer is approximately 0.07.

From Figure 9, we can see that strategies 1 and 2 lead to low trust values where strategy 2 is even less accurate than strategy 1 as each peer's credibility is less than 1.0 resulting in $c_i * T_i < T_i$. In strategy 3, the trust values become more and more accurate as the requesting peer's experience becomes more important. But the trust values in strategy 5 can be improved earlier as c_i is replaced by w_i and low credibility peers are ignored (see equation (13)). Strategy 4 slightly improves strategy 3. But it is inferior to strategy 5 when $k > 50$.

Figure 10 depicts the results from another case where 50% peers are negatively exaggerating. In this case, strategies 1 and 2 obtain lower values than those in Figure 10. In contrast, strategy 5 outperforms other strategies.

Figure 8. c_i in Experiment 2 (s=2, $c_i^{(0)}$ =0.5)

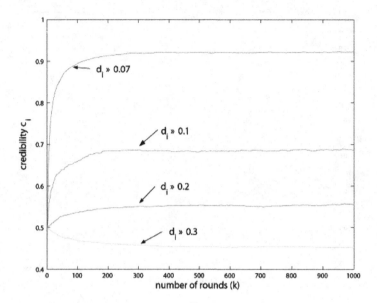

Figure 9. Experiment 2 - 30% Negatively Exaggerated Peers (s=2, tt=0.65)

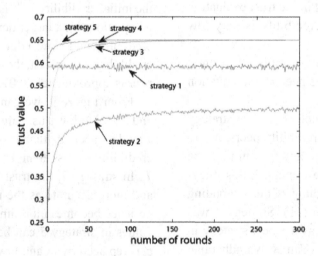

Experiment 3

In this experiment, we continue to compare five strategies with positively exaggerating peers.

The results with 30% and 50% positively exaggerating peers are plotted in Figure 11 and Figure 12 where we compare the same 5 strategies and tt=0.65. In strategy 1, as there are some positively exaggerating peers, the mean is greater than 0.65. The values in strategy 2 are lower as each peer's credibility (less than 1.0) is taken into account. The result of strategy 3 is improved as w_r takes effect. Strategy 4 improves strategy 3 slightly when $k > 50$. But in both cases strategy 5 leads to more accurate values.

Figure 10. Experiment 2 - 50% Negatively Exaggerating Peers (s=2, tt=0.65)

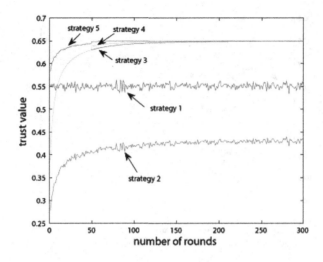

Figure 11. Experiment 3 - 30% Positively Exaggerating Peers (s=2, tt=0.65)}

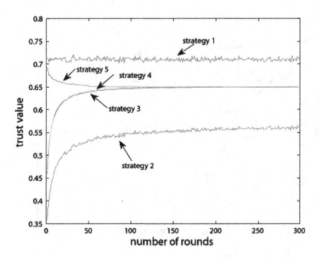

Experiment 4

In this experiment, we continue to compare five strategies with randomly exaggerating peers.

Figure 13 depicts the result with 30% randomly exaggerating peers. The result with 50% randomly exaggerating peers is plotted in Figure 14. In both cases, in strategy 1, the mean of trust values in a series of rounds is close to the true value while it has much deviation. Similar to the case in Figure 13, $c_i * T_i$ in strategy 2 results in lower trust values. Strategy 3 improves Strategy 2 and Strategy 4 slightly outperforms Strategy 3. But strategy 5 leads to accurate values with less deviations as peers with low credibility have been ignored and the impact of $c_i^{(k-1)} * T_i$ is also replaced by $w_i^{(k-1)} * T_i$.

In order to illustrate the difference of strategies more clearly, the results of strategies 3, 4 and 5 are plotted in Figures 15 and 16.

Figure 12. Experiment 3 - 50% Positively Exaggerating Peers (s=2, tt=0.65)

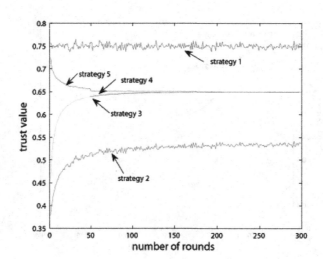

Figure 13. Experiment 4 - 30% Randomly Exaggerating Peers (s=2, tt=0.65)

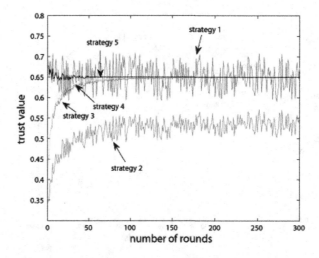

Comparison

In this section, we qualitatively compare our proposed model with several related models in the field. These models all incorporate the ratings from both the requesting peer and responding peers in the final trust evaluation of a target peer. However, they are different in other aspects, such as rating system, temporal property in trust evaluation, the consideration and measurement of trust recom-

mendation. These are fundamental and important aspects in trust evaluation.

In *EigenTrust* (Kamvar et al 2003), a model is proposed aiming at calculating the global trust value that reflects the experiences of all peers in the network with the target peer. The global trust is calculated by a requesting peer incorporating the responses of other peers and its own experience. In the trust calculation, a weight a is set for the requesting peer's local trust while $1-a$ is

Figure 14. Experiment 4 - 50% Randomly Exaggerating Peers (s=2, tt=0.65)

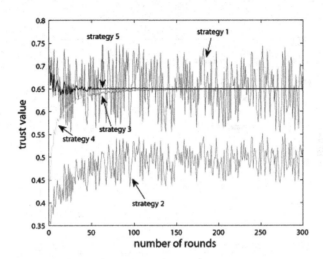

Figure 15. Experiment 4 - difference of strategies 3, 4 and 5, 30% Randomly Exaggerating Peers (s=2, tt=0.65)

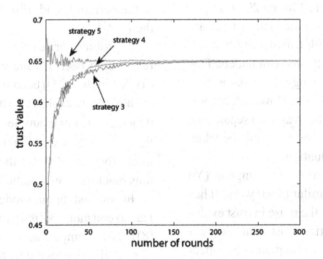

the weight for responding peers. The trust of the requesting peer on a responding peer is also taken into account.

Marti and Garcia-Molina (Marti & Garcia-Molina 2004) propose a model to calculate the aggregated trust value for P2P file-sharing environments, which incorporates both the requesting peer's experience and responding peers' recommendations with different weights. The trust on

responding peers are also taken into account when computing the aggregated trust value. There are two methods to determine the responding peer set (Marti & Garcia-Molina 2004). One method is that each requesting peer's neighbor can be a responding peer. The other one is that a peer with whom the requesting peer has good transaction (e.g. provide complete files) is asked to provide trust values (recommendations).

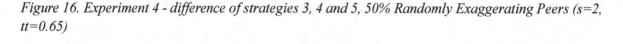

Figure 16. Experiment 4 - difference of strategies 3, 4 and 5, 50% Randomly Exaggerating Peers (s=2, tt=0.65)

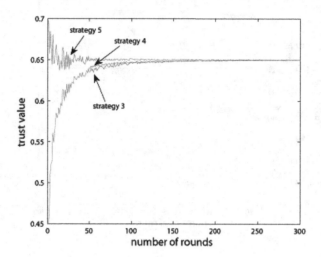

The common problem in both works (Kamvar et al 2003; Marti & Garcia-Molina 2004) is that transaction trust and recommendation trust are mixed. Namely, peers with trustworthy transactions are taken as trustworthy recommenders. This may be the compelled strategy if the requesting peer newly joins the network. However, recommendation trust needs to be evaluated separately. In addition, temporal dimension should be taken into account in trust evaluation.

In contrast, the work of Yu and Singh in (Yu & Singh 2004) is quite similar to our work. It has a mechanism to calculate the noise in trust evaluations and recommendation trust. But different from our model, it has a complementary peer class instead of random exaggeration peer class. We argue that a random exaggeration peer class is more realistic and the complementary class is covered in positive exaggeration class, negative exaggeration class or random exaggeration class. In addition, the credibility of a responding peer is taken into account when calculating aggregated trust values. The method can be described as follows:

$$c_i^{(k)} = c_i^{(k-1)} \cdot \theta$$

where $\theta \in [0,1]$ results from the deviation $d_i^{(k)}$ in the current round. If $d_i = 0$, then $\theta = 1$. If $d_i \leq 0$, then $\theta < 1$.

A problem arises that c_i (denoted as w_i for responding peer i in the work of Yu and Singh (Yu & Singh 2004)) becomes less round by round even for an honest peer with $d_i \neq 0$ because if $d_i \neq 0$ then $\theta < 1$. For example, if $c_i^{(1)} = 1$ and $d_i = 0.07$, then $c_i^{(10)} = 0.7$ and $c_i^{(20)} = 0.45$. Therefore, it is not likely for c_i to indicate the credibility level and thus blacklist low credibility responding peers.

In contrast, in our model, constant deviations lead to constant credibility values (refer to Figure (8)). For example, as we mentioned in section "Credibility Evaluation", a significant deviation decreases the credibility value. But only constant large deviations in multiple rounds lead to low credibility values (e.g. peer class with $d_i = 0.3$ in Figure (8)). Meanwhile constant accurate evaluations with low deviations lead to a high credibility level. For example, in Figure (8), though the initial credibility is 0.5 (a neutral level) for honest peer class with $d_i = 0.07$, after multiple rounds, c_i reaches approximately 0.9, which is a high credibility level. Therefore, a good credibility is the result of accumulative accurate evaluations with

Table 1. Comparison of trust evaluation models

	binary rating	aggregated trust value[1]	temporal dimension	recommendation trust considered in trust evaluation	measurement of recommendation trust
EigenTrust	yes	yes	no	partial[2]	no
model in Marti et al 2004	yes	yes	no	partial[2]	no
Model by Yu and Singh 2004	no	yes	yes	partial[3]	partial[3]
our model	no	yes	yes	yes	yes

1. The aggregated trust value incorporates the experience of both the requesting peer and responding peers.

2. Peers with good transaction trust are taken as trustworthy responding peers. Transaction trust and recommendation trust are mixed.

3. The proposed method cannot reflect the credibility level in some circumstances.

less deviation. A bad credibility is the result of accumulative evaluations with much deviation.

The comparison of several models is listed in Table 1.

CONCLUSION

In this chapter, we present a model for trust evaluation in P2P environments. A method for recommendation trust evaluation has been presented, which is based on recommendation history and the deviation in recommendations. The proposed trust evaluation model takes into account of the credibility of responding peers and hence is valuable to identify inaccurate recommendations and improve the precision of trust evaluations. Moreover, the final trust value results from both the requesting peer's evaluation and other peers' evaluations while the former one becomes more and more important. This is realistic in real applications and helps obtain more objective trust values.

However, due to the nature of P2P networks, it is impractical to obtain global trust values as it is impossible to collect trust values given by all peers. Thus the aggregated trust value is also a local value to the requesting peer. In addition, if the requesting peer is honest and objective, those responding peers who were given high credibility by the responding peer are objective. The final

trust value computed by the requesting peer is also objective. On the contrary, if the requesting peer is not honest, it's computed final trust value would not be objective as it trusts those responding peers who are not honest and objective.

Furthermore, the proposed approach requires history trust data for multiple rounds. It may occur communication overhead for feedback collection between the requesting peer and responding peers. This is the common drawback in P2P trust management systems. The overhead can be reduced when the data is collected after one request, not multiple requests in multiple rounds. Meanwhile, the proposed approach can be applied to a centralized trust management environment, where a respond can return all necessary trust data.

REFERENCES

Anancha, S., D'souza, P., Perich, F., Joshi, A., & Yesha, Y. (2003, January). P2P M-commerce in pervasive environments. *ACM SIGecom Exchange, 3*(4), 1-9.

Berth, M. B. T., & Klein, B. (1994). Valuation of trust in open networks. In *Proceedings of the European Symposium on Computer Security (ESORICS)* (LNCS 875 pp. 3-18). Berlin, Germany: Springer-Verlag.

Bishop, M. (2003). *Computer Security: Art and Science*. Reading, MA: Addition-Wesley Press.

Damiani, E., di Vimercati, S. D. C., Paraboschi, S., Samarati, P., & Violante, F. (2002). A reputation based approach for choosing reliable resources in PeertoPeer networks. In *Proceedings of ACM CCS'02* (pp. 207-216).

International Telecommunication Union. (1997). *X.509-Information Technology-Open Systems Interconnection-The Directory: Authentication Framework*.

Jøsang, A., Ismail, R., & Boyd, C. (2007). A survey of trust and reputation systems for online service provision. *Decision Support Systems, 43*(2), 618–644. doi:10.1016/j.dss.2005.05.019

Kamvar, S. D., Schlosser, M. T., & Garcia-Molina, H. (2003). The EigenTrust algorithm for reputation management in p2p networks. In *Proceedings of the 12th International WWW Conference* (pp. 640-651).

Knight, D. H., & Chervany, N. L. (1966). The meaning of trust (Technical Report WP9604). University of Minnesota, Management Information Systems Research Center.

Marsh, S. (1994). *Formalising trust as a computational concept*. Unpublished doctoral dissertation, Department of Computer Science, University of Sterling

Marti, S., & Garcia-Molina, H. (2004). Limited reputation sharing in p2p systems. In *Proceedings of ACM EC'04* (pp. 91-101).

Mui, L., Mohtashemi, M., & Halberstadt, A. (2002). A computational model of trust and reputation. In *Proceedings of the 35th Hawaii International Conference on System Sciences* (pp. 2431-2439).

Nooteboom, B. (2002). *Trust: Foundations, Functions, Failure and Figures*. Cheltenham, UK: Edward Elgar Publishing Inc. *P2PBazaar*. (n.d.). Retrieved from http://www.p2pbazaar.com/index.html/

Resnick, P., Kuwabara, K., Zeckhauser, R., & Friedman, E. (2000). Reputation systems. *Communications of the ACM, 43*(12), 45–48. doi:10.1145/355112.355122

Wang, Y., Lin, K.-J., Wong, D. S., & Varadharajan, V. (2007). The design of a rule-based and event-driven trust management framework. In *Proceedings of The IEEE International Conference on e-Business Engineering (ICEBE 2007)* (pp. 97-104).

Wang, Y., & Varadharajan, V. (2004a). Interaction trust evaluation in decentralized environments. In *Proceedings of 5th International Conference on Electronic Commerce and Web Technologies (EC-Web04)* (LNCS 3182, pp. 144-153).

Wang, Y., & Varadharajan, V. (2004b). A time-based peer trust evaluation in p2p e-commerce environments. In *Proceedings of 5th International Conference on Web Information Systems Engineering (WISE'04)* (LNCS 3306, pp. 730-735). Berlin, Germany: Springer-Verlag.

Wang, Y., & Varadharajan, V. (2005). Trust^2: Developing trust in peer-to-peer environments. In *Proceedings of 2005 IEEE International Conference on Services Computing (SCC 2005)* (pp. 24-31).

Xiong, L., & Liu, L. (2002). *PeerTrust: A trust mechanism for an open peer-to-peer information system* (Technical Report GIT-CC-02-29). Georgia Institute of Technology.

Xiong, L., & Liu, L. (2004). PeerTrust: Supporting reputation-based trust for peer-to-peer electronic communities. *IEEE Transactions on Knowledge and Data Engineering, 16*(7), 843–857. doi:10.1109/TKDE.2004.1318566

Yu, B., & Singh, M. P. (2002). An evidential model of distributed reputation management. In *Proceedings of First International Joint Conference on Autonomous Agents and Multiagent Systems* (pp. 294-301).

Yu, B., & Singh, M. P. (2003). Detecting deception in reputation management. In *Proceedings of Second International Joint Conference on Autonomous Agents and Multiagent Systems* (pp. 73-80).

Yu, B., Singh, M. P., & Sycara, K. (2004). Developing trust in large-scale peer-to-peer systems. In *Proceedings of 2004 IEEE First Symposium on Multi-Agent Security and Survivability* (pp. 1-10).

Yu, T., Winslett, M., & Seamons, K. E. (2001). Interoperable strategies in automated trust negotiation. In *Proceedings of ACM Conference on Computer and Communications Security 2001* (pp. 146-155).

Zimmerman, P. (1994). *PGP User's Guide*. Cambridge, MA: MIT Press.

Chapter 10
Trust Management in Ad Hoc Networks

Rafael Timóteo de Sousa Júnior
University of Brasília, Brazil

Ricardo Staciarini Puttini
University of Brasília, Brazil

ABSTRACT

Mobile ad hoc networks (MANETs) are wireless networks whose mobile nodes exchange information without the help of a predefined network infrastructure. MANET services, such as auto-configuration and ad hoc routing, must be provided in a distributed and self-organizing manner, by collaboration between network nodes and requiring each participant to both provide its own resources and exploit others' resources. As the nodes may, continually and at any time, appear, disappear or move around within the network, the structure of a MANET is constructed dynamically and the network topology is subject to frequent and unforeseeable changes. In this situation traditional security solutions are insufficient to exhaustively address all security requirements. The distinctive characteristics of ad hoc networks imply the need for distributed collaboration solutions that are based on some form of trust. In this chapter, the authors survey the modes of utilization of trust as means for providing, with network security mechanisms or as an alternative to them, the necessary services in MANETs.

INTRODUCTION

Mobile Ad Hoc Networks (MANETs), also known as spontaneous networks, are natural places for applying computational trust. Indeed, the distinctive characteristics of ad hoc networks imply the need for distributed collaboration solutions that implicitly are based on some form of trust.

MANETs are wireless networks whose mobile nodes exchange information without the help of a predefined network infrastructure (Corson & Marker, 1999). In these networks the nodes communicate directly with the others, in a peer-to-peer communications architecture. Since there is no supporting infrastructure, the routing services are established cooperatively and each node taking part in the network acts as a possible router for the others. Thus, when a node needs to communicate with another

DOI: 10.4018/978-1-61520-682-7.ch010

that is not within its transmission range, it relays its packets via a neighbor node that is closer to the destination node, which in turn relays the packet onward. Therefore, MANETs are multi-hop mobile networks in which the connectivity between nodes is ensured by collaborative routing (Chun, Qin, Yong & Meilin, 2000; Royer & Toh, 1999).

In a MANET, the nodes may, continually and at any time, appear, disappear or move around within the network. As a result, the structure of the MANET is constructed dynamically and the network topology is subject to frequent and unforeseeable changes. This characteristic linked to the mobility of the nodes, allied to the limited bandwidth and unreliability of wireless links, means that the availability of a specific node cannot be ensured. In this way, the services in a MANET cannot be concentrated in centralized entities. Conversely, the services in a MANET must be provided in a distributed and self-organizing manner, by collaboration between network nodes. This collaboration normally makes use of the natural redundancies resulting from the communication model which, to a certain extent, compensates for the lack of certainty regarding the availability of individual nodes.

In MANETs, as presented above, two basic services are necessary to form the networks and ensure the continuity of operations: auto-configuration (Mohsin & Prakash, 2002; Nesargi & Prakash, 2002; Perkins, Malinen, Wakikawa, Royer & Sun, 2001) and ad hoc routing (Clausen & Jacquet, 2003; Johnson, Maltz & Hu, 2004; Ogier, Templin & Lewis, 2004; Perkins & Royer, 2003). While the auto-configuration service is related to the association of the nodes to the network, allowing rapid set-up with little or no user intervention, the routing service is related to the multi-hop nature of MANETs. Thus, configuration and routing protocols must be designed to take into account the constant changes in the network topology due to the mobility of the nodes.

Given these specificities of ad hoc networks, their relation to trust aspects can be discussed

and the possible roles of trust technologies in this context can be identified as means for providing, with other mechanisms or as an alternative to them, the necessary services in MANETs.

The objective of this chapter is to present the modes of utilization of trust in ad hoc networks. We begin by describing the distinctive characteristics of ad hoc networks, discussing how the concept of trust can be useful to deal with the issues related to these characteristics and presenting the possible roles of trust technologies in this context.

We then present an overview of the underlying technologies and protocols for ad hoc networks so as to establish the basis for describing vulnerabilities of these networks. This leads to the description of attacks exploiting these vulnerabilities and to the discussion on the utilization of trust to mitigate these attacks. This issue is approached both from the point of view of autonomic trust reasoning by each node and the collaboration among nodes regarding trust aspects, based on the specification of an ad hoc trust management architecture. This approach allows the description of formal methods and languages to express the concept of trust, the presentation of trust models, including evidence management and trust calculation, and the collaboration for managing and exchanging information about reputation.

The chapter is concluded with other applications of trust in ad hoc networks, such as the utilization of trust for choosing alternative routes, and visualization of trust as a human oriented metric of the behavior and performance of ad hoc networks.

TRUST ASPECTS WITHIN AD HOC NETWORK OPERATIONS

In this section we examine some of the ad hoc operations and explain in which aspects trust technologies can be applied to perform these operations.

Node Auto-Configuration

A node arriving at an ad hoc network does not know any neighbors; therefore it does not have any view of the network. The node starts actions to acquire its identification within the network (usually the IP address) and to begin collaboration for management of available identification and address spaces. The node can broadcast requests for helping from other already present nodes or alternatively can hear from the network and discover available servers.

The first contact among nodes and the obtaining of the required identification is in fact a process of trust establishment, i.e. the process for establishing a trust relationship between a provider and a requesting node, as this node (playing the role of a trustor) must believe that the provider (in the role of trustee) is acting as specified in some protocol and has the necessary authorization for distributing identifications. This trust relationship is associated to a dual and reversed trust relationship, as the provider of the identification (now as a trustor) must believe that the arriving node will be a collaborating and correctly behaving node in conformance to ad hoc protocols.

As there is no way to ensure that preventive security mechanisms, even cryptography based ones, will be effective during all the following operations, both nodes are required to monitor each other to collect useful evidence of the respective correct expected behavior. This corresponds indeed to a mutual trust monitoring process that aims to collect useful evidence for mutual trust assessment, i.e. the evaluating of the trustworthiness of the trustee by the trustor. Each node assessing the current trust relationship can decide if the relationship has changed and make a decision about a measure that should be taken.

Although the active entity in a typical ad hoc node is not required to reason in terms of trust, the implicit idea of trust is in the specification of the auto-configuration actions. Moreover, as services in a MANET must be provided in a distributed

and self-organizing manner, by collaboration between network nodes, a node that acquires an identification becomes itself another responsible for managing the identification and addressing space and even will have to manage the entry (and exit) of other nodes in the ad hoc network, thus propagating the trust acquired from the first providing node. This way, there is a chaining of trust relationships that continuously appear and disappear in the network.

Neighbor Discovery

Independent and complementary to auto-configuration needs, useful interactions in ad hoc networks will depend in general on an arbitrary number of nodes being able to collaborate both locally and remotely through the intermediation of some nodes. This brings the issue of systematically discovering neighbors.

As with auto-configuration, initially a node does not know any neighbor, therefore it does not have any view of the network. The node must start to build its view with the exchange of specific messages (usually named HELLO messages) with the neighbors, so as to allow the node to detect links to other nodes within the transmission range. This process allows each node to obtain a link set containing both asymmetrical and symmetrical links, i.e., respectively allowing unidirectional and bidirectional message transmissions. Also, each node can announce its link set so as to allow the neighbors to calculate the best candidates for sending messages to 2-hop neighbors and for routing to nodes faraway. This way, the individual views of links are the base for future decisions which will be taken by the nodes both about the neighborhood (small world), and also, indirectly, for the possible interactions (for example, routing) towards the big world through forwarded messages.

As these actions require that a node to collaborate before acquiring certainty about the other identities and capacities, they need some form of basic trust from the node and imply a node behavior that includes trust monitoring and trust assessment among nodes.

Collaboration for Routing

Routes are obtained, and even complete routing tables are computed, from the information coming from the neighborhood. As the ad hoc topology is expected to change, previously known routes, or the routing table, must be recalculated if the node detects a change in the set of neighbors.

In this context, the inherent risk in the choice of routes towards any destination is to choose a corrupted or misbehaving node to be a router. Naturally, this vulnerability can be exploited by the attackers, who give false information about the network topology in order to direct large amounts of the network traffic towards themselves and/or to disturb the operation of the network.

The selection of intermediary nodes for routing towards a destination implies that a node, not only trusts some neighbor for routing, but also the choices of routes made by this neighbor and, successively, the chain of chosen intermediary neighbors of neighbors until the destination. Actually, there is a chain of this indirect trust relation between a node and any router forwarding its packets to the destination. This chain has the particularity that the last router before the destination, being a neighbor of this target node, is the sole node that directly exchanges discovery messages with the destination (HELLO messages). The existence of these forwarding chains expresses the fact that there is a form of trust transitivity among nodes and that the routing information exchange is in fact a kind of recommendation system in ad hoc networks. By the way, this also means that the destination node is itself the starting point of the trust chain, given that the destination is responsible for the neighborhood discovery process that ensures that every other node can correctly communicate with this destination node.

Given the existence of a spreading of the trust placed in the neighbor, it is understandable that certain attacks against ad hoc networks exploit the vulnerability resulting from the absence of validation of this derived trust chain, as is the case with the two main ad hoc routing protocols described hereafter. This brings the idea that a node should have a degree of mistrust concerning the information used for the calculation of the routes or the recommendations about routes. This mistrust could be associated to the use of a procedure for validating the routing information which is spread in network.

However, as the notions of trust and mistrust are not built into the main ad hoc routing protocols, the routing operations generate information related to trust and present implicit trust rules that, as such, are not taken into account by the nodes, although trust rules and trust related information could be actually exploited to contribute to the security of routing. As a consequence, in bare ad hoc protocols the nodes create trust relationships without validated evidence, not measuring the consequences of these relationships and thus without any mistrust in their choices.

Adaptation of Node Behavior

As discussed above, the notions of trust and mistrust, and the associated processes of trust monitoring, trust assessment and trust based decisions, are not explicitly taken into account in basic ad hoc protocols. But it is possible to put forward the conditions to use trust-based reasoning as a means for the adaptation of node behavior in ad hoc networks.

As discussed above, enabling the node to reasoning on trust can be a solution to mitigate certain vulnerabilities of ad hoc protocols. Mistrust-based controls can be set up to detect suspect behavior using the correlation between information provided in the subsequent received messages. For example, the discovery of a neighborhood, which is limited to the information provided by local messages, can be strengthened by exploiting the topological information obtained from messages coming from remote notes, so as to validate the acquired knowledge and deduce other criteria which a node can use to select routes.

Indeed, the trust assessment of routing chains is one possible measure to obtain more reliable choices and to compare alternative routes and this by means of operations and information already existing in the normal ad hoc operation, without resorting to cryptographic mechanisms. So it is also possible to consider the use of trust as an additional criterion to calculate routes, besides the traditional metric of distance.

It is also possible for a node to discover the information about the trust the other nodes place on it, so any node could by principle consider the possibility of having a behavior of reciprocity towards these trustor nodes.

Mobility

Mobility brings the possibility of neighborhood modification; consequently with possible effects such as the isolation of nodes, the splitting of a neighborhood and the merging of neighborhoods (these last two events may even concern an entire network).

These events in turn bring the issue of dynamically managing the identification and addressing spaces, as well as the question of continuously rediscovering the neighborhood and obtaining new routes towards the big world.

Then, mobility increases the possibilities of profitably using the notions of trust, mistrust and the process of trust management in ad hoc networks.

Distributed Network Management and Distributed Security Services

In general, trust can be considered as being beyond security; it is a solution for enhanced security (Yan

& Holtmanns, 2007). The interest of trust within the context of ad hoc network management and security can be put forward by the analysis of the characteristics peculiar to MANETs and related requirements for the design of any distributed service for this type of network. These requirements include:

- Because there is no concentration points and no guarantee of individual nodes availability, the MANET services must follow a distributed approach;
- The mobility and the topology dynamics imply that the distributed services must be self-organizing and cooperative, so as to avoid service interruptions when node connectivity changes and to take advantage of node and path redundancies to optimize service availability;
- The bandwidth and power-supply limitations require that the services must not generate excessive overheads in the network, so that services should be provided locally wherever possible, avoiding relaying and retransmission of messages.

The above requirements must also be satisfied when designing security services. However, with the exception of some security services that execute in isolation within hosts, most security techniques and protections used in traditional networks are not suited to ad hoc networks (Hubaux, Buttyan & Capkuny, 2001; Kong, Zerfos, Luo, Lu & Zhang, 2001; Zhou & Haas, 1999). In conventional architectures, services such as access control, authentication, authorization, network monitoring and security management are associated with clearly defined devices, such as authentication servers or firewall systems. These components cannot exist as individual devices in MANETs. Therefore, the security services in these networks have to follow a distributed approach through cooperation and self-organization. Moreover, wherever possible this cooperation must be completely local, so restricting the communication and processing overheads to the area around the nodes involved.

Various approaches are presented for the definition of security requirements in MANETs (Balfanz, Smetters, Stewart & Wong, 2002; Capkuny, Buttyan & Hubaux, 2003; Dahill, Sanzgiri, Levine, Shields & Royer, 2002; Feeney, Ahlgren & Westerlund, 2001; Guerrero & Asokan, 2002; Hu, Johnson & Perrig, 2002; Hu, Perrig & Johnson, 2002; Hubaux et al., 2001; Kong et al., 2001; Papadimitratos & Haas, 2002; Prigent, Bidan, Andreaux & Heen, 2003; Zhou & Haas, 1999). As a common aspect, they consider the combination of two basic requirements: distinguishing trusted and untrusted MANET nodes, and the identification and subsequent isolation of compromised or misbehaving nodes.

Nodes are distinguished by the definition and application of a trust model that lays down conditions for nodes to join the network. Joining the network, as discussed above, is considered as the establishment of a relationship of mutual trust between nodes, and is required of nodes as a first line of defense for cooperative services. Indeed, this requires the nodes to firstly become registered members of an ad hoc network and then to restrict cooperation to nodes which are correctly behaving network members. In this scenario, control and packet-relaying information is exchanged only among the set of nodes that have established and maintain mutual trust. The prior requirement for explicitly joining the network is justified, in particular, by the promiscuous nature of wireless communications, whereby any device configured with a wireless interface can communicate over the network. This ease of access characteristic of wireless networks is even more critical in MANET scenarios, owing to their spontaneous nature. Once membership has been established, a node must be able to validate the other members of the joined group, just as it must be possible for the other network nodes to check that its membership is valid.

Another fundamental requirement relates to the existence of malfunctioning or compromised entities in a MANET. Since the occurrence of such entities cannot be neglected, the security services must be designed to remain robust even in the presence of compromised or misbehaving nodes. In this respect, we can only allow degraded performance caused by the presence of nodes that are incorrectly integrated with the network to be temporary, and incorrect nodes must be identified and isolated from the cooperative services before the robustness of the service is compromised.

Finally, as there are a number of contexts for applying MANETs, different contexts will certainly require different levels of security and trust. For example, a MANET set up to enable cooperative working in a classroom presents different requirement levels from a MANET set up to provide communication and information services for a rescue operation in a disaster area. Similarly, these levels would be even stricter in a MANET set up between troops maneuvering on a battlefield. In general, these requirements can be expressed in terms of a security policy that specifies the levels of security required in each case. Trust is then used to ensure that security services can be quickly adapted to the security policy defined for each specific application context.

OVERVIEW OF AD HOC NETWORK TECHNOLOGIES AND PROTOCOLS

Although considerable effort has gone into designing and standardizing routing protocols for mobile ad hoc networks, auto-configuration protocols design is still a challenge. As a result, proposals for improving security in MANET routing protocols have been consolidated, whereas the literature on secure protocols for MANET auto-configuration is somewhat rare. We present an overview of the main proposals in these domains.

Protocols for Auto-Configuration

MANET auto-configuration issues require approaches that are different from those traditionally employed in structured networks. The conventional alternatives for auto-configuration in TCP/IP networks involve dynamic distribution of addresses using the DHCP protocol (Droms, 1997) and auto-configuration by random address allocation as proposed by the IETF's Zeroconf Working Group (Cheshire, Aboba & Guttman, 2004). However, the use of DHCP requires a central server for distributing information such as the IP address, network mask, standard gateway, DNS server address and other additional data. As we have seen, the use of central servers is a problem in ad hoc networks and so the mechanisms adopted in conventional networks are not suited for use in ad hoc environments.

Consequently, new auto-configuration solutions specially designed and suited for MANETs have appeared. The auto-configuration protocol is required to automatically allocate IP addresses and distribute related parameters, as well as being responsible for controlling potential problems such as duplicate addresses and network merging and splitting. According to the address configuration process, auto-configuration protocols can be classified as:

- **Stateless:** the node is required to compose its own IP address, based on either the hardware identifier or a random number. In this process the node does not depend on a second entity to carry out auto-configuration, but after the IP address is chosen, a duplicate-address detection (DAD) mechanism is needed to ensure that the composed address is unique;
- **Stateful:** each network node is required to maintain a set of IP addresses. This implies the need for a node to interact with a second entity to obtain a new IP address and to receive a sub-set of IP addresses

whose distribution will be managed by the node. Furthermore, this process maintains a common distributed structure for the entire network which consumes bandwidth mostly when there is frequent merging and splitting of ad hoc networks. Again, a DAD mechanism is need if networks are merging.

The DAD mechanisms, depending on how and when the duplicate addresses are detected, can be classified as:

- **Allocation with conflict detection:** using the trial-and-error principle, a node attempts to select an IP address and requests the approval of its choice from all the nodes in the ad hoc network. If any network node gives a negative response, this means that the chosen IP address is already being used;
- **Best-effort allocation:** each network node is responsible for assigning IP addresses to newly arriving nodes, attempting to assign a free address that is not in use by any other network node. All the network nodes maintain a table of IP addresses, each one marked as allocated or free, so when a new node arrives on the network, its nearest neighbor selects a free IP address to assign to it. The problem is that two or mode nodes may arrive at the same time and get the same IP address. However this protocol works very well with proactive routing protocols, since the nodes frequently broadcast details of the network addresses already in use;
- **Conflict-free allocation:** based on the concept of binary division, each node has different sets of IP addresses. Each node can assign an IP address without the need to consult other nodes for approval. In this way, all the network nodes are equally responsible for assigning IP addresses, with

the benefit that the protocol does not broadcast messages to assign these addresses.

Some authors classify DAD protocols as active or passive (Weniger, 2003). Active protocols are those that broadcast additional information onto the network, with a need for additional control packets to ensure that the protocol works properly, whereas passive protocols are those that detect duplicate addresses without the need to broadcast additional control packets onto the network, but just by monitoring the routing protocol traffic. However, with this latter method there is a period of time in which packets can be delivered to the wrong destination, known as the vulnerability period.

As an example of a MANET auto-configuration protocol, we present DCDP, one of the proposals for address auto-configuration in ad hoc networks.

Dynamic Configuration Distribution Protocol (DCDP)

This protocol proposed by (Misra, Das, McAuley & Das, 2001) presents a conflict-free allocation process in which each node maintains a set of IP addresses that are used to configure new nodes joining the network, without having to consult any other node already configured. These sets of addresses are different from each other within the same ad hoc network.

DCDP uses a buddy system model (Shamir, 1999) to supply different sets of IP addresses to network nodes. This model adopts a mechanism for binary division of the address block. A node wishing to join a network (a client node) broadcasts a request for an IP address (Address Request message). Existing configured neighbors respond to the request (Address Reply message), notifying the size of their block of available addresses (free_ip_block). The client node then selects the neighbor with the largest free_ip_block (Server Pool message). The selected neighbor (server

node) divides its set of IP addresses into two halves and sends one half to the client node (IP_Assigned message), keeping the other half for itself to handle future requests. When the client receives the set of addresses, it assigns the first one to itself and keeps the rest as a set of available addresses. The client node then sends a message confirming the success of the operation (IP_Assignment_OK message). A complete specification for the DCDP protocol is given in (Buiati, Puttini, De Sousa Jr., Abbas & Garcia-Villalba, 2004), a proposal that integrates the works of (Misra et al., 2001) and (Mohsin & Prakash, 2002) and takes into account the merging and splitting of ad hoc networks so as to maintain distinct sets of IP addresses in the configured network nodes.

Routing in Ad Hoc Networks

Routing in ad hoc networks is rather different from routing in wired networks, given the requirements regarding topology dynamics, router selection criteria and the heuristics to calculate the best or fastest path for delivering data.

The routing protocol design is predictably required to manage scarce resources and make efficient use of the available bandwidth, allowing energy saving wherever possible.

Ad hoc routing must operate in the presence of symmetrical and asymmetrical links. A link is known as symmetrical when two nodes are within one another's transmission area, with the same routing characteristics in both directions. When this is not the case, the link is called asymmetrical and routing becomes a difficult task so that most ad hoc routing protocols are exclusively based on symmetrical links.

In ad hoc networks some nodes are highly mobile while others can be fixed or move slowly, then it is difficult to predict the mobility pattern of nodes. Besides, the number of nodes can be very high and the task of finding a route to the destination will result in frequent exchanges of control information between nodes, leading routing traffic overloads, so that there is no bandwidth left for transmitting data packets. As expected, scalability is a requirement for the routing protocol which must function effectively in small networks, with a few dozen nodes, as well as in large-scale networks with hundreds of nodes and multi-hop topology.

Given the particular features of the ad hoc network environment, the IETF set up the MANET working group aimed at researching and developing specifications for MANET routing and proposing internet standards in this domain. These works lead to peer-to-peer routing solutions in purely mobile and wireless environment, with the specification of the two main MANET routing protocols that provide a comprehensive and flexible routing service in the various MANET application scenarios. These protocols are: Optimized Link State Routing Protocol – OLSR (Clausen & Jacquet, 2003), and Ad Hoc On-Demand Distance Vector Routing – AODV (Perkins & Royer, 2003), which are described hereafter.

Optimised Link State Routing (OLSR)

OLSR is a proactive routing protocol that uses a link-state type routing algorithm. The key feature of this protocol is the use of multipoint relays (MPRs), which are nodes selected to relay the broadcast messages in the routing protocol flooding process. Only nodes selected as MPRs broadcast information onto the network in this way. MPRs combined with the local elimination of duplication are used to minimize the number of control packets sent onto the network. OLSR is designed for use in large-scale networks, where traffic between a specific set of nodes is random and sporadic. As a proactive protocol, OLSR is also suited to scenarios where pairs of communicating nodes are constantly changing.

OLSR nodes use HELLO messages, exchanged between one-hop neighbors, to detect and update their neighbor set. Each node periodically broadcasts these messages giving information about

heard neighbor interfaces and their link status. The link status may either be "symmetric" (link has been verified to be symmetrical), "asymmetric" (communication has been verified in one direction only), "MPR" (neighboring node has been selected as one of the broadcaster's MPRs, in which case the link must also be symmetric) or "lost" (neighbor has moved away and is no longer being heard). HELLO messages are not relayed to other nodes.

Each node independently selects its own MPR set (MPRS) from among its symmetric neighborhood. The MPRS must be computed in such a way that, through the neighboring nodes in that set, it can reach all two-hop neighbors.

For provision of routes to nodes more than two hops away, each node maintains topological information about the network. This information is acquired by means of topology control (TC) messages. Nodes that have been selected as MPRs by other nodes periodically generate TC messages, which contain the list of all selector nodes (MPR Selector Set - MPRSS). TC messages are flooded to the whole network by the MPR nodes. A message sequence number (SN) field is used to avoid duplicated message processing. This field is generated as a sequence of integers, incremented monotonically each time a message is generated.

Ad Hoc On-Demand Distance Vector Routing (AODV)

AODV is a reactive routing protocol that uses a distance vector routing algorithm. As a general rule, AODV attempts to eliminate the need to broadcast routing messages, which could limit its scalability.

Route Requests (RREQs), Route Replies (RREPs), and Route Errors (RERRs) are the messages used by AODV. If a node needs a route to a destination, this node broadcasts a RREQ to find one such a route. When the RREQ reaches either the destination itself, or an intermediate node that posses a fresh route to the destination, then a unicast RREP is sent back to the origination of the RREQ. This process is possible because each node receiving the request caches a route back to the originator of the request. Moreover the nodes are required to monitor the link status of next hops in active routes, so when a node detects a link break in an active route then a RERR message is used to notify other nodes that the loss of that link has occurred and that the concerned destinations are no longer reachable through the broken link.

In fact, given that AODV attempts to minimize latency when new routes are requested, this protocol provides an intermediate solution between reactive and proactive routing. In reactive routing latency is high, since it is necessary to wait for a response to a routing request. In proactive routing, the volume of data exchanged may be very high for an ad hoc network with high mobility. In comparison with conventional routing algorithms, such as distance vector and link status, AODV substantially reduces the number of routing messages broadcast onto the network. This is due to its reactive approach. Also, AODV operates similarly to conventional algorithms, which can help where an ad hoc network is interconnected with a fixed network. Although it works similarly to conventional algorithms, AODV can support multicast and unicast traffic. However, the protocol offers a single route to each destination, a characteristic that may compromise availability.

Behavior of TCP/IP Protocols in Ad Hoc Networks

Although mobility, limitation of range, link packet loss rate, network latency, and other ad hoc network characteristic can pose particular performance and fault management challenges for transport and application layer protocols, as well as for collaborative distributed applications, the general behavior of these protocols in ad hoc networks is almost the same as traditional structured networks.

Indeed, with ad hoc solutions being in place for auto-configuration and routing, it is expected that the other higher level protocols being not modified for correct operation.

MITIGATION OF ATTACKS USING TRUST

Vulnerabilities and Attacks in Mobile Ad Hoc Networks

Many of the vulnerabilities of conventional network architectures also apply to MANETs and are even accentuated since MANET environments offer new ways in which they can be exploited. Moreover, MANETs have their own peculiar vulnerabilities which do not affect other network architectures (Kong et al., 2001; Zhou & Haas, 1999).

Due to the wireless link service, attacker nodes can monitor the use of the network through adjacent nodes that are within range of their receiver and attackers can communicate directly with one another. The possible attack target nodes depend upon one another to establish and maintain network connectivity, which is difficult given that mobility implies dynamic modification of the ad hoc network topology. Besides, service monitoring and control imply discharging power sources. Together, these characteristics make MANETs more susceptible than wired networks to a broad spectrum of attacks, such as described below.

Passive Listening

An adversary can listen promiscuously to transmissions from nearby nodes. Moreover, the attacker is generally able to move to collect information on the activity of other more distant nodes or to escape monitoring by nearby nodes. This way, the attacker can simply collect information without any authorization, but also can scan the network looking for service providers, considered as interesting targets for future attacks.

Impersonation, Black Hole and Sybil Attack

Impersonation is the situation where one entity assumes the identity of another; this possibility is leveraged by the fact that a node is able to communicate directly with any node that is within its transmission range, thus presenting a false identity within the whole neighborhood. This is a first step to more dangerous attacks, such as the black hole attack through which the attacker convinces the neighborhood that it is an interesting relay to send messages to nodes outside the neighborhood; the attacker in this position attracts the traffic and, besides getting the information, is able to not forward the messages, so acting as sink for these messages. The attacker can also disturb the routing operation by broadcasting incorrect topological information, compromising the construction of routing table, which is the primary goal of routing protocols. Moreover, impersonation is further exploited in the Sybil attack, where an entity assumes an arbitrary number of other identities; then coordinating the attack with different actions apparently from different entities.

Collusion Attacks and Wormhole

Collusion is when an arbitrary number of different nodes act together to proceed an attack, as is the case of the utilization of a hidden channel by two nodes to circumvent the n, as is the case of the utilization of a hidden channel by two nodes to circumvent the normal ad hoc routing structure;

Misbehavior and Denial of Services

Many forms of misbehavior can be used against ad hoc nodes, in which generally the attacker will both practice non-cooperation (e.g. to save its own battery power or to provoke dysfunctions in relay-

ing of network packets) and provoke unnecessary activity so as to discharge other nodes' power sources more quickly or to slow down and even break services provision. As above, these attacks can be leveraged by the fact that the attacker is generally able to move to collect information on the activity of other more distant nodes or to escape monitoring by nearby nodes, besides the fact that a node is able to communicate directly with any node that is within its transmission range.

Deficiencies of Traditional Security Measures Regarding Attacks in Mobile Ad Hoc Networks

Even cryptography based measures can be of no-interest in ad hoc networks. Besides the fact that cryptography in general implies more processing power consuming and incurs in processing delays, the utilization of it as an effective measure is not assured due to particularities of the ad hoc environment. For instance, the use of digital signatures to bind a node's IP address to its public key seems inadequate, since addressing in ad hoc networks is bound to follow the trend towards dynamic address allocation and auto-configuration (Guerrero & Asokan, 2002).

Additionally, in conventional networks, services such as routing and auto-configuration are delegated to entities designed to be secure (e.g. routers and auto-configuration servers). These entities perform a controlled set of functions and have a special position in the network topology that affords them effective protection. Thus, these entities present a reduced set of vulnerabilities, since they do not have generic functions, unnecessary functions can be deactivated and they can activate protection, logical or physical, relating to their position within the network architecture, generally at points of concentration or centralization within controlled parts of the network. In MANETs, on the other hand, the basic services, as well as the other network services, are provided in decentralized form and with potential partici-

Figure 1. Model for distributed, collaborative and self-organized services

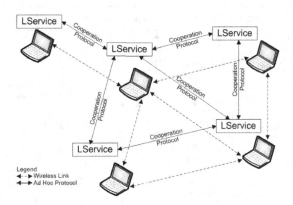

pation by all the network nodes. These nodes are often implemented in computer equipment using generic hardware and software that is subject to a series of vulnerabilities related to their operating system, software bugs, backdoors, viruses, etc. Furthermore, a MANET node that does not have proper physical protection may be captured (Luo, Zerfos, Kong, Lu & Zhang, 2002).

Thus it is not uncommon to have malfunctioning or compromised entities in the network. Regarding the existence of incorrect entities, a node that is making attacks on the MANET can even move, either to attack other parts of the network or to escape monitoring by its neighbors. This characteristic makes it difficult to detect attacks and to distinguish the misbehaving node(s) from the other correct nodes in the network.

Architecture of Ad Hoc Trust-Based Services

Trust-based services in mobile ad hoc networks must follow a distributed and self-organized approach, with a general architecture as presented in Figure 1 (Puttini, 2004). Each MANET node has an autonomous and active instance of the service. One such instance, that is generally called Local Service (L-Service), collaborates with L-Services from nearby nodes, by means of some cooperation

protocol. Collaboration may start at any time with any available L-Service peer. This is an important feature, as the availability of individual nodes may not be assumed, given that nodes may simply move out from the wireless communication range.

This sense of self-organization is exactly the same used in the very conception of the MANET routing services described above, the L-Service being represented by the MANET routing daemon, which is autonomously executed in each node, and the collaboration protocol being represented by the routing protocol.

Trust-based services must also employ a local component, given the error prone nature and the limited bandwidth of the wireless links. Thus, the node must comprise an autonomous trust-based reasoning engine that uses observations obtained from the neighborhood to take decisions, such as calculating trustful next hops for routing, or to constitute trust based defenses, such as trust based intrusion detection, as described hereafter.

Additionally, collaboration regarding trust should be done by nearby nodes, most often by 1-hop neighbor nodes, limiting the overhead due to communications among L-Services. The evaluation and use of trust through collaboration among nodes involve both the direct observations by a node and the second hand opinions on reputation of other ad hoc nodes. Such collaboration leads

Figure 2. Protocol and service architecture for trust and security in ad hoc networks

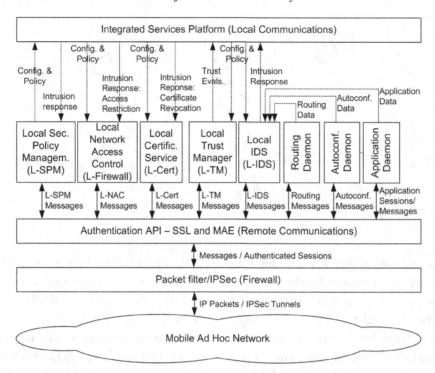

to requirements associated to securely sharing information regarding trust and reputation. Security solutions by themselves must also be robust in the existence of compromised nodes in the MANET, given the non-negligible probability for node break-ins in network, it is necessary to combine trust and security services, both as preventive services, that try to avoid the attacks to be successful, and as corrective services, that ensure the elimination of compromised nodes from the network.

Therefore, Figure 2 illustrates the service and protocol architecture of the associated trust and security services that must be enabled in each MANET node.

The fundamental security service in any distributed solution relates to unique identification of network nodes. A Local Certification Service (L-Cert) instance runs on each node, in order to implement a collaborative certification service to uniquely identify each node. Additionally, messages/sessions related to secured protocols can

be authenticated using a specific protocol. And a Local Network Access Control (L-NAC) can be used to implement distributed firewall-like services and to establish cryptographic tunnels between two or more MANET nodes. These are preventive security services. Otherwise, the corrective security services are provided in terms of intrusion detection and response system (L-IDS). The local trust manager produces evaluations that can be used by all the other services. Finally, a distributed trust and security policy management (L-SPM) deals with setting up and updating the services policy, collaborative monitoring and reporting (log) and recovering and restarting in case of serious failures.

The operations specific to trust in this architecture, both concerning autonomous reasoning by the nodes and collaboration amongst nodes, are described hereafter.

Autonomic Node Based Reasoning on Trust

In the domain of computer networks, in general, network devices must implement some basic or implicit trust behavior (Adnane, De Sousa Jr., Bidan & Mé, 2007) to start to send packets and exchange information about the network. Even when security devices, protocols and other measures are implemented, the network administrator must set some a priori configuration and operation rules based on different levels of trust.

In mobile ad hoc networks, all the nodes need to cooperate in network operation, so they assume at first that all nodes are trustful. But, given the absence of infrastructure, it is difficult to guarantee the correctness of received information, and so to manage the knowledge about network topology. The presence of misbehaving nodes could lead to the generation of compromised messages and, as a result, the nodes can experiment communication problems and message loss. Solutions based on classical security techniques such as message authentication and node certification, were proposed for these problems (Puttini, Mé & De Sousa, 2004; Raffo, 2005), though implying important communications and processing costs.

An alternative approach for MANETs is to explicitly treat the concept of trust and acquire some guarantee that the received data comes from a trustful node and that the nodes are acting as expected in view of the protocol specifications. This later point of view is the fundamental idea behind node autonomic reasoning on trust.

A model of trust to assure good interactions amongst autonomous software agents in complex, networked environments is presented in (Patel, 2007; see also Patel, Teacy, Jennings & Luck, 2005). In this model, trust calculations are based on past interactions with other entities and the reputation of these entities. Although useful in many contexts, this model does not correspond well to a MANET behavior given that an ad hoc node is essentially trustful and seeks for collaboration every time.

Certainly, in the domain of ad hoc networks, trust has been used as a means to enforce collaboration among nodes. In (Adnane, De Sousa Jr., Bidan & Mé, 2008), the effectiveness of autonomic trust-based reasoning for misbehavior detection is demonstrated, specifically for the OLSR routing protocol. This application of trust is extended in (Adnane, Bidan & De Sousa Jr., 2008), which compares simulation results regarding total nodes in the network and nodes concerned by an attack. Regarding the AODV protocol, a similar approach is presented in (Ayachi, Bidan, Abbes & Bouhoula, 2009). These referenced papers are taken as examples for the following description of elements that allow autonomic reasoning on trust in MANETs.

Formal Languages for Reasoning on Trust

The language proposed by (Yahalom, Klein & Beth, 1993) is one of the first languages for expressing the clauses concerning trust in a networking protocol. The concept of trust subjacent to this language is expressed by the fact that if an entity A trusts an entity B in some respect, informally means that A believes that B will behave in a certain way and will perform some action in certain specific circumstances.

According to the considered action and its circumstances of execution, it is necessary to distinguish various trust classes as defined by (Yahalom et al., 1993) and (Grandison & Sloman, 2000). Thus, for the sake of precision on the formalization of trust relations in MANETs, it is necessary to propose appropriate classes for the actions performed in this environment, such as the trust in another entity to present a correct identity (identification trust – id), behave according to an ad hoc protocol (non-interfering trust – ni) or route messages (routing trust – rt). Still in accordance with (Yahalom et al., 1993), there is a distinction between direct trust relations and derived trust relations, the last ones being established from recommendations of other entities. Given the presence of several types of entities in the execution environment of a protocol and the existence of indirect relationship between the entities, it is necessary to distinguish these two types of trust relations. Thus, the clauses relating to trust are expressed with the following notations:

- Each entity is identified by a single name; the terms *A*, *B* and *C* indicate specific entities, or alternatively sets of entities;

- A specific class of trust is noted *cc* and the expression *A trusts$_{cc}$(B)* means that *A* trusts *B* with respect to the action *cc*; thus *A trusts$_{id}$(B)* means that *A* trusts *B* with respect to *B* identification;

- The expression *A trusts.rec$_{cc}$(B)when. path[S]when.target[R]* means that *A* trusts the recommendations of entity *B* about the capacity of entities *R* to perform action *cc*. The *when* clause allows the specification of constraints on the recommendations. The trust recommendation *when.path* is a sequence of entities such that each one is recommended by its predecessor, so the *when.path* specifies the only set of entities to be considered, at each point in some trust recommendation path, as candidates for the next step in the path. The *when.target* clause specifies the only set of entities to be considered as candidates for becoming target entities in some recommendation path.

Trust Evaluation Models

As formally expressed in the trust language above, the trust relation is taken into account if the possibility of realization by an entity *B* of a protocol operation (the action) is evaluated by entity *A* on the basis of what *A* knows about entity *B* and the circumstances of this operation. This brings

the issue of an entity observing the other entity behavior and the circumstances of operations. The expected behavior is specified in the ad hoc protocol rules and the actual behavior of a node can be observed to verify conformity to the expected behavior. For instance, as pointed in (Adnane et al., 2007) for the OLSR protocol, the sets that compose the mind state of a node represent the vision that this node has on its neighborhood and network topology. This information set represents the circumstances for observing the protocol actions made by neighbors. So, as described above for OLSR, some intrinsic properties of this protocol can be deduced, such as:

- If a node *A* has chosen another node *B* as a router, the MPRS of *A* contains an entry for *B* and *A* expects that *B* generate timely TC messages announcing its ability to route towards the node *A*;

- If node *A* is itself a router, *A* expects *B* to forward TC messages generated by *A*.

These protocol rules can be expressed with usual mathematical logic and notations for representing sets and message exchange. Given that the OLSR node collects information about link configuration and routing topology from the exchanges of respectively HELLO and TC messages, the expected protocol operations are noted as follows (Adnane et al., 2007):

- $X \leftarrow HELLO_Y$ Y, X TC_Y Y represent, respectively, the reception by node X of HELLO and TC messages from node Y;

- $X \leftarrow (TC_Z)_Y$ Y represents the reception by X of a TC message originated in Z and forwarded by Y;

- X $TC_X \rightarrow *$, X $DATA_X \rightarrow *$ are the broadcasts by X of a TC or respectively a DATA message to be forwarded only by the MPRs of X;

- X $\neg TC_Y$ Y represents the absence of an awaited TC message from node Y, which is detected by expiration of a timer held by X;

- $X \neg (DATA_X)_Y Y$ is the notation that, supposing that Y is MPR of X, indicates the absence of an awaited DATA message generated by X and forwarded by node Y, which is detected by expiration of a timer held by X.

As the node collects and records the received information so as to maintain its vision of the network, this information can be used to derive metrics that allow trust calculation both using a discrete or a continuous trust model. For instance, (Adnane et al., 2007) proposes a binary model where, based on observation of the others behavior, a node decides simply to trust or to not trust the other, relations that are formally noted as for instance:

- $X \leftarrow HELLO Y, X \notin LS_Y \Rightarrow X \neg trusts\ (Y)$: if X receives HELLO messages from Y, but is not declared in these messages as pertaining to the link set of Y (LS_Y), then X does not trust Y neither to be a symmetrical neighbor, nor to be a MPR;
- $X \leftarrow HELLO Y, X \in LS_Y \Rightarrow X\ trusts\ (Y)$: if Y acts according to the protocol and sends HELLO messages informing that it has a link with X, then X trusts Y and regards Y as its symmetrical neighbor, and the symmetrical neighbors of Y as 2-hop neighbors.

The same observations can be considered as metrics of utility and information loss (for instance, the number of correctly generated TC announcements, the number of correct TC and data forwarding operations) and treated as random variables whose future behavior can be previewed from past observations (positive and negative outcomes) using for example the beta distribution.

Evidence Gathering and Management

The continuous observation of trust metrics implies that each node maintains a database for the possible observed metrics indexed by the identification of the observed node. Now, the management of this database requires the choice of configuration parameters and the associated management processes. This brings the issues of choosing the intervals for sampling variables, intervals for resetting observations, minimal number of observations to have valid metrics, maximum number of observations before aging, and so. These issues are associated to questions that are still object of research regarding long term metrics tracking and history, distributed logging services and processes, automatic interpretation and reaction to behavior changes.

Misbehavior Detection and Trust Based Decisions

Most of the research on MANET security has been devoted to the provision of preventive protection of the basic protocols, specially routing protocols (Dahill et al., 2002; Guerrero & Asokan, 2002; Papadimitratos & Haas, 2002; Puttini et al., 2004). Generally these solutions are not tolerant, in isolation, to the presence of compromised nodes in the network. These security mechanisms can be reinforced by proactive security services, such as intrusion detection systems.

Intrusion detection systems are designed to detect attacks against computer systems and networks or against information systems in general. It is quite difficult, if not impossible, to set up demonstrably secure information systems and keep them secure throughout their working life. Therefore intrusion detection systems are designed to monitor the use of these systems to detect the appearance of insecure states.

Generally speaking, the interest in intrusion detection can be divided into three basic processes: data collection, design of the detection algorithm (analysis) and alert management. The IETF's Intrusion Detection Working Group (IDWG) defines the components that perform these tasks (Wood & Erlinger, 2003): the sensor collects raw data about the operation of the system being monitored (e.g. audit traces, network packets) and these data are pre-processed to give events that are sent to the analyzer, where the events generated are assessed in terms of an intrusion detection mechanism. If these events are sensitive, the analyzer manages alerts, which are fed to the manager. Finally, this component, in addition to correlating and classifying the alerts in order to refine previous analyses, provides the information needed to respond to any attacks detected.

The design of IDS for MANETs has been broadly tackled (Albers, Camp, Percher, Jouga, Mé & Puttini, 2002; Huang, Fan, Lee & Yu, 2003; Marti, Giuli, Lai & Baker, 2000; Mittal & Vigna, 2002; Tseng, Balasubramanyam, Ko, Limprasittiporn, Rowe & Levitt, 2003; Zhang & Lee, 2000). The basic requirements for this type of IDS are introduced in (Zhang & Lee, 2000) and the IDS architecture concepts in (Albers et al., 2002; Percher, Puttini, Mé, Camp, Jouga & Albers, 2004; Puttini, Percher, Mé, Camp & De Sousa Jr., 2003).

In (Vigna, Gwalani, Srinivasan, Belding-Royer & Kemmerer, 2004), an IDS for AODV is designed essentially to reinforce the security of the routing protocol. However, this IDS has a centralized architecture.

In (Mittal & Vigna, 2002), the IDS comprises various sensors which promiscuously monitor the network links for detecting attacks against the routing protocol. This IDS uses collaboration concepts though the detection mechanism assumes that information on the global topology is available. But, in MANET, it would be most appropriate to use localized topology information, since the topology is dynamic and the global topology information may not be completely up to date.

In (Huang et al., 2003) and (Tseng et al., 2003), the MANET IDS design is based on a strategy of anomaly detection. The drawback of these works lies in the absence of cooperation between nodes, as each node acts in isolation to detect attacks.

A strategy for intrusion detection and response to combat uncooperative nodes in ad hoc networks is presented by (Marti et al., 2000). However, this approach does not include any notion of collaborative security services. The work (Yang, Meng & Lu, 2002) presents a security solution based on a modified version of AODV, using an intrusion detection mechanism combined with a system of tokens used to ensure that the nodes have access to the routing services. However, this solution does not incorporate any preventive protection, such as authentication. On the contrary, only a simple neighborhood verification system is used. Unfortunately, as mentioned above, this mechanism is based on the incorrect hypothesis that MAC addresses cannot be spoofed. Moreover, the intrusion detection mechanism is restricted to flooding RREP messages only, not generalizing to combat all the attacks described in terms of generating, modifying and spoofing other routing protocol messages.

A fully distributed intrusion detection system is proposed in (Puttini, Percher, Mé & De Sousa Jr., 2004), in the sense that the data collection, analysis (detection) and alert-management processes work in a distributed mode, i.e., no central entity is required. In this design, a local IDS (LIDS) is placed in each MANET node. The LIDS intercommunicate using a mechanism that takes account of the restrictions on bandwidth and connectivity. A platform of mobile agents provides self-organization. Moreover, the collaborative detection process basically takes place in the neighborhood or in a restricted number of nodes involved in an attack in multiple phases, so restricting the communication and processing overhead to the local level or between selected network nodes. Finally, contrary to the majority of works discussed above, the IDS presented in this work allows an effective strategy of active responses to detected attacks, as it is fully integrated with the other security services.

The above strategies are not based on the notion of trust, although autonomic trust-based reasoning enables misbehavior detection in ad hoc networks, as showed in (Adnane et al., 2008) for OLSR. In this trust based approach, first the intrinsic properties of the protocol, as pointed out by (Wang, Lamont, Mason & Gorlatova, 2005), are expressed formally as trust rules to be observed by the nodes regarding the expected correct behavior in message processing and routing organization. Then, the concept of mistrust is introduced formally considering the possibilities for an attacker to abuse these properties, what constitute the basic vulnerabilities of the protocol. The trust rules are reformulated to express a mistrust behavior that could be used by a node for self-protection against misbehaving neighbors, giving way to a mistrust-based anomaly detection mechanism. For instance:

- $X \leftarrow HELLO_Y Y, X \leftarrow TC_Y Y \Rightarrow TC_Y \subseteq NS_Y$: this trust rule asserts that if X receives HELLO and TC messages from Y, the protocol coherence requires that the topology information declared in the TC messages must pertain to the neighbor set of Y (LS_Y) declared in the HELLO messages;
- $X \leftarrow HELLO_Y Y, X \leftarrow TC_Y Y, TC_Y \not\subset NS_Y \Rightarrow X \neg trusts (Y)$: conversely, the mistrust-based anomaly detection rule asserts that if X receives HELLO and TC messages from Y, and asserts the incoherence between the TC messages content and the neighbor set declared in the HELLO messages, then X must mistrust Y.

Mistrust-based anomaly detection, based on a set of these rules, is showed by simulation to be an effective means for assessing the correct behavior of nodes in the operations of neighbor discovery, choice of routers and calculation of routes (Adnane et al., 2008).

Trust Through Collaboration Among Nodes

Now we consider the issue of reputation management and the associated requirements to sharing information regarding trust and reputation in an ad hoc environment. As described previously a source node must rely on intermediate nodes to forward its packets along multihop routes to the destination node and, due to the lack of infrastructure in ad hoc networks, secure and reliable packet delivery is difficult to achieve. Therefore, as discussed in (Zouridaki, Mark, Hejmo & Thomas, 2006) it is necessary a robust cooperative trust establishment scheme able particularly to succeed in the presence of malicious nodes.

Various approaches are presented for the definition of such cooperative trust-model in MANETs (Buchegger & Le Boudec, 2005; Li, Lyu & Liu, 2004; Meka, Virendra & Upadhyaya, 2006; Michiardi & Molva, 2002; Pirzada & Mcdonald, 2004). As a common aspect, they combine two basic operations: a watchdog mechanism allows a node to monitor the behavior of its neighbors in order to form an opinion, expressed as a numerical value, about the neighborhood; this opinion is then used to calculate the reputation of the nodes and to take decisions about routing and other ad hoc services, as well as to provide recommendations concerning the behavior of the other nodes. Hence, in general, each node performs a trust-based reasoning that evaluates the trustworthiness of the other nodes by combining first-hand trust information obtained independently of other nodes and second-hand trust information obtained via recommendations from other nodes. As expected, the collaborative trust scheme must resist against the propagation of false trust information by malicious nodes.

The discussion of a particular a solution to these questions puts some light on the problems of ensuring trust through collaboration among nodes in ad hoc networks. Hereafter, we adopt the point of view of (Areal, Puttini & De Sousa

Jr., 2008) and consider the trust as related to the action of forwarding packets in conformity to a given protocol specification. Regarding OLSR, as described above, a node sends packets and overhears the link to verify if the selected MPRs succeed or fail in forwarding these packets. This allows each node to compute a direct trust measure for each one of its neighbors. Information regarding the direct trust of neighbors is disseminated through slightly modified HELLO messages. Each node also considers information collected from neighbors concerning their opinion on the other nodes, i.e., the reputation of these ones. With this process in place, the nodes can evaluate the trust related to each of the neighbors, determining the untrustworthy ones and excluding them from the selected MPR set (and, thus from the routing table).

As usual, different approaches are possible when defining a trust model and this one has some interesting characteristics, according to criteria defined in (Sabater & Sierra, 2005):

- Single context (i.e. OLSR routing): indeed it seems difficult to obtain a protocol independent approach, as the very metrics are directly related to the expected behavior of the protocol being considered;
- Information sources include both experiences (direct trust) and witness (reputation);
- Visibility is not global in the sense that trust and reputation are locally updated only;
- Game-theoretical conceptual model: trust and reputation are the result of pragmatic game utility functions and numerical aggregation of past interactions.

The utility function used to observe and evaluate behavior of the peers is related to packet forward and takes advantage of the broadcast nature of the wireless link, which allows one node to monitor the behavior of a neighbor whenever one packet is due to be forwarded by it. Moreover,

it considers that TC messages should be always forwarded by MPR nodes, which are also responsible for forwarding data packets. Each time a TC (or data packet) is sent to an MPR in order to be further forwarded in the network one interaction is observed. The interaction is successful if the MPR forward the packet as expected and it is considered unsuccessful otherwise.

As designed, the trust model is aimed at improving the MPR selection based on trust and reputation information about neighbors. Non-trusted nodes (e.g. nodes that do not succeed to forward packets as expected) should not be selected as MPRs and they are excluded from the 2-hop neighbor set population and so are not used in the MPR selection algorithms.

Although information about trust can be announced for the whole network via modifications in TC messages, the trust model uses information exchanged only in neighborhood via HELLO messages. There are two main reasons to justify this choice. First, if a non-trusted node is excluded both from 2-hops neighbor set population and MPR selection processes, it is expected that other trusted nodes in the neighborhood should provide the connectivity that is avoided through the non-trusted nodes. Second, HELLO messages have an 8-bit RESERVED field which is used to exchange information about direct trust among neighbors, without major concerns on compatibility with other standard OLSR instances in the network, allowing coexistence of both standard and trust-aware OLSR instances. This is not the case for TC messages, which should be completely redefined in order to carry trust information.

A trust metric is generated for each neighbor combining both direct trust and reputation. If this trust metric in regard to a neighbor is bellow a pre-defined threshold, the node is considered to be non-trusted. A certainty calculation is also made, in order to provide a measure of how reliable is the trust/reputation value used in the model. The initial value of direct trust (before any past interaction) is always set to completely trusted, a measure that corresponds to the OLSR initial behavior, given that the node looks for collaboration immediately, even without identifying its neighbors.

A node maintains local metrics of the direct trust (D) regarding each one of the other neighbor nodes in the network, based on observation of direct interaction between them. Initially, as one node has no evidences about the behavior of others, D is set to 1 meaning "completely trusted". Each time (t) a new observation about the behavior is made, this direct trust metric is updated using a formula that pounders the previous and current time of estimation (for the new observation, the value is 1 if interaction is successful and 0 otherwise). The parameter that pounder the influence of the previous estimation is in the interval [0, 1] and is related to the memory of D estimation (Whitby, Jøsang & Indulska, 2004). Each node also computes an estimate for a certainty (C) measure of D which is simply evaluated as a function of quantity of the past interactions accumulated in the D measure.

Each node disseminates its direct trust evaluations and respective certainty measures in the neighborhood, through HELLO messages. With this information, the neighbors calculate the reputation R of other nodes, which measures the trust each node has in regard to others. The reputation measure R is actually formed by the sum of all direct trust measures made available through the HELLO messages that have a non-zero certainty, weighted by the direct trust measure that the node has itself for the node providing the information. This way, the information that comes from non-trusted nodes is minimized or excluded in the average reputation evaluation, supposing that the number of non-trusted nodes is far less than that of trusted ones. Finally, the trust metric which is used in the final decision about trustworthiness of a node is computed by combining both direct trust and reputation of a node using a formula with weighting factors that balance the influence of the direct trust measure and the reputation (third party).

As described before, this approach requires a solution for evidence gathering and management, which involves the issues of choosing the intervals for sampling variables, intervals for resetting observations, minimal number of observations to have valid metrics, maximum number of observations before aging, and so. These issues are associated to questions regarding long term metrics tracking and history, distributed logging services and processes, automatic interpretation and reaction to behavior changes, subjects that are still object of research.

OTHER APPLICATIONS OF TRUST IN MOBILE AD HOC NETWORKS

Although we focused on the use of trust as a means to enhance security, it is worth to point out that trust-based reasoning and decision are interesting for general collaboration in mobile ad hoc networks.

The same observations that a node performs prior to using trust for secure collaboration are useful for ensuring survivability of an ad hoc structure and the consideration of alternative routes and services within this environment.

It seems interesting to point out also that the notion of trust can contribute with integrated views on network management indicators. Indeed, in every network management areas, namely configuration, fault, performance, security and cost management, there are metrics with values that represent a normal expected behavior and some thresholds to be observed as indicators of some behavior not expected or desired. This corresponds to the operational notions of trust and mistrust described herein, so that very similar reasoning on trust can be applied in these areas.

Of course, trust management is associated to the costs of gathering and managing evidence, a task that presents hard challenges in ad hoc networks. But, there are the benefits of trust compared to other models, particularly the simplicity and performance of trust calculations, their effectiveness and the integrated views they bring about complex operations. We briefly discuss the question of visualization of trust metrics, as an example of the potential of trust to present this sort of intuitive and integrated views.

Visualization of Trust Metrics and Intuitive Management of Ad Hoc Networks

Using for instance OLSR as described, we consider the possibility of local visualization to check the trust between neighbors. The selection of routers (MPRs) leads to a trust relation that allows (for example) the verification of TC message forwarding: if a node X has chosen a node Y as a MPR, and X sends a TC message, but X do not hear Y forwarding this TC message, then X must not trust Y as MPR (at least, X must present some mistrust about this choice of MPR).

Now, let X take into account a metric related to this trust relation, requiring that X count:

- The number of its TC messages: $\#TC_X$;
- And the number of its TC messages forwarded by Y: $\#TC_{Xfw-Y}$.

And let X continuously gather the values and visualize these variables together in a graph which enables X to see the possible evolution of its trust relationship towards Y (Figure 3).

The simple visualization of the metric shows intuitively how the misbehavior takes place (graph d in Figure 3), but also shows the limits of trust-based reasoning, as the graph c in the Figure 3 indicates an undesirable behavior, but the propositions on trust specific to the routing service are not able to characterize it as misbehavior or as having another cause. This undecidable problem brings out to the idea that a meta-trust system must be in place to answer whether in a determined context a system can trust the trust technologies, which is

a particular instance of an important and general issue related to trust (Gambetta, 2000).

Other research questions arise on local visualization, as regarding the confidence range of the visualized values, the understanding of the inflections in curves as indicators of behavior modifications and the already discussed questions on evidence gathering and management for visualized metrics.

CONCLUSION

In the spontaneous self-organized environment of MANETs the management of trust is essential in order to allow the collaboration between network nodes to provide the necessary auto-configuration and ad hoc routing services. This collaboration requires some form of trust to enable the sharing of resources among participants so as to provide the ad hoc services in a way that meets the security requirements of all those involved.

In this chapter, we have presented an overview of some of the current modes of utilization of trust in ad hoc networks, showing how the concept of trust respond to challenges related to the distinctive characteristics of ad hoc networks. The overview of the underlying technologies and protocols for ad hoc networks has been used as the basis for describing vulnerabilities of these networks. This has led to the description of attacks exploiting these vulnerabilities and to the discussion on how trust, or conversely mistrust, is used to mitigate these attacks. This issue was approached both from the point of view of autonomic trust reasoning by each node and the collaboration among nodes regarding trust aspects, based on the specification of an ad hoc trust management architecture. This approach went along with the description of formal methods and languages to express the concept of trust, the presentation of trust models, including evidence management and trust calculation, and the collaboration for manag-

Figure 3. Visualization of a trust metric related to message forwarding in OLSR

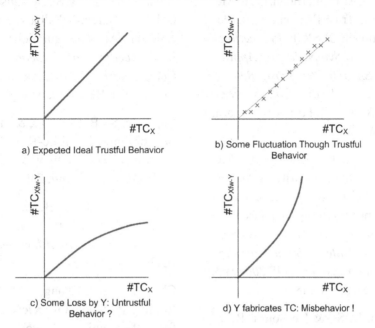

a) Expected Ideal Trustful Behavior

b) Some Fluctuation Though Trustful Behavior

c) Some Loss by Y: Untrustful Behavior ?

d) Y fabricates TC: Misbehavior !

ing and exchanging information about reputation in ad hoc networks.

Although we have focused on the use of trust as a means to enhance security, it was pointed out that trust-based decisions are interesting for general collaboration in ad hoc networks. For instance, the concept of trust was showed to be useful for choosing alternative routes, and the visualization of trust as a human oriented metric to contribute to network management purposes being an intuitive representation of the behavior and performance of ad hoc networks.

Throughout the chapter, existing challenges and limitations of trust-based reasoning in ad hoc networks were discussed. This was the case of trust metrics and the related questions of choosing the intervals for sampling variables, intervals for resetting observations, minimal number of observations to have valid metrics, maximum number of observations before aging, and so. Research efforts are still needed to answer questions regarding long term metrics tracking and history, distributed logging services, automatic interpretation of metrics and reaction to behavior changes

in ad hoc networks. Also, trust management will also be an essential part of further research into the idea of meta-trust which must be in place both to answer whether in a determined context the ad hoc trust technologies can effectively be trusted and to enable the correlation of trust information coming from different contexts for purposes of trust-based decisions.

REFERENCES

Adnane, A., Bidan, C., & De Sousa, R. T., Jr. (2008). Effectiveness of Trust Reasoning for Attack Detection in OLSR. In *Proceedings of the 6th International Workshop on Security in Information Systems (WOSIS-2008)*, Barcelona, Spain.

Adnane, A., De Sousa, R. T., Jr., Bidan, C., & Mé, L. (2007). Analysis of the implicit trust within the OLSR protocol. In *Proceedings of the IFIPTM-2007 Joint iTrust and PST Conferences on Privacy, Trust Management and Security*, Moncton, New Brunswick, Canada. Berlin, Germany: Springer.

Adnane, A., De Sousa, R. T., Jr., Bidan, C., & Mé, L. (2008). Autonomic Trust Reasoning Enables Misbehavior Detection in OLSR. In *Proceedings of the 23rd Annual ACM Symposium on Applied Computing (ACM SAC 2008): Trust, Recommendations, Evidence and other Collaboration Know-how (TRECK track)*, Fortaleza, Ceará, Brazil. New York: ACM.

Albers, P., Camp, O., Percher, J., Jouga, B., Mé, L., & Puttini, R. S. (2002). Security in Ad hoc Networks: a General Intrusion Detection Architecture Enhancing Trust Based Approaches. In Q. H. Mahmoud (Ed.), *Wireless Information Systems, Proceedings of the 1st International Workshop on Wireless Information Systems, WIS 2002* (pp. 1-12). Ciudad Real, Spain: ICEIS Press.

Areal, J. L., Puttini, R. S., & De Sousa, R. T., Jr. (2008). A New Trust-Based Extension to the HELLO Message Improves the Choice of Routes in OLSR Networks. In *Proceedings of the 7th International Information and Telecommunication Technologies Symposium I2TS'2008*, Foz do Iguaçu, Brazil.

Ayachi, M. A., Bidan, C., Abbes, T., & Bouhoula, A. (2009). Analyse de la confiance dans AODV. In *Actes de la 4ème Conférence sur la Sécurité des Architectures Réseaux et des Systèmes d'Information*. France: Publibook.

Balfanz, D., Smetters, D., Stewart, P., & Wong, H. (2002). Talking to Strangers: Authentication in Adhoc Wireless Networks. In *Proceedings of the ISOC Network and Distributed Systems Security Symposium*.

Buchegger, S., & Le Boudec, J. Y. (2005). Self-policing mobile ad hoc networks by reputation systems. *Communications Magazine, 43*(7), 101–107. doi:10.1109/MCOM.2005.1470831

Buiati, F., Puttini, R. S., De Sousa, R. T., Jr., Abbas, C. J. B., & Garcia-Villalba, L. J. (2004). Authentication and Autoconfiguration for MANET Nodes. In *Proceedings of Embedded and Ubiquitous Computing EUC 2004*, Aizu-Wakamatsu, Japan (pp. 41-52). Berlin, Germany: Springer.

Capkuny, S., Buttyan, L., & Hubaux, J. (2003). Self-organized Public-Key Management for Mobile Ad Hoc Networks. *IEEE Transactions on Mobile Computing, 2*(1).

Cheshire, S., Aboba, B., & Guttman, E. (2004). *IETF Internet Draft – Dynamic Configuration of IPv4 Link-Local Addresses*. Fremont, CA: IETF.

Chun, Y., Qin, L., Yong, L., & Meilin, S. (2000). Routing Protocols Overview and Design Issues for Self-Organized Network. In *Proceedings of 2000 IEEE International Conference on Communication Technology ICCT 2000* (pp. 1298-1303). Washington, DC: IEEE.

Clausen, T., & Jacquet, P. (2003). *IETF RFC 3626 – Optimized Link State Routing Protocol (OLSR)*. Fremont, CA: IETF.

Corson, S., & Marker, J. (1999). *IETF RFC 2501 – Mobile Ad Hoc Networking (MANET): Routing Protocol Performance Issues and Evaluation Consideration*. Fremont, CA: IETF.

Dahill, B., Sanzgiri, K., Levine, B. N., Shields, C., & Royer, E. (2002). A Secure Routing Protocol for Ad Hoc Networks. In *Proceedings of the 2002 IEEE International Conference on Network Protocols INCP 2002*. Washington, DC: IEEE.

Droms, R. (1997). *IETF RFC 2131 – Dynamic Host Configuration Protocol*. IETF.

Feeney, L., Ahlgren, B., & Westerlund, A. (2001). Spontaneous Networking: an Application-Oriented Approach to Ad Hoc Networking. *IEEE Communications Magazine, 39*(6). doi:10.1109/35.925687

Gambetta, D. (2000). Can We Trust Trust? In D. Gambetta (Ed.), *Trust: Making and Breaking Cooperative Relations* (pp. 213-237). University of Oxford, Department of Sociology.

Grandison, T., & Sloman, M. (2000). A Survey of Trust in Internet Applications. *IEEE Communications Surveys and Tutorials, 3*(4), 2–16. doi:10.1109/COMST.2000.5340804

Guerrero, M., & Asokan, N. (2002). Securing Ad Hoc Routing Protocols. In *Proceedings of 2002 ACM Workshop on Wireless Security WiSe '2002*. New York: ACM.

Hu, Y. C., Johnson, D., & Perrig, A. (2002). SEAD: Secure efficient distance vector routing for mobile wireless ad hoc networks. In *Proceedings of the Fourth IEEE Workshop on Mobile Computing Systems and Applications WMCSA '02* (pp. 3-13). Washington, DC: IEEE.

Hu, Y. C., Perrig, A., & Johnson, D. B. (2002). Ariadne: A secure On-demand routing protocol for ad hoc networks. In *Proceedings of ACM MobiCom 2002*. New York: ACM.

Huang, Y., Fan, W., Lee, W., & Yu, P. (2003). Cross-feature analysis for detecting ad-hoc routing anomalies. In *Proceedings of the 23rd International Conference on Distributed Computing Systems*. Washington, DC: IEEE Computer Society.

Hubaux, J., Buttyan, L., & Capkuny, S. (2001). The quest for security in mobile ad hoc networks. In *Proceedings of ACM MobiHOC*. New York: ACM.

Johnson, D. B., Maltz, D. A., & Hu, Y. C. (2004). *Autoconf WG Internet-Draft – The Dynamic Source Routing Protocol for Mobile Ad Hoc Networks (DSR)*. Fremont, CA: IETF.

Kong, J., Zerfos, P., Luo, H., Lu, S., & Zhang, L. (2001). Providing robust and ubiquitous security support for MANET. In *Proceedings of IEEE ICNP 2001*. Washington, DC: IEEE.

Li, X., Lyu, M. R., & Liu, J. (2004). A trust model based routing protocol for secure ad hoc networks. In *Proceedings of the Aerospace Conference IEEEAC'04*.

Luo, H., Zerfos, P., Kong, J., Lu, S., & Zhang, L. (2002). Self-securing Ad Hoc Wireless Networks. In *Proceedings of the Seventh IEEE International Symposium on Computers and Communications (ISCC'02)*. Washington, DC: IEEE.

Marti, S., Giuli, T. J., Lai, K., & Baker, M. (2000). Mitigating routing misbehaviour in mobile ad hoc networks. In *Proceedings of the Sixth Annual International Conference on Mobile Computing and Networking*, Boston, MA, USA.

Meka, K., Virendra, M., & Upadhyaya, S. (2006). Trust based routing decisions in mobile ad-hoc networks. In *Proceedings of the Workshop on Secure Knowledge Management SKM 2006*.

Michiardi, P., & Molva, R. (2002). Core: A collaborative reputation mechanism to enforce node cooperation in mobile ad hoc networks. In *Proceedings of IFIP TC6/TC11 6th Joint Working Conference on Communications and Multimedia Security CMS'02* (pp. 107-121). Berlin, Germany; Springer.

Misra, A., Das, S., McAuley, A., & Das, S. K. (2001). Autoconfiguration, Registration and Mobility Management for Pervasive Computing. *IEEE Personal Communications, 8*(4).

Mittal, V., & Vigna, G. (2002). Sensor-based intrusion detection for intra-domain distance-vector routing. In R. Sandhu (Ed.), *Proceedings of the ACM Conference on Computer and Communication Security (CCS'02)*. Washington, DC, USA: ACM Press.

Mohsin, M., & Prakash, R. (2002). IP Address Assignment in a Mobile Ad Hoc Network. In *Proceedings of IEEE Milcom*. Washington, DC: IEEE.

Nesargi, S., & Prakash, R. (2002). MANETconf: Configuration of hosts in a mobile ad hoc network. In *Proceedings of INFOCOM 2002 Assurance Workshop* (pp. 60-65).

Ogier, R., Templin, F., & Lewis, M. (2004). *IETF RFC 3684 – Topology Dissemination Based on Reverse-Path Forwarding (TBRPF)*. Fremont, CA: IETF.

Papadimitratos, P., & Haas, Z. J. (2002). Secure routing for mobile ad hoc networks. In *Proceedings of SCS Communication Networks and Distributed Systems Modeling and Simulation Conference (CNDS 2002)*.

Patel, J. (2007). *A Trust and Reputation Model for Agent-Based Virtual Organizations*. Unpublished doctoral dissertation, University of Southampton, School of Electronics and Computer Science, Faculty of Engineering and Applied Science, Southampton, UK.

Patel, J., Teacy, W. T. L., Jennings, N. R., & Luck, M. (2005). A Probabilistic Trust Model for Handling Inaccurate Reputation Sources. In P. Herrmann, V. Issarny, & S. Shiu (Eds.), *Proceedings of Third International Conference on Trust Management*, Rocquencourt, France (pp. 193-209). Berlin, Germany: Springer.

Percher, J. M., Puttini, R. S., Mé, L., Camp, O., Jouga, B., & Albers, P. (2004). *Un système de détection d'intrusion distribué pour réseaux ad hoc*. France: TSI.

Perkins, C. E., Malinen, J., Wakikawa, R., Royer, E. M., & Sun, Y. (2001). *MANET WG Internet-Draft – IP Address Autoconfiguration for Ad hoc Networks*. Fremont, CA: IETF.

Perkins, C. E., & Royer, E. M. (2003). *IETF RFC 3561 – Ad hoc on-demand distance vector (AODV) Routing*. Fremont, CA: IETF.

Pirzada, A. A., & Mcdonald, C. (2004). Establishing trust in pure ad-hoc networks. *Proceedings of the 27th conference on Australasian computer science (ACSC'04), 26*(1), 47-54.

Prigent, N., Bidan, C., Andreaux, J. P., & Heen, O. (2003). Secure Long Term Communities in Ad Hoc Networks. In *Proceedings of ACM SASN*. New York: ACM.

Puttini, R. S. (2004). *Um Modelo de Segurança para Redes Móveis Ad Hoc*. Unpublished, doctoral dissertation, University of Brasília, Brazil.

Puttini, R. S., Mé, L., & De Sousa, R. T., Jr. (2004). On the Vulnerabilities and Protection of Mobile Ad Hoc Network Routing Protocols. In *Proceedings of the 3rd International Conference on Networking ICN2004* (pp. 676-684). New Jersey, USA: IEEE.

Puttini, R. S., Mé, L., & De Sousa, R. T., Jr. (2004). Preventive and Corrective Protection for Mobile Ad Hoc Network Routing Protocols. In *Proceedings of the 1st International Conference on Wireless On-demand Network Systems*. Berlin, Germany: Springer.

Puttini, R. S., Percher, J. M., Mé, L., Camp, O., & De Sousa, R. T., Jr. (2003). A Modular Architecture for a Distributed IDS for Mobile Ad Hoc Networks. In *Proceedings of the International Conference on Computer Science and Applications* (pp. 105-113). Berlin, Germany: Springer.

Puttini, R. S., Percher, J. M., Mé, L., & De Sousa, R. T., Jr. (2004). A Fully Distributed IDS for MANET. In *Proceedings of 9th IEEE International Symposium on Computers Communications*. Washington, DC: IEEE.

Raffo, D. (2005). *Security Schemes for the OLSR Protocol for Ad Hoc Networks*. Unpublished doctoral dissertation, University of Paris 6 Pierre et Marie Curie, Paris, France.

Royer, E., & Toh, C. (1999). A review of current routing protocols for ad hoc mobile wireless networks. *IEEE Personal Communications Magazine*, 46-55.

Sabater, J., & Sierra, C. (2005). Review on Computational Trust and Reputation Models. *Artificial Intelligence Review*, *24*, 33–60. doi:10.1007/s10462-004-0041-5

Shamir, A. (1999). How to Share a Secret. *Communications of the ACM*, *22*(11), 612–613. doi:10.1145/359168.359176

Tseng, C. Y., Balasubramanyam, P., Ko, C., Limprasittiporn, R., Rowe, J., & Levitt, K. (2003). A specification-based intrusion detection system for AODV. In *Proceedings of the ACM Workshop on Security of Ad Hoc and Sensor Networks (SASN'03)*. New York: ACM.

Vigna, G., Gwalani, S., Srinivasan, K., Belding-Royer, E. M., & Kemmerer, R. A. (2004). An intrusion detection tool for AODV-based ad hoc wireless networks. In [Washington, DC: IEEE.]. *Proceedings of the IEEE ACSAC*, *04*, 16–27.

Wang, M., Lamont, L., Mason, P., & Gorlatova, M. (2005). An Effective Intrusion Detection Approach for OLSR MANET Protocol. In *Proceedings of the First Workshop on Secure Network Protocols (NPSec)*, Boston, Massachusetts, USA.

Weniger, K. (2003). Passive Duplicate Address Detection in Mobile Ad Hoc Networks. In *Proceedings of the IEEE WCNC 2003*. Washington, DC: IEEE.

Whitby, A., Jøsang, A., & Indulska, J. (2004). Filtering out unfair ratings in bayesian reputation systems. In *Proceedings of the 7th International Workshop on Trust in Agent Societies*.

Wood, M., & Erlinger, M. (2003). *IETF Internet Draft – Intrusion Detection Message Exchange Requirements*. Fremont, CA: IETF.

Yahalom, R., Klein, B., & Beth, T. (1993). Trust Relationships in Secure Systems – A Distributed Authentication Perspective. In *Proceedings of the 1993 IEEE Symposium on Security and Privacy SP'93*. Washington, DC: IEEE Computer Society.

Yan, Z., & Holtmanns, S. (2007). Trust Modeling and Management: from Social Trust to Digital Trust. In R. Subramanian (Ed.), *Computer Security, Privacy and Politics: Current Issues, Challenges and Solutions*. Hershey, PA: IGI Global.

Yang, H., Meng, X., & Lu, S. (2002). Self-Organized Network Layer Security in Mobile Ad Hoc Networks. In *Proceedings of ACM Workshop on Wireless Security 2002 (WiSe'2002)*. New York: ACM Press.

Zhang, Y., & Lee, W. (2000). Intrusion detection in wireless ad hoc networks. In *Proceedings of 6th ACM Annual International Conference on Mobile Computing and Networking (MOBICOM 2000)*. New York: ACM Press.

Zhou, H., Ni, L., & Mutka, M. (2003). Prophet Address Allocation for Large Scale MANETs. In *Proceedings of IEEE INFOCOM 2003*. Washington, DC: IEEE.

Zhou, L., & Haas, Z. J. (1999). Securing ad hoc networks. *IEEE Network Magazine*, *13*(6), 22–30.

Zouridaki, C., Mark, B. L., Hejmo, M., & Thomas, R. K. (2006). Robust cooperative trust establishment for MANETs. In *Proceedings of the fourth ACM workshop on Security of ad hoc and sensor networks SASN '06*. New York: ACM.

Chapter 11

A Context–Aware Model of Trust for Facilitating Secure Ad Hoc Collaborations

Indrajit Ray
Colorado State University, USA

Indrakshi Ray
Colorado State University, USA

Sudip Chakraborty
Valdosta State University, USA

ABSTRACT

Ad hoc collaborations often necessitate impromptu sharing of sensitive information or resources between member organizations. Each member of resulting collaboration needs to carefully assess and tradeoff the requirements of protecting its own sensitive information against the requirements of sharing some or all of them. The challenge is that no policies have been previously arrived at for such secure sharing (since the collaboration has been formed in an ad hoc manner). Thus, it needs to be done based on an evaluation of the trustworthiness of the recipient of the information or resources. In this chapter, the authors discuss some previously proposed trust models to determine if they can be effectively used to compute trustworthiness for such sharing purposes in ad hoc collaborations. Unfortunately, none of these models appear to be completely satisfactory. Almost all of them fail to satisfy one or more of the following requirements: (i) well defined techniques and procedures to evaluate and/or measure trust relationships, (ii) techniques to compare and compose trust values which are needed in the formation of collaborations, and (iii) techniques to evaluate trust in the face of incomplete information. This prompts the authors to propose a new vector (we use the term "vector" loosely; vector in this work means a tuple) model of trust that is suitable for reasoning about the trustworthiness of systems built from the integration of multiple subsystems, such as ad hoc collaborations. They identify three parameters on which trust depends and formulate how to evaluate trust relationships. The trust relationship between

DOI: 10.4018/978-1-61520-682-7.ch011

a truster and a trustee is associated with a context and depends on the experience, knowledge, and recommendation that the truster has with respect to the trustee in the given context. The authors show how their model can measure trust in a given context. Sometimes enough information is not available about a given context to calculate the trust value. Towards this end the authors show how the relationships between different contexts can be captured using a context graph. Formalizing the relationships between contexts allows us to extrapolate values from related contexts to approximate a trust value of an entity even when all the information needed to calculate the trust value is not available. Finally, the authors develop formalisms to compare two trust relationships and to compose two or more of the same – features that are invaluable in ad hoc collaborations.

INTRODUCTION

When two or more organizations collaborate, each of them needs to properly assess and tradeoff the requirements of protecting its own sensitive information and resources against the requirements of sharing some or all of them with others. Traditionally, organizational information security policies are formulated to specify who to share information and resources with, what individual pieces to share, under what circumstances, and any other restrictions on the sharing of such sensitive information and/or resources. When conventional collaborations are formed, such security policies of individual organizations are compared against each other. Any conflict between policies needs to be resolved, giving rise to a new set of security policies for the collaboration as a whole. Unfortunately, ad hoc collaborations by their very nature preclude such premeditated security policies. Such collaborations are very dynamic in nature. They can form and break down within very short periods of time. A typical example of an ad hoc collaboration is a virtual sensor network that is formed during the occurrence of an earthquake to monitor disturbances in chemical plumes owing to the earthquakes. The virtual sensor network is sustained for a small period of time by the co-operation of two special purpose sensor networks – one for monitoring chemical plumes, and the other for monitoring seismic activities. During regular times, each of these sensor networks is administered by a different entity and nothing is shared between the two. During the earthquake each sensor network needs to update its own security policies, on the spur of the moment at the time of the formation of the collaboration, to adjust to possible conflicting goals – a challenging situation. It appears that the concept of *trust* can be used to support such ad hoc adaptation of security policies. This is because the sharing of information and resources can be guided to a considerable by questions such as, who to trust, why to trust, and how much to trust. However, even today, there are no well-accepted formalisms or techniques for the specification of trust in such collaborative environments, and for reasoning about trust relationships. Secure collaborations are often built under the premise that concepts like "trustworthiness" or "trusted" are well understood, unfortunately without even agreeing on what "trust" means, how to measure it, how to compare two trust values and how to compose the same. This creates a number of inferential ambiguities in building secure systems, particularly those that are composed from several different components.

Consider the following example. Let us assume two financial organizations have decided to join hands to fight financial fraud. Each organization has previously generated its own information bases about fraud perpetrators, their activities, their ways and means, a fraud level rating and so on. As part of this collaboration, these information bases need to be merged. Typically each organization would have created its information base with the accumulation of information from several sources. Some of these sources are under the direct administrative control of the organization and thus are considered trustworthy. Other sources are "friendly" sources. Information originating directly from these sources is also considered trustworthy. However, these "friendly" organizations may, in turn, have obtained information from their own sources. The current organization may not have any firsthand knowledge about these other sources. If such third-hand information is made available to the corporation, then the corporation has no real basis for determining the quality of that information. It will be rather naïve for the organization to trust this information to the same extent that it trusts information from sources under its direct control. Similarly, not trusting this information at all may severely constrain the functionalities of the organization. Let us assume that somehow each organization has been able to rate the trustworthiness of various pieces of information in their own information bases in terms of qualitative measures such as high, medium or low. The question then remains how to compare "high trustworthy" for one organization with "high trustworthy" in the other. Or, what will be the trust level of the merged information. Note that this is not a limitation of the qualitative measures. The same problem arises when existing quantitative measures of trust are used.

The above example leads us to observe the following minimum requirements of any trust model for evaluating trustworthiness of entities for ad hoc collaborations:

1. The candidate trust model must define procedures and techniques to measure the degree of trust that a truster can have on a trustee.

2. The trust model must define procedures to compare entities at different degrees of trust.

3. The trust model must define methods that allow one to combine entities belonging to different trust levels and determine the trust level of the resulting entity.

In this chapter, we investigate several well-known trust models that have been proposed over the past several years and discuss how well they satisfy these criteria. Unfortunately, we conclude that most existing trust models are deficient in one or more of the above criteria. We also observe that the trust relationship between a truster and a trustee is never absolute. Almost always, the truster trusts the trustee with respect to the latter's ability to perform a specific action or provide a specific service. For example, a truster, *A*, may trust a trustee, *B*, about the latter's ability to keep a secret. However, this does not necessarily mean that if *A* wants a job done efficiently, *A* will trust *B* with it. Similarly, if we want to compare two trust relationships, we just cannot compare two arbitrarily picked one. We need to compare the trust relationships that serve similar purposes. We call this concept the trust *context*. Only recently have researchers started to recognize this concept of trust contexts and propose trust models that use contexts in reasoning with trust relationships. We discuss some such recently proposed models in an attempt to identify one that is suitable for ad hoc collaborations. Here also, we find none that is completely satisfactory although the vector trust model proposed by Ray and Chakraborty (2004), two of the co-authors of this work, appears closest to satisfying most of these requirements.

Ray and Chakraborty define trust between a truster and a trustee in a specific context as a vector (actually a tuple) of numeric values. Each element of the vector (or tuple) specifies a parameter for determining the value of trust. Most models prior to this one define trust as synonymous to either reputation (alternately called recommendation) or experience (exclusive). The authors, in contrast, specify three parameters, namely, *experience*, *recommendation*, and *knowledge* as contributing to the formation of a trust relationship. They define methods for determining the values of these parameters. In addition, they formulate operators that show how trust relationships expressed as vectors could be compared. Often times, a single scalar value is more intuitive than a 3-element vector. Towards this end, they authors show how the trust vector can be converted to a scalar value in the range $[-1, 1] \cup \{\perp\}$. (A positive value, a negative value, a zero, and $\perp$ indicate trust, distrust, neutrality, and uncertainty, respectively.) Further, the authors observe that trust relationships are not static but changes with time. They explore this dynamic nature of trust – how trust (or distrust) changes over time. Finally, they observe that trust depends on trust itself – that is, a trust relationship established at some point of time in the past will influence the computation of trust at the current time.

The model described in (Ray & Chakraborty, 2004) has two shortcomings. First, although the authors observe that trust relationships are not absolute but rather depend on context, they did not quite formalize the notion of context. Their formulation of context is as discreet values (strings). The model can reason about trust relationships only with respect to a given context. It allows trust values to be compared or combined only when there is an exact match on the context; that is, only when the contexts are defined using the same terms. This, in general, is a problem with several new models of trust that sets context as a parameter in trust computation (see Section on "Related Works" for discussion on some of these works). This assumption, unfortunately, is not realistic in most ad hoc collaborations. For example, two organizations may respectively specify the function of a manager as "administration" and "management". Semantically they mean the same or at least very close. Thus, it seems, if these organizations collaborate, similar trust levels can be expected from each. At a minimum, their trust levels can be compared. However, from the purely syntactic point of view of the Ray and

Chakraborty and some of the other context-aware models, these contexts are completely different. Thus, the trust relationships cannot be compared or composed. Second, it is not possible to compute a useful trust value if the truster does not have any experience, knowledge, or recommendation about a trustee in a given context. The model returns the value $\perp$ – undefined. In this case, the truster cannot establish a useful trust relationship with the trustee. However, it appears that a model providing such features will be useful in ad hoc collaborations. For example, let a user A (the truster) trust a software developer B (the trustee) to a degree T to produce excellent quality firewall software (the context). Now the software developer joins hand with a team of other developers to develop anti-virus software. Assuming that expertise to develop an anti-virus software (a related context) is comparable to the expertise needed to develop firewall software with some differences, it seems natural that the trustee A would want to determine how much to trust the combined group of B and others for the different (but related) context.

Toivonen, Lenzini and Uusitalo (2006) attempt to address the problem of computed trust from related contexts by introducing the notion of *context ontology*. Context, in this model, characterizes certain aspects of the truster, the trustee, and the environment around them. Different context attributes that share a generalization specialization relation are connected with each other to form the context ontology. Using a notion of semantic distance (Stojanovic, Maedche, Staab, Studer, & Sure, 2001) the authors determine how "close" one context is to another in the ontology. The degree of closeness is then used to evaluate a trust relationship on a new context when the trust value on a related context is known. This work is important in the sense that it is among the first to suggest an approach to extrapolate trust values from related contexts. However, the formulation of the context ontology is not rich. It does not address the problem that there may be semantic mismatches in the terms used for the contexts by different entities such as the one discussed earlier (to wit, administration versus management). In addition, the issues of trust comparison and composition needed for ad hoc collaboration have not been addressed. Thus, this model is not quite suitable for ad hoc collaborations.

In a recent work (Ray, Ray, & Chakraborty, 2009) we extended the vector model of trust by Ray and Chakraborty (2004) by formalizing the notion of context in somewhat along similar lines as (Stojanovic, et al., 2001). However, we address the issue of semantic mismatches. A context in the new model is described by a set of keywords. Multiple contexts may be related using generalization/specialization relationships or composition relationships (which is missing from the model of Stojanovic, et al. We show how these different relationships can be captured using a new data structure that we term as the *context graph*. Information obtained from different sources cannot, in general, be combined if they use different context graphs. However, we identify the relationships that can exist between different context graphs, and propose algorithms that enable us to combine different context graphs. Such formalization enables us to compare information obtained from different sources not all of which use the same terminology to describe a context. Moreover, when sufficient information is not available to calculate the trust value in a given context, we show how to extrapolate the trust value from a related context. This extrapolated value can then be used to make some important trust related decisions.

In the current work, we extend this context-sensitive trust model to make it suitable for ad hoc collaborations. The major extensions that we make are as follows. (i) We introduce the dominance relation between two trust relationships. This allows one to compare two trust relationships (and by repeated application, compare a number of trust relationships) and determine which of them represents more trustworthiness of the trustee. (ii) We define a set of composition operators on trust relationships. These operations allow one

to determine the effective trustworthiness when groups are formed between a set trustees or a set of trusters or both as well as when such groups are changing dynamically.

The rest of the chapter is organized as follows: Section "Related Works" briefly describes some of the works in the area of trust models. We discuss these works and investigate how well they are suited for evaluating trust relationships for ad hoc collaborations. Section titled "Overview of the Context-Aware Trust Model" gives our definition of trust and provides an overview of our model. The section "Trust Evaluation" defines the parameters on which trust depends and proposes techniques for assessing them. It also describes the concepts of normalized trust and the value of trust and discusses trust dynamics – the dependence of trust on time. Following section, "Reasoning About Trust Relationships in Different Contexts", formalizes the notion of trust context that will enable one to reason about trust relationships in different contexts. Section on "Evaluating Trust Without Complete Information" discusses how trust value can be extrapolated when some information needed to compute the trust value is missing. "Comparison Operation on Trust Vectors" presents the dominance relation between trust vectors that help one compare two trust relationships. Section "Combining Trust Vectors for Collaborations" defines operators for combining two or more trust relationships. Finally, "Conclusions and Future Directions" concludes the chapter with a discussion of some future research possible in this area.

RELATED WORKS

Researchers have proposed a number of logic-based formalisms of trust. Almost all of these view trust as a binary relation. Forms of first order logic (Abdul-Rahman & Hailes, 2000; Burrows, Abadi, & Needham, 1990; Jajodia, Samarati, & Subrahmanian, 1997) and modal logic or its modification (Rangan, 1988) have been variously used to model trust in these cases. Simple relational formulae like 'A trusts B' are used to model trust between two entities. Each formalism extends this primitive construct to include features such as temporal constraints and predicate arguments. Given these primitives and the traditional conjunction, disjunction, negation and implication operators, these logical frameworks express trust rules in some language and reason about these properties. Abdul-Rahman and Hailes (2000) propose a trust model, based on "reputation" that allows artificial agents to reason about trustworthiness and allows real people to automate that process. In (Jones & Firozabadi, 2000) the authors model trust as the issue of reliability of an agent's transmission. They use a variant of modal logic to model various trust scenarios. They also use their language to model the concepts of deception and an entity's trust in another entity. Unfortunately, none of these logic-based formalisms address the core issues of trust comparison, composition operations, or the association of trust and context.

The authors in (Yahalom & Klein, 1994; Yahalom, Klein, & Beth, 1993) propose a formal model for deriving new trust relationships from existing ones. In (Yahalom, et al., 1993) the authors propose a model for expressing trust relations in authentication protocols, together with an algorithm for deriving trust relations from recommendations. In (Yahalom & Klein, 1994) rules and algorithms for obtaining public keys based on trust relationships are developed. Neither of these works defines what is meant by trust. Nor do they address the core requirements that need to be satisfied for application to ad hoc collaborations. The authors of (Beth, Borcherding, & Klein, 1994) extend the ideas presented by Yahalom et al. to include relative trust. This work proposes a method for extracting trust values based on experiences and recommendations and also a method for deriving new trust values from existing ones within a network of trust relationships. The concept of trust context is missing though. Jøsang (1997,

1998, 1999) proposes a model for trust based on a general model for expressing relatively uncertain beliefs about the truth of statements. Trust is an opinion, which is expressed as a triplet $\langle b, d, u \rangle$. Here b, d, and u are respectively measures of one's belief, disbelief, and uncertainty in a proposition. We believe that Jøsang's model provides a sound formalism for a subjective concept such as trust and thus use it in our trust model. However, a major shortcoming of this model is that it has no mechanism for monitoring trust relationships to re-evaluate their constraints. It does not specify how to measure trust, and compare and compose the same. These are some of the shortcomings that we address in our model. The authors in (Cohen, Parasuraman, Serfaty, & Andes, 1997) propose an alternative, more differentiated conception of trust, called Argument-based Probabilistic Trust model (APT). The most important use of APT is to chart how trust varies, from one user, decision, or situation to another, and across phases of decision aid use. Model components to address the challenges of ad hoc collaborations are missing from this work.

Li and Liu (2003) present a coherent adaptive trust model for quantifying and comparing the trustworthiness of peers based on a transaction-based feedback system. They propose three basic trust parameters – peer feedback through transactions, total number of transactions a peer performs, and credibility of the feedback sources. The authors address factors that influence peer-to-peer trust, like reputation systems and misbehavior of peers by giving false feedback. The authors also provide a trust metric for predicting a given peer's likelihood of a successful transaction in the future. This work is very restrictive in the sense that it is applicable to only peer-to-peer systems. Purser (2001) presents a simple, graphical approach to model trust. He points out the relationship between trust and risk and argues that for every trust relationship, there exists a risk associated with a breach of the trust extended. Trust relationships are modeled as directed graphs where trust is a unidirectional directed edge from the trusting entity to the trusted entity. The author includes context (to define scope of trust), associated confidence level, associated risk, and transitivity value. This work provides some novel concepts in the formulation of trust models. However, the models applicability for ad hoc collaborations is not clear. Bacharach and Gambetta in (Bacharach & Gambetta, 2000) embark on a re-orientation of the theory of trust. They define trust as a particular belief, which arises in games with a certain payoff structure. They also identify the source of the primary trust problem in the uncertainty about the payoffs of the trustee. According to the authors, the truster must judge whether apparent signs of trustworthiness are themselves to be trusted. This is a very novel concept that has not been addressed by most researchers in the definition of trust models. We show later how this issue is addressed in our trust model.

Marsh (1994) introduces a computational model for trust in the distributed artificial intelligence community. In this model trust is represented as a real number in the range [-1, 1]. The author, however, does not consider what factors determine the value of trust. The operators and algebra for manipulating trust values are limited and have trouble dealing with negative trust values. The authors in (Guha, Kumar, Raghavan, & Tomkins, 2004) develop a formal framework for trust propagation. They are also one of the first to formally propose distrust as different from trust. They assume that a universe of users express some level of trust and distrust for any other user. However, the model does not provide a way to express neutrality. In addition, the authors do not elaborate on how to actually measure trust.

The idea of trust depending on knowledge, recommendation, and experience has been proposed by Ray and Chakraborty (2004). In this work, the authors argue that trust between a truster and trustee is associated with a context and this trust value depends on experience, knowledge, and recommendation. The authors propose a model in which trust is represented as a 3-element vector where the elements correspond to experience, knowledge, and recommendation. Each of these elements has a numeric value in the range [-1, 1] and the authors describe realistic policies that can be used to determine the values corresponding to these elements. The authors also show how to normalize the trust vector to obtain a scalar value on the basis of which a user can obtain some idea about the trustworthiness of an entity or compare the trustworthiness of different entities. One limitation of the above work is that the model relies on having experience, recommendation, and experience values pertaining to that context. Often times, this may not be the case – one or more values may be missing. In the worst case, if there are no experience, knowledge, and recommendation for some particular context, the model fails to find a trust value. This situation is not uncommon – often times, we have to evaluate the trustworthiness of a new entity for which very little information is available. We eliminate this limitation in our current work. We formalize the notion of contexts and show how different contexts are related with each other. Thus, for a certain context if the truster cannot find a value corresponding to the recommendation, experience, and knowledge, he can still evaluate the trust based on the values obtained from related contexts.

Other researchers have also proposed context aware trust models. In (Liu & Issamy, 2004) the authors define the term "context" as service category. Theirs is a reputation model for trust. They use an ontology tree of services using the DAML-S language to evaluate the semantic relation between different contexts. Each node in the ontology tree represents a type of service and is a sub-category of its parent node. Given two nodes in the tree, the distance between the two nodes is used as a degree of similarity between the contexts. The distance is defined as the least number of intermediate nodes to traverse to go from one node to the other. Toivonen et al. (2006) introduce the notion of *context ontology* in a similar manner as (Liu & Issamy, 2004). Context, in this model, characterizes certain aspects of the truster, the trustee, and the environment around them. This notion of context is closer to ours. Different context attributes that share a generalization-specialization relation are connected with each other to form the context ontology. Using a notion of semantic distance (Stojanovic, et al., 2001) the authors determine how "close" one context is to another in the ontology. The degree of closeness is then used to evaluate a trust relationship on a new context when the trust value on a related context is known. However, the formulation of the context ontology in this work as in the work by Liu and Issamy (2004) is not very rich. None of these works addresses the problem that there may be semantic mismatches in the terms used for the contexts by different entities such as the one discussed earlier (to wit, administration versus management). In addition, the issues of trust comparison and composition needed for ad hoc collaboration have not been addressed in either work. Thus, these two models are not quite suitable for ad hoc collaborations.

Quercia, Hailes, and Capra (2006) propose using context as an element of trust tuple. However, context information does not play any significant role in the computation of trust other than that ratings only from the same context can be considered in the computation of trust. Moreover, it does not appear that this model can be easily adapted to compute trust relationships in ad ho collaborations since no techniques is proposed to compare and compose trust values. In (Neisse, Wegdam, van Sinderen, & Lenzini, 2007), the authors propose a model to compute trust value for context aware services. The emphasis in this work is the development of a trust management framework. Like us, the authors adapt Jøsang's subjective logic framework for the computation of trust values. However, extrapolating trust values for newer contexts based on trust values for older contexts is not addressed in this paper. In addition, the issues of trust comparison and

composition are also not addressed. Thus, the suitability of this model for ad hoc collaborations is not clear. Wang, et al. (2008) propose a context-aware trust model for multi-agent systems. Their model uses Bayesian networks for computing trust values. The definition of context is similar to that of Toivonen, et al. (2006). However, the authors predefine the set of contexts to be limited to some *m* types. Each context within the scope of a trust relationship is a tuple whose members are instances of one of these types. Thus the same problems related to context appear in this work as in (Ray & Chakraborty, 2004). No sophisticated composition or comparison operation can be performed on trust relationships based on context information.

Blaze, Feigenbaum, & Lacy (1996) first introduced the trust management problem as a distinct and important component of security in network services. According to Blaze et al., aspects of the trust management problem include formulating security policies and security credentials, determining whether particular sets of credentials satisfy the relevant policies. The *PolicyMaker* trust management system (Blaze, et al., 1996; Blaze, Feigenbaum, & Strauss, 1998) is a framework which is able to express in a common language the authorization policies, certificates and trust relationships, thus integrating all these concepts. Here, public keys are bound to predicates that describe the actions they are trusted to sign for, rather than the names of the key-holders. *PolicyMaker* is suggested as general security certificates; filters are associated with public keys and may be written in a variety of interpreted languages. Also, any public key system may be used and signatures may be verified by external applications. Trust is decentralized, but if a local policy is not defined or available, a trusted third party may be used to issue credentials for others. One design goal of *PolicyMaker* is to separate generic mechanism from application-specific policy. The *PolicyMaker* service appears to applications very much like a database query engine. *PolicyMaker* is the first trust management system intended to be applied to any service in which cryptography is needed. Blaze et al. treat the trust management problem more like authorization; on the contrary, we think of trust in a more abstract way. *PolicyMaker* is not able to address negative policies, which limits its usage in complicated systems.

KeyNote (Blaze, Feigenbaum, Ioannidis, & Keromytis, 1999) derives from *PolicyMaker* and was designed to improve the weakness of *PolicyMaker*. *KeyNote* provides a simple language for describing and implementing security policies, trust relationships, and digitally-signed credentials. Users of applications built with the *KeyNote* system have access to a powerful, standardized language for writing security policies and credentials that can control potentially dangerous actions requested across un-trusted networks. However, *KeyNote* was designed to simplify the integration of the service with the client applications. Thus *KeyNote* has a built-in credential verification system and a simple notation to express authorization predicates.

The conventional view of the trust management problem has not focused on trust at an abstract level, but has focused on how one can make authorization and access control more efficient (Grandison, 2001). Unlike *PolicyMaker*/*KeyNote* trust management systems and the conventional view of trust proposed by Blaze et al., Grandison defined trust as "the quantified belief by a truster with respect to the competence, honesty, security and dependability of a trustee within a specified context" (Grandison, 2001). Apparently, the definition of trust is very close to the general meaning of trust and is not restricted only to authorization and access control. Grandison also proposed *SULTAN* (Simple Universal Logic-oriented Trust Analysis Notation) that is an abstract, logic-oriented framework designed to facilitate the specification, analysis and management of trust relationships.

The IBM Trust Management System (Herzberg, Mass, Mihaeli, Naor, & Ravid, 2000)

presents a novel approach, which constructs trust management system on top of the Role-Based Access Control (RBAC) (Ferraiolo, Sandhu, Gavrila, Kuhn, & Chandramouli, 2001) model. This greatly simplifies the overall system design. The Trust Policy Language is expressed in XML which also leveraging proven technology. However, there are some problems with this system. The trust model behind the system is essentially based on *recommendation*. Malicious recommenders could potentially abuse the system by adding un-trusted entities. Unlike Herzberg et al., we believe that other factors, such as, *experience* and *knowledge* should also be taken into consideration while evaluating trust. The underlying trust model in the IBM Trust Management System is binary; an entity is either allowed to be added into a trusted group, or denied. There is nothing between the two states. In our system, we model trust quantitatively. The Trust Policy Language is flexible and can be easily expanded. But when we try to model complex situations, we will have to define our own XML tags. The semantic of these tags can be ambiguous. A separate mechanism is necessary to associate the XML syntax with its semantic. In our system, we use standard syntax to express different kinds of language constructs that will not cause any ambiguity.

A number of research projects have investigated the problem of trust negotiations for web-based applications (Bonatti & Samarati, 2000; Winsborough & Li, 2006; Yu & Winslett, 2003; Yu, Winslett, & Seamons, 2003). Portfolio and Service Protection Language (PSPL) (Bonatti & Samarati, 2000) provides a language to express access control policies for services and release policies for client and server. It includes a policy filtering mechanism to provide policy disclosure and protect privacy during the process. However, PSPL does not address the problem of estimating the level of threat to individual privacy. Thus it cannot help the user decide what information to release and to whom. TrustBuilder (Yu, et al., 2003) defines a set of negotiation protocols that define the ordering of messages and the type of information the messages will contain. It aims at establishing trust through the exchange of digital credentials and the use of access control policies that specify what combination of credentials a user must disclose in order to gain access at the service provider. Bertino, Ferrari, & Squicciarini (2004) proposes Trust-*X* as a comprehensive framework for trust negotiations. They provide both a language for encoding policies and certificates, and a system architecture. They have defined a broad variety of approaches to carry out negotiations and to achieve protection of disclosure policies.

Overview of the Context-Aware Trust Model

We adopt the definition of trust as provided by Grandison and Sloman (2000).

Definition 1: Trust is defined to be the firm belief in the competence of an entity to act dependably, reliably and securely within a specific context.

In the same work, Grandison and Sloman define distrust as the "lack of firm belief in the competence of an entity to act dependably, securely and reliably". However, we believe distrust is somewhat stronger than just "lacking a belief". Grandison and Sloman's definition suggests the possibility of ambivalence in making a decision regarding distrust. We choose to be more precise and thus define distrust as follows.

Definition 2: Distrust is defined as the firm disbelief in the competence of an entity to act dependably, securely and reliably within a specified context.

In our model, trust is specified as a trust relationship between a truster, say entity *A*, – an entity that trusts the target entity – and a trustee, say entity *B*, – the entity that is trusted. The truster *A* is always an active entity (for example, a human being or a subject). The trustee *B* can either be an active entity or a passive entity (for example, a piece of information or a software).

The trust relationship between a truster, *A*, and a trustee, *B*, is seldom absolute (Grandison & Sloman, 2000). Almost always, the truster trusts the trustee with respect to its ability to perform a specific action or provide a specific service. For example, the entity *A* may trust the other entity *B* about the latter's ability to keep a secret. However, this does not mean if that *A* wants a job done efficiently, *A* will trust *B* to do it. Similarly, if we want to compare two trust values, we just cannot compare two arbitrary trust values. We need to compare the values for trust that serves similar purposes. This leads us to associate a notion of *context* with a trust relationship. Examples of contexts are (i) to *provide a service*, (ii) to *make decisions* on behalf of a truster, and (iii) to *access resources* of a truster. (The formal definition of context appears in Section "Reasoning About Trust Relationships in Different Contexts".)

We adapt Jøsang's *opinion model* (Jøsang, 1997), to model trust. The opinion model appears to be a good choice to represent trust relations because of its ability to model and reason about uncertainties very well. In (Jøsang, 1997), an opinion is represented as a triple (*b, d, u*) where *b* represents *belief*, *d* represents *disbelief* and *u* represents *uncertainty*. Each of these components has a value between [0, 1] and sum of the three components is 1. Thus, an opinion (*b, d, u*) is represented as a point in the *opinion space* which Jøsang represents by a unit equilateral triangle (see Figure 1 which is adapted from (Jøsang, 1997)). The three vertices of this triangle represent complete disbelief, complete belief and complete uncertainty respectively. For example, in Figure 1 if the opinion has a value X, it indicates a high disbelief in the proposition being true but correspondingly a high amount of uncertainty. Values Y and Z are similarly interpreted. We adapt this model to represent a truster A's trust on a trustee B on some context c as a triple $\left({}_A b_B^c, {}_A d_B^c, {}_A u_B^c \right)$

Figure 1. Unit side equilateral triangle representation of opinion space

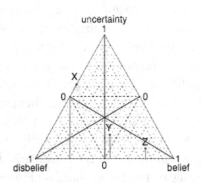

X: High disbelief in proposition being true, but high uncertainty also
Y: Almost equal belief and disbelief in proposition being true, but some uncertainty
Z: High belief in proposition being true, and slightly uncertain

where $_A b_B^c$ is A's belief on B in context c, $_A d_B^c$ is A's disbelief on B in context c, and $_A u_B^c$ is truster A's uncertainty about B in the context c.

We posit that a trust relationship is not static but changes over time. Even if there is no change in the underlying factors that influence trust over a time period, the value of the trust relationship at the end of the period is not the same as that at the beginning of the period. Thus, we need to specify time when describing a trust relationship. The trust relationship between truster A and trustee B pertaining to context c at time t is formally denoted as $(A \xrightarrow{\ c\ } B)_t$.

The trust relationship $(A \xrightarrow{\ c\ } B)_t$ is a 3 × 3 matrix. The rows of the matrix correspond to the three parameters, namely, *experience*, *knowledge*, and *recommendation*, on which trust depends. (formal definition of these parameters and methods for evaluating them are given in section "Trust Evaluation".) Each of these parameters is represented in terms of the opinion triple (b, d, u) where b represents the belief on the parameter for evaluating trust, d specifies disbelief on the parameter, and u represents uncertainty about the parameter to evaluate the trust. These three terms constitute the columns of the trust matrix and are interpreted as follows. We specify that if the belief value in any opinion triple is larger than the corresponding disbelief value, then the corresponding parameter is contributing towards an increase in the trust level. Let us assume that during the evaluation of a trust relationship the opinion triple for experience is computed to be (0.6, 0.3, 0.1). This indicates that the truster believes with a level 0.6 on a scale of 0 to 1 that her experience with the trustee has been positive and enhances her trust in the trustee; at the same time she also disbelieves with a level of 0.3 on the same scale that her experiences have been positive, and to a level of 0.1 she is not certain what to make of her experiences with the trustee.

The three parameters may not have equal importance for evaluating trust. Some truster may choose to give more importance to her personal experience with the trustee for the purpose of assessing the trustworthiness of the latter, while others may choose to give more importance to recommendations from third parties. To accommodate this concept we need to normalize the trust matrix. The *trust policy vector* specifies the normalization factor that gives the relative weight of each parameter. Applying the normalization factor to the trust relationship gives a *normalized trust relationship*. The normalized trust relationship between truster A and trustee B pertaining to context c at time t is formally denoted as $(A \xrightarrow{\ c\ } B)_t^N$. It specifies A's normalized trust on B at a given time t for a particular context c. This normalized trust is represented as a single triple $(_A \hat{b}_B^c, _A \hat{d}_B^c, _A \hat{u}_B^c)$.

Trust Evaluation

We next describe in details how trust evaluation takes place in our model. We begin by formally defining the three parameters on which trust relationship depends, namely, experience, knowledge, and recommendation.

Definition 3: The *experience* of truster about a trustee is defined as the measure of the cumulative effect of a number of events that were encountered by the truster with respect to the trustee in a particular context and over a specified period of time.

The trust of a truster on a trustee can change because of the truster's *experiences* with the trustee in the particular context. The experience depends on the type of events, namely, positive, negative or neutral, that have been encountered by the truster.

Definition 4: The *knowledge* of the truster regarding a trustee for a particular context is defined as a measure of the condition of awareness of the truster through acquaintance with, familiarity of or understanding of a science, art or technique.

The trust of a truster on a trustee can change because of some *knowledge* that the truster comes to posses regarding the trustee for the particular context. Knowledge can be of two types – *direct knowledge* and *indirect knowledge*. Direct knowledge is one which the truster acquires by itself. It may be obtained by the truster in some earlier time for some purpose or, it may be a piece of information about the trustee for which the truster has a concrete proof to be true. Indirect knowledge, on the other hand, is something that the truster does not acquire by itself. The source of indirect knowledge is the *reputation* of the trustee in the context. The truster may get the idea about the reputation of trustee from various sources like reviews, journals, news bulletin, people's opinion etc.

Definition 5: A *recommendation* about a trustee is defined as a measure of the subjective or objective judgment of a recommender about the trustee to the truster.

The trust value of a truster on a trustee can change because of a *recommendation* for the trustee. A recommender sends her opinion, in terms of a triple (b, d, u), on the trustee in the speci-fied context as the recommendation. Moreover, recommendation can be obtained by the truster from more than one source.

In the following sections, we describe how experience, knowledge, and recommendation, can be evaluated.

Evaluating Experience

We model experience in terms of the number of events encountered by a truster, A, regarding a trustee, B in the context c within a specified period of time $[t_0, t_n]$. We assume that A has a record of the events since time t_0. An event can be positive or negative or neutral. Positive events contribute towards increasing the belief component of experience. Negative events increase the disbelief component of experience. Neutral events increase both belief and disbelief components equally. No experience contributes towards the uncertainty component of experience. In the following, we describe how to calculate the experience that a truster A has about trustee B with respect to context c. This is formally denoted as $_A E_B^c = (b_E, d_E, u_E)$ where b_E, d_E, u_E represent belief, disbelief and uncertainty components respectively with respect to the experience that A has towards B.

Let $\mathbf{N}$ denote the set of natural numbers. The set of time instances $(t_0, t_1, ..., t_n)$ is a totally ordered set. The ordering relation, called the *precedes-in-time* relation and denoted by $\prec$, is defined as follows: $\forall\ i, j \in \mathbf{N}, t_i \prec t_j \Leftrightarrow i < j$. For example, time instance t_1 precedes time instance t_2, which in turn preceded time instance t_3 and so on. We use the symbol $t_i \preceq t_j$ to signify either $t_i \prec t_j$ or $t_i = t_j$.

Consecutive time instances are grouped into an interval. We use the temporal notation $[t_i, t_j]$ for describing a time interval where $t_i \preceq t_j$. The time interval $[t_i, t_j]$ describes the set of consecutive time instances where t_i is the first instance and t_j is the last one. We denote the time period of interest as $[t_0, t_n]$. This is divided into a set of n sub-intervals

$[t_0, t_1], [t_1, t_2], ..., [t_{n-1}, t_n]$. The intervals overlap at the boundary points only. That is, $\forall\ i,j,k,l \in \mathbf{N}$, where i, j, k, l are all distinct, $[t_i, t_j] \cap [t_k, t_l] = \varnothing$. Also, $\forall\ i, j, k \in \mathbf{N}$, where i, j, k are all distinct, $[t_i, t_j] \cap [t_j, t_k] = t_j$. That is, all instances, except t_0 and t_n, that occur at the boundary of an interval is a part of two intervals. We refer to the interval $[t_{k-1}, t_k]$ as the kth interval where $0 \leq k \leq n\text{-}1$.

We assume that events occur at time instances. The function *ET*, referred to as the event-occurrence-time function, returns the time instance t_j at which a given event e_k occurred. Formally, $ET(e_k) = t_j$. Moreover, if $ET(e_k) = t_j$ and $t_j \in [t_i, t_k]$ and $j \neq i$ and $j \neq k$, then e_k is said to occur in the interval $[t_i, t_k]$. For two consecutive intervals $[t_i, t_j]$ and $[t_j, t_k]$ if $ET(e_l) = t_j$ then we assume e_k occurs in the interval $[t_i, t_j]$.

Let the experience acquired at interval i, $1 \leq i \leq n\text{-}1$, be represented as (b_i, d_i, u_i) where b_i, d_i, u_i denote belief, disbelief, and uncertainty respectively. When no event occurs during some particular time interval i, this corresponds to the fact that $u_i = 1$ and $b_i = d_i = 0$. The next case is when events occur at the interval i. Let P_i denote the set of all positive events, Q_i denote the set of all negative events, and N_i denote the set of all neutral events that occur in the interval i. Each positive event increases b_i, each negative event increases d_i, and each neutral event increase both b_i and d_i. The values for b_i, d_i and u_i are computed as follows: $b_i = \dfrac{|P_i| + |N_i/2|}{|P_i| + |Q_i| + |N_i|}$,

$d_i = \dfrac{|Q_i| + |N_i/2|}{|P_i| + |Q_i| + |N_i|}$, and $u_i = 0$, where the symbol $|R_i|$ denotes the cardinality of the set R_i. The intuition is that each positive event contributes to the belief component by $\dfrac{1}{|P_i| + |Q_i| + |N_i|}$. Similarly, each negative event contributes to the disbelief component by $\dfrac{1}{|P_i| + |Q_i| + |N_i|}$. Each neutral event

contributes equally to both belief and disbelief component by $\dfrac{0.5 \times |N_i|}{|P_i| + |Q_i| + |N_i|}$. Moreover, since at least events have occurred in the interval, the uncertainty component is 0.

Note that, in real world, events occurring in the distant past have less effect than those that have recently occurred. More importance must be given to recent events than past ones. To accommodate this in our model, we assign a *non-negative* weight w_i to the ith interval such that $w_i > w_j$ whenever $j < i$, $i, j \in \mathbf{N}$. We use the formula $w_i = i/S\ \forall\ i = 1, 2, ..., n$, where $S = n(n+1)/2$, to evaluate weights of the intervals, satisfying the above condition.

The experience of A about B in context c is finally expressed as $_AE_B^c = (b_E, d_E, u_E)$. The values of b_E, d_E, and u_E are given by $b_E = \sum_{i=1}^{n} w_i \times b_i$, $d_E = \sum_{i=1}^{n} w_i \times d_i$ and $u_E = \sum_{i=1}^{n} w_i \times u_i$ respectively.

Example: Consider the timeline diagram shown in Figure 2 that represents the different encounters between a truster, *A*, and a trustee, *B*. A "+" symbol is used to denote the occurrence of a positive event in an interval, a "-" symbol to denote a negative event, and a "*" symbol to denote a neutral event. We divide the time period into 6 intervals $[t_0, t_1]$, $[t_1, t_2], ... [t_5, t_6]$. Thus $S = 21$.

During the interval $[t_1, t_2]$ no events occurred between the truster and the trustee. The weights for the different intervals are as follows: w_1 (for the interval $[t_0, t_1]$) = 0.05, w_2 (for interval $[t_1, t_2]$) = 0.09, $w_3 = 0.14$, $w_4 = 0.19$, $w_5 = 0.25$, and $w_6 = 0.29$. The values for P_i, Q_i, and N_i for the different intervals $i = 1... 6$ are respectively as follows: $i = 1$: (3, 2, 1), $i = 2$: (0, 0, 0), $i = 3$: (5, 0, 1), $i = 4$: (2, 3, 2), $i = 5$: (5, 0, 0) and $i = 6$: (2, 3, 1). This leads to values of b_i, d_i and u_i for the different intervals as: $i = 1$: (0.58, 0.42, 0), $i = 2$: (0, 0, 1), $i = 3$: (0.92, 0.08, 0), $i = 4$: (0.43, 0.57, 0), $i = 5$: (1, 0, 0) and $i = 6$: (0.42, 0.58, 0). Finally,

Figure 2. Example illustrating computation of experience

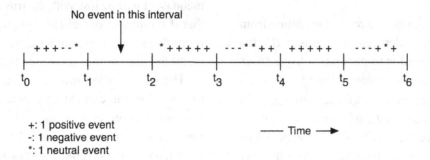

the experience value of the truster computes to (0.61, 0.30, 0.09).

Evaluating Knowledge

The knowledge factor is made up of two parts: *direct knowledge* and *indirect knowledge*. Direct knowledge can be formally assessed or evaluated. Indirect knowledge is more subjective. Direct knowledge can be evaluated via physically measureable properties of entities, credentials, and certificates. For example, operational questions about ad hoc collaborations such as how information is distributed among collaborators, where it is stored and how, failure rates of collaborators, security technology adapted by them, and so on, can be used to measure direct knowledge. Note that, algorithms to measure these are outside the scope of this work. In addition, the values arrived at for these parameters can be subjective. However, this is not of much concern since trust itself is a subjective attribute.

Indirect knowledge can be obtained from reputation. There are numerous reputation models that can be suitably adapted for this purpose. Direct knowledge and indirect knowledge are associated with triples $K_D = (b_D, d_D, u_D)$ and $K_I = (b_I, d_I, u_I)$ respectively. Each item of direct (indirect) knowledge is categorized into positive,

negative, or neutral. The elements of the triple (b_D, d_D, u_D) can be computed as follows:

$$b_D = \frac{\#\,of\;positive\;direct\;knowledge\;items + \#\,of\;neutral\;direct\;knowledge/2}{\#\,of\;direct\;knowledge\;items}$$

$$d_D = \frac{\#\,of\;negative\;direct\;knowledge\;items + \#\,of\;neutral\;direct\;knowledge/2}{\#\,of\;direct\;knowledge\;items}$$

$u_D = 0,$ *if there is some direct knowledge item,* $=1$ *otherwise.*

Similar formulae can be written for indirect knowledge. The weight that a truster assigns to each of these knowledge types depends on the problem context. The truster assigns the relative weights w_D, w_I for these two types of knowledge, where $w_D, w_I \in [0, 1]$ and $w_D + w_I = 1$. The weights are determined by the underlying policy. Truster A's knowledge about trustee B in the context c is computed as

$$_A K_B^c = w_D \times K_D + w_I \times K_I =$$
$$w_D \times (b_D, d_D, u_D) + w_I \times (b_I, d_I, u_I) = (b_K, d_K, u_K)$$

where

$$b_K = w_D \times b_D + w_I \times b_I, d_K = w_D \times d_D + w_I \times d_I,$$
$$u_K = w_D \times u_D + w_I \times u_I$$

Evaluating Recommendation

The truster A may obtain a recommendation from multiple recommenders regarding trustee B in the context c. The goal is to generate a triple (b, d, u) from each recommender and use these to get (b_R, d_R, u_R) which represents the recommendation that A has received about B with respect to context c. First, we give the details about how the triple is computed for each recommender. Later, we describe how these results are aggregated.

Let M be one such recommender. The recommender M may or may not have a trust relationship with trustee B regarding context c. The truster A can provide a questionnaire to the recommender. The recommender is allowed to use the values +1, -1, 0, or $\perp$ in filling this questionnaire. The value +1 indicates belief, -1 indicates disbelief, 0 indicates neutral, and $\perp$ indicates unknown. The number of $\perp$s with respect to the total number of values will give a measure of uncertainty. The ratio of the number of +1s together with half the number of 0s to the total number of values gives the value for belief. The ratio of the number of -1s together with half the number of 0s to the total number of values gives the value for disbelief. If the recommender does not return a recommendation, the truster uses $(0, 0, 1)$ as a recommendation from M.

The truster A will have a trust relationship with the recommender M. The context of this trust relationship will be to act "reliably to provide a service (recommendation, in this case)". This trust relationship will affect the opinion of the recommendation provided by the recommender. The truster scales the recommender's opinion about the trustee with this trust value. Scaling the recommendation score based on the trust relationship between the truster and the recommender has one important benefit. Suppose that the recommender tells a lie about the trustee in the recommendation in order to gain an advantage with the truster. If the truster does not have belief on the recommender

to a great degree then the belief on the recommendation will be low with the truster. Note also that if the truster disbelieves a recommender to properly provide a recommendation, it will most likely not ask for the recommendation.

The trust relationship that truster A has with trustee M in the context of providing a recommendation is represented as a 3×3 matrix. The rows of the matrix correspond to experience, knowledge, and recommendation and the columns correspond to belief, disbelief, and uncertainty. This matrix is normalized as outlined in section "Normalization of Trust Vector" and converted into a triple of the form (b, d, u). This triple will be used for the scaling operation.

To do this scaling, we borrow the concept of "discounting" proposed in (Jøsang, 2001; Jøsang, Gray, & Kinateder, 2006). According to Jøsang's proposition, if the recommender M disbelieves the trustee B or is uncertain about B, then A also disbelieves B or is uncertain about B; however, this opinion is scaled down by A's belief on M. In addition, A's disbelief and uncertainty about M's opinion, contribute towards A's uncertainty about B. If M sends the triple $(_M b_B, {}_M d_B, {}_M u_B)$ as a recommendation about B, and A has the trust on M as $(_A b_M, {}_A d_M, {}_A u_M)$, then the recommendation $_M R_B^c$ of a recommender M for an entity B to the truster A in a context c is given by $(_{AM} b_B^R, {}_{AM} d_B^R, {}_{AM} u_B^R)$. The values of $_{AM} b_B^R, {}_{AM} d_B^R, {}_{AM} u_B^R$ computed as per Jøsang's formula are:

$$_{AM} b_B^R = {}_A b_M \times {}_M b_B,$$
$$_{AM} d_B^R = {}_A b_M \times {}_M d_B,$$
$$_{AM} u_B^R = {}_A d_M + {}_A u_M + {}_A b_M \times {}_M u_B.$$

Recall that the truster A may get recommendations about the trustee B from many different recommenders. Then A's belief on the recommendation about B is the average of the belief values of all recommendations and A's disbelief is the average of the disbelief values of the recommendations. The same is true for

A's uncertainty about the recommendations. Therefore, if ψ is a group of n recommenders then $_{A\psi}b_R = (\sum_{i=1}^{n} {}_{A_i}b_B^R) / n$, $_{A\psi}d_R = (\sum_{i=1}^{n} {}_{A_i}d_B^R) / n$, and $_{A\psi}u_R = (\sum_{i=1}^{n} {}_{A_i}u_B^R) / n$. Hence, the recommendation component is expressed by the triple $\left(_{A\psi}b_R, \, _{A\psi}d_R, \, _{A\psi}u_R\right)$.

Example. Let us assume that a truster A solicits recommendations for trustee B, from 5 potential recommenders: $R_1, R_2, R_3, R_4,$ and R_5. Every recommender except R_3 sends a recommendation score back to A. The trust relationships between A and each of the recommenders, and the recommendation score submitted by each is summarized in Table 1, which also shows the discounted recommendation computed as per (Jøsang, 2001).

Normalization of Trust Vector

Having determined the triples for each component of trust we specify the simple trust relationship between the truster A and the trustee B in a context c at time t as

$$(A \xrightarrow{\;c\;} B)_t = \begin{pmatrix} b_B & d_B & u_B \\ b_K & d_K & u_K \\ _{A\psi}b_R & _{A\psi}d_R & _{A\psi}u_R \end{pmatrix} \quad (1)$$

Given the same set of values for the factors that influence trust, two trusters may come up with two different trusts for the same trustee. Grandison and Sloman (Grandison & Sloman, 2000) refer to this

characteristic as propensity to trust. This may happen because a truster may assign different weights to the different factors that influence trust. A truster may give more weight to one of the parameters than another in computing a trust relationship. For example, a truster A may choose to lay more emphasis on experience than recommendation in computing trust. Alternatively, a truster may be quite skeptical regarding a recommendation about the trustee. In that case, the truster may want to consider the recommendation factor to a lesser extent in computing trust than experience and knowledge about the trustee. Which particular component needs to be emphasized more than the others, is a matter of trust evaluation policy of the truster. The policy is represented as a trust policy vector by the truster.

Definition 6: The *trust policy vector*, $_AW_B^c$, is a vector that has the same number of components as the simple-trust vector. The elements are real numbers in the range [0, 1] and the sum of all elements is equal to 1.

The elements of this vector are weights corresponding to the parameters of trust relationship. Let $(A \xrightarrow{\;c\;} B)_t$ be the simple trust relationship between truster A and trustee B in context c at time t. Let also $_AW_B^c = (W_E, W_K, W_R)$ be the corresponding trust evaluation policy vector elements such that $W_E + W_K + W_R = 1$ and $(W_E, W_K, W_R \in [0, 1]$. Therefore, the normalized trust relationship between a truster A and a trustee B at a time t and for a particular context c is given by

Table 1. The computed recommendation triple of truster A for trustee B is then (0.26, 0.14, 0.60).

	$(A \xrightarrow{reco} R_i)_t^N$	Recommendation about B	Discounted recommendation
R_1	(0.7, 0.2, 0.1)	(0.8, 0.1, 0.1)	(0.56, 0.07, 0.37)
R_2	(0.5, 0.3, 0.2)	(0.2, 0.7, 0.1)	(0.10, 0.35, 0.55)
R_3	(0.6, 0.3, 0.1)	(0.0, 0.0, 1.0)	(0.00, 0.00, 1.00)
R_4	(0.3, 0.5, 0.2)	(0.5, 0.2, 0.3)	(0.15, 0.06, 0.79)
R_5	(0.8, 0.0, 0.2)	(0.6, 0.3, 0.1)	(0.48, 0.24, 0.28)

$$(A \xrightarrow{\;\;c\;\;} B)_t^N = {}_A W_B^c \times (A \xrightarrow{\;\;c\;\;} B)_t$$

$$= (W_B, W_K, W_R) \times \begin{pmatrix} b_B & d_B & u_B \\ b_K & d_K & u_K \\ {}_{A\psi}b_R & {}_{A\psi}d_R & {}_{A\psi}u_R \end{pmatrix}$$

$$= ({}_A\hat{b}_B^c, \; {}_A\hat{d}_B^c, \; {}_A\hat{u}_B^c)$$

where ${}_A\hat{b}_B^c = W_E \times b_E + W_K \times b_K + W_R \times {}_{A\psi}b_R$, ${}_A\hat{d}_B^c = W_E \times d_E + W_K \times d_K + W_R \times {}_{A\psi}d_R$, and ${}_A\hat{u}_B^c = W_E \times u_E + W_K \times u_K + W_R \times {}_{A\psi}u_R$.

It follows from the above that each element ${}_A\hat{b}_B^c, {}_A\hat{d}_B^c, {}_A\hat{u}_B^c$ of the normalized trust relationship lies within [0, 1] and ${}_A\hat{b}_B^c + {}_A\hat{d}_B^c + {}_A\hat{u}_B^c = 1$.

Trust Dynamics

Belief, disbelief, and uncertainty change over time. Thus, trust also changes over time. Let us suppose that we have initially computed a trust relationship T_{t_i} at time t_i, based on the values of the belief, disbelief, and uncertainty component of underlying parameters at that time. Suppose now that we try to recompute the trust relationship T_{t_n} at time t_n. We claim that even if the underlying parameters do not change between times t_i and t_n, the belief, disbelief, and uncertainty of the trust relationship will change, thereby changing the trust relationship. This change of trust over time is often called *trust dynamics*.

To model trust dynamics we refer to the old adage – time the great healer. The general tendency is to forget about past happenings. This leads us to claim that belief (and disbelief) tends towards zero as time increases, thereby increasing uncertainty. Initially, the value does not change much; after a certain period the change is more rapid; finally the change becomes more stable as the value approaches the 0 level. Also we assert that $\lim_{t\to\infty} b = 0$ and $\lim_{t\to\infty} d = 0$.

How fast belief (or disbelief) will decay over time, is, we believe, dependent on the truster's policy. The truster may choose to forget about his belief (or disbelief) which is 3 years old or 5

years old. The model cannot dictate this. Our goal is to provide a basis by which the truster can at least estimate, based on the truster's individual perception about this, the trust at time t_n. We further believe that trust relationship at present time is not only dependent on the values of the underlying parameters, but also on the "decayed" values of the previous trust. We discuss this in more details in the next section.

Let b_{t_i} be the value of 'belief' component of a trust relationship T_{t_i} at time t_i, and b_{t_n} be the decayed value of the same at time t_n. Then the *time-dependent value* of b_{t_i} s defined as follows:

Definition 7: The *time-dependent value* of belief of a trust relationship T_{t_i} from time t_i, computed at present time t_n, is given by

$$b_{t_n} = b_{t_i} \times e^{-((b_{t_i})^{-1}\Delta t)^{2k}} \tag{2}$$

where $\Delta t = t_n - t_i$ and k is any small integer $\geq 1^1$.

Similarly, we define time-dependent value of disbelief. Hence, the time-dependent value of uncertainty is obtained as $u_{t_n} = 1 - b_{t_n} - d_{t_n}$. This equation shows that, as belief and disbelief decrease over time, uncertainty increases. Figure 3(a) shows the nature of decay in different belief values with the same decay rate k = 1 and figure 3(b) shows the nature of decay of disbelief value 0.9 with different k.

The value of k determines the rate of change of belief (or, disbelief) with time and is assigned by the truster based on its perception about the change. If $\Delta t = 0$ that is at $t_n = t_i$, $e^{-((b_{t_i})^{-1}\Delta t)^{2k}} = 1$ and hence $b_{t_n} = b_{t_i}$. When $\Delta t \to \infty$, then $e^{-((b_{t_i})^{-1}\Delta t)^{2k}} \to 0$ and hence $b_{t_n} \to 0$. This corroborates the fact the time-dependent value of the last known belief (or, disbelief) value is asymptotic to zero at infinite time. Thus, the trust relationship T_{t_n} at time t_n is specified as $b_{t_n}, d_{t_n}, u_{t_n}$.

Figure 3. Graphs illustrating nature of trust decay over time. (a) Decay in different belief values for same k = 1; (b) Decay in disbelief value 0.9 for different k

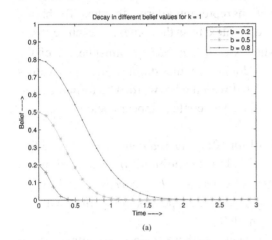

(a)

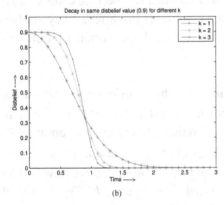

(b)

Note: it is not necessary to have the same decay rate for belief and disbelief. A truster may choose to have two different values k and k' for belief and disbelief respectively.

Trust Vector at Present Time

As indicated earlier, the trust of a truster A on a trustee B in a context c at time t_n depends not only on the underlying components of the trust relationship but also on the trust established earlier at time t_i. Consider for example that at time t_i Alice trusts Bob to the fullest extent (1, 0, 0). At time t_n Alice re-evaluates the trust relationship and determines

the value to be (0.2, 0.5, 0.3). However, we believe that Alice will lay some importance to the previous trust and will not distrust Bob as much as the new trust relationship. So, the normalized trust vector at t_n is a linear combination of time-dependent trust and the normalized trust calculated at present time. The weight Alice will give to old trust vector and present normalized trust vector is, again, a matter of policy. However, this leads us to refine the expression for normalized trust vector at time t_n as follows. This refinement is given by the following definition where α and β are the weights corresponding to present normalized trust vector $({}_A\hat{b}^c_B, {}_A\hat{d}^c_B, {}_A\hat{u}^c_B)$ and time-dependent trust vector $(b_{t_n}, d_{t_n}, u_{t_n})$ respectively.

Definition 8: The normalized trust relationship between a truster A and a trustee B at time t_n in a particular context c taking into account the old trust values is given by

$$(A \xrightarrow{c} B)^N_{t_n} = \alpha \times ({}_A\hat{b}^c_B, {}_A\hat{d}^c_B, {}_A\hat{u}^c_B) + \beta \times (b_{t_n}, d_{t_n}, u_{t_n})$$
$$= (\alpha \times {}_A\hat{b}^c_B + \beta \times b_{t_n}, \quad \alpha \times {}_A\hat{d}^c_B + \beta \times d_{t_n}, \quad \alpha \times {}_A\hat{u}^c_B + \beta \times u_{t_n})$$
$$= ({}_A b^c_B, {}_A d^c_B, {}_A u^c_B)$$

where

$${}_A b^c_B = \alpha \times {}_A\hat{b}^c_B + \beta \times b_{t_n}, \quad {}_A d^c_B = \alpha \times {}_A\hat{d}^c_B + \beta \times d_{t_n},$$

$${}_A u^c_B = \alpha \times {}_A\hat{u}^c_B + \beta \times u_{t_n}$$

and α + β = 1, α, β ∈ [0, 1].

Reasoning about Trust Relationships in Different Contexts

The model described so far has two shortcomings that need to be overcome if the model is to be useful for real-world collaborations. First, it is not possible to compute a useful trust value if the truster does not have any experience, knowledge, or recommendation about a trustee in a given context. The model returns the value ⊥ – undefined. Second, the model developed so far can reason about trust relationships only with respect to a given context. It allows trust values to be compared only if there is an exact match on the context. This requirement is not realistic in most situations. It is extremely unlikely that different trusters will specify a given context in exactly the same manner. This prevents our model from being interoperable. At this stage, we formalize the notion of context and the relationships that exist between different contexts.

We observe that we must define contexts in such a manner that makes our model interoperable. Different entities often use different words to describe the same context. Alternately, the same word can be used for describing different contexts. These are example of semantic conflicts in the use of terminology. To solve these problems we borrow some ideas from the work on ontologies (Gruber, 1993; Uschold & Gruninger, 1996). Our ontology consists of a set of contexts together with relationships defined among them. We begin by giving a formal definition of context and later describe the relationships between contexts.

Definition 9: A *context* C_i is represented by a set of keywords that is denoted by $KeywordSet_{C_i}$.

Each keyword in $KeywordSet_{C_i}$ is used to describe the context C_i. The keywords in $KeywordSet_{C_i}$ are semantically equivalent because they express the same context. For each context C_i, we require that the $KeywordSet_{C_i}$ should be non-empty and finite. For any two distinct contexts C and C', $KeywordSet_C \cap KeywordSet_{C'} = \{\}$. In other words, any keyword belongs to exactly one context. As an example, the context "age" can be expressed by the keywords {age, yearOfBirth}.

Consider the two contexts "doing a job" and "doing a job well". Modeling them as distinct concepts increases the total number of contexts that must be managed. To solve this problem, we specify "doing a job" as a context and associate a

set of values with it. The values in this case can be, for example, {badly, reasonably well, well, very well}. Using these values, we can specify different conditions on the context. Each of these conditions represents a derived context. To obtain a derived context from the context C_i, each keyword k, where $k \in KeywordSet_{C_i}$, must be associated with a domain D_k that defines the set of values associated with the keyword. The formal definition of derived context appears below.

Definition 10: A *derived context* DC_i is one that is specified by a condition k *op* v defined over a context C_i where $k \in KeywordSet_{C_i}$ and $v \in D_k$ and *op* is a logical operator compatible with the domain of D_k.

To check whether two derived contexts specified using conditions on different keywords are equivalent, we need the notion of translation functions.

Definition 11: The *translation function* associated with a context C_i, denoted as TF_{C_i}, is a total function that takes as input a condition k *op* v ($k \in KeywordSet_{C_i}$) and a keyword k' ($k' \in KeywordSet_{C_i}$) and produces an equivalent condition defined over keyword k'. This is formally expressed as follows:

$$TF_{C_i} : Cond_{C_i} \times KeywordSet_{C_i} \rightarrow Cond_{C_i}$$

where $Cond_{C_i}$ is the set of all valid conditions specified over the keywords in $KeywordSet_{C_i}$.

Since the translation function is total, for every given valid condition and keyword there exists an equivalent condition defined on the given keyword. Several steps are involved in developing the translation function. To express k *op* v in terms of k', we need to first convert the value k to an equivalent value that is in the domain of k'. This step is performed by conversion functions which convert the value of one keyword to an equivalent value of another keyword. The second step is to convert the operator *op* into an equivalent operator *op'* that is suitable for the domain of *k'*. The definition of the conversion function together with the domain of the keyword can determine how the operator must be changed.

Relationships between Contexts

Two kinds of relationships may exist between distinct contexts. One is the generalization / specialization relationship between related contexts. The other is the composition relationship between possibly unrelated contexts.

Specialization Relationship

Distinct contexts may be related by the specialization relationship. The specialization relation is anti-symmetric and transitive. We use the notation $C_i \subset C_j$ to indicate that the context C_i is a generalization of context C_j. Alternately, context C_j is referred to as the specialization of context C_i. For instance, the contexts *makes decisions* and *makes financial decisions* are related by the specialization relationship, that is, *makes decisions $\subset$ makes financial decisions*. Also, *makes financial decisions $\subset$ makes payment decisions*. By transitivity, *makes decisions $\subset$ makes payment decisions*.

Each specialization relationship is associated with a degree of specialization. This indicates the closeness of the two concepts. For instance, *makes payment decisions* is a specialization of *makes decisions*, and *makes payment decisions* is also a specialization of *makes financial decisions*. However, the degree of specialization is different in the two cases. *makes payment decision* is closer to *makes financial decision* than *makes decision*s. The *degree of specialization* captures this difference. Since two contexts related by specialization will not be exactly identical, the degree of specialization will be denoted as a fraction. The

exact value of the fraction will be determined using domain knowledge.

The specialization relationship will be used in trust evaluation when information cannot be obtained for a particular context, and the values obtained from the generalized or specialized context will need to be extrapolated.

Composition Relationship

Specialization captures the relationship between contexts that are related. Sometimes unrelated contexts can be linked together using the composition relation. We now describe this composition relation. A context in our model can either be an *elementary* context or a *composite* context. An elementary context is one which cannot be subdivided into other contexts. A composite context is one that is composed from other contexts using the logical and operation. The individual contexts that form a composite context are referred to as the *component* contexts. A component context can either be composite or elementary.

We use the notation $C_i << C_j$ to indicate that the context C_i is a component of context C_j. In such cases, C_i is referred to as the component context and C_j is the composite context. For instance, we may have the component contexts *secure key generation* and *secure key distribution* that can be combined to form the composite context *secure key generation and distribution*. This is denoted as *secure key generation << secure key generation and distribution*.

Sometimes a composite context C_i may be composed from the individual contexts C_j, C_k and C_m. All these contexts may not contribute equally to form C_i. The *degree of composition* captures this idea. A degree of composition is associated with each composition relation. Since two contexts related by composition will not be exactly identical, the degree of composition is denoted as a fraction. The sum of all these fractions equals one if C_i is composed of C_j, C_k and C_m only. If

C_i is composed of C_j, C_k and C_m and also other component contexts, then the sum of fractions associated with C_j, C_k and C_m must be equal to or less than one. The exact value of the fraction representing the degree of composition will be determined by domain knowledge.

The composition relationship is important. When trust information cannot be computed for the composite context because of missing recommendation, experience, or knowledge values, the related information obtained from the components can be used to compute the trust value. Alternately, if we cannot calculate the trust value for a component context, we can use the trust value for the composite context and extrapolate it. Later, we show how we do this.

Context Graphs

The specialization and the composition relations can be described using one single graph which we refer to as the *context graph*. Each node n_i in this graph corresponds to a context. There are two kinds of weighted edges in this graph: composition edges and specialization edges. A composition edge (n_i, n_j), denoted by a solid arrow from node n_i to node n_j, indicates that the context represented by node n_i is a component of the context represented by node n_j. The weight on this edge indicates what percentage of the component context comprises

the composite context. A specialization edge (n_p, n_q), shown by a dashed arrow from node n_p to node n_q, indicates that the context represented by node n_p is a specialization of the context represented by node n_q. The weight on the edge indicates the degree of specialization of a context.

Unrelated contexts correspond to nodes in different context graphs. Each context corresponds to only one node in the set of context graphs. We denote the context graph associated with context C_i as CG_{C_i}.

Figure 4 shows an example of a context graph that is associated with the context *cryptographic key establishment*. The solid arrows in this graph indicate composition relationships and the dashed arrows indicate generalization/specialization relationships. The context *cryptographic key establishment* can have two specializations, namely, *symmetric key establishment* and *asymmetric key establishment*. The weight on the edge connecting this *symmetric key establishment* with *cryptographic key establishment* indicates the degree of specialization. For instance, if symmetric key establishment is very closely related to key establishment, the degree of specialization may be labeled as 4/5. Similarly, the edge connecting *asymmetric key establishment* to *key establishment* may be labeled as 4/5. Each of these specific contexts is a composition of some component contexts. *Generation and distribution of symmetric*

Figure 4. An example of specialization and composition relationship

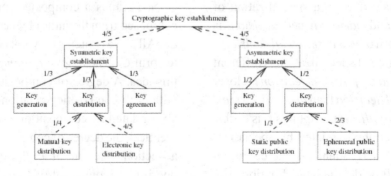

* Dotted lines represent 'generalization–specialization' relationship

* Solid lines represet 'composition–component' relationship

keys has three components – *key generation, key distribution*, and *key agreement*. A weight of ⅓ can be assigned to each of these components contexts. Similarly, *generation and distribution of asymmetric keys* can have components *key generation* and *key distribution* with weights ½ each.

A component context can also be a generalization of some specialized contexts. In the above example the context *key distribution* has two categories – *manual key distribution* and *electronic key distribution*. Similarly *key distribution* in asymmetric keys can be thought of as generalization of *static public key distribution* and *ephemeral public key distribution*.

Consider two contexts C_i and C_j where $C_i \subset C_j$, that is, C_j is a specialization of C_i. The degree of specialization is computed as follows. Let n_i, n_j be the nodes corresponding to contexts C_i and C_j in the weighted graph. Let the path from n_i to n_j consisting of specialization edges be denoted as $(n_i, n_{i+1}, n_{i+2}, ..., n_{j-1}, n_j)$. The degree of specialization is $\prod_{p=i}^{j-1} w(n_p, n_{p+1})$. This corresponds to our notion that the similarity decreases as the length of the path from the generalized node to the specialized node increases. Note that, in real world there may be multiple paths from C_i to C_j. In such cases, it is important that the degree of specialization yield the same values when any of these paths are used for computation.

Consider two contexts C_i and C_j such that C_j is a component of C_i. Degree of composition captures what portion of C_i is made up of C_j. The degree of composition is computed as follows. Let n_i, n_j be the nodes corresponding to contexts C_i and C_j in the context graph. Let there be m paths consisting of composition edges from n_i to n_j. Let the qth path ($1 \le q \le m$) from n_i to n_j be denoted as $(n_i, n_{i_q+1}, n_{i_q+2}, ..., n_{j_q-1}, n_j)$. The degree of composition is $= \sum_{q=1}^{m} (w(n_i, n_{i_q+1}) \times w(n_{j_q-1}, n_j) \times \prod_{p=i_q+1}^{j_q-2} w(n_p, n_{p+1}))$.

A context may be related to several other contexts through specialization and composition relationships. However, we need to find out which context or set of contexts is conceptually closest to the given context. The closest context is a singleton set if the context is a generalization or specialization of context c. It is also a singleton set if it is a composite context in which c is a component. However, if c is a composite context, then the closest concept can also be a set that contains the components of c. The formal definition appears below.

Definition 12: Let c be a context. The set of contexts $S = \{c_1, c_2, ..., c_n\}$ is defined to be *closest* to c if the following relation holds:

- **Case 1:** The elements in S are the components of c:
  - for all contexts n_i that are specializations of c
    - degree of specialization $(n_i, c) \le \sum_{j=1}^{n}$ degree of composition (c_j, c)
  - for all contexts n_i that are generalizations of c
    - degree of specialization $(c, n_i) \le \sum_{j=1}^{n}$ degree of composition (c_j, c)
  - for all contexts n_i in which c is a component
    - degree of composition$(c, n_i) \le \sum_{j=1}^{n}$ degree of composition (c_j, c)
- **Case 2:** S is a singleton set containing c_1 and c as component of c_1:
  - for all contexts n_i that are specializations of c
    - degree of specialization $(n_i, c) \le$ degree of composition (c, c_1)
  - for all contexts n_i that are generalizations of c
    - degree of specialization $(c, n_i) \le$ degree of composition (c, c_1)
  - for all contexts $n_1, n_2, ..., n_m$ that are components of c

- $\sum_{i=1}^{m}$ degree of composition (n_i, c) $\leq$ degree of composition (c, c_j)
  - for all composite contexts n_i in which c is a component
    - degree of specialization $(c, n_i) \leq$ degree of composition (c, c_j)
- **Case 3:** S is a singleton set containing c_j and c is a specialization of c_j:
  - for all component contexts $n_1, n_2, ..., n_m$ of c
    - $\sum_{i=1}^{m}$ degree of composition $(n_i, c) \leq$ degree of specialization (c, c_j)
  - for all contexts n_i that are specializations of c
    - degree of specialization $(n_i, c) \leq$ degree of specialization (c, c_j)
  - for all contexts n_i that are generalizations of c
    - degree of specialization $(c, n_i) \leq$ degree of specialization (c, c_j)
  - for all composite contexts n_i in which c is a component
    - degree of composition $(c, n_i) \leq$ degree of composition (c, c_j)
- **Case 4:** S is a singleton set containing c_j and c is a generalization of c_j:
  - for all component contexts $n_1, n_2, ..., n_m$ of c
    - $\sum_{i=1}^{m}$ degree of composition $(n_i, c) \leq$ degree of specialization (c_j, c)
  - for all composite contexts n_i in which c is a component
    - degree of composition $(c, n_i) \leq$ degree of specialization (c_j, c)
  - for all contexts n_i that are specializations of c
    - degree of specialization $(n_i, c) \leq$ degree of specialization (c_j, c)
  - for all contexts n_i that are generalizations of c
    - degree of specialization $(c, n_i) \leq$ degree of specialization (c_j, c)

Evaluating Trust without Complete Information

The model presented so far describes how trust pertaining to some context is evaluated, how trust changes with time, and how different trust values can be compared. All this relies on the assumption that the trust value can be determined in a given context. This may not be possible when complete information is not available. For instance, the trust evaluation policy vector may assign a weight of 0.5 to the recommendation component and it may not be possible to obtain any recommendation about the trustee under the given context. In the worst case, it may not be possible to obtain information about any of the components for a given context. This situation is not very uncommon -- suppose a truster is trying to determine the trustworthiness of a new software product. In such a case, the truster may not have any experience or knowledge pertaining to this product. Obtaining a recommendation is also not possible. In such a case, the model that we have presented so far, cannot determine the trust value of the software product. In this section, we present an approach using which a truster can obtain an approximate trust value of the given software product. Our approach exploits the relationships between contexts in order to extrapolate the trust value.

Extrapolating Trust Values from Different Contexts

When a truster A cannot determine the trust value of truster B for a context C, we show how the trust value can be obtained from one or more related contexts, say, C_i. The first issue that we must resolve is what value we should use from the related context C_i. We use the individual values for recommendation, experience, and knowledge from C_i and use these to compute the trust value for C. The second issue is that a context C may be related to many other contexts, say, C_i, C_j, and C_k. Which contexts do we refer to in order to evaluate the trust value for context *C*? Many strategies are possible and different strategies may be needed in different real-world situations. In this chapter, we propose a very simple strategy for choosing related contexts. The algorithm given below describes this strategy. This algorithm has three inputs. One is the context *c* whose closest context we are trying to determine. The other is the context graph *CG* in which *c* is a context. The third input is the set of contexts that we should not consider. We term this as the prohibited set of contexts. The algorithm uses a variable *total_weight* that is used for evaluating the closest context. The algorithm proceeds by checking the component contexts of *c*. If these are not prohibited, then the total weight of all these component contexts makes up the variable *total_weight*. These component contexts are inserted into the set *closest* which contains the closest context. We then check each generalized parent and each specialized children whether the weight on the edge is greater than the *total_weight*. If so, *total_weight* is assigned this new weight and closest is initialized with this parent or children. The algorithm returns the set *closest* which gives the set of contexts closest to *c*.

Algorithm 1: Get the Closest Context

Input: (i) *c* – the context whose closest one needs to be determined. (ii) *CG* – the context graph in which *c* is a context. (iii) *S* – set of contexts that should not be considered.

Output: *closest* – set of contexts closest to *c*

Procedure *ChooseContext(c, CG, S)*

begin

closest = {}; total_weight = 0

let *CC* be the set of component contexts of *c*

for each $c_i \in CC(c)$

if $c_i \in/ S$

total_weight = total_weight + w(c_i,c);

closest = closest $\cup$ {c_i};

for each generalization or composite con-

text p_i of *c*

if $p_i \in/ S$ and *total_weight* < w(c, p_i)

total_weight = w(c, p_i); closest = {p_i}

for each specialization r_i of *c*

if $r_i \in/ S$ and *total_weight* < w(r_i, c)

total_weight = w(r_i, c); closest = {r_i}

return *closest*

end

Once the set of closest contexts has been identified we can easily extrapolate the trust relationship between the truster and the trustee for this closest context to the new context. For this purpose we individually extrapolate the experience, knowledge and recommendation components corresponding to the closest contexts to the new context. We provide an algorithm that shows how recommendation about trustee B can be obtained from the closest context. Similar algorithms can be developed for extrapolating the knowledge and experience values.

Algorithm 2: Get Recommendation about Trustee B from the Closest Context

Input: (i) *c* – the context whose recommendation value needs to be determined. (ii) *CG* – the context graph in which *c* is a context.

Procedure *GetRecommendation(c, CG)*

begin

if $_\psi R_B^c \neq \perp$ **return** $_\psi R_B^c$

else

S = {}; closest = {c}

while $_\psi R_B^c = \perp$ and *closest* $\neq$ {} **do**

closest = ChooseClosest(c, CG, S)

if *closest* ={ c_i} and *c* is a component or specialization of c_i **then**

if $_\psi R_B^{c_i} \neq \perp$ **then** $_\psi R_B^c = w(c, c_i) \times {}_\psi R_B^{c_i}$

else S = S $\cup$ {c_i}

if *closest* ={c_i} and *c* is a generalization of c_i **then**

if $_\psi R_B^{c_i} \neq \perp$ **then** $_\psi R_B^c = w(c_i, c) \times {}_\psi R_B^{c_i}$

```
else S = S ∪ {c_i}
if closest = {c_1, c_2, …, c_n} and c is com-
posed of c_i (i =1, 2, …, n)
for each c_i ∈ closest
if _ψR_B^{c_i} ≠⊥ then
```

$$_\psi R_B^c = {_\psi R_B^c} + w(c_i,c) \times {_\psi R_B^{c_i}}$$ **else** S = S ∪ {c_i}

```
end
```

Comparison Operation on Trust Vectors

In many real life scenarios we need to determine the relative trustworthiness of two trustees. Consider the following example. Suppose entity A gets two conflicting pieces of information from two different sources B and C. In this case A will probably want to compare its trust relationships with entities B and C and accept the information that originated from the "more" trustworthy entity. This leads us to define a comparison operator on trust relationships. Note that not all trust relationships can be directly compared. To compare two trust relationships directly they must be for the same truster and on the same context. We define such trust relationships to be compatible. More formally,

Definition 13: Let $T = (A \xrightarrow{\dot{c}} B)_{t_n}^N$ and $T' = (A \xrightarrow{\ddot{c}} C)_{t_n}^N$ be two normalized trust relationships. The trust relationships, T and T', are said to be *compatible* if the trust relationships have been defined under the same trust evaluation policy vector and the contexts $\dot{c}$ and $\ddot{c}$ are the same. Otherwise the two trust relationships are called *incompatible*.

Sometimes, we can compare two trust relationships that are not for the same context. If we can extrapolate the trust relationship of one of the contexts to a trust relationship of the other context as discussed in section "Extrapolating Trust Values From Different Contexts", then we can use the extrapolated trust relationship for the comparison operation.

The most intuitive way to compare two trust relationships is to compare the strengths of the truster's trust levels in the trustees. One indicator of the strength of the trust level is the value of the belief component in the trust vector. More the belief the greater is the trustworthiness of the trustee. This leads us to our first comparison operator for trust relationships.

Definition 14: Consider two trust relationships $T = (A \xrightarrow{\dot{c}} B)_{t_n}^N$ and $T' = (A \xrightarrow{\ddot{c}} C)_{t_n}^N$ that have been defined over the same context and using the same policy vector. Let b_X, d_X and u_X, represent the corresponding component of the trust tuple X, where X is either T or T'. We say T dominates T', denoted by $T \succ T'$, if any of the following conditions hold.

1. $b_T > b_{T'}$
2. $b_T = b_{T'} \wedge d_T < d_{T'}$

The dominance relation compares the two trust relationships using the belief component. The relationship with the higher belief value is said to dominate the other. When the two relationships have identical beliefs, we compare them on the basis of disbelief. However, owing to the uncertainty component in our model it is quite possible that a trust relationship with a somewhat smaller belief component actually represents more trustworthiness. This is because the uncertainty component can be transformed into greater belief. It is equally possible that the uncertainty component is indicative of greater disbelief in the trustworthiness. We may choose to ignore the uncertainty components. On the other hand, to address this dichotomy we rely on a notion of average strength of trust level. We assign a rank to each trust relationship based on average level of trustworthiness of the truster. The rank is computed by the following algorithm which is based on Jøsang's work on subjective logic [Jøsang 1997].

Algorithm 3: Compute Rank of Trust Relationship

Input: A normalized trust relationship $T = (A \xrightarrow{\dot{c}} B)^N_{t_n} = ({}_A b^{\dot{c}}_B, {}_A d^{\dot{c}}_B, {}_A u^{\dot{c}}_B)$

Output: A rank of T.

Procedure ComputeRank(T)

begin

$$rank = \frac{{}_A b^{\dot{c}}_B + {}_A u^{\dot{c}}_B}{{}_A b^{\dot{c}}_B + {}_A d^{\dot{c}}_B + 2 \times {}_A u^{\dot{c}}_B}$$

return rank

end

Let two compatible trust relationships $T = (A \xrightarrow{\dot{c}} B)^N_{t_n}$ and $T' = (A \xrightarrow{\ddot{c}} C)^N_{t_n}$ have ranks T_{rank} and T'_{rank} respectively. We say trust relationship T *dominates* trust relationship T', given by $T \succ T'$ if $T_{rank} > T'_{rank}$. If $T_{rank} = T'_{rank}$ then $T \succ T'$ if $u_T < u_{T''}$.

Combining Trust Vectors for Collaborations

Ad hoc collaborations typically involve many cooperative entities in a relationship within a specific context. Combination of trust is needed for the interoperability of these cooperating agents. Whenever a group of agents are working together, combining their individual trust relationships is necessary to have an idea about the expected behavior of the group. Keeping this in mind we now formalize combination operators for trust relationships. Different possibilities like one-to-many, many-to-one, and many-to-many relationships are addressed. We also formalize the effect of reconfiguration of these groups on the corresponding trust relationships. As in the comparison operation between trust relationships, we assume that the contexts of the trust relationships are the same. If needed and possible, we can extrapolate trust relationships as per section "Extrapolating Trust Values from Different Contexts".

Trust Relationship between a Truster and a Group of Trustee

In real life, we often encounter situations where we have to take decisions based on information coming from different sources. Consider the scenario where an entity has existing trust relationships with different service providers for a particular service. The truster expects some service which is provided collectively by the service providers. The truster has some expectation from each individual provider. To have an idea about the service provided by the group, the combined trust of the service providers needs to be estimated. Therefore, the receiver needs a mechanism to combine the existing trust relationships to estimate an initial *composite trust relationship*. The group of service providers is considered as a single entity (trustee). Once the combination is done, the truster no longer considers the trust relationships with individual trustee. The truster begins with the combined group as a single entity and subsequently a trust relationship with the group evolves.

Assume a truster A has trust relationships $T = (A \xrightarrow{c} B)^N_{t_n} = (b_T, d_T, u_T)$ and $T' = (A \xrightarrow{c} C)^N_{t_n} = (b_{T'}, d_{T'}, u_{T'})$ with two trustees B and C at the same time t_n and in the same context c. A decides to have a trust relationship with the combined group BC in the same context. Based on the disjunction operator of subjective logic we define the *initial* trust relationship between A and BC as follows: $(A \xrightarrow{c} BC)^N_{t_n} = (\hat{b}, \hat{d}, \hat{u})$ where $\hat{b} = b_T + b_{T'} - b_T \times b_{T'}$, $\hat{d} = d_T \times d_{T'}$, and $\hat{u} = d_T \times u_{T'} + d_{T'} \times u_T + u_T \times u_{T'}$.

Trust Relationship between a Group of Trusters and a Single Trustee

Next, we address the situation where different trusters having different trust relationships with the same trustee decide to form a group. After forming the group the trusters behave as a single truster. We need to define a way to combine these different trust relationships to get the initial trust for the group. This initial trust gives the starting point of a trust relationship between the two entities. Thereafter, this trust evolves as before. But before the collaboration can succeed all trusters need to agree to a common policy as to how to continue to evaluate the trustee as a single group.

Let trusters A and B have independent trust relationships $T = (A \xrightarrow{\ c\ } B)_{t_n}^N$ and $T' = (B \xrightarrow{\ c\ } C)_{t_n}^N$ with a trustee C in the same context. Before forming the group AB the members need to agree about the following: (i) a common interval length to determine experience as well as trust, (ii) a common set of recommenders whom the group consider suitable for recommendation purposes, (iii) a common policy for evaluating trust relationships with recommenders, and (iv) a common trust evaluation policy vector to assign weights to each component. Based on this agreement each truster needs to go back and revaluate their individual trust relationships. Let the updated trust relationships be $\hat{T} = (\hat{b}_T, \hat{d}_T, \hat{u}_T)$ and $\hat{T}' = (\hat{b}_{T'}, \hat{d}_{T'}, \hat{u}_{T'})$ respectively. We use the consensus operation in subjective logic to define the combined trust relationship between the group AB and the trustee C, as $\bar{T} = (AB \xrightarrow{\ c\ } C)_{t_n}^N = (b_{\bar{T}}, d_{\bar{T}}, u_{\bar{T}})$ where

$$b_{\bar{T}} = \frac{\hat{b}_T \times \hat{u}_{T'} + \hat{b}_{T'} \times \hat{u}_T}{\hat{u}_T + \hat{u}_{T'} - \hat{u}_T \times \hat{u}_{T'}}, \ d_{\bar{T}} = \frac{\hat{d}_T \times \hat{u}_{T'} + \hat{d}_{T'} \times \hat{u}_T}{\hat{u}_T + \hat{u}_{T'} - \hat{u}_T \times \hat{u}_{T'}} \text{ and}$$

$$u_{\bar{T}} = \frac{\hat{u}_T \times \hat{u}_{T'}}{\hat{u}_T + \hat{u}_{T'} - \hat{u}_T \times \hat{u}_{T'}}.$$

When more than two trusters need to form a collaboration, the composite trust relationship is formed by first combining two of the trusters to form a smaller group and then enlarging the group one more truster at a time till every one of them has been included.

Trust Relationship between a Group of Trusters and a Group of Trustees

We now explore the situation when a group of trusters G_r forms a trust relationship with a group of trustees G_e in some common context c. We can formalize this by combining the above two cases. Combination can take place in different ways.

1. If the group of trustees G_e already exists, then each truster A_i must already have, or must build a trust relationship $(A_i \xrightarrow{\ c\ } G_e)_t^N$ as described in section "Trust Relationship between a Truster and a Group of Trustee". Then A_i's form the truster group G_r with G_e, considering G_e as a single trustee, as described in section "Trust Relationship between a Group of Trusters and a Single Trustee".

2. If the truster group G_r already exists with m different trust relationships like $(G_r \xrightarrow{\ c\ } B_i)_t^N$ for i = 1, 2, …, m, then $(G_r \xrightarrow{\ c\ } G_e)_{t_n}^N$ can be formed as in section "Trust Relationship between a Truster and a Group of Trustee".

3. If neither the group of trusters nor the group of trustees exists then one of the groups has to be formed first after which then the other group is formed as explained above.

Next we examine the effect of reconfiguration of a group on the trust relationship.

Reconfiguration of a Group

Ad hoc collaborations are very dynamic in nature. Consequently, anytime after a group is formed one or more members may leave or a new member may join necessitating re-evaluation of corresponding trust relationships. We have two cases to consider, namely, (i) re-evaluation owing to reorganization of trustee group, and (ii) re-evaluation owing to reorganization of truster group.

We consider the case where a new trustee, C joins an existing group of trustees G at a time t_0. For the purpose of re-evaluation of the trust relationship the truster, A, assumes the group G as a single trustee. The new trust relationship is then computed in the manner discussed in section "Trust Relationship between a Truster and a Group of Trustee". If a trustee leaves a group the re-evaluation of the trust relationship proceeds as follows. Assume C, the exiting trustee, had joined the group G at time t_0 and is leaving the group G' at time t_n. When C leaves the group it is as if a dummy trustee $\hat{C}$ with a trust relationship diametrically opposite to that of C joins the group such that the effects of C is mitigated in the group. However, at time t_n C's effective trust value has degraded from T_C to some value $T'_C = (b'_C, d'_C, u'_C)$. This is the value that needs to be mitigated. A trust relationship that is diametrically opposite to T'_C is $\hat{T}_C = (\hat{b}_C, \hat{d}_C, \hat{u}_C)$ where $\hat{b}_C = d'_C, \hat{d}_C = b'_C, \hat{u}_C = u'_C$.

The new trust relationship between the group G'–C is then obtained by assuming that the dummy trustee $\hat{C}$ joins the group. The exit of a group member may or may not necessitate a change in the trust evaluation policy. If the rank of the trust relationship T_C was greater than the rank of the trust relationship T_G (G being the group that C joined) then the trust evaluation policy needs to be changed after C leaves. The next re-evaluation of the trust relationship $T_{G'-C}$ will be based on the new policy.

When a truster B joins an existing group of trusters, G', the trust relationship is re-evaluated by considering the group G' as a single truster and then following the principles discussed in section "Trust Relationship between a Group of Trusters and a Group of Trustees". Removal of a truster from the group does not affect the group trust relationship. However, the remaining group members may decide to revisit the policy for trust evaluation. The new policy will henceforth decide how the trust relationship is re-evaluated the next time.

CONCLUSION AND FUTURE DIRECTIONS

In this chapter we introduce a new model of trust for ad hoc collaborations. Trust is specified as a trust relationship between a truster and a trustee at a particular time instance and for a particular context. We identify three parameters namely, experience, knowledge and recommendation that contribute towards defining this trust relationship. We propose expression for evaluating these factors. A novel feature of our model is that it is easily adaptable if the underlying parameters are changed to include more than the current three parameters (the parameters all need to be orthogonal to each other). Next we introduce the concept of normalized trust. We show how to factor in a notion of trust policy in computing the trust vector. We also model the notion of trust dynamics that is, the change of trust with time. Incorporating all these different notions we finally provide an expression to compute a trust vector that also includes the effect of a previous trust relationship between the same truster, trustee in the same context.

In order to make our trust model interoperable, an important requirement for applicability to ad hoc collaborations, we formalize the notion of context. A context in our model is described by a set of keywords. Distinct contexts are related using generalization/specialization or composition relationships. Understanding this relationship is important for several reasons. First, it allows one to reason about trust relationships in different contexts, or in cases where the same context is described by different terms. Second, it allows one to extrapolate trust value even when certain information is missing for a given context. Finally, we define ways by which we can compare two trust relationships and combine them. The latter, in particular, is a very important operation for collaborations.

There are a number of open issues in the area of trust models for ad hoc collaborations that researchers (including us) need to address. First and foremost is the issue of defining the set of keywords that represents a specific context. Domain experts will typically develop the context ontology. However, domain experts often differ with each other regarding use of terms for defining various concepts. This becomes a serious issue when multiple organizations need to collaborate as two domain experts may use the same word to mean two completely different things. Thus, when collaboration is formed, the first challenge is to reconcile these semantic mismatches. This is a challenging problem that needs to be addressed.

The next issue related to extending the trust model itself, namely, how to formalize the notion of trust chains. Most researchers take the position that trust relationships can often be transitive. If an entity A trusts another entity B who, in turn, trusts entity C, it can be the case that entity A ends up trusting C. Had trust been a binary relation then such trust chains are easy to model. However, in non-binary models like ours, it is more difficult. Currently, in our model, we support partially, the notion of trust transitivity to one level via the notion of recommendations. However, how to formalize this for chains of arbitrary lengths remains to be seen.

Trust, by nature, is a subjective attribute. That is precisely the reason we have adopted the formalisms of subjective logic and we introduced the notion of trust evaluation policy. However, we are yet to come across any research that addresses the issues related to determining trust policy. We have assumed that there exits an underlying trust policy that helps one to assign weights to the various components of the model. However, what is good way to assign these weights? What will be an appropriate guideline for that? What are the factors that should be considered in assigning these weights? There is also a concept of "gullibility" that often influences a human being's trusting another. Some human beings are more trusting than others. Is there a need to model a similar concept in ad hoc collaborations? We do not have a clear answer to this as yet. We believe an answer will be forthcoming only after there have been serious attempts to incorporate such models in real world applications – such as access control.

A formal language to manage and manipulate trust relationships is another area of research that is much needed. A trust model, such as the one described in this chapter, will purportedly be used as a support tool in decision-making. Without a language to support query and manipulation of trust relationships, such a model will be of limited value. Moreover, a language for this purpose should be as close to natural language as possible. What are the required features of such a language? How to develop a trust management system around this language? These are all some open challenges.

Last but not the least, there is a need to investigate specific application requirements on a trust model. Our model, for instance, require measuring direct knowledge for evaluation of trust relationships. What constitutes knowledge in this case? How does one determine what constitutes positive experience and what negative experience? How does one ensure that a recommender does not exploit the nature of an application to falsify recommendation score for a competitor? How does a truster identify such problems? These are some open research issues that need to be investigated.

ACKNOWLEDGMENT

This work was partially supported by the U.S. Air Force Office of Scientific Research under contract FA9550-07-1-0042. The views presented here are solely those of the authors and do not necessarily represent those of the U.S. Air Force, the U.S. DoD or other federal government agencies or their affiliates.

REFERENCES

Abdul-Rahman, A., & Hailes, S. (2000, January). *Supporting Trust in Virtual Communities.* Paper presented at the 33rd Annual Hawaii International Conference on System Sciences, Maui, Hawaii.

Bacharach, M., & Gambetta, D. (2000). Trust as Type Identification. In C. Castelfranchi & Y. Tan (Eds.), *Trust and Deception in Virtual Societies* (pp. 1-26). Amsterdam: Kluwer Academic Publishers.

Bertino, E., Ferrari, E., & Squicciarini, A. (2004). Trust-X A Peer to Peer Framework for Trust Establishment. *IEEE Transactions on Knowledge and Data Engineering, 16*(7), 827–842. doi:doi:10.1109/TKDE.2004.1318565

Beth, T., Borcherding, M., & Klein, B. (1994, November). *Valuation of Trust in Open Networks.* Paper presented at the Third European Symposium on Research in Computer Security, Brighton, UK.

Blaze, M., Feigenbaum, J., Ioannidis, J., & Keromytis, A. (1999). *The KeyNote Trust Management System (version 2).* Retrieved from http://www.crypto.com/papers/rfc2704.txt

Blaze, M., Feigenbaum, J., & Lacy, J. (1996, May). *Decentralized Trust Management.* Paper presented at the Seventeenth Annual IEEE Symposium on Security and Privacy, Oakland, California, USA.

Blaze, M., Feigenbaum, J., & Strauss, M. (1998, February). *Compliance Checking in the Policy-Maker Trust Management System.* Paper presented at the Second Financial Cryptography Conference, Anguilla.

Bonatti, P., & Samarati, P. (2000, November). *Regulating Access Services and Information Release on the Web.* Paper presented at the Seventh ACM Conference on Computer and Communications Security, Athens, Greece.

Burrows, M., Abadi, M., & Needham, R. M. (1990). A Logic of Authentication. *ACM Transactions on Computer Systems, 8*(1), 18–36. doi:doi:10.1145/77648.77649

Cohen, M. S., Parasuraman, R., Serfaty, R. S., & Andes, R. C. (1997). *Trust in Decision Aids: A Model and a Training Strategy* (No. USAAT-COM TR 97-D-4). Fort Eustis, VA: Cognitive Technologies Inc.

Ferraiolo, D. F., Sandhu, R., Gavrila, S., Kuhn, D. R., & Chandramouli, R. (2001). Proposed NIST Standard for Role-Based Access Control. *ACM Transactions on Information and System Security, 4*(3), 224–274. doi:doi:10.1145/501978.501980

Grandison, T. (2001). *Trust Specification and Analysis for Internet Applications.* London, UK.

Grandison, T., & Sloman, M. (2000). A Survey of Trust in Internet Applications. *IEEE Communications Surveys and Tutorials, 3*(4), 2–16. doi:doi:10.1109/COMST.2000.5340804

Gruber, T. R. (1993). A translation approach to portable ontology specifications. *Knowledge Acquisition, 5*(2), 199–220. doi:doi:10.1006/knac.1993.1008

Guha, R., Kumar, R., Raghavan, P., & Tomkins, A. (2004, May). *Propagation of Trust and Distrust.* Paper presented at the Thirteenth International World Wide Web Conference, New York, NY.

Herzberg, A., Mass, Y., Mihaeli, J., Naor, O., & Ravid, Y. (2000, May). *Access Control Meets Public Key Infrastructure, Or: Assigning Roles to Strangers.* Paper presented at the Annual IEEE Symposium on Security and Privacy, Oakland, California, USA.

Jajodia, S., Samarati, P., & Subrahmanian, V. (1997, May). *A Logical Language for Expressing Authorizations.* Paper presented at the Annual IEEE Symposium on Security and Privacy, Oakland, CA, USA.

Jones, A. J. I., & Firozabadi, B. S. (2000). On the Characterization of a Trusting Agent -- Aspects of a Formal Approach. In C. Castelfranchi & Y. Tan (Eds.), *Trust and Deception in Virtual Societies* (pp. 163-174). Amsterdam: Kluwer Academic Publishers.

Jøsang, A. (1997, December). *Artificial Reasoning with Subjective Logic.* Paper presented at the Second Australian Workshop on Commonsense Reasoning, Perth, Australia.

Jøsang, A. (1998, September). *A Subjective Metric of Authentication.* Paper presented at the Fifth European Symposium on Research in Computer Security Louvain-la-Neuve, Belgium.

Jøsang, A. (1999, February). *An Algebra for Assessing Trust in Certification Chains.* Paper presented at the Network and Distributed Systems Security Symposium(NDSS'99), San Diego, California.

Jøsang, A. (2001). A Logic for Uncertain Probabilities. *International Journal of Uncertainty. Fuzziness and Knowledge-Based Systems, 9*(3), 279–311.

Jøsang, A., Gray, E., & Kinateder, M. (2006). Simplification and Analysis of Transitive Trust Networks. *Web Intelligence and Agent Systems Journal, 4*(2), 139–161.

Li, L. X., & Liu, L. (2003, June). *A Reputation-Based Trust Model For Peer-To-Peer Ecommerce Communities.* Paper presented at the IEEE Conference on E-Commerce (CEC'03), Newport Beach, California.

Liu, J., & Issamy, V. (2004, March-April). *Enhanced Reputation Mechanism for Mobile Ad Hoc Networks.* Paper presented at the Second International Conference on Trust Management, Oxford, UK.

Marsh, S. (1994). *Formalising Trust as a Computational Concept.* University of Stirling.

Neisse, R., Wegdam, M., van Sinderen, M., & Lenzini, G. (2007). *Trust Management Model and Architecture for Context-Aware Service Platforms.* Paper presented at the On the Move to Meaningful Internet Systems 2007: CoopIS, DOA, ODBASE, GADA, and IS.

Purser, S. (2001). A Simple Graphical Tool For Modelling Trust. *Computers & Security, 20*(6), 479–484.doi:doi:10.1016/S0167-4048(01)00605-8

Quercia, D., Hailes, S., & Capra, L. (2006, May). *B-trust: Bayesian Trust Framework for Pervasive Computing.* Paper presented at the Fourth International Conference on Trust Management, Pisa, Italy.

Rangan, P. V. (1988, April). *An Axiomatic Basis of Trust in Distributed Systems.* Paper presented at the Annual IEEE Symposium on Security and Privacy, Oakland, California.

Ray, I., & Chakraborty, S. (2004, September). *A Vector Model of Trust for Developing Trustworthy Systems.* Paper presented at the Ninth European Symposium on Research in Computer Security, Sophia Antipolis, Frech Riviera, France.

Ray, I., Ray, I., & Chakraborty, S. (2009). An Interoperable Context-Sensitive Model of Trust. *Journal of Intelligent Information Systems, 32*(1). doi:doi:10.1007/s10844-007-0049-9

Stevens, M., & Williams, P. D. (2007, April). *Use of Trust Vectors for CyberCraft and the Limits of Usable Data History for Trust Vectors.* Paper presented at the IEEE Conference on Computational Intelligence for Security and Defense Applications, Honululu, Hawaii.

Stojanovic, N., Maedche, A., Staab, S., Studer, R., & Sure, Y. (2001, October). *SEAL - A Framework for Developing Semantic Portals.* Paper presented at the First International Conference on Knowledge Capture, Victoria, Canada.

Toivonen, S., Lenzini, G., & Uusitalo, I. (2006). *Contex-taware Trust Evaluation Functions for Dynamic Reconfigurable Systems.* Paper presented at the Annual World Wide Web Conference.

Uschold, M., & Gruninger, M. (1996). Ontologies: Principles, Methods, and Applications. *The Knowledge Engineering Review, 11*(2), 93–155. doi:doi:10.1017/S0269888900007797

Wang, Y., Li, M., Dillon, E., Cui, L., Hu, J., & Liao, L. (2008, April). *A Context-aware Computational Trust Model for Multi-agent Systems.* Paper presented at the IEEE International Conference on Network, Sensing and Control, Sanya, China.

Winsborough, W. H., & Li, N. (2006). Safety in Automated Trust Negotiation. *ACM Transactions on Information and System Security, 9*(3), 352–390.doi:doi:10.1145/1178618.1178623

Yahalom, R., & Klein, B. (1994). Trust-based Navigation in Distributed Systems. *Computing Systems, 7*(1), 45–73.

Yahalom, R., Klein, B., & Beth, T. (1993, May). *Trust Relationship in Secure Systems: A Distributed Authentication Perspective.* Paper presented at the Annual IEEE Symposium on Security and Privacy, Oakland, California.

Yu, T., & Winslett, M. (2003, May). *A Unified Scheme for Resource Protection in Automated Trust Negotiation.* Paper presented at the Annual IEEE Symposium on Security and Privacy, Oakland, CA.

Yu, T., Winslett, M., & Seamons, K. E. (2003). Supporting Structured Credentials and Sensitive Policies through Interoperable Strategies for Automated Trust Negotiation. *ACM Transactions on Information and System Security, 6*(1).

ENDNOTE

[1] We would like to thank Michael Stevens and Paul D. Williams (Stevens & Williams, 2007) for suggesting a better modification of the equation for time dependent value.

Chapter 12
An Evaluation Framework for Reputation Management Systems*

Andrew G. West
University of Pennsylvania, USA

Sampath Kannan
University of Pennsylvania, USA

Insup Lee
University of Pennsylvania, USA

Oleg Sokolsky
University of Pennsylvania, USA

ABSTRACT

Reputation management (RM) is employed in distributed and peer-to-peer networks to help users compute a measure of trust in other users based on initial belief, observed behavior, and run-time feedback. These trust values influence how, or with whom, a user will interact. Existing literature on RM focuses primarily on algorithm development, not comparative analysis. To remedy this, the authors propose an evaluation framework based on the trace-simulator paradigm. Trace file generation emulates a variety of network configurations, and particular attention is given to modeling malicious user behavior. Simulation is trace-based and incremental trust calculation techniques are developed to allow experimentation with networks of substantial size. The described framework is available as open source so that researchers can evaluate the effectiveness of other reputation management techniques and/or extend functionality. This chapter reports on the authors' framework's design decisions. Their goal being to build a general-purpose simulator, the authors have the opportunity to characterize the breadth of existing RM systems. Further, they demonstrate their tool using two reputation algorithms (EigenTrust and a modified TNA-SL) under varied network conditions. The authors' analysis permits them to make claims about the algorithms' comparative merits. They conclude that such systems, assuming their distribution is secure, are highly effective at managing trust, even against adversarial collectives.

DOI: 10.4018/978-1-61520-682-7.ch012

INTRODUCTION

At the start of the network-age the client-server (centralized) model was the dominant topology. Trust in these servers was implicit and security measures focused on access control and user permissions. More recently, new network architectures and computing paradigms have emerged such as distributed systems, peer-to-peer (P2P) networks, and ad-hoc mobile computing. Frequently, all network nodes have the ability to both request services from *and* provide services to other users. This is inherently risky since decentralized models typically lack the notions of authenticity, reliability, and accountability that monolithic servers provide. Nonetheless, well-behaved decentralized systems are beneficial in comparison to their client-server counterparts. Advantages include increased service diversity, availability, scalability, and bandwidth.

Enforcing good behavior is the task of a *trust management* (TM) system. The seminal work of Blaze, Feigenbaum, and Lacy (1996) introduced the term -- their system consisted of using cryptographically delegated credentials and policies to specify static access control rights. In *reputation management*[1] (RM), rather than determining if a user has the authority/permission to do some action, we instead ask: Given permission, how do we expect a user to behave (*i.e.*, what is his/her reputation)? A systems treatment of these expectations gives rise to a *dynamic* access control mechanism which is categorically different than that provided by TM. Reputation management is implemented by a *RM system* or *reputation algorithm*[2] (RA).

Almost universally, RAs work by using past behavior as a basis for future conduct. Transitive trust is often exploited, especially in the absence of prior interaction between two parties. To promote a well-intentioned network either bad behavior is punished, good behavior rewarded, or both. EigenTrust (Kamvar, Schlosser, & Garcia-molina, 2003) and Trust Network Analysis with Subjective Logic (TNA-SL) (Jøsang, 2001; Jøsang, Hayward, & Pope, 2006) are two RAs that will be given particular attention herein. For a broader survey of available systems, readers should review the work of Li and Singhai (2007). One should note that the need for RM is not confined to purely digital dealings. In fact, eBay manages one of the largest RM systems (Resnick, & Zeckhauser, 2001), pertaining to the exchange of physical commodities.

Research concerning RM has been focused on algorithm development with little attention given to *quantitative* comparative analysis between existing RAs (*qualitative* analyses are often seen, but we feel, insufficient). Tests on some systems, like EigenTrust, use briefly-described, proprietary, or closed-source simulators (Schlosser, Condie, & Kamvar, 2003). Others, like TNA-SL, opt for a more theoretical description with no evaluation results. In order to compare systems such as these and verify author's claims, an objective simulator is needed. While network and P2P simulators exist, having the additional overheard of simulating Distributed Hash Tables (DHTs), latency, network hops, *etc.*, in addition to trust calculation make their use computationally inappropriate. Furthermore, such simulators offer little abstraction, making the implementation of RAs inconvenient. Therefore, in this chapter we describe the construction of an evaluation framework specific to reputation management.

This chapter is organized as follows: We will begin by standardizing terminology and justifying our architecture of choice. Trace generation and simulation under this architecture will then be discussed. Next, evaluation metrics with regard to effectiveness and efficiency will be introduced. Then, test runs will be used to exemplify behavior and identify potential shortcomings in our design. Finally, future work will be noted and concluding remarks made.

OVERVIEW OF EVALUATION FRAMEWORK

There are many challenges in building a general-purpose evaluation framework for RM systems. First, RM is used in a variety of network architectures such as, peer-to-peer (P2P), service-oriented (SOA), and social networks. Second, there is a tension between simulating realistic behavior and excessive parameterization. We must find a tractable compromise that yields accurate trust values. Third, it is a challenge to define user behavior models, especially those pertaining to malicious users. While good users behave in a predictable manner, malicious users, especially those acting in a collective manner, may behave in erratic and dynamic ways.

In this chapter we will address precisely these challenges. Though many approaches are possible, we will present one that our research and intuition has found most appropriate – while still giving attention to alternative strategies.

Terminology

We consider systems that consist of *users*, *nodes*, or *peers*. These users are part of a *network*. Certain pairs of users have a communication channel between them. In graph theoretic terms, users are the nodes and these channels are the edges. The graph need not be connected. At any time, a user may be acting as a *provider* (server), a *requester* (client), or both. The items being requested and traded are termed *files* but could be representative of services or remote-procedure calls. Files are either *valid* or *invalid* and we assume this is a determination users can make accurately. A file's validity is permanent, and multiple copies of the same file can exist on a network. Users are evaluated according to the quality of files they provide to other users. Files are stored in a user's *library* and a user enters the network with an *initial library*. Broadcasting to determine the set of owners who possess some file is termed a *query* and the actual

request and acquisition a *transaction*. Following each transaction, binary[3] *feedback* is expected. Finally, a user is able to remove files from his/her library, an action we term *clean-up*.

Architectural Justification

We now describe the infrastructure on which our implementation is based. As our terminology may have hinted, we believe an underlying P2P network (*e.g.*, a file trading network, akin to Gnutella) is most appropriate because of its expressiveness. Such an architecture is capable of emulating several other system models by limiting functionality appropriately.

For example, suppose one wants to test a system with a mutually exclusive set of clients and service providers where clients use RM to determine provider reliability. With only slight modification a P2P framework can simulate such a model. The *files* being traded become representative of *services*. Service providers enter a network with an initial library (of services) but never make requests. Clients enter the network with an empty initial library, request and receive services, but *clean-up* (do not store) every service they receive. By cleaning up, clients prevent themselves from becoming providers. *Feedback* can then encode not only if services are valid or invalid, but also a measure of the quality of service (QoS) provided. Other emulation scenarios are possible but not described here. For a survey of reputation strategies grouped by application-domain, see the work of Zhang, Yu, and Irwin (2004).

Comparability of reputation algorithms is realized via our trace-simulator approach. Crucially, traces are *static* in nature; they are pre-generated and not modified during the simulation phase. The generation of trace files encodes network parameters and is independent of the RA being tested. These traces are then given to the simulator, which implements the RA, and other, minimal, dynamic considerations. Thus, multiple simulations, implementing different RAs, can be run

Figure 1. Overview of evaluation architecture

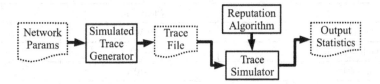

from the same trace. Figure 1 shows this overall architecture.

By fixing every aspect of a network run except those specific to RAs, the only differences between runs will be reputation-algorithm specific – ideal for comparison. Adherence to the static constraint does present some problems, as we will later describe. Nonetheless, comparability should not be sacrificed as it is precisely the motivation/objective of this work.

TRACE GENERATION

The trace generator is a program that takes network parameters and outputs a static script of a network run. There is a tension between simplicity and modeling realistic behavior. On one hand, a rich feature set can model the most complex and subtle of behaviors. On the other, excessive parameterization might obfuscate results or make it difficult to derive useful statistical inferences. Also, such exacting detail may be unnecessary for comparing the merits of different RM methods. We opt for a reasonably simple design and describe it in depth below.

Trace Generation Summary

In our generations/simulations we model a network of users. We have a library of user models, some corresponding to *good* users and others to *malicious* ones. Input parameters tell us how many users to pick per model. In this paper we assume there is a link between every pair of users. Each user is also given an initial endowment of files,

some *valid* and others *invalid*. There can be many copies of any file. The initial file distribution is also governed by input parameters.

Generally speaking, a trace is a sequence of queries. Each query specifies a filename and the user seeking that file (the client). The choice of server from which to download the file will be made at simulation runtime, taking into account input from the reputation algorithm.

Users have behavioral choices along two dimensions. First, for each file they download they can choose to clean-up, *i.e.*, get rid of the file. Good users will tend to clean up invalid files with high probability to reduce the proliferation of bad files. Malicious users may do just the opposite. We assume that no clean-up happens on the initial endowment and that users have just one opportunity to clean-up a file -- immediately after they download it. Second, after each transaction the client provides universally-observable feedback regarding the server with respect to the nature of the file served. Good users will tend to provide honest feedback, submitting positive marks if they received a valid file. Malicious users may tend to do the reverse.

To account for the rich variety of strategies and motives for adversarial behavior we have many malicious user models. These models vary with respect to clean-up and honest-feedback probabilities. We also allow for more subtle malicious behaviors where users behave badly only some of the time. Malicious collusion is a complex topic reserved for a later section. We also make the simplifying assumption that malicious behavior is purely probabilistic and independent of the client or file requested in a particular transaction. We

Table 1. User initialization parameters

User Type	Clean-up%	Honesty%
Good	90-100%	100%
Purely Malicious	0-10%	0%
Malicious Provider	0-10%	100%
Feedback Malicious	90-100%	0%
Disguised Malicious	50-100%	50-100%
Sybil Attack	0-10%	Irrelevant

now proceed with a more in-depth discussion of the trace generation process, beginning with the physical file format.

Trace Files

Our goal is to use the minimum parameterization necessary to realistically exercise the RM systems being evaluated. Given at the command-line, the most critical arguments are:

1. Number of users in network
2. Behavior model for each user
3. Number of distinct files
4. Probability of file ownership
5. Number of queries / transactions to simulate
6. Maximum number of user connections
7. Bandwidth period, in time units

These topics will be covered in greater depth in their respective sections. The output of trace generation is a terse text file with four distinct types of data:

1. **Header:** The command line arguments are printed. The simulator needs these to size data structures so they are provided upfront.
2. **User Initializations:** Triples of the form (u, c, h) where u is the user being initialized, c is the percentage of the time the user removes an *invalid* file from his/her library (clean-up), and h is the percentage of the time the

user provides honest feedback. Derived from this tuple, inverse clean-up, $(100 - c)$, is the percentage of the time a user removes a *valid* file from his/her library.

3. **Library Initializations:** Triples of the form (u, f, v) that state that user u has file f in his/her initial library with validity v (a Boolean).
4. **Static Queries:** Pairs of form (u, f) stating user u wishes to obtain file f.

User Models

As alluded to in the previous section, there are only two dimensions of user behavior, the feedback-honesty and clean-up rates. Table 1 describes the initializations of several user models. Our selection of user models is not comprehensive. Additional user models can be imagined and easily implemented in our framework.

It should be noted that several of these models were inspired by the threats detailed by Kamvar *et al.* (2003) and Hoffman, Zage, & Nita-Rotaru (2008). Because clean-up is a passive action, clean-up rates are expressed as a range – a precise percentage assignment is made when a user is initialized. Feedback, meanwhile, is required following each transaction so we expect that most user models will provide feedback according to a strict pattern.

We should pause to consider the motivations behind user behavior. A good user simply wants to *obtain* a valid copy of the file they query for.

Bad users want to *deliver* invalid files. The notion of *invalidity* will vary based on the intentions of the malicious user. Files that are corrupt or contain viruses will be traded by users who wish to instigate havoc, as these behaviors are not self-serving. However, the intentional mislabeling and distribution of a music file as a guerilla advertising tactic could constitute a selfish form of invalidity. Stepping outside of the P2P realm, manipulation of RM systems can prove much more profitable. Subverting eBay's RA could have large monetary consequences. We now describe our user models in detail:

- **Good:** Initializing well-behaved users is straightforward. First, they will provide honest feedback. Secondly, they will be attentive about their file libraries, removing invalid files that reside there. A clean-up rate between 90-100% permits some degree of apathy, as we cannot expect *good* users to be ideal ones.

- **Purely Malicious:** A user misbehaving in both dimensions is termed *purely malicious*. Such users retain invalid files, dispose of valid ones, and consistently lie about the nature of the files they receive. Because they misbehave with such consistency a RA may quickly identify such users and take preventive measures.

- **Single Dimension Malicious:** *Malicious providers* and *feedback malicious* are complementary user models that misbehave along a single axis. Such strategies can be devastating in systems where trust is evaluated along only one dimension. For example, providing dishonest feedback is not of first order consequence (*i.e.*, liars are not punished) in a system like EigenTrust. Feedback dishonesty seems particularly hard to detect because systems rely on non-automated and user-provided *soft-feedback*[4]. The deficiencies and game-theoretic strategies of soft-feedback are well

investigated by Resnick and Zeckhauser (2001) in their analysis of the eBay system. The DIRECT (Zhang, Lin, & Klefstad, 2006) and TrustGuard (Srivatsa, Xiong, & Liu, 2005) approaches attempt to discover outlying feedback patterns but require continuous feedback variables. However, the *feedback-malicious* model that exploits this weakness does not directly benefit the user implementing it. Because the *feedback-malicious* user maintains a valid library he/she cannot distribute the invalid files of his/her choice (*i.e.*, the motive). Instead, by exploiting transitive trust such users can act as a gateway, using the trust others likely have in them to direct users to invalid libraries. This is a malicious approach we later validate in our description of cooperative strategies. In contrast, effective strategies involving *malicious providers* are harder to envision. Trust can still be managed in networks overrun with such users because they are honest about where bad files reside. Thus, it is trivial to avoid downloading from such providers (for those who desire to do so). Nonetheless, the model is included for completeness.

- **Disguised Malicious:** In the absence of a sophisticated collective strategy (see below), users consistently distributing invalid files will likely be identified as such. Often, this means they will be sent a smaller amount of request traffic from *good* users and be unable to distribute their files. An effective strategy may be to act well-behaved slightly more often than bad. This way, systems that rely on normalization and casual relationships between positive and negative feedbacks will think of them as (weakly) *good* users. This is the strategy of the *disguised malicious* user. Some systems, like TNA-SL combat this by using beta-PDF strategies that consider the raw number of feedbacks.

- **Sybil Attacker:** Based on the model described by Douceur (2002), the *Sybil attacker* takes advantage of the low-entry threshold present in most networks. With an invalid library, the attacker waits until he/she is a provider in some transaction, deletes his/her account, and then reappears on the network under a different username. The neutral trust associated with the new account is preferable to the (presumably) negative trust of the old one. For implementation purposes we simply prohibit feedback from being recorded by Sybil users, or concerning them. This prevents expansive network growth from disposable 'single-use' users. Having the *Sybil attacker* model could help analyze the effectiveness of RM systems that give preference to experienced users.

- **Malicious Collectives:** A group of cooperating malicious users presents the most severe threat to a decentralized system. Isolated malicious users participate in *casual* cooperation, for example, when they provide positive feedback to an anonymous user that sent them an invalid file. However, organized *tight* cooperation, characterized by intelligent and peer-aware strategies, is the real danger. RM systems deter this threat by using anonymous identifiers and DHTs with local voting to blur the network topology. Thus, such users may have an out-of-band communication method to coordinate their activities. Effectively modeling such behavior is a topic given considerable attention in a later section entitled 'Empowering Malicious Collectives'.

Of course, the raw number of users in a trace is dependent on the needs of whoever is generating it. Simulating larger networks will produce more consistent results, while sacrificing efficiency. Similarly, the number of users per model will vary depending on the trust scenario being tested. We can, however, offer some guidance in this selection. We should assume we are modeling a network organized with good intentions. Malicious users rarely create networks; they try to infiltrate existing ones[5]. Therefore, we wish to study an infection model and invalid file propagation. Furthermore, no RA will be able to revive a network that is severely compromised from the outset. For these reasons, individuals should not generate traces that are initially amok with invalidity, *i.e.*, with an excess of malicious peers.

Library Initialization

Library composition is modeled as a Zipf distribution (Zipf, 1949). Many studies have been completed, including that of Breslau, Cao, Fan, Phillips, and Shenker (1999) that demonstrate Zipf frequencies accurately model file/service popularity in many Internet domains. Zipf parameter α is provided at the command line such that file i has a $(1 / i^{\alpha})$ probability of being owned by a particular user[6]. The validity of an initial file copy is determined by the clean-up-rate of the user who owns it. For example, a user with cleanup-rate c has a c percent chance of an initial file being valid. Clean-up is *not* performed during initial library construction.

Under such a distribution every user will have an initial library of identical expected size. This is an unrealistic assumption but one we are willing to make for the sake of simplicity and because we believe that it will not affect our empirical results significantly.

Choosing a good α value is a challenge. Arguments can be made for both a high and low α value. On one hand, studies like that of Breslau *et al.* (1999) suggest $\alpha=0.8$ or higher is the best reflection of real-life data patterns. On the other, such a high α value may be problematic. If one wants to 'schedule' a large number of queries/transactions there must be sufficient resources such that every user does not acquire every file. A high α value makes initial libraries small and non-diverse (due to the Zipf distribution's tail), exacerbating such a problem. There are three remedies. First, more users can be added, but this creates an acute efficiency problem. Second, the file set can be made larger. However, the nature of Zipf's law is such that the file set would need a substantial increase, and substantial memory footprint, to make user's libraries marginally more diverse. Third, α can be decreased. We prefer this course of action and default to $\alpha=0.4$, a value simulation has shown to be a good compromise.

Query Generation

The final consideration is who should be requesting files, which files, and in what quantity? Our generator supports two modes, which we call *naïve* and *intelligent* query generation. In the naïve version, a random user requests a random file, and this is recorded as a query in the trace file. The intelligent version adds stipulations to prevent a large number of incomplete-able transactions at runtime. First, a user may not request a file they already possess or requested in the past. This eliminates the need for any user to store multiple copies of the same file or determine which copy should persist. Second, a requested file must exist in the network. A query which returns no results is inconsequential. This is not, however, a guarantee a file will be available when it is requested as all owners may have no bandwidth (see below).

Every user has an equal probability of being a file requester. Though some user models may request files at varying rates, this is not something we attempt to model here. Which file is requested is dictated by the same Zipf distribution used to populate initial libraries.

We envision several future improvements in this area. First, P2P interactions usually occur in *cliques*, with users only interested in some genres of files as opposed to all those available. This is a point revisited in the 'Future Work' section. Second, it is intuitive to expect a good user

who receives a bad file to re-query and attempt to obtain a valid copy. Unfortunately, the static nature of our trace nature cannot support such an operation.

TRACE SIMULATION

We next describe the *simulator* wherein the trace is dynamically run and relevant statistics are output. After initialization is complete the simulator proceeds in the following simplified loop:

```
While more queries remain:
    Read query from trace file
    Broadcast query to determine poten-
tial providers
    Compute trust-values for relevant
user pairs
    Select bandwidth-available source
user
    Copy source file to requester's li-
brary
    Requester submits feedback concerning
source
End
```

Bandwidth & Load Distribution

With RAs it is possible for the global trust view to converge and identify a single or small set of users as 'most trustworthy.' These nodes are likely to be overwhelmed with provider requests. Bandwidth limitations will prevent some of these requests from being fulfilled or will serve the files at a very slow rate (poor QoS) (Papaioannou & Stamoulis, 2004). Some notion of *load distribution* is needed. Systems like EigenTrust handle this implicitly in their reputation management systems. Others, like TNA-SL, give the topic no attention. Load balancing inherently lowers reputation algorithm performance. Decreasing the load of the most trusted users means the load will increase for less trusted users, and probabilistically speaking, more invalid files will be traded. Even so, load balance is a practical necessity.

We propose that one should ignore load balancing suggestions when implementing a RM system for the simulator. Instead, the RA should export a relative ordering of users based on trust values. The simulator's included bandwidth manager will then objectively handle load balancing by allowing only bandwidth-available users to participate in transactions.

Bandwidth restrictions are set by two command-line parameters. Summarily, a user may have at maximum x connections at any time, and the transaction of a single file requires y time units. Our simulator has a weak notion of time that permits this description, namely, each query requires a single *time unit* and there is only one query per clock tick. A *connection* is a distinct upload/download. For example, if $x = 2$ and $y = 100$, a user who begins a download at time 21 and another at time 56 will have no download bandwidth available until time 121 when a single connection becomes available. Since file transmission is not instantaneous, feedback is delayed until the transaction is complete. Separate upload and download queues are maintained.

Indeed, our approach to load distribution is a basic one. If one wishes to model variable file sizes, connection speeds, *etc.*, matters get very (and perhaps unnecessarily) complex. However, it succeeds in enforcing a tunable and objective model of load balance.

Source Selection

After trust computation it is the requester's responsibility to use the relative ordering to choose a source/provider. As Table 2 shows, the desired source varies depending on user model.

The *worst* option is chosen by users who wish to increase the scope of their invalid libraries, whereas a *random* approach allows feedback-focused malicious users to boost the global opinion

Table 2. Source selection by requester model

Requester Model	Source
Good	BEST
Purely Malicious	WORST
Feedback Malicious	RANDOM
Malicious Provider	WORST
Disguised Malicious	RANDOM
Sybil Attacker	WORST

of other bad users and mar that of good ones. Intuitively, *good* users want the *best* provider. Recall that only bandwidth-available users can serve as providers. Ties between users with identical trust values are broken randomly.

Feedback Database

Reputation algorithms aggregate interaction histories to produce a trust value characterizing some user-to-user relationship. We now describe how these interaction histories are stored. In our architecture the feedback database (DB) is *centralized*, so it appears identical from every user's viewpoint. A centralized DB means trust computation can be centralized, as well. Our framework will assume such a centralized *trust service* exists, for the time being.

In practice, P2P networks (among other topologies) are not centralized and the DB and/or computation must be distributed. Nonetheless, when feasible (and responsibly hosted) centralized DBs are secure and convenient, as distribution may expose holes for exploitation. In later sections we relax our fully-centralized approach to aid in describing malicious attacks.

Minimally, a feedback DB needs to store the number of positive and negative prior interactions between directed (non-symmetric) user pairs. Other data may also be stored, as required by different RAs. For example, associating a time-stamp with each feedback might allow an algorithm to weigh recent interactions more heavily than those occurring long ago. Similarly, context information might be entered, *e.g.*, user X had a negative experience with user Y with respect to his download of file Z. Such entries may permit trust to be computed at fine granularity. By querying the DB and retrieving only those rows where Z was the file involved, and letting the RA aggregate over only these entries, it may be possible to compute trust in individual files. This is a complex topic we revisit in our 'Future Work' section.

Because we have control over the environment in which our feedback DB operates its security can be assumed. Real DBs would be afforded no such luxury. It is likely DBs will be interfaced via a RPC. Ballot-stuffing attacks (Srivatsa *et al.*, 2005) and identity management are two practical challenges that must be addressed, but are beyond the scope of this work.

REPUTATION ALGORITHMS

There are many RAs in existence (Li & Singhai, 2007) though we will only give attention to EigenTrust (Kamvar *et al.*, 2003) and a modified TNA-SL (Jøsang *et al.*, 2006). Precise details of these systems can be found in their respective papers; our concern is with their general behavior and efficiency. Why these two algorithms? One (EigenTrust) is terse, scalable, efficient, implementation-ready, and designed with P2P in mind. The other (TNA-SL) is theoretical, expressive, and inefficient in a P2P setting. By designing our framework with these two radically different systems in mind, we believe our work will be applicable to the vast expanse of other RAs that lie between them. Furthermore, the significant differences will make for more interesting test runs in forthcoming sections.

The simulator is designed to promote the easy addition of new RAs; a simple calling interface is used. Most important is the interfaced computeTrust() method. Given a source user and access to feedback data, it returns a vector quantifying the trust user *source* has in other users in the network. At a high-level, we will now describe three RAs for the sake of familiarizing the reader with their basic operation and implementation.

None (No RA Present)

None simulates the absence of a reputation system and uses exclusively random file-providers. At initialization all trust values are set to an identical value; every call thereafter allows these original trust values to persist. Thus, a user model selecting the best/worst source will result in a tie between all available users that will be broken randomly. This 'system' is of little interest, aside from providing a baseline for comparison purposes.

EigenTrust

EigenTrust (Kamvar *et al.*, 2003) is a system that uses local normalization combined with global convergence via vector-matrix multiplication. Prior interaction is best visualized as an $n \times n$ matrix where n is the number of peers. Vectors are local to users. For example, the entry in the i-th row and j-th column describes user j's directed dealings with user i. We will next describe how trust is calculated in EigenTrust. Figure 2 provides a concrete example.

A *relation* stores the number of positive (pos) and negative (neg) interactions between two users. For each relation, a single feedback integer is calculated as $\max(0,(pos-neg))$ as in example matrix A. Next, these values are normalized on a vector basis (example A'). Normalized vector p of size n is then initialized to encode a-priori notions of trust. Next, t_k is calculated using the above formulae. For sufficiently high k, vector t_k will converge to the left principal eigenvector of A', the *global trust vector* (t_∞). The i-th position of t_∞ is i's trust value. For our purposes, k need only be so high that the relative order of trust values is fixed.

The proper initialization of p is critical to EigenTrust success. Greater weight is given to

Figure 2. An example EigenTrust computation

$$A = \begin{bmatrix} \left(\begin{array}{c} pos:0 \\ neg:0 \end{array}\right)=0 & \left(\begin{array}{c} pos:3 \\ neg:1 \end{array}\right)=2 & \left(\begin{array}{c} pos:3 \\ neg:2 \end{array}\right)=1 \\ \left(\begin{array}{c} pos:9 \\ neg:3 \end{array}\right)=6 & \left(\begin{array}{c} pos:0 \\ neg:0 \end{array}\right)=0 & \left(\begin{array}{c} pos:8 \\ neg:1 \end{array}\right)=7 \\ \left(\begin{array}{c} pos:2 \\ neg:4 \end{array}\right)=0 & \left(\begin{array}{c} pos:5 \\ neg:4 \end{array}\right)=1 & \left(\begin{array}{c} pos:0 \\ neg:0 \end{array}\right)=0 \end{bmatrix}$$

$$A' = \begin{bmatrix} {}^0/_6 & {}^2/_3 & {}^1/_8 \\ {}^6/_6 & {}^0/_3 & {}^7/_8 \\ {}^0/_6 & {}^1/_3 & {}^0/_8 \end{bmatrix} \quad p = \begin{bmatrix} {}^1/_3 \\ {}^1/_3 \\ {}^1/_3 \end{bmatrix} \quad t_\infty = \begin{bmatrix} 0.35 \\ 0.49 \\ 0.16 \end{bmatrix}$$

Where $t_0 = p$ and $t_{k+1} = (0.5 \times A'^T \times t_k) + (0.5 \times p)$

those users deemed 'pre-trusted'. In practice, a small but highly trusted subset of z users are designated pre-trusted. Then, $p_i = (1/z)$ if user i is pre-trusted, and $p_i = 0$, otherwise.

Trust Network Analysis with Subjective Logic (TNA-SL)

Trust Network Analysis with Subjective Logic (TNA-SL) (Jøsang, 2001; Jøsang *et al.*, 2003) is a system that places greater emphasis on prior direct interaction. Here, trust is stored as an *opinion*, a 4-tuple (b, d, u, α) that represents belief, disbelief, uncertainty, and a base-rate, respectively. At all times $(b + d + u) = 1$ and α (a real) in [0...1] is used to store a-priori notions of trust. Converting past interaction into an opinion is done as shown in Table 3. Though there are many logical operators, two, *discount* and *consensus*, are of note. Table 4 shows their calculation.

Discount is used to evaluate transitive chains. Discount would be used, for example, if user A wanted to calculate an opinion about user C using information at intermediate user B. Notionally this would be written as

$$\omega_C^{A:B} = \omega_B^A \otimes \omega_C^B.$$

Consensus is used to average together two opinions. Suppose user A and user B both have opinions about user C. To consolidate these, consensus would be used, with notation

$$\omega_C^{A \Diamond B} = \omega_C^A \oplus \omega_C^B.$$

Computing trust given these operations and a digraph of opinions (constructed from a feedback DB) is not straightforward. The approach given in the describing paper (Jøsang *et al.*, 2003) re-

Table 3. Calculating opinions from prior interaction

belief	=	$(pos / (pos + neg + 2.0))$
disbelief	=	$(neg / (pos + neg + 2.0))$
uncertainty	=	$(2.0 / (pos + neg + 2.0))$
base-rate	=	1.0 – if user is pre-trusted 0.5 – otherwise

Table 4. Defining discount and consensus operators

Discount : $\otimes$	Consensus : $\oplus$
$b_C^{A:B} = b_B^A b_C^B$	$b_C^{A\Diamond B} = b_C^A u_C^B + b_C^B u_C^A \,/\, denominator$
$d_C^{A:B} = b_B^A d_C^B$	$d_C^{A\Diamond B} = d_C^A u_C^B + d_C^B u_C^A \,/\, denominator$
$u_C^{A:B} = d_B^A + u_B^A + b_B^A u_C^B$	$u_C^{A\Diamond B} = u_C^A u_C^B \,/\, denominator$
$\alpha_C^{A:B} = \alpha_C^B$	$\alpha_C^{A\Diamond B} = \alpha_C^A$
Where $denominator = u_C^A + u_C^B - u_C^A u_C^B$	

quires one to find an acyclic direct series-parallel graph (DSPG) between the requester and potential source that minimizes uncertainty. Then, given that DSPG, a single characterizing opinion is derived by applying the SL-operators (note that *discount* corresponds to series composition and *consensus* to parallel composition). For export to a single trust value, the *expected value* of that opinion is calculated as $EV = b + \alpha u$.

While theoretically sound, applying this approach to our simulator is computationally infeasible for three reasons. (1) Our network is fully connected, yielding an exponential number of paths. (2) The DSPG recognition problem, while solvable in linear time[7], becomes burdensome due to the sheer number of times it must be called (though caching can help). (3) The described procedure computes trust between just two users. To populate the output vector the above reduction and analysis would need to be computed n times.

While the DSPG approach does not apply well to this scenario, the expressiveness of opinion objects could be beneficial if harnessed in a different manner. How to best and efficiently aggregate trust remains an open question. When cycles are present it is difficult to exhaustively analyze a graph. Finding a single most-trusted (or most certain) path is possible, but ignores data the other (perhaps contrary) paths provide. We have found it effective to use an aggregation strategy that *maximizes the consensus certainty at some depth of search*. We do not claim this is the best means by which to evaluate trust – rather, that it is a reasonable one. Our method requires no graph refinement, is mathematically elegant, and takes a large amount of global opinion into account. Furthermore, simulations will demonstrate our technique's effectiveness.

To compute trust for a network of n users, a matrix, A, of opinion objects with dimension $n \times n$ is created. Just as in the EigenTrust example, each matrix element defines a user-user relationship. Table 3 describes how to compute opinions from feedback histories. Then, compute A^x for large x, using the *discount* and *consensus* operators to overload multiplication and addition, respectively. Because of the non-monotonic nature of the consensus operator and our lack of normalization, taking A to a high power will not result in convergence (as with EigenTrust). Instead, *belief* values will tend towards 0 because the discount operator weakens trust, and thus, many discounts in a long transitive chain will severely weaken it. Instead, we create a separate opinion matrix A', to store the opinion with maximum confidence seen at each position throughout the multiplication process. We define *EV(A')* to be the global trust matrix and $EV(A'_{i,j})$ represents the trust user *j* has in user *i*.

Because our technique uses the subjective logic (SL) operators to analyze opinion digraphs, *TNA-SL* remains our term of choice for the modified strategy. The majority of TNA-SL behavior (in either case) is captured by the SL-operators, not the method by which they are applied. Thus, we see foresee no serious conflict arising from our redundant terminology. In situations where a significant difference is foreseen between our approach and the original, note will be made.

EVALUATION METRICS

The primary thrust of our simulator is to compare RA effectiveness. Below, we define a succinct metric for this purpose. However, the framework affords us other assessment opportunities. In particular, algorithm efficiency can be examined and speed-up strategies tested.

Effectiveness Metric

When comparing the effectiveness of RM simulations it is helpful to have a single evaluation metric, which we define as:

$$\text{Metric} = \frac{\#\text{ valid files received by 'good' users}}{\#\text{ transactions attempted by 'good' users}}$$

Effective RM systems do not clean-up networks; they only provide *accurate* trust information. Such a system will not only help good users find good providers, it will succeed in helping malicious users find bad providers. However, we do not care about the success of malicious users so our objective function is based solely on the *good* user success rate.

Simulation Efficiency

Through examination of simulation run times one can gain insight into the efficiency/scalability of the implemented RAs. Timings of simulations run over realistic data are arguably more useful than the asymptotic complexity analysis found in the papers describing these systems. Additionally, speed-up strategies can be developed and their effectiveness can be validated. Such strategies have been given considerable attention in our simulator development because inefficient algorithms create inefficient simulations. We now describe why efficiency is a particularly acute problem and introduce a general-purpose strategy for improving it.

For a network of *n* users, there are n^2 user-to-user relationships, each with their own trust value. Since RAs often exploit transitive trust, there are a multitude of network paths to explore, often implemented as matrix multiplication. Examining long transitive chains takes many multiplications and trust is recomputed after every transaction. As a result, some reputation systems, especially expressive and theoretic ones, pose a large computational burden. This inhibits experimentation with large networks and high transaction counts.

EigenTrust is quite scalable because of its globally convergent values via vector-matrix multiply. TNA-SL (our version), with its user-centric trust values and matrix-matrix multiplication is not so fortunate[8]. For example, the 50-user 50k transaction traces like those analyzed herein take ≈ 2 seconds to run under EigenTrust but 2.5 minutes under TNA-SL. An increase to 100 users takes 5 seconds for EigenTrust and over 10 minutes for TNA-SL.

Our framework's scalability is disadvantaged in two ways. First, trust computation is often distributed among nodes, a notion our centralized simulator cannot take advantage of. Second, our network's fully-connected nature may lead to an unrealistic explosion of network paths.

While burdensome, these difficulties pale in comparison to the efficiency hurdles faced in actual networks. Consider that a popular P2P application might have hundreds-of-thousands of users. Exhaustive trust analysis in such situations is impossible and approximation techniques must be used. For example, a RA may consider only feedbacks from a random subset of users, utilize feedbacks from only the most experienced users, or limit path search-depth. The first approach is one tested and advocated in the work of Papaioannou and Stamoulis (2004).

Fortunately, as Kamvar *et al.* (2003) suggests and our own work confirms, simulations scale intuitively. That is, an x user simulation with y malicious peers produces statistical ratios and evaluation metrics comparable to that of a $2x$ user simulation with $2y$ malicious peers. This fact, combined with our (simulator-based) heuristic efficiency improvements introduced below, allow the production of meaningful results in a reasonable time frame.

Heuristically Improving Simulation Efficiency

By taking advantage of the static nature of traces and the preponderance of consistent behavior in simulations, efficiency improvements can be made while maintaining near-correctness. First, consider that user models are constant during a run, *i.e.*, users behave in consistent ways. Second, as a test run progresses each successive feedback has less influence because it is being considered along with a growing body of previous feedbacks. Over time the network becomes 'solved' and trust values change very little. This allows one to use slightly aged trust-values with minimal consequence and not have to recompute trust after every transaction.

As a preliminary experiment, we decided to confirm that the trust networks we generate are indeed solvable. To do so, we generated 50-user, 50k transaction traces with between 0-100%

purely malicious users. We then ran the traces (using TNA-SL) and recomputed trust after every cycle for the first $n = \{0, 250, 1k, 2.5k, 5k, 50k\}$ cycles. After that point, transactions were executed until all 50k were complete, but the persistent (aged) trust values were used for source selection. The trials where $n = 50k$ act as a control and define correctness, since trust is always recomputed in that case. Figure 3 displays how lower n values fared[9].

By approximately $n = 2.5k$, and certainly by $n = 5k$, the margin of error is < 1% at all data points. Therefore, about 90% of the trust computations performed are unnecessary on runs of this nature, which were designed to difficult to 'solve.' In practice, only computing trust up to some point is not the best idea, instead, an evaluation interval should be used, which we term *skip*. Initially skip:=1 and every time transac_num % skip == 0, trust is recomputed and a snapshot of the trust values taken. At each recalculation, the new trust values are compared against those of the previous snapshot. If each entry deviates less than some ε, then skip *= 2, else skip /=2. Bounding skip to [1...32] helps maintain correctness.

Tests have shown that at the beginning of a run the value of skip fluctuates and remains low, but quickly saturates leading to a speedup of ≈ 32×. The adaptive nature of this technique should make it conducive for use with any algorithm. Furthermore, this adaptivity would permit speed-ups in more dynamic systems, perhaps even those present in real-life.

Indeed, the described strategy is an approximation. Those trust (re-)calculations skipped over may have changed the relative trust ordering, and thus source selection, and the resulting metric. Our tests have found this gap to be minimal. Since correctness is not guaranteed, however, the performance graphs presented later in this chapter were not generated using the described heuristic. The approximation, however, was helpful in the rapid prototyping of test runs.

Figure 3. Trust convergence rate (TNA-SL)

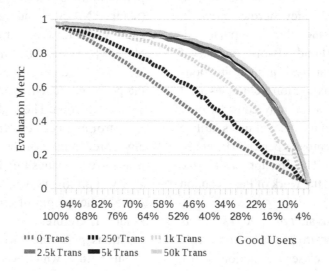

More subtle speed-up strategies are often algorithm-specific. Lots of persistent storage is used to minimize redundant calculations at each call. For matrix-multiplication strategies it is important to do the minimal amount of multiplies necessary to reach convergence/saturation. The static approach of simply doing x multiplies each time is unacceptable because x must be high enough to buffer for worst-case behavior. In the EigenTrust case, multiplication ceases once convergence is indicated via a precision ε on the global vector. For (our version of) TNA-SL, if a multiplication makes no update to the maximal matrix, no more are needed.

TEST RUNS AND OBSERVATIONS

Using simulator runs we will now exemplify behavioral aspects of RAs. This gives us an opportunity not only to test RAs but our simulator itself. We begin by examining how RAs manage adversarial user models, like the *purely malicious* one, and then look at how varying network conditions, *i.e.*, bandwidth and interaction density, affect the evaluation metric.

Simple Test Runs

The simplest test is how a RA handles *malicious providers*; those that own and acquire invalid files but give honest feedback. Figure 4 demonstrates how trivially managed such a system is.

The graph was produced from 50-user, 50k transaction traces with no pre-trusted peers, and infinite bandwidth. The *y*-axis corresponds to the evaluation metric of the previous section. The *x*-axis represents the number of malicious users present, *i.e.*, a data point with 72% malicious providers has $(0.72*50)=36$ *malicious providers*, and the remaining $(50-36) = 14$ users are *good* ones. The data sets correspond to the different reputation algorithms being evaluated.

As shown, NONE always regresses in linear fashion. As expected, all RAs converge to a metric near 0% when the network is completely saturated with bad users, since they remove good files from their libraries. Any RA with a metric scoring above control line NONE is considered a success. *Malicious providers* do not present a serious threat to a network because they are honest about their poor intentions. Thus, the algorithm success demonstrated in Figure 4 is not seen as

Figure 4. RAs vs. Malicious Providers

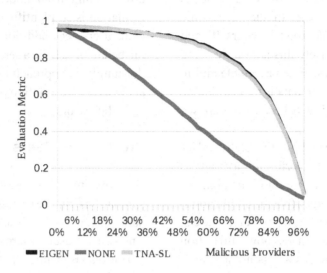

significant, but rather, a sanity-check on implementation correctness.

Figure 5 shows a more interesting graph where invalid files *and* feedback dishonesty are present. It is parameterized just as Figure 4, except that *purely malicious* users now replace *malicious providers*. While TNA-SL is still very successful, EigenTrust is less impressive, narrowly improving upon the control metric. Why does EigenTrust perform so poorly?

As we shall see, the notion of *pre-trusted peers* corrects this EigenTrust deficiency. For now, we concentrate on the simpler case where they are not included. So then, why does TNA-SL so dramatically outperform EigenTrust in this example? TNA-SL weighs local (*i.e.*, direct) interaction history more heavily than transitive feedback data due to the nature of the discount operator. In contrast, EigenTrust computes a global 'average.' From a *good* user's perspective, the average

Figure 5. RAs vs. Purely Malicious users

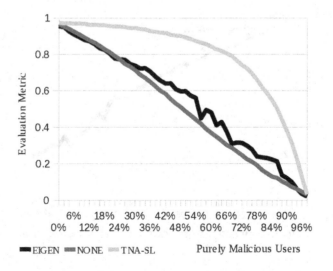

global view of a network overrun with malice is probably an inaccurate one. In such cases, the only person you should trust is yourself, and TNA-SL encodes precisely this notion by using user-centric trust values. When available and in quantity, direct interaction data is more valuable than that received transitively because it is known to be accurate.

EigenTrust has the capability to weigh local information more heavily. By performing a weighted average of the normalized (pre-multiplication) local vector with the converged (post-multiplication) global trust vector, the local:global preference can be shifted. This average is a less powerful notion than that TNA-SL provides and is not a feature we examine in this chapter.

Another surprising aspect of Figure 5 is that EigenTrust still provides improvements over NONE even when the network is overwhelmed by malicious users. It is unintuitive a super-majority of bad users can't manipulate the system for their benefit. Recall these users are in non-organized *casual* cooperation. Purely malicious users lie, making bad guys appear good, and good guys appear bad. With lots of bad guys the whole notion of good and bad becomes reversed. Bad guys trying to download from other bad guys end up

downloading from good users because misinformation is so plentiful. As we shall see, malicious users need additional capabilities for their misbehavior to have a serious effect. Fortunately, the simplistic approach of simulator permits the analysis and description of such second and third order behaviors.

Pre-Trusted Peers

We now introduce *pre-trusted peers* into our simulations. Figure 6 presents just such a test run, parameterized precisely as those above except with n pre-trusted users where n in $\{0, 5\}$. Note when $n = 0$ the data is identical to that presented in Figure 5. For implementation purposes, pre-trusted peers are a subset of *good* users. For EigenTrust, the inclusion of pre-trusted peers produces a staggering improvement. Pre-trust makes global aggregation less naïve and permits other subtle improvements discussed by Kamvar *et al.* (2003). For example, new users with *no* network experience place all of their initial trust in the pre-trusted user set.

For TNA-SL the gain is minimal, however, there is little room to improve. When $n = 5$, both algorithms perform near-ideally, that is, the evaluation metrics are the highest attainable when

Figure 6. Introducing pre-trusted nodes

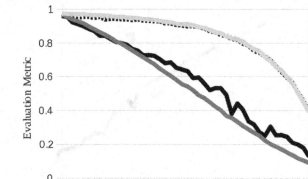

one considers valid file copies may be scarce in malice networks. Notice in Figure 6 that the evaluation metric begins a rapid decline for the high performing algorithms, *i.e.*, datasets EIGEN-5 and TNA-SL-5, when the network has 66% or more *purely malicious* users. These low metrics are a side effect of our constraint that transactions must be completed, when possible. Thus, *good* users are likely aware that they are about to download from a poor user, but simply have no better alternative. Enabling users to 'decline' a transaction after examination of trust values would present a myriad of challenges. Not only would this strain the simulator's static nature, but trust values would need an absolute interpretation (EigenTrust's are relative).

Reduced Interaction Density

The 'near-ideal' performance exhibited to this point is unsatisfactory. More interesting are the parameterizations that challenge the RAs. Let us begin with interaction density. The 50-user, 50k transaction traces we have been examining produce ≈ 20 interactions between each user pair; an abundance of direct experience. While such densities do allow us to study convergent algorithm

behavior, actual P2P networks are far sparser. A reduced transaction count will simulate a sparse network, and the less complete information should test the transitive functionality of the RAs.

Figure 7 is set up just as Figure 6 except there are only 500 transactions, leading to $\approx (1/5)$ interactions between each user pair. The graph shows that pre-trust is particularly important when data is not plentiful. Without it, both algorithms perform comparably to the control line.

It is possible for EigenTrust to outperform TNA-SL, as Figure 7 shows at many data points. In general, however, TNA-SL's expressiveness (*e.g.*, the ability to quantify negative trust) compared to EigenTrust results in higher evaluation metrics while sacrificing efficiency.

Tightening Bandwidth Constraints

To this point, we have only examined parameterizations with unlimited bandwidth. Just as with plentiful interaction densities, this condition is unrealistically beneficial to the RA being studied. When bandwidth constraints are enforced, users may be unable to source-select their most satisfactory choice. We demonstrate that bandwidth limitations are necessary via Figure 8; the cumu-

Figure 7. RAs in a sparse network

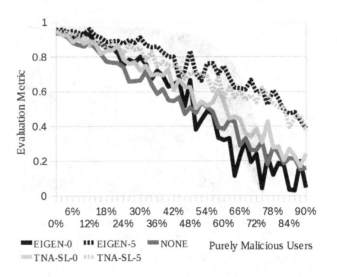

lative distribution function (CDF) of uploads per the percentage of network participants.

Figure 8 is parameterized with 50 *good* users and unlimited bandwidth over 50k transactions.

As the graph shows, during EigenTrust runs just 20% of users account for 90% of all uploads; evidence that a subset of users become identified as 'most trusted.' While good for trust metrics this is clearly not the best utilization of network bandwidth. More interesting is the graph of Figure 9, showing how identical traces fared under varying upload bandwidth availability.

As Figure 9 shows, tight bandwidth inhibits RA performance. The percentages associated with data sets are indicative of the bandwidth utilization, *i.e.*, dataset '100%-BW' means the trace could be run with no incomplete-able transactions if-and-only-if every user utilized the full allotment (100%) of bandwidth given to them. Tighter bandwidth constraints make RA performance tend towards the control line (NONE). Just as bandwidth may force *good* users to select *less trusted* providers, malicious users may have to select *more trusted* ones. Bandwidth, important for realism, is largely uninteresting from a trust perspective; only acting as a scalar on the metric gap between systems. Bandwidth constraints also produce incomplete-

able transactions from which no useful statistics can be derived. For these reasons, we have -- and will continue to -- present scenarios with unlimited bandwidth.

EMPOWERING MALICIOUS USERS

To this point test runs have shown impressive RA performance. However, the fact that networks with upwards of 75% malicious users can still be managed may suggest our malicious user models are not sufficiently powerful. Rather than being an endorsement of RAs our simulator should strive to find their breaking points, even if by unrealistic means.

Assumptions Benefiting Bad Users

Starting on the complementary end, several of our assumptions are *beneficial* to malicious users. First, our simulator has a 'closed world.' Users do not come and go from the network; all participants are available to participate in transactions from the outset. In a more realistic setting, networks would be built by well-intentioned users and some basis of trust would be established between *good* users

Figure 8. CDF of upload frequency

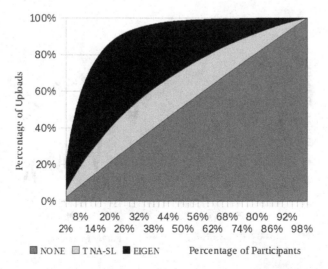

Figure 9. RAs under varying bandwidth constraints

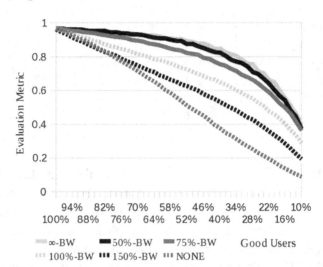

before malicious ones appeared. Furthermore, it is unlikely a significant number of bad users will enter the network at a single time. Therefore the RA would be able to 'cast aside' malicious users as they are identified and not have to deal with the cumulative effect of simultaneous arrival. Secondly, as discussed previously, complete-able transactions must complete. Thus, when limited file copies exist or in tight bandwidth situations, users further down the relative ordering (*i.e.*, less trustworthy) will be given the chance to disseminate files.

Distributed Schema

On the other hand, some of our assumptions *inhibit* malicious users from gaining an advantage. First, RAs are usually implemented in a distributed setting and thus interaction and trust value storage are distributed, as well. It is insecure to let users store and report their own data. In practice, *score management systems*, like TrustMe (Singh & Liu, 2003) or that of Yang, Kamvar, and Garcia-molina (2003) are used. For security reasons, data is stored redundantly. When discrepancies arise,

a vote determines how to proceed. Thus, a large and cooperative group of malicious users can agree on dishonest values and subvert a reputation framework entirely.

Our simulator uses a centralized feedback-store and trust service, and therefore cannot fall prey to such subversion. This fact may unfairly hamper malicious user efforts. However, a centralized approach is simple and efficient for simulation purposes. Also, readers must realize that an RA and the distribution scheme it employs are two separate entities. While the EigenTrust paper uses MOTHERS (Yang *et al.*, 2003) for secure distribution, other score managers may work just as well. One should be careful not to apply the deficiencies of distribution strategies to reputation management algorithms.

A centralized reputation database does have a severe weakness; everyone has a consistent view of the network. Intuitively, malicious users want to lie to *good* users but provide their malicious colleagues good information. We now describe how such differing perspectives can be realized without having to implement score managers or distribution schema.

Figure 10. Overwriting global feedback data

$$A = \begin{bmatrix} \begin{pmatrix} pos:0 \\ neg:0 \end{pmatrix} & \begin{pmatrix} pos:3 \\ neg:1 \end{pmatrix} & \begin{pmatrix} pos:3 \\ neg:2 \end{pmatrix} \\ \begin{pmatrix} pos:9 \\ neg:3 \end{pmatrix} & \begin{pmatrix} pos:0 \\ neg:0 \end{pmatrix} & \begin{pmatrix} pos:8 \\ neg:1 \end{pmatrix} \\ \begin{pmatrix} pos:2 \\ neg:4 \end{pmatrix} & \begin{pmatrix} pos:5 \\ neg:4 \end{pmatrix} & \begin{pmatrix} pos:0 \\ neg:0 \end{pmatrix} \end{bmatrix}, \ w = \begin{bmatrix} \begin{pmatrix} pos:0 \\ neg:0 \end{pmatrix} \\ \begin{pmatrix} pos:3 \\ neg:9 \end{pmatrix} \\ \begin{pmatrix} pos:4 \\ neg:2 \end{pmatrix} \end{bmatrix}, \ A' = \begin{bmatrix} w_{0,0} & A_{0,1} & A_{0,2} \\ w_{1,0} & A_{1,1} & A_{1,2} \\ w_{2,0} & A_{2,1} & A_{2,2} \end{bmatrix}$$

Empowering Isolated Malicious Users

To exemplify our architecture's weakness, let us examine the case of a single, isolated, *purely malicious* user, *u*. Suppose TNA-SL, with its preference for direct experience, is the RA being used. User *u* receives a valid file from a *good* user, *v*, and dishonestly submits negative feedback. Now, the next time user *u* queries and needs to compute trust he will go the feedback database and aggregate over feedback(s), including those that he/she previously submitted. In particular, trust(*u*->*v*) may be low as it is characterized by one or more negative feedbacks. User *u*, being malicious, is then likely to use *v* as a source. However, *v* is actually a good user, *u* gets a good file, *u* has less bad files, and the network is slightly better on the whole. Our (static) source selection criteria (Table 2) operate on the assumption that stored interactions are honest – behavioral patterns become uncharacteristic when this is not the case.

Luckily, this it is not difficult to correct. We previously assumed the feedback DB and trust computation were centralized. Relaxing this to allow *distributed trust computation* gives malicious users more power. Now, we assume a user who wants to make a trust inquiry will export a copy of the centralized feedback DB to his/her own machine and perform trust computation locally. Further, in addition to submitting (perhaps dishonest) feedbacks to the global-DB, users will also locally store a vector of *completely honest* interaction history.

After the centralized feedback DB has been imported, and before trust computation is done, users will override 'their' vector in the global matrix with their local honest one. For example, in Figure 10, we assume user *u* (ID=0) is computing trust. Therein, *A* is the (summarized) feedback DB, *w* is *u*'s local honest vector, and *A'* is subsequently given to the RA to compute trust[10].

Test runs have demonstrated this benefits malicious users by the *smallest* of margins. This is intuitive: The local vectors of *good* users are identical to those in the global-DB. *Good* users compute trust and source-select precisely as before. Malicious users compute trust differently, but the evaluation metric does not concern them. For malicious users to deteriorate the evaluation metric, they must skew the opinions of *good* users. Enter the malicious collective.

Empowering Malicious Collectives

A *malicious collective* is a set of nodes cooperating to increase the number of invalid files *good* users receive. Assume collective members are aware of all other participating members. Now, malicious users do not just use their *honest interaction vector* for local trust computation, they also broadcast it to others in the collective so they may gain a more accurate network view.

This capability alone is insufficient for a malicious collective to deliver invalid files. Imagine a network has a set of *good* users and a group of *purely malicious* ones. Simulation shows the two groups become disjoint subgraphs. Good users

Figure 11. Simulating the malicious gateway strategy

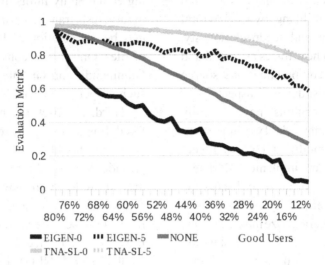

trade with other good users, with great success, and because of the enhanced capability, bad users become really good at finding bad files. Still, interaction rarely crosses this boundary, as is necessary for the metric to decrease.

For a malicious collective to succeed its members need to have well-defined and coordinated roles. We now describe one such strategy. Suppose a network has a set of good users, *G*, and malicious collective, *M,* which consists of a set of *feedback malicious* users, *FM*, and a set of *purely malicious* users, *PM*. The nodes of *FM* distribute good files and therefore trust(*G->FM*) is high. *FM* members are also liars so their global vectors indicate trust(*FM->PM*)is high. Now, from a transitive perspective trust(*G->FM->PM*) is high, so in the absence of contrary direct experience of the form trust(*G->PM*), *good* users are likely to obtain bad files in this scenario, which we term the *malicious gateway* strategy.

Simulation confirms we have alas given malicious users sufficient power to subvert a reputation algorithm. Figure 11, implementing the *malicious gateway* strategy, shows Eigen-Trust (w/o pre-trust) is particularly vulnerable to this approach. The addition of pre-trusted peers corrects this deficiency (by-in-large) and seems to suggest that networks implementing well-chosen pre-trusted peers are robust to even collective attacks.

Having demonstrated our simulator has sufficient power to model a group of cooperating malicious users overtaking a network -- albeit one managed by a slightly naïve global average algorithm -- our examination concludes. We leave the invention, implementation, and testing of other collective strategies as an exercise for the reader. Our own attempts have shown this task to be a difficult one. When confined to only algorithm-based attacks, (*i.e.*, not attacking feedback mechanisms or distribution strategies) RAs appear remarkably robust.

CONCLUSION

Emerging decentralized topologies offer benefits over their centralized counterparts. However, to take advantage of these, reputation management needs used to limit corruption and malicious behavior. Though many such RM systems exist, prior to our proposal of one in this chapter, there was no convenient means to objectively compare them or verify authors' claims.

Herein, we reported on our framework's design decisions. First, we explained static network trace generation. Particular attention was given to user initialization; utilizing two behavioral dimensions – clean-up and feedback-honesty. Next, we demonstrated how traces are simulated with bandwidth, trust computation, and source selection among the most dynamic aspects.

New reputation algorithms may be easily interfaced into our framework. Two in particular (EigenTrust and a modified TNA-SL) were discussed and have been implemented. These RAs provided us the opportunity to discuss the implementation details, efficiency hurdles, and behavioral qualities that characterize many systems. Example analyses increased our understanding of existing RAs and helped us refine malicious user strategies.

These test simulations were an endorsement of the current state of RAs. Malicious collectives, even large ones, were unable to subvert the robust forms of either algorithm. Further, in the vast majority of parameterizations, the systems enforced near ideal behavior. Though we did not intend this study to be an endorsement of the current methodology, it ended up being just that, as we encountered significant challenges in deteriorating algorithm performance.

Future Work

Though RA analysis with the simulator has been beneficial, improvements could make it an even more powerful tool. Though it was our intention to simulate simplified networks, some of our departures from realism may be too significant. First, our 'closed world' approach may need re-thinking. Allowing users to enter and exit the network, change user models mid-trace (Srivatsa *et al.*, 2005), and insert new files into the network are all future considerations. While possible, such notions strain the framework's static nature[11]. Similarly, our notion of time needs enhanced.

Second, network connectivity/topology needs examined. In our simulator, we assume everyone trades with *everyone* else in the network. Limit-

ing connectivity limits direct experience, which in turn, tests transitive trust propagation. *Cliques* may be one solution to the problem, *i.e.*, genres of files. One should consult the work of Saroiu, Gummandi, and Gribble (2002) to learn about such properties in actual P2P networks.

Third, feedback mechanisms need to be refined. It is clear that the receiver (client) of a file (service) should enter feedback regarding the provider (server). Entry of additional feedbacks may allow for more powerful methods of trust computation. Suppose user A downloaded a bad file from B, because users C and D suggested that B was a good choice. In addition to the obvious feedback(A->B, NEG), A may also want to submit feedbacks indicating that B and C were poor referrers. With entries of this style, one can determine referral trust of users. Properly implemented, this could defend against the *malicious gateway* strategy. Similarly, trust in individual files may be calculated via context and feedback filtering. Such analysis can likely be performed to infinite specificity, but less relevant feedback will exist as scope narrows. Adaptive approaches will need to be developed to consolidate values from varying granularities.

Similarly, we need to develop methods to verify that whoever is entering feedback in a DB is justified in doing so. Perhaps a token issued at service completion will need to be presented at feedback submittal in order to verify this fact. Still, this does not entirely prevent ballot stuffing attacks. When the costs and risks of an exchange are high, cost-benefit analyses and decision meta-policies might need to be implemented.

Fifth, we have demonstrated that pre-trusted peers can be critical to the effectiveness of a RA. Research needs focused on how such users should be selected and how varying quantities affect algorithm metrics. From the malicious perspective, it would be interesting to examine how pre-trust can be exploited. For example, malicious users may choose to always deliver valid files to pre-trusted users (if they can identify them), dramatically boosting global opinion. Lastly, out-of-band manipulation of a pre-trusted peer, *i.e.* a botnet takeover, could prove significant.

Sixth, additional RAs need interfaced into our framework, allowing us to confirm the applicability of our design. Furthermore, small, algorithm-specific, enhancements might need made. For example, EigenTrust and TNA-SL both encode the notion of pre-trust. What about algorithms that cannot take advantage of pre-trust, but are dependent on other properties? For example, an RA may want to store feedback timestamps and treat older entries as less relevant. Such properties should be included, so long as they are perceived as being realistic.

Finally, we would like to note the above identification of shortcomings does not invalidate the significance of our simulation results or the usefulness of our current implementation. Rather, they are a series of improvements that should be simple additions to our modular design.

Source Availability

The evaluation framework described herein has been implemented in both C and Java; their functionality is equivalent. The Java code is fully documented and intuitive -- it is the suggested viewing for anyone with casual interest. The C code is not as straightforward but is significantly quicker. The source code and supporting documents are available at http://rtg.cis.upenn.edu/qtm/

REFERENCES

Blaze, M., Feigenbaum, J., & Lacy, J. (1996). Decentralized Trust Management. In *Proceedings of the 1996 IEEE Symposium on Security and Privacy* (pp. 164-173). Washington, DC: IEEE Computer Society Press.

Breslau, L., Cao, P., Fan, L., Phillips, G., & Shenker, S. (1999). Web Caching and Zipf-like Distributions: Evidence and Implications. In *Proceedings of INFOCOM '99: Eighteenth Annual Conference of the IEEE Computer and Communications Societies* (pp. 126-134).

Douceur, J. R., & Donath, J. S. (2002). The Sybil Attack. In *Proceedings of the First IPTPS* (pp. 251-260).

Hoffman, K., Zage, D., & Nita-Rotaru, C. (2008). A Survey of Attack and Defense Techniques for Reputation Systems. *ACM Computing Surveys*.

Jøsang, A. (2001). A Logic for Uncertain Probabilities. *International Journal of Uncertainty, Fuzziness, and Knowledge Based Systems, 9*(3), 279–311.

Jøsang, A., Hayward, R., & Pope, S. (2006). Trust Network Analysis with Subjective Logic. In *Proceedings of the 29th Australasian Computer Science Conference*.

Kamvar, S. D., Schlosser, M. T., & Garcia-molina, H. (2003). The EigenTrust Algorithm for Reputation Management in P2P Networks. In *Proceedings of the Twelfth International World Wide Web Conference* (pp. 640-651). New York: ACM Press.

Li, H., & Singhai, M. (2007). Trust Management in Distributed Systems. *IEEE Computer, 40*(2).

Papaioannou, T. G., & Stamoulis, G. D. (2004). Effective Use of Reputation in Peer-to-Peer Environments. In *Proceedings of the Fourth International Scientific Workshop on Global and Peer-to-Peer Computing* (pp. 259-268).

Resnick, P., & Zeckhauser, R. (2001). Trust Among Strangers in Internet Transactions: Empirical Analysis of eBay's Reputation System [working paper]. In *Proceedings of the NBER Workshop on Empirical Studies of Electronic Commerce*.

Saroiu, S., Gummadi, P. K., & Gribble, S. D. (2002). A Measurement Study of Peer-to-Peer File Sharing Systems. In *Proceedings of Multimedia Computing and Networking*.

Schlosser, M. T., Condie, T. E., & Kamvar, S. D. (2003). Simulating a File-Sharing P2P Network. In *Proceedings of the Workshop on Semantics in Peer-to-Peer and Grid Computing*.

Singh, A., & Liu, L. (2003). TrustMe: Anonymous Management of Trust Relationships in Decentralized P2P Systems. In . *Proceedings of the Peer-to-Peer Computing, 2003*, 142–149.

Srivatsa, M., Xiong, L., & Liu, L. (2005). TrustGuard: Countering Vulnerabilities in Reputation Management for Decentralized Overlay Networks. In *Proceedings of the International World Wide Web Conference*.

Valdes, J., Tarjan, R. E., & Lawler, E. L. (1979). The Recognition of Series Parallel Digraphs. In *Proceedings of the 11th Annual ACM Symposium on Theory of Computing* (pp. 1-12).

West, A. G., Aviv, A. J., Chang, J., Prabhu, V. S., Blaze, M., Kannan, S., et al. (2009). QuanTM: A Quantified Trust Management System. In *EUROSEC 2009*, Nuremberg, Germany (pp. 28-35).

Yang, B., Kamvar, S. D., & Garcia-molina, H. (2003). *Secure Score Management for P2P Systems* (Technical report). Stanford University.

Zhang, Q., Yu, T., & Irwin, K. (2004). A Classification Scheme for Trust Functions in Reputation-Based Trust Management. In *Proceedings of the ISWC Workshop on Trust, Security, and Reputation on the Semantic Web*.

Zhang, Y., Lin, K. J., & Klefstad, R. (2006). DIRECT: A Robust Distributed Broker Framework for Trust and Reputation Management. In *Proceedings of the 8th IEEE Conference on E-Commerce Technology*.

Zipf, G. K. (1949). *Human Behavior and the Principle of Least Effort*. Reading, MA: Addison-Wesley Press.

ADDITIONAL READING

Aberer, K., & Despotovic, Z. (2001). Managing Trust in a Peer-2-Peer Information System. In *Proceedings of the 9th Intl. Conference on Information and Knowledge Management*.

Aringhieri, R., Damiani, E., De, S., Vimercati, C., Paraboschi, S., & Samarati, P. (2006). Fuzzy Techniques for Trust and Reputation Management in Anonymous Peer-to-Peer Systems. *Journal of the American Society for Information Science and Technology*, 57(4), 528–537. doi:10.1002/asi.20307

Buchegger, S., & Boudec, J. V. (2004). A Robust Reputation System for Peer-to-Peer and Mobile Ad-hoc Networks. In *Proceedings of P2PEcon 2004*.

Cornelli, F., Damiani, E., Capitani, S., & Paraboschi, S. (2002). Choosing Reputable Servants in a P2P Network. In *Proceedings of the 11th World Wide Web Conference* (pp. 376-386).

Garg, A., & Battiti, R. (2005). *WikiRep: Digital Reputations in Virtual Communities* (Technical Report). University of Trento, Italy.

Grandison, T., & Sloman, M. (2009). A Survey of Trust in Internet Applications. In *IEEE Communications Surveys and Tutorials, 3*(4), 2-16.

Gutscher, A., Heesen, J., & Siemoneit, O. (2008). Possibilities and Limitations of Modeling Trust and Reputation. In *Proceedings of the WSPI 2008*.

Jøsang, A., Bhuiyan, T., Xu, Y., & Cox, C. (2008). Combining Trust and Reputation Management for Web-Based Services. In . *Proceedings of TrustBus, 2008*, 69–75.

Jurca, R., & Faltings, B. (2003). An Incentive Compatible Reputation Mechanism. In . *Proceedings of the IEEE Conference on E-Commerce, 2003*, 285–293.

Kinateder, M., & Rothermel, K. (2003). Architecture and Algorithms for a Distributed Reputation System. In *Proceedings of the 1st International Conference on Trust Management* (pp. 1-16).

Lin, K., Lu, H., Yu, T., & Tai, C. (2005). A Reputation and Trust Management Broker Framework for Web Applications. In *Proceedings of the International Conference on e-Technology, e-Commerce, and e-Services* (pp. 262-269). Washington, DC: IEEE Press.

Marti, S., & Garcia-molina, H. (2006). Taxonomy of Trust: Categorizing P2P Reputation Systems. *Computer Networks, 50*(4), 472–484. doi:10.1016/j.comnet.2005.07.011

Vu, L. H., Hauswirth, M., & Aberer, K. (2005). QoS-Based Service Selection and Ranking with Trust and Reputation Management. In *Proceedings of the OTM Confederated International Conferences 2005* (pp. 446-483).

Xiong, L., & Liu, L. (2004). PeerTrust: Supporting Reputation-Based Trust for Peer-to-Peer Electronic Communities. *IEEE Transactions on Knowledge and Data Engineering, 16*(7).

ENDNOTES

[*] This research was supported in part by ONR MURI N00014-07-1-0907.

[1] Systems in the *reputation management* domain are sometimes (erroneously, we believe) called *trust management systems*. We prefer the term *reputation management* since *trust management* was coined to describe policy-based access control. No matter what these systems are called, the values computed by them are almost always called *trust values*. Further complicating the terminology, so called *quantitative trust management* (QTM) systems have been developed, selectively combining desirable TM/RM features (West *et al.*, 2009).

[2] We will use these terms interchangeably. Indeed, *reputation manager* is a convenient term common in literature, but this is avoided as it would introduce acronymic confusion.

[3] RM systems are by no means limited to binary feedback. Continuous variables or ordered sets are also common. We use only positive/negative feedback because it interfaces well will the two RM systems we discuss and it simplifies discussion.

[4] The major challenge is not so much getting users to provide *honest* feedback, as it is getting users to provide *any* feedback. Feedback submission is optional in almost all applications implementing it. Our simulator makes the assumption that feedback is *always* provided.

[5] To support this notion, our simulator allows a *warm-up* period to be specified, in which trust relationships/values can stabilize before statistics begin to be tabulated.

[6] Files are labeled numerically [1…NUM_ FILES].

[7] Efficient (linear-time) DSPG recognition is a rather complex topic. The casual reader may find the earlier work of Valdes, Tarjan, and Lawler (1979) to be helpful.

[8] Attempting to bring the DSPG approach to bear on a fully-connected, 50-user network is not the wisest approach. Consider the fact 1.12×10^{15} paths would exist between each user pair.

[9] All data points on the graphs herein are the average of 5+ simulations, where each simulation is produced from a different trace, and each trace is generated using an identical parameterization (aside from the random seed). This is an attempt to reduce

variance and produce the most characterizing plots possible. The speed-up heuristic was not used for graph generation.

10   Distributed trust computation complicates our speed-up heuristic. To adapt, every user would need to store his/her own snapshots and skip values. This is not a feature we explore.

11   Such 'strains' on the static nature are not difficult to overcome, but they would massively increase trace file size. Comparability must be preserved. For example, stating a user will be present x% of the time, then letting this presence be determined randomly at runtime is insufficient. Instead, every user entry-to/exit-from the network needs written to the trace.

Chapter 13
Observation–Based Trust Management for Services in Mobile Networks

André Paul
Fraunhofer Institute for Open Communication Systems (FOKUS), Germany

Carsten Jacob
Fraunhofer Institute for Open Communication Systems (FOKUS), Germany

Heiko Pfeffer
Technische Universität Berlin, Germany

Stephan Steglich
Technische Universität Berlin, Germany

ABSTRACT

The growing availability of well-equipped handheld devices and the increasing mobility of users influence the way today's services can be used. In the future, services provided by different devices can be used on an ad-hoc basis to fulfill user-specified tasks. This chapter proposes an infrastructure for mobile networks that allows for the rating of nodes with respect to their provided functionalities. Thus, it is possible to create reputation relationships and trust assessments between service requesters and service providers. One means for making use of trust relationships is in the reduction and the prevention of interactions with misbehaving or inaccurate nodes. The authors' work also factors in the subjectivity of users by allowing different service quality perceptions for each user. Thus, each user can base his or her cooperation behavior on their own service behavior preferences instead on the aggregated preferences of all users.

INTRODUCTION

The growing availability and usage of well-equipped handheld devices such as mobile phones, personal digital assistants (PDAs), and mobile computers, and the increasing mobility of users influence the way today's services can be used. For example, "service communities" (Jacob et. Al, 2008) allow for a number of distributed services hosted on mobile

DOI: 10.4018/978-1-61520-682-7.ch013

or fixed nodes to temporarily communicate with each other for joint fulfillment of a task specified by the user.

Increasing mobility results in an intense transformation of the network topology. Thus, nodes of mobile ad hoc networks often have no access to central and continuously accessible control instances. As service providers cannot perform their tasks as expected (providing inaccurate, insufficient, false, or no service results at all) mechanisms are needed to detect misuse or misbehavior. Usage of such mechanisms in mobile environments means that they must be independent of central and always available instances.

Indeed, since inaccurate or insufficient results may refer to the subjective perception of a user in terms of his or her personal preferences, a service's quality and performance rating may be different for each service consumer.

Reputation-based trust can handle all these issues. Service consumers have to trust in expected service behavior to prevent negative effects during cooperation, i.e., service consumers have to trust that requested services will be executed properly or that granted access rights won't be misused. Creating trust relationships based on the reputation of nodes allows for the detection of the quality of services. Thus, a service requester can be supported within the service selection by proposing services with a good reputation.

This work deals with the representation and evaluation of trust in mobile ad hoc networks. Its focus is set to the modeling of a framework that allows for the creation of trust relationships between peers and its services with regard to the special requirements of interest in distributed service environments.

The presented approach is based on a dynamic service behavior observation model which is applied either to find and propose the most suitable and reliable service or to restrict access to local services. Moreover, misbehaving peers can be identified and excluded from the network's knowledge about other peers.

Two main issues are of particular importance. First, a proper service rating model to get knowledge about the behavior of nodes is needed. Second, the dissemination of information about other nodes is required to achieve a broader decision basis, i.e. to get priori knowledge about unknown nodes and to keep up-to-date.

The proposed observation approach describes mechanisms that support the creation and usage of "observers". These software modules are responsible for the validation, rating, and evaluation of services with respect to their functionality and user preferences. Thus, the proposed trust management framework can provide a distributed service rating and evaluation infrastructure in which service evaluations are either based on a peer's estimated reputation or can be based on trust recommendations received from trusted nodes.

To extend the information basis about available services, the knowledge obtained is shared with trusted network peers. Querying trusted nodes for their recommendations and disseminating own observations to trusted peers are the approaches applied. Dissemination of observations allows for a service evaluation based on the receiver's user preferences instead of those of the sender.

BACKGROUND

Since trust is a broad research topic with a variety of specializations (Artz & Gil, 2007), the understanding of reputation, trust, and recommendation as used in this work needs definition. Reputation-based trust refers to the so-called "soft" way of determining trust by measuring reputations and sharing them in distributed environments. Reputations are assessments about someone's past behavior. The reputation notion used in this work is modified from that given by Mui, Mohatashemi, & Halberstadt in 2002:

Reputation is a perception that an entity has about another's intentions and norms.

This definition places no restrictions on how reputation is originated. Rating of information or service providers is one possibility used in this work. The association between reputation and trust can be formulated as follows; adjusted from (Maresch, 2005):

An entity A trusts an entity B based on the reputation RAB, where RAB is A's reputation perception about B, if A believes from RAB that B acts correspondent to A's expectations.

This shows that trust provides the possibility of interaction with someone under the condition of accepting risk in situations of incomplete or uncertain information. In this work, trust is defined as follows in line with (Gambetta, 1988):

Trust (or, symmetrically, distrust) is a particular level of the subjective probability with which an agent assesses that another agent or group of agents will perform a particular action, both before he can monitor such action (or independently or his capacity ever to be able to monitor it) and in a context in which it affects his own action.

Gambetta's definition of trust covers both elemental features of trust: subjectivity, i.e., each agent can have different trust assessments about others, and contextualization, i.e., trust is related to the scope of the trust relationship. Furthermore, the definition considers that agents can trust other agents even if the agent has not previously rated, or cannot rate, the behavior of the other one, e.g., due to the lack of monitoring capabilities.

Trust Metrics

To determine the trustworthiness of nodes, different kinds of trust models and metrics can be used. These models are necessary to allow nodes to base their cooperation behavior on the evaluation of measured values. In addition, trust must be classified to make trust values interpretable

and comparable. This section gives a brief overview about works that deal with the creation of trust relationships between nodes. For our work the subjectivity of ratings, the rating source, and the differentiation between nodes and their functionalities are of critical importance. The PeerTrust algorithm (Liu & Xiong, 2002) makes use of transaction and feedback information. The calculation of a peer's trustworthiness is based on five factors:

- The feedback as amount of satisfaction.
- The number of transactions.
- The credibility of feedback.
- The context of transactions to weight the type or size of transactions.
- The community context factor to allow influencing of reputations according to the status of entities, e.g., entities that are known a priori as trustworthy or entities that are authorized through the usage of other security mechanisms.

An entity in PeerTrust is trustworthy if the result value of a calculation is bigger than a minimal threshold value. Accordingly it is possible to set a second threshold that determines the minimum of done transactions to achieve an expressive calculation.

The calculation is based on all known past transactions. It is not restricted to local gathered, requested, or received information. Thus, Peer-Trust is a global trust metric that makes global assumptions about the trustworthiness of entities. The trust computation is based on all transactions between all peers. PeerTrust considers different functionalities and aging through the use of weighting factors. However, trust assessments about a specific functionality are not possible because ratings are about the whole node.

The EigenTrust (Kamvar, Schlosser, Garcia-Molina, 2003) algorithm aims for the identification and exclusion of nodes that perform bad services in peer-to-peer file-sharing networks, e.g., render

Table 1. Poblano Trust Components

Trust Component	Description
CodatConfidence	Evaluates trust in a Codat according to a keyword. Four elements are used: a keyword, a Codat identifier, a flag that indicates local or remote availability, and a confidence value.
PeerConfidence	Evaluates trust in a peer by using all CodatConfidences about Codats that are known as available at the regarded peer. Three elements are used: a keyword, a peer identifier, and the confidence value.
Risk	Contains measureable properties known from traditional trust concepts. Examples of this include availability and performance.

corrupt or false data. To achieve this, a distributed method that assigns global trust values to each peer was developed. The global trust value of a peer reflects the experiences of all peers in the network with that particular peer. To address the initialization problem EigenTrust assumes a set of pre-trusted peers.

Each peer rates transactions as being positive or negative. Given the ratings, a local trust value is computed through the sum of all local created ratings. The global reputation of a peer is calculated by using the local trust values of each peer where the local values are weighted by the global reputation of the local value provider.

Due to the usage of distributed data pools, PeerTrust and EigenTrust are not applicable in mobile environments. Furthermore, PeerTrust only use global trust assessments which means that the subjectivity of a service's quality is not taken into consideration.

B. Yu and M. P. Singh (Yu & Singh, 2002) proposed a calculation model based on belief functions and plausible reasoning. Accordingly, the *Dempster-Shafer-Theory (Shafer, 1976)* is taken for the use and combination of information about past service behaviors so that uncertainty about trust classifications can be directly considered. If a set of peers has different assessments about the trustworthiness of another peer, these uncertainties are used to create a combined result that may be more precise than each individual result. Furthermore, in contrast to EigenTrust, the evidential model distinguishes between peers with no reputation and peers with a bad reputation.

The Poblano project (Chen & Yeager, 2001) introduces a trust model as part of the JXTA[1] protocol architecture. The project aims at the rating of received information and therewith at the rating of the information providers. The notion Codat was introduced as a neologism that combines the meanings of "code" and "data" in one word. The concepts of Poblano are described with the help of a demonstration application. The scope of this application is geared to find Codats that meet the user interests. Therefore, the interests are represented by keywords. Codats are also annotated with keywords represent the content of the particular Codat. Thus, Codats can be found that match the user's interest.

The three trust components shown in Table 1 are combined to calculate trust classifications. To determine if a peer is trustworthy or not and, thus if it is able to cooperate, the PeerConfidence and the Risk are used together. Poblano grades the relevance of received Codats in six classes ranging between "Distrust" and "Complete Trust".

Poblano along with EigenTrust and the evidence-based model take no account of interaction types. Ratings are about the whole node without regard to the performance of different services hosted on the same node. Because each user may have his or her own subjective performance and behavior expectations about services, all functionalities of nodes must be considered as well as the whole node itself.

Fuzzy Service Property Model

Most of the trust metrics described above assume that peers are either trustworthy or not. Indeed, in reality a clear distinction is often difficult to make. One approach to accounting for this difficulty is that of the fuzzy set theory. The common set theory assumes that entities can be classified as either a definitive part of a set or a definitive non part of a set. In contrast to this, the fuzzy set theory allows entities to be a member of a set with a probability between 0 to 100 percent. Thus, entities can be members of multiple disjointed sets.

In our approach we will use and extend the fuzzy function from Pfeffer et al. (2008). In this work measured service properties are represented by fuzzy functions. These representations are used to compare the performance of different services and to select the most suitable ones. Therefore, service properties like "response time" or "availability" are measured and added as "*records*" to the fuzzy representation related to a service/ function pair. Records consist of the following five parameters:

- *Context*: the current state of the user's device to differentiate between a service's behavior according to the context of the device.
- *Service*: the identifier of the corresponding service, typically its URI.
- *Value:* the measured value.
- *Domain*: the type of the measured value, e.g. response time.
- *Weight*: an optional weighting factor that specifies how often the record should be added.

The proposed model generates triangular fuzzy sets that are based on the inserted records. To make assessments about service behaviors according to a user-defined preferred performance, the fuzzy model supports the creation of user profiles that describe the importance of particular parameters for users. In the evaluation process the fuzzy model searches for the lowest and the highest inserted values within the domain in question. The user profile is then fitted to the interval that has the lowest and the highest inserted value as boarders.

The result of the fuzzy evaluation - which can be between 0 and 1 - is the similarity between a service property representation and the given user profile. If the result is 1, the service can be used because it matches the user profile and is assumed to match it in the future as well. Otherwise, if the result is 0, there is no clue that the service will behave as the desired user profile specifies.

The fuzzy model is appropriate for calculations based on first hand information. Compared with the other models, the advantage of the fuzzy model is that user preferences can be changed with immediate effect. Thus, trust assessments can be rapidly changed if preferences are changed. Since changing subjective preferences and service behavior classifications are important parts of this work, the fuzzy model is taken and adapted as the core of the calculation model.

OBSERVATION-BASED TRUST FOR SERVICES IN MOBILE NETWORKS

To establish trust relationships in mobile and ad hoc networks it is essential to pay attention to the absence of global instances that may provide network nodes with information about others. Our work introduces an observation and dissemination system for the rating of nodes and node services. Thus, it is possible to reduce or ignore interactions with services or nodes classified as untrustworthy, misbehaving or inaccurate.

The conceptual part of this work is divided into the three sections *information gathering*, *information processing*, and *information usage*. Information gathering refers to the acquisition of data about nodes.

Information processing denotes the rating, representation, and storage of data received from the different information sources while information usage refers to applications that make use of, or take advantage of, the available knowledge.

Information Gathering

We distinguish three information sources: observation, dissemination, and querying. An observation is evidence gathering about the behavior of another node. Observation also refers to the detection and rating of interactions between nodes. Observation systems are widely used in intrusion detection systems, whereby intrusion detection systems can be divided in two types (Ruohomaa & Kutvonen, 2005): anomaly (Teng, Chen, & Lu, 2005), (Forrest, Hofmeyr, Somaya, & Longstaff, 1996) and misuse detection (Kumar & Spafford, 1994).

Observation over time allows for the creation of reputation values. Thus, a peer can base its future cooperation behavior on its opinions about others. Reputation systems are typically used to reduce uncertainty about social interactions to a tolerable level (Resnick, Zeckhause, Friedman, & Kuwabara, 2000) (Josang, Hird, & Faccer, 2003) or to motivate nodes to cooperate, i.e. to motivate them to abstain from cheating and to penalize nodes if they are cheating (Michiardi & Molva, 2002) (Bansal & Baker, 2003) (Buchegger & Le Boudec, 2002).

The Observer Management System

The observer management system (OMS) handles the usage of specialized software programs, termed *observers*. Observers can be defined as software programs that detect insufficient or incorrect service behavior and evaluate a satisfaction value in terms of a performed service. Whether a service is classified as insufficient or not depends on current user preferences about preferred service properties. In dependence on the observer's capabilities it can be responsible for unique services or for service categories.

Because the OMS allows for the dynamic deployment of observers, methods are needed to identify the observers responsible for given services. To this end, an observer has to publish a description on the observation system that describes the services it can handle, i.e., services it can validate, rate and evaluate. The counterparts to observer descriptions are service descriptions that describe service functionalities. To create a relation between these, the trust framework must provide methods that can evaluate the descriptions and decide if an observer is responsible or not. In addition, observers may implement their own responsibility checks that can be dynamically added to the trust framework.

Services are commonly annotated with syntactic or semantic descriptions that describe their functionalities, data type bindings, invocation conditions, etc. Thus, service descriptions can be used to describe an observer's responsibility for certain services and to create description-matching modules. Each observer has to implement three capabilities:

1. Observation
2. Rating
3. Evaluation

An observer must be capable of processing and understanding information related to the observer's own specific responsibility. This means that an observer must understand the messages of services that it can observe. Thus, observers can validate service results by detecting deviations from the service's promised functionality.

To allow observers to rate service interactions, they must be provided with four mandatory parameters.

- The service description,
- The node identifier,
- The content,
- A direction flag.

The service description is either about the service that was used remotely or about an own service requested by a remote node. Service description enables the selection of responsible observers for the validation process. The identifier of the involved node is used to connect the rating created to a unique identity.

To rate a service execution the content of the service request and response may be needed. This can be the complete communication dialog needed to invoke the service in question. The expected effects of a service execution can be determined by responsible observers through a service description and request parameter analysis. The service can be rated through a comparison of the expected effects and the occurred effects. Once the observer's specialized analysis procedure is completed, the results can be stored within the framework for future trust assessments about the service provider.

The trust framework provides a unified data storage and evaluation mechanism, - the introduced fuzzy model - to support the evaluation of an unrestricted number of different service property ratings. Thus, observers can evaluate an unrestricted set of service properties including response time, availability and correctness.

To evaluate the measured service properties, the trust framework provides access to the fuzzy evaluation mechanisms. Thus, observers can calculate overall satisfaction about a service with regard to user preferences for each of the observed service properties. If only one service property is observed, the fuzzy evaluation of this property is the service evaluation result. If more than one service property is observed, the results of each corresponding fuzzy evaluation must be combined by the observer to give an overall result.

Dissemination and Querying

Sharing observations about nodes with others may increase the node assessment quality. Dissemination of observations helps other nodes to keep up-to-date even if these nodes have no direct interaction with the reported node. Querying remote nodes for information helps to achieve knowledge if no data about a considered node is locally available.

A dissemination management system (DMS) can distribute observations to nodes assessed as trustworthy. Whether a node is classified as trustworthy or not according to the DMS should be determined by a preconfigured threshold whereby the number of destination nodes can be limited to save system resources like bandwidth and batteries and distrusted nodes are excluded from observation knowledge.

The querying mechanism can be used if own experiences about a considered node are insufficient, e.g., too old, or if the node is unknown to the assessing node. Since concrete trust recommendation as query result is independent of a node's internal data representation, i.e. fuzzy triangular functions, multiple distributed recommendations can be freely combined to create own trust assessments that are based on a set of trust recommendations.

Trust Management Framework Observation Reports

To represent queried, disseminated, and observed information we introduce *observation reports*. Observation reports contain all the information needed for trust calculations. We distinguish between two report types:

- Reputation reports that are created by local or remote observers and are about observations,
- Recommendation reports that are created by the trust calculation system and are about received trust recommendations.

A report consists of the following five attributes:

- The unique identifier of the reported node.
- The service type of the reported interaction as textural representation.
- The timestamp on creation time and date.
- The unique identifier of the report source that also includes an identifier of the observer that created the report. Thus the influence of reports can be adjusted according to the trustworthiness of the report provider.
- The rating which is either a set of observed service property values with an additional rating on the measured properties or the actual trust assessment of the report provider on the reported node according to a node's functionality.

We store service properties rather than final ratings to allow for changing service behavior preferences and to allow remote evaluations based on the requestor's preferences. A pre-calculated rating about the observation is also stored. This rating may be used if a report receiver has no observers that can handle or understand the received measurements.

Moreover, each observer may create an unrestricted number of its own fuzzy representations per service. Thus, observers can decide which value range they are willing to use to represent measured service properties, and how many different service properties they want to observe. For example, if an observer wants to store a satisfaction rating and a cost rating it may use two fuzzy representations. At a later juncture, in the trust evaluation process the observer is queried to evaluate whether the measured service properties are sufficient or not according to the current user's preferences about quality and costs. Moreover, users can change their views about price and quality at any time through the use of user profiles which have immediate effect.

Information Processing

The information about nodes collected through the three information gathering methods must be categorized to allow for the evaluation of trust in relation to the information type and source. According to the data gathered, we can categorize ratings and measurement values in five trust bases. To use observation reports as a calculation base for the fuzzy model, reports are transformed into "fuzzy model records". Additionally, during transformation the information is weighted in terms of the credibility of the information source and the actuality of information.

Trust Classification

This work differentiates between two types of trust classification - *reputation-based trust* and *recommendation-based trust*. Reputation-based trust refers to trust calculations based on service observations. Recommendation-based trust refers to trust calculations based on trust assessments of remote nodes about other nodes.

Moreover, as different data for trust calculations is also used according to received and locally gathered information, reputation-based trust can be based on local and remote information. Recommendation-based trust, however, is only based on remote information. Three data bases for reputation based trust are introduced:

- *Local measurements*
- *Remote measurements*
- *Remote reputation*

The local measurement is used for evaluations based on locally observed service behavior. The remote measurement is used for evaluations based on observations of remotely measured service behaviors. The remote reputation data basis is used if received remote measurements cannot be understood by the receiver. In this case, a normalized rating about the measurements is deployed.

Table 2. Trust Bases

Data Basis Name	Trust Classification	Source
Local Measurements	Reputation based trust	Locally measured data about an interaction.
Remote Measurements	Reputation based trust	Remotely measured data about an interaction.
Remote Reputation	Reputation based trust	Remotely created ratings about an interaction.
Profile Based Recommendation	Recommendation based trust	Requested remote trust evaluation.
Recommendation	Recommendation based trust	Trust assessment of remote nodes.

Since this work assumes that each entity mostly trusts itself, it strictly differentiates between own information and received information. If a sufficient number of observations are available, the framework is restricted to local observation information. A configurable threshold defines the minimum number of needed observations.

Depending on the available observation modules, recommendation-based trust can either be based on the preferred service behavior of the recommendation requester or on the preferred service behavior of the requested node. Accordingly, received information is either classified as *profile-based recommendation* or only as *recommendation*. Table 2 summarizes the trust classifications introduced and the corresponding data sets and sources.

Fuzzy Model Integration

Since each observer needs to store and evaluate its measured values according to a specific service, the framework offers integrative support for storage and evaluation. The fuzzy models internal data representation is based on *records*. This means that the system must map *reports* to *records* so that the five *record* attributes - *context*, *service*, *value*, *domain*, and *weight* must be set.

The context is the condition a node/service is currently situated in. Hence, the rating type, i.e. reputation report or recommendation report, can be interpreted as context. Thus, the data basis names listed in Table 2 are used as context selectors.

The service attribute is used as unique identifier for monitored services. Thus, this attribute can be mapped to the reported node which is the unique identifier within the trust framework. The value attribute directly corresponds to the observation report's rating or measurement values. The report's service description specifies the observed service, and also specifies the observer that created the report if it is a reputation report. Hence, the service description is mapped to the domain. Since each observer has its own fuzzy representation according to a node/service pair, the observer ID and the property ID of the measured values must be encoded within the domain property as well. Table 3 summarizes mappings between observation reports and fuzzy model records.

Observation Report Weighting

The trust framework uses two weighting methods to determine the influence of new records - the source of records, and the elapsed time since the previous record was inserted. As mentioned above, the fuzzy model supports the adding of a weight to new records. The weight of a record is mapped within the fuzzy model to the number of equal records added at the same time.

Since the received reports may be false or not authentic, a credibility assessment about the report provider to weight its reports increases the quality of received information. The framework uses the current trust assessment about the report provider as the record weighting parameter, thus

Table 3. Observation Report / Fuzzy Record Mappings

Observation Report	Fuzzy Model Record
Rating type and report source	Context
Unique identifier of the reported node	Service
Measured value	Value
Service description, observer type identifier and measured service property identifier	Domain
Credibility of the report provider	Weight

reducing the influence of reports provided by distrusted nodes. Determination and evaluation of more sophisticated credibility approaches is not within the scope of this work.

The second weighting factor is determined by an aging method that accounts for the up-to-dateness of information where records are weighted higher the more up-to-date they are. Thus, contemporary changes in the behavior of nodes are regarded earlier than they would be without the use of aging mechanisms. The proposed aging algorithm uses time spans between the latest record and new records to determine the weighting to be applied. Every time a new record is inserted into the system the aging algorithm is applied.

The aging algorithm introduces a divisor that is used to divide the internal fuzzy representation. The division has no effect on the probability distribution of the property memberships while the aging algorithm also assumes that the time spans for each service type are preconfigured. In this context a time span denotes the time that elapses before a record is halved in weight. The computation of the fuzzy representation devisor (D) is presented in Equation 1.

$$D = 2^{\left\lceil \frac{T_C - T_L}{T_s} \right\rceil}$$

(1)

The first step of the algorithm determines the elapsed time between the current record (T_C) and the last added record (T_L). The number of elapsed intervals is determined by dividing the elapsed time by the preconfigured time span (T_s). To determine the decreasing devisor in terms of half weightings per time span, the power of 2 and the number of elapsed time spans is calculated. Thus, the next value inserted has a higher weighting, in particular a $2^{intrevals}$ higher weighting than the latest value.

The length of the used time span influences the record distributions within the fuzzy model. If the time span's length is set to a short interval, e.g., two seconds, and new records are only added every minute, the previous records have nearly no effect on the fuzzy representation. This stems from the fact that the influence of stored records is halved every 2nd second. Thus, the influence is halved 60 times.

As it is difficult to automatically determine a time span appropriate for a specific service type, the framework provides an interface that allows for the definition of aging time spans, e.g., by the user. If no time span is provided, a preconfigured value may be used.

Information Usage

So far we have shown how information about nodes in mobile environments can be gathered and also discussed the persistence model of observation reports and the influence of two weighting methods - the concepts needed to allow for the evaluation of trust. This section introduces the calculation principles that use observation reports to determine trust values about nodes. Two applications that make use of the calculated results are also presented.

Figure 1. Trust Calculation Process

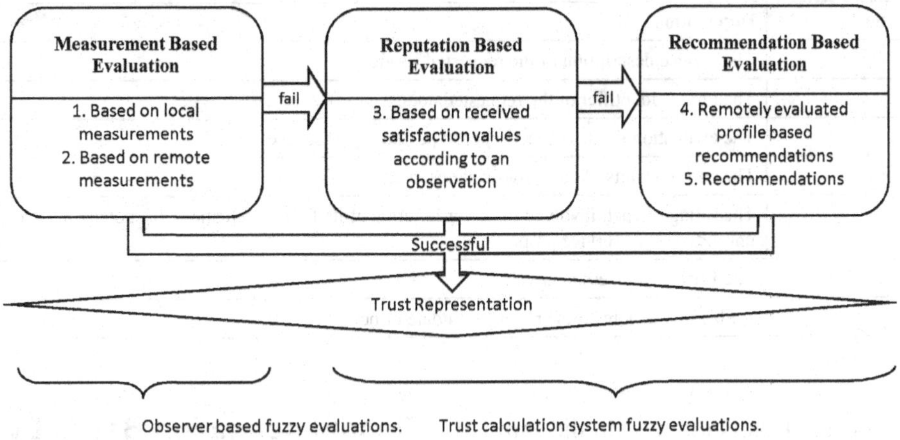

| Observer based fuzzy evaluations. | Trust calculation system fuzzy evaluations. |

Trust Assessment

Trust assessments can either pertain to a specific service offered by a node or to the node itself. The five fuzzy record contexts or trust data bases introduced above are successively used to calculate trust assessments as shown in Figure 1. If one step succeeds, the algorithm stops and gives the result.

Measurement Based Evaluation

The first step uses the local measurement context that only contains records about local observations. At first, the framework determines locally available observers for the given service. If no observer is available, the algorithm jumps to the third step because measured values cannot be evaluated.

If observers are available, each of them is queried for its current satisfaction. Observers have to evaluate each of their observable service properties using the fuzzy evaluation mechanism with respect to the deployed user profiles. Afterwards, they have to create an overall satisfaction value that has to be between 0 and 1. The returned results are checked for two conditions. The "number of available records" condition checks the number of records used. The second condition, i.e., the

"outdated" condition, checks whether used fuzzy representations are outdated.

A fuzzy data representation is *outdated* if sufficient records for an evaluation are available and a new record dominates the whole representation.

A new record dominates a fuzzy data representation when the influence it exerts on the evaluation result is strong enough to negate all previous records.

The number of sufficient records depends on the environment, i.e. on the importance of the respective service or the frequency of service invocations, and can be predefined. A calculation based on outdated data is dropped unless it is the only one within the complete evaluation process, i.e., within all five evaluation steps.

Evaluation results, which are still valid after the condition check, are used to create the final trust assessment. If more than one observer has provided evaluations, the values are averaged for the final trust assessment. Additionally, to inform the user about the assessment composition, the partial results are retrained as part of the trust assessment representation. Table 4 shows all trust assessment parameters (see Table 4).

If no result can be provided by the local measurement context evaluation, perhaps due to a lack of sufficient data, the remote measurement context is evaluated in the next step of the trust

Table 4. Trust Assessment Result Parameters

Result Parameter	Description
Service Type	The service description of the requested service.
About	The unique identifier of the requested node.
Context	The evaluation's data source (report type and report source).
Fuzzy evaluations	The partial results of each involved observer.
Satisfactions	The rating of each involved observer in terms of its fuzzy evaluations (as noted, an observer may rate an unlimited set of service properties).
Total Value	The final trust assessment value.
Valid	A Flag that denotes if the report is outdate or not.

assessment process. This is realized in the same way as in step one with one significant difference: the remote measurement context is used instead of the local measurement context.

Reputation Based Evaluation

If both measurement-based methods have no success or are based on outdated records, the third trust assessment step is used. As shown above, reputation reports contain a satisfaction value according to the observed interaction. The remote reputation evaluation makes use of these values so that the fuzzy model is queried for an evaluation within the remote reputation context according to a node/service pair. Since the inserted record values are between 0 and 1 - the higher the value the better - the user profile deployed in this evaluation describes a function with a linear gradient of factor 1.

Before the evaluation is requested, the two conditions "outdated" and "number of available records" are checked. If the checks are passed, the fuzzy evaluation result is used to create the trust assessment result by using the introduced result attributes. Since no observers are used within the remote reputation evaluation the observer parameter is empty.

Recommendation Based Evaluation

If local data for evaluations is insufficient, remote nodes are queried for support. Firstly, the trust calculation request including the desired user profiles is forwarded to trusted nodes only. This limitation is based on the assumption that trusted nodes have a tendency to be more reliable than distrusted nodes. Adding the user profiles to the request allows for the remote evaluation while results can be based on the profiles of the queried node if, for instance, no suitable observer is available. Accordingly, results are either added to the profile-based recommendation context or to the recommendation context of the fuzzy model for future use.

If trusted nodes cannot provide results, the algorithm queries unknown nodes if available. For example, an unknown node may answer if it assesses the requesting node as trustworthy or because it wants to improve its reputation. The trust assessment algorithm fails if all five trust assessment options cannot provide results.

General Trust Assessment

In addition to trust assessments based on service functionality, it is also possible to get a "general trust assessment". This is based on all available information about a considered node and may be used as a decision-making aid if no information about a specific service/node pair is available. The general trust assessment is calculated by averaging the available service-based trust assessments of the considered node.

Furthermore, it is also possible to use additional information to consider different possible weightings between service types. This may help to account for the performance of services that are more or less risky or are of particular interest for the requester. By default, each service type may be weighted with 1.

This work proposes to use two automatic service type weighting methods for general trust assessment. Since the importance relationship between different service types is not a measurable quantity, both methods have their own advantages and disadvantages. Besides using user-defined weightings, the number of requests per service type may also be used to determine weightings. Frequently used services should be weighted higher since they are of special interest to the user.

A second method to automatically determine weightings between service types is to consider the availability of services responsible for specific functionalities. Thus, service providers are rewarded for providing rare services or penalized if they take advantage of their unique services. However, both methods cannot be used to compare general trust assessments of multiple nodes because the weightings used are unknown to the trust recommendation requestors.

Risk and Service Invocation

With knowledge about a node's past behavior it is possible to decide if a node should be allowed to use local services or if a requested service should be executed at a given node. Hence, nodes have more access rights the more trustful they are. To realize a "risk assessment" the user has to provide a service description for the accessed service, the node identifier of the involved node, the direction, i.e., if it is about an incoming or

outgoing request, and, as an optional value, the content of the request message, e.g., the body of HTTP messages.

With knowledge about the service type and the trust assessment on the remote node involved, an observer responsible for the given functionality can execute its specialized risk assessment calculation. The result is either an access permission level for incoming requests or a usage recommendation for outgoing ones.

If no suitable local observer is available, the observer management tries to find trusted remote nodes that can process the risk assessment request. Thus, all necessary data is transmitted to the queried trusted remote nodes. In this case, the same risk assessment procedure is executed on the remote node without requesting nodes yet again. The queried node may rather propose to refer the query to its trusted nodes. A "risk assessment" result consists of four properties:

- The proposed access level or usage recommendation,
- The observer identifier of the observer that provides the result,
- The node that hosts the used observer, i.e. the local node itself or a remote one,
- The trust representations used for the risk assessment.

If more than one result is available, i.e., if more than one observer is responsible, all results are collected and returned to the requestor.

In addition to risk assessment, the trust management framework also provides a service selection mechanism that can be used to select the most appropriate service provider for a given service type. The calculation system is queried for trust assessments about each node/service pair within a given set of nodes, and the trust assessments of the calculation results are then compared and the node with the highest rating is given as the service selection result. This result does not mean that the service can be used without any risk; the service is merely the best choice according to the given set of nodes. The given set of nodes may be a set of all currently available nodes in terms of the requested service type.

The service selection approach can be complemented with risk assessment. Thus, the result is not only the best available choice, but is also assessed as being "not risky". The use of the risk assessment mechanism can thus result in a "failed service selection process" if all services are assessed as risky.

Realization

For a reference implementation of the proposed framework JAVA (Sun Microsystems, 2008) was chosen as the programming language with implementation being Java 1.3 code compliant to make the framework compatible with mobile devices using CDC (Sun Microsystems, 2008) compliant JAVA virtual machines. Since REST (Fielding, 2000) offers concepts to address and manipulate resources by using URIs, the open source RESTAC ("A Java REST Framework", 2008) framework was selected as communication middleware.

As shown in Figure 2, the introduced concepts were summarized in four main building blocks. The trust management system (TMS) component is responsible for handling the logical dependencies between the other components. The TMS is the central interface from the user's perspective. Trust assessments, risk assessments, rating requests, and service selection requests are invoked from here. As the TMS forwards each request to the appropriate subsystems,. trust assessment requests are forwarded to the trust calculation system (TCS), risk assessment or rating requests are forwarded to the observer management system (OMS), while locally created observation reports are forwarded to the dissemination management system (DMS) for distribution to trusted nodes. Service selection is performed directly by the TMS and adding

new reports and determining their weight is also processed in the TMS.

The observer management system (OMS) is responsible for the realization of the proposed observation approach. It provides all needed functionalities to load, unload, and invoke observers at runtime. Furthermore, if no suitable observers are locally available, this component forwards risk assessment and rating requests to trustworthy remote peers.

Once an observer is loaded, it is queried for its responsibilities to complete the deployment process. The "responsibility descriptions" are used later on to find responsible observers for given service types with he introduced description comparison modules being used to find responsible observers for rating, evaluation, and risk requests. The framework contains a default module that checks two given service descriptions for equality. Other modules can also be dynamically added so that each observer may provide its own specialized module if desired.

To forward requests to remote nodes, the OMS uses a list that contains trusted nodes and node identifiers. A "who is" component may responsible for discovering the current logical endpoint address of a node according to its identifier, i.e. its URL.

Figure 2. Design Overview

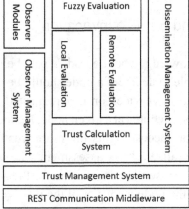

Since the framework supports remote evaluations based on measured or observed service behavior, two further OMS functionalities are exposed to the TMS:

- Providing user profiles used by a given observer to make remote evaluations possible,
- Providing a central evaluation function that forwards observer-based evaluations to responsible observers using either local user profiles or given profiles, i.e. those received from a remote node for remote measurement-based evaluation requests.

The dissemination management system (DMS) component is responsible for the distribution of locally created observation reports to trusted nodes. If a node is currently unavailable, its identifier and the respective reports are stored for later retries. Resending is either tried in configurable intervals or if a new dissemination request is made. To differentiate between own and received reports the context of received reports is set to "Remote Measurement".

Received reports are weighted by using the trust assessment on the report provider. If a trust assessment is not available, a default weight for unknown providers can be used. The proposed aging algorithm is then applied and the observation report added to the fuzzy model.

As the trust calculation system (TCS) is responsible for the creation of trust representations for a requested node/service pair, it may be necessary to query remote nodes for their trust assessments. What's more, trust calculations can be limited to being based on locally available information only which allows the system to query other nodes for trust assessments if another node queried the requestor itself. Since the framework supports remote evaluations of user profiles, the calculation can also be restricted to evaluations of a specific observer and the corresponding user profiles.

Evaluation

To evaluate the concepts of the proposed framework a simulation environment was realized. This application allows for the management and monitoring of simulated networks of nodes. Thus, it is possible to show the world view of nodes and create various statistics. A world view shows the current trust assessments of one node about all the other nodes. Exemplary statistics are the number of positive or negative rated interactions, the number of received recommendations, the number of interactions needed until each node is known and the trust assessment about other nodes.

The main parameters of each simulation are the number of nodes and the number of used clusters. A cluster can be defined as a set of nodes in transmission range of each other. A node that belongs to one cluster is only able to communicate with nodes belonging to the same cluster. Thus, mobility of nodes can be simulated by changing the cluster memberships of nodes. The simulation environment provides the possibility of adjusting further parameters such as those for "probability of misbehavior" or "rate of mobility" to define an initial simulation setup.

Simulations

The basic simulation parameters are set as follows:

- Each simulation is based on the results of 1,000 runs.
- Each node provides the same service.
- Negative and positive reports are classified as reports that are rated either as less than or equal to 0.5, or greater than 0.5.
- Whether a service of a remote node can be used or not is determined by the risk assessment mechanism. To enable the usage of a service its trust value must be greater than 0.5.

Some simulations use adaptations to the standard calculation schemes and information gathering concepts. For this reason certain notions are introduced:

- "Risky" is used to find the most suitable service. This means that unknown services are favored over positively rated services.
- "Best" is used to get the "best known" service. Thus, unknown services are not used if another positively rated service is already known.
- "No DMS" refers to the usage of the "Risky" model with a disabled dissemination mechanism. Thus, observation reports are not disseminated.
- "No TCS" refers to the usage of the "Risky" model with a disabled trust querying mechanism. Thus, the calculation mechanism is restricted to locally available information only.
- "Random" refers to pseudo-random-based service selection.

The first simulation evaluates the different introduced approaches. The following simulation parameters were used:

- Number of Nodes: 20, 10 well behaving, cooperating, and active and up to 10 badly behaving.

- Number of service requests: 20 at each active node, 200 altogether.
- Variable parameter: number of bad behaving services between 5% and 50%.
- Measurement: badly rated service executions.

As shown in Figure 3, the number of bad service executions increases if the number of badly behaving nodes increases. Our framework outscores a random selection between 60% and 90% according to the referred trust calculation model.

In another simulation we found that the number of messages received by the dissemination system increases linearly with an increasing number of cooperating nodes. This is because each observation is propagated to each trusted node even if the receiver does not need the provided information since it gets its own information through its own interactions. The more well behaving nodes are available, the more nodes must be informed about new observations.

In addition, the simulation showed that the number of received trust calculation system messages stagnates with an increasing number of cooperating nodes. This is because recommendations are only requested until a sufficient number of answers are received or until own observations are made. The number of needed recommendation requests is higher if fewer cooperating nodes are available. This is because trust assessment requests

Figure 3. Performance Comparison

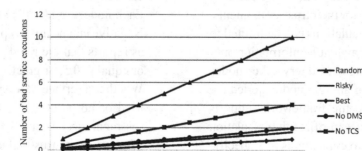

must be repeated more often until a complete world view becomes available.

The following simulation considers the influence of mobility. Each node here is a member of a cluster with cluster memberships changing over time. The following setup was used:

- Number of Nodes: 20; 10 well behaving and 10 badly behaving.
- Number of service requests: 20 for each active or cooperating node (overall 200 requests).
- Pseudo randomly selected start cluster for each node.
- Mobility: pseudo random clusters change after each node has requested a service. A service request fails if no service is available or authorized for use in the current cluster.
- Used calculation model: Risky.
- Variable parameter: number of Clusters 1 – 10.

The number of negatively rated service executions in the first simulation is of interest. The "risky" and "random" service-proposing mechanisms are used to evaluate the advantages our work offers when compared to standard service selection schemes. In this simulation, an increasing number of clusters is used to simulate the mobility of nodes. As shown in Figure 4, the probability of negatively rated service executions is noticeable

lower when our approach is used. Even with high mobility, our approach performs about 140% better than randomly chosen services. The "random" service selection also seems to perform better with an increasing number of clusters. But this is a false conclusion - the number of negatively rated service executions decreases because of the increasing probability of failed requests in cases where no service is available in the current cluster.

The second observation considers the influence of mobility on the availability of services. Figure 5 shows three types of request results. The "successful request" rate refers to the number of service requests that are successfully made. This is the case either if an unknown service provider was available and used or if a known node assessed as trustworthy was available and used. "No service allowed" refers to the number of service requests that could not be fulfilled because only distrusted services were available. In contrast, "no service available" refers to the number of service requests that could not be fulfilled because no service provider was available. Finally, failed requests illustrate the sum of both cases.

As shown, the absence of trusted services or the availability of distrusted services appears if more than two clusters are available. In this case, a random service selection mechanism would use the poorly rated service because no one else can be randomly chosen. In such cases, the trust framework proposes to abstain from using these services.

Figure 4. Mobility and Negative Reports

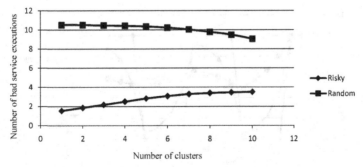

Figure 5. Mobility Service Requests

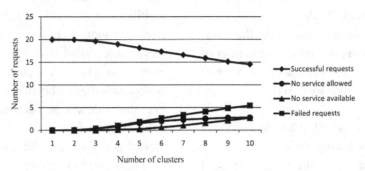

The last mobility simulation deals with the ratio between services rated as "good" and "bad", and the needed requests to detect all poorly rated services. The following simulation setup was used:

- Number of Nodes: 20
- Used calculation model: Risky.
- Variable parameter: ratio between good and poorly rated nodes from 95%:5% to 5%:95%.
- Measurement: number of needed interactions until each poorly rated service is known by each cooperating node.

If the number of cooperating nodes increases while, the number of poorly rated services simultaneously decreases, the number of needed reports decreases by approx. 25% until the amount of cooperating nodes reaches 25%. The detection speed then begins to stagnate. This effect has two reasons: the less poorly rated nodes are available, the more time is needed to detect them. Furthermore, the creation of trust relationships between all cooperating nodes requires some interactions. The trust algorithm is most effective if all cooperating nodes are known among one another.

To reduce complexity, only nodes with a fixed personality have been used thus far, i.e. each node and its services are positive or negative. The next simulation deals with the reaction of the algorithm to oscillating service behavior.

The first dynamic service behavior simulation shown in Figure 6 refers to the benefits of using an aging mechanism as introduced in the main section of this chapter. The service behavior function describes the real behavior of a considered node. As shown, the node changes its behavior after four cycles. One cycle refers to the time elapsed between two service requests made by another node to the considered node.

Figure 6. Oscillating Service Behavior 1

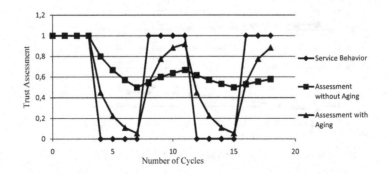

To illustrate the adaptation of the trust computation results to real service behavior, services are requested even if a negative rating is expected. If no aging mechanism is used, the computed trust values converge to the value 0.5 during the elapsed time. As noted, 0.5 specifies the threshold that determines whether or not a service can be used within the simulations. If no aging mechanism is used, there is no chance of falling below the threshold due to the majority of positively rated interactions. Hence, the service is always assessed as being useable even if it behaves in a negative way.

The aging algorithm deployed is configured to use a doubled weight for each new rating. Thus, the trust assessment falls below the service selection threshold after the first negative experience. It also passes the threshold after only one positive observation. As shown in Figure 6, the computed trust influenced by the ageing mechanism comes closer to the real service behavior.

The second dynamic service behavior simulation permits the usage of negatively rated services except those services with outdated ratings. Thus, a bad rated service can be used again or additional information about the service can be collected since it may have changed its behavior. As introduced, the algorithm allows for the configuration of time spans that specify when a trust assessment result is classified as outdated.

Beside the real service behavior, Figure 7 shows the usage of two "outdated" configurations.

The first uses an outdate configuration that is set to one cycle. The second configuration is set to four cycles which corresponds to the service's oscillating behavior frequency.

For this simulation the observer risk assessment used allows the execution of services with outdated ratings. As shown, the service requestor gets the benefit of using the service if it behaves positively. However, this is only achieved at the risk of some negatively rated service executions. As also shown in Figure 7, if the oscillating behavior frequency of a service is known, the trust computation for positive ratings comes close to the real service behavior. In short, the simulation has shown that dynamic service behavior can have a significant impact on trust assessments. Thus, dynamic service behavior is a field that would well repay investigation.

CONCLUSION

The simulations have shown that misbehaving, inaccurate, or insufficient services can be identified. Here, "inaccurate" and "insufficient" are subjective preferences about a service's behavior, e.g., the service quality such as response time or availability. Identified nodes and their services are successively excluded from usage and the service requestor's knowledge. Moreover, remote nodes can be assessed even if no direct interactions are made. Reputation-based trust assessments can

Figure 7. Oscillating Service Behavior 2

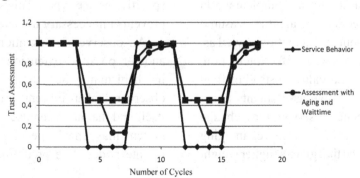

be used to prevent the usage of services with unwanted behavior while the cooperation of nodes results in a decreasing number of negatively rated service executions.

SUMMARY

This work proposes a trust management framework especially designed for usage in mobile service environments. Due to the lack of centrally available instances to support trust computations at each node, the principles of observation-based trust and reputation systems are used.

The "observer" concept that allows for the automatic rating of services was introduced. Observers are responsible for detecting misbehavior or inaccuracy in service executions and for rating them according to user preferences. Observers can also be responsible for determining the risk of interactions. Thus, observers can propose whether or not to use a service. Alternatively, allowing or denying an incoming service request is also possible. If no responsible observers are available locally, remote nodes can be queried for their assessments.

If the framework is queried for trust assessments about an unknown node, it actively tries to collect information from remote nodes. The subjectivity of trust assessments is dealt with by the distinction between the node's own observations and information received from other nodes. Thus, the node mainly trusts its own information.

Observations can be disseminated to trusted nodes to get a more accurate and complete world view. The disseminated data contains the measured service properties about an interaction as well as, a satisfaction degree in terms of the interaction. Distribution of measured values instead of final ratings allows services own assessments about a node's behavior. Since a service may change its behavior from positive to negative, an aging mechanism is proposed that gives a higher weight

to more recent information. Thus, nodes can react quickly to bad behavior.

To evaluate the proposed framework a simulation environment was implemented. It was shown that the proposed trust management framework can reduce interactions with poorly rated services. Furthermore, its use in mobile environments and the influence of dynamically behaving nodes was evaluated.

FUTURE WORK

This section proposes three mechanisms that may help to reduce bandwidth and CPU resource consumption and to increase the response times of the concepts proposed.

To prevent the framework - and especially the OMS - from re-querying remote nodes with equal requests in relatively short time intervals, a request hash code may be created and mapped to the received results. The hash code/result mapping can be used for future OMS requests instead of re-querying remote nodes yet again. This means savings in bandwidth and battery power without any lose of accuracy. Moreover, the response time of the OMS mechanism is also decreased. Mapping may be valid until a predefined timeout threshold is reached.

The framework may also store nodes that were able to fulfill requests for specific service types by providing answers - making it possible to use the services of these nodes before other nodes because they are known to have capability for specific service types. This saves resources and prevents unnecessary transmissions.

An observer immigration system feature is another possible extension to the OMS. This mechanism may be responsible for downloading observers that are currently unavailable on a node itself and that are often used remotely. Thus, the system may check the number of re-querying remote nodes. If a predefined threshold is exceeded, remote nodes that have provided results are requested for downloading suitable observers, avoiding bandwidth consumption for the service type in question, .

To increase the framework's response time a trust cache may be used. This cache may contain trust assessments about a set of nodes, i.e., about each node that has corresponding representations within the fuzzy model or nodes that are often used for their functionalities. Recalculations about a node can automatically be initiated every time new information about this node is received and the received information is assessed as useful and added to the fuzzy model.

Open Issues

The evaluation has shown that the general requirements, as presented in the introduction, can indeed be realized. Even so, some of the aspects introduced still need consideration.

Since it may be possible to misuse remote evaluation concepts, the effects of false recommendations should be analyzed. For example, it should not be allowed that the requesting node itself determines the risk of an incoming service request by using remote risk assessments.

The evaluation has shown that the dissemination mechanism creates a linearly increasing number of exchanged messages. Strategies to reduce the resource consumption of the dissemination mechanism should be developed to deal with possible resource restrictions in mobile networks.

The performed simulations are not concerned with the cooperation of badly behaving nodes. It may well be possible that numerous nodes are cooperating and distributing false ratings about another node. The behavior of the framework when under such attacks must be analyzed. It may be necessary to change the weighting method used from the general trust assessment about a node to a similarity method that takes account of the dif-

ferent trust assessments of a report provider and a report receiver about a third node. Liu and Xiong (Liu & Xiong, 2002) provide a model for this.

The simulations have shown that the framework can indeed rapidly react to the changing behavior of nodes. For the detection of misbehaving nodes this is certainly of great advantage. However, since a node may build and milk its reputation, the creation of good reputation needs more appropriate strategies to make bad behavior less alluring.

REFERENCES

Artz, D., & Gil, Y. (2007). A Survey of Trust in Computer Science and the Semantic Web. In *Web Semantics: Science, Services and Agents on the World Wide Web*. Retrieved November, 2008, from http://www.isi.edu/~gil/papers/jws-trust-07.pdf

Bansal, S., & Baker, M. (2003). *Observation-based cooperation enforcement in ad hoc networks*. Retrieved October 2008, from http://arxiv.org/pdf/cs.NI/0307012

Buchegger, S., & Le Boudec, J.-Y. (2002). Performance Analysis of the CONFIDANT Protocol: Cooperation Of Nodes – Fairness In Dynamic Ad-hoc Networks. In *Proceedings of the IEEE/ACM Symposium on Mobile Ad Hoc Networking and Computing (MobiHOC)*, Lausanne, CH.

Chen, R., & Yeager, W. (2001). *Poblano – A Distributed Trust Model for Peer to Peer Networks*. *Sun Microsystems*. Retrieved May, 2008, from http://gnunet.org/papers/jxtatrust.pdf

Connected Device Configuration (CDC). *Sun Microsystems*. (n.d.). Retrieved August 2008, from http://java.sun.com/javame/technology/cdc/index.jsp

Fielding, R. T. (2000). *Architectural Styles and the Design of Network based Software Architectures*. Retrieved July 2008, from http://www. ics.uci.edu/~fielding/pubs/dissertation/fielding_dissertation_2up.pdf orrest, S., Hofmeyr, S., Somaya, A., & Longstaff, T. (1996) A sense of for self UNIX processes. In *Proceedings of the 1996 Symposium on Security and Privacy*.

Gambetta, D. (1988). *Can We Trust Trust?* Oxford, UK: Basil Blackwell.

Jacob, C., Pfeffer, H., Zhang, L., & Steglich, S. (2008). *Establishing service communities in Peer-to-Peer Networks*. Paper presented at the 1st IEEE Internation Peer-to-Peer for Handheld Devices Workshop CCNC 2008, Las Vegas, NV, USA.

Josang, A., Hird, S., & Faccer, E. (2003). Simulating the effect of reputation systems on e-markets. In *Proceedings of the Trust Management: First Internationl Conference, iTrust 2003* (LNCS 2692, pp. 179-194). Retrieved May, 2008, from http://sky.fit.qut.edu.au/~josang/papers/JHF2003-iTrust.pdf

Kamvar, S. D., Schlosser, M. T., & Garcia-Molina, H. (2003). The EigenTrust Algorithm for Reputation Management in P2P Networks. In *Proceedings of the 12th International conference on World Wide Web*.

Kumar, S., & Spafford, E. H. (1994). A Pattern Matching Model for Misuse Intrusion Detection In *Proceedings of the 7th Nation Computer Security Conference*, Baltimore, Maryland (pp. 11-21).

Liu, L., & Xiong, L. (2002). Building Trust in Decentralized Peer to Peer Electronic Communities. In *Proceedings of the fifth International Conference on Electronic Commerce Research*.

Maresch, O. M. (2005). *Reputationsbasierte Trust Metriken im Kontext des Semantik Web*. Unpublished diploma thesis, Technische Universität Berlin, Germany.

Michiardi, P., & Molva, R. (2002). *Core: A COllaborative REputation mechanism to enforce node cooperation in Mobile Ad Hoc Networks*. Paper presented at the IFIP-Communication and Multimedia Securtiy Conference 2002.

Microsystems, S. (n.d.). *JAVA*. Retrieved August 2008, from http://java.sun.com/

Mui, L., Mohatashemi, M., & Halberstadt, A. (2002). A computational model of trust and reputation. In *proceedings of the 35th International Conference on System Science* (pp. 280-287).

Pfeffer, H., Krüssel, S., & Steglich, S. (2008). *A Fuzzy Logic based Model for Representing and Evaluating Service Composition Properties*. Paper presented at the International Conference on Advances in Human-oriented and Personalized Mechanisms, Technologies, and Services (I-CENTRIC 2008), Sliema, Malta.

Resnick, P., Zeckhause, R., Friedman, E., & Kuwabara, K. (2000). Reputation Systems. *Communications of the ACM, 43*, 45-48. Retrieved May 2008, from http://portal.acm.org/citation.cfm?id=355122&coll=portal&dl=ACM&CFID=27694799&CFTOKEN=36804746

RESTAC. *a Java REST framework for Rest-style interactions*. (n.d.). Retrieved August 2008, from https://developer.berlios.de/projects/restac/

Ruohomaa, S., & Kutvonen, L. (2005). Trust Management Survey. In P. Herrmann, et al. (Eds.), *Proceedings of the iTrust 2005* (pp. 77-92). Berlin, Germany: Springer.

Shafer, G. (1976). *A Mathematical Theory of Evidence*. Princeton, NJ: Princeton University Press.

Teng, H. S., Chen, K., & Lu, S. C. Y. (1990). Adaptive real-time anomaly detection using inductively generated sequential patterns. In *Proceedings of the 1990 IEEE Symposium on Research in Security and Privacy* (pp. 278-284). Washington, DC: IEEE Computer Society.

Yu, B., & Singh, M. P. (2002). An Evidential Model of Distributed Reputation Management. In *Proceedings of the first International Joint Conference on Autonomous Agents and Multiagent Systems*.

ENDNOTE

[1] JXTA is a project initiated by Sun Microsystems that standardizes peer-to-peer applications. JXTA provides specifications for protocols that cover all functionalities needed for the realization of interoperability in peer-to-peer applications.

Chapter 14
Risk–Based Trust Management for E–Commerce

Soon-Keow Chong
Deakin University, Australia

Jemal H. Abawajy
Deakin University, Australia

ABSTRACT

Electronic commerce (e-commerce) offers enormous opportunities for online trading while at the same time presenting potential risks. Although various mechanisms have been developed to elevate trust in e-commerce, research shows that shoppers continue to be skeptical about buying online and lack of trust is often cited as the main reason for it. Thus, enhancing success in e-commerce requires eliminating or reducing the risks. In this chapter, we present a multi-attribute trust management model that incorporates trust, transaction costs and product warranties. The new trust management system enables potential buyers to determine the risk level of a product before committing to proceed with the transaction. This is useful to online buyers as it allows them to be aware of the risk level and subsequently take the appropriate actions to minimize potential risks before engaging in risky businesses. Results of various simulation experiments show that the proposed multi-attribute trust management system can be highly effective in identifying risky transaction in electronic market places.

INTRODUCTION

E-commerce is a relatively new form of trading and it is now a major strategic issue for many organizations. It has grown at a rapid pace over the last few years and has changed the way in which trading parties transact and businesses conducted. E-commerce has brought about a new set of opportunities and

challenges to businesses. E-commerce has the capability of providing continuous service by offering access to information around the clock and globe in multiple languages. Theoretically, both consumers and businesses stand to benefit from e-commerce. For businesses, e-commerce enables them to target a wider variety of consumers as well as easily and cost effectively reaches a worldwide market. By enabling businesses to expand their customer base internationally, e-commerce opens markets and

DOI: 10.4018/978-1-61520-682-7.ch014

potential customers that were once inaccessible to businesses. As it permits the instant establishment of virtual branches anywhere, it removes the need for physical presence at every location where the business wants to conduct sales as such saving the businesses on the lease of expensive retail space and outfit stores. Also, it allows direct and immediate overseas market entry thus eroding the competitive advantages of scale economies while improving business competitiveness locally, nationally and internationally.

The consumers gain greater choice amongst a wider and more diverse range of products and services thus making them to no longer be restricted to what are available in their local store. E-commerce gives the consumers the ability to browse and purchase from many different service providers at competitive prices and greater value, making it easier to find exactly what they are looking for. However, for the on-line consumer, e-commerce has many characteristics which make it different from shop-front purchases. In an in-store purchase scenario, consumers generally carry their product with them, knowing what they have purchased, the size and texture all previewed to check the contents. This is usually not possible with an e-commerce purchase where the customer must wait until delivery to ascertain exactly what they have purchased and if it meets their expectations of quality and specifications.

On the negative side, e-commerce has also opened up more opportunities for unlawful activities. The open and anonymous nature of an e-commerce makes it an ideal medium for malicious activities. As a result, e-commerce is fraught with a whole new type of fraud, deception, theft and extortion. In addition to the illicit activities, factors such as the increased uncertainty about the identity and address of the retailer, inability to inspect goods prior to purchase, the requirements to pay in advance of receipt of goods have elevated uncertainty about the performance of the product. These factors have generally reduced

consumer confidence that made establishing trust between retailers and consumers difficult (Cho, Cheon & Kang, 2006; eMarketer, 2007). As a result, it has hindered the uptake of electronic commerce and retarded e-commerce from reaching its full potential (Cho et al., 2006; Greenleaf & Lehmann, 1995).

The promises of the e-commerce are currently being constrained by their risks, be they real or perceived. Research shows that if for some reason the perceived risk (potential loss of resources) in a transaction is too high, consumers are likely to delay the transaction until some form of institutional mechanism is in place to reduce the associated risks. This explains the fact that also millions of consumers browse thousands of e-commerce sites daily, the majority of these consumers decide to buy the products or services from their local stores rather than completing the purchase process online (Salam, Iyer, Palvia & Singh, 2005). To mitigate this risk, mechanisms based on trust management systems to increase the confidence of online buyers have been suggested in the literature. We believe that exiting trust management systems are simplistic in a sense that they focus only on a single parameter to compute trust values. This is fine for services that are inexpensive as a buyer might not worry about losing nominal amount of money. Research shows that customers are more comfortable buying small items with greater frequency. There is very little work to make customers more comfortable buying larger ticket items with greater frequency. For example, many buyers are relatively comfortable buying simple services such as booking an event ticket that cost $10. However, a recent report shows that online shoppers are now venturing into expensive product buying online (eMarketer, 2007). For such products, the current trust management systems will not be sufficient and need to be extended. All consumers are generally risk averse, and will always attempt to try to reduce risk during the purchasing process. This is no different when dealing with an e-commerce customer. Therefore there is a need for the retailer to consider and deal with areas that help to reduce risk or perceived risk in the eyes of the consumer.

This chapter discusses a mechanism that help reduce the risk being met by the consumers and assist them in making an informed decision, as much as it is possible, when purchasing less predictable (more risky) products on the e-commerce. Our focus is on augmenting the potential online buyers' decision making process by exposing the potential risk levels of a given transaction to them. To this end, we propose a multi-attribute risk management approach that takes important properties of the product or services as well as the trustworthiness of the service providers to compute the risk levels. To the best of our knowledge, we are the first to merge such product properties with trust value in computing the risk level of a particular product. The advantage of the proposed approach is that it helps consumers identify transaction risks much earlier than using other system such as reputation-based systems.

The rest of the chapter is organized as follows. First an overview of e-commerce along the basic architecture, threats and approaches to counter the threats is discussed. Then a risk- based Trust Management model is proposed and the trust management approach is explained. We quantify three real-life parameters in order to be used efficiently in transaction risk evaluation. We present an experimental evaluation of the effectiveness of the proposed approach in a variety of e-commerce environment scenarios. Results of various simulation experiments show that the proposed multi-attribute trust management system can be highly effective in identifying risky transaction in electronic market places. The areas that warrant further research attention are discussed and finally, conclude with a discussion of the findings and implications.

ELECTRONIC COMMERCE OVERVIEW

With the ever increasing use of the Internet worldwide, e-commerce has become important for businesses to consider. This section presents a high-level e-commerce architecture and outlines the various e-commerce modes of operations. We will also discuss threats to e-commerce and relevant trust models that support users or their agents with different behavioral profiles.

E-Commerce Architecture

Electronic commerce is an emerging and exciting field that requires the integration of Internet, telecommunication, audio/video technologies, computing hardware and software, and business models. E-commerce consists primarily of distributing, buying, selling, marketing, and servicing of products or services over the Internet. It brings many new ways for businesses and consumers to communicate and conduct business on line from anywhere at any time. By offering products and services on-line, businesses can gain unique benefits such as new customers, cost-effective delivery channel, streamlined enrolment and better marketing through better customer knowledge. Similarly, people can interact with businesses at any hour of the day that is convenient to them.

As shown in Figure 1, in its simplest form, e-commerce is composed of buyers, service providers, products and payment processing centre. These components collectively cover most, if not all, phases of e-commerce business transactions such as orders and payments, marketing and distribution. They enable service providers to advertise products and services, and deliver goods and services electronically and provide ongoing customer support. These components also enable buyers to enquire about products and services, place orders, pay for it and receive goods and services online. Service providers have web site that displays and describes to the customers

Figure 1. High level architecture of electronic commerce

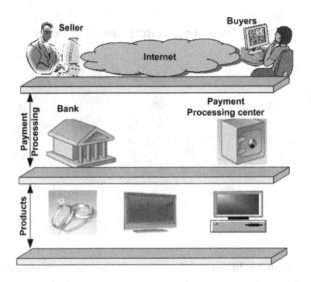

all of the information about the products, prices, manufacturers, product warranties, etc. Buyers browse the catalogue of the merchandise, choose one or more products and pay for the order. The payment processing components enable funds to be transferred electronically to anywhere in the world.

The last decade has witnessed a considerable increase in the use of e-commerce by a wide range of businesses, organizations and institutions globally. As a new business can start trading online for as little as $2000 (Web Transitions Inc, 2004),

there is an explosion of online traders in every sphere of trading. As shown in Figure 2, there is a steady growth in online sales and this trend is expected to grow for the next few years (U.S. Census Bureau, 2007). Online retail in the US reached $175 billion in 2007 and is projected to grow to $335 billion by 2012 (Forrester, 2007).

Risks Associated with E-Commerce

Despite its huge growth, e-commerce has not reached its full potential (Standifer & James, 2003).

Figure 2. Prediction of e-commerce growth

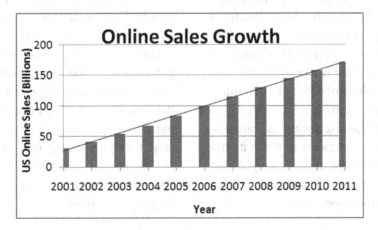

Figure 3. Comparison of yearly dollar loss of referred complaints

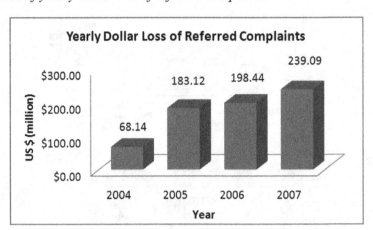

For example, the number of online buyers globally increased only by 9.2% in 2006 compared to an average annual growth rate of 21.3% between 2002 and 2005. The open and anonymous nature of e-commerce presents potential risks to the online buyers. From the customers' prospective, risk becomes an important factor in electronic shopping (Jarvenpaa & Todd, 1996). The risk can be the risk of monetary loss arising from online shopping due to the unreliability of vendors or about whether the purchased goods or services are able to meet customers' expectations (Jarvenpaa & Todd, 1996). There is evidence that consumers consider product perceptions as more important in completing transactions (Jarvenpaa & Todd, 1996).

The consumer's perception of risk associated with the transaction will tend to predominate in customers decision to engage in a transaction (Salam, et. al., 2005). The increasing online fraud is but one factor for eroding online customer confidences in e-commerce. According to the Internet Crime watch, online fraud is increasing and cost online businesses millions of dollars. For example, the total loss to fraud in 2007 was $239.09 million (IC3, 2008) and has been growing as shown in Figure 3. Thus, for e-commerce to reach its full potential, an approach that address the growing erosion of the consumer confidence is needed (Federal Trade Commission, 2000).

There is a high degree of uncertainty in e-commerce as buyers and service providers are geographically separated and anonymous from one another (Benassi. 1999). Although transaction risk is always present in all businesses and e-commerce is no exception, there are many uncertainties that could diminish potential buyers' confidence (Luhmann, 1990). Since e-commerce enables transactions among trading parties who have never transacted before, it changes the business engagement rules on many aspects. Unlike the traditional store environment where payment and delivery can be effected concurrently, many purchases are delivered after payment is made. Also, the lack of face-to-face interaction between the consumers and the traders constitutes a problem for choosing a suitable trading partner. In brick-and-mortar environments, a wide range of informal mechanisms (e.g., meeting face-to-face) and formal institutions (e.g., written contracts and commercial law) have been established to reduce potential risks and thus facilitate trade between the trading partners. Moreover, consumers accept the risks of purchasing because they can see and touch the products and make judgments about the store they purchasing from. Also, often rational but sometimes purely intuitive cues such as appearance, the tone of trading partner voice or body language are used to trust or distrust potential trading partners. Without these cues, it is much more difficult to assess the safety of a business on the Internet.

This suggests that perceived risk is an important ingredient in the consumer decision-making process and often translates into their reluctance to engage in online transactions. Customers purchase online because it is convenient, without sales pressure, and saves time (Henderson, Rickwood & Roberts, 1998). However, a substantial number of customers often browse items online but with no intention to buy. Statistics Canada found that 57% of Internet users like to window shop online, while a quarter less are willing to buy online (eMarketer, 2007) and up to 75 percent of online shoppers do not complete the purchases (Vu, Smith & Bennett, 1999). In Australia, it is estimated that almost half of Australian consumers have experience being online, only slightly more than 5% of them are willing to actually complete an online purchase (Love, 2001). These evidences clearly suggest that consumers need to feel a greater degree of trust in e-commerce if e-commerce is ever going to become a mainstream way of conducting Business-to-Consumer (B2C) transactions.

Trust and Reputation Management

E-Commerce, as any other form of commerce, depends on a level of trust to exist between a buyer and a service provider. Trust plays an important role in our daily life and it forms a basic condition for cooperative activities and working relationships (Gambetta, 1990). Moreover, it is critical in forming new organisation relationships (McKnight, Cummings & Chervany, 1988) and it is a central strategic asset for organisations (Mayer, Davis & Schoorman, 1995). It has been shown that, with respect to an e-commerce transaction, the level of trust has an approximate inverse relationship to the degree of risk (Konrad, Fuchs & Bathel, 1999). However, trust is a complex subject encompassing concepts such as honesty, truthfulness, competence and reliability. As a result, trust

has been defined in a broad range of disciplines for different purposes. Mishra (1996) defines trust as the willingness of one party to be vulnerable to another party based on what he/she beliefs. Chopra & Wallace (2003) define trust as an attitude held by an individual and is influenced by the personality of participants. Grandison & Sloman (2000) define the context of a trust relationship as a set of actions which must be evaluated for the trust relationship to apply. Trust is described as the assurance for a long term relationship between business trading partners (Morgan & Hunt, 1994; Shankar, 1994). Also, trust is often described as relevant to risky situations (Padmanabhan, 1997) or as a risk management approach where future interactions are difficult to predict (Balachander, 2001). Thus, trust can mean different things to different people.

One facet of the trust management architecture is focused on the authentication and authorization security mechanisms (Blaze, Feigenbaum, 1998 & Keromytis; Blaze, Feigenbaun & Strauss, 1988; Chu, Feigenbaum, LaMacchia, Resnick & Strauss, 1997). These trust-management systems act as a standard interface for applications, web servers, etc. to ensure only authorised request action should be allowed. Another class of trust management systems and the most widely used mechanisms in e-commerce is the reputation-based systems (Resnick & Zeckhauser, 2002; Jurca & Faltings, 2003). The basic idea behind the reputation-based system is that trading partners rate each other after the conclusion of the transaction and the system aggregates the ratings and makes them available to interested users. It is also intended to make the service providers to be trustworthy to keep their customer base and attract new once. eBay is one of the prominent systems that use reputation-based system in which buyers and service providers rate one another, after successful transactions, based on the service quality or behaviors during transactions. It also allows the trading partners to leave a short comment. eBay makes the cumulative ratings of its members, as well as all individual comments publicly available to every registered user. However, reputation systems suffer from numerous problems such as lack of rating for aggregating trust (Miller, Resnick, & Zeckhauser, 2003) and bias or unfair rating (Resnick & Zeckhauser, 2002). Several approaches such as financial incentive based schemes for eliciting truthful ratings from the trading partners (Miller, et al., 2003; Jurca & Faltings, 2003); detecting ratings that are likely to be unfair (Dellarocas, 2000; Yu & Singh 2003) and a filtering scheme for grouping raters according to the ratings they provided (Chen & Singh, 2001) have been proposed in the literature. Our work differs from the exiting trust management systems in that we attempt to connect risk and trust management systems in an e-market environment. To this end, we proposes a trust model that incorporates both trust value and service information in assessing online transaction risk in order to enhance the mechanism of buying decision. Moreover, this chapter quantifies three real-life parameters in order to be used efficiently in transaction risk evaluation.

Recommender systems help users identify items of interest in an online setting. Recommender system is used in many applications such as travel agents (Lorenzi, 2007). Amazon is a well-known example of a recommender system. recommendation algorithms use customers' interest to generate a list of recommended items to users (Linden, Smith & York, 2003). These recommendations are generally made in two ways. The first method calculates the similarity between items and recommending items related to those in which the user has expressed interest. The second method calculates the similarity between users in the system and recommending items that are liked by similar users. This latter method is also known as collaborative filtering, which is the most widely used technique in recommender system (Breese, 1998; Adomavicius & Tuzhilin, 2005). Our work is unlike the approach taken in the recommender systems in that its goal is not to present a list of good items to users; rather, to

enables potential buyers to determine the risk level of a product before committing to proceed with the transaction. This is useful to online buyers as it allows them to be aware of the risk level and subsequently take the appropriate actions to minimize potential risks before engaging in risky businesses. Results of various simulation experiments show that the proposed multi-attribute trust management system can be highly effective in identifying risky transaction in electronic market places. The work of Manchala (2000) and Jøsang & LoPresti (2004) are closely related to our work. The model of Manchala (2000) uses risk analysis based on a fuzzy logic to measure a risk of a transaction. Jøsang & LoPresti (2004) extended the work of Manchala (2000) model. This model considers an agent's probability of success, transaction's expected gain and buyers risk attitude to determine whether or not to transact with a particular party. However, our work differs from the previous models in various ways. For example, we take into account warranty as an element of risk reduction factor. Our work is also independent of transaction history. As a buyer may make complaint after several months of receiving the goods, transaction history based systems fail to capture such cases. Also, as sellers' behavior is difficult to predict, we think the property of a product to be purchased should be considered in every product or services. To address this shortfall, we propose a new multi-attribute risk technique that can inform potential buyers the risk level associated with a given product. This helps the buyers to make informed decision before proceeding with the purchase of the product.

RISK-BASED TRUST MANAGEMENT MODEL

The sustained growth of the e-commerce will be influenced by factors such as the level of trust that exist between buyers and retailers as well as the quality level of the products relative to the

Figure 4. The proposed risk evaluator

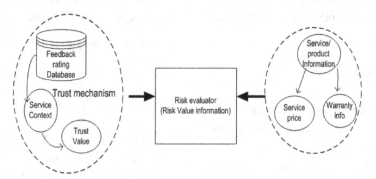

purchase price. In this section, we discuss a multi-attribute risk management system which takes important properties of the product or services such as price, quality and the reliability as well as the trustworthiness of the service providers to compute the risk levels into account.

Highlight of the Framework

Figure 4 shows the basic component of the proposed risk evaluator. We believe that trust, product price and quality are some of the important parameters that should be considered in the design of trust management systems. The purchase of a high ticket items requires a great deal of information as the risks involved in such a purchase are substantial (Jarvenpaa & Todd, 1996). Trust is relevant to risky situations (Gambetta, 1990) and helps deal with uncertainty (Benassi, 1999). As risk is a function of the cost of goods and services (Manchala, 2000), the price of the product generally has direct influence on the level of trust. Although, many people shop on price, but the willingness of a consumer to pay a high price depends on his/her being convinced about the quality of a product (Huang, Liu & Murthy, 2007). Therefore, trust, price and quality of the product are three important and inter-related variables that need to be taken into account in the design and development of a trust management system to help online buyer's concern to make a purchase decision.

In e-commerce, like any business transaction, at least two sources of risk and two types of claims can be associated with a given product. The first risk is that the product does not meet the specified (promised by the service provider) properties, during the specified period of its life. The second risk is that the product does not meet the expectations of the buyer. Precise assessment of these risks is critical for the success in e-commerce. Warranty addresses this kind of risks and helps online transaction to reduce perceived risk (Murthy & Blischke, 2005). According to marketing signal theory, product warranty is a tool that serves as a signal to provide information about the quality and reliability of the product or service (Padmanabhan, 1997). Warranty can also represent how fragile (delicate) or robust a product is. The longer the warranty period indicates the better quality of a product (Huang et al., 2007). Many online retailers sell warranted goods and research suggests that people felt comfortable buying online using e-commerce website if they see product warranty on the website (Lee, 2002). For example, a search of the eBay site using the word warranty returns 16,072 matches. Individual service providers usually list the terms of their warranties, if warranties are on offer, or if they are transferrable from the original buyer to the next owner. Warranties supplied by manufacturers or service providers help to limit risks, the loss will be small when the expectations are not fulfilled since it assure by the warranty (Konrad et al.,

1999). As a result, the warranty of a product is able to create trust even under the overall condition of distrust.

Risk Formulation

In this section, we present our risk formulation. Instead of considering all parameters equally, each parameter is weighted separately so that applications may hand pick different value for each parameter as needed.

Computing Trust Value Risk

In our model, trust value is weighted according to the freshness of the feedback ratings. Trust can be used to measure our confidence that a service provider in an e-commerce environment behaves as expected. However, due to the dynamic nature of trust, the value of trust at the beginning and the end of a time slot will not be the same. We consider the feedback rating received is more accurate if it is relevant to the product of the potential transaction. Therefore, the feedback rating is based on the relevancy and the time difference as Manchala (2000) pointed out transactions conducted during a certain period of time could reflect a change of trust state. The feedback rating of the service provider is grouped into two subsets as relevant and irrelevant. This allows us to select the right subset of ratings for trust evaluation. In other words, we obtain feedback rating from the relevant group for calculating the trust value. However, when no relevant ratings are found, we used the other group of feedback ratings that is not relevant to the service enquired.

In order to determine trust as a prediction of the future behavior, it is possible to specify, that the latest experiences ought to weigh more than older experiences. The rational for this is that the quality of trustees is not necessarily fixed but may change over time, for example due to gathered experience in a certain field. Let r_i be a feedback rating submitted by a buyer (b_n) after a successful transaction with a service provider s_j on a product $p_{s_j}^i$. The cumulative feedback rating for the service provider is computed as follows:

$$F_{p_{s_j}^i}^n = r_i . e^{\dfrac{-\Delta t(r_i)}{\lambda}} \mid F_{p_{s_j}^i}^n \in [0,1] \qquad (1.1)$$

In Eq. 1.1, $\Delta t \mid 0 \leq -\Delta t(r_i) \leq 1$ denotes the difference between the current time and the time when the rating r_i is recorded. The parameter $\lambda \mid 0 \leq \lambda \leq 1$ is the aging factor mainly used to decide how much previous history of the service providers trust level should be taken into the account when calculating the current trust value. For example, a user could decide that a feedback rating obtained 10 weeks earlier to contribute only half the effect of a new rating obtained today. The metric used for the trust measure in our proposed trust model is a real number in the interval of [0, 1]. Complete distrust is represented by 0 whereas 1 corresponds to full trust.

Let $T_{p_{s_j}^i}$ denote the trust value of the service providers in the online market. Thus, $F_{p_{s_j}^i}^n$ is an indication of the weighted rating feedback assigned by buyers who have previously conducted business with the service provider s_j

$$T_{p_{s_j}^i} = \frac{1}{m} . \sum_{n=1}^{m} F_{p_{s_j}^i}^n \qquad (1.2)$$

where m is the total submission of weighted rating and $n \in [1, m]$. Thus, it is clear that the measuring of the trust value $T_{p_{s_j}^i}$ is dependence on the freshness of the feedback ratings which can be adjusted according to the desire of the application.

Thus, the risk $D_{p_{s_j}^i}$ on trust value $T_{p_{s_j}^i}$ of the product $p_{s_j}^i$ is given as follows:

$$D_{p_{s_j}^i} = 1 - T_{p_{s_j}^i} \qquad (1.3)$$

Computing Service Cost

Transaction price is scaled according to the size of the unit cost. As risk is a function of the cost of goods and services (Manchala, 2000), the price of the product generally has direct influence on the level of trust. In general, consumers are more cautious when buying a product at higher price compared to a cheaper product.

Let β_i be the price of a given product $p_{s_j}^i$ sold by a given service provider s_j and α is the scale factor of the product cost. The risk associated with the given product price, $A_{p_{s_j}^i}$ is computed as follows:

$$A_{p_{s_j}^i} = 1 - e^{-\alpha\beta_i} \mid 0 \le -\alpha\beta_i \le 1$$

$$(1.4)$$

Eq. 1.3 allows users to adjust the risk level based on the amount of the product. For example, users can set the risk level to 1.0 when the price of the product exceeds $10K.

Computing Warranty Value

Warranty value is weighted separately according to the length and the type. The willingness of a consumer to pay a high price depends on shoppers being convinced about the quality of a product (Huang, Liu & Murthy, 2007). In general, online shoppers demand assurance that the purchased product will perform satisfactorily over its expected life. As a result, many consumers are known to have a higher tendency to buy a product that comes with a warranty program (Murthy and Blischke, 2006). Warranties may reduce perceived performance risk by providing against product defects and premature malfunction of the product during the time that the warranty is in force. Financial risk may be reduced by a warranty protecting consumer against a large repair bill or having to replace the product during the warrant period. Thus warranties play a vitally important role in providing the assurance to the online buyers. Because online shoppers order goods without being able to handle or test them first, the product warranty offered by retailers is likely to help enhance in buyers trust in respect to the products quality (Bearden and Shimp, 1982).

Let *wl* and *wt* be the warranty length and the type of warranty coverage of a product $p_{s_j}^i$ respectively. The purpose of measuring product warranty is to obtain the appropriate warranty value $w_{p_{s_j}^i}$ which for a given product $p_{s_j}^i$. The risk on product warranty $w_{p_{s_j}^i}$ is measured as

$$w_{p_{s_j}^i} = 1 - wl_{p_{s_j}^i} + wt_{p_{s_j}^i}$$

$$(1.5)$$

Warranty length defines the duration of the warranty period while warranty type is the warranty coverage type: (A) product parts only, (B) product parts and service charge only or (C) parts, service charge and other compensation, such as extended warranty duration, gift voucher, replacement of new product, etc. Different weight of the warranty risk is given according to the different warranty's coverage type, where (A) > (B) > (C).

The information shown in Table 1 is the measurement of the warranty length and warranty type. To simplify the calculation, the percentage obtained in Table 1 is divided by 100. To decide the percentage of the warranty length and warranty type, an average coverage type of a product is taken into account. For instance, when we buy a laptop, the maximum warranty coverage will be three years. According to the Consumer reports (2008), the average warranty coverage of electronics and electrical appliances is approximately three year. Nevertheless, the weighing scale can be adjusted according to the service average life span. Note that we do not take into account extended warranty coverage. In this example, since three years is the average warranty coverage for a laptop, any warranty duration offered that is three years

Table 1. Product warranty and weight

Product	wl	wt	Total Warranty	(Weight)
1	1	C =1	0.865	0.135
2	0.66	C=1	0.810	0.190
3	0.33	C=1	0.736	0.264
4	1	B=0.66	0.810	0.190
5	0.66	B=0.66	0.736	0.264
6	0.33	B=0.66	0.628	0.372
7	1	A=0.33	0.736	0.264
8	0.66	A=0.33	0.628	0.372
9	0.33	A=0.33	0.484	0.516

(36 months) or more will receive the minimum risk value 1/3. Warranty duration of one year will have the maximum risk value of 1, and two year duration but less than three years will have the two third of the maximum rate. Similarly, to obtain the percentage of warranty type, we set C = 1/3, B = 2/3 and A has the maximum risk value of 1. From this explanation, the item 1 have both warranty duration and warranty type as maximum of 1, and weight given to the item indicates a value of 0.135 compared with the item 9 of 0.516 which has the lowest total warranty. The information also shows that an item has maximum warranty duration of 1 and it does not necessarily have a lower risk. From the above information, it is clear that the weight of warranty is depending on both duration and coverage type.

Computing Transaction Risk

The transaction risk is computed based on the trust, product price and warranty parameters. The goal is to produce a risk indication of a product for potential buyers in the present of unknown online e-commerce environment. The overall risk level of a given transaction is computed as follows:

$$R = w_1 D_{p^i_{s_j}} + w_2 w_{p^i_{s_j}} + w_3 A_{p^i_{s_j}} \mid (w_1 + w_2 + w_3 = 1)$$

(1.6)

The highest value of the risk indicates the highest risk of the transaction. The parameters $D_{p^i_{s_j}}$, $w_{p^i_{s_j}}$ and $A_{p^i_{s_j}}$ represent the risk of trust level, the risks to warranty and the price levels respectively. The parameters w_1, w_2 and w_3 are used to scale the risk to trust level, the risks to warranty and the price levels. The purpose of differently weighting $D_{p^i_{s_j}}$, $w_{p^i_{s_j}}$ and $A_{p^i_{s_j}}$ is to have the flexibility and improve risk indication levels when there is no feedback rating for new service providers and when the feedback rating are irrelevant to the product.

PERFORMANCE ANALYSIS

To verify the effectiveness of the proposed trust model, we have carried out analysis of the risk-based trust management system using simulation. We also compared the proposed scheme with the reputation-based systems commonly used in systems such as eBay. In this section, we discuss the simulation setup and the results of the experiments.

We tested the performance of the proposed model with simulations in different e-commerce scenarios. Although it is not possible to exhaust all potential scenarios types, testing the protocol with a variety of scenarios gives an idea on the effectiveness of the proposed trust management system. In the simulation, the risk of trust value, $D_{p_{s_j}^i}$ is generated randomly for each provider in the range of [0, 1]. We used a 100 service providers selling the same product. Among them there are some with high trust value (trustworthy) and some with low trust value (untrustworthy). Participants are randomly chosen for the assessment. Average results of 100 interactions are simulated for assessing the risk value. We carried out several experiments. The first set of the experiments is to study the impact of the three different weighing scales we used. The weighing scale of feedback rating is conducted using different time length and different scale factor in the range of 0.1, 0.5, 0.7 and 1.0. For the service cost, we used $0.1K to $10K. A warranty length of 3 years is set as the maximum with any service that are equal or more than 3 years will have the minimum risk value.

The second set of the experiments is to compare the proposed model with standard reputation-based system. One well-known such system is the rating scheme used by the eBay on-line auction site. Reputation-based systems are used to establish trust in e-market places where transacting parties with no prior knowledge of each other use the feedback from the participants to assess the trustworthiness of the service providers in the e-market place. In particular, we focus

on the stability of both models when the number of untrustworthy service providers increasingly varies in the system. Another experiment is carried out to study cases such as when the service providers are new in the market.

Simulation Result and Discussion

Impact of Weighing Scales

In order to determine trust as a prediction of the future behavior, it is possible to specify, that the latest experiences ought to weigh more than older experiences. The rational for this is that the quality of trustees is not necessarily fixed but may change over time. The parameter $\lambda | 0 \leq \lambda \leq 1$ is the aging factor mainly used to decide how much previous history of the service providers trust level should be taken into the account when calculating the current trust value. For example, a user could decide that a feedback rating obtained 10 weeks earlier to contribute only half the effect of a new rating obtained today. That is the newest rating should have the maximum weight of 1 and any rating of 10 weeks and older should have the weight of 0.5.

Figure 5 shows the impact of the aging factor on the selection of the feedbacks. The aging factor in the interval of [0, 1] determines the ratio of a new experience to previous experiences in the update computation.

Figure 5. Measure of feedback rating over time

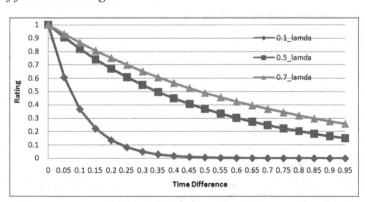

The result demonstrates that the recent feedbacks weigh more than older feedbacks. Proposed time is gives not only higher values to the most recent ratings, it also gives higher values to the higher λ.

Table 2 shows the different weights obtained from the product price when $100K and $10K is set as maximum respectively. In both cases (i.e., $100K and $10K), the product price is set to $5K and the weight is set to 0.05 and 1 respectively. Then the weighted values $A_{p_{s_j}^i}$ of product cost $p_{s_j}^i$

are 0.0488 and 0.632 respectively. We can observe form Figure 6 that when product cost increases the weight of risk is also increases. This shows that the proposed weighting scale is dependent on the size of the product cost.

Comparative Analysis

We compared the proposed model with the standard reputation-based system. In particular,

we focus on the stability of both models when the number of untrustworthy service providers increasingly varies in the system. We created 100 service providers that are in the online market selling the same product. Among them there are some with high trust value (trustworthy) and some with low trust value (untrustworthy). All one hundred of service providers participate on the assign product. Participants are randomly chosen for the assessment.

Figure 7 shows the result of the simulations of the two models. It shows the comparison of both models in terms of the total risk indication when service providers are randomly chosen. The risk indication of our proposed model is rather consistent. The trust - value only model is very sensitive. This is because the trust value only model predicts the future behavior depends on the past behavior of service providers. It totally depends on the trust value of service providers, and did not take into account of the service information when assessing the risk value.

Table 2. Scale of Service Cost

Product	cost β	(1) α	value	(2) α	Value
1	10-99	0.00001	0.0001	0.001	0.01
2	100-499	0.00001	0.001	0.001	0.1
3	500-999	0.00001	0.01	0.001	1
4	1k -4999	0.00001	0.1	0.001	1
5	5k -9999	0.00001	0.5	0.001	1
6	≥ 10k	0.00001	1	0.001	1

Figure 6. Measure of risk value against service cost

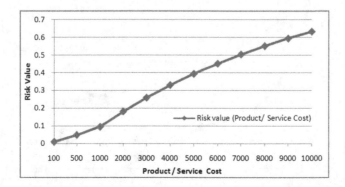

Figure 7. Risk Comparison

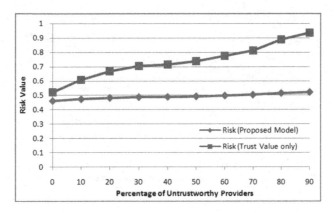

When buying in the open electronics market there are both trustworthy and untrustworthy service providers. Thus, buyers are more likely to conduct business with the service providers with a higher trust value. However, when service providers with high trust level change their behavior, most trust models could not correctly indicates the transaction risk when a potential buyer needs it. For example, a service provider that has been in the e-market business for a while can build up his trustworthiness and at a sometime can decide to cheat. The reputation-based system could not predict the change in the service provider and will indicate to the potential buyers that the risk of the transaction is minimal. On the other hand, the proposed model considers, in addition to the trust value of service providers, product

properties namely the price and warranty as well. Thus, when the trust level of the service providers changes their behavior, the risk indication will not have much influence in the proposed trust management system.

Figures 8, 9, 10, 11, and 12 show the results of experiments when the values of the various parameters varied. The proposed model is able to indicate the risk value of a potential transaction.

Figure 8 shows the results of risk value when trust value is relevant to the potential transaction. However, the value of product cost and the warranty are both set as constant to the highest level of 1. We can see that the risk values computed by both models show an increase when the percentage of malicious or untrustworthy service providers increases. The proposed model however

Figure 8. Risk result when weighted service cost =1, Warranty =1 and trust value = Random

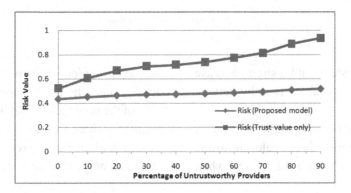

Figure 9. Risk result when weighted service cost=0.1, Warranty =1 and trust value = not relevant

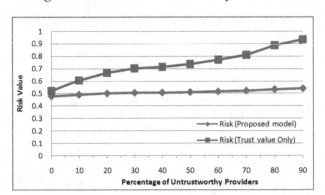

Figure 10. Risk result when weighted service cost =1, Warranty =1 and trust value = not relevant

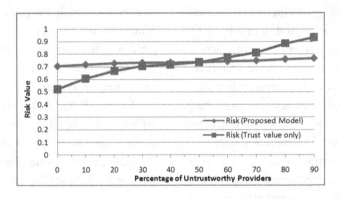

Figure 11. Risk result when weighted service cost=1, Warranty =0.33 and trust value = not relevant

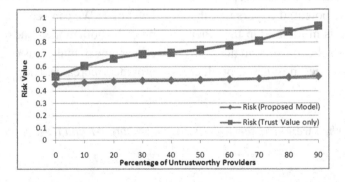

performs fairly consistent with a slight increase as the percentage of the untrustworthy service providers' increases.

Figure 9 to Figure 11 show results when trust value of service providers is not relevant to the potential transaction. Figure 12 shows when service providers are new in the marker with no trust value. The result shows that the risk indication of the proposed model is higher than the trust reputation-based model at the first half of the result. And all the figures also show that when the percentage of untrustworthy service provid-

Figure 12. Risk result when weighted service cost=0.1, Warranty =1 and trust value =0

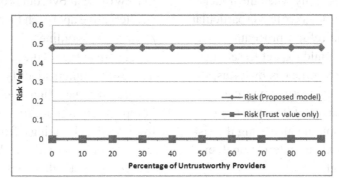

FUTURE RESEARCH DIRECTIONS

ers increases the differences of the resulting risk value of the two models increases as well. This is because of the fact that although trust value is one of the important parameters in transaction risk value assessment, it should not be the only parameter used in transaction risk assessment in online environments. Also, the consistency of the risk values under varying percentage of untrustworthy service providers demonstrates the importance of the product properties (i.e., cost and warranty) when computing the transaction risk values. It also demonstrates the advantage of the proposed model, which shows its ability to produce a risk level even when there is no trust value of service providers such as a new service provider. For example, in reputation-based systems, trust value is accumulated from feedback ratings from buyers who have transaction experience with the service providers. These trust value is used to estimate the risk of buying from the individual service provider. The higher the trust value of a service provider indicates the lower the risk of future transaction. However, when service providers change their behavior, buyers might not have immediate information as the trust values take time to accumulate. This model will enable buyers to use the risk indicator to have immediate result rather than cumulative, and does enhance the accuracy of risk information.

To take advantage of the opportunities of e-commerce and avoid the risks of communicating and transacting business online, every business must address practical problems and questions involving privacy, security, and overall confidence in the underlying features of the system. This constitutes our future work. If e-commerce is to become a mainstream way of conducting online transactions, consumers will necessarily need to feel that they enjoy at least the same degree of protection while conducting business via the Internet as they do at the local store. However, with emergence of e-commerce, a whole new type of fraud, deception, theft and extortion have also emerged. These give rise to issues for consumers, including increased uncertainty about the identity and address of the service provider, the inability to inspect goods prior to purchase, payment in advance of receipt of goods, uncertainty about delivery arrangements, and redress difficulties where purchases are made across borders. Only if there is a healthy balance between the consumer's need for protection and the business' need to be able to conduct business in an effective manner, will e-commerce reach its full potential. Cognitive response research suggests that a consumer may respond to warranty information in several ways. Therefore, another question that we are currently tackling is to find out how consumers process warranty information. Even though online buyers' warranties and refund rights can in some cases apply when the trader is overseas, consumers must realize that in particular cases the warranty and refund procedures may be different and they should expect to see these rights stated. Also, if the trader is overseas, the consumer's chances of getting a warranty or refund will be considerably weakened. Therefore, how to integrate this information in calculating the risk level of warranty at local and international level will be an open problem.

There is also a need for a robust approach against malicious attacks, which are quite common in e-commerce. We also need to study how the proposed model behaves when under malicious attacks such as Sybil attacks. Another area to be addressed is to look other factors such as security of the delivery, location of the merchant, available recourses, payment methods, availability of credit etc as input to the decision-making process.

CONCLUSION

In this chapter, we proposed a risk-based trust management system that helps online shoppers decide whether or not to proceed with a given transaction. Unlike the existing systems that solely depend on a single value to determine the trustworthiness of a product, we proposed a multi-attribute trust management system that takes into account both product properties and the service providers historical trust in computing the risk level of the transaction. The novelty of the system is that it enables potential users identify the risk associated with a given transaction much earlier than using the reputation system. We have studied the effectiveness of the system through simulation and compared it with a standard reputation based systems. The results of the experiment demonstrate that the multiattribute-based system outperforms the tradition reputation-based systems. Furthermore, multiattribute-based system is able to provide risk indication for online buyer when there is no trust value of a new service provider.

In view of the above, our proposed model presents an alternative approach to avoid financial loss on buying goods online.

The advantage of the proposed approach is that it helps consumers identify the risk of transaction much earlier than using other system. For example, in reputation system, trust value is accumulated from feedback ratings from buyers who have transaction experience with the service providers. These trust value is used to estimate the risk of buying from the individual service provider. The higher the trust value of a service provider indicates the lower the risk of future transaction. However, when service providers change their behaviour, buyers might not have immediate information as the trust values take time to accumulate. This model will enable buyers to use the risk indicator to have immediate result rather than cumulative, and does enhance the accuracy of risk information.

REFERENCES

Adomavicius, G., & Tuzhilin, A. (2005). Toward the next generation of recommender system: a survey of the state-of-the-art and possible extensions. *IEEE Transactions on Knowledge and Data Engineering, 17*(6), 734–749. doi:10.1109/TKDE.2005.99

Balachander, S. (2001). Warranty signaling and reputation. *Management Science, 47*(9), 1282–1289. doi:10.1287/mnsc.47.9.1282.9783

Bearden, W. O., & Shimp, T. A. (1982). The use of extrinsic cues to facilitate product adoption. *JMR, Journal of Marketing Research, 19*(5), 229–239. doi:10.2307/3151623

Benassi, P. (1999). TRUSTe: An online privacy seal program. *Communications of the ACM, 42*(2), 56. doi:10.1145/293411.293461

Blaze, M., Feigenbaum, J., & Keromytis, A. D. (1998). *KeyNote: Trust Management for Public-Key Infrastructures*. Paper presented at the inSecurity Protocols International Workshop, Cambridge, UK.

Blaze, M., Feigenbaum, J., & Lacy, J. (1996). Decentralized trust management. In *Proceedings of the 17th Symposium on Security and Privacy* (pp. 164-173). Washington, DC: IEEE Computer Society Press.

Blaze, M., Feigenbaum, J., & Strauss, M. (1998). Compliance Checking in the PolicyMaker Trust Management System. In *Proceedings of the the Financial Cryptography: Second International Conference. Lecture Notes in Computer Science* (pp. 625). Berlin, Germany: Springer.

Breese, J., Heckerman, D., & Kadie, C. (1998). Empirical analysis of predictive algorithms for collaborative filtering. In *Proceedings of the Fourteenth Conference on Uncertainty in Artificial Intelligence* (pp. 43-52). San Francisco: Morgan Kaufmann Publisher.

Chen, M., & Singh, J. (2001). Computing and using reputations for internet ratings. In *EC '01: Proceedings of the 3rd ACM conference on Electronic Commerce* (pp. 154-162). New York: ACM Press.

Cho, C. H., Cheon, H. J., & Kang, J. (2006). Online Shopping Hesitation. *Cyberpsychology & Behavior, 9*(3), 261–274. doi:10.1089/cpb.2006.9.261

Chopra, K., & Wallace, W. (2003). Trust in Electronic Environments. In *Proceedings of the 36th Annual Hawaii International Conference on System Sciences* (pp. 331.1). Washington, DC: IEEE Computer Society.

Chu, Y. H., Feigenbaum, J., LaMacchia, B., Resnick, P., & Strauss, M. (1997). *REFEREE: Trust Management for Web Applications*. Retrieved December 10, 2008, from http://www.farcaster.com/papers/www6-referee/www6-referee.htm

Consumer Reports. (2008). *Why don't you need an extended warranty.* Retrieved August 20, 2008, from http://www.consumerreports.org/cro/money/news/november-2006/why-you-dont-need-an-extended-warranty-11-06/overview/extended-warranty-11-06.htm

Dellarocas, C. (2000). Immunizing online reputation reporting systems against unfair ratings and discriminatory behavior. In *Proceedings of the 2nd ACM conference on Electronic commerce* (pp. 150 - 157).

eMarketer. (2007). *Canada B2C E-Commerce.* Mindbranch. Retrieved December 10, 2008, from http://www.mindbranch.com/Canada-B2C-Commerce-R203-462/

Federal Trade Commission. (2000). *U.S. Implementation of the OECD E-Commerce Guidelines Remarks on TACD 2000 Meeting.* Retreived March 28, 2009, from http://www.ftc.gov/speeches/thompson/thomtacdremarks.shtm

Forrester Research. (2007). *Total Online Sales Expected To Hit $259 Billion In 2007 Washington.* Retrieved January 5, 2009, from http://www.forrester.com/ER/Press/Release/0,1769,1145,00.html

Gambetta, D. (1990). *Can We Trust Trust?* Oxford, UK: Basil Blackwell.

Grandison, T., & Sloman, M. (2000). A Survey of Trust in Internet Applications. *IEEE Communications Survey and Tutorials, 3*(4), 2–16. doi:10.1109/COMST.2000.5340804

Greenleaf, E. A., & Lehmann, D. R. (1995). Reasons for substantial delay in consumer decision making. *The Journal of Consumer Research, 22*, 186–199. doi:10.1086/209444

Henderson, R., Rickwood, D., & Roberts, P. (1998). The beta test of an electronic supermarket. *Interacting with Computers, 10*, 385–399. doi:10.1016/S0953-5438(98)00037-X

Huang, L. H., Zhong, Z. J., & Murthy, D. N. P. (2007). Optimal reliability, warranty and price for new products. *IIE Transactions, 39*(8), 819–827. doi:10.1080/07408170601091907

Ic3. (2008). *Reported Dollar Loss From Internet Crime Reaches All Time High*. Retrieved January 10, 2009, from http://www.ic3.gov/media/annualreport/2007_IC3Report.pdf

Jarvenpaa, S. L., & Todd, P. A. (1996). Consumer reactions to electronic shopping on the World Wide Web. *International Journal of Electronic Commerce, 1*(2), 59–88.

Jøsang, A., & LoPresti, S. (2004). Analysing the Relationship between Risk and Trust. In *Trust Management* (pp. 135-145). Berlin, Germany: Springer.

Jurca, R., & Faltings, B. (2003). An Incentive Compatible Reputation Mechanism. In *Proceedings of the 6th International Workshop on Deception Fraud and Trust in Agent Societies (at AAMAS '03)* (pp. 1026-1027).

Konrad, K., Fuchs, G., & Bathcl, J. (1999). Trust and Electronic Commerce - More than a Technical Problem. In *Proceedings of the 18th Symp. Reliable Distributed Systems. Lausanne, Switzerland.* Retrieved March 3, 2009, from http://ftp.informatik.rwth-aachen.de/dblp/db/conf/srds/srds99.html

Lee, P. M. (2002). Behavioral Model of Online Purchasers in E-Commerce Environment. *Electronic Commerce Research, 2*(1-2), 75–85. doi:10.1023/A:1013340118965

Linden, G., Smith, B., & York, J. (2003). Amazon. Com Recommendations: Item-To-Item Collaborative Filtering. *IEEE Internet Computing, 7*(1), 76–80. doi:10.1109/MIC.2003.1167344

Lorenzi, F. (2007). A multiagent knowledge-based recommender approach with truth maintenance. In *RecSys07: Proceedings of the ACM conference on Recommender systems* (pp. 195-198).

Love, J. (2001). *Comments to the Australian AG's on the proposed Hague Convention on Jurisdiction and Foreign Judgments* (Issues paper 3). Australian Consumers' Association. Retrieved March 3, 2009, from http://lists.essential.org/pipermail/hague-jur-commercial-law/2001-February/000009.html

Luhmann, N. (Ed.). (1990). *Trust: making and breaking cooperative relations*. Oxford, UK: Blackwell.

Manchala, D. W. (2000). E-commerce trust metrics and models. *Journal Internet Computing, 4*(2), 36–44. doi:10.1109/4236.832944

Mayer, R. C., Davis, J. H., & Schoorman, F. D. (1995). An Integrative Model of Organizational Trust. *Academy of Management Review, 20*(3), 709–734. doi:10.2307/258792

McKnight, D. H., Cummings, L. L., & Chervany, N. L. (1988). Initial Trust Formation in New Organizational Relationships. *Academy of Management Review, 23*(3), 472–490.

Miller, N., Resnick, P., & Zeckhauser, R. (2003). *Eliciting Honest Feedback in Electronic Markets in Kennedy School of Government Working paper originally prepared for the SITE '02 workshop.* Retrieved January 5, 2009, from http://ksgnotes1.harvard.edu/Research/wpaper.nsf/46ad8749e613af608525693c0014d6cc/d997a59b1cb907cb85256c39004c241c/$FILE/elicit.pdf

Mishra, A. K. (Ed.). (1996). *Trust in Organizational responses to crisis: The centrality of trust.* Thousand Oaks, CA: Sage Publications.

Morgan, R. M., & Hunt, S. D. (1994). The commitment - trust theory of relationship marketing. *Journal of Marketing, 58*(3), 20–38. doi:10.2307/1252308

Murthy, D. N. P., & Blischke, W. R. (Eds.). (2005). *Warranty Management and Product Manufacture.* London: Springer Verlag.

Padmanabhan, V. (1997). Manufacturers Returns Policies and Retail. *Competition Marketing Science*, *16*(1), 81–94.

Resnick, P., & Zeckhauser, R. (Eds.). (2002). *Trust among strangers in internet transactions: empirical analysis of eBay's reputation system* (Vol. 11).

Salam, A., Iyer, L., Palvia, P., & Singh, R. (2005). Trust in e-commerce. *Communications of the ACM*, *48*(2), 72–77. doi:10.1145/1042091.1042093

Schneider, G. P. (2003). *Electronic Commerce-Fourth Annual Edition*. Boston, MA.

Shankar, G. (1994). Detweminants of long - term orientation in buyer - service provider relationships. *Journal of Marketing*, *58*(1), 1–19. doi:10.2307/1252247

Standifera, R. L., & James, A. W. Jr. (2003). Managing conflict in B2B e-commerce. *Business Horizons*, *46*(2), 65–70. doi:10.1016/S0007-6813(03)00011-9

U.S. Census Bureau. (2007). *Annual Retail Trade Survey–2007*. Retreived December 10, 2008, from http://www.census.gov/svsd/www/artstbl.html

Vu, T., Smith, P., & Bennett, T. (1999). *BizRate.com, NPD Joint Survey Reveals 75 percent of Online Customers are Abandoning Shopping Cart*. Retrieved March 5, 2009, from http://www.highbeam.com/doc/1G1-56901280.html

Web Transitions, Inc. (2004). *Advantages of an e-commerce website*. Virginia: Boons Mill. Retrieved March 5, 2009, from http://www.letme-shop.com/ecommerce-design-info/advantages-of-ecommerce.asp

Yu, B., & Singh, M. P. (2003). Detecting Deception in Reputation Management. In *Proceedings of the Second Int. Joint Conference on Autonomous Agents & Multiagent Systems (AAMAS)*. New York: ACM

Chapter 15
Privacy and Trust Issues in Context–Aware Pervasive Computing:
State–of–the–Art and Future Directions

Pierre E. Abi-Char
Institut Telecom SudParis, France

Abdallah M'hamed
Institut Telecom SudParis, France

Bachar El-Hassan
Lebanese University, Lebanon

Mounir Mokhtari
Institut Telecom SudParis, France

ABSTRACT

The growing evolution of information and communication technology (ICT) systems towards more pervasive and ubiquitous infrastructures contribute significantly to the deployment of services anywhere, at anytime and for anyone. To provide personalized services in such infrastructures, we should consider both user's privacy and security requirements and context-awareness environment. This can be really achieved owing to context awareness systems which allow us to benefit from sensing and mobile technologies to derive more accurate data about the user and his/her location. While the availability of contextual information may introduce new threats against security and privacy, it can also be used to improve dynamic, adaptive and autonomic aspects of security, and user privacy. Moreover, context-aware information offers new opportunities for the establishment of trust relationship among involved entities (e.g., users, devices, and platforms). As context awareness represents new challenges and new opportunities regarding privacy, trust and security of users in pervasive computing environments (PCE), the main purpose of this chapter aims to survey each of the involved issues to understand and address the interdependencies among them.

DOI: 10.4018/978-1-61520-682-7.ch015

INTRODUCTION

Besides *Security, Privacy* and *Trust* in pervasive computing are currently hot issues in digital information technology area. As observed by (Saltzer & Schroeder, 1975), security is used to describe techniques that control who may use or modify private data and context information, privacy is viewed as the ability of an entity to determine whether, when, and to whom information is to be released and finally trust denotes the grounds for confidence that a system will meet its security objectives. Privacy preservation has been identified as an important factor to the success and acceptance of pervasive computing systems. The development of mobile communications technologies and ubiquitous computing paradigm and the convergence of m-healthcare, m-business, m-entertainment and m-education services have raised the urgency of dealing with privacy threats (i.e. personal information, etc.). These threats are caused by the detection of personal sensitive information such as location, preferences, and activities about individuals through sensors or invisible computing devices, gathering collating data and deriving user context, available anywhere and at any time and for anyone. Organizations and service providers collect large amounts of personal information about individuals in order to deliver suitable services to them; this could lead to a conflict between personal information owners (*individuals*) and information collectors (e.g. *service providers*) regarding privacy control. This conflict is mainly caused by the confrontation between service providers, aiming to collect more information about users in order to provide personalized services, and users' requirements of controlling their privacy attributes. In (Cranor, Reagle & Ackerman, 1999) it is mentioned that people dislike automatic transfer of identifiable and personal data, especially when information is spread to other entities beyond their control. Context-aware computing environments may use information provided by many sensors to acquire knowledge about the users' context. These sensors can be invisible to users who consider the act of gathering information about them without being notified as a great threat to their privacy. If the risks of privacy violation when using a context-aware application can not be estimated, users may be unwilling to use such systems. *This is why privacy control is essential to be integrated in the design of any new context-aware computing platform.* However, the quests for authentication, access control, and user privacy protection conflict with each other in many aspects and the problem is highly complex as the context information of users is more of a concern. On one hand, service providers want to authenticate legitimate users and make sure they are accessing their authorized services in a legal way. On the other hand, users want to maintain the necessary privacy without being tracked down for wherever they are and whatever they are doing. Furthermore, new provided services generally depend on the user identity information, context-awareness information and corresponding pre-established and context-aware dynamically evaluated trust relationship to accomplish user privacy and authentication and to conduct access control. The tradeoff between privacy and authentication poses great challenges to security designers. *This is why the conflict between user privacy protection and user authentication process makes security design in Pervasive Computing Environments (PCE) a very challenging task.*

The rest of the chapter is organized as below. We firstly introduce the features, security challenges and requirements of pervasive computing. Then, we give an overview of context-aware computing. Furthermore, the privacy issue is discussed, followed by the trust researches in pervasive computing. In addition, we specify the requirements of achieving authentication in the PCE, especially for supporting context awareness and privacy. Finally we review the related work conducted in this area and conclude the chapter by proposing a number of future directions.

PERVASIVE COMPUTING

Pervasive computing refers to the emerging trend toward *numerous, casually, accessible, often invisible computing devices*, frequently mobile or embedded in the environment, and finally connected to an increasingly ubiquitous network infrastructure composed of a wired core and wireless edges (NIST, 2001). Pervasive computing is expected to enter more and more everyday life in the foreseeable future. It will surround users with a comfortable and convenient information environment that merges physical and computational infrastructures into an integrated environment.

Properties and Features

The pervasive computing environment will feature a proliferation of hundreds or thousands of computing devices and sensors that will provide new functionalities, offer specialized services, enhance management and control, expand usability and efficiency, and improve interaction. Before addressing the challenges associated with security in pervasive computing environments, we list the salient features of pervasive computing, which were observed by (Campbell, Al-Muhtadi, Nadldurg, Sampemane & Mickunas, 2002):

- **Extend Computing Boundaries:** The pervasive computing should be able to transform traditional computing environment into interactive, dynamic, and programmable environment.
- **Invisibility and Non-Intrusiveness:** In pervasive computing, computers should blend in the background allowing people to perform their duties without having machines at the center of their focus.
- **Creating Smart and Sentient Spaces:** The pervasive computing environment should become intelligent enough to understand users' intent and become an integral part of users' everyday life.

- **Context Awareness:** The pervasive computing environment should be able to automatically tailor itself, by capturing and integrating different contexts with users and devices, to meet users' expectations and preferences.
- **Mobility and Adaptability:** The pervasive computing environment should be mobile as its users and should be able to adapt itself to evolve and extend once more resources become available.

The vision of ubiquitous computing bears (among others) an obvious problem: privacy (i.e. the capability to determine what one wants to reveal and how accessible one wants to be (Bellotti, 1997) is under great risk. Ubiquitous or pervasive Computing essentially relies on intensive collection, processing and dissemination of large amounts of data. Much of this data is related to users (e.g., personal information) and can be very sensitive and of great value for other parties. Langheinrich (2001) had identified four key properties of Ubiquitous Computing:

- **Ubiquity:** The infrastructure will be everywhere consequently affecting every aspect of life.
- **Invisibility:** The infrastructure will be cognitively or physically invisible to the user. The users will have no ideas when or where they are using computer.
- **Sensing:** Input to the ever-present invisible computer will be everything we do or say, rather than everything we type.
- **Memory Amplification:** Every aspect of these interactions, no matter how personal, has the potential to be stored, queried and replayed.

The descriptions of these key properties show that the pervasive computing environment is characterized by massive numbers of almost invisible miniature sensing devices that can potentially observe, collect and store personal information.

Requirements

To deal with the new vulnerabilities introduced by pervasive computing, security and privacy guarantees in pervasive computing environments should be specified and drafted early into the design process. Previous efforts in retrofitting security, privacy, authentication, access control, and anonymity into existing systems have proved to be inefficient and ineffective. In the following, we will outline some of security requirements for building security and privacy based infrastructures, which have been addressed in (Campbell, Al-Muhtadi, Nadldurg, Sampemane & Mickunas, 2002):

- **Multilevel:** The design for new security architectures should be able to provide different levels of security services based on system policies, preferences, rules, context information, environmental situations, temporal circumstances, available resources, etc.

- **Context-Awareness:** Traditional security systems are somewhat static and context insensitive. Pervasive computing integrates context information, transforming the computing environment into a sentient space. Security services should make extensive use of context information available. Security policies must be able to change dynamically regarding the environment changes. In addition, there is a need to verify the authenticity and integrity of the context information acquired.

- **Flexibility and customizability:** The security subsystem should be flexible, adaptable, and customizable. It must be able to adapt to environment changes by evolving and providing additional functionality when more or new resources become available.

- **Interoperability:** The security architecture should be able to support multiple security mechanisms and levels (e.g. policy discovery, authentication and access control, etc.) and to negotiate security requirements.

- **Extend Boundaries:** While traditional information security was restricted to the virtual world, security now should incorporate some aspects of the physical world, e.g. preventing intruders from accessing physical spaces. In essence, virtual and physical security becomes interdependent.

- **Scalability:** The security services should be able to scale to the dust of mobile and embedded devices available at some particular instant of time. In addition, the security services need to be able to support huge numbers of users with different roles and privileges, under different situational information.

Security Challenges

Recent research on pervasive computing focuses on building infrastructures for managing smart spaces, connecting new devices, and providing useful applications and services. Privacy, trust, and security issues in such environments, however, have not been explored in depth. Indeed, several researchers (Langheinrich, 2002; Langheinrich, 2001; Stefano, 2002) have admitted that pervasive computing environments are vulnerable to security and privacy threats and that securing pervasive computing (Kagal, Finin & Joshi, 2001; Kagal, Undercoffer & Perich, 2002) presents critical challenges at many levels. Below, we will outline the privacy and security challenges which have been addressed in (Campbell, Al-Muhtadi, Nadldurg, Sampemane & Mickunas, 2002):

- **Privacy Issues:** Increasing active spaces with active sensor and actuators enables the construction of more intelligent capabilities. Unfortunately, these devices could threaten the privacy of users severely because they can be exploited by intruders, malicious insiders, or tracking systems. Thus the privacy aspects have to be considered to protect personal and confidential data of users.

- **Users Interaction Issues:** One of the main characteristics of pervasive applications is a richer user interface for interaction between users and the environment. The access control mechanisms have to be integrated in a way allowing users and devices to use the environment in a manner that facilitates collaboration, while enforcing the appropriate access control policies and preventing the unauthorized users.

- **Security Policies:** Another characteristic of pervasive computing is to have a suitable and convenient method for defining and managing security policies in a dynamic and flexible fashion. Policy management tools provide administrators the ability to specify, implement, and enforce rules to exercise advanced control over the behavior of entities in their systems.

In addition to the security challenges introduced above, and based on deep relevant research (Tentori, Favela, Gonzalez & Rodriguez, 2005; Xiao, Malcolm, Christianson & Zhang, 2007), we argue the necessity to introduce two more security challenges that should be added to the above list and which are:

- **Quality of Privacy:** It is important in pervasive computing to have a flexible and convenient method in order to satisfy the level of Quality of Privacy (QoP). This flexible method should allow balancing the trade-off between the amount of privacy a user is willing to concede and the value of the services that can be provided by the Ubiquitous Computing (UbiComp) application.

- **Trustworthy authentication:** Trustworthy authentication is defined as entity authentication accompanied by an assurance of trustworthy behavior of the authenticated entity. For example, a wireless printer should provide a trustworthy authentication to a user who wishes to use it. Trustworthy means that this printer ensures that no other party has access to the data which it is resident on the printer and that the printer itself will not use the data in a malicious way. Moreover, the concept of trustworthy authentication can be generalized for security devices and servers such as portals, firewalls, and intrusion detection systems (IDS).

CONTEXT-AWARE COMPUTING

Context-Aware computing is an emerging computing paradigm that tries to exploit information about the context of its users to provide new or improved services. (Dey & Abowd, 2000) have defined context as "*any information that can be used to characterize the situation of an entity. An entity is a person, place, or object that is considered relevant to the interaction between a user and an application, including the user and applications themselves*". This definition is widely used in literature today. Nowadays, the increasing interested in using context awareness information (Dey, 2001; Dey & Abowd, 2000; Zimmer, 2004) is turning up to become an important factor for future mobile information systems requiring more advanced mobile context based applications and services. Context information can have a strong impact on application adaptation. Models like ambient intelligence and pervasive computing systems rely on context information in order to personalize services provided to their end users.

Several terminologies and classifications for context-aware computing have been proposed.

Terminology

As observed in (Worna & Gomez, 2005), context information is defined as any kind of information, which can be used to characterize the state of an entity. An entity might be any kind of assets of a computing system such as user, software, hardware, media storage or data (Pfleeger, 1997). Moreover, a Context Information Source (CIS) is defined as any kind of entity which delivers context information. A CIS can be a thermometer, GPS, etc. A context-aware system is defined as a backend system that uses any kind of information before or during service provisioning, including, e.g., service design, implementation, and delivery.

Life-Cycle of Context-Aware Information

Context information provider delivers context information to a context-aware system following the life-cycle process. As it is outlined in (Worna & Gomez, 2005), the main steps in a life cycle are:

- **Discovery of context information:** In this step, a context-aware system discovers available context information providers. The discovery can be performed either in a push or a pull mode (Siljeee & Bosloper, 2004)), i.e. the context-aware system can actively look for CISs or can passively receive information about available CISs.

- **Acquisition of Context Information:** In this step, a context-aware system collects context information from the discovered context information providers and stores it in a context information repository for further reasoning. The process of acquisition is performed either in a pull or a push mode. In pull mode, the context-aware

system explicitly requests for context information whereas in a push mode, context information providers push context information to the context-aware system.

- **Reasoning about context Information:** Reasoning mechanisms enable applications to take the advantage of the available context information. The reasoning can be performed based on a single piece of context information or on a collection of such information.

Context Taxonomy

In general, context information can consist of very different information including, e.g., user's location (Hengartner & Steenkiste, 2004), user's identity, activity pattern, IP address, time, role, etc. In (Chen & Kotz, 2000; Schilit, Adams & Want, 1994; Worna & Gomez, 2005), the main basic categories for context information can be classified as:

- **System Context:** A mobile application has to take into account context information related to both the computing system it is running on, e.g. the particular type of mobile device, and to communications system being used, e.g. the particular type of wireless network. System context deals with any kind of context information related to a computing system, e.g. computer CPU, network, IP address, status of a workflow, wireless network, etc.

- **User Context:** Refers to any kind of context information related to the user and characterizing him. User context information can be user's age, location, medical history, etc. User context can also include context information related to user's tasks, social connections, personal state, and spatial-temporal information.

- **Environmental Context:** Consists of any kind of context information related to the physical environment, which is not covered by system and user context. Environment context information include, e.g., lighting, temperature, weather, etc.

- **Temporal Context:** Defines any kind of context information related to time. Time and day are typical temporal context information.

Reasoning about Uncertain Contexts in Pervasive Computing

In Pervasive computing, context-aware systems can not always identify the current context precisely, so it is crucial that these systems might be integrated with formal decision-making process for handling uncertainty. These systems allow applications and services to reason about uncertainty using new mechanisms such as ontology and fuzzy logic.

Ontology Reasoning in Context-Aware Computing

The term ontology originates from philosophy and refers to the discipline that deals with existence and the things that exist. In computer science, things that exist are those which can be represented by data. Different definitions for ontology in computer science can be found. As an example the definition by (Feruzan, 2007) is given as follow: *"Ontology is a formally defined system of concepts and relations between these concepts. Ontology contains, at least implicitly, rules"*.

Ontology in context is needed in order to deal with a heterogeneous character of context information. Ontology focuses on identifying objects by classifying and characterizing them with properties (Chandrasekaran, Josephson & Benjamins, 1999). Context-awareness is important for pervasive computing environments to adapt computational entities to changing situations such as the users' needs and technical capabilities. The fundament for context-awareness is a formal con-

text model which is needed to represent the context in a way computers can interpret it, and a formal context reasoning which is needed to reason on the context knowledge. Context modeling is the specification of all entities and relations between these entities which are needed to describe the context e.g., information on location, time, current or planned activity, etc. Context reasoning means to automatically deduce further previously implicit facts from explicitly given context information.

A context model is a system of concepts (entities) and relations, which makes ontology a possible mean for context modeling. An ontology is formally defined, which is a precondition for a computer to interpret it, e.g., for reasoning purposes. Rules can be used to implement context reasoning. There are three main areas of application of ontology in context-aware computing (Gruninger & Lee, 2002):

- **Communication and knowledge sharing:** Ontology serves as a common vocabulary of different agents (computational entities and human).
- **Logic interfering / reasoning:** Ontology can be used to deduce implicit knowledge from explicit knowledge by applying rules.
- **Knowledge reuse:** Common ontology (e.g., on time and spatial concepts) can be reused when building domain specific ontology.

Moreover, the real benefit of using ontology for context information in pervasive computing environments will not become effective before there is widely-accepted standard context ontology.

Fuzzy Logic Reasoning in Context-Aware Computing

Fuzzy logic theory is used to express fuzzy information, human's experience, human brain concepts, and cognitive process. It has been widely used in decision field. The use of fuzzy logic helps in supporting reasoning under uncertainty. The concept of fuzzy logic was first introduced by (Zadeh, 1973). Fuzzy logic employs fuzzy sets to deal with imprecise and incomplete phenomena (Bojadziev, 1997). A fuzzy set is defined by a so-called membership function. The study of fuzzy sets differs from the study of the probability theory because fuzzy sets depend on subjectivity in perceiving and representing concepts with member functions and not on randomness as in probability theory and statistics (Konar, 2000). Moreover, trust and risk play a very important role in the field of trusted decision. Risk will evaluate the security of the interaction process between trustor and trustee. Currently, fuzzy logic theory is used to integrate privacy, trust, and risk into trusted decision for providing robust trust models.

However, although people have recognized the importance of security and privacy for their personal information; they remain uncertain when they have to define and enforce their own access control rules or have to handle indirect information. The trust relationships in pervasive computing environments are hard to assess due to the uncertainties involved. If the trust relationship relies on subjective judgment based on indirect information, it will be very uncertain and any operations related to that relationship may cause unexpected results. The theory of fuzzy logic extends ontology's concepts and theories to be a composite which leverages quality and quantity, and which contains certain fuzziness. With the help of fuzzy operations and rules, we can form a formal decision-making process for handling the imprecise nature and uncertainty in trust management, and for modeling trust representation, trust aggregation, and trust evolution.

Trust management provides trust systems designers the flexibility to manage the enforcement of trust policies. According to (Wu & Weaver, 2006), this flexibility could be achieved by applying fuzzy logic which can help handling uncertainty and fuzziness in trust management models. More-

over, fuzzy set theory has been used to improve user-role assignment in role-based access control (RBAC). In (Berrached & Korvin, 2006), authors presented an algorithm for reinforcing access control based on heuristic information about the user, the data being accessed, and the various system components. The model uses fuzzy set theory to access the risks involved in granting the requested services based on uncertain information. (Takabi, Amini & Jalili, 2006) apply fuzzy relations into the RBAC model. Their proposed model extends RBAC with fuzzy parameters to allow imprecise access control policies using the concept of trust and trustworthiness. Authors have used fuzzy set theory for measurement and prediction of trustworthiness. Moreover, (Rehak, Foltyn, Pechoucek & Benda 2005) showed that trust can be represented by using fuzzy numbers to capture the trust value and its uncertainty. They used the fuzzy rule computation and fuzzy control domain to take trusting decision. In (Almenarez, Marin, Diaz & Sanchez, 2006), authors expressed trust relationships by using fuzzy logic. They presented a mathematical and probabilistic trust evolution model to decrease the uncertainty for making decisions in pervasive computing environments.

PRIVACY IN PERVASIVE COMPUTING

This section gives the background information which helps to understand the growing needs of user privacy involved by ubiquitous computing. It presents privacy aspects, privacy laws and technology, and general principles supporting privacy control and management.

Clearly, privacy is a social, ethical and legal issue, beyond technical threats. In order to establish acceptance of Ubiquitous Computing vision, protecting the privacy of users is of central importance. If those privacy concerns are not addressed appropriately, the continuous surveillance through countless sensors may be perceived as a serious downside for those living and working in smart environments like dependant people in a medical center, tourists and visitors in public locations and museums, medical staff moving in their workspace, public users in an airport or public locations, etc.

Privacy Definition

Many definitions have been given for privacy. One of these definitions that seem to cover the most of the aspects of privacy was given by the *British Committee on Privacy and related Matters* (Calcutt, 1990):

The right of the individual to be protected against intrusion into his personal life or affairs, or those of his family, by direct physical means or by publication of information.

Privacy is divided into the following aspects which were identified as new technologies or social changes providing new ways of intrusion (Langheinrich, 2001):

- **Behavioral or Media Privacy:** The right to know whom is gathering information about a user.
- **Territorial Privacy:** This aspect of privacy relates to the right to have one's own place, where nobody can enter without permission.
- **Communication Privacy:** As direct personal communications through the telephone system became more frequently used, the possibility to tap conversations led to privacy concerns.
- **Bodily Privacy:** This form of privacy relates to physical intrusion, and expresses individual's right not to safeguard. One example is medical experiments conducted without permission.
- **Information Privacy:** With the increase of electronically stored data, ease and speed

of access and the possibility of data mining also raised the issue of privacy.

As this last aspect of Privacy is most relevant when dealing with a context-aware system, a definition for privacy has been chosen accordingly (Westin, 1967):

Privacy is the claim of individuals, groups, and institutions to determine for themselves, when, how and what extent information about them is communicated to others.

General Principles and Privacy Requirements

Based on previous work addressed by (Westin, 1967), Langheinrich (2001) has pointed to the *Principles of Fair Information Practices*:

- **Openness and Transparency:** No secret record should be kept.
- **Individual Participation:** The subject of a record should have the privilege to see and correct the record.
- **Collection Limitation:** Record collection should be appropriate for the application.
- **Data quality:** Data record should be accurate and relevant to the purposes for which they are collected and also should be kept up to date.
- **Use Limitation:** Record should only be used for their well specified purpose and only by relevant authorized people.
- **Reasonable Security:** Appropriate security safeguards should be deployed regarding the sensitivity of these records.
- **Accountability:** Record keepers must be accountable.

Privacy-Aware Design Guidelines

This paragraph tries to serve as an introductory reading to give a comprehensive set of guidelines for designing *Privacy-Aware Pervasive Systems*. In order to design a general architecture of a privacy awareness system, we should follow six principles set out earlier for preserving privacy in ubiquitous computing (Langheinrich, 2001). These principles, which are based on the well-known *Fair Information Practices* (OECD, 1980), have been adopted as general rules for the development of privacy enhanced pervasive systems (e.g. *European Disappearing Computer Privacy Design Guidelines*) (Lahlou & Jegou, 2004). In the following, we will outline each of these concepts as observed by (Langheinrich, 2001; Lahlou & Jegou, 2004):

- **Notice:** Given a ubiquitous environment where it is often difficult for data subjects to realize that data collection is actually taking place, we will need not only mechanisms to declare collection practices (i.e., privacy policies), but also efficient ways to communicate these data to the user (i.e., policy announcement).

- **Choice and Consent:** In order to give users a true choice, we need to provide a selection mechanism (i.e., privacy agreements) so that users can indicate which services they prefer. These principles state that a user must not only be informed about data collection, but also be offered a choice whether or not to use a data-collecting service.

- **Anonymity and Pseudonymity:** Data should not be linked to individuals and one should be able to conceal one's true identity with pseudonyms. Moreover, a service provider should not collect more data than absolutely necessary for performing the service a user requests. Thus, wherever possible anonymous data should be gathered if this kind of data does not pose a threat to privacy.

- **Proximity and Locality:** The system should support mechanisms to encode and use locality information for collected data that can enforce access restrictions based on the location of the person wanting to use the data.

- **Access and recourse:** Any new system needs to provide a way for users to access their personal information in a simple way through standardized interfaces (i.e., data access). Users should be informed about the usage of their data once it is stored. Moreover, and in order to gain trust, users must be aware of what information is stored about them. Basically, users should be in control of their own data.

- **Adequate Security:** To achieve confidentiality in information and communication technology, cryptography is classically regarded as the main mechanism used. However, this is a difficult trade-off for simple, small, and low power devices which will not be able to use robust encryption techniques because of limited systems resources, e.g. computational overhead.

TRUST IN PERVASIVE COMPUTING

Trust in pervasive computing is a complex subject relating to belief in the honesty, trustfulness, competence, and reliability of entities and agents participating in the network activities. In the context of pervasive computing, trust is usually specified as a set of relations between a resource or service requester and a resource or service provider. These trust relations are based on previous behaviors of agents and entities. To trust pervasive computing systems, we must be able to manage the privacy, confidentiality, availability, and controlled access to digital information as it flows through the system. Trust forms the basis for allowing a requester to use services or manipulate resources owned by a service provider. Also, it may influence a requester's decision to use a service or resource from a provider. Moreover, the mechanisms required to effectively enforce and deploy trust-based strategies across distributed network are becoming increasingly complex. This complexity arises not only because of the size of distributed users accessing needed services but also because of the fact these trust-based systems should be able to capture security-relevant contextual information, such as time, location, behavioral history, personal characteristics, and capability (e.g. user's intelligent, skills, etc.) at the time access requests are made. These context parameters directly affect the level of trust associated with a user, and hence the decision-making consequence granted to him/her.

Trust Management in Pervasive Computing

Trust management was first introduced by (Blaze, Feigenbaum & Lacy, 1996). With the application of trust management in research for network security, a more general definition is proposed by Grandison (Grandison, 2003): "*Trust Management is the activity of collecting, encoding, analyzing, and presenting evidence relating to competence, honesty, security or dependability with the purpose of making assessments and decision regarding trust relationships.*" Trust management has been introduced in the context of access control (Li & Mitchell, 2003), public key architecture (Caronni, 2000), and peer-to-peer reputation systems (Duma, Shahmehri & Caronni, 2005).

Trust management is a multifunctional control mechanism. We can consider several important key aspects of trust management, including trust establishment, trust negotiation, trust delegation, trust based on reputation, etc. Trust management enables security systems designers to increase the security and privacy of shared resources and collaborative activities without increasing workload. In order to manage a collection of trusted-related activities, flexibility is needed in the enforcement of trust policies. This flexibility could be achieved

by applying fuzzy logic to trust management systems in order to reasoning about uncertain contexts in pervasive network environment.

Trust Establishment in Pervasive Computing

Due to the mobility of pervasive computing environment, trust management and modeling are identified nowadays as one of the important issues. Moreover, pervasive computing applications may need to interact with entities that are not known a priori and therefore can not be trusted. One of the critical trust management processes is trust establishment (Xiu & Liu, 2004). Trust establishment is mainly achieved in the following way (English, Nixon, Terzis, McGettick & Lowe, 2002): the system collects the trust evidence of the clients, defines the trust policies, and builds up the trust level of the clients based on the trust evidence and policies. As more evidence becomes available, the system iteratively updates the trust information including trust evidence and policies. Because there are different application scenarios and trust polices specified by the systems, different kinds of trust evidence are needed. So are different trust strategies for the trust establishment. For trust establishment in the pervasive computing environments, the mobility and uncertainty of the systems and clients need more dynamic and flexible trust strategies. In addition to the traditional trust strategies such as access control and PKI, other trust strategies are proposed and used for trust establishment and management in pervasive computing environments (Xiu & Liu, 2004). These trust strategies are:

* **Trust Negotiation:** Is needed when system does not have the client information and there is no third party to consult with on the trustworthiness of the client. In this case, it is only reasonable and practical for the client and system to build their trust

relationship by disclosing their credentials gradually to meet the access control policies of each other.

- **Trust Delegation:** Is needed when one entity in the system trusts the client and can assign its rights to the clients.

- **Trust Based on Reputation:** Is used when the system can derive the clients' trustworthiness from the client's behavior records. Because the system may need to collect the clients' reputation from other peer systems, the trust level of the network and the peers systems are taken into account when deciding the trust reputation of the clients.

- **Trust Based on Context and Ontology:** Can be used when clients and the systems may have the smart sensing devices. This ontology information can help the system to determine the trust levels of its clients or assign them trust rights in the given context.

- **Securing Dataflow and Information Privacy:** Is used to ensure that the sensitive information is not disclosed and the privacy of the clients is kept.

Privacy in Trust Negotiation

Trust negotiation is a compromising approach for establishing trust in open systems, where sensitive interactions may often occur between entities with no prior knowledge of each other. However, although several efficient and powerful negotiations systems have been developed so far, few of them provide a comprehensive solution to protect privacy during the negotiation process. In particular, few of them support *Privacy Preferences* (P3P) policies, where P3P is the platform for privacy preferences designed to help users express their requirements and preferences in a standard way (Cranor & Wenning, 2002). During trust negotiations credentials play a key role, in that they represent the means to prove parties properties required to establish trust. Moreover,

one of the major concerns users have in adopting negotiation systems is that trust negotiation does not control or safeguard personal information once it has been disclosed. Another potential vulnerability of trust negotiation arises because of the common strategy of postponing actual credential disclosure. Indeed, during the policy evaluation phase, privacy can be compromised in several ways, since there are no guarantees about counterpart honesty until the end of the process. Policy disclosure can be used to determine the value of sensitive attributes without the credential ever being disclosed. Furthermore, during policy exchange it is not to determine whether a party is a legitimate party or not until the credentials are actually disclosed. According to (Squicciarini, Bertino, Ferrari & Ray, 2006), trust negotiations systems allow different subjects to securely exchange protected resources and services. This process is achieved by first establishing trust through a bilateral, iterative process of requesting and disclosing user attributes and policies. Attributes are exchanged through the disclosure of digital credentials. Digital credentials can collect several attributes which can be used to verify identification information. The second key issue of any trust negotiation system is represented by disclosure policies, protecting sensitive resources, credentials, and even other policies from unauthorized accesses. However, trust negotiation systems may represent a threat to privacy in that credentials, exchanged during negotiations, often contain sensitive personal information that may need to be selectively released. In addition, users may need to minimize the released information, thus enforcing the need to know principle in disclosing relevant credentials to other parties.

AUTHENTICATION IN PERVASIVE COMPUTING

Pervasive Computing Environments, (PCE), change constantly by sensing and processing information about users and their environments. This environment is considered intelligent, since it is equipped with sensory means to be aware of changes in the environment. An intelligent environment is also referred to as a smart space in the computer literature. In this environment, user authentication should be an integral part of security of the whole system. In PCE, user authentication may include context authentication in addition to the entity authentication. The concept of context authentication and access control is to collect and recognize the user's current situation and to generate and control a secure user environment based on the current context. In such an environment, protecting the privacy of users is no longer optional, and it must be integrated within authentication service. Additionally, conventional authentication systems usually operate on a fixed set of rules and do not have to track and respond to changes in the environment. Therefore, the conventional authentication schemes are incompetent in satisfying the needs in a context-aware environment that is composed of heterogeneous parts and systems.

Authentication Requirements

Most traditional authentication methods either do not scale well in massively distributed environments, with hundreds or thousands of embedded devices like smart spaces, or they are inconvenient for users roaming around within smart environments. In addition, authentication in smart environments can not use a one-size-fits-all approach, as authentication requirements differ greatly among different spaces and different applications and contexts within the same smart space. In general, users must be able to authenticate with other entities with a varied level of confidence, in a transparent, convenient, and private manner. Therefore, any proposed privacy preserving authentication framework must satisfy the following requirements (Ren & Lou, 2007; Ren, Lou, Kim & Dang, 2006):

- **Identity Anonymity:** The identity of the users should be transparent to an Authentication System (AS) whenever an authentication procedure is processed. This can prevent the ASs from mapping a user's identity with its location.
- **Mutual Authentication:** During an authentication process, a mutual authentication process is required and needed. On one hand, a user is required to be authenticated as a legal and legitimate user. On the other hand, the user needs to authenticate the pervasive environment through the AS.
- **Context Privacy:** Neither the service nor other users of the services should be able to learn the exact context information (e.g., location, duration, type of service request, etc.) of the user, unless the user decides to disclose such information. Users' context information should be protected against both outsiders and services providers they interact with.
- **Confidentiality and Integrity:** During the authentication process, users should be ensured that their transactions cannot be read by unauthorized parties, and the authenticator should be able to detect any intentional or unintentional changes to data that occur in transit.
- **Fast Authentication:** The authentication latency must be very short; otherwise, the long authentication delay will disrupt the continuity of the current session or connection.
- **Non-Linkability:** The moving route of a particular user should be protected, even if the identities are hidden. The AS should not be able to figure out the relationship between the user and the pervasive environment whenever the authentication mechanism is processed.

Designing Privacy-Based Context-Aware Authentication Systems

An inherent tension exists between authentication and privacy because the act of authentication often involves some disclosure or confirmation of personal information. System designers sometimes fail to consider the myriad impact that authentication affects privacy. When designing an authentication system, selecting one for use, or developing policies for one, we should authenticate only for necessary (well-defined purposes), minimize the scope of the data collected, articulate what entities will have access to the collected data, articulate what kinds of access to and use of the data will be allowed, and finally provide means for individuals to check on and correct any information held about them for use in authentication. Context-aware services should be able to trust context data provided to them from these various sources and to respond to changes.

The dynamic nature of a context-aware environment necessitates the need for a very active and flexible authentication mechanism that allows members across different domains to identify and communicate with each other with a reasonable level of trust. More generally, systems architects' developers should focus more on reconciling authentication and privacy goals when designing, developing, and deploying systems. Understanding security needs and developing appropriate threat models are keys for determining whether and what authentication are necessary and what kind is needed. According to (Malek, Miri & Karmouch, 2008) the context-aware authentication service has to hold the following distinguishing properties:

- **Context-Awareness:** A context-aware service has to use context data to provide relevant services to users. The security system adapts itself to match with the dynamism of context information. It also has to be able to prune its services accordingly to

changes in context data, such as changes in time, location, activity, etc. Therefore, it is critical to check the authenticity and integrity of the context data from context-providers.

- **Autonomy:** The context-aware service should involve the last human intervention possible. The security may improvise new policies based on the available or new context data.

- **Scalability:** The authentication service has to be capable of bootstrapping trust and authentication across heterogeneous domains.

- **Flexibility:** In an open, massively distributed, pervasive computing system, using different means of authentication should be made possible, and it does not have to be constrained to a specific format. Therefore, the system has to be able to provide a great level of customization to each individual.

- **Privacy-Preserving:** In a context-aware environment, there will be thousands of sensors recording every type of important information about users. They will silently track user's location, preferences, and activities in the environment. Therefore, protecting privacy of the user is important, and there has to be a provision to protect it against abuse.

RELATED WORK

Recently, many papers have been published to address mechanisms designed against security, privacy threats, and trust in pervasive computing environments. However, most of these designs fall in the scope of establishing a general security framework identifying general security and privacy requirements. Some of these efforts focused on designing security infrastructures to protect users' personal information such as Mix-Network architecture, Mist system, Aware Home Architecture, Solar, etc. Others focused on designing identity management approach. Some efforts focused on providing privacy control through integrating privacy preferences (P3P), policies and context-aware systems. Various trust management strategies including, trust negotiations and trust establishments, have been proposed to prevent unauthorized disclosure of any relevant information that can be used for inferring sensitive credentials. This section discusses these diverse studies, approaches and architectures.

Security Infrastructure

Mist (is an infrastructure that preserves privacy in ubiquitous environments Al-Muhtadi, Campbell, Kapadia, Mickunas & Yi, 2002). Mist facilitates the separation of location from identity. This allows authorized entities to access services while at the same time preventing the disclosure of their location privacy. Mist's operation is based on Mist routers and Mist circuits. As drawback, Mist has an architectural limitation as it has a limited application area and therefore can not address all privacy issues. In addition, Mist is not a context-aware system and do not deal with user preferences and policies. In all context-aware systems, context information is only handled if the user gives its consent to the system and the user is able to define whether his personal information may flow to third-parties or not by using privacy preferences.

The Aware Home System is integrated into a house with a rich computation and communication infrastructure (Covington, Long, Srinivasan, Dey, Ahamad & Abowd, 2001). The system allows users to control and manage resources in the house from a variety of location. The system takes a privacy approach towards access control by using Role Based Access Control (RBAC). The Aware Home System provides means to define who can access what types of information or services at specific times. As drawback, the system does not deal with other services than the one inside the house and thus have limited application scope. In

addition, the system has no means to protect the kind of information that is given to application. Information needed to active services is more privacy-sensitive than the others that are protected by the system itself. Moreover, the system does not give consent to users.

Solar is a middleware that supports the collection, processing and dissemination of context information for context-aware applications (Minami & Kotz, 2002). To preserve privacy in Solar, an Access Control list (ACL) is combined with different roles. The system combines access restriction with policy preference. As drawback, the third parties and services providers are contacted directly without looking at the privacy preference of the user which could cause a security threat regarding user's privacy.

Privacy Related Researches

The Privacy Preferences (P3P) helps web sites announce their privacy practices while letting users automate their acceptance or rejection decision (Cranor & Wenning, 2002). P3P specifies an architecture comprising user agents, privacy reference files and privacy policies. Although P3P provides a technical mechanism for helping inform Web site visitors about privacy policies before they release personal information, it does not provide a mechanism for ensuring that sites act according to their policies. However, P3P was designed for static environment such as Internet where users' privacy preferences are not expected to change. Several existing projects and architectures have extended P3P research with providing security services in context-aware environments. Langheinrich (2002) proposed a privacy-awareness system for ubiquitous environments (pawS) that uses P3P for privacy policy description. Langheinrich expresses the need to extend P3P with the capability to describe contextual information. APPEL (A P3P Preference Exchange Language) is proposed as the language for expressing user preferences. PawS aims to allow data collector to announce and implement adequate privacy policies, as well as to provide users with the capability to be aware of how their personal data are processed. As drawback, the system does not propose solutions that support anonymity and pseudonymity. Therefore, although pawS does not offer a high level of anonymity by itself, its effectiveness, regarding the level of anonymity, is proportional to the level offered by the underlying infrastructure solutions adopted by it. Jiang & Landay (2002) proposed a privacy control system based on defining information spaces. Zuidweg (2003) developed a privacy control architecture based on P3P. The architecture aims at providing privacy control for a context-aware application platform developed in the Web Architectures for Services Platforms (WASP) project. Another context-aware system using P3P was proposed by (Myles, Friday & Davies, 2003). The system focuses on requests for location information of users initiated by services providers. The system uses a modified version of P3P in order to not specify the gathered data in the privacy policy.

(Hong & Landay, 2004) proposed Confab architecture for privacy-sensitive UbiComp. They assume that a user is in control of his context data by devising an infrastructure that captures, stores, and processes personal information on the user's devices. In case a user decides to disseminate personal data, e.g., his location determined by his GPS system, to a third party, he specifies his privacy preferences and attached them as metadata. Moreover, Confab implements a social component of privacy protection, i.e. users are able to provide white lies (Requested data unknown), to hide their real privacy preferences. Hong and Landay called this ability plausible deniability. As a severe drawback, the Confab architecture does not address the cases, in which context is acquired by external sensors. This underlying assumption does not hold for the vision of smart UbiComp environments.

Hull et al. (2004) proposed another privacy preferences mechanism based control system. It is based mainly on users self-provisioning of preferences and rules. In this approach, users are assumed to be heavily involved which represents a challenge when considered for a context aware mobile environment due to the time strictness and complexity of manually managing preferences. Kapadia et al. (2007) described the concept of virtual walls, i.e. usable policy abstractions. Like a physical wall controls physical access, a virtual wall controls access to acquired sensor data. Users are enabled to setup their privacy preferences using three predefined levels of configuration, namely transparent, translucent and opaque. As a severe drawback the translucent level, which allows some private data to be accessed from outside, preferably chosen in most cases, does certainly need adjustment to personal demands.

Privacy-Enhanced Identity Management Systems

Jendricke, Kreutzer & Zugenmaier (2002) introduced an identity management system for PCE where users are issued multiples identities, and the user uses them depending on applications. The paper presents a general framework of using multiple identities to protect users when performing access control and authentication, but did not give any concrete solutions. (He, Wu & Khosla, 2004) proposed a simple anonymous ID mechanism for pervasive computing. As drawbacks, the scheme cannot prevent double spending problem and the scheme does not provide differentiated services access control. In addition, the scheme does not achieve Non-Linkability feature. Moreover, (Ren & Lou, 2005; Ren, Lou, Kim & Deng, 2006; Kim, 2007) proposed novel schemes which can satisfy the requirements for PCE. These schemes provide differentiated services access control, mutual authentication, and Non-Linkability. As a drawback, these schemes do not provide service discovery mechanism which is nowadays an essential element to access network services.

Trust Researches

Herzberg, Mass & Michaeli (2000) developed a system for establishing trust between entities based on a trust Policy Language with XML syntax to map these entities to predefined business roles. English et al. (2002) described the dynamic aspects for the dynamic trusts models in pervasive computing and provided ideas for trust management processes including trust formation, trust evolution and trust exploitation. Kagal, Finin & Joshi (2001) and Kagal, Undercoffer, Perich, Joshi & Finin (2002) proposed a distributed trust model based on trust delegation in which access rights can be assigned dynamically through delegations. His model also uses ontology to help specify the access rights for users. Yu (2003) defined the concepts for trust negotiations, strategies and protocols, and proposed a couple of strategies for automated trust negotiation between two unknown entities. Winsborough & Li (2002) and Li, Winsborough & Mitchell (2003) provided trust negotiation models that focus on trust negotiation concepts, strategies and their mathematical interpretation. In trust negotiation, establishment, and management systems, Xiu & Liu (2004) proposed a formal dynamic trust model for providing a comprehensive solution to solve the trust establishment problems in PCE. Their trust model is a distributed model and works by incorporating different trust strategies in one system. Each trust strategy is implemented by a trust application. When a client requests to access a resource, the trust model determines the trust application modules based on trust policies for the resource.

Seigneur & Jensen (2004) argued an inherent conflict between trust and privacy because both depend on knowledge about an entity. The more knowledge a first entity knows about a second entity, the more accurate should be the trustworthiness assessment; the more knowledge is know about this second entity, the less privacy is left to this entity. This conflict needs to be addressed because both trust and privacy are essential ele-

ments for a smart environment. They proposed a solution to achieve the right trade-off between trust and privacy by ensuring minimal trade of privacy for the required trust. They proposed a model for privacy/trust trade based on linkability of pieces of evidence. They proposed to use pseudonymity as a level of indirection, which allows the formation of trust without exposing the real-world identity. They introduced the liseng algorithm to ensure that the minimal linkability principle is taken into account.

A formal framework for trust negotiations has been proposed by (Winsborough & Li, 2004). The authors provided an approach for safe enforcement of policies that focus on credentials exchange. A formal notion of safety in automated trust negotiations is given which is based on the possibility by third parties of inferring information on negotiation parties' profiles. However, the framework does not support the development of credentials and policy language based on ontology. (Bertino, Ferrari & Squicciarini, 2004a) presented a system for trust negotiation specifically designed for preserving privacy during a negotiation. The system provides a support for P3P policies, which can be exchanged at various steps of the negotiation, and for different credentials formats, providing different degrees of privacy protection. The authors have extended the recent work done by (Bertino, Ferrari & Squicciarini, 2004b) and (Seamons, Winslett & Yu, 2001) by adding techniques for preserving privacy, such as the selective disclosure of credentials and the integration with P3P platform. However, the authors did not introduce the notion of trust requirements or the notion of reference ontologies. Trust-X is a comprehensive framework for trust negotiations, providing both a language for encoding policies and certificates, and system architecture (Bertino, Ferrari & Squicciarini, 2004b). In (Dimmock et al. 2004; Dimmock et al. 2005) authors extend the existing access control architecture (RBAC) to incorporate trust-based evaluation and reasoning in order to have a more dynamic form of policy that can reason with uncertainty. Both of these approaches are risk-aware. Huynh et al. (2004) introduced a trust model, called FIRE, which has four components: interaction trust, role-based trust, witness reputation, and certified reputation. FIRE incorporates all those components to provide a combined trust framework. However, FIRE is not a risk-aware.

Ray, Bertino, Squicciarini & Ferrari (2005) proposed anonymization techniques, generalization and substitution techniques, where a subject can transform its disclosure set into an anonymous one. They proposed that trust negotiation requirements can be expressed using property-based policies where a property-based policy can be implemented by a number of disclosure policies. The property-based policy lists the properties the counterpart has to provide and the conditions it must satisfy in order to obtain some resource. A disclosure policy lists the attributes and credentials types needed to obtain a given resources. In addition, as anonymity may present an important requirement for trust negotiating subjects, the authors included the concept of identity disclosure. An identity disclosure is said to occur for the subject who submits the credentials if the data released to the counterpart contain attributes and credentials that uniquely identify her. Identity disclosure happens when either the identity of an individual is directly revealed or it can de derived from the released data. Trust management and negotiation are a key aspect of secure knowledge management (Bertino, Khan, Sandhu & Thuraisingham, 2006). Secure knowledge-management technologies include technologies for secure data management and information management including databases, information systems, and data mining. Therefore, only authorized individuals must be permitted to execute various operations and functions. Moreover, the work presented by (Squicciarini, Bertino, Ferrari & Ray, 2006) is developed in the system context of (Bertino, Ferrari & Squicciarini, 2004a) and (Bertino, Ferrari & Squicciarini, 2004b). The authors addressed

the problem of preserving privacy in trust negotiations by proposing three orthogonal privacy preserving mechanisms that can be used in trust negotiations. They have addressed the notion of privacy preserving disclosure by introducing substitution and generalization techniques. In Bertino et al (2006), authors discussed trust management and negotiation by establishing different trust negotiation rules for collaboration between different parties. Squicciarini et al. (2006) proposed a protocol that supports anonymization in trust negotiations. They mentioned that credentials, exchanged during trust negotiations, often contain sensitive attributes that attest to the properties of the credential owner. Uncontrolled disclosure of such sensitive attributes may cause grave damage to the credential owner. The proposed protocol gives assurance to the credentials submitter that his disclosure set is k-anonymous. Moreover, their protocol ensures that the credentials submitted by a subject cannot be linked to the ones previously submitted by him. In (Yuan et al. 2006a; Yuan et al. 2006b) authors propose a context-based method for trust model to find reliable recommendations and filter out unfair recommendations in PCE. Context is exploited to analyze users' behavior, state and intention. Moreover, authors use learning based neural network to cope with the context to catch doubtful recommendations.

(Ries, 2007) developed a new trust model that can easily be interpreted and adjusted by users and software agents. One key feature is that it is capable of expressing the certainty of a trust opinion by using contexts which are associated with different levels of risk in interactions. In (Wang & Singh, 2007), trust and recommendations are formally defined and analyzed by incorporating belief, disbelief and uncertainty to each interaction. Xu et al. (2007) proposed a novel trust framework for pervasive computing. They presented a hybrid model including a trust model, a security model, and a risk model. The proposed framework is dynamic and lightweight enough to be applicable in PCE. However, the proposed protocol does not

Table 1. Protocol Security features comparison

	MA	UCP	NL	LA	DCI	DSAC	QoP	CA	TM	RA
MIST	Partially	N.A.	Yes	High	Yes	No	No	No	No	No
Aware Home	Yes	Yes	N.A.	N.A.	Yes	No	No	No	No	No
Solar	N.A.	No	N.A.	N.A.	N.A.	N.A.	No	No	No	No
pawS	Partially	Yes	N.A.	High	Yes	No	No	Yes	No	No
Jend, 2002	No	No	No	Medium	No	Yes	No	No	No	No
He, 2004	Yes	Yes	No	Medium	No	No	No	Yes	No	No
Ren, 2005	Yes	Yes	Partially	High	Yes	Yes	No	Yes	No	No
Ren, 2006	Yes	Yes	Partially	High	No	Yes	No	Yes	No	No
Kim, 2007	Yes	Yes	Yes	High	Yes	Yes	No	Yes	No	No
Ren, 2007	Yes	Yes	Yes	High	Yes	Yes	No	Yes	No	No
FIRE (2004)	No	Yes	N.A.	N.A.	N.A.	No	No	Yes	Yes	No
Dimmock 04	No	N.A.	N.A.	N.A.	Yes	No	No	Yes	Yes	Yes
Dimmock 05	No	No	N.A.	N.A.	N.A.	No	No	No	Yes	Yes
Yuan 2006a	No	Yes	N.A.	N.A.	N.A	N.A.	No	Yes	Yes	No
Yuan 2006b	No	Yes	N.A.	N.A.	N.A.	N.A.	No	Yes	Yes	No
Ries 2007	No	No	N.A.	N.A.	N.A.	N.A.	No	Yes	Yes	Yes
Xu 2007	No	No	N.A.	N.A.	N.A.	N.A.	No	No	Yes	Yes
Uddin 2008	No	Yes	N.A.	N.A.	N.A.	N.A.	No	Yes	Yes	No
Mohan 2008	No	Yes	N.A.	N.A.	N.A.	N.A.	o	Yes	Yes	No

address users' role and context factors. Squicciarini et al. (2007) investigated privacy in the context of trust negotiations. They proposed a framework for negotiating the release of sensitive attributes. Authors proposed a set of privacy-preserving features such as the support for the P3P. They discuss several interoperable negotiation strategies for improving privacy and efficiency. Uddin et al. (2008) proposed a context-based trust model for open and dynamic systems called CAT. Authors presented an interaction-based context-aware trust model by considering services as contexts. The proposed protocol uses rule-based trust calculation, direct trust calculation, and direct and indirect recommendation calculation. However, in CAT, it is considered that the network is secure from malicious attacks, and therefore CAT presents a major drawback. Moreover, CAT can not perform authentication process. Mohan et al. (2008) proposed a framework for evaluating trust. They presented attribute trust, a policy-based enhanced framework, for aggregating user attributes and evaluating confidence in these attributes. Authors addressed the problem by integrating a reputation system model based on transitive trust.

In the table below (Table 1), we compare some of the most important features for the above schemes. The comparison is done based on privacy and security related features. The following comparison cover these features: Trust Management (TM), Context-Awareness (CA), Mutual Authentication (MA), User Context Privacy (UCP), Non-Linkability (NL), Data Confidentiality and Integrity (DCI), Differentiated Service Access Control (DSAC), Level of Anonymity (LA), Quality of Privacy (QoP), and Risk Awareness (RA).

From this table, we can deduce that much research still needs to be done concerning privacy, trust, and security. To overcome these limitations, a deep study is required and a cohesive model should be created to reflect user's real world and its perception on privacy, trust, and risk in different situations and environments. However, a full exhaustive comparison study including trust features (i.e. Trustworthy Authentication (TA), Trust Management (TM), Trust Establishment (TE), Trust Negotiation (TN), Risk Awareness, etc.) and performance analysis (i.e. computation and communication overhead) will be addressed in detailed in a later coming work.

CONCLUSION AND FUTURE DIRECTIONS

In this survey, we have outlined challenges facing developers of UbiComp applications with regard toward privacy, security and trust. The main contribution for this chapter is the notion of security, privacy, and trust enhancing services. Privacy and trust adaptively provide protection for users as they enter UbiComp environments which allow for continued transparent use of services without compromising neither the users privacy nor the services ability to provide services. In pervasive computing environments, the deployment for a robust and dynamic security framework should be conditioned by privacy and trust needs so users can be confident by using available services within the environment.

New researches should focus on understanding these services in order to design a global architecture which preserve privacy, provide flexible authentication, enhance context-aware access control, and ensure the enforcement of dynamic authorization. These new designs and architecture should express privacy practices regarding the collection, use and distribution of personal information gathered from users and their agents. System developers should implement guidelines to limit the amount of personal information collected and privacy policies that require disclosure on a "need-to-know". In addition, identity management

solutions should further be studied and extended to support role-based access control (RBAC) and authentication. Moreover, authentication and context-aware should be integrated within any trust and privacy-based access control models. RBAC should require user authentication as a prerequisite and should be strong and efficient. Privacy-based enhanced access control should also be more explored and extended to support privacy preferences. These designs should be incorporated into distributed and dynamic environments.

Moreover, there are new areas that need further work. Trust needs to be integrated into the design of any new context-based framework. We need to develop a methodology for investigating trust modeling (i.e. trust management and trust negotiations), trust value establishment, trust propagation, trust synthesizing, etc. By incorporating all these trust strategies into a formal model, this trust model can adapt to the different application scenarios, environment changes, and trust evidence types. It further resolves the limitations of current existing trust models in handling different trust management requirements. These researches and studies should focus on integrating privacy policies and references that can be automatically retrieved and interpreted by users' agents, who accept or reject services according to user's stated preference policy. Beside trust, any new methodology should be based on a dynamic hybrid model that should integrate risk analysis, risk management and reputation mechanisms. The risk and reputation factors are little considered in trust model, thus we should further evaluate the influence of these factors to trusted decision systems by exploring mechanisms and integrating them into trusted decision mechanisms. In addition, trust model based on users' roles, capabilities, behavior, and context factors, etc., should be further investigated to improve the hybrid model.

Other primary goal scheme is to increase quality of privacy, (QoP), by giving users more time to react adequately to dangerous situations. The concept of Quality of Privacy (QoP) allows balancing the trade-off between the amount of privacy a user is willing to concede and the value of the services that can be provided by UbiComp applications. This concept should be explored in any new trust and risk-based framework in pervasive computing. We need to explore the incorporation of new additional policy specifications into trust negotiations and management strategies. For example, we need to examine the P3P specified by the World Wide Web Consortium and determine how we can enforce such a policy within the framework of trust strategies. Moreover, we should plan to further explore the use of fuzzy set theory and ontologies in trust negotiation systems to make suitable decisions despite the imperfect knowledge. We should further explore the use of the methods from the fuzzy rule computation and fuzzy control domain to take trusting decisions, to model separation of duty policies, to model trust representation, trust aggregation and trust evolution.

REFERENCES

Al-Muhtadi, J., Campell, R., Kapadia, A., Mickunas, M., & Yi, S. (2002). Routing Through the Mist: Privacy Preserving Communication In Ubiquitous Computing Environments. In *Proceedings of the International Conference of Distributed Computing Systems (ICDCS 2002)*, Vienna, Austria (pp. 65-74).

Almenarez, F., Marin, A., Diaz, D., & Sanchez, J. (2006). Developing a Model for Trust Management in Pervasive Devices. In *Proceeding of the fourth Annual IEEE International Conference on Pervasive Computing and Communications Workshops (PERCOM'06)*, Italy (pp. 267-271).

Bellotti, V. (1997). Design for Privacy in Multimedia Computing and Communications Environments. In *Technology and Privacy: The New Landscape* (pp. 63-98).

Berrached, A., & Korvin, A. (2006). Reinforcing Access Control Using Fuzzy Relation Equations. In *Proceedings of the 2006 International Conference on Security and Management (SAM06)* (pp. 489-493).

Bertino, E., Ferrari, E., & Squicciarini, A. (2004a). Privacy Preserving Trust Negotiations. In *Proceedings of the fourth International workshop Privacy Enhancing Technologies* (pp. 283-301).

Bertino, E., Ferrari, E., & Squicciarini, A. (2004b). Trust-X: A Peer to Peer Framework for Trust Establishment. *IEEE Transactions on Knowledge and Data Engineering, 16*(7), 827–842. doi:10.1109/TKDE.2004.1318565

Bertino, E., Khan, L., Sandhu, R., & Thuraisingham, B. (2006). Secure Knowledge Management: Confidentiality, Trust, and Privacy. *IEEE Transactions on Systems, Man, and Cybernetics . Systems and Humans, 36*(3), 429–438.

Blaze, M., Feigenbaum, J., & Lacy, J. (1996). Decentralized Trust Management. In *Proceedings of the 1996 IEEE Symposium on Security and Privacy* (pp. 164-173).

Bojadziev, G., & Bojadziev, M. (1997). *Fuzzy Logic for Business, Finance, and Management*. Singapore: World Scientific.

Calcutt, D. (1990). *British House of Commons, Committee on Privacy and Related Matters* (Report of the Committee on Privacy and Related Matters, Cm 1102). London.

Campbell, R., Al-Muhtadi, J., Nadldurg, P., Sampemane, G., & Mickunas, M. (2002). Towards Security and Privacy for Pervasive Computing. In *Proceedings of the ISSS*, Tokyo, Japan (pp. 1-15).

Caronni, G. (2000). Walking the Web of Trust. In *Proceedings of the 9th IEEE International Workshops on Enabling Technologies* (pp. 153-158).

Chandrasekaran, B., Josephson, J., & Benjamins, V. (1999). What are ontologies, and why do we need them? *IEEE Intelligent Systems and Applications*, *14*, 20–26. doi:10.1109/5254.747902

Chen, G., & Kotz, D. (2000). *A Survey of Context-Aware Mobile Computing Research* (Tech. Rep. Dartmouth Computer Science Technical Report TR2000-381).

Covington, M., Long, W., Srinivasan, S., Dey, A., Ahamad, M., & Abowd, D. G. (2001). Securing Context-Aware Applications Using Environments Roles. In *Proceedings of the sixth ACM Symposium on Access Controls Models and Technologies* (pp. 10-20).

Cranor, L., Reagle, J., & Ackerman, S. M. (1999). *Beyond Concern: Understanding net USERS' attitudes about online privacy* (Technical report TR 99.4.3). AT&T Labs Research.

Cranor, L., & Wenning, R. (2002). *Platform for Privacy Preferences (P3P) Project*. Retrieved March 4, 2009, from http://www.w3.org/P3P/

Dey, A. K. (2001). Understanding and using context. *Personal and Ubiquitous Computing Journal*, *5*(1), 4-7. Retrieved February 23, 2009, from http://www.cc.gatech.edu/fce/ctk/pubs/PeTe5-1.pdf

Dey, A. K., & Abowd, G. D. (2000). Towards a better understanding of context and context-awareness. The *Proceedings of the CHI 2000 Workshop on the What, Who, when, and How of Context-Awareness*, The Hague, The Netherlands. Retrieved January 8, 2009, from ftp://ftp.cc.gatech.edu/pub/gvu/tr/1999/92-22.pdf

Dimmock, N., Bacon, J., Ingram, D., & Moody, k. (2005). Risk Models for Trust-Based Access Control (TBAC). In *Proceeding of the 3rd Annual Conference on Trust Management*, France (pp. 364-371).

Dimmock, N., Belokosztolski, A., Eyers, D., Bacon, J., Ingram, D., & Moody, k. (2004). Using Trust and Risk in Role-Based Access Control Policies. In *Proceeding of the 9th ACM Symposium on Access Control Models and technologies* (pp. 156-162). New York: ACM Press.

Duma, C., Shahmehri, N., & Caronni, G. (2005). Dynamic Trust Metrics for Peer-to-Peer Systems. In *Proc. of the 2nd IEEE Workshop on P2P Data Management, Security and Trust*.

English, C., Nixon, P., Terzis, S., McGettrick, A., & Lowe, H. (2002). Dynamic Trust Models for Ubiquitous Computing Environments. In *Proceedings of the UBICOMP 2002-Workshop on Security in Ubiquitous Computing*, Goteborg, Sweden.

Feruzan, A. (2007). *Context Modeling and Reasoning using Ontologies*. Retrieved February 15, 2009, from http://www.ponnuki.de/cmaruo/cmaruo.pdf

Grandison, T. (2003). *Trust Management for Internet Application*. Unpublished doctoral dissertation, Imperial College London.

Gruninger, M., & Lee, J. (2002). Ontology-Applications and Design. *Communications of the ACM*, *45*(2), 39–65. doi:10.1145/503124.503146

He, Q., Wu, L., & Khosla, P. (2004). Quest for Personal Control over Mobile Location Privacy. *IEEE Communications Magazine*, *42*(5), 130–136. doi:10.1109/MCOM.2004.1299356

Hengartner, U., & Steenkiste, P. (2004). Implementing access control to people location information. In *SACMAT '04, Proceedings of the 9th ACM symposium on Access Control Models and Technologies* (pp. 11-20). New York: ACM.

Herzberg, A., Mass, Y., & Michaeli, J. (2000). Access Control Meets Public Key Infrastructure, or: Assigning Roles to Strangers. In *Proceedings of the 2000 IEEE Symposium on Security and Privacy* (pp. 2-14).

Hong, I. J., & Landay, A. L. (2004). An Architecture for Privacy-Sensitive Ubiquitous Computing. In *Proceeding of the Second International Conference on Mobile Systems, Applications and Services (MobiSys 2004)* (pp. 177-189).

Hull, R., Kumar, B., Lieuwen, D., Patel-Schneider, P. F., Shuguet, A., Varadarajan, S., & Vyas, A. (2004). Enabling Context-Aware and Privacy-Conscious User Data Sharing. In *Proc. of the 2004 IEEE International Conference on Mobile Data Management* (pp.187-198).

Huynh, T., Jennings, N., & Shadbolt, N. (2004). FIRE: An integrated trust and reputation model for open multi-agent systems. In *Proceeding of the 16th European Conference on Artificial Intelligence,* Spain (pp. 18-22).

Jendricke, U., Kreutzer, M., & Zugenmair, A. (2002). Pervasive Privacy with Identity Management. In *Proceedings of the 1st Workshop Security, UbiComp.*

Jiang, X., & Landay, J. A. (2002). Modeling Privacy Control in Context-Aware Systems. *Pervasive Computing, 1*(3), 59–63. doi:10.1109/MPRV.2002.1037723

Kagal, L., Finin, T., & Joshi, A. (2001). Trusted-based Secuirty in Pervasive Computing Environments. *IEEE Computer Society Press, 34*(12), 154–157.

Kagal, L., Undercoffer, J., Perich, F., Joshi, A., & Finin, T. (2002). Vigil: Enforcing Security in Ubiquitous Environments. In *Proceedings of the Grace Hopper Celebration of Women in Computing 2002.*

Kagal, L., Undercoffer, J., Perich, F., Joshi, A., & Finin, T. (2002). A Security Architecture Based on Trust Management for Pervasive Computing. In *Proceeding of the Grace Hopper Celebration of Women in Computing.*

Kapadia, A., Henderson, T., Fielding, J. J., & Kotz, D. (2007). Virtual Walls: Protecting Digital Privacy in Pervasive Environments. In *Proceedings of the Fifth International Conference on Pervasive Computing (Pervasive)* (pp. 162-179). Berlin, Germany: Springer-Verlag.

Kim, J., Kim, Z., & Kim, K. (2007). A lightweight Privacy Preserving Authentication and Access Control Scheme for Ubiquitous Environment. In *Proceeding of the 10th international Conference on Information Security and Cryptography, ICISC 2007* (pp. 37-48).

Konar, A. (2000). *Artificial Intelligence and Soft Computing: Behavioral and Cognitive Modeling of the Human Brain.* Boca Raton, FL: CRC Press.

Lahlou, S., & Jegou, F. (2004). *European Disappearing Computer Privacy Design Guidelines (version 1.1), Ambient Agoras Programme Report* (IST-2000-25134). Disappearing Computer Initiative.

Langheinrich, M. (2001). Privacy by Design-Principles of Privacy-Aware Ubiquitous Systems. In *Proceeding of the 3rd International Conference on Ubiquitous Computing (UbiComp 2001)* (LNCS 2201, pp. 273-291). Berlin, Germany: Springer.

Langheinrich, M. (2002). A Privacy Awareness System for Ubiquitous Computing Environments. In *Proceeding of the 4th International Conference on Ubiquitous Computing (UbiComp2002),* (LNCS 2498, pp. 237-245). Berlin, Germany: Springer.

Li, N., & Mitchell, J. C. (2003). Datalog with Constraints: A Foundation for Trust-Management Languages. In *Proc. of the Fifth International Symposium on Practical aspects of Declarative Languages* (pp. 58-73).

Li, N., Winsborough, W., & Mitchell, J. (2003). Distributed Credential Chain Discovery in Trust Management. *Journal of Computer Security, 11*(1), 35–86.

Malek, B., Miri, A., & Karmouch, A. (2008). A Framework for Context-Aware Authentication. In *Proceedings of the IET 4th International Conference on Intelligent Environments* (pp. 1-8). Washington, DC: IEEE Computer Society Press.

Minami, K., & Kotz, D. (2002). *Controlling Access to Pervasive Information in the "Solar" system* (Dartmouth Computer Science Technical Report TR2002-422).

Mohan, A., & Blough, M. (2008). Attribute Trust-a Framework for Evaluating Trust in Aggregated Attributes via a Reputation System. In *Proceeding of the 6th Annual Conference on Privacy, Security and Trust* (pp. 201-212). Washington, DC: IEEE Computer Society Press.

Myles, G., Friday, A., & Davies, N. (2003). Preserving Privacy in Environments with Location-Based Applications. *IEEE Pervasive Computing / IEEE Computer Society [and] IEEE Communications Society, 2*(1), 56–64. doi:10.1109/MPRV.2003.1186726

NIST. (2001). *National Institute of Standards and Technologies, About Pervasive Computing*. Retrieved December 13, 2008, from http://www.nist.gov/pc2001/about-pervasive.html

OECD. (1980). *Organization for Economic Co-operation and Development, Recommendation of the council concerning guidelines on the Protection of Privacy and Transborder Flows of Personal Data*. Retrieved December 14, 2008, from http://www.oecd.org/document

Pfleeger, P. C. (1997). *Security in Computing*. Upper Saddle River, NJ: Prentice-Hall, Inc.

Ray, I., Bertino, E., Squicciarini, A., & Ferrari, E. (2005). Anonymity Preserving Techniques in Trust Negotiations. In *Proceedings of the 5th International Workshop on Privacy Enhancing Technologies (PET)*, Cavtat, Croatia (pp. 93-109).

Rehak, M., Foltyn, M., Pechoucek, M., & Benda, P. (2005). Trust Model for Open Ubiquitous agent systems. In *Proceedings of the IEEE/WIC/ACM/ International Conference on Intelligent Agent Technology (IAT)*, Compiegne University of Technology, France (pp. 536-542).

Ren, K., & Lou, W. (2005). Privacy Enhanced Access Control in Ubiquitous Computing Environments. In *Proceedings of the 2nd International Conference of Broadband Networks* 2005 (Vol. 1, pp. 356-365).

Ren, K., & Lou, W. (2007). Privacy-Enhanced, Attack-Resilient Access Control in Pervasive Computing Environments with Optional Context Authentication Capability. *Mobile Networks and Applications, 12*(1), 79–92. doi:10.1007/s11036-006-0008-7

Ren, K., Lou, W., Kim, K., & Deng, R. (2006). A Novel Privacy Preserving Authentication and Access Control Scheme for Pervasive Computing Environments. *IEEE Transactions on Vehicular Technology, 55*(4), 1373–1384. doi:10.1109/TVT.2006.877704

Ries, S. (2007). Certain Trust: A Trust Model for Users and Agents. In *Proceeding of the 22nd Annual ACM Symposium on Applied Computing* (pp. 1599-1604). New York: ACM Press.

Saltzer, J., & Schroeder, M. (1975). The protection of information in computer systems. *Proceedings of the IEEE Computer Society Press, 63*(9).

Schilit, B., Adams, N., & Want, R. (1994). Context-Aware Computer Applications. In *Proceedings of the Workshop on Mobile Computing Systems and Applications* (pp. 85-90).

Seamons, K. E., Winslett, M., & Yu, T. (2001). Limiting the Disclosure of Access Control Policies During Automated Trust Negotiation. In *Proceedings of the Network and Distributed System Security Symposium*, San Diego, CA.

Seigneur, J., & Jensen, C. (2004). Trading Privacy for Trust. In *Proceedings of the 2nd International Conference on Trust Management* (pp. 93-107).

Siljeee, B. I. J., & Bosloper, I. E. (2004). A classification framework for storage and retrieved of context. In *Proceedings of the First International Workshop on Modeling and Retrieval of Context (MRC2004)*.

Squicciarini, A., Bertino, E., Ferrari, E., Paci, F., & Thuraisinghm, B. (2007). PP-Trust-X: A system for Privacy Preserving Trust Negotiations. [TISSEC]. *ACM Transactions on Information and System Security, 10*(3). doi:10.1145/1266977.1266981

Squicciarini, A., Bertino, E., Ferrari, E., & Ray, I. (2006). Achieving Privacy in Trust Negotiations with an Ontology-Based Approach. *IEEE Transactions on Dependable and Secure Computing, 3*(1), 13–30. doi:10.1109/TDSC.2006.3

Squicciarini, A., Spantzel, A., Bertino, E., Ferrari, E., & Ray, I. (2006). Trust Negotiations with Customizable Anonymity. In *Proceedings of the IEEE/WIC/ACM International Conference on Web Intelligence and Intelligent Agent Technology (WI-ATW06)* (pp. 69-72).

Stajano, F. (2002). *Security for Ubiquitous Computing*. New York: Halsted Press.

Takabi, H., Amini, M., & Jalili, R. (2006). Enhancing Role-Based Access Control Model through Fuzzy Relations. In *Proceedings of the third International Conference on Information Assurance and Security (IAS07)* (pp. 131-136). Washington, DC: IEEE Computer Society Press.

Tentori, M., Favela, J., Gonzalez, V., & Rodriguez, M. (2005). Supporting Quality of Privacy (QOP) in Pervasive Computing. In *Proceeding of the Sixth Mexican International Conference on Computer Science* (pp. 58-67). New York: ACM Press.

Wang, Y., & Singh, M. (2007). Formal Trust Model for Multiagent Systems. In *Proceeding of the 20th International Joint Conference on Artificial Intelligence,* Boston (pp. 1-6).

Westin, F. A. (1967). *Privacy and Freedom*. New York: Atheneum.

Winsborough, W., & Li, N. (2002). Towards Practical Automated Trust Negotiation. In *Proceedings of the 3rd International Workshop on Policies for Distributed Systems and Networks* (pp. 92-103). Washington, DC: IEEE Computer Society Press.

Worna, K., & Gomez, L. (2005). Context-Aware Security and Secure Context-Awareness in Ubiquitous Computing Environments. In *SAP research, XXI Autumn Meeting of Polish Information Processing Society Conference Proceedings* (pp. 255-265).

Wu, Z., & Weaver, A. (2006). Application of Fuzzy Logic in Federated Trust Management for Pervasive Computing. In *Proceeding of the 30th Annual International Computer Software and Applications Conferences (COMPSAC06)* (pp. 215-222). Washington, DC: IEEE Computer Society Press.

Xia, H., Malcolm, J., Christianson, B., & Zhang, Y. (2007). Hierarchical Trustworthy Authentication for Pervasive Computing. In Proceedings 4th Annual International Conference on Mobile and Ubiquitous Systems: Networking and Services (pp. 1-3). Washington, DC: IEEE Society Press.

Xiu, D., & Liu, Z. (2004). *A Dynamic Trust Model for Pervasive Computing Environments. A Research Paper. Research Supported by the NSF Grant0406325*. Retrieved from http://coitweb.uncc.edu/~zhliu/Research/Papers/asc.pdf

Xu, W., Xin, Y., & Lu, G. (2007). A Trust Framework for Pervasive Computing Environments. In Proceeding of the International Conference on Wireless Communications, Networking and Mobile Computing (WiCom 07) (pp. 2222-2225). Washington, DC: IEEE Society Press.

Yu, T. (2003). *Automated Trust Establishment In Open Systems*. Unpublished doctoral dissertation, University of Illinois at Urbana-Champaign.

Yuan, W., Guan, D., Lee, S., Lee, Y., & Gavrilov, A. (2006a). Finding Reliable Recommendations for trust model. In *Proceeding of the 7ᵗʰ International Conference on Web Information Systems Engineering (WISE06)* (pp. 375-386).

Yuan, W., Guan, D., Lee, S., Lee, Y., & Lee, H. (2006b). Filtering out unfair recommendations Finding for trust model in ubiquitous environments. In *Proceeding of the second International Conference on Information Systems Security (ICISS '06)* (pp. 258-263).

Zadeh, L. A. (1973). Outline of a new Approach to the Analysis of Complex Systems and Decision Processes. *IEEE Transactions on Systems, Man, and Cybernetics, 3*(1), 28–44.

Zimmer, T. (2004). Toward a better understanding of Context attributes. In *Proceedings of the second IEEE Annual Conference on Pervasive Computing and Communications Workshops (PERCOMMW04)* (pp. 23). Washington, DC: IEEE Computer Society.

Zuidweg, M. (2003). Using P3P in a Web Services-Based context-aware Application Platform. In *Proc. of 9th Open European Summer School and IFIP Workshop on Next Generation Networks (EUNICE 2003)*, Hungary.

Chapter 16
Trust and Stability in Heterogeneous Multimedia Networks

Dimitrios Koukopoulos
University of Ioannina, Greece

ABSTRACT

In this chapter, the author views trust as the confidence in the association of a stable network execution to the efficient distribution of multimedia products in the final user. A network is stable under a greedy protocol (or a composition of protocols) if, for any adversary of injection rate less than 1, the number of packets in the network remains bounded at all times. The author focuses on a basic adversarial model for packet arrival and path determination for which the time-averaged arrival rate of packets requiring a single edge is no more than 1. Within this framework, the author studies the property of stability under various compositions of contention-resolution protocols and different packet trajectories trying to characterize this property in terms of network topologies. Furthermore, the author enhances the adversary allowing the monitoring of network link capacities/slowdowns. Within this context, the author shows how the stability properties of network topologies change when network link slowdowns/capacities can change dynamically. Interestingly, his results indicate that a composition of protocols leads to worst stability behaviour than having a single unstable protocol for contention-resolution. This suggests that the potential for instability incurred by the composition of protocols may be worse than that of some single protocol. Consequently, this study could help on the design and maintainance of trustworthy heterogeneous multimedia systems.

INTRODUCTION

Nowadays, there is a necessity for the development of fast and reliable large-scale communica-

DOI: 10.4018/978-1-61520-682-7.ch016

tion platforms for the distribution of commercial multimedia products. Within this context, it is important the presence of a trust relationship among all the entities that cooperate (vendors, consumers, network infrastructure). However, in a distributed system or a network, the entities involved in a trust relationship may have no direct knowledge of each other so there is a need for mechanisms to support trust among them. A trust relationship has specific properties (Grandison & Sloman, 2000): (i) It is not absolute. (ii) It may not be symmetric. (iii) It should not be transitive. However, some trust scenarios do exhibit transitivity. (iv) It is associated with a level of trust. Some entities may be trusted more than others with respect to performing an action. We should take into account these properties in order to design trustworthy multimedia networks.

An important problem of multimedia networks is their vulnerability to denial of service attacks that attempt to degrade network performance (Levine & Kessler, 2002). Such attacks can jeopardise the user's confidence in (or specifically distrusts) the standard of quality of service provided by the network. Therefore, in distributed environments the required service trust is directly related to the reliability or integrity properties of the network infrastructure. Especially, in e-commerce and e-banking network applications, the customer or vendor trusts the network to support mechanisms that will ensure that all the transactions will be handled fast and reliable.

The performance and reliability properties of multimedia networks are closely related to stability. Stability requires that the number of packets in the network remains bounded at all times against any adversary under a single contention-resolution protocol or a composition of protocols. (By composition of contention-resolution protocols, we mean the simultaneous use of different such protocols at different queues of the network.). Adversarial attacks that can lead a network to instability can be seen as a type of denial of service attacks since their purpose is to flood the network (or a subnetwork) with packets whose sole purpose is to overload the local system in order to hamper (or prevent) legitimate users from having access to the system. If a network is proven to be stable its users are ensured that the network services are trusted against adversarial attacks. Therefore, the

users can develop a trust relationship with the network infrastructure.

Studying the stability behaviour of a network is not an easy task. The complexity of this study increases taking into account the heterogeneity that characterises modern large-scale communication platforms, such as the Internet. Heterogeneity comes around in many different flavours. For example, different traffic sources over the Internet (due to varying mechanisms for supporting different service qualities) result in a heterogeneous mix of traffic traces. Moreover, although, conceptually, the Internet uses a unified set of protocols, in practice each protocol has been implemented with widely varying features (Clark, 1988; Floyd & Paxson, 2001). Thus, heterogeneity is a crucial feature that makes it difficult to model, verify and analyze the behaviour of such large-scale multimedia networks. As the Internet evolves into a ubiquitous communication infrastructure that supports multiple protocols running on different network hosts, its dependability in the presence of various adversarial attacks becomes critical. These attacks can degrade system performance and lead to service disruption. Therefore, the study of performance properties of heterogeneous systems which suffer from adversarial attacks can help to certify the trust properties of such systems. Thus, the researchers will not only be informed of a better design for establishing and maintaining a trustworthy heterogeneous multimedia system, but they will also be assisted in the understanding of the concept of trust in a heterogeneous multimedia environment.

A fundamental question that arises in heterogeneous multimedia systems concerns the presence (or not) of stability properties when individual greedy, contention-resolution protocols are simultaneously running over different hosts in a large packet-switched multimedia network. Stability received a lot of interest recently in the study of performance issues of large-scale heterogeneous networks against various types of adversarial attacks. Trust, on the other hand, is an important property for the reliability and the viability of networks when used for commercial purposes. In such a context, trust can be interpreted as the confidence in the association of a stable network execution to the efficient distribution of multimedia products in the final user. Naturally, achieving stability in a heterogeneous packet-switched multimedia network depends on the network topology, the capacity (which is the packet service rate on a link) or slowdown (that is the time delay an outgoing packet suffers on a link) of network links, the rate at which packets are injected into the system, and the employed contention-resolution protocols on the different network queues. Our goal is to show how stability can be used as a vehicle to build efficient heterogeneous multimedia networks which people can trust for multimedia distribution.

The rest of this chapter is organized as follows. In significance and research questions section we explain the significance of the study of the relationship between trust and stability. Review of literature section presents related works to the concepts of trust management, heterogeneous multimedia networks and network stability. Theoretical framework section presents adversarial models definitions. Stability behavior of heterogeneous networks section demonstrates the stability properties of various types of network topologies under specific compositions of protocols running on top of them in contrast to different types of adversarial attacks. Network simulation platform section proposes an innovative platform for conducting network simulations in adversarial environments. Evaluation section makes an experimental evaluation of the stability behavior of heterogeneous multimedia networks under various adversarial attacks. Potential use section presents how instability is translated in terms of trust in heterogeneous nultimedia networks and how trustworthiness is evaluated from network instability behavior. Conclusions and discussions section concludes our results and discusses some open problems.

SIGNIFICANCE AND RESEARCH QUESTIONS

In this work we will investigate the relationship between trust and stability in heterogeneous multimedia networks facing various types of adversarial attacks. Especially, we are interested in the trust behavior of heterogeneous packet-switched multimedia networks in which packets arrive dynamically at the nodes and they are routed in discrete time steps across the links. We aim at revealing how the knowledge of the stability properties of heterogeneous networks can enhance trust management assisting in the understanding of the concept of trust in a heterogeneous multimedia network.

First, we will describe the specifications of already proposed adversarial attacks in heterogeneous multimedia networks. We will mainly focus on attacks that can manipulate the network topology parameters, change the capacity or slowdown of network links or monitor the rate at which packets are injected into the system. These attacks are real-life scenarios and their handling from a trust management system is critical in order to maintain efficient multimedia networks with guaranteed end-user quality of service.

Then, we will analyse the stability properties of various types of network topologies under specific compositions of protocols running on top of them in contrast to different types of adversarial attacks. Thus, we will present adversarial constructions that exploit network topology, control the rates of packet injections and determine packet paths to lead the set of subgraphs that are forbidden for universal stability and simple-path universal stability under a single protocol to instability when different compositions of contention-resolution protocols are composed on the network nodes. These results show that the forbidden subgraphs for universal stability and simple-path universal stability under a single protocol are also unstable when a specific protocol composition is employed for contention-resolution on network queues. Surprisingly, the usage of protocol compositions for contention-resolution in some networks results in lower bounds on the injection rate for instability compared to the instability bounds obtained using a single protocol on the same networks.

Moreover, we will prove that when the network size increases, an adversary that can change dynamically the network link slowdowns can drop to arbitrarily low values the lower bound on injection rate that guarantees instability for heterogeneous networks. Furthermore, we will consider heterogeneous networks facing adversarial attacks where the adversary can control the packet injection rate and network link capacities. Within this context, we will provide interesting combinatorial constructions of heterogeneous networks proving that they can become unstable. These results show that enhancing the power of the adversary with the ability to change dynamically network link capacities/slowdowns leads to worst instability behaviour networks than in the case all the network links have unit capacities/slowdowns at all times. This may suggest that not only do the trust properties of a network degrade when different contention-resolution protocols are composed on different network hosts, but they become even worse when the network faces adversarial attacks that can change dynamically network link capacities/slowdowns.

In order to evaluate the stability behavior of heterogeneous multimedia networks under various adversarial attacks, we will use an innovative platform for conducting network simulations. This platform assumes that the adversary controls the rate of packet injections, determines packet paths and monitors the capacity or slowdown of network links. Our results suggest that the instability properties of a protocol that is not universally stable can become worse when it is composed with another protocol on the same network. One of the main open issues, however, is the development of design criteria, i.e. sets of properties that can be employed in order to construct stable heterogeneous networks. Characterizing the sta-

bility of specific compositions of protocols that have been proved unstable for specific networks remains a very interesting problem in the field of network stability and we believe that it can be successfully applied to trust management assisting in the understanding of the concept of trust in a heterogeneous multimedia network.

REVIEW OF LITERATURE

Trust is an important concept in distributed computing systems due to the use of trust management for enhancing system security (Wobber, Abadi, Burrows & Lampson, 1994; Chu, Feigenbaum, LaMacchia, Resnick & Strauss, 1997). However, the notion of trust is interpreted differently among the various research communities depending on the specific problem they deal with: access control (Sandhu, Coyne, Feinstein & Youman, 1996; Dimmock, Belokosztolszki, Eyers, Bacon & Moody, 2004), trust negotiation (Winslett, Yu, Seamons, Hess, Jacobson, Jarvis, Smith & Yu, 2002), trust reputation (Shmatikov & Talcott, 2005), dynamic trust management systems (Xiu & Liu, 2005). Two popular approaches are either trust to be interpreted as access rights aiming at developing efficient access control schemes (Li & Mitchell, 2003) or trust to be interpreted as reliability using the probability theory (Josang & Knapskog, 1998). Traditional access control mechanisms are centralized and operate under a closed world assumption in which all of the parties are known. Trust management systems generalize traditional mechanisms by operating in distributed systems and eliminating the closed world assumption.

The concept of trust management was defined as a coherent framework for the study of security policies, security credentials and trust relationships (Blaze, Feigenbaum & Lacy, 1996). Two of the first trust management systems were PolicyMaker (Blaze, Feigenbaum & Strauss, 1998) and KeyNote (Blaze, Feigenbaum & Keromytis,

1998). There are two types of trust management models: the certificate-based models, which have been widely deployed in e-commerce (Blaze, Feigenbaum & Strauss, 1998; Blaze, Feigenbaum & Keromytis, 1998) and the reputation-based models (Abdul-Rahman & Hailes, 2000; Aberer & Despotovic, 2001; Richardson, Agrawal & Domingos, 2003). These two categories of approaches have been developed in different environments with different assumptions, but address the same problem – establishing trust among interacting parties in distributed and decentralized systems. The certificate-based approaches are for structured organizational environments and use certificate authorities as the source of trust. On the other hand, the reputation-based approaches address the unstructured user community, such as peer-to-peer systems, and use community opinions as the course of trust.

The main problems a trust management system handles are service provision and routing. As far as concerns service provision a number of trust management system have been proposed in the literature (Blaze, Feigenbaum & Strauss, 1998; Blaze, Feigenbaum & Keromytis, 1998; Abdul-Rahman & Hailes, 2000; Aberer & Despotovic, 2001; Capra, 2004; Quercia & Hailes, 2007). On the other hand routing problems are handled by trust management systems like CONFIDANT (Buchegger & Le Boudec, 2002), SECURE (Cahill, Gray, Seigneur, Jensen, Chen, Shand, Dimmock, Twigg, Bacon, English, Wagealla, Terzis, Nixon, Serugendo, Bryce, Carbone, Krukow& Nielsen, 2003) and STRUDEL (Quercia, Lad, Hailes, Capra & Bhatti, 2006). Last years all the proposed trust management systems follow one of three trust management approaches: distributed trust models (Capra, 2004; Quercia, & Hailes, 2007), global trust where each peer in the system has a unique global trust value that other peers can access (Kamvar, Schlosser & Garcia-Molina, 2003; Donato, Paniccia, Selis, Castillo, Cortese & Leonardi, 2007) and federated trust where there is management of trust-related activities across multiple and heterogeneous security domains and autonomous systems and it deals with strategies for managing inter-domain behaviors (Chun & Bavier, 2004; Bhargav-Spantzel, Squicciarini & Bertino, 2007). In this work, we attempt to interpret trust as stability in order to handle the establishment of a trustworthy heterogeneous multimedia network.

One of the most important features of contemporary large-scale networks for multimedia distribution and communication, such as the Internet, is their heterogeneity. In multimedia networks heterogeneity comes around in many different flavours. For example, the specifics of how the computers in different parts of the network are connected (directly or indirectly) with each other, and the properties of the links that foster the interconnection, is difficult to characterize uniformly. Second, different traffic sources over the Internet (due to varying mechanisms for supporting different classes and qualities of service) result in a heterogeneous mix of traffic traces. Especially, an increasing number of web sites are providing rich multimedia content in the form of integrated text, graphics, audio and video. Third but not least, although, conceptually, the Internet uses a unified set of protocols, in practice each protocol has been implemented with widely varying features (Floyd & Paxson, 2001). Tchepnda & Riguidel (2006) propose a distributed trust infrastructure for heterogeneous networks which assumes that heterogeneous networks involve various security domains and therefore various security policies implementations. Within each security domain, it sets up a trust entity in charge of negotiating and exchanging trust parameters with the trust entities of other security domains.

The Internet is a dynamic multimedia network of heterogeneous transmission media with widely varying bandwidth capacities and latency characteristics. The tremendous popularity of the Internet has led to the emergence of a new generation of applications with widely varying characteristics and requirements. An important class among these is distributed multimedia applications such as multimedia conferencing, video-on-demand and IP telephony (Deering, Estrin, Farinacci, Jacobson, Liu & Wei, 1994; Floyd, Jacobson, McCanne, Liu & Zhang, 1995; McCanne, Jacobson & Vetterli, 1996).

Heterogeneous multimedia networks have been studied extensively in the context of quality of service management that depends on a number of parameters such as network topology, traffic, capacity, available queueing policies (Goyal, Lam & Vin, 1997; Alpcan & Basar, 2003; Jeong, Shin & Choi, 2005; Rong & Burnett, 2006). Such networks rely on traffic engineering techniques to control the flow of IP data packets (Alpcan, Singh & Basar, 2007). Szwabe, Schorr, Hauck & Kassler (2006) studied the rate adaptation of multimedia streams in heterogeneous networks. Jurca & Frossard (2006) presented a media-aware rate allocation scheme that takes into account the impact of both packet loss rates and available bandwidth over each link, on the end-to-end video quality of a single stream. Rate allocation among multiple traffic flows over shared network resources is an important and well-studied problem (Floyd & Fal, 1999; Handley, Floyd, Pahdye & Widmer, 2003; Zhu, Singh & Girod, 2006). Rate allocation for flows with different utility can be solved using distributed solutions (Kelly, Maulloo & Tan, 1998; La & Anantharam, 2002).

Algorithms, protocols and techniques to deliver multimedia content over large-scale networks have been the focus of intensive research in the last 20 years, especially in ATM wired and wireless networks (Libman, Midani & Nguyen, 1995; Fowler & Murphy, 1996; Balboni & Bosco, 1996). Examples of commercial products and research prototypes in the area of content delivery under heterogeneous clients and network conditions include OnLineAnywhere, Spyglass, Intel QuickWeb, ProxiNet and IBM Transcoding proxy (Shaha, Desai & Parashar, 2001).

Heterogeneous wireless multimedia networks have recently received a lot of interest (Li & Chao, 2007; TalebiFard & Leung, 2008). An interesting type of heterogeneous multimedia networks is wireless multimedia sensor networks (Akyildiz, Melodia & Chowdhury, 2006; Akyildiz, Su, Sankarasubramaniam & Cayirci, 2002; Gurses & Akan, 2005), i.e., networks of wirelessly interconnected devices that allow retrieving video and audio streams, still images, and scalar sensor data..

Adversarial environments can be used to model intrusion attacks as an intruder can behave like an adversary that tries to change network environment parameters (network topology, packet service rate, packet injection rate or the used contention-resolution protocols). In particular, adversarial attacks that attempt to lead a network to instability aiming at flooding the network with dummy packets. If adversarial attacks succeed the network is overloaded and its quality of service is degraded. In the community of Security, the study of intrusion detection and the proposal of methods for guaranteed quality service against various attacks received a lot of interest (Moore, Shannon, Brown, Voelker & Savage, 2006; Oh, Park, Jang & Jeon, 2005; Yau, Lui, Liang & Yam, 2005).

In the community of stability, adversarial queueing theory model (Borodin, Kleinberg, Raghavan, Sudan & Williamson, 2001) received a lot of interest in the study of network performance issues. It was developed as a more realistic model that replaces traditional stochastic assumptions made in queueing theory by more robust, worst-case ones. It considers a packet-switched network in which packets arrive dynamically at the nodes with predetermined paths, and they are routed at discrete time steps across the edges. Roughly speaking, this model views the time evolution of a packet-switched communication network as a game between an adversary and a protocol. At each time step, the adversary may inject a set of packets into some nodes. For each packet, the adversary specifies a simple path (including an origin and destination) that the packet must traverse. When more than one packets wish to cross a queue at a given time step, a contention-resolution protocol is employed to resolve the conflict. A crucial parameter of the adversary is its injection rate r, where $0 < r < 1$. Among the packets that the adversary injects in any time interval I, at most $r|I|$ can have paths that contain any particular edge.

Andrews, Awerbuch, Fernandez, Kleinberg, Leighton & Liu (2001) studied the universal stability of various natural greedy protocols (stability against every adversary and every network). FIFO, FFS and NTG protocols have been proved unstable (Andrews, Awerbuch, Fernandez, Kleinberg, Leighton & Liu, 2001). Koukopoulos, Mavronicolas, Nikoletseas & Spirakis (2002) introduced the subfield of study of the stability properties of compositions of protocols where the compositions of LIS with any of SIS, NTS and FTG protocols have been proved unstable. Alvarez, Blesa & Serna (2004a) gave a characterization for the universal stability of directed networks (stability against every adversary) under any single contention-resolution protocol when the packets follow simple paths (paths do not contain repeated edges and vertices) and non-simple paths (paths do not contain repeated edges, but they can contain repeated vertices). According to this characterization, a directed network graph where packets are injected in non-simple paths is universally stable if and only if it does not contain as subgraph any extension of two specific subgraphs U1 or U2; while a directed graph where packets are injected in simple paths is simple-path universally stable if and only if it does not contain as subgraph any extension of four specific subgraphs S1 or S2 or S3 or S4 (Alvarez, Blesa & Serna, 2004a).

Borodin, Ostrovsky & Rabani (2001) proposed two enhanced types of adversarial attacks in which the adversary can change dynamically the capacities or slowdowns of the network links. A packet-switched network can contain different types of links, which is common especially in large-scale networks like Internet. Then, it is well motivated to assign a capacity to each link (which is the rate at which a link forwards outgoing packets). Also,

a real network can suffer from link failures due to natural disasters (like hurricanes), human action (like hacker attacks) or by unintentional software failures. Then, it is well motivated to assign a slowdown to each link (which is the time delay which is suffered by outgoing packets in order to be forwarded on a link). It has been proved that the universal stability of networks is preserved under this varying context (Borodin, Ostrovsky & Rabani, 2001). Also, it was shown that many well-known universally stable protocols (SIS, NTS, FTG) do maintain their universal stability when the link capacity or slowdown is changing dynamically, whereas the universal stability of LIS is not preserved (Borodin, Ostrovsky & Rabani, 2001). Koukopoulos (2005) studied the impact of dynamic link slowdowns on network stability when a single protocol is used or a forbidden subgraph for universal stability is induced. Also, Koukopoulos, Mavronicolas & Spirakis (2007) studied the impact of dynamic link capacities on network stability. Moreover, there have been proposed generalizations of the adversarial queueing theory to networks with dynamic failures (Alvarez, Blesa, & Serna, 2003; Alvarez, Blesa & Serna, 2004b) and networks where the traffic flow is continuous in time and arbitrary packet lengths, link speeds and link propagation delays are allowed (Blesa, Calzada, Fernandez, Lopez, Martinez, Santos & Serna, 2005).

THEORETICAL FRAMEWORK

In this section, we will focus on the basic ideas underlying the Adversarial Queueing Theory Model. The model definitions are patterned after those defined by Borodin, Kleinberg, Raghavan, Sudan & Williamson (2001). We consider that a routing network is modelled by a directed graph G on n vertices and m edges, $G = (V, E)$. Each vertex $x \in V$ represents a communication switch (node), and each edge $e \in E$ represents a link between two switches. In each node, there is a queue associated with each outgoing link. Time proceeds in discrete time steps. Queues store packets that are injected into the network with a route, which is a simple directed path in G. A packet is an atomic entity that resides at a queue at the end of any step. It must travel along paths in the network from its source to its destination, both of which are nodes in the network. When a packet is injected, it is placed in the queue of the first link on its route. When a packet reaches its destination, we say that it is *absorbed*. During each step, a packet may be sent from its current node along one of the outgoing edges from that node.

Any packets that wish to travel along an edge *e* at a particular time step, but they are not sent, they wait in a queue for the edge *e*. At each step, an *adversary* generates a set of requests. A *request* is a *path* specifying the route that will be followed by a packet. In this work, it is assumed, as it is common in packet routing, that there are two types of paths: simple paths where edges and vertices cannot be overlapped and non-simple paths where edges cannot be overlapped, while vertices can be overlapped (Alvarez, Blesa & Serna, 2004a). We say that the adversary generates a set of packets when it generates a set of requested paths. Also, we say that a packet *p requires* an edge *e* at time *t* if the edge *e* lies on the path from its position to its destination at time *t*. We restrict our study to the case of non-adaptive routing, where the path that is traversed by each packet is fixed at the time of injection, so that we are able to focus on queueing rather than routing aspects of the problem. (Aiello, Kushilevitz, Ostrovsky & Rosen (2000) propose an extension of the adversarial model to the case of adaptive routing.) There are no computational restrictions on how the adversary chooses its requests at any given time step.

The definition of a *bounded adversary A* of rate (r, b) (where $b \geq 1$ is a natural number and $0 < r < 1$) (Borodin, Kleinberg, Raghavan, Sudan & Williamson, 2001) requires that for any edge *e* and any interval *I*, the adversary injects no more than $r |I| + b$ packets during *I* that require edge *e*

at their time of injection. Such a model allows for adversarial injection of packets that are bursty' using the integer $b > 0$.

Roughly speaking, a protocol (or a composition of protocols) P is stable on a network G against an adversary *A* of rate *r* if there is a constant *B* for which the number of packets in the system is bounded at all times by *B* (Borodin, Kleinberg, Raghavan, Sudan & Williamson, 2001). On the other hand, a protocol (or a composition of protocols) P is universally stable, if it is stable against any adversary of rate less than 1 and on any network (Borodin, Kleinberg, Raghavan, Sudan & Williamson, 2001). We also say that a network G is universally stable, if any greedy protocol is stable against any adversary of rate less than 1 on G (Borodin, Kleinberg, Raghavan, Sudan & Williamson, 2001).

When we consider adversarial constructions for proving instability of compositions of specific protocols in which we want to derive lower bounds, it is advantageous to have an adversary that is as weak as possible. Thus, for these purposes, we say that an adversary *A* has injection rate *r* if for every $t \geq 1$, every interval *I* of *t* steps, and every edge *e*, it injects no more than $r |t|$ packets during *I* that require edge *e* at the time of their injection.

In order to formalize the behaviour of a network, we use the notions of *system* and *system configuration*. A triple of the form <G, *A*, P> where G is a network, *A* is an adversary and P is the used protocol (or composition of protocols) on the network queues is called a system. The execution of the system proceeds in global time steps numbered 0, 1,…. Each time-step is divided in two sub-steps. In the first sub-step, one packet is sent from each non-empty buffer over its corresponding link. In the second sub-step, packets are received by the nodes at the other end of the links; they are absorbed (eliminated) if that node is their destination, and otherwise they are placed in the buffer of the next link on their respective routes. New packets are injected in the second sub-step.

In every time step t, the current configuration C^t of a system a system <G, A, P> is a collection of sets $\{S_e^t : e \in G\}$, such that S_e^t is the set of packets waiting in the queue of the edge e at the end of step t. If the current system configuration is C^t, we obtain the system configuration C^{t+1} for the next time step as follows: (i) Addition of new packets to some of the sets S_e^t, each of which has an assigned path in G, and (ii) for each non-empty set S_e^t deletion of a single packet $p \in S_e^t$ and its insertion into the S_f^{t+1} where f is the edge following e on its assigned path (if e is the last edge on the path of p, then p is not inserted into any set.). A time evolution of the system is a sequence of such configurations C^1, C^2,.... An execution of the adversary's construction on a system <G, A, P> determines the time evolution of the system configuration.

Extension of Adversarial Queueing Theory Model with Dynamic Slowdowns. The definitions of the extension of adversarial queueing theory with dynamic slowdowns are patterned after those defined by Borodin, Kleinberg, Raghavan, Sudan & Williamson (2001), adjusted to reflect the fact that the edge slowdowns may vary arbitrarily as was proposed by Borodin, Ostrovsky & Rabani (2001), but we address the weakest possible model of changing slowdowns. During each step, a packet may be sent from its current node along one of the outgoing edges from that node. Edges can have different integer slowdowns, which may or may not vary over time. Denote $D_e(t)$ the *slowdown* of the edge e at time step t. That is, we assume that if a packet p is scheduled to traverse the edge e at time t, then packet p completes the traversal of e at time $t + D_e(t)$ and during this time interval, no other packet can be scheduled on e.

Let $D > 1$ be an integer parameter. We demand that $\forall e$ and $\forall t$, $D_e(t) \in \{1, D\}$ (i.e. each edge slowdown can get only two values, high and low). We also demand for each edge e that $D_e(t)$ stays at some value for a continuous period of time at least equal to $f(r, D)$ s time steps, where s is the number of packets in the system at the time of

setting the link capacity to the value and $f(r, D)$ is a function of the injection rate r of the adversary in the network and the high link slowdown D.

Fix any arbitrary positive integer $w \geq 1$. For any edge e of the network and any sequence of w consecutive time steps, define $N(w, e)$ to be the number of paths that are injected by the adversary during the time interval of w consecutive time steps requiring to traverse the edge e. For any constant r, $0 < r \leq 1$, a (w, r)-adversary} is an adversary that injects packets subject to the following load condition: For every edge e and for every sequence τ of w consecutive time steps,

$$N(\tau, e) \leq r \sum_{t \in \tau} \frac{1}{D_e(t)} \qquad (1)$$

We say that a (w, r)-adversary injects packets at rate r with *window size* w. The assumption that $r \geq 1$ ensures that it is not necessary a priori that some edge of the network is congested (that happens when $r > 1$).

Extension of Adversarial Queueing Theory Model with Dynamic Capacities. The definitions of the extension of adversarial queueing theory with dynamic capacities are patterned after those defined by Borodin, Kleinberg, Raghavan, Sudan & Williamson (2001), they are adjusted to reflect the fact that the edge capacities may vary arbitrarily as was proposed by Borodin, Ostrovsky & Rabani (2001), but we address the weakest possible model of changing capacities. Edges can have different integer capacities, which may or may not vary over time. Denote $C_e(t)$ the *capacity* of the edge e at time step t. That is, we assume that the edge e is capable of simultaneously transmitting up to $C_e(t)$ packets at time t.

Let $C > 1$ be an integer parameter. We demand that $\forall e$ and $\forall t$, $C_e(t) \in \{1, C\}$ (i.e. each edge capacity can get only two values, high and low). We also demand for each edge e that $C_e(t)$ stays at some value for a continuous period of time at least equal to $f(r, C)$ s time steps, where s is the number of packets in the system at the time of setting the link capacity to the value and $f(r, C)$ is a function of the injection rate r of the adversary in the network and the high link capacity C.

Fix any arbitrary positive integer $w \geq 1$. For any edge e of the network and any sequence of w consecutive time steps, define $N(w, e)$ to be the number of paths that are injected by the adversary during the time interval of w consecutive time steps requiring to traverse the edge e. For any constant r, $0 < r \leq 1$, a (w, r)-*adversary* is an adversary that injects packets subject to the following load condition: For every edge e and for every sequence τ of w consecutive time steps,

$$N(\tau, e) \leq r \sum_{t \in \tau} C_e(t) \tag{2}$$

We say that a (w, r)-adversary injects packets at rate r with *window size w*. The assumption that $r \geq 1$ ensures that it is not necessary a priori that some edge of the network is congested (that happens when $r > 1$).

Contention-resolution Protocols. A *contention-resolution* protocol specifies, for each pair of an edge e and a time step, which packet among those waiting at the tail of the edge e will be moved along the edge e. A *greedy* contention-resolution protocol always specifies some packet to move along the edge e if there are packets waiting to use the edge e. In this work, we restrict attention to deterministic, greedy contention-resolution protocols. In particular, we consider:

- SIS (Shortest-in-System) gives priority to the most recently injected packet into the network;
- LIS (Longest-in-System) gives priority to the least recently injected packet into the network;
- FTG (Furthest-to-Go) gives priority to the packet that has to traverse the largest number of edges to its destination;

- NTS (Nearest-to-Source) gives priority to the packet that has traversed the smallest number of edges from its origin;
- FFS (Furthest-from-Source) gives priority to the packet that has traversed the largest number of edges from its origin;
- FIFO (First-In-First-Out) gives priority to the packet that has arrived first at the queue;
- NTG (Nearest-To-Go) gives priority to the nearest packet to its destination.

All these contention-resolution protocols require some tie-breaking rule in order to be unambiguously defined. In this work, we can assume any well-determined tie breaking rule for the adversary.

STABILITY BEHAVIOR OF HETEROGENEOUS NETWORKS

In the adversarial constructions we study here for proving instability, we split time into *phases*. In each phase, we study the evolution of the system configuration by considering corresponding *time rounds*. For each phase, we inductively prove that the number of packets of a specific subset of queues in the system increases in order to guarantee instability. This inductive argument can be applied repeatedly, thus showing instability. Furthermore, we assume that there is a sufficiently large number of packets s_0 in the initial system configuration. This will imply instability results for networks with an empty initial configuration (Andrews, Awerbuch, Fernandez, Kleinberg, Leighton & Liu, 2001). For simplicity, we omit floors and ceilings from our analysis, and we, sometimes, count time steps and packets only roughly. This may only result to loosing small additive constants, while it implies a gain in clarity.

Figure 1. Forbidden subgraphs for universal stability

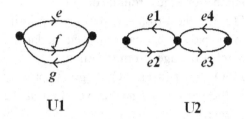

U1   U2

Unstable Heterogeneous Networks under Classical Adversarial Attacks

We consider all compositions of NTG with LIS and FFS protocols. We examine whether the corresponding composition is stable on the set of forbidden subgraphs for universal stability (Figure 1) and simple-path universal stability (Figure 2) for the basic adversarial model (Koukopoulos, 2008). For each forbidden subgraph, we demonstrate an adversary such that the composition is not stable on the subgraph. In addition, in order to qualitatively evaluate how unstable are the compositions, we consider the FIFO protocol, which is known not to be universally stable in general, but it is stable against the network U1. We measure the instability of the composition of FIFO with NTG against that of FIFO (Koukopoulos, 2008). Finally, we present an experimental evaluation of the stability properties of the set of forbidden subgraphs for universal stability and simple-path universal stability with different protocol compositions under an adversarial strategy in order to strengthen our theoretical results.

Unstable Compositions of NTG with FFS and LIS

In this section we show lower bounds on injection rate that guarantee instability for specific networks (Figure 1, Figure 2) under the composition of NTG with FFS and LIS protocols when packets are injected with non-simple and simple paths.

Stability Behavior of U1 Network

First, consider the network U1 (Figure 1) that uses the composition of NTG with LIS protocol where packets are injected with non-simple paths. We have:

Theorem 1. For the network U1, there is an adversary A of rate $r \geq 0.841$ such that the system $<U1, A, (NTG, LIS)>$ is unstable.

Proof. The edge f uses LIS protocol, while the edges e, g use NTG protocol. *Inductive hypothesis*: At the beginning of phase j, there are s_j packets (called S set of packets) in the queues e, f requiring to traverse the edges e, g and f, g correspondingly. *Induction Step*: At the beginning of phase $j+1$ there will be more than s_j packets, $s_{j+1} > s_j$, in the queues e, f requiring to traverse the edges e, g and f, g correspondingly.

We will construct an adversary A such that the induction step will hold. Proving that the induction step holds, we ensure that the induction hypothesis will hold at the beginning of phase $j+1$ with an increased value of s_j, $s_{j+1} > s_j$. In order to prove that the inductive argument works, we consider that there is a large enough number of packets s_j in the initial system configuration. During phase j the adversary plays four rounds of injections.

Figure 2. Forbidden subgraphs for simple-path universal stability

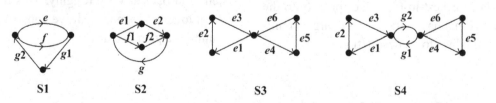

S1   S2   S3   S4

- *Round* 1: It lasts $|T1| = s_j$ time steps. During this round, the adversary injects in g a set Z1 of $|Z1| = r|T1|$ packets wanting to traverse the edges g, f. S packets have priority over Z1 packets in g.

- *Round* 2: It lasts $|T2| = r|T1|$ time steps. During this round, the adversary injects a set Z2 of $|Z2| = r|T2|$ packets in g requiring to traverse the edges g, e and a set Z3 of $|Z3| = r|T2|$ packets in f requiring to traverse f. Z1 packets have priority over Z2 packets in g. All Z1 packets arrive at queue f along with Z3 packets. The total number of packets arriving at f during this round is $|Z1| + |Z3|$ packets. However, the duration of the round is $|T2|$ time steps. Therefore, $|T2|$ packets traverse f during this round. Thus, at the end of this round, there will be a set X of $|X| = r|T2|$ packets in f wanting to traverse f and $|Z2| = r|T2|$ packets in g wanting to traverse g, e.

- *Round* 3: It lasts $|T3| = r|T2|$ time steps. During this round, the adversary injects a set Z4 of $|Z4| = r|T3|$ packets in f requiring to traverse f and a set Z5 of $|Z5| = r|T3|$ packets in e requiring to traverse e, g. X packets have priority over Z4 packets in f because X packets are longer in system than Z4 packets. Thus at the end of this round, there are $|Z4| = r|T3|$ packets in f wanting to traverse f. Also, the Z2 packets have priority over Z5 packets in e. Thus, at the end of this round, there will be $|Z5|$ packets in e wanting to traverse e, g.

- *Round* 4: It lasts $|T4| = r|T3|$ time steps. During this round, the adversary injects a set Z6 of $|Z6| = r|T4|$ packets in e requiring to traverse e and a set Z7 of $|Z7| = r|T4|$ packets in f requiring to traverse f, g. Z4 packets have priority over Z7 packets in f because they are longer in the system. Also, Z6 packets have priority over Z5 packets in e, because Z6 packets are nearest to their destination than Z5 packets. At the end of

round 4, there are $|Y| = |Z5| + |Z6| - |T4| = r|T4|$ packets in e wanting to traverse e, g. At the end of round 4, the number of packets in e, f requiring to traverse e, g and f, g is $s_{j+1} = |Z7| + |Y| = 2r|T4|$.

In order to have instability, we must have $s_{j+1} > s_j$. This holds for $2r|T4| > |T1|$, i.e. $r \geq 0.841$. This argument can be repeated for an infinite and unbounded number of phases ensuring that the number of packets in e, f requiring to traverse e, g and f, g at the end of a phase is larger than at the beginning of the phase. $\square$

Similarly to Theorem 1 we can prove Theorem 2. For the system <U1, A, (NTG, FFS)> the queue f of U1 uses FFS and e, g use NTG. For the system <U1, A, (NTG, LIS, FFS)> the queue f uses LIS, g uses FFS and e uses NTG. The strategy of the adversary is the same in both of the systems.

Adversary's strategy. We consider that each phase consists of four distinguished time rounds. The inductive argument states that if at the beginning of a phase j, there are s_j packets in the queues e, f requiring to traverse the edges e, g and f, g correspondingly, then at the beginning of phase $j+1$ there will be more than s_j packets in the same queues requiring to traverse the same edges. The adversary's strategy during a phase j follows:

- *Round 1*: It lasts $|T1| = s_j$ time steps. During this round, the adversary injects in g a set Z1 of $|Z1| = r|T1|$ packets wanting to traverse the edges g, f.

- *Round 2*: It lasts $|T2| = r|T1|$ time steps. During this round, the adversary injects a set Z2 of $|Z2| = r|T2|$ packets in g requiring to traverse the edges g, e and a set Z3 of $|Z3| = r|T2|$ packets in f requiring to traverse f.

- *Round 3*: It lasts $|T3| = r|T2|$ time steps. During this round, the adversary injects a set Z4 of $|Z4| = r|T3|$ packets in f requiring to traverse f and a set Z5 of $|Z5| = r|T3|$ packets in e requiring to traverse e, g.

- *Round 4*: It lasts $|T4| = r|T3|$ time steps. During this round, the adversary injects a set Z6 of $|Z6| = r|T4|$ packets in e requiring to traverse e and a set Z7 of $|Z7|=r|T4|$ packets in f requiring to traverse f, g.

Theorem 2. For the network U1 there is an adversary A of rate $r \geq 0.841$ such that the system <U1, A, Ni> is unstable where i={1, 2} and Ni={(NTG, FFS), (NTG, FFS, LIS)}.

Stability Behavior of U2 Network
We consider network U2 (Figure 1). Similarly to Theorem 1 we can prove Theorem 3. For the system <U2, $A2$, (NTG, LIS)> and the system <U2,$A2$,(NTG,FFS)> the queue $e4$ uses LIS and FFS protocol correspondingly and the rest queues use NTG. For the system <U2, $A2$, (NTG, LIS, FFS)> the queue $e4$ uses LIS, $e1$ uses FFS and $e2$, $e3$ use NTG. The strategy of the adversary is the same in these three systems.

Adversary's strategy. We consider that each phase consists of three distinguished time rounds. The inductive argument states that if at the beginning of a phase j, there are s_j packets in the queues $e2$, $e3$ requiring to traverse the edges $e2$, $e1$ and $e3$, $e4$, $e1$, then at the beginning of phase $j+1$ there will be more than s_j packets in the same queues requiring to traverse the same edges. We consider that each phase consists of three distinguished time rounds. The adversary's strategy during a phase j follows:

- *Round 1*: It lasts $|T1| = s_j$ time steps. During this round, the adversary injects in $e1$ a set Z1 of $|Z1| = r|T1|$ packets wanting to traverse $e1$, $e2$, $e3$.
- *Round 2*: It lasts $|T2| = r|T1|$ time steps. During this round, the adversary injects a set Z2 of $|Z2| = r|T2|$ packets in e2 requiring to traverse $e2$ and a set Z3 of $|Z3| = r|T2|$ packets in $e3$ requiring to traverse $e3$, $e4$, $e1$.
- *Round 3*: It lasts $|T3| = r|T2|$ time steps. During this round, the adversary injects a

set Z4 of $|Z4| = r|T3|$ packets in $e2$ requiring to traverse $e2$, $e1$ and a set Z5 of $|Z5|$ = $r|T3|$ packets in $e3$ requiring to traverse $e3$.

Theorem 3. For the network U2 there is an adversary A of rate $r \geq 0.794$ such that the system <U2, $A2$, Ni> is unstable where i={1, 2, 3} and Ni={(NTG, LIS), (NTG, FFS), (NTG, FFS, LIS)}.

Stability Behavior of S1, S2, S3, S4 Networks
Now, we consider the networks S1, S2, S3 and S4 (Figure 2). Then, similarly to Theorem 1 we can prove Theorem 4.

Adversary's strategy in network S1. For the system <S1,$A1$,(NTG,LIS)> and the system <S1, $A1$, (NTG, FFS)> the queue f uses LIS and FFS protocol correspondingly and the rest queues use NTG. For the system <S1, $A1$, (NTG, LIS, FFS)> the queue f uses LIS, $g1$ uses FFS and e, $g2$ use NTG. The strategy of the adversary is the same in these three systems. We consider that each phase consists of four distinguished time rounds. The inductive argument states that if at the beginning of a phase j, there are s_j packets in the queues e, f requiring to traverse the edges e, $g1$ and f, $g1$, then at the beginning of phase $j+1$ there will be more than s_j packets in the same queues requiring to traverse the same edges. The adversary's strategy during a phase j follows:

- *Round 1*: It lasts $|T1| = s_j$ time steps. During this round, the adversary injects in $g1$ a set Z1 of $|Z1| = r|T1|$ packets wanting to traverse $g1$, $g2$.
- *Round 2*: It lasts $|T2| = r|T1|$ time steps. During this round, the adversary injects a set Z2 of $|Z2| = r|T2|$ packets in $g2$ requiring to traverse $g2$, e.
- *Round 3*: It lasts $|T3| = r|T2|$ time steps. During this round, the adversary injects a set Z3 of $|Z3| = r|T3|$ packets in $g2$ requiring to traverse $g2$, f and a set Z4 of $|Z4| =$

$r|T3|$ packets in e requiring to traverse e, $g1$.

- *Round 4*: It lasts $|T4| = r|T3|$ time steps. During this round, the adversary injects a set Z5 of $|Z5| = r|T4|$ packets in e requiring to traverse e and a set Z6 of $|Z6| = r|T4|$ packets in f requiring to traverse f, $g1$.

Adversary's strategy in network S2. For the system <S2, A2, (NTG, LIS)> and the system <S2, A2, (NTG, FFS)> the queue g uses LIS and FFS protocol correspondingly and the rest queues use NTG. For the system <S2, A2, (NTG, LIS, FFS)> the queue g uses FFS, $f2$ uses LIS and $e1$, $e2$, $f1$ use NTG. The strategy of the adversary is the same in these three systems. We consider that each phase consists of four distinguished time rounds. The inductive argument states that if at the beginning of a phase j, there are s_j packets in the queues $e2$, $f2$ requiring to traverse the edges $e2$, g and $f2$, g correspondingly, then at the beginning of phase $j+1$ there will be more than s_j packets in the same queues requiring to traverse the same edges. The adversary's strategy during a phase j follows:

- *Round 1*: It lasts $|T1| = s_j$ time steps. During this round, the adversary injects in g a set Z1 of $|Z1| = r|T1|$ packets wanting to traverse g, $e1$.
- *Round 2*: It lasts $|T2| = r|T1|$ time steps. During this round, the adversary injects a set Z2 of $|Z2| = r|T2|$ packets in queue $e1$ requiring to traverse $e1$, $e2$ and a set Z3 of $|Z3| = r|T2|$ packets in queue g requiring to traverse g, $f1$.
- *Round 3*: It lasts $|T3| = r|T2|$ time steps. During this round, the adversary injects a set Z4 of $|Z4| = r|T3|$ packets in $f1$ requiring to traverse $f1$, $f2$ and a set Z5 of $|Z5| = r|T3|$ packets in $e2$ requiring to traverse $e2$, g.
- *Round 4*: It lasts $|T4| = r|T3|$ time steps. During this round, the adversary injects a set Z6 of $|Z6| = r|T4|$ packets in $e2$ requiring

to traverse $e2$ and a set Z7 of $|Z7| = r|T4|$ packets in $f2$ requiring to traverse $f2$, g.

Adversary's strategy in network S3. For the system <S3, A3, (NTG, LIS)> the queues $e1$, $e2$ use LIS protocol and the rest queues use NTG. For the system <S3, A3, (NTG, FFS)> the queues $e1$, $e2$ use FFS protocol and the rest queues use NTG. For the system <S3, A3, (NTG, LIS, FFS)> the queue $e6$ uses LIS, the queues $e1$, $e2$ use FFS and the queues $e3$, $e4$, $e5$ use NTG. The strategy of the adversary is the same in these three systems. We consider that each phase consists of four distinguished time rounds. The inductive argument states that if at the beginning of a phase j, there are s_j packets in the queues $e3$, $e5$ requiring to traverse the edges $e3$, $e1$ and $e5$, $e6$, $e1$, then at the beginning of phase $j+1$ there will be more than s_j packets in the same queues requiring to traverse the same edges. The adversary's strategy during a phase j follows:

- *Round 1*: It lasts $|T1| = s_j$ time steps. During this round, the adversary injects in $e1$ a set Z1 of $|Z1| = r|T1|$ packets wanting to traverse $e1$, $e2$.
- *Round 2*: It lasts $|T2| = r|T1|$ time steps. During this round, the adversary injects a set Z2 of $|Z2| = r|T2|$ packets in $e2$ requiring to traverse $e2$, $e3$, $e4$, $e5$.
- *Round 3*: It lasts $|T3| = r|T2|$ time steps. During this round, the adversary injects a set Z3 of $|Z3|=r|T3|$ packets in $e2$ requiring to traverse $e2$, $e3$ and a set Z4 of $|Z4| = r|T3|$ packets in $e5$ requiring to traverse $e5$, $e6$, $e1$.
- *Round 4*: It lasts $|T4| = r|T3|$ time steps. During this round, the adversary injects a set Z5 of $|Z5| = r|T4|$ packets in $e3$ requiring to traverse $e3$, $e1$ and a set Z6 of $|Z6| = r|T4|$ packets in $e5$ requiring to traverse $e5$.

Adversary's strategy in network S4. For the system <S4, A4, (NTG, LIS)> the queues $e1$, $e2$

use LIS protocol and the rest queues use NTG. For the system <S4, *A*4, (NTG, FFS)> the queues *e*1, *e*2 use FFS protocol and the rest queues use NTG. For the system <S4, *A*4, (NTG, LIS, FFS)> the queue *e*6 uses LIS, the queues *e*1, *e*2 use FFS and the queues *e*3, *e*4, *e*5, *g*1, *g*2 use NTG. The strategy of the adversary is the same in these three systems. We consider that each phase consists of four distinguished time rounds. The inductive argument states that if at the beginning of a phase *j*, there are s_j packets in the queues *e*3, *e*5 requiring to traverse the edges *e*3, *e*1 and *e*5, *e*6, *g*1, *e*1, then at the beginning of phase *j*+1 there will be more than s_j packets in the same queues requiring to traverse the same edges. The adversary's strategy during a phase *j* follows:

- *Round 1*: It lasts $|T1| = s_j$ time steps. During this round, the adversary injects in *e*1 a set Z1 of $|Z1| = r|T1|$ packets wanting to traverse *e*1, *e*2.
- *Round 2*: It lasts $|T2| = r|T1|$ time steps. During this round, the adversary injects a set Z2 of $|Z2| = r|T2|$ packets in *e*2 requiring to traverse *e*2, *e*3, *g*2, *e*4, *e*5.
- *Round 3*: It lasts $|T3| = r|T2|$ time steps. During this round, the adversary injects a set Z3 of $|Z3| = r|T3|$ packets in *e*2 requiring to traverse *e*2, *e*3 and a set Z4 of $|Z4| = r|T3|$ packets in *e*5 requiring to traverse *e*5, *e*6, *g*1, *e*1.
- *Round 4*: It lasts $|T4| = r|T3|$ time steps. During this round, the adversary injects a set Z5 of $|Z5| = r|T4|$ packets in *e*3 requiring to traverse *e*3, *e*1 and a set Z6 of $|Z6| = r|T4|$ packets in *e*5 requiring to traverse *e*5.

Theorem 4. For the network Si there is an adversary *A*i of rate $r \geq 0.841$ such that the systems <Si, *A*i, (NTG, LIS)>, <Si, *A*i, (NTG, FFS)> and <Si, *A*i, (NTG, LIS, FFS)> are unstable where i={1,2,3,4}.

Instability of FIFO and NTG Compositions

In this section we show lower bounds on injection rate that guarantee instability for specific networks (Figure 1, Figure 2)] under the composition of FIFO and NTG protocols when packets are injected with non-simple and simple paths. First, consider the network U1 (Figure 1) where packets are injected with non-simple paths. We have:

Theorem 5. For the network U1 there is an adversary *A* of rate $r \geq 0.841$ such that the system <U1, *A*, (NTG, FIFO)> is unstable.

Proof. The edge *e* uses FIFO protocol, while the edges *f*, *g* use NTG protocol. *Inductive hypothesis*: At the beginning of phase *j*, there are s_j packets (called *S* set of packets) in the queues *e*, *f* requiring to traverse the edges *e*, *g* and *f*, *g* correspondingly. *Induction Step*: At the beginning of phase *j*+1 there will be more than s_j packets, $s_{j+1} > s_j$, in the queues *e*, *f* requiring to traverse the edges *e*, *g* and *f*, *g* correspondingly.

We will construct an adversary *A* such that the induction step will hold. Proving that the induction step holds, we ensure that the induction hypothesis will hold at the beginning of phase *j*+1 with an increased value of s_j, $s_{j+1} > s_j$. In order to prove that the inductive argument works, we consider that there is a large enough number of packets s_j in the initial system configuration. During phase *j* the adversary plays four rounds of injections.

- *Round 1*: It lasts $|T1| = s_j$ time steps. During this round, the adversary injects in queue *g* a set Z1 of $|Z1| = r|T1|$ packets wanting to traverse the edges *g*, *f*. *S* packets have priority over Z1 packets in *g*.
- *Round 2*: It lasts $|T2| = r|T1|$ time steps. During this round, the adversary injects a set Z2 of $|Z2| = r|T2|$ packets in queue *g* requiring to traverse the edges *g*, *e* and a set Z3 of $|Z3| = r|T2|$ packets in queue *f* requiring to traverse the edge *f*. Z1 packets have priority over Z2 packets in *g*. Therefore, all Z1 packets arrive at *f* along with Z3 packets. The total number of packets arriving at

f during this round is $|Z1| + |Z3|$ packets. However, the duration of this round is $|T2|$ time steps. Therefore, $|T2|$ packets traverse f during this round. At the end of the round, there will be a set X of $|X| = r|T2|$ packets in f wanting to traverse f and $|Z2| = r|T2|$ packets in g wanting to traverse the edges g, e.

- *Round* 3: It lasts $|T3| = r|T2|$ time steps. During this round, the adversary injects a set Z4 of $|Z4| = r|T3|$ packets in queue e requiring to traverse e and a set Z5 of $|Z5| = r|T3|$ packets in f requiring to traverse the edges f, g. X packets have priority over Z5 packets in f. At the end of this round, there are $|Z5| = r|T3|$ packets in f wanting to traverse f, g. Also, the Z4 packets arrive at e along with Z2 packets. The total number of packets arriving at e during round 3 is $|Z4| + |Z2|$ packets. However, the duration of this round is $|T3|$ time steps. Therefore, $|T3|$ packets traverse e during this round. Thus, at the end of round 3, there will be a set Y of $|Y| = r|T3|$ packets in e wanting to traverse e and $|Z5| = r|T3|$ packets in f wanting to traverse f, g.

- *Round* 4: It lasts $|T4| = r|T3|$ time steps. During round 4, the adversary injects a set Z6 of $|Z6| = r|T4|$ packets in e requiring to traverse the edges e, g and a set Z7 of $|Z7| = r|T4|$ packets in f requiring to traverse the edge f. Z7 packets have priority over Z5 packets in f. Thus at the end of round 4, there are $|Z8| = r|T4|$ packets in f wanting to traverse f, g. Also, Y packets have priority over Z6 packets in e, because Y packets are longer time in e than Z6 packets. At the end of round 4, there are $s_{j+1} = |Z6| + |Z8| = 2r|T4|$ packets in e, f requiring to traverse e, g and f, g.

In order to have instability, we must have $s_{j+1} > s_j$. This holds for $2r|T4| > |T1|$, i.e. $r \geq 0.841$. This argument can be repeated for an infinite and unbounded number of phases ensuring that the number of packets in e, f requiring to traverse e, g and f, g at the end of a phase is larger than at the beginning of the phase forever. $\square$

Now, consider the network U2 (Figure 1). Similarly to Theorem 5 we can prove Theorem 6. For the system <U2, $A2$, (NTG, FIFO)> the queues $e2, e4$ use FIFO, and the queues $e1, e3$ use NTG. The inductive argument and the adversary's strategy for the system <U2, $A2$, (NTG, FIFO)> during a phase j is the same as for the systems <U2, $A2$, Ni> in Theorem 3.

Theorem 6. For the network U2 there is an adversary $A2$ of rate $r \geq 0.867$ such that the system <U2, $A2$, (NTG, FIFO)> is unstable.

Now, we consider the networks S1 and S2, (Figure 2). Then, similarly to Theorem 5 we can prove Theorem 7. For the system <S1, $A1$, (NTG, FIFO)> the queue f uses FIFO and $e, g1, g2$ use NTG. For the system <S2, $A2$, (NTG, FIFO)> the queue $f2$ uses FIFO and the queues $f1, g, e1, e2$ use NTG. The inductive argument and the adversary's strategy for the systems <S1, $A1$, (NTG, FIFO)> and <S2, $A2$, (NTG, FIFO)> is the same as for the systems <S1, $A1$, (NTG, LIS)> and <S2, $A2$, (NTG, LIS)> in Theorem 4 correspondingly.

Theorem 7. For the network Si there is an adversary Ai of rate $r \geq 0.908$ such that the system <Si, Ai, (NTG, FIFO)> is unstable where i={1, 2}.

Now, we consider the networks S3 and S4 (Figure 2). Then, similarly to Theorem 5 we can prove Theorem 8. For the system <S3, $A3$, (NTG, FIFO)> the queues $e3, e6$ use FIFO and the queues $e1, e2, e4, e5$ use NTG. For the system <S4, $A4$, (NTG, FIFO)> the queues $e3, e6$ use FIFO and the queues $e1, e2, e4, e5, g1, g2$ use NTG. We consider that each phase consists of four distinguished time rounds. For the system <S3, $A3$, (NTG, FIFO)> (<S4, $A4$, (NTG, FIFO)>) the inductive argument states that if at the beginning of a phase j, there are s_j packets in the queues $e3, e5$ ($e3, e5$) requiring to traverse the edges $e3, e1$ ($e3, e1$) and $e5, e6, e1$ ($e5, e6, g1, e1$) correspondingly, then at the beginning of phase $j+1$ there will be more than s_j packets in the same queues requiring to traverse the same edges. The adversary's strategy for the systems <S3, $A3$, (NTG, FIFO)> and <S4, $A4$, (NTG, FIFO)> during the first two rounds of a phase j is the same as for the systems <S3, $A4$, (NTG, LIS)> and <S4, $A4$, (NTG, LIS)> in Theorem 4 correspondingly.

For the system <S3, $A3$, (NTG, FIFO)> the adversary's construction during the last two rounds of a phase j is as follows:

- *Round 3*: It lasts $|T3| = r|T2| = r^2 s_j$ time steps. During this round, the adversary injects a set Z3 of $|Z3| = r|T3|$ packets in $e3$ requiring to traverse $e3$ and a set Z4 of $|Z4| = r|T3|$ packets in $e5$ requiring to traverse $e5, e6, e1$.
- *Round 4*: It lasts $|T4| = r|T3|$ time steps. During this round, the adversary injects a set Z5 of $|Z5| = r|T4|$ packets in $e3$ requiring to traverse $e3, e1$ and a set Z6 of $|Z6| = |T4|-|T3|+|T3|^2 / (|T3|+|Z3|)$ packets in $e5$ requiring to traverse $e5$.

For the system <S4, $A4$, (NTG, FIFO)> the adversary's construction during the last two rounds of a phase j is as follows:

- *Round 3*: It lasts $|T3| = r|T2| = r^2 s_j$ time steps. During this round, the adversary injects a set Z3 of $|Z3| = r|T3|$ packets in $e3$ requiring to traverse $e3$ and a set Z4 of $|Z4| = r|T3|$ packets in $e5$ requiring to traverse $e5, e6, g1, e1$.
- *Round 4*: It lasts $|T4| = r|T3|$ time steps. During this round, the adversary injects a set Z5 of $|Z5| = r|T4|$ packets in $e3$ requiring to traverse $e3, e1$ and a set Z6 of $|Z6| = |T4| - |T3| + |T3|^2 / (|T3|+|Z3|)$ packets in $e5$ requiring to traverse $e5$.

Theorem 8. For the network Si there is an adversary Ai of rate $r \geq 0.9$ such that the system <Si, Ai, (NTG, FIFO)> is unstable where i={3, 4}.

Unstable Heterogeneous Networks under Adversarial Attacks with Dynamic Slowdowns

Instability Behavior of Size-Parameterized Networks

In this section, we prove that the composition of the LIS protocol with any of SIS, NTS and FTG protocols can become unstable for arbitrarily low injection rates (Koukopoulos & Nikolopoulos, 2006). Before proceeding to the adversarial constructions for proving instability we give two basic definitions.

Definition 1. We denote by Xi the set of packets that are injected into the system in the ith round of a phase. These packet sets are characterized as *investing flows* because only packets from these sets will remain in the system at the beginning of the next phase contributing in packet accumulation.

Definition 2. We denote by Si the set of packets the adversary injects into the system in the ith round of a phase. These packet sets are characterized as *short flows* because they are injected on judiciously chosen links of the network for delaying investing flows.

A Parameterized Network Family G_l. We provide here a parameterized family of networks G_l (see Figure 3). The motivation that led us to such a parameterization in the network topology is two-fold: (a) The existence of many pairs of parallel queues in the network allows the adversary to inject an investing flow at a time round over a path with unit slowdown edges, while the previously injected investing flows are delayed in another queue due to its high slowdown D. Also, this structure permits the simultaneous injection of an investing flow on one queue of a pair, and a short flow on the other, without violating the rule of the restricted adversarial model. (b) Such a parameterized network topology construction enables a parameterized analysis of the system configuration evolution into distinguished rounds

Figure 3. The network G_l

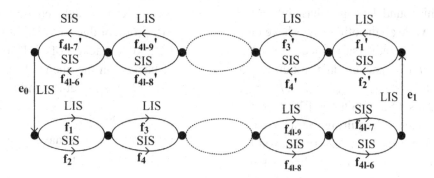

whose number depends on the parameterized network topology. In (LIS, FTG) composition, the parameterization, besides the parallel edges, includes additional chains of queues for the exploitation of FTG in blocking investing flows.

Parameterized Adversarial Constructions. The main ideas of the adversarial constructions we present are: (a) the accurate tuning of the duration of each round of every phase j (as a function of the high slowdown D, the injection rate r and the number of packets in the system at the beginning of phase j, s_j) to maximize the growth of the packet population in the system, (b) the careful setting of the slowdowns of some edges to D for specified time intervals in order to accumulate packets, and (c) the careful injections of packets that guarantee that the load condition is satisfied.

Theorem 9. Let $r' = 0.0056$. For the network G_l where $l > 1000$ is a parameter linear to the number of network queues there is an adversary $A1$ of rate r that can change the link slowdowns of G_l between the two integer values 1 and $D > 1000$ such that the system $<G_l, A1, (LIS, SIS)>$ is unstable for every $r > r'$. When $\{D, l\}$ tend to infinity the system $<G_l, A1, (LIS, SIS)>$ is unstable for $r > 0$.

Proof. Consider an instance of the parameterized network family (network G_l, see Figure 3). The edges $e_0, e_1, f_1, f_3, f_7, \ldots, f_{4l-9}, f_1', f_3', f_7', \ldots, f_{4l-9}'$ of G_l use the LIS protocol, while the remaining edges of G_l use the SIS protocol. *Inductive Hypothesis*: At the beginning of phase j (suppose j is even),

there are s_j packets (called S set of packets) that are queued in the queues f_{4l-9}', f_{4l-6}' (in total) requiring to traverse the edges e_0, f_1. *Induction Step*: At the beginning of phase $j+1$, there will be $s_{j+1} > s_j$ packets that will be queued in the queues f_{4l-9}, f_{4l-6} (in total) requiring to traverse the edges e_1, f_1'.

We will construct an adversary $A1$ such that the induction step will hold. Proving that the induction step holds, we ensure that the inductive hypothesis will hold at the beginning of phase $j+1$ for the symmetric edges with an increased value of s_j, $s_{j+1} > s_j$. By the symmetry of the network, repeating the phase construction an unbounded number of times, we will create an unbounded number of packets in the network.. During phase j, the adversary plays l rounds of injections as follows:

* *Round 1*: It lasts $|T1| = s_j$ time steps. During this round the edge f_1 has high slowdown D, while all the other edges have unit slowdown. The adversary injects a set $X1$ of $|X1| = r |T1|$ packets in the queue e_0 wanting to traverse the edges $e_0, f_2, f_3, f_6, f_7, f_{10}, \ldots, f_{4l-9}, f_{4l-6}, e_1, f_1'$. The packets of the set S delay the packets of the set X1 in the queue e_0 that uses the LIS protocol. At the same time, the packets of the set S are delayed in f_1 due to the high slowdown of the edge f_1. At the end of this round, the remaining packets of S in f_1 are $|S'| = |S|-(|T1| / D)$.

- *Round 2*: It lasts $|T2| = |S'|$ time steps. During this round the edge f_2 has high slowdown D, while all the other edges have unit slowdown. The adversary injects a set X2 of $|X2| = r\,|T2|$ packets in f_1 requiring to traverse the edges $f_1, f_3, f_6, f_7, f_{10}, \ldots, f_{4l-9}, f_{4l-6}$, e_1, f_1' and a set S2 of $|S2| = r\,|T2|\,/\,D$ packets in the queue f_2 requiring to traverse the edge f_2. The packets of X2 are delayed by the packets of the set S' in f_1 that uses the LIS protocol. At the same time, the packets of X1 are delayed in f_2 that uses the SIS protocol due to its high slowdown D and the packets of S2. Therefore, the remaining packets of X1 in f_2 are $|X1| + (r-1)\,|T2|/D$.

- *Round 3*: It lasts $|T3| = |X1| + |X2| + (r-1)\,|T2|\,/\,D$ time steps. During this round the edge f_6 has high slowdown D, while all the other edges have unit slowdown. The adversary injects a set X3 of $|X3| = r\,|T3|$ packets in f_3 requiring to traverse the edges $f_3, f_5, f_7, f_{10}, \ldots, f_{4l-9}, f_{4l-6}, e_1, f_1'$ and a set S3 of $|S3| = r\,|T3|\,/\,D$ packets in the queue f_6 requiring to traverse the edge f_6. The packets of X1, X2 delay the packets of the set X3 in f_3 that uses the LIS protocol. At the same time, the packets of X1, X2 are delayed in f_6 that uses the SIS protocol due to the high slowdown of f_6 and the packets of S3. Therefore, the remaining packets of the sets X1, X2 in f_6 are $|X1| + |X2| + (r-1)$ $(|T2| + |T3|)\,/\,D$.

- *Round l*: It lasts $|Tl| = \sum_{i=1}^{l-1} |Xi| - (r-1) \sum_{i=2}^{l-1} \dfrac{|Ti|}{D}$ time steps. During this round the edge f_{4l-6} has high slowdown D, while all the other edges have unit slowdown. The adversary injects a set Xl of $|Xl| = r\,|Tl|$ packets in the queue f_{4l-9} requiring to traverse the edges $f_{4l-9}, f_{4l-7}, e_1, f_1'$ and a set Sl of $|Sl| = r\,|Tl|$ $/\,D$ packets in the queue f_{4l-6} requiring to traverse the edge f_{4l-6}. The packets of the sets X1,…,Xl-1 delay the packets of Xl in the queue f_{4l-9} that uses the LIS protocol.

At the same time, the packets of the sets X1,…, Xl-1 are delayed in f_{4l-6} that uses the SIS protocol due to the high slowdown of f_{4l-6} and the packets of Sl. Thus, the number of packets in the queues f_{4l-9}, f_{4l-6} requiring to traverse e_1, f_1' at the end of this round is $s_{j+1} = rs_j + \left(r + \dfrac{r-1}{D}\right) \sum_{i=2}^{l} |Ti|$. In order to have instability, we must have $s_{j+1} > s_j$. Therefore, for instability it suffices:

$$r + \left(r + \frac{r-1}{D}\right)\frac{D-1}{D} + \left(r + \frac{r-1}{D}\right)\left(2r - \frac{1}{D} - \frac{r-1}{D^2}\right)\frac{1 - \left(r + \frac{D+r-1}{D}\right)^{l-2}}{\frac{1-(D+1)r}{D}} > 1$$

(3)

If we let $r = 0.0056$, $D = 1000$ and $l = 1000$, the inequality holds. Thus, for $\{D, l\} > 1000$ the inequality holds, too. When $D \rightarrow \infty$, it holds that $(1/D^k) \rightarrow 0$ for all $k \geq 1$. Then, the inequality becomes $r > 1/(2(r+1)^{l-2})$. When $l \rightarrow \infty$, and $x > 0$, it holds that $(1 + x)^{l-2} \rightarrow \infty$. Therefore, for $\{D, l\} \rightarrow \infty$ the inequality $r > 1/(2(r+1)^{l-2})$ holds for $r > 0$. Note that if we have a sequence of equations $f_{\{D,l\}}(r)$ and there exists the limit $lim_{\{D,l\} \rightarrow \infty} f_{\{D,l\}}(r) = f_\infty(r)$, then it holds fundamentally by the theory of function limits that if $r(D, l)$ is the root of $f_{\{D,l\}}(r) = 0$, the $lim_{\{D,l\} \rightarrow \infty} r(D, l)$ is the root of $f_\infty(r)$. Therefore, for $r > 0$ the system is unstable. This argument can be repeated for an infinite number of phases showing that the number of packets in the system increases forever for $r > 0$. □

With a similar adversarial construction to Theorem 9, we show that the composition of the LIS and NTS protocols can become unstable for arbitrarily low injection rates considering an instance of the parameterized network family (network G_l, see Figure 3). The network G_l is also used for proving the instability of the composition of the LIS and SIS protocols. However in this case, the edges e_0, $e_1, f_1, f_3, f_7, \ldots, f_{4l-9}, f_1', f_3', f_7', \ldots, f_{4l-9}'$ of G_l use the LIS protocol, while the remaining edges of G_l use the NTS protocol. Thus, the following theorem, analogous to Theorem 9, holds.

Theorem 10. Let $r' = 0.0056$. For the network G_l where $l>1000$ is a parameter linear to the number of network queues there is an adversary $A2$ of rate r that can change the link slowdowns of G_l between the two integer values 1 and $D>1000$ such that the system $<G_l, A2, (LIS, NTS)>$ is unstable for every $r > r'$. When $\{D, l\} \to \infty$ the system $<G_l, A2, (LIS, NTS)>$ is unstable for $r>0$.

Similarly, we show that the composition of the LIS and FTG protocols can become unstable for arbitrarily low injection rates considering an instance G_l' of the parameterized network family G_l (see Figure 4). The topology of the network G_l' has a significant difference with the networks that are used for proving Theorems 9 and 10. The network G_l' contains additional paths, comparing to the other three cases, that start at queues that use the FTG protocol. These paths have sufficient lengths, such that the injected short flows have the same blocking effects over the injected investing flows when they conflict in queues that use FTG, as happens in (LIS, SIS) and (LIS, NTS) cases. Thus, the following theorem, analogous to Theorem 9 and Theorem 10, holds.

Theorem 11. Let $r' = 0.0056$. For the network G_l' where $l>1000$ is a parameter linear to the number of network queues there is an adversary $A3$ of rate r that can change the link slowdowns of G_l' between the two integer values 1 and $D>1000$ such that the system $<G_l', A3, (LIS, FTG)>$ is unstable for every $r > r'$. When $\{D, l\} \to \infty$ the system $<G_l', A3, (LIS, FTG)>$ is unstable for $r>0$.

Instability Bounds for Forbidden Subgraphs

In this section, we present lower bounds on the injection rate that guarantee instability for forbidden subgraphs. We consider the networks U1, U2 (see Figure 1) that use the composition of (NTG, LIS) protocols. We show:

Theorem 12. Let $r = 0.769$. For the network U1 there is an adversary A of rate r that can change the link slowdowns of U1 between the two inte-

ger values 1 and $D > 1000$ such that the system $<U1, A, (NTG, LIS)>$ is unstable. When $D \to \infty$ the system $<U1, A, (NTG, LIS)>$ is unstable for $r > 0.769$.

Proof. The edge g uses LIS protocol, while the edges f, e use NTG protocol. *Inductive Hypothesis*: At the beginning of phase j, there are s_j packets (called S set of packets) that are queued in the queues f, e requiring to traverse the edge g. *Induction Step*: At the beginning of phase $j+1$, there will be $s_{j+1} > s_j$ packets that will be queued in the queues f, e requiring to traverse the edge g.

We will construct an adversary A such that the induction step will hold. Proving that the induction step holds, we ensure that the inductive hypothesis will hold at the beginning of phase $j + 1$ with an increased value of s_j, $s_{j+1} > s_j$. During phase j the adversary plays four rounds of injections as follows:

- *Round 1*: It lasts $|T1| = s_j$ time steps. During this round all the network edges have unit slowdown and the adversary injects in the queue g a set X of $|X| = r |T1|$ packets wanting to traverse the edges g, f. The packets of the set S delay the packets of the set X in the queue g.

- *Round 2*: It lasts $|T2| = |T1|$ time steps. During this round the edge f has high slowdown D, while all the other network edges have unit slowdown. Also, the adversary injects a set Y of $|Y| = r |T2|$ packets in the queue g requiring to traverse the edges g, e. The packets of the set X delay the packets of the set Y in the queue g. Thus, the remaining packets of the set Y in the queue g is a set Y1 of $|Y1| = |Y| + |X| - |T2|$ packets. Furthermore, the packets of X are delayed in the queue f due to the high slowdown of the edge f. Thus, the remaining packets of the set X in the queue f is a set X1 of $|X1| = |X| - |T2| / D$ packets.

- *Round 3*: It lasts $|T3| = |Y1|$ time steps. During this round the edge f has high

Figure 4. The network G_l'

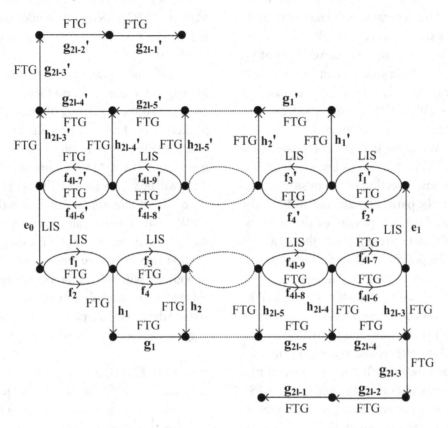

slowdown D, while all the other network edges have unit slowdown. Also, the adversary injects a set Z of $|Z| = r\,|T3|$ packets in the queue e requiring to traverse the edges e, g. The packets of the set Y1 delay the packets of the set Z in the queue e. Furthermore, the packets of the set X1 are delayed in f due to the high slowdown of the edge f during this round. Thus, the remaining packets of the set X1 in the queue f at the end of this round is a set X2 of $|X2| = |X1| - |T3| / D$ packets.

- *Round 4*: It lasts $|T4| = |X2|$ time steps. During this round the edge e has high slowdown D, while all the other edges have unit slowdown. Also, the adversary injects a set L of $|L| = r\,|T4|$ packets in the queue f requiring to traverse the edges f, g.

The packets of the set X2 delay the packets of the set L in the queue f. Moreover, the packets of Z are delayed in e due to the high slowdown D of the edge e during this round. Therefore, the packets of the set Z in e at the end of this round is a set Z1 of $|Z1| = |Z| - |T4| / D$ packets. Thus, the number of packets in the queues f, e requiring to traverse e at the end of this round is $s_{j+1} = |L| + |Z1|$.

In order to have instability, we must have $s_{j+1} > s_j$, that is $r^2[3-2/D] + r\,[-1-1/D + 2/D^2] > 1$. If we let $D = 1000$ and $r = 0.769$, the inequality holds. Thus, for $D > 1000$ and $r = 0.769$ the inequality holds, too. When $D \to \infty$, it holds that $(1 / D^k) \to 0$ for all $k \geq 1$. Then, our inequality becomes $3\,r^2 - r > 1$ which holds for $r > 0.769$. This argument can be repeated for an infinite number of phases showing that the number of packets in the system increases forever for $r > 0.769$. □

Theorem 13. Let $r = 0.733$. For the network U2 there is an adversary A' of rate r that can change the link slowdowns of U2 between the two integer values 1 and $D > 1000$ such that the system <U2, A', (NTG, LIS)> is unstable. When $D \rightarrow \infty$ the system <U2, A', (NTG, LIS)> is unstable for $r > 0.733$.

Proof. The edge $e2$ uses LIS protocol and the rest queues use NTG protocol. *Inductive Hypothesis*: At the beginning of phase j, there are s_j packets (called S set of packets) that are queued in the queues $e2$, $e4$ requiring to traverse the edge $e1$. *Induction Step*: At the beginning of phase $j + 1$ there will be $s_{j+1} > s_j$ packets which will be queued in the queues $e2$, $e4$ requiring to traverse the edge $e1$.

We will construct an adversary A' such that the induction step will hold. Proving that the induction step holds, we ensure that the inductive hypothesis will hold at the beginning of phase j + 1 with an increased value of s_j, $s_{j+1} > s_j$. During phase j the adversary plays three rounds of injections as follows:

- *Round 1*: It lasts $|T1| = s_j$ time steps. During this round all the network edges have unit capacity and the adversary injects in the queue $e1$ a set X of $|X| = r |T1|$ packets wanting to traverse the edges $e1$, $e2$, $e3$, $e4$. The packets of the set S delay the packets of X in $e1$.
- *Round 2*: It lasts $|T2| = |T1|$ time steps. During this round the edge $e3$ has high slowdown D, while all the other network edges have unit capacity. Also, the adversary injects a set Y of $|Y| = r |T2|$ packets in the queue $e2$ requiring to traverse the edges $e2$, $e1$. The packets of the set X delay the packets of the set Y in the queue $e2$. Therefore, a set Y1 of $|Y1| = |Y| + |X| - |T2|$ packets remain in $e2$ at the end of this

round. Furthermore, the packets of the set X are delayed in the queue $e3$ due to the high slowdown of $e3$. Therefore, a set X1 of $|X1| = |X| - |T2| / D$ packets remain in $e3$ at the end of this round.

- *Round 3*: It lasts $|T3| = |X1|$ time steps. During this round the edge $e2$ has high slowdown D, while all the other edges have unit slowdown. The adversary injects a set Z of $|Z| = r |T3|$ packets in the queue $e4$ requiring to traverse the edges $e4$, $e1$. The packets of the set X1 delay the packets of the set Z in the queue $e4$. Moreover, the packets of Y1 are delayed in $e2$ due to the high slowdown of $e2$ during this round. Therefore, the packets of the set Y1 in $e2$ at the end of this round is a set Y2 of $|Y2| = |Y1| - |T3| / D$ packets. Thus, the number of packets in the queues $e2$, $e4$ requiring to traverse the edge $e1$ at the end of this round is $s_{j+1} = |Z| + |Y2|$.

In order to have instability, we must have $s_{j+1} > s_j$, that is, $r^2 + r (2 - 2 / D) > 2 + 1 / D^2$. If we let $D = 1000$ and $r = 0.733$, the inequality holds. Thus, for $D > 1000$ and $r = 0.733$ the inequality holds, too. When $D \rightarrow \infty$, it holds that $(1 / D^k) \rightarrow 0$ for all $k \geq 1$. Then, the inequality becomes $r^2 + 2 r > 2$, which holds for $r > 0.733$. This argument can be repeated for an infinite number of phases showing that the number of packets in the system increases forever for $r > 0.733$. □

Unstable Heterogeneous Networks under Adversarial Attacks with Dynamic Capacities

In this section, we present lower bounds on the injection rate that guarantee instability for forbidden subgraphs. First, we consider the simple-path networks S1, S2, S3, S4 (Figure 2) that use the (NTG, LIS) protocol composition. We show:

Theorem 14. Let $r \geq 0.82$. For the network S1 there is an adversary $A1$ of rate r that can change the link capacities of S1 between the two integer values 1 and $C > 1000$ such that the system $<$S1, $A1$, (LIS, NTG)$>$ is unstable. When $C \rightarrow \infty$, the system $<$S1, $A1$, (LIS, NTG)$>$ is unstable for $r > 0.8191$.

Proof. The edge $g2$ uses LIS protocol and the rest queues use NTG protocol. *Inductive Hypothesis*: At the beginning of phase j, there are s_j packets (called S set of packets) that are queued in the queues e, f requiring to traverse the edge $g1$. *Induction Step*: At the beginning of phase $j+1$, there will be $s_{j+1} > s_j$ packets that will be queued in the queues e, f requiring to traverse the edge $g1$.

We will construct an adversary $A1$ such that the induction step will hold. Proving that the induction step holds, we ensure that the inductive hypothesis will hold at the beginning of phase $j+1$ with an increased value of s_j, $s_{j+1} > s_j$. During phase j, the adversary plays four rounds of injections as follows:

- *Round 1:* It lasts $|T1| = s_j / C$ time steps. During this round all the network edges have high capacity C and the adversary injects in the queue $g1$ a set X of $|X| = r\, C\, |T1|$ packets wanting to traverse the edges $g1, g2$. The packets of S delay the packets of X in the queue $g1$.

- *Round 2:* It lasts $|T2| = |X| / C$ time steps. During this round all the network edges have high capacity C and the adversary injects a set Y of $|Y| = r\, C\, |T2|$ packets in the queue $g2$ requiring to traverse the edges $g2, e$. The packets of X delay the packets of Y in the queue $g2$.

- *Round 3:* It lasts $|T3| = |Y| / C$ time steps. During this round all the network edges have high capacity C and the adversary injects a set Z of $|Z| = r\, C\, |T3|$ packets in the queue $g2$ requiring to traverse the edges $g2, f$. Also, it injects a set Z1 of $|Z1| = r\, C\, |T3|$ packets in the queue e requiring to traverse the edges $e, g1$. The packets of the

set Y delay the packets of the set Z in the queue $g2$. Moreover, the packets of Y delay the packets of Z1 in the queue e.

- *Round 4:* It lasts $|T4| = |Z| / C$ time steps. During this round the edge e has unit capacity, while all the other edges have high capacity C. The adversary injects a set Z2 of $|Z2| = r\, C\, |T4|$ packets in the queue f requiring to traverse the edges $e, g1$. The packets of the set Z delay the packets of the set Z2 in the queue f. The packets of the set Z1 are delayed in the queue e due to the unit capacity of the edge e during this round. Thus, the number of packets in the queues e, f requiring to traverse the edge $g1$ at the end of this round is $s_{j+1} = |Z2| + |Z1| - |T4|$.

In order to have instability, we must have $s_{j+1} > s_j$, that is $r^4 + r^3\,(1 - (1 / C)) > 1$. If we let $C=1000$ and $r = 0.82$, the inequality holds. Thus, for $C > 1000$ and $r = 0.82$ the inequality holds, too. When $C \rightarrow \infty$, it holds that $(1/C^k) \rightarrow 0$ for all $k \geq 1$. Then, our inequality becomes $r^4 + r^3 -1>0$ which holds for $r > 0.8191$. This argument can be repeated for an infinite number of phases showing that the number of packets in the system increases forever for $r > 0.8191$. $\square$

Theorem 15. Let $r \geq 0.82$. For the network S2 there is an adversary $A2$ of rate r that can change the link capacities of S2 between the two integer values 1 and $C > 1000$ such that the system $<$S2, $A2$, (LIS, NTG)$>$ is unstable. When $C \rightarrow \infty$, the system $<$S2, $A2$, (LIS, NTG)$>$ is unstable for $r > 0.8191$.

Proof. The edge g uses LIS protocol and the rest queues use NTG protocol. *Inductive Hypothesis*: At the beginning of phase j, there are s_j packets (called S set of packets) that are queued in the queues $e2, f2$ requiring to traverse the edge g. *Induction Step*: At the beginning of phase $j+1$, there will be $s_{j+1} > s_j$ packets that will be queued in the queues $e2, f2$ requiring to traverse the edge g.

We will construct an adversary $A2$ such that the induction step will hold. Proving that the induction step holds, we ensure that the inductive hypothesis will hold at the beginning of phase $j+1$ with an increased value of of s_j, $s_{j+1} > s_j$. During phase j, the adversary plays four rounds of injections as follows:

- *Round 1:* It lasts $|T1| = s_j / C$ time steps. During this round all the network edges have high capacity C and the adversary injects in the queue g a set X of $|X| = r\, C\, |T1|$ packets wanting to traverse the edges $g, f1$. The packets of the set S delay the packets of the set X in the queue g.

- *Round 2:* It lasts $|T2| = |X| / C$ time steps. During this round all the network edges have high capacity C and the adversary injects a set Y of $|Y| = r\, C\, |T2|$ packets in the queue $f1$ requiring to traverse the edges $f1$, $f2$ and a set Z of $|Z| = r\, C\, |T2|$ packets in the queue g requiring to traverse the edges g, $e1$. The packets of the set X delay the packets of Z in g. The packets of the set X delay the packets of the set Y in the queue $f1$.

- *Round 3:* It lasts $|T3| = |Y| / C$ time steps. During this round all the network edges have high capacity C. Also, the adversary injects a set Z1 of $|Z1| = r\, C\, |T3|$ packets in the queue $f2$ requiring to traverse the edges $f2$, g and a set Z2 of $|Z2| = r\, C\, |T3|$ packets in $e1$ requiring to traverse the edges $e1$, $e2$. The packets of the set Y delay the packets of Z1 in $f2$. The packets of Z delay the packets of the set Z2 in the queue $e1$.

- *Round 4:* It lasts $|T4| = |Z1| / C$ time steps. During this round the edge $e4$ has unit capacity, while all the other edges have high capacity C. Also, the adversary injects a set Z3 of $|Z3| = r\, C\, |T4|$ packets in the queue $e2$ requiring to traverse the edges $e2$, g. The packets of the set Z2 delay the packets of the set Z3 in the queue $e2$. The packets of the set Z1 are delayed in $f2$ due to the unit

capacity of the edge $f2$ during this round. Thus, the number of packets in the queues $e2, f2$ requiring to traverse the edge g at the end of this round is $s_{j+1} = |Z3| + |Z1| - |T4|$.

In order to have instability, we must have $s_{j+1} > s_j$, that is $r^4 + r^3 (1 - (1 / C)) > 1$. If we let $C = 1000$ and $r = 0.82$, the inequality holds. Thus, for $C > 1000$ and $r = 0.82$ the inequality holds, too. When $C \to \infty$, it holds that $(1/C^k) \to 0$ for all $k \geq 1$. Then, our inequality becomes $r^4 + r^3 - 1 > 0$ which holds for $r > 0.8191$. This argument can be repeated for an infinite number of phases showing that the number of packets in the system increases forever for $r > 0.8191$. $\square$

Theorem 16. Let $r \geq 0.82$. For the network S3 there is an adversary $A3$ of rate r that can change the link capacities of S3 between the two integer values 1 and $C > 1000$ such that the system <S3, $A3$, (LIS, NTG)> is unstable. When $C \to \infty$, the system <S3, $A3$, (LIS, NTG)> is unstable for $r > 0.8191$.

Proof. The edge $e3$ uses LIS protocol and the rest queues use NTG protocol. *Inductive Hypothesis*: At the beginning of phase j, there are s_j packets (called S set of packets) that are queued in the queues $e3, e5$ requiring to traverse the edges $e3, e1$ and $e5, e6, e1$ correspondingly. *Induction Step*: At the beginning of phase $j+1$ there will be $s_{j+1} > s_j$ packets that will be queued in the queues $e3, e5$ requiring to traverse the edges $e3, e1$ and $e5, e6, e1$ correspondingly.

We will construct an adversary $A3$ such that the induction step will hold. Proving that the induction step holds, we ensure that the inductive hypothesis will hold at the beginning of phase $j+1$ with an increased value of s_j, $s_{j+1} > s_j$. During phase j, the adversary plays four rounds of injections as follows:

- *Round 1:* It lasts $|T1| = s_j / C$ time steps. During this round all the network edges have high capacity C and the adversary injects in the queue $e1$ a set X of $|X| = r\, C$

|T1| packets wanting to traverse the edges $e1$, $e2$. The packets of the set S delay the packets of the set X in the queue $e1$.

- *Round 2*: It lasts $|T2| = |X| / C$ time steps. During this round all the network edges have high capacity C and the adversary injects a set Y of $|Y| = r\,C\,|T2|$ packets in the queue $e2$ requiring to traverse the edges $e2$, $e3$, $e4$. The packets of the set X delay the packets of the set Y in the queue $e2$.

- *Round 3:* It lasts $|T3| = |Y| / C$ time steps. During this round all the network edges have high capacity C. Also, the adversary injects a set Z of $|Z| = r\,C\,|T3|$ packets in the queue $e3$ requiring to traverse the edges $e3$, $e1$ and a set Z1 of $|Z1| = r\,C\,|T3|$ packets in $e4$ requiring to traverse the edges $e4$, $e5$. The packets of the set Y delay the packets of the set Z in $e3$. Furthermore, the packets of the set Y delay the packets of the set Z1 in the queue $e4$.

- *Round 4*: It lasts $|T4| = |Z| / C$ time steps. During this round the edge $e3$ has unit capacity, while all the other edges have high capacity C. Also, the adversary injects a set Z2 of $|Z2| = r\,C\,|T4|$ packets in the queue $e5$ requiring to traverse the edges $e5$, $e6$, $e1$. The packets of the set Z1 delay the packets of the set Z2 in the queue $e6$. Moreover, the packets of the set Z are delayed in $e3$ due to the unit capacity of the edge $e3$ during this round. Thus, the number of packets in the queues $e3$, $e5$ requiring to traverse the edges $e3$, $e1$ and $e5$, $e6$, $e1$ correspondingly at the end of this round is $s_{j+1} = |Z2| + |Z| - |T4|$.

In order to have instability, we must have $s_{j+1} > s_j$, that is $r^4 + r^3 (1 - (1 / C)) > 1$. If we let $C = 1000$ and $r = 0.82$, the inequality holds. Thus, for $C > 1000$ and $r = 0.82$ the inequality holds, too. When $C \to \infty$, it holds that $(1/C^k) \to 0$ for all $k \geq 1$. Then, our inequality becomes $r^4 + r^3 - 1 > 0$ which holds for $r > 0.8191$. This argument can be

repeated for an infinite number of phases showing that the number of packets in the system increases forever for $r > 0.8191$. $\square$

Theorem 17. Let $r \geq 0.82$. For the network S4 there is an adversary $A4$ of rate r that can change the link capacities of S4 between the two integer values 1 and $C > 1000$ such that the system <S4 $A4$, (LIS, NTG)> is unstable. When $C \to \infty$, the system <S4, $A4$, (LIS, NTG)> is unstable for $r > 0.8191$.

Proof. The edge $e3$ uses LIS protocol and the rest queues use NTG protocol. *Inductive Hypothesis*: At the beginning of phase j, there are s_j packets (called S set of packets) that are queued in the queues $e3$, $e5$ requiring to traverse the edges $e3$, $e1$ and $e5$, $e6$, $g1$, $e1$ correspondingly. *Induction Step*: At the beginning of phase $j+1$ there will be $s_{j+1} > s_j$ packets that will be queued in the queues $e3$, $e5$ requiring to traverse the edges $e3$, $e1$ and $e5$, $e6$, $g1$, $e1$ correspondingly.

We will construct an adversary $A4$ such that the induction step will hold. Proving that the induction step holds, we ensure that the inductive hypothesis will hold at the beginning of phase $j+1$ with an increased value of s_j, $s_{j+1} > s_j$. During phase j, the adversary plays four rounds of injections as follows:

- *Round 1:* It lasts $|T1| = s_j / C$ time steps. During this round all the network edges have high capacity C and the adversary injects in the queue $e1$ a set X of $|X| = r\,C$ $|T1|$ packets wanting to traverse the edges $e1$, $e2$. The packets of the set S delay the packets of the set X in the queue $e1$.

- *Round 2*: It lasts $|T2| = |X| / C$ time steps. During this round all the network edges have high capacity C and the adversary injects a set Y of $|Y| = r\,C\,|T2|$ packets in the queue $e2$ requiring to traverse the edges $e2$, $e3$, $g2$. The packets of the set X delay the packets of Y in the queue $e2$.

- *Round 3*: It lasts $|T3| = |Y| / C$ time steps. During this round all the network edges have high capacity C. Also, the adversary injects a set Z1 of $|Z1| = r\,C\,|T3|$ packets in the queue $e3$ requiring to traverse the edges $e3$, $e1$ and a set Z2 of $|Z2| = r\,C\,|T3|$ packets in $g2$ requiring to traverse the edges $g2$, $e4$, $e5$. The packets of the set Y delay the packets of Z1 in $e3$. The packets of the set Y delay the packets of Z2 in the queue $g2$.

- *Round 4*: It lasts $|T4| = |Z1| / C$ time steps. During this round the edge $e3$ has unit capacity, while all the other edges have high capacity C. Also, the adversary injects a set Z3 of $|Z3| = r\,C\,|T4|$ packets in the queue $e5$ requiring to traverse the edges $e5$, $e6$, $g1$, $e1$. The packets of the set Z2 delay the packets of Z3 in the queue $e5$. The packets of the set Z1 are delayed in $e3$ due to the unit capacity of the edge $e3$ during this round. Thus, the number of packets in the queues $e3$, $e5$ requiring to traverse the edges $e3$, $e1$ and $e5$, $e6$, $g1$, $e1$ correspondingly at the end of this round is $s_{j+1} = |Z3| + |Z1| - |T4|$.

In order to have instability, we must have $s_{j+1} > s_j$, that is $r^4 + r^3 (1 - (1 / C)) > 1$. If we let $C = 1000$ and $r = 0.82$, the inequality holds. Thus, for $C > 1000$ and $r = 0.82$ the inequality holds, too. When $C \to \infty$, it holds that $(1/C^k) \to 0$ for all $k \geq 1$. Then, our inequality becomes $r^4 + r^3 - 1 > 0$ which holds for $r > 0.8191$. This argument can be repeated for an infinite number of phases showing that the number of packets in the system increases forever for $r > 0.8191$. □

Now, we consider the networks U1, U2 (Figure 1) that use the (NTG, LIS) protocol composition.

Theorem 18. Let $r = 0.8$. For the network U1 there is an adversary A of rate r that can change the link capacities of U1 between the two integer values 1 and $C > 1000$ such that the system $<U1, A, (LIS, NTG)>$ is unstable. When $C \to \infty$, the system $<U1, A, (LIS, NTG)>$ is unstable for $r > \sqrt[3]{0.5}$.

Proof. The edges g, f use LIS protocol and the queue e uses NTG protocol. *Inductive Hypothesis*: At the beginning of phase j, there are s_j packets (called S set of packets) that are queued in the queues f, e requiring to traverse the edge g. *Induction Step*: At the beginning of phase $j+1$ there will be $s_{j+1} > s_j$ packets that will be queued in the queues f, e requiring to traverse the edge g.

We will construct an adversary A such that the induction step will hold. Proving that the induction step holds, we ensure that the inductive hypothesis will hold at the beginning of phase $j+1$ with an increased value of s_j, $s_{j+1} > s_j$. During phase j the adversary plays four rounds of injections as follows:

- *Round 1*: It lasts $|T1| = s_j / C$ time steps. During this round all the network edges have high capacity C and the adversary injects in the queue g a set X of $|X| = r\,C\,|T1|$ packets wanting to traverse the edges g, f. The packets of the set S delay the packets of the set X in the queue g.

- *Round 2*: It lasts $|T2| = |X| / C$ time steps. During this round all the network edges have high capacity C. Also, the adversary injects a set Y of $|Y| = r\,C\,|T2|$ packets in the queue g requiring to traverse the edges g, e and a set Z of $|Z| = r\,C\,|T2|$ packets in the queue f requiring to traverse the edge f. The packets of the set X delay the packets of the set Y and the set Z in g and f correspondingly.

- *Round 3*: It lasts $|T3| = |Y| / C$ time steps. During this round the edge e has unit capacity, while all the network edges have high capacity C. Also, the adversary injects a set Z1 of $|Z1| = r\,C\,|T3|$ packets in the queue f requiring to traverse the edges f, g. The packets of the set Z delay the packets of the set Z1 in the queue f. Furthermore, the packets of the set Y are delayed in e due to the unit capacity of the edge e during this round. Thus, the remaining packets of

Y in e at the end of this round is a set Y' of $|Y'| = |Y| - |T3|$ packets.

- *Round 4*: It lasts $|T4| = |Y'| / C$ time steps. During this round the edge f has unit capacity, while all the other edges have high capacity C. Also, the adversary injects a set Z2 of $|Z2| = r C |T4|$ packets in the queue e requiring to traverse the edges e, g. The packets of the set Y' delay the packets of the set Z2 in the queue e. Moreover, the packets of the set Z1 are delayed in the queue f due to the unit capacity of the edge f during this round. Thus, the number of packets in the queues f, e requiring to traverse the edge g at the end of this round is $s_{j+1} = |Z2| + |Z1| - |T4|$.

In order to have instability, we must have $s_{j+1} > s_j$, that is $r^3 (2-1/C) - r^2 ((1/C)-(1/C^2)) > 1$. If we let $C = 1000$ and $r = 0.8$, the inequality holds. Thus, for $C > 1000$ and $r = 0.8$ the inequality holds, too. When $C \to \infty$, it holds that $(1/C^k) \to 0$ for all $k \geq 1$. Then, our inequality becomes $2 r^3 - 1 > 0$ which holds for $r > \sqrt[3]{0.5}$. This argument can be repeated for an infinite number of phases showing that the number of packets in the system increases forever for $r > \sqrt[3]{0.5}$. □

Theorem 19. Let $r = 0.76$. For the network U2 there is an adversary A' of rate r that can change the link capacities of U2 between the two integer values 1 and $C > 1000$ such that the system <U2, A', (LIS, NTG)> is unstable. When $C \to \infty$, the system <U2, A', (LIS, NTG)> is unstable for $r > 0.754$.

Proof. The edge $e2$ uses LIS protocol and the rest queues use NTG protocol. *Inductive Hypothesis*: At the beginning of phase j, there are s_j packets (called S set of packets) that are queued in the queues $e2$, $e4$ requiring to traverse the edge $e1$. *Induction Step*: At the beginning of phase $j+1$ there will be $s_{j+1} > s_j$ packets which will be queued in the queues $e2$, $e4$ requiring to traverse the edge $e1$.

We will construct an adversary A' such that the induction step will hold. Proving that the induction step holds, we ensure that the inductive hypothesis will hold at the beginning of phase $j+1$ with an increased value of s_j, $s_{j+1} > s_j$. During phase j the adversary plays three rounds of injections as follows:

- *Round 1*: It lasts $|T1| = s_j / C$ time steps. During this round all the network edges have high capacity C and the adversary injects in the queue $e1$ a set X of $|X| = r C |T1|$ packets wanting to traverse the edges $e1$, $e2$, $e3$. The packets of the set S delay the packets of the set X in the queue $e1$.

- *Round 2*: It lasts $|T2| = |X| / C$ time steps. During this round all the network edges have high capacity C. Also, the adversary injects a set Y of $|Y| = r C |T2|$ packets in the queue $e2$ requiring to traverse the edges $e2$, $e1$ and a set Z of $|Z| = r C |T2|$ packets in the queue $e3$ requiring to traverse the edges $e3$, $e4$. The packets of the set X delay the packets of Y in the queue $e2$. Furthermore, the packets of the set X delay the packets of Z in the queue $e3$.

- *Round 3:* It lasts $|T3| = |Y| / C$ time steps. During this round the edge $e2$ has unit capacity, while all the other edges have high capacity C. Also, the adversary injects a set Z1 of $|Z1| = r C |T3|$ packets in the queue $e4$ requiring to traverse the edges $e4$, $e1$. The packets of Z delay the packets of Z1 in the queue $e4$. Moreover, the packets of Y are delayed in $e2$ due to the unit capacity of $e2$ during this round. Thus, the number of packets in the queues $e2$, $e4$ requiring to traverse the edge $e1$ at the end of this round is $s_{j+1} = |Z1| + |Y| - |T3|$.

In order to have instability, we must have $s_{j+1} > s_j$, that is $r^3 + r^2 (1 - 1 / C) > 1$. If we let $C = 1000$ and $r = 0.76$, the inequality holds. Thus, for $C > 1000$ and $r = 0.76$ the inequality holds, too.

When $C \to \infty$, it holds that $(1/C^k) \to 0$ for all $k \geq 1$. Then, our inequality becomes $r^3 + r^2 - 1 > 0$, which holds for $r > 0.754$. This argument can be repeated for an infinite number of phases showing that the number of packets in the system increases forever for $r > 0.754$. $\square$

NETWORK SIMULATION PLATFORM

The simulation environment that we developed supports the types of adversarial attacks described in this chapter. It can simulate symmetric and non-symmetric networks according to different scenarios proving the stability or not of a network. Our platform was built by using C++ Builder due to its friendliness for developing Windows applications. There are several network simulators in the academic community, such as NS-2, and OPNET. All the existing network simulators try to simulate real situations. In this attempt they take into account characteristics like the amount of data transferred from one place to another (throughput), the amount of data that can be transmitted in a fixed amount of time (bandwidth), the delay. However, to check if a network is unstable or not there is no need to define such kind of characteristics. Moreover, for the network simulators NS-2 and OPNET, time is counted in seconds, but in Adversarial Queueing theory, time is counted in time steps. Our system respects these characteristics. We only need the network topology, the injection rate, the link capacities/slowdowns, the contention-resolution protocol used in each queue, the amount of the initial packets in the network along with their placement into the network queues and the adversary's injection strategy. As far as it concerns queueing disciplines.

The simulation of the stability behavior of a network through the implemented platform consists of the following steps:

1. Design of the network topology as a directed graph using the platform's editor. It should be explicitly indicated if the topology is symmetric or non-symmetric.is is used for bulleted / numbered lists.

2. Definition of the initial configuration of the system (how many packets contained in each queue and their paths).

3. Construction of the adversary's strategy.

4. Specification of the queueing discipline implemented in each queue.

5. Execution.

The description of the usage scenario steps follows:

- *Network topology design*. On the main form of the platform the user draws on the canvas nodes and directed edges and indicates whether the network is symmetric or non-symmetric. All nodes and edges have unique labels.

- *Initial system configuration*. The user specifies the adversary's injection rate r and the total number of the initial packets that are already in the network. Furthermore, the user determines the number of packets contained in each queue and the path that the packets must traverse to reach their destination.

- *Adversary's strategy*. The user determines the number of the rounds each phase consists of and the duration of the rounds. Also, the user specifies the number of packets that the adversary injects in the network queues in each round, and the paths these packets will traverse. Moreover, the capacity/slowdown of any edge during each round of a phase is specified.

- *Queueing discipline*s. We have developed the following queueing disciplines: FIFO, LIS, SIS, FTG, NTG, FFS, NTS. For homogeneous networks the user selects one queueing discipline for all the network queues. For heterogeneous networks the user specifies for each queue the used queueing discipline.

- *Execution*. The user gives the number of phases the system is going to run. The results of the system are depicted with graphical representations. One graphical representation depicts the total number of packets that remain in the network queues at the end of each phase. The second one shows the evolution of the number of packets in specific queues for specific intervals of time that are defined by the user.

EVALUATION

In order to evaluate our theoretical results about the stability properties of heterogeneous networks under various protocol compositions and different types of adversarial attacks we carried an experimental study. All of our implementations follow closely the network constructions, the adversarial strategies and the properties of contention-resolution protocols we described in previous sections. The experiments were conducted on a Windows box (Windows XP, Pentium III at 933MHz, with 512MB memory at 133MHz) using C++ Builder ver. They have been implemented as C++ classes by using C++ Builder.

We are interested in the behaviour of the number of packets of all the network queues in successive phases for various compositions of protocols under the three presented types of adversarial attacks in this chapter. If the total number of packets in the network queues increases at any times, then the network is unstable. Figures 5, 6 and 7 illustrate our experiments considering the worst injection rate we estimated with respect to instability for any composition of protocols we studied under classical adversarial attacks. The results of our experiments in the classical adversarial model are summarized in Tables 1 and 2.

Figure 5. Instability Curves of U1 and U2 under a protocol or a composition of protocols in the classical adversarial model: (a) NTG and FIFO in U1, (b) compositions of NTG with LIS, FFS, (LIS, FFS), FIFO in U1, (c) NTG and FIFO in U2, (d) compositions of NTG with LIS, FFS, (LIS, FFS), FIFO in U2

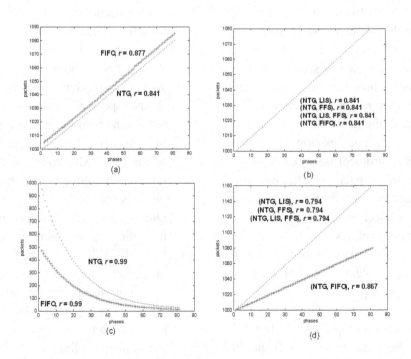

Figure 6. Instability Curves of S1 and S2 under a protocol or a composition of protocols: (a) NTG and FIFO in S1, (b) compositions (NTG, LIS), (NTG, FFS), (NTG, LIS, FFS), (NTG, FIFO) in S1, (c) NTG and FIFO in S2, (d) compositions (NTG, LIS), (NTG, FFS), (NTG, LIS, FFS), (NTG, FIFO) in S2

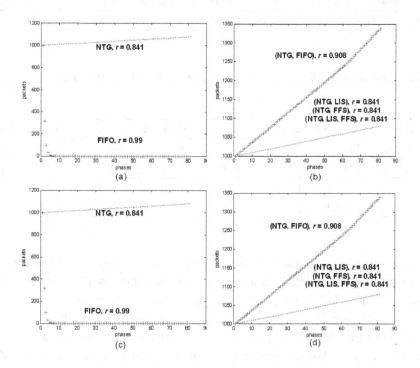

Figure 7. Instability Curves of S3 and S4 under a protocol or a composition of protocols: (a) NTG and FIFO in S3, (b) compositions (NTG, LIS), (NTG, FFS), (NTG, LIS, FFS), (NTG, FIFO) in S3, (c) NTG and FIFO in S4, (d) compositions (NTG, LIS), (NTG, FFS), (NTG, LIS, FFS), (NTG, FIFO) in S4

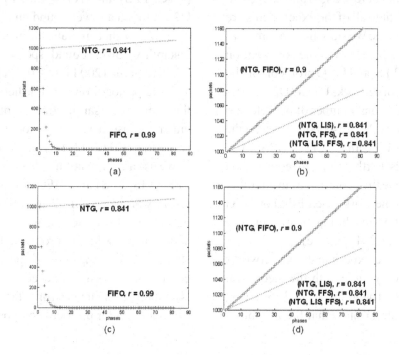

Table 1. Instability of forbidden subgraphs for universal stability under basic adversarial attacks

	(NTG, LIS)	**(NTG, FFS)**	**(NTG, LIS, FFS)**	**(NTG, FIFO)**
U1	LIS: [*f*] ($r \geq 0.841$)	FFS: [*f*], ($r \geq 0.841$)	LIS: [*f*], FFS: [*g*], ($r \geq 0.841$)	FIFO: [*e*], ($r \geq 0.841$)
U2	LIS: [*e4*], ($r \geq 0.794$)	FFS: [*e4*], ($r \geq 0.794$)	LIS: [*e4*], FFS: [*e1*], ($r \geq 0.794$)	FIFO: [*e2, e4*], ($r \geq 0.867$)

Table 2. Instability of forbidden subgraphs for simple-path universal stability under classical adversarial attacks

	<NTG, LIS>	**<NTG, FFS>**	**<NTG, LIS, FFS>**	**<NTG, FIFO>**
S1	LIS: [*f*], ($r \geq 0.841$)	FFS: [*f*], ($r \geq 0.841$)	LIS: [*f*], FFS: [*g1*], ($r \geq 0.841$)	FIFO: [*f*], ($r \geq 0.908$)
S2	LIS: [*g*], ($r \geq 0.841$)	FFS: [*g*], ($r \geq 0.841$)	LIS: [*f2*], FFS: [*g*], ($r \geq 0.841$)	FIFO: [*f2*], ($r \geq 0.908$)
S3	LIS: [*e1, e2*], ($r \geq 0.841$)	FFS: [*e1, e2*], ($r \geq 0.841$)	LIS: [*e6*], FFS: [*e1, e2*], ($r \geq 0.841$)	FIFO: [*e3, e6*], ($r \geq 0.9$)
S4	LIS: [*e1, e2*], ($r \geq 0.841$)	FFS: [*e1, e2*], ($r \geq 0.841$)	LIS: [*e6*], FFS: [*e1, e2*], ($r \geq 0.841$)	FIFO: [*e3, e6*], ($r \geq 0.9$)

The information of which protocol is used in each queue for contention-resolution is included into the tables. For example, in Table 2, in the cell that corresponds to the composition (NTG, LIS} the line LIS: [*f*], ($r \geq 0.841$) means that all the queues use NTG except from the queue *f* which uses LIS protocol and the injection rate lower bound that guarantees instability is $r \geq 0.841$.

Generally, we formulated our experiments assuming that initially there are $s_0 = 1000$ packets in the system. In addition, all of the experiments are executed for 80 phases. We start the experimentation by considering the effect of the composition of NTG with LIS, FFS, and FIFO protocols on the stability properties of networks U1 and U2. Figures 5b and 5d depict the total number of packets into the queues of U1 and U2 correspondingly under the compositions of NTG with LIS, FFS, (LIS, FFS) and FIFO protocols. Furthermore, for comparison reasons, we estimate the evolution of the number of packets into the network when FIFO or NTG is used for contention-resolution on all queues of U1 (Figure 5a) and U2 (Figure 5c).

The results of the experiments on networks U1 and U2 (Table 1) agree with the theoretical results obtained in Theorems 1, 2, 3, 5 and 6. Those results (Table 1) show that the instability

properties of the set of forbidden subgraphs for universal stability (U1 and U2) under a single protocol are maintained, even though we use protocol compositions for contention resolution on different network queues. Even in the case of composing an unstable protocol (NTG) with a universally stable protocol (LIS) on networks U1 and U2 we obtain instability. Surprisingly, in the case of the composition pairs (NTG, LIS), (NTG, FFS) and (NTG, LIS, FFS) on network U2 we found a lower bound on the injection rate ($r \geq 0.794$) that guarantees instability than the instability lower bound specified by Alvarez, Blesa & Serna (2004a) ($r \geq 0.841$) applying only a single protocol on U2. Furthermore, applying the same adversarial strategy on network U2, either we use a single protocol for contention resolution (FIFO or NTG) on all network queues, or we use a composition of NTG with any of LIS, FFS, (LIS, FFS) and FIFO, we observe that the stability properties of U2 are different (Figure 5c, Figure 5d). In particular, when we use a single contention-resolution protocol, the network is stable, while using any of the above protocol compositions the network becomes unstable. This is an indication that networks face worst stability behaviour under protocol compositions.

After studying the stability properties of networks U1 and U2, we study the effect of composing protocols NTG with LIS, FFS, and FIFO on networks S1 and S2 under classical adversarial attacks. Figures 6b and 6d depict the total number of packets into the queues of S1 and S2 correspondingly under the compositions of NTG with LIS, FFS, (LIS, FFS), and FIFO protocols. Furthermore, for comparison reasons, we estimate the evolution of the number of packets into the network when FIFO or NTG is used for contention-resolution on all queues of S1 (Figure 6a) and S2 (Figure 6c).

The results of the experiments on networks S1 and S2 (Table 2) agree with the theoretical results obtained in Theorems 4 and 7. Those results (Table 3) show that the instability properties of the subset of forbidden subgraphs for simple-path universal stability (S1 and S2) under a single protocol are maintained, even though we use protocol compositions for contention resolution on different network queues. Even in the case of composing an unstable protocol (NTG) with a universally stable protocol (LIS) on networks S1 and S2 we obtain instability. Surprisingly, in the case of the composition pairs (NTG, LIS), (NTG, FFS) and (NTG, LIS, FFS) on network S1 we found a lower bound on the injection rate ($r \geq 0.841$) that guarantees instability than the instability lower bound specified by Alvarez, Blesa & Serna (2004a) ($r \geq 0.871$) applying only a single protocol on S1.

Furthermore, applying the same adversarial strategy on network S1 when we use FIFO on all network queues for contention resolution and when we use the composition of NTG with FIFO, we observe that the stability properties of S1 are different (Figure 6a, Figure 6b). In particular,

when we use only FIFO for contention resolution S1 is stable, while composing NTG with FIFO makes the network unstable. The same observation holds in the case of network S2 (Figure 6c, Figure 6d). This is an indication that networks face worst stability behaviour under protocol compositions. Then, we experiment with the effect of composing protocols NTG with LIS, FFS, (LIS, FFS) and FIFO on networks S3 and S4 under classical adversarial attacks. Figure 7b and Figure 7d depict the total number of packets into the queues of S3 and S4 correspondingly under the compositions of NTG with LIS, FFS, (LIS, FFS), and FIFO. Also, for comparison reasons, we estimate the evolution of the number of packets into the network when FIFO or NTG is used for contention-resolution on all queues of S3 (Figure 7a) and S4 (Figure 7c).

The results of the experiments on networks S3 and S4 (Table 2) agree with the theoretical results obtained in Theorems 4 and 8. Those results (Table 2) show that the instability properties of the subset of forbidden subgraphs for simple-path universal stability (S3 and S4) under a single protocol are maintained, even though we use protocol compositions for contention resolution on different network queues. Even in the case of composing an unstable protocol (NTG) with a universally stable protocol (LIS) on networks S3 and S4 we obtain instability. Furthermore, applying the same adversarial strategy on network S3 when we use FIFO on all network queues for contention resolution and when we compose FIFO with NTG for contention resolution, we observe that the stability properties of S3 are different (Figure 7a, Figure 7b). In particular, when we use only FIFO for contention resolution S3 is stable, while

Table 3. Instability of heterogeneous networks under adversarial attacks with dynamic slowdowns

U1	U2	G_i	G_i'
(LIS, NTG), LIS: [g2], ($r \geq 0.769$)	(LIS, NTG), LIS: [e2], ($r \geq 0.733$)	(LIS, SIS), and (LIS, NTS), LIS: [e_0, $e_1, f_1, f_3, f_7, \ldots, f_{4l\text{-}7}, f_1', f_3', f_7', \ldots f_{4l\text{-}7}'$], ($r \geq 0.0056$)	(LIS, FTG), LIS: [$e_0, e_1, f_1, f_3, f_7, \ldots, f_{4l\text{-}7}, f_1', f_3', f_7', \ldots f_{4l\text{-}7}'$], ($r \geq 0.0056$)

composing NTG with FIFO makes the network unstable. The same observation holds in the case of network S4 (Figure 7c, Figure 7d). This is another indication that networks face worst stability behaviour under protocol compositions.

The results of our experiments in the adversarial model with dynamic slowdowns are summarized in Table 3. The information of which protocol is used in each queue for contention-resolution is included into the tables. For example, in Table 3, in the cell that corresponds to network U1, the line (NTG, LIS), LIS: [f], ($r \geq 0.769$) means that the composition (NTG, LIS) is used, all the queues use NTG except from the queue f which uses LIS protocol and the injection rate lower bound that guarantees instability is $r \geq 0.769$. In those experiments we assume that initially there are $s_0 = 1000$ packets in the system. In addition, all of the experiments are executed for 80 phases.

Figure 8 illustrates our experiments considering the worst injection rate we estimated with respect to instability for any composition of protocols we studied under adversarial attacks with dynamic slowdowns. The results of the experiments on networks U1, U2, G_l and G_l' (Table 3) agree with the theoretical results obtained in Theorems 9, 10, 11, 12 and 13. Those results (Table 3) show that the instability properties of the set of forbidden subgraphs for universal stability (U1 and U2) under a single protocol are maintained, even though we use protocol compositions for contention resolution on different network queues. Even in the case of composing an unstable protocol NTG with a universally stable protocol LIS on networks U1 and U2 we obtain instability. Surprisingly, we not only found lower bounds on the injection rate for networks U1 and U2 that guarantee instability than the instability lower bounds specified by Alvarez, Blesa & Serna (2004a) ($r \geq 0.841$) applying only a single protocol on U1 and U2, but they are also lower than the instability bounds specified in Theorem 1 and Theorem 3 for the classical adversarial model. Furthemore, the instability

results for the size-parameterized networks G_l and G_l' under the composition of LIS with any of SIS, NTS and FTG are the first ones which show instability at arbitrarily low injection rates. This is an indication that networks face worst stability behaviour under adversarial attacks with dynamic slowdowns.

Figure 8a depicts the total number of packets into the queues of U1 and U2 correspondingly for the same value of high slowdown D. Figures 8b and 8c depict the total number of packets into the queues of U1 and U2 correspondingly for two values of high slowdown D in each case. Figure 8d shows the total number of packets into the queues of G_l and G_l' for the same values of packet injection rates and network size parameter l when high slowdown D takes different values.

The results of our experiments in the adversarial model with dynamic capacities are summarized in Table 4. In those experiments we assume that initially there are $s_0 = 1000$ packets in the system. In addition, all of the experiments are executed for 80 phases. Figure 9 illustrates our experiments considering the worst injection rate we estimated with respect to instability for any composition of protocols we studied under adversarial attacks with dynamic capacities.

The results of the experiments on networks U1, U2, S1, S2, S3, S4 (Table 4) agree with the theoretical results obtained in Theorems 14, 15, 16, 17, 18, 19. Those results (Table 4) suggest that the instability properties of heterogeneous networks facing adversarial attacks with dynamic capacities are worse than case the heterogeneous networks face classical adversarial attacks and better than the case they face adversarial attacks with dynamic slowdowns. Figure 9a and Figure 9b depict the total number of packets into the queues of U1 and U2 correspondingly. Figure 9c depicts the total number of packets into the queues of S1, S2, S3 and S4 for two values of high capacity C showing that higher capacity value C leads to worse instability behavior. Figure

Figure 8. Instability behaviour of the composition of protocols (LIS, NTG) (a) in U1 and U2 for D=1000, (b) in U1 for D=1000 and D=500, (c) in U2 for D=1000 and D=500, and (d) instability behaviour of the protocol compositions (LIS, SIS), (LIS, NTS) in G_l and (LIS, FTG) in G_l'

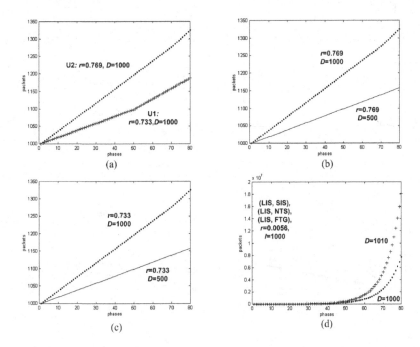

9d shows that networks S1, S2, S3 and S4 can lead to instability for $r=0.8192$ for large values of high capacity C.

POTENTIAL USE

Trust in computing systems is usually specified in terms of a relationship between a trustor and a trustee. A trustor is the entity that trusts a target entity and a trustee is the entity that is trusted.

Roughly speaking, trust is the system property that gives confidence to the trustor to use a service provided by a trustee. Different forms of trust are proposed by Grandison & Sloman (2000) relating to whether access is being provided to the trustor's resources, the trustee is providing a service, the trustworthiness of a trustee is certified, the trust is being delegated or the trustor trusts its own infrastructure. We believe that the study of the stability behaviour of heterogeneous multimedia networks contributes to service provision trust,

Table 4. Instability of heterogeneous networks under adversarial attacks with dynamic capacities

U1	(NTG, LIS), LIS: [g2] ($r > \sqrt[3]{0.5}$)
U2	(NTG, LIS), LIS: [e2], ($r \geq 0.756$)
S1	(NTG, LIS), LIS: [e2], ($r \geq 0.82$)
S2	(NTG, LIS), LIS: [e2], ($r \geq 0.82$)
S3	(NTG, LIS), LIS: [e2], ($r \geq 0.82$)
S4	(NTG, LIS), LIS: [e2], ($r \geq 0.82$)

Figure 9. Instability behaviour of the composition of protocols (LIS, NTG) in (a) U1, (b) U2, (c) S1, S2, S3, S4 for C=1000 and C=200, and (d) S1, S2, S3, S4, for C=1000 and C=5000

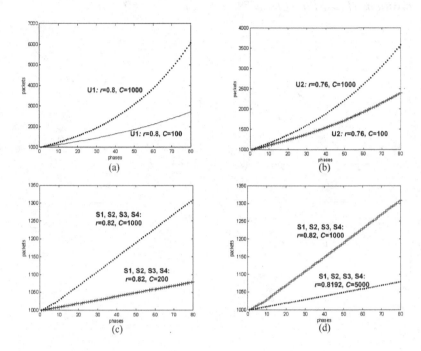

certification of the trustworthiness of a trustee and infrastructure trust.

Service provision trust in multimedia networks mainly depends on how confident is the trustor that the trustee will satisfy the standard of service that has been guaranteed for the satisfaction of the trustor service requests. Such a guarantee of efficient service provision is not possible in network environments where a malicious user can flood the network with dummy packets exploiting specific network system parameters like the network topology, the link capacities/slowdowns, the contention-resolution protocols employed on network queues, the number of network links or the packet injection rate into the network. Thus, it is important to develop a trust mechanism that can specify in advance the network system parameters that may lead to undesirable network behavior (instability) and detect any change in those parameters that may happen during the system execution that can be exploited by a malicious user in order to degrade the performance of the provided services.

Such a trust mechanism would be very useful in dynamically changing network environments like radio-LANs or wireless networks, in general, where the links between any two network nodes can be active or inactive depending on the distance between the nodes or the change in enviromental parameters. The results presented in this work can be very helpful towards this direction because they determine specific network system parameters that can lead a heterogeneous multimedia network to bad behaviour. In particular, our results show that the existence of specific network topologies as subnetworks in large-scale networks under certain compositions of contention-resolution protocols on different network nodes when link capacities/slowdowns change dynamically between certain values and the packet injection rate takes values in a certain domain may lead a network to instability behaviour interrupting any guaranteed service provision. Detecting such conditions we are sure that our system is vulnerable to adversarial attacks. Therefore, we make the appropriate actions in time in order to avoid them enhancinge the service provision trust of our system.

Another domain where the results presented in this work would be valuable is e-banking, e-commerce and e-government applications, all the applications that need real-time processing in general. Such applications are distributed from their nature and it is common to use large-scale heterogeneous networks like Internet in order to communicate with the end-user. Also, they are security sensitive and require more security services (authentication, integrity, confidentiality services). The administrator of networks supporting those applications wants to avoid in advance or detects as soon as possible during system execution any possibility for degradation in system performance due to the resource overloading of a node or a slow connection that result in slow response before it really happens, because this is critical for the reputation of the system. The customer or vendor should trust the network to support mechanisms that will ensure that all the transactions will be handled fast and reliable.In such situations, our results can operate as a first attempt towards eastablishing design criteria to the system administrator for avoiding vulnerability due to adversarial attacks.

Moreover, the trust of system infrastructure is equivalently important with service provision trust. System infrastructure trust in multimedia networks mainly depends on how confident is the trustor that the provided network system infrastructure is not vulnerable to malicious attacks. Our results contribute to this direction because they give us the ability to check very quickly our network infrastructure before we actually use it for possible holes in security or other services we use in order to protect our infrastructure from specific adversarial attacks. This is critical especially in military systems where the trustor wants enhanced trust from the used system infrastructure.

Finally, our results can be used by a third party in order to certify the trustworthiness of the used network system. In this case trust will be based on the set of certificates presented by the trustee to the trustor. Those certificates will be related on metrics that are based on network system parameters that affect the stability behaviour of networks like packet injection rate into the network, employed compositions of contention-resolution protocols on network queues, link capacities/ slowdowns and network topology. Certificates are commonly used in Internet applications for authentication purposes.

Our goal in this study is the deployment of efficient design and maintainance criteria towards establishing a trustworthy heterogeneous multimedia network. The designer/administrator of a heterogeneous multimedia network can use our results before and during system execution. Based on our results the designer/administrator of such a network can choose a network topology that fits to the final users needs without be vulnerable to adversarial attacks. In the case the administrator should use a pre-exist network, he can detect the network for the existence of forbidden subgraphs for network stability and modify appropriately the network. In particular, this will be realized with the use of our results for the stability behavior of forbidden subgraphs for stability. After the choice of the appropriate network topology the designer/ administrator can use our results in order to choose the suitable protocols for contention-resolution on different network queues based on their stability properties when they are composed with other protocols. All these actions should be taken in advance. During the execution of the system, the administrator should monitor the packet injection rate into the network based on our results for unstable thresholds in packet injection rates. At the same time, the administrator should control and handle efficiently the dynamic changing of network link slowdowns/capacities because they can make worse the network stability properties and degrade the overall system performance.

CONCLUSION AND DISCUSSIONS

In this chapter, we studied how efficiently the property of stability under the composition of specific protocols ((NTG, LIS), (NTG, FFS), (NTG, LIS, FFS), (NTG, FIFO)) can be characterized considering directed graphs where packets are injected with non-simple or simple paths under a basic adversarial model. In particular, we proved that the set of subgraphs that are forbidden for universal stability and simple-path universal stability under a single protocol maintain their instability when specific compositions of contention-resolution protocols are composed on the network queues. Interestingly, some of the compositions in some network constructions result in lower bounds on injection rate for network instability comparing to the usage of a single protocol. Also, we showed that the stability properties of FIFO networks are not preserved when FIFO is composed with NTG. In particular, network constructions that are stable when FIFO is used as the only contention-resolution protocol become unstable when FIFO is composed with NTG under the same adversarial constructions. Even, the subgraph U1 that is stable for FIFO under any adversarial construction (Weinard, 2006) becomes unstable composing FIFO with NTG. Thus, we can suggest that the instability properties of a protocol that is not universally stable can become worse when it is composed with another protocol on the same network.

Furthermore, we proved that enhancing the power of the adversary with the ability to monitor the network link capacities / slowdowns may lead to worse instability properties heterogeneous networks that are unstable under the basic adversarial model. In particular, we studied the instability behavior which is induced by all the known forbidden subgraphs on networks running a composition of NTG and LIS protocols when the link capacities change dynamically showing lower instability bounds than their counterparts in the classical adversarial model (Alvarez, Blesa &

Serna, 2004). Also, we studied how the dynamic changing of link slowdowns affects the instability properties of compositions of contention-resolution protocols that include LIS when network size tends to infinity. Our results suggest that, for every unstable network with network link slowdowns that change dynamically, its instability bound may be lower than for the classical adversarial model or other dynamic adversarial model. Proving (or disproving) this remains an open problem.

Finally, in order to evaluate our theoretical results we proceeded in the experimental analysis of the stability behavior of heterogeneous networks under different adversarial strategies and various scenarios of protocol compositions. We feel that this study is a nice complement to our theoretical analysis and gives a better understanding to how an adversary/intruder can exploit the topological structure of a large-scale heterogeneous multimedia network in order to flood the network with packets degrading system performance and leading to service disruption.

By now, the interplay among all the concepts outlined in this chapter, towards the goal designing and maintaining a trustworthy heterogeneous multimedia network, should be apparent: (i) Each designer/administrator of a heterogeneous multimedia network first chooses a network topology that fits to the final users needs. (ii) Then, the designer/administrator should detect the existence or not of forbidden subgraphs for stability at the network topology. (iii) At the same time, the appropriate contention-resolution protocols will be chosen based on their stability properties when they are composed with other protocols. (iv) During the operation of the network the administrator should monitor the packet injection rate into the network. (v) At the same time, the administrator should control and handle efficiently the appearance of dynamic network link slowdowns/capacities situations because they can make worse the network stability properties.

Of course, the above brief description is too general and avoids many important technological issues. For instance, how fast can we detect if an increase in packet injection rate leads the network to instability? How can we exclude forbidden network subgraphs without affecting the guaranteed quality of service to the final user? How much deviation of network link capacity/ slowdown can we afford without facing service disruption? And the list is endless. We believe that these issues, although important in practice, can always be settled given the advances in hardware as well as control software.

Apart from purely technological issues mentioned above, there is another, more important one that is also an open question in network stability: the *characterization* of stability giving a network topology and an adversary's injection rate. Until now, all such characterizations are either of a heuristic nature or too theoretical to be used in practice and, thus, it is not possible to guarantee network stability using an algorithmic method.

REFERENCES

Abdul-Rahman, A., & Hailes, S. (2000). Supporting Trust in Virtual Communities. In *Proceedings of the 33rd Annual Hawaii International Conference on System Sciences* (pp. 1-9).

Aberer, K., & Despotovic, Z. (2001). Managing trust in a peer-2-peer information system. In *Proceedings of the 10th International Conference on Information and Knowledge Management* (pp. 310-317).

Aiello, W., Kushilevitz, E., Ostrovsky, R., & Rosen, A. (2000). Adaptive packet routing for bursty adversarial traffic. *Journal of Computer and System Sciences*, *60*(3), 482–509. doi:10.1006/jcss.1999.1681

Akyildiz, I. F., Melodia, T., & Chowdhury, K. R. (2006). A survey on wireless multimedia sensor networks. *Journal of Computer Networks*, *51*(4), 921–960. doi:10.1016/j.comnet.2006.10.002

Akyildiz, I. F., Su, W., Sankarasubramaniam, Y., & Cayirci, E. (2002). Wireless sensor networks: a survey. *Journal of Computer Networks*, *38*(4), 393–422. doi:10.1016/S1389-1286(01)00302-4

Alpcan, T., & Basar, T. (2003). Global stability analysis of an end-to-end congestion control scheme for general topology networks with delay. In *Proceedings of the 42nd IEEE Conference on Decision and Control* (pp. 1092-1097).

Alpcan, T., Singh, J. P., & Basar, T. (2007). A robust flow control framework for heterogenous network access. In *Proceedings of the 5th Intl. Symposium on Modeling and Optimization in Mobile, Ad Hoc, and Wireless Networks* (pp. 1-8).

Alvarez, C., Blesa, M., Diaz, J., Fernandez, A., & Serna, M. (2003). Adversarial Models for Priority-Based Networks. In *Proceedings of the 28th International Symposium on Mathematical Foundations of Computer Science Vol. 2747* (pp. 142-151).

Alvarez, C., Blesa, M., & Serna, M. (2004a). A Characterization of Universal Stability in the Adversarial Queuing Model. *SIAM Journal on Computing*, *34*, 41–66. doi:10.1137/S0097539703435522

Alvarez, C., Blesa, M., & Serna, M. (2004b). The Impact of Failure Management on the Stability of Communication Networks. In *Proceedings of the 10th International Conference on Parallel and Distributed Systems* (pp. 153-160).

Andrews, M., Awerbuch, B., Fernandez, A., Kleinberg, J., Leighton, T., & Liu, Z. (2001). Universal Stability Results for Greedy Contention-Resolution Protocols. *Journal of the ACM*, *48*, 39–69. doi:10.1145/363647.363677

Balboni, G. P., & Bosco, P. G. (1996). *A TINA Structured Service Gateway*. Paper presented at the Telecommunications Information Networking Architecture Conference.

Bhargav-Spantzel, A., Squicciarini, A., & Bertino, E. (2007). Trust Negotiation in Identity Management. *IEEE Security and Privacy, 5*(2), 55–63. doi:10.1109/MSP.2007.46

Blaze, M., Feigenbaum, F., & Keromytis, A. D. (1998). KeyNote: Trust Management for Public-Key Infrastructures. In *Proceedings of the 1998 International Workshop of Security Protocols* (LNCS 1550, pp. 59-63).

Blaze, M., Feigenbaum, J., & Lacy, J. (1996). Decentralized Trust Management. In *Proceedings of the IEEE Symposium on Security and Privacy* (pp. 164-173).

Blaze, M., Feigenbaum, J., & Strauss, M. (1998). Compliance Checking in the PolicyMaker Trust Management System. In *Proceedings of the 2nd International Conference of Financial Cryptography* (pp. 254-274).

Blesa, M., Calzada, D., Fernandez, A., Lopez, A., Martinez, A., Santos, A., & Serna, M. (2005). Adversarial Queueing Model for Continuous Network Dynamics. In *Proceedings of the 30th International Symposium on Mathematical Foundations of Computer Science Vol. 3618* (pp. 144-155).

Borodin, A., Kleinberg, J., Raghavan, P., Sudan, M., & Williamson, D. (2001). Adversarial Queueing Theory. *Journal of the ACM, 48*, 13–38. doi:10.1145/363647.363659

Borodin, A., Ostrovsky, R., & Rabani, Y. (2001). Stability Preserving Transformations: Packet Routing Networks with Edge Capacities and Speeds Adversarial Queueing Theory. In *Proceedings of the 12th Annual ACM-SIAM Symposium on Discrete Algorithms* (pp. 601-610).

Buchegger, S., & Le Boudec, J. (2002). Performance Analysis of the CONFIDANT Protocol: Cooperation of Nodes — Fairness in Dynamic Ad-hoc Networks. In *Proceedings of the IEEE/ACM Symposium on Mobile Ad Hoc Networking and Computing* (pp. 226-236).

Cahill, V., Gray, E., Seigneur, J., Jensen, C., Chen, Y., & Shand, B. (2003). Using Trust for Secure Collaboration in Uncertain Environments. *IEEE Pervasive Computing Mobile and Ubiquitous Computing, 2*(3), 52–61.

Capra, L. (2004). Engineering human trust in mobile system collaborations. In *Proceedings of the 12th International Symposium on Foundations of Software Engineering* (pp. 107-116).

Chu, Y.-H., Feigenbaum, J., LaMacchia, B., Resnick, P., & Strauss, M. (1997). REFEREE: Trust management for Web applications. *Computer Networks and ISDN Systems, 29*(8-13), 953-964.

Chun, B., & Bavier, A. (2004). Decentralized Trust Management and Accountability in Federated Systems. In *Proceedings of the 37th Hawaii International Conference of System Sciences Vol. 9* (90279a).

Clark, D. (1988). The Design Philosophy of the DARPA Internet Protocols. *ACM Computer Communication Reviews, 18*, 106–114. doi:10.1145/52325.52336

Deering, S., Estrin, D., Farinacci, D., Jacobson, V., Liu, C.-G., & Wei, L. (1994). An Architecture for Wide Area Multicast Routing. In *Proceedings of the ACM SIGCOMM* (pp. 126-135).

Dimmock, N., Belokosztolszki, A., Eyers, D., Bacon, J., & Moody, K. (2004). Using trust and risk in role-based access control policies. In *Proceedings of the ninth ACM symposium on Access control models and technologies* (pp. 156-162).

Donato, D., Paniccia, M., Selis, M., Castillo, C., Cortese, G., & Leonardi, S. (2007). *New metrics for reputation Management in P2P networks*. Paper presented at the 3rd International Workshop on Adversarial Information retrieval on the web.

Floyd, S., & Fal, K. (1999). Promoting the use of end-to-end congestion control in the internet. *IEEE/ACM Transactions on Networking, 7*, 458-472.

Floyd, S., Jacobson, V., McCanne, S., Liu, C.-G., & Zhang, L. (1995). A Reliable Multicast Framework for Light-weight Sessions and Application Level Framing. In *Proceedings of the ACM SIGCOMM* (pp. 342-356).

Floyd, S., & Paxson, V. (2001). Difficulties in Simulating the Internet. *IEEE/ACM Transactions on Networking, 9*, 392-403.

Fowler, H. J., & Murphy, J. W. (1996). Network Management Considerations for Interworking ATM Networks with Non-ATM Services. *IEEE Communications Magazine, 34*(6), 102–106. doi:10.1109/35.506816

Goyal, P., Lam, S., & Vin, H. M. (1997). Determining end-to-end delay bounds in heterogeneous networks. *Multimedia Systems, 5*, 157–163. doi:10.1007/s005300050052

Grandison, T., & Sloman, M. (2000). A Survey of Trust in Internet Applications. *IEEE Communications Surveys and Tutorials, 3*(4), 2–16. doi:10.1109/COMST.2000.5340804

Gurses, E., & Akan, O. B. (2005). Multimedia communication in wireless sensor networks. *Annales des Télécommunications, 60*(7-8), 799–827.

Handley, M., Floyd, S., Pahdye, J., & Widmer, J. (2003). *TCP Friendly Rate Control (TFRC): Protocol Specification* (RFC 3448).

Herlihy, M. P., & Wing, J. (1990). Linearizability: A Correctness Condition for Concurrent Objects. *ACM Transactions on Programming Languages and Systems, 12*(3), 463–492. doi:10.1145/78969.78972

Jeong, Y., Shin, J., & Choi, H.-K. (2005). Channel-Adaptive GPS Scheduling for Heterogeneous Multimedia in CDMA Networks. In. *Proceedings of the ICCNMC, 3619*, 93–101.

Josang, A., & Knapskog, S. J. (1998). A Metric for Trusted Systems. In *Proceedings of the 21st NIST-NCSC National Information Systems Security Conference* (pp. 16-29).

Jurca, D., & Frossard, P. (2006). Media-specific rate allocation in heterogeneous wireless networks. In *Proceedings of the 15th International Packet Video Workshop Vol. 7* (pp. 713-726).

Kamvar, S., Schlosser, M., & Garcia-Molina, H. (2003). The Eigentrust Algorithm for Reputation Management in P2P Networks. In *Proceedings of the 12th International Conference on WWW* (pp. 640-651).

Kelly, F., Maulloo, A., & Tan, D. (1998). Rate control for communication networks: Shadow prices, proportional fairness and stability. *The Journal of the Operational Research Society, 49*(3), 237–252.

Koukopoulos, D. (2005). The Impact of Dynamic Link Slowdowns on Network Stability. In *Proceedings of the 8th International Symposium on Parallel Architectures, Algorithms and Networks* (pp. 340-345).

Koukopoulos, D. (2008). Stability of Heterogeneous Multimedia Networks against Adversarial Attacks. In *Proceedings of the 3rd International Conference on Communications and Networking* (pp. 1259-1263).

Koukopoulos, D., Mavronicolas, M., Nikoletseas, S., & Spirakis, P. (2002). On the Stability of Compositions of Universally Stable, Greedy, Contention-Resolution Protocols. In *Proceedings of the 16th Int. Symposium on DIStributed Computing Vol. 2508* (pp. 88-102).

Koukopoulos, D., Mavronicolas, M., Nikoletseas, S., & Spirakis, P. (2005). The Impact of Network Structure on the Stability of Greedy Protocols. *Journal Theory of Computing Systems, 38,* 425–460. doi:10.1007/s00224-004-1181-3

Koukopoulos, D., Mavronikolas, M., & Spirakis, P. (2007). The Increase of the Instability of Networks due to Quasi-Static Link Capacities. *Journal Theoretical Computer Science, 381,* 44–56. doi:10.1016/j.tcs.2007.04.008

Koukopoulos, D., & Nikolopoulos, S. D. (2006). Heterogenous Networks Can Be Unstable at Arbitrarily Low Injection Rates. In *Proceedings of the 6th International Conference on Algorithms and Complexity* (pp. 93-104).

Kumar, S. (1995). *Classification and detection of computer intrusions.* Unpublished doctoral dissertation, Dept. Computer Science, Purdue University. La, R. J., & Anantharam, V. (2002). Utility-based rate control in the internet for elastic traffic. *IEEE Transactions. on Networking, 10*(2), 272-285.

Levine, D., & Kessler, G. (2002). Denial of Service Attacks. In *Computer Security Handbook* (4th ed.). John Wiley & Sons.

Li, N., & Mitchell, J. C. (2003). RT: A Role-based Trust-management Framework. In *Proceedings of the 3rd DARPA Information Survivability Conference and Exposition* (pp. 201-212).

Li, W., & Chao, X. (2007). Call Admission Control for an Adaptive Heterogeneous Multimedia Mobile Network. *IEEE Transactions on Wireless Communications, 6*(2), 515–525. doi:10.1109/TWC.2006.05192

Libman, R. E., Midani, M. T., & Nguyen, H. T. (1995). The Interactive Video Network: An Overview of the Video Manger and the V Protocol. *AT&T Tech. Journal, 74*(5), 92–105.

Lynch, N. (1996). *Distributed Algorithms.* San Francisco: Morgan Kaufmann.

McCanne, S., Jacobson, V., & Vetterli, M. (1996). Receiver-driven Layered Multicast. In *Proceedings of the ACM SIGCOMM* (pp. 117-130).

Moore, D., Shannon, C., Brown, D. J., Voelker, G. M., & Savage, S. (2006). Inferring Internet Denial-of-Service Activity. *ACM Transactions on Computer Systems, 24*(2), 115–139. doi:10.1145/1132026.1132027

Oh, J.-T., Park, S. K., Jang, J.-S., & Jeon, Y.-H. (2005). Detection of DDoS and IDS Evasion Attacks in a High-Speed Networks Environment. *International Journal of Computer Science and Network Security, 7*(6), 124–131.

Quercia, D., & Hailes, S. (2007). MATE: Mobility and Adaptation with Trust and Expected-utility. *International Journal Internet Technology and Secured Transactions, 1.*

Quercia, D., Lad, M., Hailes, S., Capra, L., & Bhatti, S. (2006). STRUDEL: Supporting Trust in the Dynamic Establishment of peering coalitions. In *Proceedings of the 21st ACM Symposium on Applied Computing* (pp. 1870-1874).

Richardson, M., Agrawal, R., & Domingos, P. (2003). Trust Management for the Semantic Web. In *Proceedings of the 2nd International Semantic Web Conference* (pp. 351-368).

Rong, L., & Burnett, I. (2006). Facilitating Universal Multimedia Adaptation (UMA) in a heterogeneous Peer-to-Peer Network. In *Proceedings of the Second International Conference on Automated Production of Cross Media Content for Multi-Channel Distribution* (pp. 105-109).

Sandhu, R. S., Coyne, E. J., Feinstein, H. L., & Youman, C. E. (1996). Role-based Access Control Models. *IEEE Computer*, *29*, 38–47.

Shaha, N., Desai, A., & Parashar, M. (2001). Multimedia Content Adapatation for QoS Mnagement over Heterogeneous Networks. In *Proceedings of the International Conference on Internet Computing* (pp. 642-648).

Shmatikov, V., & Talcott, C. (2005). Reputation-Based Trust Management. *Journal of Computer Security*, *13*(1), 167–190.

Szwabe, A., Schorr, A., Hauck, F. J., & Kassler, A. J. (2006). Dynamic multimedia stream adaptation and rate control for heterogeneous networks. In *Proceedings of the 15th International Packet Video Workshop Vol. 7* (pp. 63-69).

TalebiFard. P., & Leung, V. C. M. (2008). Efficient Multimedia Call Delivery over IP-Based Heterogeneous Wireless Access Networks. In *Proceedings of the MobiWac* (pp. 85-92).

Tchepnda, C., & Riguidel, M. (2006). Distributed Trust Infrastructure and Trust-Security Articulation: Application to Heterogeneous Networks. In *Proceedings of the 20th International Conference on Advanced Information Networking and Applications* (pp. 33-38).

Weinard, M. (2006). Deciding the FIFO Stability of Networks in Polynomial Time. In *Proceedings of the 8th International Conference on Algorithms and Complexity Vol. 3998* (pp. 81-92).

Winslett, M., Yu, T., Seamons, K. E., Hess, A., Jacobson, J., & Jarvis, R. (2002). Negotiating Trust on the Web. *IEEE Internet Computing*, *6*(6), 30–37. doi:10.1109/MIC.2002.1067734

Wobber, E., Abadi, M., Burrows, M., & Lampson, B. (1994). Authentication in the Taos operating system. *ACM Transactions on Computer Systems*, *12*(1), 3–32. doi:10.1145/174613.174614

Xiu, D., & Liu, Z. (2005). *A Dynamic Trust Model for Pervasive Computing Environments*. Paper presented at the 4th Annual Security Conference.

Yau, D. K. Y., Lui, J.C.S., Liang, F., & Yam, Y. (2005). Defending against Distributed Denial-of-Service Attacks with Max-Min Fair Server-Centric Router Throttles. *IEEE/ACM Transactions on Networking*, *13*(1), 29-42.

Zhu, X., Singh, J. P., & Girod, B. (2006). Joint routing and rate allocation for multiple video streams in ad hoc wireless networks. In *Proceedings of the 15th International Packet Video Workshop Vol. 7* (pp. 727-736).

Section 3
Trust Modeling and Management
Driven by Social Study

Chapter 17
The Role of Trust in Social Life

Yan Dong
Renmin University of China, China

ABSTRACT

This chapter reviews the literature of trust in sociology and psychology. By introducing the conception, theory model and measurement of trust, we discuss trust in three important social contexts: interpersonal situation, organizational settings and Internet life. Furthermore, the author proposes a synthetic trust model with a multi-disciplinary approach as a future research direction and described its implications for trust study.

INTRODUCTION

Trust plays an important role in our social life not only for individuals but also for organizations. It is an essential component of social capital, especially for adults (Paxton, 1999). Trust is also very important for children's development. Children who fail to trust others might fall into the risk of developing a defensive or antagonistic posture and may view social relations as "get them before they get you." Lack of trust has been consistently implicated in the development of maladjustment including socially irresponsible criminal and delinquent behavior (Rotenberg, 1984). On the other hand,

recent research has highlighted trust's potential value in understanding the performance of health care organizations (Goold, 2001) and health systems (Gilson, 2003; Goudge, 2005). Particularly, trust has been identified as an important aspect of prosocial human behavior and experience at individual and organizational level (Schindler & Thomas, 1993). With regard to organization, the trust that individuals have with each other is the foundation of organizational effectiveness (Ferrin & Dirks, 2006). Indeed, recent evidence indicates that interpersonal trust has direct or indirect effects on a number of desired outcomes such as individuals' work performance, organizational commitment, turnover intentions, and working group's performance (Dirks & Ferrin, 2001, 2002; Kramer, 1999).

DOI: 10.4018/978-1-61520-682-7.ch017

Moreover, trust also plays in a crucial role in virtual life. Nowadays, many researches have been focusing on trust issues in electronic commerce. As accepted in the literature, trust is an indispensable component of online exchange and communications (e.g. friend-making), which are characterized by uncertainty, anonymity, lack of control, and potential opportunism (Dirks, 1999).

This book chapter studies the role of trust in social life and reviews the state art of trust research in the areas of psychology and sociology. We aim to help readers understand why trust is very important in social life by evaluating it in three important social contexts: interpersonal situation, organizational settings, and internet life. We also present our perspectives on the issues and controversies in this area, as well as solutions. Finally, the implications for future studies are discussed.

BACKGROUND

Trust issues in social life have led to many researches. Different researches are based on different concepts, theories, models and measurement methods in order to examine the role of trust in social life.

Conception of Trust

Trust is a key concept in many social situations ranging from interpersonal relationships to economic exchange (Miller, 2003). However, trust is a very complicated phenomenon attached to multiple disciplines and influenced by many factors. It is hard to say what trust exactly is and there is no well-established definition of trust. We can find various definitions of trust in the literature (Rotenberg, 2005). For example, it can be loosely defined as "a state involving confident positive expectations about another's motives with respect to oneself in situations entailing risk" (Boon & Holmes, 1991). Deutsch (1958, pp. 266) asserted that "an individual may be said to have trust in the

occurrence of an event if he expects its occurrence and his expectation lead to a behavior which he perceives to have greater negative motivational consequences if the expectation is not confirmed than positive motivational consequences if it is confirmed." In developmental psychology, although trust has been defined in very different ways over the past four decades, most researches are consistent with either Erikson's or Rotter's theories (Bernath, 1995). Erikson (1950) viewed trust as a foundation for identity development, as a pervasive way of sensing and behaving within the world, and as a critical step for the subsequent emergence of positive self-esteem and general psychological health. Rotter (1967, 1971) held the opinion that trust is integral to individuals' social functioning, the organization, survival, and the efficiency of society, as well as societies' local, national, and international relations. Rotter (1967) defined trust as the generalized expectancy that other individuals will keep their word or promises. Overall, the definition of trust broadly accepted is presented by Mayer (1995). Mayer, Davis, & Schoorman (1995) defined trust as "the willingness of a party to be vulnerable to the actions of another party based on the expectation that the other party will perform a particular action important to the trustor, irrespective of the ability to monitor or control that other party."

Although the concept of trust has gained popularity in public debate and academic analysis over recent years and it is still difficult to define and to investigate, these definitions of trust are nonetheless related to each other (Mayer et al., 1995; Goudge, 2005). Lewicki, Tomlinson, & Gillespie (2006) concluded the theoretical approaches and empirical evidence of trust. They conceptualized trust from the view of behavioral and psychological approach development.

In the Behavior Tradition

Trust is often defined in terms of choice behavior, which is derived from confidence and expecta-

Table 1. Two views of trust conception

Trust is a link to object	Trust is a link to general objects	Trust is defined as the general expectation of goodwill in general people, society or world (Rotter, 1967; Wrightsman, 1992).
	Trust is a link to specific objects (parents, friends, co-worker, etc.)	Generally, this view involves situation. Trustors also form a "standard estimate" of the trustworthiness of a person, who is not a friend or even an acquaintance (Glanville, 2007). Yamagishi & Yamagishi (1994, pp. 139) called this type of trust "general trust," as it reflects "a belief in the benevolence of human nature in general."
Trust is emphasized by psychological processes	Conceptualize trust based on cognition	For example, Mayer (1995) believed perceived trustworthiness is the key to predict trust;
	Conceptualize trust by emphasizing effects	For example, McAllister (2005) found that the affective foundations upon which trust between managers are built as an essential counterpart to other foundations for interpersonal trust and highlight affect-based trust's role in facilitating effective coordinated action in organizations.
	Conceptualize trust by emphasizing behavior tendency	For example, Gambetta (1990) defined trust as "trust (or, symmetrically distrust) is a particular level of the subjective probability with which an agent will perform a particular action, both before [we] can monitor such action (or independently of his capacity of ever to be able to monitor it) and in a context in which it affects [our] we action."

tions, and the choice is assumed rational. The essence of trust is the choice to cooperate or not to cooperate. Most of definitions of trust in this approach are from Deutsch's conception.

In the Psychological Approach

In a unidimensional model, trust and distrust is bipolar opposites (Jones & George, 1998; Mayer et al., 1995; McAllister, 1995). Trust is defined as confident expectations and/or willingness to be vulnerable, including cognitive, affective, behavioral intention elements. In a two-dimensional model, trust and distrust are two distinctly differentiable dimensions that can vary independently (Lewicki, McAllister, & Bies, 1998). Furthermore, trust is defined as positive confidence and negative expectations. In a transformational model, trust has different forms that develop and emerge over time (Lewicki & Bunker, 1995, 1996; Shapiro, Sheppard, & Cheraskin, 1992). Moreover, trust is defined in terms of the basis of trust (i.e. expected

costs and benefits, knowledge of the other, degree of shared values and identity).

Although the richness of the concept, we can still summarize the concept from the multitudinous definitions of trust into two views: (a) trust is a link to the object (including the general and specific object); (b) trust is emphasized by psychological process, including cognition, affect and behavior, as shown in Table 1.

From the role of trust in social life, we consider trust as a psychological process, including cognition, affect and behavior and trust is link to context. Therefore, trust is conceptualized that a trustor has confidence belief, expectations and particular action tendency to a trustee in a context.

Theory and Model of Trust

We synthesize four main theories of trust in social life according to the researches conducted in this area.

Psychological Trait Theory

This perspective views trust to be driven by a highly stable psychological propensity, unlikely to be appreciably modified by commonplace experiences. Trust is seen as a psychological predisposition, a propensity that is either innate or formulated in early life to believe in other people (e.g., Becker, 1996; Jones, 1996; Wrightsman, 1992). Generally, we can summarize two main variants of psychological propensity to trust: (a) trust as a psychological trait (Deutsch, 1958; Costa & McCrae, 1992; Counch & Jones, 1997); (b) trust is developmentally learned in early life (Wrigthtsman, 1992). These two views of trust as a psychological predisposition lead to a similar conclusion: a general propensity to trust, either innate or learned in early life, influences all contemporary trust decisions (Glanville, 2007).

Social Learning Theory

From the social learning perspective, people extrapolate from localized experiences to produce their estimates of generalized trust (Hardin, 2002; Rotter, 1971; Yosano & Hayashi, 2005). "Each individual encounters a variety of others who treat him positively or negatively, who keep their promises or do not. Each person generalizes from his/her past experiences in the process of developing expectancies about how the next person will treat him/her" (Stack, 1978, pp. 563). For example, we can learn trust from family, neighbors, coworkers, members of church, members of clubs and store workers to inform the belief of generalized trust concerning which person can be trusted, if people are helpful and fair, etc.

Glanville's Theory

Glanville (2007) examined whether individuals decide that people are generally trustworthy of untrustworthy by extrapolating from their experiences in localized interactions or whether a more fixed predisposition drives assessments of trustworthiness. These thoughts were then tested in confirmatory tetrad analysis, and it was found that individuals develop a generalized expectation of trustworthiness based on their experiences with different groups of people in localized settings. Results support the utility of the social learning model of generalized trust over the psychological propensity model across two separate datasets, in two nationally representative samples, and in an urban sample. That is to say, individuals generalize from experiences in particular domains in formulating their assessments of the trustworthiness of people in general.

Rotenberg's Theory

Rotenberg proposed a 3 (bases) × 2 (domains) × 2 (target dimensions) model of trust (Rotenberg, 1994, 2001, 2005). According to the model, there are three fundamental *bases* of interpersonal trust: (a) reliability, which refers to the fulfillment of personal words or promise (Hochreich, 1973; Johnson-George & Swap, 1982; Rotenberg, 1980, 1986, 1995; Rotter, 1967, 1971, 1980; Schlenker, Helm & Tedeschi, 1973); (b) emotional, which refers to the reliance on others to refrain from causing emotional harm, such as being receptive to disclosures, maintaining confidentiality of them, refraining from criticism, and avoiding acts that elicit embarrassment (Johnson-George & Swap, 1982; Rotenberg, 1986, 1995); and (c) honesty, which refers to telling the truth and engaging in behaviors that are guided by benign rather than malicious intent and by genuine rather than manipulative strategies (Giffin, 1967; Rotenberg, 1991). This model can be described by a cube (Rotenberg, 2005). The preceding bases of trust are further differentiated with respect to two *domains*: cognitive/affective and behavioral. The cognitive/affective domain pertains to individuals' beliefs/attributions and accompanies with emotional experiences concerning the three bases of trust. The behavioral domain pertains to individuals' behavioral tendencies to rely on others to engage in reliable, emotional, and honest behaviors. The bases and domains are differentiated by *dimensions of the target of trust*, comprising specific qualities of trusted-distrusted persons. The dimensions of the target of trust are (a) specificity, which ranges from generalized to a specific person, and (b) familiarity, which ranges from somewhat unfamiliar to very familiar. In addition, this framework emphasizes the reciprocal and dyadic nature of trust, notably from the relations between familiar and specific persons.

We found that there are controversies among these four main theories of trust in social life. In fact, everyone has the general trust tendency for others in the earlier life. And with experience, we can learn how to construct our trust system. Facing to different context and various objects, we can induce our experience into the trust tendency, and integrate them, and then we could decide whether to trust or distrust the object.

Measurement of Trust in Sociology and Psychology

There are many methods to measure trust in different disciplines. For example, questionnaire survey, setting experimental situation, interview method, etc. In what follows, we describe the main methods applied to measure trust in the literature of psychology and sociology.

Questionnaire Survey

Questionnaire is a common tool to investigate trust. Several omnibus self-report personality inventories have been published, such as, Interpersonal Trust Scale (Rotter, 1971; 1976), Philosophies of Human Nature Scale (Wrightsman, 1974), and Company Trust Scale (CTS, Remoel & Holmes, 1986).

Rotter's (1976) Interpersonal Trust Scale (ITS) was mostly used as a tool for researches concerning trust. However, this measure defines trust rather broadly as an expectation that other people's behavior, promises, or verbal and written statements can be relied on. Rotter's scale apparently has three underlying dimensions, or factors: credibility of social institutions, belief in others' sincerity, and caution. Heretick (1981) criticized Rotter's (1976) scale as confounded with another construct and locus of control (refers to whether people tend to locate that responsibility internally, within themselves, or externally, in fate, luck, or chance). So Heretick developed his own 6-item Trust-Suspiciousness Scale (T-SS) to measure "expectancies concerning the motives of other individuals" (p. 269). The T-SS overlaps much with the MMPI (Minnesota Multiphasic Personality Inventory) and was reliable, weakly correlated with locus of control, according to Heretick's report. However, no other evidence of the validity of the T-SS has been reported. Rosenberg (1957) published a 5-item scale measuring individuals' general levels of confidence in the trustworthiness, honesty, goodness, generosity, and brotherliness of people in general. The scale was reported to be highly reliable, but validity data were limited to a finding that students with a high level of faith in people, compared with those with a low level of faith in people, were more likely to endorse a preference for people-oriented occupations (Omodei, 2000). Wrightsman (1964) constructed an 84-item Philosophies of Human Nature measure, which incorporated a Trustworthiness subscale. A subsequent factor-analytic study led Wrightsman (1974) to propose a revised measure comprising two 10-item scales, one measuring beliefs that people are conventionally good, the other measuring cynicism.

The participants of all above scales are adults. Therefore, in order to investigate children's trust and its implications, researchers have developed scales to assess children's generalized trust beliefs (CGTB) (Rotenberg, 2005). There are two empirically based scales reported in the literature: Hochreich's (1973) Children's Interpersonal Trust Scale (HCITS), and Imber's (1973) Children's

Trust Scale (ICTS). Its reliability and validity were assessed with 77 children from sixth graders. In support of the consistency of the HCITS, its split-half reliability was .88 and, in support of the validity of the scale, the scores were associated with children's choice of a delayed rather than an immediate reward. The ICTS is composed of 40 items designed to assess generalized trust in four target groups: father, mother, teacher, and peer. Children answered each item by selecting one of two alternatives. The development of the ICTS was guided by Imber's definition of trust beliefs as children's confidence "in an individual's words and actions, and expectancy that a person will do what he promises to do, dependability, responsibility, trustworthiness, confidentiality, and a security that arises from a communication of those variables'" (Imber, 1973, pp. 145). There are six limitations with HCITS and ICTS that prompted revision of those scales for current use (Rotenberg, 2005). Therefore, a scale was constructed to assess children's generalized trust beliefs (CGTB) in four target groups (mother, father, teacher and peer) with respect to three bases of trust: reliability, emotionality, and honesty. Exploratory and confirmatory factor analyses yielded evidence for the expected factor structure of the CGTB Scale. The total CGTB Scale and subscales demonstrate acceptable internal consistency and expected levels of stability across time. In support of validity, 6-aged participants' scores on the CGTB peer subscale were correlated with their trust beliefs in classmates, assessed a year earlier.

Researches explore the validity of a survey question commonly used for measuring generalized trust. The accuracy with which it is measured has profound implications for many studies (Miller, 2003). Miller (2003) suggested that ambiguous wording on this survey item has led to misinterpretations concerning actual trust levels, especially in a cross-cultural context. We must pay more attention to the purpose of validity research of trust questionnaire which data analytic procedures would be desirable. Another problem is that small sample sizes could cause severe problems concerning the adequacy and applicability of certain analytic techniques, e.g. structural equation modeling.

Experimental Method

Experimental study is very important in psychological research because it can explore the causality. However, few studies apply experimental methods in their investigation of trust. For example, some methods were applied to gather information on interpersonal trust from participants around a setting event, game, or experiment. After the intervention, further data are collected to assess whether they changes at the level of interpersonal trust. A laboratory style approach could reduce the influence of context over trust, as the experiment may separate individuals from their context. However, such an approach appears to be of limited use where the influence of the setting is an important determinant of trust. The laboratory situation is often, and intentionally, artificial and context-free, frequently using induced valuations rather than real goods and regularly relying on abstract terminology (Danielson, 2007). Field experiments complement the standard set-up by making the context less artificial and by often using non-students as the subject pool. Hall, Dugan, Balkrishnan, & Bradley (2002) offered an interesting alternative because the intervention took place in a real setting, comparing responses between an intervention and control group. Trust (or co-operation) has been investigated through a task or game approach. For example, Dirks (1999) employed a tower building task to investigate trust. Each group of participations is asked to build a tower from wooden blocks, with each person in the group using blocks of a unique color. The objective is to place as many blocks on the tower as possible (a) as an individual and (b) as a group. Trust was manipulated by providing participants with differing perceptions about the other team members. The authors counted the number of blocks of each tower, reported the number of times the tower fell and computed an efficiency measure as a ratio of the group's actual performance to its expected performance. Each group was scored by a range of variables such as co-ordination, helping, intensity of effort, direction of effort and commitment to a plan. Data was used in regression analysis to examine the effect of the game and the manipulations on trust. Taking another example, Hall et al. (2002) investigated how the knowledge of physicians' financial incentives affects patient trust. They distributed information about physicians' payment incentives (capitation and fee-for service payments) to two groups of members of healthcare management organizations. The two intervention groups were compared with a control group who were given no information. More knowledge about incentives did not have a negative impact on patient's trust in their physicians, suggesting that patients had already taken into account the effect of financial incentives in the assessment of physicians' trustworthiness.

Besides field experiments, versions of the Trust Game have been used for a long time. For example, in the research of Holm and Danielson (2005, henceforth HD), participants may or may not be given a participation fee. They are divided into equally sized two groups, Proposers (P) and Responders (R), and each P is (usually anonymously) matched to an R. Proposers are given a sum of money and given the opportunity of investing all or part of this (what is not invested and retained by P). The rate of return is r. The proceeds of the investment accrue to R, so if P decides to invest an amount x, R receives x (1 + r). Receivers are then asked whether they would like to return to P part of the proceeds, a sum between 0 and x (1 + r). This is a pure transfer, so the rate of return on what R decides to send to P is zero. R retains the part of the proceeds that he or she decides not to return at the end of game. These rules, including P's initial endowment and the rate of return, are common knowledge. Interpretation is straightfor-

ward. To maximize a pair's sum, P should invest everything. However, since R does not have any pecuniary incentive to return any money, P risks ending up with zero. Consequently, P might be expected to invest a positive amount only if he believes that R will return a positive amount. The amount that P invests, consequently, is interpreted as the extent to which P trusts R, a completely anonymous co-player. Similarly, since R does not have any pecuniary incentive for returning any money, the amount that R returns is interpreted as the extent to which R is trustworthy. In several experiments, Proposers send well over half of the initial sum and Responders return around one-third (Camerer, 2003). This suggests, given the interpretations of the game above, that people tend to trust strangers (if only from the same peer group, given that most subject pools are students), and that trust tends to be reciprocated (i.e. the more R receives, the more R will return). One challenge faced by experimenters is to find the factors that determine the extent of trust and trustworthiness (Danielson, 2007).

Overall, researchers who work within the behavioral tradition observe behavior in simulated interactions and games, such as the Prisoner's Dilemma (Kiesler & Waters, 1996), under laboratory conditions that minimize interpersonal interaction. Typically, cooperative behavior is accepted as an observable manifestation of trust.

Qualitative Research Method

The review of trust researches suggests that appropriate definitions of trust are highly context dependent (Goudge, 2005). Whereas little is known about how trust functions, qualitative research explores how respondents view trust and 'trusted' behavior important in advance of quantitative investigation. The results of qualitative inquiry facilitate the development and refinement of hypotheses about how trust functions and can be used to generate questions in structured questionnaires. Quantitative inquiry is valuable because it allows larger scale investigation and generates data that can be used, for example, to assess the statistical significance of different determinants to overall levels of trust. The majority of studies using purely qualitative research methods to investigate trust applied semi-structured interviews (e.g. Mechanic & Meyer, 2000), although some used ethnographic techniques (Newell & Swan, 2000) and a diary of social relations in which the respondents recorded who they met each day and what they discussed with each other (Lonkila, 1997). Only one study used a range of data collection approaches, in order to broaden the types of opportunities to gather data (Lyon, 2000).

Remarks

Overall, each method has its own advantage and disadvantage. Using questionnaire survey, we can get amount of data in the same time, but we only get the statement of participants in general. It is quite possible the participants may have another trust behavior in a specific context. Although we can observe actual trust behaviors using field experiment, we have to spend more money and time in order to get enough data. Interview is a good method to study the process of trust construct and the factors that influence trust. However, we can only get qualitative results in common with this method.

TRUST IN SOCIAL LIFE

Issues, Controversies and Problems

We classified the amount of research of trust in sociology and psychology based on three main social contexts: interpersonal trust, organizational trust and internet trust.

Interpersonal Trust

Interpersonal trust is an individual's belief about the integrity and dependability of another. Perhaps the most fundamental judgment one can make about another individual is a judgment concerning his or her degree of trustworthiness (Ferrin & Dirks, 2006). For individual, interpersonal trust is linked to individuals' wellbeing (DeNeve & Cooper, 1998) and associated with health and longevity (Barefoot et al., 1998). Trust between people can be seen as a key component to facilitate coordination and cooperation for mutual benefits (Yan, 2007). For society, interpersonal trust has been regarded by various researchers as the cornerstone, the 'glue' that maintains social order (Rotenberg, 1991, 1995; Rotenberg & Cerda, 1995; Rotter, 1967). Therefore, the study of interpersonal trust is very important for scholars attempting to better understand the dynamics of cooperation and competition (Deutsch, 1958, 1962; Gambetta, 1988), the resolution of conflicts (Deutsch, 1973; Lewicki & Stevenson, 1998), and the facilitation of economic exchange (Granovetter, 1985). Researches in this domain have explored the relationships between trust and such factors as social interaction, physical and psychological trauma, psychosocial maladjustment, psychotherapeutic and medical treatment, sociopolitical relations, and business, organizational, and economic practices in adult populations. Trust is not only very important for adults but also is regarded as a significant variable in children's personality, social and intellectual development. According to Erikson's (1963) psychosocial theory, basic trust versus mistrust is the critical stage of development during infancy that affects social functioning throughout the course of development. So the early interpersonal trust is postulated to be necessary for children to develop healthy self-esteem, creative intellect, and adequate peer relationships (Rotenberg, 2005). Some researches support these views, interpersonal trust has been found to be associated with children's moral behaviour (Wright

& Kirmani, 1977), friendship (Rotenberg, 1986), social competence (Buzzelli, 1988; Wentzel, 1991), and academic achievement (Imber, 1973; Wentzel, 1991).

The majority of research on the construct examines trust in adults. In contrast, only some authors have recognized the significance of trust for children (Bernath & Feshbach, 1995; Rotter, 1967; Bernath, 1995). The interpersonal trust of children concerns teacher-students trust, parent-child trust and peers trust. Teacher is the important people for students. Trust is the bridge of teacher and students. When students trust in their teacher, they would learn more knowledge from the teacher. At the same time, when the teacher trusts his/her students, he/she can in turn pay more attention to teaching. Most people believe that teacher-students trust can predict the prosocial behavior, social responsibility, and affect the academic achievement. Furthermore, according to attachment theory, the quality of interaction between infants and caregivers influences cognitive models of interpersonal trust that, in turn, affect their subsequent social relationships (Bridges, 2003; Rotenberg, 2005). Bernath & Feshbach (1995) proposed that children need to be able to trust that their caregivers will protect and support them and believe that their peers will be honest, cooperative and benevolent. The resulting trust is postulated to be necessary for children to develop healthy self-esteem, creative intellect, and adequate peer relationships (supportive, cooperative and intimate). Other researchers have found that children who attain unsatisfactory relationships with the peer group (e.g., are rejected by peers) are at risk for later problems in psychosocial adjustment (e.g., depression and conduct disorders) (Parker & Asher, 1987, Rotenberg et al., 2004). If children holding low reliability trust beliefs in peers establish unsatisfactory peer group relationships, then they should also be at risk for problems in psychosocial adjustment. Children who hold *very* low trust beliefs in peers and those who hold *very* high trust beliefs in peers substantively deviate

from norms of the peer group and therefore are at risk for being rejected and excluded by them. Specifically, children who hold very low trust beliefs in peers display a *cynical* orientation in comparison to the group norm by believing and behaving as though their peers will not fulfill promises and maintain confidentiality. Children who hold very high trust beliefs in peers display a naive orientation in comparison to the group norm by believing and behaving as though peers almost always fulfill promises and maintain confidentiality (Rotenberg, 2005).

There are three main problems in this domain. Firstly, few researches studied children's trust, especially, for teacher-students trust. For example, only CGTB scale and the questionnaire of Li & Liu (2007) considered the trust between teacher and students (Rotenberg, 2005). Rotenberg (1995) remarked, "Despite the apparent importance of socialization of trust, it has received little empirical attention" (p. 713). Noack, Kerr, & Olah (1999) commented that "trust in the family has never really attracted scholarly attention" (p. 714). Secondly, most researches of interpersonal trust only take the cross-sectional study into account. So these studies can't explore the change or evolution of children's interpersonal trust. Thirdly, the research for the interpersonal trust of people with disadvantage situation is scarce. For example, researchers who have studied adolescents with economic disadvantage have failed to examine mutual trust between parents and have not considered children's readiness to communicate with both parents, although there are an increasing number of related studies, which have been conducted focusing on childhood children.

Trust in Organization

Recent developments in the organizational sciences reflect the importance of interpersonal trust relationships for sustaining individual and organizational effectiveness (McAllister, 1995). Many studies have recognized that trust is a multidimensional construct and have also examined the types of trust; most of them were conducted in organizational settings (Abrams et al., 2003; Corritore, 2003; Gefen et al., 2003; McAllister, 1995; McDaniel, 2004; Ratnasingam, 2005; Hsu, 2006). Trust is known as a good predictor of behavior for individual or group performance (Dirks, 1999; Paul & McDaniel, 2004). For decades, many studies have documented that when the level of trust is increased in an organization, positive work outcomes result, among them, cooperation (Coleman, 1990), organizational citizenship behaviors (McAllister, 1995), reduced monitoring (Langfred, 2004), and enhanced group performance (Dirks, 2000) and organizational performance (Davis, Schoorman, Mayer, & Tan, 2000; Lau, 2008). Most of the trust-related researches have direct (main) effects on work group process and performance. The results of these studies show that trust increases the ability of group members to work together both in terms of effectiveness and efficiency (Dirks, 1999). However, not all researchers believe that there is no sufficient evidence to the positive direct relation between trust and performance. Dirks (1999) used an experimental method to examine the role of trust through which interpersonal trust could affect group performance: a main effect and a moderating effect. The data collected do not support the main effect that has dominated the literature on interpersonal trust. However, the data do support the moderating role: trust seems to influence how motivation is converted into work group processes and performance. On the basis of these findings, Dirks suggested that trust may be best understood as a construct that influences group performance indirectly by channeling the group member's energy toward reaching alternative goals.

In fact, past studies of the determinants of interpersonal trust have focused primarily on how trust forms in isolated dyads. Yet within organizations, trust typically develops between individuals who are embedded in a complex web of existing and potential relationships. Ferrin, Dirks & Shah (2006) examined the role of third parties in the trust of coworkers. In their research, they identified 3 alternative ways in which a trustor and a trustee may be linked to each other via third parties: network closure (linked via social interactions with the third parties), trust transferability (linked via trusted third parties), and structural equivalence (linked via the similarity of their relationships with all potential third parties within the organization) (Ferrin, 2006). They found that network closure and structural equivalence would predict interpersonal trust indirectly via their impact on interpersonal organizational citizenship behaviors performed within the interpersonal relationship, whereas trust transferability would predict trust directly. In 2001, Dirks developed an alternative model that describes how trust functions as a moderator, facilitating or hindering the effect of other determinants on outcomes of interest.

There are still some additional research issues in this domain. In general, despite the well-developed literature on trust in leaders, relatively few studies have examined trust for coworkers (Ferres, Connell, & Travaglione, 2004; Parker, Williams, & Turner, 2006). Moreover, the few studies that have examined coworker trust have emphasized its role as an independent variable (Alge, Wiethoff, & Klein, 2003; Ladebo, 2006). Only Lau & Liden (2008) focused their investigation on coworker trust as a dependent variable, that is, on the determinants of the extent to which coworkers trust one another. Another issue is few researches concerned the connection about trust at both the individual and the organizational level. Trust in people and trust in their organization are related to the roles that people play in their organization, organizational processes of motivation and monitoring, and organization culture. Finally, most researches of trust in organization only take the method of questionnaire survey. As we have discussed already, this methodology has some shortcomings. It is preferred various methodologies are applied to explore trust issues in organizational context.

Trust in Virtual Reality

With the rapid growth of internet technologies, people's life is highly linked with virtual reality, such as making friends, chatting, and shopping. Electric commerce has been an important part of people's life nowadays, especially for young people. However, lack of trust is treated as one of the most important reasons that retard Internet activities, e.g. on-line shopping. Thus, the role of trust in virtual reality is not negligible. Although a relative young field, there are many different constructs based on diversified trust theories and eclectic research models to study trust in e-commerce. McKnight (2002) justified a parsimonious interdisciplinary typology and related trust constructs to e-commerce consumer actions, defining both conceptual-level and operational-level trust constructs. Conceptual-level constructs consist of disposition to trust (primarily from psychology), institution-based trust (from sociology), and trusting beliefs and trusting intentions (primarily from social psychology). McKnight and his team examined the constructs of trust using a questionnaire and provided a model to explain the relationship of these constructs and sub-constructs. Their model could help researchers examine e-commerce customer relationships in new ways, since it includes personal, institutional and interpersonal concepts. Other studies found that trust is known as a good predictor of behavior in prior research, such as e-commerce adoption (Gefen et al., 2003; Pavlou & Fygenson, 2006; Hsu, 2006) and business cooperative relationship (Pavlou & Gefen, 2004). Given the differences between a virtual and a conventional marketplace, antecedents and consequences of trust merit were re-examined. Corbitt, Thanasankit, & Yi (2003) identified a number of key factors related to trust in the B2C (Business To Consumer) context and proposed a framework based on a series of underpinning relationships among these factors. The findings in their research suggest that people are more likely to purchase from the web if they perceive a higher degree of trust in e-commerce and have more experience in using the web. Customer's trust levels are likely to be influenced by the level of perceived market orientation, site quality, trustworthiness of technologies, and user's web experience. Research on trust in e-commerce also found that the willingness of on-line consumers to use the Internet for economic transactions and even more actual risk taking behavior require both system trust and transactional trust (Grabner-Krauter, 2003). Naquin (2003) explored the effect of interacting over the Internet on interpersonal trust when bargaining online. Results suggested that relative to face-to-face negotiations, online negotiations were characterized by (a) lower levels of pre-negotiation trust and (b) lower levels of post-negotiation trust. The reduced levels of pre-negotiation trust in online negotiations (i.e., before any interaction took place) demonstrate that negotiators bring different expectations to the electronic bargaining table than to the face-to-face negotiations. Those who negotiated online reported less desire for future interactions with the other party. Online negotiators were also less satisfied with their outcome and less confident in the quality of their performance, despite the absence of observable differences in economic outcome quality.

In general, trust is an important factor in many social interactions, involving uncertainty and dependency. "The need for trust only arises in a risky situation" (Mayer et al., 1995, pp. 711), Logically, trust would not be needed if actions could be undertaken with complete certainty and no risk. On-line transactions and exchange relationships are not only characterized by uncertainty, but also by anonymity, lack of control and potential opportunism, making risk and trust crucial elements of electronic commerce (Grabner-Krauter, 2003). Buying on the Internet presents numerous risks for consumers over and above the transaction process itself being perceived as risky (Einwiller et al., 2000; Einwiller & Will, 2001). Moreover, having only limited cognitive resources available, it is more difficult to accumulate accurate information for trust purposes in remote digital communications where information can be easily distorted or faked identities can be created.

Trust can serve as a mechanism to reduce the complexity of human conduct in situations where people have to cope with uncertainty (Luhmann, 1989). Siau & Shen (2003) proposed that cultivating trust in electronic commerce is a dynamic and time-consuming process that involves initial trust formation and repeated trials until a firm loyalty is established. Establishing a trust relationship in digital networking environment involves more aspects than in the social world. This is because communications in the computing network rely on not only relevant human beings and their relationships, but also digital components. Therefore, researchers on one hand focus on the test of hypothesized relationships in trust and e-commerce, on the other hand primarily consider the importance of trust in design and analysis of secure distributed and electronic commerce. In particular, for some emerging technologies, such as MANET (Mobile Ad Hoc Networks), P2P (peer-to-peer) computing, and GRID virtual systems, trust management has been proposed as a useful solution to break through new challenges of security and privacy (Yan, Zhang & Virtanen 2003; Yan 2006; Yan, 2007).

Although a lot of researches have been conducted to study trust in e-commerce, we notice that there are still some limitations. A large number of participants in the empirical research on trust in e-commerce are students. As students are not representative of the entire on-line consumer population, the results may not be generalized to other types of customers. Another problem of trust research in e-commerce is that some potential variables influencing on-line trust is excluded by researchers. For example, Koufaris & Hampton-Sosa (2002) pointed out prior experience with the Web and trust in on-line shopping in general, but variables supposed to influence trust in the Internet merchant were not controlled in the

study. Some researches on trust in e-commerce are absence of external validity. The frequently used trust scales are neither theoretically derived nor rigorously validated (Bhattacherjee, 2002; Grabner-Krauter, 2003). These researchers usually conduct questionnaires to understand the trust in e-commerce and the antecedents of trust. However, participants were not required or even not allowed to actually perform a shopping transaction, most likely because of limited research budgets. These shortcomings should be addressed in the future research on trust in ecommerce.

Solutions and Recommendations

Interpersonal Trust

Firstly, studies onr children's trust, especially for teacher-students trust are expected and significant. Because children are company with teachers in most daytime, the teachers definitely influence the students on both their personality and behavior. For example, Rotenberg (2005) found a relation between children's helpfulness to classmates and trust beliefs in teachers. Therefore, it is very valuable to do some research on it. Secondly, in order to explore the change of interpersonal trust we need to do some longitudinal study. Longitudinal study can indicate the change of interpersonal trust with time, especially for children. We could know what is the key period for children to form their trust attitude; at what time their trust is disappeared and why the change happens. Moreover, through the longitudinal study, we will found the causality of trust. That is to say, what factors can enhance or decrease trust and what results could be led by increasing trust, etc. In addition, we can examine whether the trust is innate or acquired in the development through the longitudinal study. The longitudinal study may also integrate the controversies of different theories of trust. Finally, interpersonal trust is more important for some people in a disadvantaged situation, than normal people. Therefore, we need to pay more attention to the trust study in this kind of situation or context and concern the mutual trust between them and the people who are in an advantaged situation.

Trust in Organization

The researches about trust in organization are abundant. But it is significant to examine trust for coworkers, which is lacked study in the current literature. Especially, we need to consider the coworker trust as an independent variable. In fact, the coworker trust affects the cooperation of work. So it is necessary to do the related study in this field. An organization includes not only leaders and employees but also organizational relationships. However, few researches concerned to connect trust at both the individual and the organizational level. The trust in different department is a key to an organization's success. Therefore, we must pay more attention to the trust in the organization level. Particularly, most researchers in this field applied questionnaires to conduct their studies. The methodology limitation is obvious. We suggest integrating other methods to make up the shortcoming of questionnaire based trust research.

Trust in Virtual Reality

Firstly, we need to enlarge the scope of participants because there are some limitations if selecting only students as participants. It seems necessary for future trust research to use more representative samples, especially for e-commerce studies. Secondly, we should introduce and study some potential variables that impacts on-line trust in the future research. For example, motivation, personality, reputation/recommendation and decision-making style are factors that could impact on-line trust. These variables should be addressed in the future research on trust in e-commerce. Finally, interview is a helpful way to explore the on-line trust. With questionnaires, we can get amount of data, but we must notify that the validity and reliability of questionnaire should be guaranteed, which is hard to ensure sometimes. With interviews, we can get more details on why people distrust or trust other people on internet and how trust will influence the behavior on internet.

FUTURE RESEARCH DIRECTIONS

Multi-Disciplinary Integration of Trust Research

Over the last several decades, researchers have increasingly recognized that trust plays an important role in many contexts. In most studies, scholars have assumed that trust has a direct, or indirect positive effect on people's daily life and have designed empirical researches to assess these direct and indirect effects. Trust is not only a psychological process, or a social phenomenon, but also a crucial element for individual development and organization governance. Because of this reason, trust is concerned by many disciplines, for example, economics, principles of management, policy-making studies and so on. However, we notice that there are a lot of controversies and problems in the trust researches in sociology and psychology caused by different applied trust conceptions, theories and measurements. Therefore, in the future, researchers should consider integrating the difference of conception, method and theory together cross multiple disciplines. We believe different views and methods in different disciplines could make up the weakness of single disciplinary study.

Applying the Results of Trust into Industry

Although there are some controversies and problems about the researches of trust in social life, we have noticed that there are more consistent results on the role of trust and how trust is informed. These results will help us in designing and implementing a trustworthy digital system, for example, in emerging distributed systems. There is a trend that trust management is important and needed in the design of new products. For example, with the mobile phone, the user must get enough information to make correct decisions on which mobile phone is trustworthy. What information is useful to increase users' trust and how to get this information are interesting research topics. One possible solution could be applying and transferring the results of trust study in sociology and psychology to industry design.

CONCLUSION

This chapter introduced the conception, theory and measurement of trust in social life. We summarized the conception of trust and pointed the shortcoming of different theories and measurements. Furthermore, we discussed the issues, controversies and problems of the trust studies in three important social contexts: interpersonal situation, organizational settings and Internet life. Solutions and recommendations were also suggested with a proposal of future research..

REFERENCES

Abrams, L. C., Cross, R., Lesser, E., & Levin, D. Z. (2003). Nurturing interpersonal trust in knowledge-sharing networks. *The Academy of Management Executive*, 17, 64–77.

Alge, B. J., Wiethoff, C., & Klein, H. J. (2003). When does the medium matter? Knowledge-building experiences and opportunities in decision making teams. *Organizational Behavior and Human Decision Processes*, 91, 26–37. doi:10.1016/S0749-5978(02)00524-1

Ardichvili, A., Page, V., & Wentling, T. (2003). Motivation and barriers to participation in virtualknowledge-sharing communities of practice. *Journal of Knowledge Management*, 7, 64–77. doi:10.1108/13673270310463626

Barefoot, J. C., Maynard, K. E., Beckham, J. C., Bramme, B. H., Hooker, K., & Siegler, I. C. (1998). Trust, health and longevity. *Journal of Behavioral Medicine*, 21, 517–526. doi:10.1023/A:1018792528008

Becker, L. C. (1996). Trust as Noncognitive Security about Motives. *Ethics*, 10, 743–761.

Bernath, M. S., & Feshbach, N. D. (1995). Children's trust: Theory,assessment, development, and research directions. *Applied & Preventive Psychology*, 4, 1–19. doi:10.1016/S0962-1849(05)80048-4

Bhattacherjee, A. (2002). Individual trust in online firms: scale development and initial trust. *Journal of Management Information Systems*, 19(1), 213–243.

Boon, S., & Holmes, J. (1991). The dynamics of interpersonal trust: Resolving uncertainty in the face of risk. In R. Hinde & J. Groebel (Eds.), *Cooperation and Prosocial Behavior* (pp. 190-211). Cambridge, UK: Cambridge University Press.

Bridges, L. J. (2003). Trust, attachment, and relatedness. In M. H. Bornstein & L. Davidson (Eds.), *Well-being: Positive development across the life course. Crosscurrents in contemporary psychology* (pp. 177-189). Mahwah, NJ: Lawrence Erlbaum Associates.

Buzzelli, C. A. (1988). The development of trust in children's relations with peers. *Child Study Journal*, 18, 33–46.

Camerer, C. (2003). *Behavioral Game Theory: Experiments in Strategic Interaction*. Princeton, NJ: Princeton University Press.

Coleman, J. S. (1990). *Foundations of social theory*. Cambridge, MA: Harvard University Press.

Corbitt, B., Thanasankit, T., & Yi, H. (2003). Trust and e-commerce: a study of consumer perceptions. *Electronic Commerce Research and Applications, 2*, 203–215. doi:10.1016/S1567-4223(03)00024-3

Corritore, C. L., Kracher, B., & Wiedenbeck, S. (2003). On-line trust: concepts, evolving themes, a model. *International Journal of Human-Computer Studies, 58*, 737–758. doi:10.1016/S1071-5819(03)00041-7

Costa, P. T., & McCrae, R. R. (1992). *Revised NEO Personality Inventory and NEW Five-Factor Inventory Professional Manual*. Odessa, FL: Psychological Assessment Resources, Inc.

Couch, L. L., & Warren, H. J. (1997). Measuring levels of trust. *Journal of Research in Personality, 31*, 319–336. doi:10.1006/jrpe.1997.2186

Danielson, A. J., & Holm, H. J. (2007). Do you trust you brethren? *Journal of Economic Behavior & Organization, 62*, 255–271. doi:10.1016/j.jebo.2004.10.011

Davis, J. H., Schoorman, F. D., Mayer, R. C., & Tan, H. H. (2000). The trusted general manager and business unit performance: Empirical evidence of a competitive advantage. *Strategic Management Journal, 21*, 563–576. doi:10.1002/(SICI)1097-0266(200005)21:5<563::AID-SMJ99>3.0.CO;2-0

DeNeve, K., & Cooper, H. (1998). The happy personality: A meta-analysis of 137 personality traits and subjective well-being. *Psychological Bulletin, 124*, 197–229. doi:10.1037/0033-2909.124.2.197

Deutsch, M. (1958). Trust and suspicion. *The Journal of Conflict Resolution, 2*, 265–279. doi:10.1177/002200275800200401

Deutsch, M. (1962). Cooperation and trust: Some theoretical notes. In *Nebraska symposium on motivation* (pp. 275-320).

Deutsch, M. (1973). *The resolution of conflict*. New Haven, CT: Yale University Press.

Dirks, K. T. (1999). The effects of interpersonal trust on work group performance. *The Journal of Applied Psychology, 84*, 445–455. doi:10.1037/0021-9010.84.3.445

Dirks, K. T., & Ferrin, D. L. (2001). The role of trust in organizational settings. *Organization Science, 12*, 450–467. doi:10.1287/orsc.12.4.450.10640

Einwiller, S., Geissler, U., & Will, M. (2000). Engendering trust in Internet businesses using elements of corporate branding. In H.M. Chung (Ed.), *Proceedings of the 2000 Americas Conference on Information Systems (AMCIS)* (pp. 33-739). Long Beach, CA: AIS.

Einwiller, S., & Will, M. (2001). The role of reputation to engender trust in electronic markets. In *Proceedings of the Fifth International Conference on Corporate Reputation, Identity, and Competitiveness*, Paris. Retrieved October 31, 2002, from http://www.communicationsmgt.org/modules/pub/view.php/communicationsmgt-11

Erikson, E. (1950). *Childhood in society*. New York: Norton.

Erikson, E. H. (1963). *Childhood and society* (2nd ed.). New York: Norton.

Ferrin, D. L., Dirks, K. T., & Shah, P. P. (2006). Direct and indirect effects of third-party relationships on interpersonal trust. *The Journal of Applied Psychology, 91*, 870–883. doi:10.1037/0021-9010.91.4.870

Gambetta, D. (1988). Can we trust trust? In D. Gambetta (Ed.), *Trust: Making and breaking cooperative relationships* (pp. 213-237). Cambridge, UK: Basil Blackwell.

Gambetta, D. (1990). Can We Trust Trust? In D. Gambetta (Ed.), *Trust: Making and Breaking Cooperative elations* (pp. 213-238). Oxford, UK: Basil Blackwell.

Gefen, D., Karahanna, E., & Straub, D. W. (2003). Trust and TAM in online shopping: an integrated model. *MIS Quarterly*, *27*(1), 51–90.

Gilson, L. (2003). Trust and the development of health care as a social institution. *Social Science & Medicine*, *56*, 1453–1468. doi:10.1016/S0277-9536(02)00142-9

Glanville, J. L., & Paxton, P. (2007). How do we learn to trust? A confirmatory tetrad analysis of the sources of the sources of generalized trust. *Social Psychology Quarterly*, *70*, 230–242.

Goold, S. D. (2001). Trust and the ethics of health care institutions. *The Hastings Center Report*, *31*(6), 26–33. doi:10.2307/3527779

Goudge, J., & Gilson, L. (2005). How can trust be investigated? Drawing lessons from past experience. *Social Science & Medicine*, *61*, 1439–1451. doi:10.1016/j.socscimed.2004.11.071

Grabner-Krauter, S., & Kaluscha, E. A. (2003). Empirical Research in on-line trust: a review and critical assessment. *Human-Computer Studies*, *58*, 783–812. doi:10.1016/S1071-5819(03)00043-0

Granovetter, M. (1985). Economic Action and Social Structure: The Problem of Embeddedness. *American Journal of Sociology*, *91*, 481. doi:10.1086/228311

Hardin, R. (2002). *Trust and Trustworthiness*. New York: Russell Sage Foundation.

Heretick, D. M. L. (1981). Gender-specific relationships between trust-suspicion, locus of control, and psychological distress. *The Journal of Psychology*, *108*, 267–274.

Hochreich, D. J. (1973). A children's scale to measure interpersonal trust. *Developmental Psychology*, *9*, 141. doi:10.1037/h0035085

Hsu, M.H., Ju, T.L., Yen, C.H., & Chang, C.M. (2007). Knowledge sharing behavior in virtual communities: The relationship between trust, self-efficacy, and outcome expectations. *Human-computer studies*, *65*, 153-169.

Imber, S. C. (1973). Relationship of trust to academic performance. *Journal of Personality and Social Psychology*, *28*, 145–150. doi:10.1037/h0035644

Jones, G. R., & George, J. M. (1998). The experience and evolution of trust: Implications for cooperation and teamwork. *Academy of Management Review*, *23*, 531–546. doi:10.2307/259293

Jones, K. (1996). Trust as an Affective Attitude. *Ethics*, *10*, 74–125.

Kiesler, S., Soroull, L., & Waters, K. (1996). A prisoner's dilemma experiment on cooperation with people and human-like computers. *Journal of Personality and Social Psychology*, *70*, 47–65. doi:10.1037/0022-3514.70.1.47

Koufaris, M., & Hampton-Sosa, W. (2002). *Customer trust online: examining the role of the experience with the Web-site* (CIS Working Paper Series). Zicklin School of Business, Baruch College, New York, NY. Retrieved October 31, 2002, from http://cisnet.baruch.cuny.edu/papers/cis200205.pdf

Kramer, R. M. (1999). Trust and distrust in organizations: Emerging perspectives, enduring questions. *Annual Review of Psychology*, *50*, 569–598. doi:10.1146/annurev.psych.50.1.569

Ladebo, O. J. (2006). Perceptions of trust and employees' attitudes: A look at Nigeria's agricultural extension workers. *Journal of Business andPsychology*, *20,* 409-427.

Langfred, C. W., & Moye, N. A. (2004). Effects of task autonomy on performance: an extended model considering motivational, informational, and structural mechanisms. *The Journal of Applied Psychology*, *89*, 934–945. doi:10.1037/0021-9010.89.6.934

Lau, D. C., & Liden, R. C. (2008). Antecedents of Coworker Trust: Leaders' Blessings. *The Journal of Applied Psychology*, *93*, 1130–1138. doi:10.1037/0021-9010.93.5.1130

Lewicki, R. J., & Bunker, B. B. (1995). Trust in relationships: A model of development and decline. In B. B. Bunker, J. Z. Rubin, & Associates (Eds.), *Conflict, cooperation and justice: Essays inspired by the work of Morton Deutsch* (pp. 133-173). San Francisco: Jossey-Bass.

Lewicki, R. J., & Bunker, B. B. (1996). Developing and maintaining trust in work relationships. In R. M. Kramer & T. R. Tyler (Eds.), *Trust in organizations: Frontiers of theory and research* (pp. 114-139). Thousand Oaks, CA: Sage Publications, Inc.

Lewicki, R. J., McAllister, D., & Bies, R. (1998). Trust and distrust: New relationships and realities. *Academy of Management Review*, *23*, 439–458. doi:10.2307/259288

Lewicki, R. J., & Stevenson, M. A. (1998). Trust development in negotiation: Proposed actions and a research agenda. *Journal of Business and Professional Ethics*, *16*(1-3), 99–132.

Lewicki, R. J., Tomlinson, E. C., & Gillespie, N. (2006). Models of Interpersonal Trust Development: Theoretical Approaches. *Empirical Evidence, and Future Directions*, *32*, 991–1022.

Li, Y., & Liu, H. (2007). Developing Questionnaire for Trust of Students in Teachers. *Psychological Development and Education*, *4*, 88-94.

Lonkila, M. (1997). Informal exchange relations in post-soviet Russia: a comparative perspective. *Sociological Review Online*. Retrieved from http://www.socresonline.org.uk/socresonlime/2/2/9.html

Luhmann, N. (1989). *Vertrauen. Ein Mechanismus der Reduktion sozialer Komplexit.at* (3rd ed.). Enke, Stuttgart.

Lyon, F. (2000). Trust, networks and norms: the creation of social capital in agricultural economies in Ghana. *World Development*, *28*(4), 663–681. doi:10.1016/S0305-750X(99)00146-1

Mayer, R. C., & Davis, J. H. (1995). An integrative model of organizational trust. *Academy of Management Review*, *20*(3), 709–735. doi:10.2307/258792

McAllister, D. J. (1995). Affect-and Cognition-Based Trust as Foundations for Interpersonal Cooperation In Organizations. *Academy of Management Journal*, *38*, 24–59. doi:10.2307/256727

McDonald, R. P., & Ho, M. R. (2002). Principles and practice in reporting structural equation analyses. *Psychological Methods*, *7*, 64–82. doi:10.1037/1082-989X.7.1.64

McKnight, D. H., Choudhury, V., & Kacmar, C. (2002). The impact of initial consumer trust on intentions to transact with a web site: a trust building mode. *The Journal of Strategic Information Systems*, *11*(3-4), 297–323. doi:10.1016/S0963-8687(02)00020-3

Mechanic, D., & Meyer, S. (2000). Concepts of trust among patients with serious illness. *Social Science & Medicine*, *51*(5), 657–668. doi:10.1016/S0277-9536(00)00014-9

Miller, A. S., & Mitamura, T. (2003). Are surveys on trust trustworthy? *Social Psychology Quarterly*, *66*, 62–70. doi:10.2307/3090141

Naquin, C. E., & Paulson, G. D. (2003). Online Bargaining and Interpersonal Trust. *The Journal of Applied Psychology*, *88*, 113–120. doi:10.1037/0021-9010.88.1.113

Newell, S., & Swan, J. (2000). Trust and inter-organizational networking. *Human Relations*, *53*, 1287–1328.

Noack, P., Kerr, M., & Olah, A. (1999). Family Relations in Adolescence. *Journal of Adolescence*, *22*, 713–717. doi:10.1006/jado.1999.0265

Omodei, M. M., & Mclennan, J. (2000). Conceptualizing and Measuring Global Interpersonal Mistrust-Trust. *The Journal of Social Psychology*, *140*(3), 279–294. doi:10.1080/00224540009600471

Park, K. A., Lay, K., & Ramsay, L. (1993). Individual differences and developmental changes in preschooler's friendships. *Developmental Psychology*, *29*, 264–270. doi:10.1037/0012-1649.29.2.264

Park, K. A., & Waters, E. (1989). Security of attachment and preschool friendships. *Child Development*, *60*, 1076–1081. doi:10.2307/1130781

Paul, D. L., & McDaniel, R. R. Jr. (2004). A field study of the effect of interpersonal trust on virtual collaborative relationship performance. *MIS Quarterly*, *28*, 183–227.

Pavlou, P. A., & Fygenson, M. (2006). Understanding and predicting electronic commerce adoption: an extension of the theory of planned behavior. *MIS Quarterly*, *30*, 115–143.

Pavlou, P. A., & Gefen, D. (2004). Building effective online marketplaces with institution-based trust. *Information Systems Research*, *15*, 35–62. doi:10.1287/isre.1040.0015

Paxton, P. (1999). "Is Social Capital Declining in the United States?" A Multiple Indicator Assessment. *American Journal of Sociology*, *105*, 88–127. doi:10.1086/210268

Ratnasingam, P. (2005). Trust in inter-organizational exchanges: a case study in business to business electronic commerce. *Decision Support Systems*, *39*(3), 525–544. doi:10.1016/j.dss.2003.12.005

Rotenberg, K. J. (1984). Sex differences in children's trust in peers. *Sex Roles*, *11*, 953–957. doi:10.1007/BF00287822

Rotenberg, K. J. (1986). Same-sex partners and same-sex differences in the trust-value basis of children's friendships. *Sex Roles*, *15*, 613–626. doi:10.1007/BF00288218

Rotenberg, K. J. (1991). Children's cue use and strategies for detecting deception. In K. J. Rotenberg (Ed.), *Children's interpersonal trust: Sensitivity to lying, deception, and promise violations*. New York: Springer-Verlag.

Rotenberg, K. J. (1991). The trust-value basis of children's friendship. In K. J. Rotenberg (Ed.), *Children's interpersonal trust: Sensitivity to lying, deception, and promise violations*. New York: Springer-Verlag.

Rotenberg, K. J. (1994). Loneliness and interpersonal trust. *Journal of Social and Clinical Psychology*, *13*, 152–173.

Rotenberg, K. J. (1995). The socialisation of trust: Parents' and children's interpersonal trust. *International Journal of Behavioral Development*, *18*, 713–726. doi:10.1177/016502549501800408

Rotenberg, K. J. (2001). Trust across the life-span. In N. J. Smelser & P. B. Baltes (Eds.), *International encyclopedia of the social and behavioural sciences* (pp. 7866-7868). New York: Pergamon.

Rotenberg, K. J., Boulton, M. J., & Fox, C. L. (2005). Cross-Sectional and Longitudinal Relations Among Children's Trust Beliefs, Psychological Maladjustment and Social Relationships: Are Very High as Well as Very Low Trusting Children at Risk? *Journal of Abnormal Child Psychology*, *33*, 595–610. doi:10.1007/s10802-005-6740-9

Rotenberg, K. J., & Cerda, C. (1995). Racially based trust expectancies of Native American and Caucasian children. *The Journal of Social Psychology, 134*, 621–631.

Rotenberg, K. J., Fox, C., & Green, S. (2005). Construction and validation of a children's interpersonal trust belief scale. *The British Journal of Developmental Psychology, 23*, 271–292. doi:10.1348/026151005X26192

Rotenberg, K. J., & Pilipenko, T. A. (1983-1984). Mutuality, temporal consistency, and helpfulness in children's trust in peers. *Social Cognition, 2*, 235–255.

Rotenberg, K. J., & Sliz, D. (1988). Children's restrictive disclosure to friends. *Merrill-Palmer Quarterly, 34*, 203–215.

Rotter, J. B. (1967). A new scale for the measurement of interpersonal trust. *Journal of Personality, 35*, 651–665. doi:10.1111/j.1467-6494.1967.tb01454.x

Rotter, J. B. (1971). Generalized expectancies for interpersonal trust. *The American Psychologist, 26*, 443–452. doi:10.1037/h0031464

Schindler, P. L., & Thomas, C. C. (1993). The structure of interpersonal trust. *Journal of Personality, 35*, 651–665.

Shapiro, D., Sheppard, B. H., & Cheraskin, L. (1992). Business on a handshake. *Negotiation Journal, 8*, 365–377. doi:10.1111/j.1571-9979.1992.tb00679.x

Shek, D. T. L. (2005). Perceived Parental Control Processes, Parent-Child Relational Qualities, and Psychological Well-Being in Chinese Adolescents With and Without Economic Disadvantage. *The Journal of Genetic Psychology, 166*, 171–188. doi:10.3200/GNTP.166.2.171-188

Siau, K., & Shen, Z. (2003). Building consumer trust in mobile commerce. *Communications of the ACM, 46*(4), 91–93. doi:10.1145/641205.641211

Tyler, T. R. (Ed.). (1996). *Trust in organizations: Frontiers of theory and research.* Thousand Oaks, CA: Sage.

Wentzel, K. R. (1991). Relations between social competence and academic achievement in early adolescence. *Child Development, 62*, 1066–1078. doi:10.2307/1131152

Wright, T. L., & Kirmani, A. (1977). Interpersonal trust, trustworthiness, and shopliing? in high-school. *Psychological Reports, 41*, 1165–1166.

Wrightsman, L. S. (1964). Measurement of philosophies of human nature. *Psychological Reports, 14*, 743–751.

Wrightsman, L. S. (1974). *Assumptions about human nature: A social psychological approach.* Monterey, CA: Brooks/Cole.

Wrightsman, L. S. (1991). *Interpersonal trust and attitudes toward human mature, and measures of personality and psychological attitudes.* San Diego, CA: Academic.

Wrightsman, L. S. (1992). *Assumptions about Human Nature: Implications for Researchers and Practitioners.* Newbury Park, CA: Sage.

Yamagishi, T., & Yamagishi, M. (1994). Trust and commitment in the united states and Japan. *Motivation and Emotion, 18*, 129–166. doi:10.1007/BF02249397

Yan, Z. (2006). A Conceptual architecture of a trusted mobile environment. In *Proceedings of IEEE SecPerU'06*, France (pp. 75-81).

Yan, Z., & Holtmanns, S. (2007). Trust Modeling and Management: from Social Trust to Digital Trust. In *Computer Security, Privacy and Politics: Current Issues, Challenges and Solutions.* Hershey, PA: IGI Global.

Yan, Z., Zhang, P., & Virtanen, T. (2003). Trust evaluation based security solution in ad hoc networks. In *Proceedings of the seventh Nordic Workshop on Secure IT Systems (NordSec03)*, Norway.

Yosano, A., & Nahoko, H. (2005). Social Stratifications, Intermediary Groups, and Creation of Trustfulness. *Sociological Theory and Methods, 20*, 27–44.

Chapter 18
Issues on Anshin and its Factors

Yuko Murayama
Iwate Prefectural University, Japan

Yasuhiro Fujihara
Iwate Prefectural University, Japan

ABSTRACT

Traditional research on security and safety has been based on the assumption that a user feels secure and safe when using objectively secure and safe systems and services. The authors investigate factors influencing users' subjective sense of security, which they call Anshin in Japanese. In this chapter, the authors introduce the concept of Anshin as an emotional trust and its research issues. They also show how to use statistical analysis methods to derive the factors of Anshin and present some results. Results using exploratory factor analysis and structural equation modeling bring us with three factors contributing to Anshin.

INTRODUCTION

In this chapter, we introduce the concept of Anshin and its research issues. We also present how to use statistical analysis methods to derive the factors of Anshin in our research presenting some results. Anshin is a Japanese term indicating an emotional state of one's mind in peace. "An" is to ease and "shin" is to mind; Anshin literally means to ease one's mind. We have introduced Anshin, and identified it as a key component of emotional trust (Murayama, Hauser, Hikage and Chakraborty, 2008).

We have tried and identified the factors of Anshin based on user surveys. This chapter introduces our research as well as some statistical analysis methods we use presenting some examples. The paper organization is as follows. The next section presents related work on Anshin and the concept of Anshin as the emotional trust. Section 3 describes how to conduct a user survey with statistical analysis, including questionnaire design issues, Factor Analysis and Structural Equation Modeling (SEM). Section 4 gives our conclusions.

DOI: 10.4018/978-1-61520-682-7.ch018

RELATED WORK ON ANSHIN AND TRUST

In this section, we introduce some related work. Most of them are introduced more thoroughly in our previous publication (Murayama, Hauser, Hikage and Chakraborty, 2008).

The sense of security is the emotional aspect of security. Since research on information security has been focused on its cognitive aspect, it is hard to find specific related work concerning the emotional aspect. On the other hand, some researchers have been looked at emotional aspects of trust. The relationship of user interfaces and trust has also been looked at by some researchers. Anshin has been studied in risk communication which is communication about the risks of nuclear power plants for a long time.

The concept of trust has been researched as a multi-disciplinary concept. From psychological viewpoint, Deutsch defined trust in an interpersonal context (Deutsch, 1960). Gambetta defined trust as a particular level of one's subjective probability that another's action would be favorable to oneself (Gambetta, 1988). Later Abdul-Rahman and Hailes used Gambetta's definition of trust and proposed a distributed model of trust based on recommendation (Abdul-Rahman & Hailes, 2000). Marsh proposed the first computational trust model with quantized trust values in the rage of -1 to +1 (Marsh, 1994).

Lewis and Weigert (Lewis & Weigert, 1985) identified that trust had two aspects, viz. cognitive trust and emotional trust. Xiao and Benbasat defined the emotional aspect of trust in terms of commerce calling the trust concepts researched so far cognitive trust (Xiao & Benbasat, 2003; Xiao Komiak & Benbasat, 2004).

Popularly, cognitive trust is defined as a trustor's rational expectation that a trustee will have the necessary competence, benevolence, and integrity to be relied upon. On the other hand, the emotional aspect of trust is defined as an emotional security, or feeling secure, or comfortable (Kuan & Bock, 2005; Xiao & Benbasat, 2003). According to Xiao and Benbasat(Xiao Komiak & Benbasat, 2004), emotional trust is feeling, while cognitive trust is cognition.

Yamagishi gives the distinct definitions of Anshin and trust from a sociological viewpoint; Anshin is the belief that we have no social uncertainty, whereas trust is needed when we have high social uncertainty. Trust is expectations of others' intentions based on trustor's judgment of others' personalities and feelings (Yamagishi, 1998).

From a human interface viewpoint, Whitten and Tygar point out that user interfaces in security systems need special interfaces (Whitten & Tygar, 1999). Stephens gives design elements, such as page layout, navigation, and graphics which affect the development of trust between buyers and sellers in e-commerce (Stephens, 2004). Pu and Chen also report that how information was presented affected trust building in user interfaces (Pu & Chen, 2006). According to Riegelsberger, Sasse and McCarthy, affective reactions influence consumer decision-making (Riegelsberger, Sasse, & McCarthy, 2003).

From the viewpoint of communication about the risks of nuclear power plants, Kikkawa et al. introduced two Anshin states, viz. one with knowledge and the other without knowledge (Kikkawa et al., 2003, pp.1-8). They suggested that it would be necessary for users to study and obtain information in an active way to get more Anshin. To create Anshin the experts on technology would need to provide information to users as well as reducing technological risks. Yamazaki and Kikkawa suggested that there is a structure in Anshin through their study on Anshin in epidemic disease 'Yamazaki & Kikkawa, 2006).

Recently Camp identified that trust included security, safety and reliability (Camp, 2003). Later Hoffman et al. presented such a structure as well with security, safety, reliability, privacy and availability (Hoffman, Lawson-Jenkins, & Blum,

Figure 1. Anshin as Emotional part of Trust

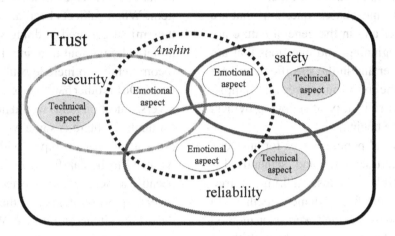

2006). Accordingly, we can deduce that the emotional trust is composed of the senses of security, safety, reliability, privacy and availability.

Indeed, in Japanese, Anshin presents the senses of security, safety, reliability and so on. Therefore, Anshin is the emotional trust. Figure 1 shows the concepts.

USER SURVEY WITH STATISTICAL ANALYSIS

Questionnaire Survey

In this section, we introduce a questionnaire technique for extracting rules of human activity as a conceptual abstract based on the observation of actions and reactions. We take our latest suevey with seven hundred and fifty six local government officers for deducing Anshin factors as an example.

When one is trying to identify such factors, in many cases, we could have enough information by literature survey on existing research results at the exploratory stage. *Psychological Abstracts* (American Psychological Association, n.d.) is a good source of information in the field of psychology. When such survey is not enough for the preparation of questionnaire, we need a data

collection as a preliminary study before the actual data collection. With the questionnaire survey, we could collect data from many subjects so as to have information in an objective manner.

Preparing a Questionnaire

When preparing a questionnaire, we need to review the past work as well as to have the feedbacks from the subjects. In our survey, we conducted a survey based on a free statement method with fifteen university students whose major was computer science. We asked what could make them feel Anshin when they use information systems so that we collected Anshin elements from the users' viewpoint. Apart from such a survey, we could have the feedbacks from the users by interviewing each subject individually. Brain storming with a small-group of subjects is useful as well.

In the next step, we produce question items based on the literature survey and the results from interview and brain streaming. The similar questions are put together into one question item, but it is necessary to be careful not to include multiple elements into one question. A question item needs to be brief and understood easily by subject. Time length required for answering each question is important. The adequate amount of question is the one that can be answered within

30 minutes including instructing time, in case of adult subjects. In most cases, questions that are simple to answer and in the general nature are placed in the beginning, and questions that are difficult to answer and in the specific nature are placed towards the end. In our survey for example, a question about reliability of service providers was placed in the beginning.

We have several popular styles for answers, such as the Likert scale method, semantic differential, multiple choices, ranking, paired comparison and the free statement method. In this section, we describe the Likert scale method because it is most popular among them. With the Likert scale, we have several levels for showing degree and frequency in each question so that a subject would answer selecting one of the levels. 5-level and 7-level scales are most popular. We recommend using at least the 5-level scale in order to avoid difficulties with later analysis. It would become difficult for subjects to answer when there are too many levels; therefore, it is necessary to decide the levels deliberately taking account of subjects and question items. The more levels, the longer time is required for subjects to answer the questions.

Moreover, the distance between levels needs to be more or less equal for degree and frequency because the interval distance plays an important role in later analysis.

In the case of the odd number levels such as 5-levels and 7-levels, an intermediate answer such as "Neither agree nor disagree" is included. There are various thoughts on this issue whether to include or not such an intermediate answer. The majority of subjects tend to choose the intermediate answer, and this might not be desirable in terms of detecting the variability of an individual (Berdie, Anderson, & Niebuhr, 1992). On the other hand, some subjects seem to feel difficult in answering questions when there is no intermediate option, which may result in increasing the number of missing answers. There is another argument among researchers over the issue whether or not

to include a reverse question item for a question item. When subjects keep answering questions, they might get tired of doing so and answer automatically without thinking. In such cases, it is recommended to include some reverse question items. On the other hand, since the answers to those reverse question items would need to be reversed for analysis, there is some worry of such results processing. For example, with factor analysis, we need to be careful to include reverse items because a factor could be often composed of the reverse question items and the other items than the original items (Johnson & Wichern, 1998). In our survey, we used factor analysis and did not include any reverse items.

Improving the Questionnaire

In the previous subsection, we described how to produce the draft questionnaire. In this subsection, we describe how to improve the questionnaire taking examples from our survey on Anshin. Quite often such a questionnaire may be missing out necessary question items whereas it may include similar items. Moreover, because subjects may not understand what a researcher expects them to answer, the draft questionnaire needs to be tested previously by those whose attributes are similar to the target subjects of the main survey. This way the questionnaire would be improved practically.

We conducted survey with four hundred fifty two students (Hikage, Hauser, & Murayama, 2007). The questionnaire was prepared based on the literature survey as well as preliminary survey with a small group of students. We had another survey with local government officers. In this case, we asked some officers in the same organization as the subjects of the main survey for a preliminary survey and obtained one hundred nine answers (Fujihara, Murayama, & Yamaguchi, 2008a). In this preliminary test, we used the questionnaire used for the survey with students. As a result, the subjects answered what items were difficult for them to answer and what else could make them feel Anshin apart from the given items. As a result, those subjects who were not familiar with information security pointed out that it was difficult for them to understand some security terms and situations.

In the preliminary test, we asked subjects to suppose two popular situations; 1) they use the internet using computer and cellular phone for a search of some information and 2) they need to input personal information when using some services and systems. For the main survey, we modified them so that the subjects could presume more specific situations such as "entering credit card information when shopping at an internet site." Moreover, each question item was modified so as to be more understandable.

If you had a certain number of subjects for a preliminary test, it would be possible to figure out what question items could be improved using some statistical methods. Firstly you would review whether there would be any extreme bias in the distribution of any items or not. You could review whether there would be frequently missing data with any items due to the ceiling effect and the floor effect, from the statistics of each question item. Secondly, you would perform G-P (Good-Poor) analysis and get I-T (Item-Test) correlation coefficient.

With G-P analysis, answers of all the question items would be summed up for each subject; each subject would be separated into upper level group or lower level group depending on the summed value. The average of the answers from the upper level group to each question item would be calculated and compared to the one from the lower level group. You would verify whether the difference is significant or not, and need to review the question items that do not have any difference.

With I-T correlation coefficient, you would calculate the correlation coefficient between the sum of the answers for all the question items and the answer for each question item. You would need to review the items that had the low correlation

because these items would be different from the overall pattern. Moreover, you could conduct factor analysis and review the items with low load for any of the factors as well as those with high load for the multiple factors. You could use the reliability coefficient that represents accuracy of the entire questionnaire. In many cases, Cronbach's α coefficient is used for reliability coefficient. You could calculate the α coefficient with all the question items, as well as the α coefficient with all but some question items; it does not matter whether one item or multiple items. You would compare those two α coefficient. If the latter is higher, you might need to eliminate the question items. In our survey, six items were eliminated from the questionnaire used in the preliminary test based on the result from these numeric data analysis. We improved twenty eight items based on the feedbacks from the free statement answers as well. In this way we improved our questionnaire for the main survey.

Kanji introduced more details about those statistical analyses (Kanji, 1999).

Conducting Survey

When you start a user survey, you need the deliberate selection of the subjects. The number of the subjects is an important issue as well. In this section, we introduce how we selected the subjects in our latest survey (Fujihara, Murayama, & Yamaguchi, 2008b). It would be best if we could have a group of the subjects so that they represent the entire population of the survey target perfectly. However, that would not be possible due to the limited time and budget for research. In our survey, random selection was not possible because the subjects were the employees of a local government. The primary reason of targeting the local government officers is that one of the officers was interested in our survey. Although those subjects might not represent the entire population of the target users, we believe that this group of subjects would represent the users to a certain extent. We asked the subjects how much they knew about computer and internet, apart from the general attributes such as age, in our questionnaire, in order to figure out the characteristics of the subject group. Researchers have various views about the required number of subjects (Hair, 2009). For our survey we collected more subjects than the number of data required for analysis; we planned to conduct factor analysis, structural equation modeling, and analysis according to the knowledge level on information security. In practice what we needed were five hundred subjects, whereas we actually had seven hundred and fifty six subjects. It is well known that the collection ratio would change according to the way how a survey request was made, answering styles and how to collect the answers (Dillman, 1978). In our survey, we asked for participating the survey through email within the office. We used the Likert scale for answers and a web-based questionnaire system for collecting them.

Exploratory Factor Analysis with Examples

Factor analysis is a statistical method that figures out a latent variable that cannot be observed directly from the observable variable, which was suggested in the beginning of 20th century (Spearman, 1904). With exploratory factor analysis we can figure out a factor that affects an observable variable from data without any specific model. With confirmatory factor analysis we can verify the correlation between the factors. In most cases, it is the former that is meant by factor analysis. We look into exploratory factor analysis in this section. Harman introduced details about factor analysis (Harman, 1976).

Selecting Factors

As the first step, we need to decide target items for factor analysis, just as we decided the question items with the improving process in the previous section, IMPROVING the QUESTIONNAIRE. In our survey, three items with the ceiling effect and two items with low I-T correlation coefficient were eliminated, and twenty three items were left for factor analysis.

In our survey we used Maximum Likelihood Method for calculating the initial Eigenvalues in order to determine the number of factors due to the normality in the distribution of the collected data. One might use Principal Factor Method and Least Square Method when the data did not have normal distribution and when the initial Eigenvalues could not be calculated by Maximum Likelihood Method.

As the next step, we need to determine the number of factors based on the calculated initial Eigenvalues. There are two popular methods for this. One is to choose the number of factors graphically with greater decrease of the Eigenvalue compared to the others (the scree test). The other is to choose the factors with Eigenvalue greater than one (The Kaiser criterion). Whatever method is used, the number of factors is determined according to how possibly interpretable the chosen factors would be. This way number of factors is determined temporarily, and it will be reviewed to what degrees it could be explained in the following section.

Figure 2 is a graph called scree plot for determining the number of factors by scree test for the Eigenvalues in our latest survey. For the analysis we used SPSS 16.0J™ for Windows. It was 7.934, 2.245, 1.805, 1.382, 1.040, 0.9258 (the rest is omitted) from the first factor. It can be imagined from this figure that two factors, three factors, and four factors are alternatives with scree test. The next section describes how to interpret when three factors would be selected. The communality for explaining the entire variance with three factors is 52.10%.

Figure 2. An example of a scree plot

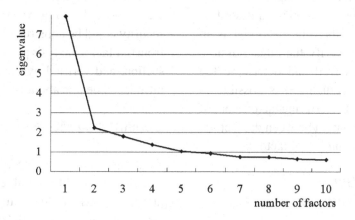

Interpreting Factors

It is possible to figure out the loading of each factor for each question item by calculating as described in the previous subsection; however, it is difficult to interpret as it is. For example, factor loading of the first factor is higher for many question items, and those with low correlation with the first factor become high correlation in many cases. Moreover, there are question items with multiple high-load factors in some cases. In such cases, axes are generally rotated in order to make loading clearer. There are two types of rotations, viz. orthogonal rotation and oblique rotation. An orthogonal rotation would be used if there was no correlation between factors. As an orthogonal rotation, Varimax rotation is popular. On the other hand, an oblique rotation would be used if there was correlation between factors. Since in our survey, we presumed that there was correlation between factors, we used Promax rotation, one of oblique rotation. If the correlation between factors is not known, oblique rotation is often used.

In the next step, we interpret three factors from the result of Promax rotation from our survey example. Factor pattern matrix after Promax rotation is shown in Table 1. Each numeric value represents factor loading of each factor on each question item. When the loading is closer to 0, its influence is smaller. When the absolute loading is larger, the influence is greater. In the case with oblique rotation, the loadings sometimes slightly exceed 1. In the case with the first factor, Q11 with the highest loading represents "Support in the case of troubles." Other question items represent the integrity of service provider, the competence of service provider to keep the system secure, and the benevolence of service provider. Therefore, this factor indicates "Cognitive Trust." The second factor, Q22 with the highest loading represents "Decent explanation how to use the system." Other question items represent the usability of the system and decent correspondence. Therefore, this factor represents "Usability and Availability of the system" from the viewpoint of users, not from the viewpoint of system reliability. The third factor, Q16 with highest loading represents "Users' understanding about information technology." Other question items represent understanding about system and security countermeasures by users. Therefore, this factor indicates "Understanding about information technology and the system." The Cronbach α coefficient described in the previous section was calculated in order to verify internal consistency of three factors, which resulted in α=0.881 for the items that belong to the first factor, α=0.823 for the second factor, and α=0.829 for the third factor. High reliability was shown. Furthermore, α coefficient is generally considered as showing high reliability when it is 0.8 or higher. We could interpret with three-factor solution as described above. We showed the three-factor model as an example, but we will verify the other possible number of factors as well and determine the number of factors eventually. It is possible to further review factors by verifying factor score of subjects, and the correlation between the factors, after determining the number of factors.

Structural Equation Modeling with Examples

Structural Equation Modeling (SEM) is a statistical technique to verify a causal model (Jöreskov, 1969). Exploratory factor analysis could be con-

sidered as a stage prior to SEM. In this section, we introduce how our Anshin model in terms of security could be constructed based on the result from our factor analysis presented in the previous section, and verified by the use of SEM. Kline introduced details about SEM (Kline, 2005).

Constructing Models

Factor analysis is conducted on the assumption that the observable variables (answers to each question item) would be influenced by the factors of latent variables. In our latest survey, at the first step, we created a model in which three question items with high factor loading have an effect on each factor. In Figure 3, *Anshin, Cogni-*

Table 1. Factor pattern matrix

	Factor 1	Factor 2	Factor 3
Q10	0.870	-0.089	0.014
Q11	0.811	0.067	-0.042
Q05	0.729	0.037	-0.082
Q07	0.648	-0.040	0.067
Q04	0.615	-0.079	0.010
Q12	0.580	0.204	0.082
Q13	0.580	0.050	0.089
Q03	0.571	-0.089	0.067
Q06	0.422	0.115	-0.132
Q09	0.419	-0.035	0.317
Q22	-0.089	0.876	0.009
Q23	0.155	0.726	-0.045
Q21	-0.053	0.696	0.044
Q24	-0.147	0.598	0.095
Q18	0.050	0.545	0.194
Q25	-0.023	0.517	0.088
Q28	-0.003	0.385	-0.107
Q27	0.098	0.382	-0.172
Q26	0.209	0.332	-0.144
Q16	-0.073	-0.064	0.941
Q17	-0.070	0.035	0.890
Q14	0.157	-0.036	0.606
Q15	0.168	0.072	0.484

tive Trust, Usability and *Understanding* are latent variables whereas observable variables are from Q10 to Q14, answers to question items. Error of answers to question items is represented in e1, e2, etc., and disturbance variables for factors are represented in d1. d2 and d3. Single-directional arrows show causal relation, and bi-directional arrows represent correlation.

At the next step, we look into parameter estimation for the model. Figure 3 shows a result from Maximum Likelihood Method. We used AMOS 16.0J™ for Windows for analysis. The weight of an arrow is the estimate value of a path coefficient that indicates the strength of a relation. The variance of observable variable was all normalized into one when calculating path coefficient.

Fitness of Models

We verify to what degrees the model could fit to the actual data. Fit assessment is conducted based on fit indexes. We introduce some fit indexes. The fitness of the model is verified by referring multiple fit indexes. Bollen and Long introduced more details about fit indexes used in SEM (Bollen & Long, 1993).

There are indexes such as Goodness of fit index (GFI), Adjusted goodness of fit index (AGFI), root mean square error of approximation (RMSEA).

and Comparative Fit Index (CFI). GFI is calculated from divergence of variance-covariance matrix estimated as data variance-covariance matrix. AGFI is a variant of GFI with a penalty on additional parameters, and its value is the same or lower than GFI. The higher the values of both GFI and AGFI become, the better they fit; the fitness is supposed to be good when the values are 0.9 or higher. RMSEA is a fit index that adjusts for the level of complexity in the model. With RMSEA, the lower the value of becomes, the better it fits; the fitness is bad when the value is 0.10 or higher. It is possible to use Akaike's information criterion (AIC) (Bollen & Long, 1993) for verifying fitness of a model. The lower the value of AIC becomes, the better it fits. It is used to compare the fitness of multiple models. CFI is an index that uses likelihood ratio test.

User Survey on Anshin

As we have presented in previous subsections, we present briefly the results from our latest survey. We conducted the survey in August 2008. The subjects were local government officers and their number was seven hundred and sixty five. We analyzed the survey responses using exploratory factor analysis using Maximum Likelihood Method under the normality assumption over the

Figure 3. The structure of Anshin with three factors

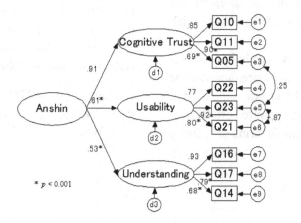

data. We used Promax rotation since the factors are co-related. As a result of the analysis, we had three factors based on the scree plot.

Three factors are *Cognitive Trust, Usability* and *Understanding* as in Figure 3. The first factor, *Cognitive Trust*, is the competence of service provider to keep the system secure, and the benevolence of service provider. The second factor, *Usability* is Usability and Availability of the system" from the viewpoint of users, not from the viewpoint of system reliability. The third factor, *Understanding* is users' understanding about information technology and the system.

Our model with three factors was verified with SEM and the fitness of our three factors model is as follows: GFI=0.978, AGFI=0.958, RMSEA=0.056, and CFI=0.983. We presume that they totally show high values.

CONCLUSION

In this chapter, we have introduced the concept of Anshin as emotional trust and its research issues as well as methods to be used for user survey presenting some results from our survey on Anshin. The concept of trust has been researched as a multi-disciplinary concept. We have presented briefly literature survey in this area. Trust has been researched to a great extent. The emotional part of security was identified firstly by Lewis and Weigert (Lewis & Weigert, 1985), and researched later by Xiao in the area of electronic commerce (Xiao & Benbasat, 2003; Xiao Komiak & Benbasat, 2004).

We introduce the user survey technique including how to produce a questionnaire, analyze the answers, produce a model and assess the model. Finally our latest survey was reported briefly. According to the result, Anshin in terms of security would be generated based on cognitive trust,

usability of a system or service in question, and users' understanding of information technology.

The research results presented show a snap shot of our research and we need to work more on figuring our Anshin. We hope that the work presented here would be useful to the researchers in this area.

REFERENCES

Abdul-Rahman, A., & Hailes, S. (2000). Supporting trust in virtual communities. In *Proceedings of the Hawaii International Conference on System Sciences 33*. Retrieved from http://ieeexplore.ieee.org/application/mdl/mdlconfirmation.jsp?arnumber=926814

American Psychological Association. (n.d.). *Psychological Abstracts*. Retrieved February 2, 2009, from http://www.apa.org/psycinfo/

Berdie, D. R., Anderson, J. F., & Niebuhr, M. A. (1992) *Questionnaires: Design and use*. Lanham, MD: Scarecrow Press.

Bollen, K. A., & Long, J. S. (1993). *Testing Structural Equation Models*. Newbury Park, CA: SAGE Publications.

Camp, L. J. (2003). Design for Trust. In R. Falcone (Ed.), *Trust, Reputation and Security: Theories and Practice* (pp. 15-29). Berlin, Germany: Springer-Verlag.

Deutsch, M. (1962). Cooperation and trust: Some theoretical notes. In M. R. Jones (Ed.), *Nebraska Symposium on Motivation* (pp. 275-319). Lincoln, NE: University of Nebraska Press.

Dillman, D. A. (1978). *Mail and Telephone Surveys: The Total Design Method*. New York, NY: John Wiley.

Fujihara, Y., Murayama, Y., & Yamaguchi, K. (2008a). A user survey on the sense of security, Anshin. In S. Jajodia, P. Samarati, & S. Cimato (Eds.), *Proceedings of The Ifip Tc 11 23rd International Information Security Conference of IFIP International Federation for Information Processing* (pp. 699-703). New York, NY: Springer.

Fujihara, Y., Murayama, Y., & Yamaguchi, K. (2008b, October). *User survey on the Anshin with civil servants for a local government* (in Japanese). Paper presented at Computer Security Symposium 2008, Okinawa, Japan.

Gambetta, D. (1988). Can we trust trust? In D. Gambetta (Ed.), *Trust: Making and breaking cooperative relations* (pp. 213-237). Oxford, UK: Basil Blackwell. Retrieved from http://www.sociology. ox.ac.uk/papers/gambetta213-237.pdf

Hair, J. F., Jr., Black, W. C., Babin, B. J., & Anderson, R. E. (2009). *Multivariate data analysis* (7th ed.). Upper Saddle River, NJ: Prentice Hall.

Harman, H. H. (1976). Modern factor analysis (3rd ed.). Chicago, IL: University of Chicago Press

Hikage, N., Hauser, C., & Murayama, Y. (2007). Joho security gijutsu ni taisuru anshinkan no kozo ni kansuru tokeiteki kento [A statistical discussion of the sense of security, Anshin]. *Information Processing Society of Japan Journal, 48*(9). (in Japanese)

Hoffman, L. J., Lawson-Jenkins, K., & Blum, J. (2006). Trust beyond security: an expanded trust model. *Communications of the ACM, 49*(7), 94–101. doi:10.1145/1139922.1139924

Johnson, R. A., & Wichern, D. W. (1998). *Applied Multivariate Statistical Analysis* (4th ed.). Upper Saddle River, NJ: Prentice Hall.

Jöreskov, K. G. (1969). A general approach to confirmatory maximum likelihood factor analysis. *Psychometrika, 21*, 85–96.

Kanji, G. K. (1999). *100 Statistical Tests*. Newbury Park, CA: SAGE Publications.

Kikkawa, T., Shirato, S., Fujii, S., & Takemura, K. (2003). Gijutsuteki anzen to shakaiteki Anshin [The pursuit of informed reassurance ('An-Shin' in Society) and technological safety ('An-Zen')] [in Japanese]. *Journal of SHAKAI-GIJUTSU, 1*, 1–8. doi:10.3392/sociotechnica.1.1

Kline, R. B. (2005). *Principles and Practice of Structural Equation Modeling*. New York, NY: The Guilford Press, Kuan, H. H., & Bock, G. W. (2005). The collective reality of trust: An investigation of social relations and networks on trust in multi-channel retailers. In *Proceedings of the 13th European Conference on Information Systems*. Retrieved February 9, 2007, from http://is2.lse.ac.uk/asp/aspecis/20050018.pdf

Komiak, S. X., & Benbasat, I. (2004). Understanding customer trust in agent-mediated electronic commerce, web-mediated electronic commerce, and traditional commerce. *Information Technology and Management, 5*(1-2), 181–207. doi:10.1023/B:ITEM.0000008081.55563.d4

Lewis, D. J., & Weigert, A. (1985). Trust as a social reality. *Social Forces, 63*(4), 967–985. doi:10.2307/2578601

Marsh, S. (1994). *Formalising trust as a computational concept*. Unpublished doctoral dissertation, University of Stirling, UK.

Murayama, Y., Hauser, C., Hikage, N., & Chakraborty, B. (2008). The Sense of Security and Trust. In M. Gupta & R. Sharman (Eds.), *Handbook of Research on Social and Organizational Liabilities in Information Security*. Hershey, PA: IGI Global.

Pu, P., & Chen, L. (2006). Trust building with explanation interfaces. In *Proceedings of the 11th international conference on Intelligent user interfaces (IUI'06)* (pp. 93-100).

Riegelsberger, J., Sasse, M. A., & McCarthy, J. D. (2003). Privacy and trust: Shiny happy people building trust? Photos on e-commerce websites and consumer trust. *Proceedings of CHI, 5*(1), 121–128.

Spearman, C. (1904). General intelligence objectively determined and measured. *The American Journal of Psychology, 15*, 201–293. doi:10.2307/1412107

Stephens, R. T. (2004). A framework for the identification of electronic commerce design elements that enable trust within the small hotel industry. In *Proceedings of ACMSE* (pp. 309-314).

Stevens, J. (2001). *Applied Multivariate Statistics for the Social Sciences* (4th ed.). Mahwah, NJ: Lawrence Erlbaum Assoc Inc.

Whitten, A., & Tygar, D. (1999). Why johnny can't encrypt: A usability evaluation of PGP 5.0. In *Proceedings of the 9th USENIX Security Symposium* (pp. 169-184).

Xiao, S., & Benbasat, I. (2003). The formation of trust and distrust in recommendation agents in repeated interactions: A process-tracing analysis. In *Proceedings of the 5th International Conference on Electronic Commerce* (pp. 287-293).

Yamagishi, T. (1998). *The structure of trust: The evolutionary games of mind and society* (in Japanese). Tokyo: Tokyo University Press. Retrieved April 2007, from http://lynx.let.hokudai.ac.jp/members/yamagishi/english.htm

Yamazaki, M., & Kikkawa, T. (2006). The Structure of Anxiety Associated with Avian Influenza and Pandemic Influenza. In *Proceedings of the 47th annual conference of the Japanese Society of Social Psychology* (in Japanese) (pp. 676-677).

Chapter 19

Trust in Identification Systems:
From Empirical Observations to Design Guidelines

Piotr Cofta
BT Innovate, UK

Hazel Lacohée
BT Innovate, UK

ABSTRACT

This chapter is concerned with methodology. The authors utilise a case study of citizen identification systems (that are adopted or are in the process of consideration for adoption in several countries throughout the world) to illustrate the continuum of trust-related considerations and technology adoption, ranging from theoretical underpinnings of trust, to empirical studies, through to practical design guidelines. The interdisciplinary nature of the research calls for a mixed methodological approach that combines the best from various disciplines. Drawing from the authors' rich experience and their numerous publications in this field, this chapter provides a practical example of a methodology that combines empirical and theoretical studies in trust and technology adoption to deliver clear operational and technical guidelines that may increase trust in identification systems.

INTRODUCTION

Trust is valuable. The introduction of trust into a relationship between people (or, for example, between customers and institutions) promises to decrease the complexity and cost of such relationships and eventually brings benefits to both parties. However, as technology becomes an increasingly important element of these relationships, the question of whether technology should be trusted, and

how others should be trusted through technology, also becomes increasingly important.

Different forms of identification and authentication have always been with us; without the ability to reliably identify ourselves, no relationship can be established and maintained. The introduction of technology has re-defined established protocols regarding identity (and its verification), introducing dis-embedding and re-embedding of social interactions (Giddens, 1988). It is a disruption rather than an evolution, and while the technology is an important factor of such disruptive change, it does

DOI: 10.4018/978-1-61520-682-7.ch019

not guarantee that a new system will be accepted on the merits of technology alone.

Citizen identification systems (commonly referred to as 'citizen cards' or 'citizen id' systems) have received mixed reception throughout the world. Some of the successes and failures of these identification systems can be attributed to the widely understood existing culture. However, there is still a question of whether certain properties of such systems result in an increase or decrease of public trust in their ability to deliver what they promise, such as increased security and improved service delivery. It is not appropriate here to engage in an in-depth discussion of the many, varied and complex issues concerning trust in identification systems but we address these in detail in chapter 5 of our book 'Understanding Public Perceptions: Trust and Engagement in ICT-Mediated Services (Lacohée, Cofta, Phippen & Furnell, 2008).

The question that is addressed in this chapter is formulated as follows:

Having a particular application area, such as a citizen identification system, what are the technical (and associated operational) properties of such a system that can be deployed that warrant citizens' justified trust in the said system?

This question is inherently interdisciplinary, for example, it spans the subject of user acceptance, social psychology, organisational science, and management, as well as technology. The methodology that is employed to answer such a question should therefore reflect its interdisciplinary nature.

This chapter discusses an example of the methodology that the authors have applied to the question presented above, together with justifications, intermediary results and resulting guidelines. While this chapter has been designed as a discussion on interdisciplinary methodology, it can be also seen as a justification for particular guidelines regarding citizen identification systems.

The chapter starts with a detailed discussion of the chosen methodology and builds to provide background information concerning trust and identification systems. From there, we introduce the outcome of an anthropological, empirical study on user's trust in technical systems, and in particular, in citizen identity systems. Such a study leads to the formulation of certain findings regarding the current state of the trust relationship between people and technology.

The chapter then explores various theoretical models that attempt to explain the relationship between society and technology, mostly for the purpose of technology adoption. Observations from empirical studies guide the selection of the theory and eventually lead to predictions regarding possible reactions to alterations of the system. Alterations that are beneficial to justified trust are then converted into technological guidelines.

METHODOLOGY

The complexity of technology adoption calls for mixed, interdisciplinary research with associated mixed, interdisciplinary methodology. We do not aspire to provide a complete methodology that will serve all possible cases of mixed interdisciplinary research; rather, our focus is on presenting the logic and outcome of a particular body of work, to demonstrate how such mixed methodologies work in practise for interdisciplinary research. As such, we would like to position our methodology as two-fold: first, against on-going methodological debates, and then against established and applicable methodologies.

As a research discipline matures, it also determines the best research methodology that serves its needs. While each discipline eventually develops a methodology that is incompatible with others, the most important differences lie along two axes: qualitative vs. quantitative and empirical vs. theoretical.

Qualitative research (Silverman, 2006) concentrates on determining descriptive properties and changes of the subject under study and can provide a deep level of understanding of the issues under investigation. Qualitative research is often criticised as being subjective because methods used to collect and analyse information call for direct involvement of the researcher but it does have considerable value in investigating complex and sensitive areas. Conversely, quantitative research attempts to capture numerical values that characterise the research subject, in a manner that strives for objectivity.

Empirical research concentrates on capturing the properties or measurements of actual research subjects, either in their natural environment or through experiments. Theoretical research concentrates on developing theories that generalise the outcome of empirical research and allow for predictions to be made.

No approach is without its drawbacks as well as its merits. While individual methodologies tend to suppress what they perceive to be inappropriate, mixed methodology (characteristic of interdisciplinary research) can be constructed in such a way as to increase the benefits and minimise the deficiencies of a chosen approach. The additional hurdle that mixed inter-disciplinary methodology has to clear is the incompatibility of vocabulary, and paradigms, both those that are used by researchers and by their subjects (for example, in the case of field studies).

Against this background, the methodology that has been applied to the research question discussed in this chapter combines empirical and theoretical research within the general qualitative approach. The purpose of this methodology is to make informed predictions that are closely relevant to the current situation, in a language that can be readily understood by potential recipients of the research.

The methodology chosen here subscribes to philosophical foundations of soft systems methodology (Checkland, 1990), applied to the specific case of technology adoption for identity systems. We acknowledge the embedded and circular nature of the process, the necessity to abstract the situation known from the real world, to seek the root problem and its logical consequences and then translate them into activities.

However, in the true spirit of soft systems methodology (Checkland, 2000), we have not followed the seven steps for which the methodology is famous (see e.g. Wilson, 2001). Instead, we have chosen to follow the development that has been adopted by creators of this methodology that has led them towards the 'four activities' model (Checkland, 1990), adapting it further to the situation at hand. Those activities relate to fact-finding, model formulation, discussion about the situation and formulating (and taking) actions. Note that such an approach is not only allowed, but even encouraged by this methodology that stresses continuous learning from past experience.

Note that the purpose of this paper is to illustrate the continuity of the problem of trust throughout the particular case study, not the comparatory study of different methodologies that might be applicable to it. The authors acknowledge the existence of alternative approaches, ranging from those that are purely anthropological to strict application of system development models, but found them unsatisfactory in addressing this particular case.

As a starting point, the outcome of an extensive empirical study has been chosen. This study, conducted using a qualitative methodological approach (Lacohée, Crane & Phippen, 2006), resulted in a wealth of observations regarding people's trust in technology in general, as well as their perception of identity schemes, privacy and security etc.

However, such empirical research may not necessarily demonstrate significant predictive values; attitudes may change over time, as may the technologies in current use. On the other hand, theories that discuss the relationship between people and technology are not always relevant to the current situation, as revealed by empirical research. Therefore, an empirical study has been used to make a decision regarding applicable theory. Taking into account the number of theories related to trust, technology, society, adoption etc., such a selection is critical to the success of this research.

The choice has been made on the basis of the explanatory power the theory can provide, i.e. the theory needs to explain all the empirical observations and should allow us to speculate on different potential developments in the future.

Having chosen the theory, the research concentrated on identifying technical choices that maximise the adoption of a particular technology - in this case a citizen identification system. A set of four scenarios (see Cofta, 2009 for detailed analysis) were used to develop recommendations, and these were then converted into practical technical guidelines. Those scenarios that were considered include: benevolent state, pragmatic state, incompetent state and finally malicious state.

TRUST

Even though the construct of trust is interdisciplinary, research in trust tends to follow a recognised structure and methodology of disciplines. The following section is a short and non-exhaustive overview of different works related to trust, structured into two main groups. For a detailed discussion see e.g. (Cofta, 2007). The first group covers the widely understood humanities (including social science, philosophy, psychology, economy and management), while the other covers technical approaches to trust, mostly within the context of information and communication technology (ICT).

Overview

Humanities approach trust from the perspective of a voluntary belief in what *may* be trusted, i.e. the intentions of the other party. Several different

perspectives on trust are available, for example, trust as a complexity reductor (Luhmann, 1979) interprets trust as a social enabler that reduces the otherwise unbearable complexity of possible futures. This approach strongly correlates with the perception that communication technology both creates trust and creates a need for trust, and that in general, usability of a given technology instils trust.

The observation that there is a link between the level of social trust, welfare and development (Fukuyama, 1996) has created interest in considering trust as a form of social capital. Current developments associated with social networking, computer supported cooperation etc. reflect this approach well. In this case, trust in technology (and associated technology adoption) is not discussed, and is assumed to be high.

Management sciences discuss trust as an important element of organisation (e.g. Solomon & Flores, 2001) There is an underlying assumption that the technology, once mastered, will facilitate the creation (or at least the sustainability) of trust.

Game theories (e.g. Berg, Dickhaut & McCabe, 1995) use the concept of trust to explain phenomena that counter the instant economic rationality of utility maximisation. The ability of economic players to go beyond the obvious self-interest, (potentially in expectation that the other party will reciprocate) became a foundation of several economic games. ICT is used here as the context-neutral enabler (most games are played with the help of a computer), and the impact of technology is not usually considered.

Within the realm of technology, trust has been associated with reliability and security (Anderson, 2001). This security-inspired approach has resulted in concentrating not on what *may* be trusted, but on what *has to* be trusted. The recognition of this nature of trust has been addressed in initiatives such as trusted computing (Pearson, 2002), where individual devices are granted reassurance over its own configuration on the basis of a high-assurance root of trust.

The understanding that trust precedes meaningful and secure communication has eventually led to the concept of trust management, a separate layer of interactions that maintains trust relationships between communicating nodes, reflecting existing social and legal arrangements. Autonomous agents (e.g. Falcone, 2006) have liberated trust management from the need for such a mandatory trust provided that identity can be assured, and has brought about the notion of imperfect trust.

Works on the impact of technically-mediated communication on trust form a separate stream. While some researchers believe that improved communication generates more trust, others are more sceptical, pointing out that technology makes deception easier, thus causing problems with proper assessment of trust-related evidence (Riegelsberger, Sasse, & McCarthy, 2005).

Another effect of the introduction of electronically-mediated communication is the development of research in user trust in digital devices, e.g. in a form of web features that facilitate the creation of perceived trust (Egger, 2000), trust in information systems (Li, Valacich & Hess, 2004) or in improvements of trust between people while communicating through digital channels.

Definition

Despite the fact that trust has 16 meanings (McKnight & Chervany, 1996), it is possible to detect common traits. There is a general agreement that trust is attributable only to intentional agents, i.e. usually only to people and that the perception of trust can be expanded to inanimate objects or organisations (Dennett, 1989). Further, there is an agreement that trust expressed through technology reflects trust that exists in society and that technology has a problem with facilitating the creation of trust between people.

The operational definition of trust that is used throughout this chapter follows the approach of humanities (i.e. it interprets trust as a voluntary belief) and is derived from typical constructs found in the literature literature (e.g. Mayer, Davis, & Schoorman, 1995).

[Trust is] the willingness of a party (trustor) to be vulnerable to the actions of another party (trustee) based on expectation that the other party will perform a particular action important to the trustor, irrespective of the ability to monitor or control that other party.

Asymmetric Trust

The kind of trust that is required for citizen identification systems is asymmetric. This form of trust is that which hopefully emerges where one entity in a relationship has a power that is significantly larger than the other. For such asymmetric relationships trust is desired, but is particularly hard to build and maintain.

Most relationships between individuals and institutions are asymmetrical; individuals, while being dependent upon institutions, seldom have any influence over how those institutions behave. Conversely, an institution is not dependent upon the relationship and may significantly influence one's life by wilful or negligent action.

Drawing from the definition provided, an individual is in the position to trust (or not) institutions, as he is both vulnerable and unable to control the relationship. Institutions do not have to trust individuals (and they usually do not); in order to control their vulnerabilities they can employ risk management rather than trust.

While a single individual can do little harm to an institution, a mass refusal to participate can impact heavily on an institution. Therefore, even if an institution may not be concerned with each and every individual, it is usually concerned with gaining a certain level of trust from the majority of those with whom it is dealing.

When it comes to such asymmetric relationships, an individual's only available strategy is to trust or not trust. Therefore, he interprets all available information about the institution in terms of trust and distrust, possibly over-interpreting some messages. Currently communication technology is quite often used to maintain a relationship. As it is placed in this position by the institution, it is the technology itself, as well as the message that is delivered through this technology that is interpreted by the individual.

Justified Trust

The intention of this research is to focus only upon justified (warranted) trust where trust matches the trustworthiness of a trustee. While too little trust leads to the under-utilisation of opportunities, too much trust makes individuals vulnerable to possible mischief on the part of the other party. It has been demonstrated that it is justified trust that drives the optimum market equilibrium (Braynov & Sandholm, 2002).

The prerequisite of justified trust is the ability to correctly determine intentions (that is, trustworthiness) of the other party, from signals that are always insufficient yet, are the only signifiers that are available. Therefore the focus of this research is not on making parties more trustworthy, but on determining how the assessment of trustworthiness can be improved, even if such an improvement may eventually lead to a decrease rather than an increase in trust.

Interestingly, deploying systems that allow for justified trust to flourish may eventually increase the overall degree of trust. This is because once individuals have learnt to trust institutions only to the extent of their trustworthiness, institutions will have no choice but to become increasingly trustworthy - assuming that they find it beneficial to be trusted.

CITIZEN IDENTIFICATION SYSTEMS

Citizen identification systems have had a rather bad press recently, specifically in the UK where the scheme has been introduced with the Identity Card Act (2006), and its deployment is being staged from November 2008 onwards (National Identity Scheme Delivery Plan, 2008). There is a heated discussion concerning the viability of such a system considering for example, associated risks, infringement of civil liberties, the potential for function creep, as well as the inevitable technical challenges. At the same time the project is also experiencing cost overruns, security blunders, sudden changes in specification, and an unclear political agenda (London School of Economics, 2005). The image of public disenchantment combined with entrenched interests looks like yet another expensive failure.

Technically, citizen identification systems are quite straightforward; they all follow the concept of trust management systems (Blaze, Ioannidis and Keromytis, 2003) that they share with e.g. access control or credit payment. While several architectures may exist, they usually follow the same pattern: a central database and 'identity cards' that are issued to citizens. Variations are related to the location and content of the database (or several distributed but cross-linked databases), the content and technology of the card (size, security, required information), and communication architecture etc. For further technical discussion please see e.g. (Windley, 2005).

Similarly, processes supported by such system are not very different from credit or loyalty card schemes. During the enrolment process an individual receives the card that can subsequently be used at participating points to obtain access to goods or services. Such processes well support what is seen as the main purpose of citizen identification systems: to improve assurance of citizen's identity in their dealings with the state, thus decreasing both cost and risk that the state must bear while dealing with individuals. This relatively narrow definition of the purpose of such a system makes it particularly irrelevant to the rich experience individuals actually have in the presentation of their identity.

There are certain perceived social benefits of a citizen identification system, yet countries differ in the way in which these are realised. Such a system is believed to significantly improve the efficiency of service delivery, decrease overall costs, improve border control, simplify everyday experience in contact with a variety of institutions etc. While its ability to contain terrorist attacks is questionable, the usefulness of a good citizen identification system should not be overlooked. Some countries have significantly benefited from the centralised identification of its citizens, and others are in the process of, or are considering the introduction of such systems. However, within the European Union, there is very limited trust in institutions that administer such schemes (Backhouse and Halperin, 2007).

Significant risks associated with improper design or operation may quite often offset any perceived benefits. Such systems do indeed pose a variety of risks, both directly (for example, if personal information is compromised leading to large scale identity theft) and indirectly (where it can be used as a platform to cross-link surveillance systems and to restrict civil rights). Both risks are real and while their likelihood may be discussed, the potential of negative impact must not be ignored. Specifically, privacy as well as other civil rights can be significantly violated either as a result of intentional information sharing, by accidental data loss, or direct attack on the system.

EMPIRICAL FINDINGS

In this section we take the qualitative methodology of the authors' core research (Lacohée, Crane, & Phippen, 2006), see also (Lacohée, Cofta, Phippen, & Furnell, 2008), combined with theoretical analysis of the subject, to reveal some surprising insights into the relationship between modern society and technology.

The work presented here is based on the research we undertook as part of the Trustguide project (Lacohée, Crane, & Phippen, 2006). The project sought to establish clear guidelines for the research, development and delivery of trustworthy ICT (information, communications technology) and to identify where the responsibilities lie in making the future ICT-enabled world a safe and trusted environment. Over a 15-month period, ending October 2006, we hosted 29 workshops across the UK. Each workshop focused on a range of trust issues that continue to arise through the development and deployment of new technologies. A mixed methodology was employed combining technology demonstrations and hands-on experience within a workshop setting, with professionally facilitated semi-structured discussions based on relevant topic areas. We recorded verbatim discussion from participants as well as more subjective cues such as reaction, body language and straw polls. The results were analysed and assessed to draw out common themes and issues and these were used to inform our recommendations. The dialogue arising from the groups was then analysed using QSR N6, a qualitative data management and analysis code-based tool for use with open-ended survey data, in depth interviews and focus group transcripts (a more detailed description can be found within the Trustguide Report pages 5-12).

We have found that citizens are experienced and articulate in voicing their opinions about privacy, security and trust in technology because it is part of their daily experience. In the course of modern day living we have a good deal of choice and control concerning when and how we interact with technology, from Internet banking at home to accessing the web from a mobile phone whilst on the move.

In some cases however we do not have a choice, and we do not have control, technology is imposed upon us as is the case with CCTV and other surveillance devices deployed in public areas. When technological systems are imposed upon citizens those systems are likely to be met with opposition, or at least, there is a tipping point beyond which acceptability cannot be achieved. This is largely due to the fact that such systems impinge on what is perceived to be the private sphere of life, and, as it is currently proposed, the UK National Identity Scheme is a prime example of the case in question.

Risk and Benefits

Technology is not consumed in a vacuum it is consumed by social beings in a social context and hence adoption, rejection and acceptability of given technologies must be examined in that context too if we are to understand the reality of technology uptake. People do not trust technology to be secure but, where choice is available, they continue to engage with it because there is some benefit to them personally, and they feel that the benefits outweigh the risks. Whilst they may not trust the technology they may have well-founded trust in the organisation or institution employing that technology to deliver products or services.

Whether or not they are consciously aware of it, citizens (if they can) engage in a risk-benefit trade off, they are looking for the 'what's in it for me?' factors. The kind of issues they consider are the severity of the risk - what do I have to lose? The probability of the risk - how likely is it that something will go wrong? How will things be put right if something does go wrong – what sort of guarantees and restitution measures are in place to mitigate the risk? And ultimately, is it worth it - do the benefits outweigh the risks?

There are many variables that have a positive impact on this process, for example, something that enables the individual to save time or provides greater convenience, or enables them to do something that could not otherwise be easily achieved by other means, or improves the quality of life. Where such factors are available they are likely to tip the balance in favour of engagement, and if such factors are available in combination, then the impact is even greater and the benefits of a given proposition are multiplied. A detailed discussion

of the ways in which trust may be improved is discussed in detail in Lacohée, Cofta, Phippen, & Furnell (2008, chapter 9).

Government agencies or service providers for example can exploit such factors to encourage engagement, and that's exactly what cyber criminals do too, it is why phishing scams work. The perpetrators play on the very reasons that people engage with such systems or services and they threaten to take those benefits away unless additional information is provided, passwords confirmed, or account details re-entered. People fall for scams because they fear losing the benefits, they are time poor, and they do not know how to easily check if they are genuine, and they want to protect whatever benefit it is they receive from such services.

Vulnerability and Scepticism

Technology, like the people who use and operate it is not infallible, and things can and do go wrong. Recent government data losses in the UK illustrate the problem; we have seen admitted losses of 658 laptops and 121 USB data drives since 2004 by the UK Ministry of Defence (BBC News, 2008), a memory stick containing personal details of 84,000 prisoners in England and Wales lost by PA Consulting working on behalf on the UK Home Office (Silicon.com 2008), the loss of two discs containing the names, addresses, dates of birth, employment and bank details of 25 million UK child benefit recipients by Her Majesty's Revenue and Customs (Telegraph News, 2008), as well as numerous other news stories reporting laptops containing sensitive information left on trains, information copied without authorisation, data stolen from cars, and even dumped at the roadside. Perhaps the most revealing aspect here is that although citizens were concerned at these data losses they were not surprised that they had occurred. One of the reasons that the public were not surprised is that they simply do not believe that electronic data can ever be held securely, and in particular they do not trust government to hold that information securely.

The effect of such events can range from mild inconvenience to having a very serious and potentially irrecoverable impact on an individual's life. Identification systems, by the very nature of the information they contain, pose a particular and significant risk; we found that the collection and use of identity data increased a sense of citizen vulnerability, particularly because they have no choice in whether or not to engage with the system, and no control over how their data is used.

Perhaps the most revealing aspect here is that although citizens are concerned at well publicised data losses they are not surprised that they occur. Citizens know that their data is valuable and they know that it is vulnerable, and the more valuable the data the more vulnerable they feel; that is one of the reasons why they do not trust government in particular – the value of the data that government holds or intends to hold about individuals, the way it could be used, either now or in the future, and the impact that might have on their lives.

Citizens consider their anxiety and scepticism concerning data security to be well founded when data losses occur. This is accompanied by a sense of powerlessness and loss of control amplified by the implications for loss of personal privacy. The undesirable consequence of that of course is that public confidence in government data gathering is seriously undermined. UK citizens are very concerned about their privacy; a recent study (European Comission, 2008) showed that we have the second highest level of concern about Internet privacy in Europe.

Another contributory factor to the sense of lack of control is the practice of outsourcing or sharing information with other organisations which makes citizens feel even more vulnerable. We found high levels of uncertainty concerning what data is held, by whom, how it is stored, shared or amalgamated, who has access to it and under what circumstances or indeed, how individuals

might be better informed about such matters and what their rights are in this respect.

Privacy and Data Loss

Privacy is a fundamental human right, and respect for privacy is one of the foundation stones of the modern democratic state. Privacy is under threat and the public know that UK legislation can do little to protect their data once it is overseas, and they know that legislation has trouble keeping pace with technological change and this increases the sense of lack of control.

UK citizens believe that their personal data belongs to them; they believe that they *own* their personal data and that it should not be perceived as a public possession. They are increasingly concerned about protecting that information and our findings are supported by the 2007 Information Commissioner's Office Annual Track report to assess awareness of the provisions of the UK Data Protection Act. That report showed that 92 per cent of respondents rated protection of personal details as the second most important issue of concern (the first was mismanagement of information in terms of passing or selling of details onto other organisations). The question of 'Who owns the data?' and the answer to that, is very important, not least because ownership infers control over how, when and where the data can be used. This also has implications for the application of the law, as well as who should benefit from the selling and usage of personal information.

Clearly there are vulnerabilities caused by human error that pose a very real threat to data security and citizen's right to privacy. We might also point to the failure of business practices, or at least, failure to comply with practices that are supposed to be laid down and adhered to in order to protect our data. The UK government does actually have strict rules about how personal data should be stored and managed. Downloading data from secure servers onto memory sticks or CDs is not allowed, but even so, data has been lost and the procedures for handling sensitive information simply are not working. We might conclude then that citizens are right not to put their trust in such systems.

In fact human error may be only the tip of the iceberg in terms of data security and threats to privacy; it is certainly the most visible part of the problem. There is a very serious danger of a black market in personal information and we can safely assume that any information that has value outside of its legitimate use is vulnerable to attack whether that is health information, financial information or identity information.

Conclusion

What becomes clear from our research is that we need a two-fold culture change in government, one that encompasses greater respect and recognition of the increased vulnerability that is imposed in increased collection and storage of citizen's personal data, and a far greater respect for privacy of that data. Security and privacy of information needs to built-in to the technology and the processes for dealing with it, not bolt-on after the damage has been done.

What emerges from our work is that there is a distinct lack of trust in the organisation imposing this system (in this case government, but it would apply equally to any other institution undertaking a similar endeavour) that is the necessary basis of the relationship. The problems inherent in the technology employed to deliver such a system are in fact only part of the equation. Where trust in the organisation behind the technology is in evidence we see very different levels of acceptability and adoption and this hinges on the ability of the institution concerned to consistently supply realistic guarantees, and where restitution measures are in place.

We found that dealing with a trusted operator was a positive enabler, greatly enhanced by the ability to push perceived risks to a third party,

or where measures are in place and are clearly spelled out to cover instances where something has gone wrong and expectations have not been met. Clearly there are cases where restitution measures are easier to supply than others, for example it is far easier to reimburse financial loss than it is to restore a stolen identity or to recover compromised privacy. In the case of identity data the severity of loss and the implications of this upon an individual's life have the potential to be far reaching and this is an aspect inherent in all identity schemes that needs to be properly addressed.

WHAT THEORY?

The methodological question that needs to be addressed next is that concerning choosing the appropriate theory. It has been said before that there are several theories that apply to the relationship between technology and society, and to the process of technology adoption etc. While all of the established theories are true (in the sense of being congruent with observed facts), not all of them equally well explain the situation that has emerged from empirical observations, i.e. not all of them are equally useful to reason about the current situation and predict the imminent future.

The decision to choose a particular theory has been reached through dialogue that has been informed by the collective expertise of researchers, captured through open discussion. While other methods can be used to capture the majority vote or group consensus, the small size of the research team did not warrant such an approach.

The following paragraphs briefly discuss the general relationship between society and technology and then explore different theories from the area of technology adoption, to demonstrate the particular theory that has been chosen, together with the implications of such a choice.

Society and Technology

Intentionally contrasting two main stances in the research of society and technology offers the opportunity to study such a relationship from the perspective of technological determinism or social constructivism. More recently, a mixed evolutionary approach is gaining acceptance.

Technological determinism (Gehlen, 1980) assumes that the development of technology is driven by forces that are generally outside of the influence of the society that uses that technology. Therefore the technology is an invariant of the change and it is provided 'as is' for societal use. The only decision left to society in this case is whether to accept or reject the technology, or how best to utilise (or avoid) the technology if it is imposed on society, potentially by evolving social structures and relationships.

Social constructivism (Pinch & Bijker, 1987) assumes that technology does not have deterministic properties of itself, but that such properties are attributed by the society during the design and adoption process, becoming part of the explanatory framework that is continuously created and accepted by social groups. Technology therefore is adopted if it stabilises existing (or emerging) social structures through its own interpretation.

Both approaches are not necessary mutually exclusive; technology may demonstrate properties that facilitate certain interpretation while desired social interpretations can be used to alter design properties. This co-evolutionary approach has been chosen as the foundation of the research presented here. As a consequence of this decision, we assume that while certain technical choices are driven by available technology, it is possible to include identified social needs and values into the discussion about particular technological choices, within the limits of those available. Further, we can see that whichever technology is chosen, there will be changes in social interpretations and practises, both intended (and possibly desirable) and unintended.

Technology Adoption

Research into technology adoption (acceptance) splits into three main streams. The first approaches the problem from the perspective of pure technological determinism as it analyses the process of personal adoption of particular technical products and services, investigating the process behind decisions made by individuals, on the assumption that those individuals are relatively free and well informed to accept or reject the given product or service. The Technology Acceptance Model (TAM) (Davis, 1989) is a well known example of the conceptualisation of this process, where ease of use is seen as a driver of adoption. The richer UTAUT model (Venkatesh, Morris, Davis, & Davis, 2003) also addresses components that relate to social influence.

Another stream belongs to technological determinism but acknowledges elements of social constructivism. Here, an individual decision to adopt is embedded into the existing structure of social relationships. Some research addresses technology adoption and diffusion (for example, Isham, 2000) to investigate how individual decisions are affected by the socially-embedded distribution of knowledge and practise. It is commonly observed that both diffusion and adoption follow social relationships, i.e. if trusted individuals and groups adopt a given technology; they are followed by those who trust in their choice.

The inadequacy of technological determinism is acknowledged by several field studies. For example, the case study provided by Bunker, Kautz, & Nguyen (2006), shows how employees innovate practises around technology that they find incompatible with their values, often contravening the original intent of the deployment. Several examples from Lacohée, Crane, & Phippen (2006) also demonstrate strong elements of social constructivism where technology is adopted only after being re-purposed to social or individual needs.

The third stream acknowledges the evolutionary approach and is close to social constructivism as it concentrates on the relationship between society (rather than individuals) and technology (rather then particular products). It acknowledges the circular relationship between society and technology [Giddens 84] and views technology as a medium and a message by which different parties express their values. It has been demonstrated that the compatibility with regards to value and structure of technology, greatly improves its adoption.

For example, a multidimensional analysis of the value compatibility of the information system within the corporate environment (Bunker, Kautz, & Nguyen, 2006) shows that adoption can be hampered by perceived cultural incompatibility. Bohmann (1989) addresses the concept of social compatibility of technology, defining a desired set of values that should be embedded in the technology, in the form of a set of propositions that should benefit the society as a whole.

Technology as a Message

The notion of technology adoption through value compatibility offers a perspective that may be particularly useful here, specifically when combined with an approach that positions technology as a socially embedded message.

This approach assumes that the technology (i.e. products with associated services, customer support etc.) is perceived as a message regarding values that are being upheld by institutions that deploy and operate such technology. If the message reassures individuals that values upheld by institutions are compatible with theirs, trust emerges and the technology is adopted. Theoretical foundations of such approaches, specifically when applied to trust, can be found e.g. in a theory of mental frames known from social psychology (e.g. Nooteboom, 2005).

The concept of 'technology as a message' resonates well with some observations on brand, products and customer loyalty where a product that may be technically inferior (for example of lower

usability or limited functionality) wins popularity amongst customers because it is believed to be delivered by a company that shares a certain set of values.

There are several striking similarities between the current situation regarding trust in technology in general and the notion of value compatibility and technology as a message. Lacohée, Crane, & Phippen (2006) deliver strong evidence that individuals look for trust beyond technology, and try to ascertain intentions of operators of such technology. As people tend to infer intentions from all available evidence, no matter how irrelevant it may seem (Dwyer & Cofta, 2008), it is not surprising that details of technical artefacts can be treated this way.

Further, technology is no longer instilling a perception of trust (as it cannot be trusted), and is no longer perceived to be infallible. One may anticipate that the role of technology is increasingly shifting from being a reliable tool that delivers solutions to being a means to upkeep the relationship between an individual and the operator of such technology, e.g. through updates, value added services etc. This again contributes to the perception of technology being a message, while its product role becomes marginalised.

Identification System as a Message

Revisiting citizen identification systems, this approach assumes that an identification system is not only a tool to achieve certain ends, but it is also a communication from the state (that is, the operator of such a system) regarding its intentions. Here, technical and operational components of the system are interpreted by citizens as signals of values that the state is willing to uphold. If they find those values compatible with theirs, the system may be willingly adopted, despite its other potential shortcomings.

As privacy seems to be a value with which citizens are concerned, the system has to demonstrate that it takes such concerns seriously in order to drive adoption, and to reflexively build trust (Cofta, 2008). Privacy-related value compatibility creates its own virtuous loop. Such privacy-related communication contributes to the perception of trustworthiness of the state, so that eventually it may alleviate the source of worries related to privacy: those of a lack of trust in the state.

This brings into question the nature of the type of privacy that is being discussed here. Indeed, considering the number of partly conflicting definitions of privacy, clarification is needed. The concept of 'privacy as contextual integrity' (Nissenbaum, 2004) defines privacy as compatibility with perceived norms of information appropriateness and distribution, i.e. privacy is preserved if information flow of personal information adheres to norms and standards as seen by an individual. Therefore, information disclosure, collection and processing that is expected and approved of by individuals does not impinge on their privacy. However, activities such as secret information sharing, use of information beyond its original purpose, information linking across domains etc. negatively impacts on privacy.

In the light of value compatibility, this definition of privacy brings an additional insight, as it is the compatibility of norms and values regarding information flow that both defines and upholds privacy - provided that there is not a great discrepancy between norms and their implementation. Should citizens and their state be in accord with the norms regarding information processing, their privacy will not be endangered. A citizen identity system is therefore not only a technical solution to certain problems, it is first and foremost, the message sent by the state describing norms and values that it wants to uphold.

Note that the specific role of the state warrants much deeper discussion regarding such values than is necessary for a similar commercial system. While there is no significant technical difference between an advanced loyalty or credit card scheme and a citizen identification system, their value proposition and the strength of the

required commitment is quite different, as commercial systems tend to communicate value that is linked to brand promise.

For customers, such value compatibility is non-obligatory and non-binding; should they become unhappy with one brand (and one scheme), they can always switch to another which promises to reflect their values more closely. In contrast, there are no competing propositions from the state, and the commitment is effectively life-long (discounting the possibility of migration).

Implications

The nature of citizen identification systems is that real benefits of such systems can be captured only when they are universally adopted. If an identification system is only one of several that must be dealt with, the system is more of a burden than a value, for the state, its citizens and potentially also for businesses. Therefore, assuming that participation in such a system is voluntary, its success depends greatly on its adoption.

The adoption of technical systems is driven by the perception of risk associated with its operation (Lacohée, Crane and Phippen, 2006), much more than by the trust in its operation, as technology itself is no longer trusted. The entity that is investigated when it comes to making a risk assessment is the operator of the technology, to verify whether such an operator is willing to uphold values that are compatible with current social values. Of several potential concerns and perceived shortcomings, those that are related to citizen's privacy are the most important (Lacohée, Crane and Phippen, 2006; Information Commissioner's Office, 2006).

Assuming that technology can be interpreted as a message about value compatibility, the implications are three-fold. First, the organisation should understand the values that it communicates through technology. The omnipresence of technology in large systems (that is at the same time the message and the medium) makes it almost impossible to permanently hide values from public scrutiny. Privacy, care, and restitution are values that individuals are seeking both in general and specifically when it comes to identification systems.

Second, if an organisation can believe in value compatibility, the challenge that it faces is to convey appropriate messages through and with technology. Understanding that digital technology is particularly susceptible to fraud, and that individuals are aware of this, makes such a task particularly challenging.

Finally, once the message is out, the final task is to continue the dialogue with individuals, by continuously investigating how and why they utilise technology, whether they receive the message appropriately, whether they believe in value compatibility etc. Necessary alterations to technology (or organisational policies) should facilitate better and more accurate reception of the message.

GUIDELINES

The final stage of the methodology addresses the creation of technically-oriented guidelines for the developer and operator of identification systems. Until now the methodology has produced a set of observations that are described in language that vaguely relates to technology, so that the challenge presented here has been to convert such guidelines into something that can be deployed to make design choices.

Those guidelines are necessarily general as they concentrate on what has to be done, not how it can be achieved. Therefore, technical implementation of guidelines has to be interpreted in the context of a specific system. The guidelines can usually be satisfied by the combination of design and operational standards and procedures, even though they are expressed here in operational terms, as they are directed towards the operator of the system (that supposedly also sets design

requirements for such a system). Some suggestions regarding technical implementation of guidelines are provided e.g. in (Cofta, 2009).

Some of the guidelines can be also implemented though procedural, economical or political means as technical implementation may not always be perceived by the operator as the simplest or cheapest option. However, technical implementation of the guidelines has a significant advantage, as the technology may be opaque but it is undeniable. While procedures can be interpreted and changed at a whim, technical measures demonstrate significant resistance to manipulation, creating a stronger message.

We have assumed that the major invariant of citizen identification systems is its general architecture, with a set of centralised databases and cards provided to citizens. While it may be tempting (and it is definitely easier) to design an optimum system from scratch, the assumption of such architectural invariants makes an exercise more realistic.

Therefore we have experimented with different possible configurations of architectural components that are known and are potentially available. In addition we have investigated components that may be added to the system without altering its architecture, drawing both from experience and from established literature. Only the most promising configurations have been selected and verified against the expectations listed above, and against possible internal conflicts.

Communicate through Technology

In the case of identification systems, the technology is both a message and a medium; it represents values and delivers a message about those values. Further, technology is only one of several communication channels that are available to the operator to convey the message.

While the technology has the advantage of being undeniable, its opacity represents the challenge. We must not underestimate people's awareness of technology but for the technology to succeed in delivering the message, it must be presented in a simplified form and made relevant to everyday experience.

The simplification of technology proposed here does not relate to the face-lifting offered by clever design of the user interface, but to the ability to explain the technology in simple terms. For identification systems, the role of the card is a key, as the card is both tangible and evocative.

The relevance of technology to everyday experience also contributes to better understanding. For identity systems, the ability to relate to the experience of mobility and the Internet is a key, as otherwise the system's usage will be too limited to allow for deeper engagement and understanding.

Set Baseline to Avoid Negative Messages

Before any positive message can be conveyed through technology, the most important guideline is to avoid negative messages. Trust can be easily destroyed through inappropriate actions that demonstrate significant value incompatibility.

The baseline that the operator should strive to achieve is simple: it is honesty. Assuming that the operator truly upholds values that are to be communicated, honesty works both as an enabler and as a protection against negative messages (or negative interpretation of messages that are deemed to be positive).

Technology, with its ability to widely distribute information makes honesty both appealing and possible. Transparency of operation, combined with cryptographically assured accountability, and ultimately linked back to citizens, delivers, reassures and enforces honesty.

Demonstrate Value Compatibility

It has been identified that citizens desire trust, even though an asymmetric relationship makes trust

particularly difficult. Citizens value their privacy, expect care, and seek restitution - and these are the values that should be communicated.

In the case of privacy, value compatibility can be demonstrated by intentionally self-constraining the operator so that citizens have a level of control over information about themselves that the operator cannot circumvent, even if it wants. Such self-constraint can come in a form of e.g. the separation of identities on the card, the use of privacy enhancing technologies, user-centric identity management, trusted third party audit etc.

General care about the citizen can be communicated together with the perception of competence by the use of appropriate security measures. Against the background of frequent unsupported claims about security, security that actually works is a very strong message.

The desire for restitution can be supported by the technology where cards are disposable, associations between citizens and their information is modifiable, and changes are amendable. The simple example of changing the identification number once the old one has been abused best illustrates the concept.

Finally, trust (that can already be built through care, privacy, etc.), can be further reinforced by embedding self-limiting measures into the technology that bind together the interest of the state and of the citizen. For example, an encryption scheme where personal data cannot be accessed if the card is not present but can be altered by the citizen himself binds the interest of the state (access to reliable data), with the interest of the citizen (control over data dissemination), so that one cannot proceed without the other.

Allow for Experimentation and Keep Learning from It

Whatever the intention of the operator, the message can and will be distorted and the technology misinterpreted. Therefore the operator should be prepared to allow for experimentation, learn from this and eventually modify the message (and the technology).

Fortunately, flexibility is built into modern technology and can be utilised for this purpose. Databases can have their schemes modified, and cards can be uploaded with new applications - if they are designed with flexibility and upgrade-ability in mind.

Experimentation is encouraged by the avail-ability of restitution measures as well as by guaranteed security. For the latter, the system should be truly fail-safe, preventing citizens from significant harm, no matter what - including a coup d'état. Cryptographic protection measures that satisfy such needs by linking databases with the card and user's control are available.

Finally, audit measures and transparency of op-eration (that are needed anyway for accountability purposes), combined with mutual communication allows for early detection of misinterpretation and establish the system as a common responsibility of the operator and citizens.

CONCLUSION

When technology is deployed in society, it is in-terpreted as a message about the intentions of its operator and determines trust in such an operator. Value compatibility determines adoption of such technology and involves an amalgamation of society's values and the operators' intentions.

The interdisciplinary nature of the problem of technology adoption requires a mixed-methodol-ogy approach. Citizen identification systems have been used to illustrate the process of developing technical guidelines from anthropological ob-servations. While the methodology is still under development, this chapter demonstrate that such a process is possible and desirable, and that it delivers results of practical importance.

It can be clearly noted that relatively simple technical design choices may have a profound impact on the way technology is adopted - or rejected. Such choices, informed by theories

built on empirical observations may significantly improve technology adoption, specifically where asymmetric trust is required.

Continued work is needed to fully develop the methodology, specifically to assure the smooth transition between its different phases. Further, the incorporation of quantitative components may enrich the methodology and better inform business decisions.

REFERENCES

Anderson, R. (2001). *Security Engineering: A Guide to Building Dependable Distributed Systems*. New York: John Wiley & Sons Inc.

Backhouse, J., & Halperin, R. (2007). A Survey on EU Citizen's Trust in ID Systems and Authorities. *FIDIS Journal, 1*(2007). Retrieved from http://journal.fidis.net/fileadmin/journal/issues/1-2007/Survey_on_Citizen_s_Trust.pdf

BBC News. (2008). *MoD Admits Loss of Secret Files*. Retrieved from http://news.bbc.co.uk/1/hi/uk/7514281.stm

Berg, J., Dickhaut, J., & McCabe, K. (1995). Trust, Reciprocity, and Social History. *Games and Economic Behavior, 10*, 122–142. doi:10.1006/game.1995.1027

Blaze, M., Ioannidis, J., & Keromytis, A. D. (2003). Experience with the KeyNote Trust Management System: Applications and Future Directions. In *Proc. of the First Int. Conf. on Trust Management iTrust 2003* (LNCS 2692, pp. 284-300). Berlin, Germany: Springer.

Bohmann, K. (1989). About the Sense of Social Compatibility. *AI & Society, 3*(4), 323–331. doi:10.1007/BF01908622

Braynov, S., & Sandholm, T. (2002). Contracting With Uncertain Level Of Trust. *Computational Intelligence, 18*(4), 501–514. doi:10.1111/1467-8640.00200

Bunker, D., Kautz, K., & Nguyen, A. L. T. (2006). The Role of Value Compatibility in Information Technology Adoption. In B. Donnellan, T. J. Larsen, L. Levine, & J. I. DeGross (Eds.), *The Transfer and Diffusion of Information Technology for Organizational Resilience, IFIP vol. 206* (pp. 53-70). Berlin, Germany: Springer.

Checkland, P. (2000). Soft Systems Methodology: A Thirty Year Retrospective. *Systems Research and Behavioral Science, 17*, 11–58. doi:10.1002/1099-1743(200011)17:1+<::AID-SRES374>3.0.CO;2-O

Checkland, P., & Scholes, J. (1990). *Soft Systems Methodology in Action*. Chichester, UK: John Wiley.

Cofta, P. (2007). *Trust, Complexity and Control: Confidence in a Convergent World*. Chichester, UK: J. Wiley & Sons.

Cofta, P. (2008) Confidence-compensating privacy protection. In *Proc. of PST2008, The Sixth Annual Conference on Privacy, Security and Trust*, Canada.

Cofta, P. (2009). Towards a better citizen identification system. *FIDIS Journal*.

Davis, F. D. (1989). Perceived usefulness, perceived ease of use, and user acceptance of information technology. *MIS Quarterly, 13*(3), 319–340. doi:10.2307/249008

Dennett, D. C. (1989). *The Intentional Stance*. Cambridge, MA: Bradford Books.

Dwyer, N., & Cofta, P. (2008). *Understanding the grounds to trust: game as a cultural probe*. Paper presented at Web 2.0 Trust (W2Trust), Trondheim, Norway in conjunction with IFIPTM 2008.

Egger, F. N. (2000). *From Interactions to Transactions: Designing the Trust Experience for Business-to-Consumer Electronic Commerce*. Unpublished, doctoral dissertation, Eindhoven University of Technology, The Netherlands.

European Comission. (2008). *Communication from the Commission to the European Parliament, the Council, the European Economic and Social Committee and the Committee of the Regions - Communication on future networks and the internet*. Retrieved December 23, 2008, from http://eur-lex.europa.eu/LexUriServ/LexUriServ.do?uri=CELEX:52008DC0594:EN:NOT.

Falcone, R. (Ed.). (2006). *Ninth Int. Workshop on Trust in Agent Societies (TRUST), Proc. of Fifth Int. Conf. on Autonomous Agents and Multiagent Systems AAMAS-06*, Hakodate, Japan.

Fukuyama, F. (1996). *Trust: The Social Virtues and the Creation of Prosperity*. Clearwater, FL: Touchstone Books.

Gehlen, A. (1980). *Man in the Age of Technology* (P. Lipscomb, Trans.). New York: Columbia University Press.

Giddens, A. (1984). *The Constitution of Society: Outline of the Theory of Structuration*. Cambridge, UK: Polity Press.

Giddens, A. (1988). *The Consequences of Modernity*. Cambridge, UK: Polity Press.

Information Commissioner's Office. (2006). *What Price Privacy?* Isham, J. (2000). *The Effect of Social Capital on Technology Adoption: Evidence from Rural Tanzania. Opportunities in Africa: Micro-evidence on Firms and Households*. Retrieved October 18, 2007, from http://www.csae.ox.ac.uk/conferences/2000-OiA/pdfpapers/isham.PDF

Lacohée, H., Cofta, P., Phippen, A., & Furnell, S. (2008). *Understanding Public Perceptions: Trust and Engagement in ICT Mediated Services*. International Engineering Consortium.

Lacohée, H., Crane, S., & Phippen, A. (2006). *Trustguide: Final Report*. Retrieved January 5, 2007, from http:// www.trustguide.org

Li, X., Valacich, J. S., & Hess, T. J. (2004). Predicting User Trust in Information Systems: A Comparison of Competing Trust Models. In *Proc. of the 37th Hawaii Int. Conf. on System Sciences HICSS2004*.

London School of Economics. (2005). *The Identity Project. An assessment of the UK Identity Cards Bill & its implications. Interim Report*. Retrieved July 14, 2006, from http://www.lse.ac.uk/collections/pressAndInformationOffice/PDF/IDreport.pdf

Luhmann, N. (1979). *Trust and Power*. New York: John Wiley & Sons.

Mayer, R. C., Davis, J. H., & Schoorman, F. D. (1995). An integrative model of organizational trust. *Academy of Management Review, 20*(3), 709–734. doi:10.2307/258792

McKnight, D. H., & Chervany, N. L. (1996). *The Meanings of Trust*. Retrieved from http://www.misrc.umn.edu/wpaper/wp96-04.htm

National Identity Scheme Delivery Plan. (2008). *Home Office*. Retrieved from http://www.ips.gov.uk/identity/downloads/national-identity-scheme-delivery-2008.pdf

Nissenbaum, H. (2004). Privacy as Contextual Integrity. *Washington Law Review, 17*, 101-139. Retrieved June 10, 2006, from http://crypto.stanford.edu/portia/papers/RevnissenbaumDTP31.pdf

Nooteboom, B. (2005). Framing, attribution and scripts in the development of trust. In *Proc. of symposium on 'Risk, trust and civility'*, Victoria College, University of Toronto.

Pearson, S., et al. (2002). *Trusted Computing Platforms: TCPA Technology In Context*. Upper Saddle River, NJ: Prentice-Hall.

Pinch, T., & Bijker, W. (1987). The Social Construction of Facts and Artifacts: Or How the Sociology of Science and the Sociology of Technology Might Benefit Each Other. *Social Studies of Science, 14*(3).

Riegelsberger, J., Sasse, M. A., & McCarthy, J. D. (2005). The Mechanics of Trust: A Framework for Research and Design. *International Journal of Human-Computer Studies, 62*(3), 381–422. doi:10.1016/j.ijhcs.2005.01.001

Silicon.com. (2008). *Home Office Loses Data on 84,000 Prisoners*. Retrieved from http://www.silicon.com/publicsector/0,3800010403,39274254,00.htm

Silverman, D. (2006). *Qualitative Research. Theory, Method and Practice*. San Francisco: Sage Publications.

Solomon, R. C., & Flores, F. (2001). *Building Trust in Business, Politics, Relationships and Life*. Oxford, UK: Oxford University Press.

Telegraph News. (2008). *Is Our Data Safe in the Government's Hands?* Retrieved from http://www.telegraph.co.uk/news/newstopics/politics/liberaldemocrats/1569947/Is-our-data-safe-in-the-Government's-hands.html

Venkatesh, V., Morris, M. G., Davis, G. B., & Davis, F. D. (2003). User acceptance of information technology: Toward a unified view. *MIS Quarterly, 27*(3), 425–478.

Wilson, B. (2001). *Soft Systems Methodology*. New York: John Wiley & Sons Ltd.

Windley, P. (2005). *Digital Identity*. Sebastopol, CA: O'Reilly Media Inc.

Chapter 20
Human–Machine Trust Interaction:
A Technical Overview

Conghui Liu
Renmin University of China, China

ABSTRACT

Improving user's trust appropriately could help in designing an intelligent system and make it work effectively, especially with the fast growth of Web-base technology. This chapter introduces the solutions of improving user's trust in human-machine interaction (HMI), especially for electronic commerce (e-commerce). The author firstly reviews the concept of trust and the main factors that affects the appropriateness of user's trust in human-machine interaction, such as the properties of machine systems, the properties of human, and context. On the basis of these, the author further discusses the current state, challenges, problems and limitations of establishing and improving the user's trust in human-machine interaction. Finally, the author summarizes and evaluates the existing solutions for improving the user's trust appropriately in e-commerce environment.

INTRODUCTION

Trust is familiar to all of us in everyday life. It plays a key role to mediate human-to-human interaction. We often talk about trust that we have in other people (e.g. family members, friends and colleagues), how much we believe what we see or are told, or how confident we are on somebody or something that could work properly. The trust relationships actually shape our social life. With the advent of complex intelligent machine systems, the relationship between human and machine need to be understood. The key factor influencing this relationship could be the human's trust in the machine. In general, trust is based on past experiences. If the machine has been able to achieve tasks as expectation all the time, you would establish sufficiently strong trust in it.

With the rapid development of modern technology such as digital computing and network technologies, human-machine interaction is becoming prevalent, appearing in all aspects of human life and work. Human-machine interaction is the study of

DOI: 10.4018/978-1-61520-682-7.ch020

interaction between people and machines, while the interaction between people and machines occurs at user interfaces. The Association for Computing Machinery gives the following definition: "Human-computer interaction is a discipline concerned with the design, evaluation and implementation of interactive computing systems for human use and with the study of major phenomena surrounding them."(ACM SIGCHI Curricula for Human-Computer Interaction) Human-machine interaction is also sometimes referred to as human-computer interaction or computer-human interaction. Human-machine interaction shows massive potential to improve human performance and enhance safety. However, it is not uniformly beneficial to people. If trust is not properly considered, there are maybe machine-assisted accidents caused by human-machine interaction. If users trust the capability of the machine even when it does not perform the task perfectly, the disaster could occur. For example the autopilot crashed the Airbus A320 (Sparaco, 1995). In addition, if people refute to utilize the machine even when it could achieve the goal very well, the advanced benefits of using the machine will be lost.

Such an improper relationship between human and machine can be described in terms of over-trusting or under-trusting of machines. These are illustrated in Figure 1. Over-trusting (too trusting) and under-trusting (not trusting enough) can lead to user misusing and disusing the machine (Parasuraman & Riley, 1997). Reducing over-trusting and under-trusting in the machine system is a very important issue in human-machine interaction. Appropriate trust can improve greatly human-machine interaction. Ideally, the human should maintain a correctly calibrated level of trust that matches the objective capability of the machine system. How to calibrate the user's trust to an appropriate level? It is essential to understand the factors influencing trust in human-machine interaction.

This book chapter studies the factors influencing the user's trust in human-machine interaction.

We believe understanding this issue is important for us to develop human's trust in the machine system at an appropriate level, neither too high nor too low. Firstly, the concept of trust and the factors influencing the user's trust in human-machine interaction are introduced. We further discuss the issues, problems and challenges in this area that are introduced by e-commerce and web services, and recommend a number of solutions in order to improve the trust in human-machine interaction based on the trust influencing factors. Finally, we propose future research directions and conclude the chapter.

BACKGROUND

It is very important to calibrate the user's trust to an appropriate level in human-machine interaction. For this purpose, we have to know what trust is, which factors influence the user's trust, and how trust is influenced. We begin by reviewing the most common definitions of trust from social science, psychological science and informational science perspectives. We then examine the main factors influencing the user's trust in human-machine interaction.

Concept of Human-Machine Trust

Trust, a social psychological concept, is examined by many researchers from a broad of disciplines, such as sociology, psychology, economics, information science, and so on. Trust has been regarded as an important research issue in the areas of psychology and sociology since late 1950s. From a social psychological perspective, trust in another person has been defined as "the confidence that one will find what is desired from another person" (Deutsch, 1973); "a generalized expectation related to the subjective probability an individual assigns to the occurrence of some set of future events" (Rempel et al., 1985); "expectations of persistence of the natural physical order, biologi-

Figure 1. Theoretical relationship between trust and performance of machine

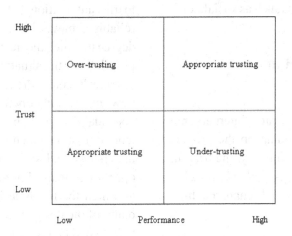

cal order, and the moral social order" (Barber, 1983); "expectations of technical competence and fiduciary responsibility" (Barber, 1983). Clearly, these definitions show the element of expectation regarding behaviors or outcomes in common.

The researches about trust between people provide a good foundation for understanding the relationships between human and machine. Muir (1994); Muir & Moray (1996) investigated the models of trust between people proposed by Remple et al. (1985) and Barber (1983). They found that the trust model between people could be applied to the trust between humans and machines. Human subjective ratings of trust in the automation were based mainly upon their perception of competence of automation. Lee and Moray (1994) developed Muir's studies. They showed that people's reliance on machine depends not only on trust in the machine, but also on the people's self-confidence in their own capability. Recently, Mui (2003) argued that trust is a subjective expectation an agent has about another agent's future behavior in multi-agent system. In the context of complex human-machine interaction, Madsen & Gregor (2000) defined trust as the extent to which a user is confident in, and willing to act on the basis of the recommendations, actions, and decisions of an artificially intelligent decision aid. Corritore et al. (2003) gave a definition of trust in the context of on-line system: "trust is an attitude of confident expectation in an online situation of risk that one's vulnerabilities will not be exploited". Just as the definition of trust between people, all of these trust definitions regarding human-machine interaction placed emphasis on expectation. Furthermore, Lee & See (2004) gave a simple definition by summarizing other researchers' definition of trust (Barber, 1983; Mayer et al., 1995; Meyer, 2001): "the attitude that an agent will help achieve individual's goals in a situation characterized by uncertainty and vulnerability".

Based on the above brief literature review on the definition of trust between people or between human and machine, we think that trust in human-machine interaction has at least three principal components. The first is the properties of operator (human), including stable personality trait (such as trust trait) and subjective state (such as attitude and expectation to trustee, and subjective standards). The second component is the properties of machine, including performance (such as ability, competence, reliability and behavior, etc.) and the style of machine. The third component is the characteristics of context, including organizational context (such as information from other people) and cultural context (such as social norm and expectation).

Factors Influencing Human-Machine Trust

Trust develops in a complicated interpersonal and cultural context, depending on the properties of trustor and trustee. Similarly, the trust in human-machine interaction is evolved in such a complicated interaction among human, machine and context.

Properties of Machine System

The properties of a machine system play a very important role in human-machine trust interaction. The properties mainly include reliability, predictability, dependability, integrity, availability, confidentiality, security, UI design (user interface design) style, brand, and so on.

Empirical researches on trust and human intervention systems started with the research conducted by Muir (1994) and Muir & Moray (1996) who investigated trust in the operation of supervisory control systems. They developed a model of human trust in machines, extending the model of trust between people to the human-machine relationship. Muir & Moray (1996) extended Muir's pioneering work over the last decade. They found that trust is strongly affected by system reliability. The people's subjective ratings of trust in human-machine interaction were based mainly on their perception of machine reliability and competence. The people only used machine they trusted.

Lee & Moray (1992) defined the factors that influence trust in automation. They identified performance, process, and purpose as main factors. Performance refers to the current and historical behavior of the machine that also includes such characteristics as reliability, predictability, and ability. Performance information describes what the machine does. The operator will be inclined to trust automation that performs in a manner that reliably achieves his or her goals. Process is the degree to which the machine's algorithms are appropriate for the situation and able to achieve the operator's goals. Process information describes how the machine operates. Process is similar to dependability and integrity. The operator will tend to trust the machine if its algorithms can be understood and seem capable of achieving the operator's goals. Purpose refers to the degree to which the machine is being used within the realm of the designer's intent. Purpose is similar to faith and benevolence. Purpose describes why the machine was developed. The operator tend to trust the machine if its designer's intention has been communicated to the operator.

Another important factor influencing trust in human-machine interaction is the UI design style. Some studies showed that machine system that displays personality characteristics similar to those of the user tends to be more readily accepted (Nass, Moon, Fogg, Reeves, & Dryer, 1995; Nass & Lee, 2001). The machine that can sense and react to the user's emotional states may greatly enhance the trust in human-machine interaction (Picard, 1997). More generally, design and style that consider the user's emotion or needs are likely to gain the acceptance and improve the productivity of the machine system (Norman, Ortony, & Russell, 2003).

Brand is another factor influencing the trust in human-machine interaction. The brand of the machine system may be a psychological factor that impacts trust. This includes the company or institution that promotes the machine system. The user tend to trust the machine if the brand of the machine system has a high reputation of credibility (Fogg & Tseng, 2001).

Properties of Human

The property of human is another important factor influencing the trust in human-machine interaction. It mainly includes stable trait (disposition to trust), state trait (attitude to an object). Deutsch (1960) found a significant correlation between trust and personal predispositions. Rotter (1967) defined trust as an enduring personality trait. He believes that trust is a kind of stable trait. He predicted that trust growing out of people's history of experiences where others had keep their promises would generalize from one situation to another. A child whose parents had been consistent would grow up to be generally trusting, while a child who had been regularly disappointed by broken promises would grow up with a generalized suspicion of people's motives and promises. Certain people have an attitude that makes them inclined to extend trust to everything and everyone - a "disposition to trust" (McKnight, Cummings, & Chervany, 1998). Lee & Moray (1992) investigated the role of operator's self-confidence in human-machine interaction as a determinant of intervention behavior. We argue that stable trust trait depends on an individual's long-term experience and his/her inherited characteristics. The personality of people affects the initial level of trust and influences how new information is interpreted. Some people are more inclined to trust than others (Gaines et al., 1997). Tendency to trust can be reliably measured and it influences behavior. Interpersonal trust scale reliably differentiates people based on their trust traits (Rotter, 1980). People with high propensity to trust are not more gullible than low-trust people (Gurtman, 1992). Interestingly, high-trust people predict others' trustworthiness better than those with a low propensity to trust. The high-trust individuals are found to trust more appropriately than low-trust individuals (Gurtman, 1992).

These findings may explain why the relationship between trust in human-machine interaction and misuse of automation is not clear. High-trust subjects can detected more failures (53.4%) in a constantly reliable condition compared with low-trust subjects (18.7%) (Singh, Molloy, & Parasuraman, 1993). Interestingly, several studies showed that trust of some people changes

substantially as the reliability of the automation changes, however, other people's trust changes relatively little (Masalonis, 2000). High-trust individuals may be better able to calibrate their trust appropriately. The influence of personality trait to trust is more important, especially when a situation is not clear, and it becomes less important as the situation becomes clear (McKnight, Cummings, & Chervany, 1998).

Except stable personality trait (disposition to trust), affective state (emotion and mood) could also influence the trust judgment. Dunn & Schweitzer (2005) found that incidental emotions significantly affect trust. Positive emotion (happiness and gratitude) increases trust, and negative emotion (anger) decreases trust. However, emotions do not influence trust when individuals are aware of the source of their emotions or when individuals are very familiar with the trustee.

Context

It is impossible that trust develop in a vacuum. Interpersonal and cultural context is an important component that affects trust and its development (Baba, Falkenburg, & Hill, 1996; Lee & See, 2004). The interpersonal context reflects the interactions between people that inform them about the trustworthiness of the machine system. The initial trust is determined by past experience in a similar situation. In addition, the prior experience that may come from others also affects the trust of people who have never had any direct contact or interaction with the trustee (for example, a machine system) (Kramer, 1999). The degree to which the interpersonal circumstance affects the development of trust depends on a person's ability to establish links between the situations experienced by others and the situation experienced by him/her (Doney et al., 1998). These findings suggest that the past experience or information from others have an important influence on trust and reliance.

Cultural context mainly includes a set of social norms and social expectations. People in different cultural background could have different level of trust. For example, some researchers found that Japanese have a generally low level of trust (Yamagishi & Yamagishi, 1994). Japanese interpersonal networks of mutually committed relations are more important in human-human interactions than that in USA. They pay more attention to exchange relationships that are based on interpersonal relationships. However, American was more trusting in general and considered reputation more important. Doney et al. (1998) argued that extreme social stability of mutually committed relationships in Japan reduces uncertainty when people are exchanging and diminishes the role of trust.

Cultural difference can influence trust in an online environment. Karvonen (2001) compared trust in e-commerce service among consumers from Finland, Sweden, and Iceland. There were substantial differences in the initial trust, with Finnish customers being the most distrusting and Icelandic customers the most trusting. More generally, the level of social trust varies substantially among countries (Huang, Keser, Leland, & Shachat, 2002). The cultural-dependent nature of trust suggests that trust in human-machine interaction might need to be verified when they are extrapolated from one culture to another. Zuboff (1988) found that the culture associated with people who had been exposed to computer leads to easy trust and acceptance of automation. Riley (1996) found that pilots, who are accustomed to using automation, trust and rely on automation more than the students who are not so familiar with automation. These results show that trust in automation, like trust in people, is culturally influenced in that it depends on the long-term experiences of a group of people (Lee & See, 2004).

In summary, the trust between human and machine depends on the properties of the machine (reliability, predictability, dependability, integrity, UI design style, brand, and so on) and the human (personality trait, attitude), as well as context (including interpersonal context and cultural context). These properties and context influence trust because these factors not only affect the initial level of trust, but also modulate the development of trust in human-machine interaction.

APPROPRIATE TRUST IN HUMAN-MACHINE INTERACTION

With the rapid development of automation technology, human-machine trust is paid special attention to (Lee & See, 2004; Parasuraman & Riley, 1997). In this section, the issues and challenges pertaining to this subject are reviewed, and the means to improve human-machine interaction are discussed.

Issue, Controversies and Problems

There is a common misconception that human operators could use machine compete task perfectly and make no mistakes. In fact, many serious accidents and incidents have been attributed to the operators' failing to use the automated systems properly (Parasuraman & Riley, 1997). Parasuraman & Riley (1997) found that the human's problematic use of automation falls into two categories: disuse and misuse of automation. Disuse of automation refers to the cases where operators fail to rely on reliable automation (e.g., Dzindole et al., 2003; Karsh et al., 1995). The benefit of automation cannot be obtained if it is disused. Misuse of automation occurs when the operators overly rely on unreliable automation (e.g., Bagheri & Jamieson, 2004). The operators who misuse automation often fail to intervene when the automation malfunctions. Clearly, the problematic uses of automation are closely related to the operators' decisions to trust or not to trust automation (Riley, 1996).

In our opinion, appropriate trust mainly includes three components. The first component is calibration, which refers to the correspondence between the individual's trust in machines and the machine's capabilities (Lee & Moray, 1994). Over-trusting means that trust exceeds the machine system's capabilities. Under-trusting means that trust falls short of the machines' capabilities. The second component is resolution that refers to how precisely the judgment of trust differentiates the level of automation capability (Cohen, Parasuraman, & Freeman, 1999). If a big change in the machine's capability leads to a small change in trust, the resolution is low. Specificity is the third component of appropriate trust (Lee & Dee, 2004). This component contains two parts. One part is functional specificity that refers to the degree to which trust is associated with the sub-functions of automation. High functional specificity means the individual's trust reflects the capabilities of the sub system. The other is temporal specificity that means whether the change in trust is a function of context or time. High temporal specificity means that the human's trust changes with the time or context. High calibration, high resolution, and high specificity can ensure appropriate trust. However, one big problem in human-machine interaction is the inappropriate relationship between the real capabilities of the machine and the level of trust.

On the other hand, with the growth of Internet and World Wide Web, human-machine interaction became popular in the field of consumer-oriented business, for example, electronic commerce. The emergence of electronic commerce has brought new challenges in digital environments, with regard to building and maintaining trust in electronic markets.

Shaw (2000) argued that the e-commerce involves four different entities: a buyer, a seller, the third party, and technology. The four different entities represent three ingredients in the trust formation process in e-commerce: trustor (buyer), trustee (seller) and environment (technology and the third party). Buyers, sellers, and the third parties can connect through an electronic market structure supported by information technology. In e-commerce, the buyers are consumers and the sellers are online vendors. The third parties are organizations who deliver business confidence through an electronic transaction by applying commercial and technical security features. The interaction among consumers, e-vendors, and environment (technology and the third party) plays as the core of online shopping. Consumers have to consider whether or not they trust the e-vendor and the Internet before the online purchase takes place.

The Internet gives the seller an easy way to set up shops for electronic commence through out the world. The customer usually pays for e-commence goods and service with a credit card. Internet security and information privacy are two key hurdles in e-commerce (Cox, 1999; Ernst & Young, 2001). To overcome these hurdles, Web site should create the climate of trust (Shneiderman, 2000). The third parties may play an important role in establishing trust. E-commerce success, especially in the business area, is determined partially by the consumers' trust in the sellers and products that they cannot see, and the machine system (the e-commerce system) with which they may have no previous experience. The relationship between the customer and the e-commerce system is a kind of relationship between human and machine. A major weakness of electronic commerce is the risk attached to the on-line transactions. Hoffman, Novak, & Peralta (1999) indicated that the lack of trust relationship between businesses and consumers in e-commerce is the main reason. In fact, many consumers are not familiar to e-commerce, which makes them hesitate to provide their personal information to a web site when being asked or trust in the ability of the vendors to fulfil their commitments because they suspect the security of web site (Hoffman, Novak, & Peralta, 1999). In an on-line shopping, trading partners have limited information about each other's reliability or the product quality during the transaction. The major issue is the information asymmetry between the buyer and the seller (Ba & Pavlou, 2002). The buyers know about their own trading behavior and the quality of the products they are expecting. On the other hand, the sellers can guess that the buyers could know their trustworthiness and reputation based on the collected information about them.

As can be seen from the above, under trusting of the consumer (disusing) is a critical barrier that impacts the success of e-commerce. The most effective way for e-commerce is to improve the user's trust to an appropriate level. Thus, appropriate trust is a critical factor influencing the success of e-commence.

Solutions and Recommendations

It is evident that trust play an important role not only in general market but also in e-commerce (Jarvenpaa, Tractinsky, & Vitale, 2000; Chellappa & Pavlou, 2002). Much recent evidence indicates that trust contributes to economic and social success (Zak, & Knack, 2001). Appropriate trust can lead to the success of e-commerce that is superior to the performance of real commercial affairs. The absence of trust among trading partners could break electronic transactions down. However, how to build up and improve the buyer's trust to an appropriate level becomes an important issue.

Several researchers developed their model of trust for e-commerce, and described the main factors influencing consumer's trust in e-commerce. Jarvenpaa, Tractinsky, & Saarinen (1999) argued the reputation of merchants had a significant effect on consumers' trust. A positive reputation is likely to increase trust in the vendors. Egger (2000) described that trust is initially determined by three factors: user knowledge of the domain and reputation of the vendor, the impression made by the interface, and the quality of the information content. Kim et al. (2001) provided a trust model for on-line exchange that includes six main characteristics, known as information content, product, transaction, technology, institutional and consumer behavior. He suggested that the different developmental experiences, personality

types, and cultural backgrounds of consumers influence their inherent propensity to trust and their ultimate placement of trust in a vendor (Kim et al, 2003).

Basing on the main factors influencing trust, we argue that appropriate trust depends on three components: content and the design of Web site, the consumer's prosperities and context in e-commerce.

Make Web Site Content Trustable

Appropriate trust depends on the Web site content (including quality, price and brand of product, identity of company, past performance, services, and so on). We provide the following suggestions in order to improve the trustworthiness of the web site contents.

Show background of product, including quality, company, price, and post performance. Information quality is a key component of e-commerce Web site. The company has responsibility to ensure that information about product, company, and price is accurate and complete (Nielsen, 1999). Accurate and up-to-date information is very important to maintain consumers' trust in the company. Without a basic understanding of the background information, consumers are unlikely to build up enough trust in the product and company.

Show services of product, including privacy and security, delivery information, and return policy. Providing privacy and security policy is essential for the development of trust (Greenspan, 2002). A privacy and security policy concerning how and what type of consumers' personal and transaction information will be collected, how it will be used, how it will be protected from unauthorized access. Such information will enable consumers to make informed decisions concerning the benefits and risks of engaging in online business transactions. In addition, Shneiderman (2000) argued that the consumers' responsibilities and obligations, guarantees and their associated compensation should be clearly stated. For example, delivery information and return policy should be clearly specified.

Make Design of Web Site Trustable

Appropriate trust depends on the design of Web site that includes professionalism, personalization, usability, reliability and security of Web site.

Professionalism, personalization and usability are important aspects that determine trust. A professionally designed and user-friendly Web site that meets consumers' needs can facilitate their shopping experience and increase their overall perception of trust and level of loyalty. A professional Web site that is easy to understand and navigate brings confidence to consumers.

In addition, as discussed earlier, reliability and security have always been major concerns of consumers (Cox, 1999; Ernst & Young, 2001). It is the responsibility of the vendor to ensure that its technology is reliable and secure, and provide security assurance to its consumers. In addition, reliability and security can ensure the accuracy of transactions, detect and prevent the occurrence of fraud and manipulation, and safeguard transaction authentication (Siau & Shen, 2002).

Consider Properties of Consumers

The properties of consumers might play an indirect role in developing trust in e-commerce. They concern stable personality and affective state.

Gefen (2000) argues that personality is strong determinant of initial trust for new relationships between a consumer and a previously unused online service. McCord & Ratnasingam (2004) found that the consumers' disposition to trust has been shown to exert a strong impact on their trust in an e-retailer and subsequently on their intention to purchase. In particular, the consumers who exhibit a greater disposition to trust will more readily trust an e-retailer given only limited information about the vendor. However, other consumers will require more information in order

to establish trusting beliefs in the vendor (Salam et al., 2005). Sutherland & Tan (2004) specified their multidimensional model of trust that also concerns the concept of dispositional trust. They argued that both institutional and interpersonal trusts are reliant on dispositional trust. If an individual has trouble in developing trust in general, then he or she is unlikely to find it easy to trust a remote third party such as an online vendor. They propose that extroversion and openness to experience lead to a higher disposition to trust. However, neuroticism and conscientiousness lead to a lower disposition to trust. Lumsden & Mackay (2006) investigated the personality's effects on trust in B2C e-commerce. They found that extroverts are more disposed to trust, that is, to trust a vendor again after their trust has been broken. Their results indicate that different personalities attribute different importance levels to each of the accepted trust triggers (such as branding, third party security seals, clearly stated policies and vendor information, professional website design, etc.).

The emotional state of consumer is an important factor influencing trust in interpersonal interaction (Dunn & Schweitzer, 2005). Positive emotions (e.g. happiness and gratitude) increase trust. However, few researches have considered how emotional state of consumers could influence trust in e-commerce. Whether or not the positive emotions could promote trust in e-commerce requests empirical investigation.

Consider Context of E-Commerce

Appropriate trust also depends on context that includes interpersonal context and cultural context.

Few researches have considered how interpersonal context influences trust in e-commerce. The interpersonal context reflects the interactions between people that exchange information about the trustworthiness of trustee. In e-commerce, the third parties maybe play a role of interpersonal context by providing certification information, the third party service, past and current users' feedback, in order to increase credibility of online service and the consumer trust in an online market (Kollock, 1999). Certifications may be obtained from professional third parties. Approvals from professional associations enhance credibility concerning the competence of the online market. For example, escrow services are often used to increase consumer trust in online markets (Kollock, 1999). The buyer firstly transfers funds to the escrow service; the seller ships the goods only after the funds have been cleared by the escrow service; the buyer approves payment to the seller after the goods have been inspected. The major disadvantage of using the escrow service is the high service charge, usually 2 to 15 percentage of total transaction cost. Thereby, the escrow services are typically used only when high-price goods are exchanged. The information from past and current users provides an effective measure to assess reputation (Shneiderman, 2000; Resnick et al., 2000). In the online environment, such reputations of online companies can be gathered from online comments and ratings posted by consumers. Reputation can serve as a feedback mechanism to help consumers assess the trustworthiness of an online company. However, it is very difficult to assess the reliability and validity of reviews. Future research is needed to overcome these problems and limitations. To our knowledge, there are few studies concerned with a third party assurance mechanism. McKnight, Choudhury, & Kacmar (2000) planed to investigate the vendor strategy in order to increase consumer trust by placing icons on their web sites by "trusted" third parties, such as the Certified Public Accountants (CPA) society, Consumer Reports, or Trust-e (which certifies that the vendor has a privacy policy). Recently, Yan et al. (in press) investigated displaying trust information's effects on mobile application usage. They found that displaying an application's reputation value and/or a user's individual trust value could assist mobile application usage.

The cultural factor may be an important variable to affect the antecedent and outcome of consumer trust. In different culture, consumers might have different expectations on what makes a web merchant trustworthy. Some researchers argued that trust is culturally sensitive, claiming that people from different cultures have different perception of trust (Jarvenpaa & Tractinsky, 2000). Different cultures have different trust beliefs; countries with different cultural properties should have different levels of e-commerce trust. For example, countries with high uncertainty avoidance and high individualism might make fewer online purchases than collectivistic countries. Gefen & Heart (2006) investigated trust and trust beliefs (trustworthiness) in U.S. and Israel and concluded that trust beliefs differ across national culture.

The above factors influencing trust in e-commerce are generally categorized in four aspects: Web site content (quality, price and brand of product, identity of company, past performance, services and so on), design of Web site (professionalism, personalization, usability, reliability and security), properties of consumer (personality, emotion and so on), and context (the third party assurance, cultural context). We can improve the buyer's trust to an appropriate level in e-commerce by calibrating or considering these factors. Showing informative and qualified content, improving the design of Web site, considering the properties of consumer and cultural difference, providing information and services from the third parties, are important means to modulate trust in e-commerce. However, mistrust should be avoided while improving the consumers' trust in e-commerce.

FUTURE RESEARCH DIRECTIONS

Up to now, the researches on the definition of trust have not yet reached a common agreement on the definition of trust, which might be the main reason why conflicting and confused results appeared in different studies. Trust is a multidimensional and inter-disciplinary concept. It is very hard to give a general definition of trust that can be applied in all disciplines and domains. Therefore, future research should make clear the definition of trust in advance, which could help in comparing the results achieved from different research fields.

The influencing factors of trust are the key to trust modeling and management. However, many studies only explored the independent effect of the factor's influence on trust. Few researches investigate the interaction among several independent factors. Which factors are more effective for trust formation and which play a key role in maintaining trust? Do people with different disposition of trust respond differently to the same user design style or the third party assurance? Which characteristics of a trusted third party assurance promote the user's trust? In different contexts, the characteristics of people might have different effects on trust decision. These might be very interesting phenomena worth being explored.

Empirical studies are needed to assess the effectiveness of factors affecting trust in human-machine interaction, especially in e-commerce. With better understanding of these factors and their interaction, we could develop more effective methods to build up a healthy and trustworthy environment. More work is needed to be done with regard to dynamic and adaptive trust formation and development in human-machine interaction. In e-commerce, many issues request further research. For achieving appropriate trust, a professional designed Web site should integrate the factors related to contents, design, consumer's properties and context. This chapter provides some basic methods that facilitate the development of trust. But we hope this is a starting point for future research.

Regarding the techniques used to measure trust, self-report is widely applied in empirical researches. The surface cues would affect trust and behavior, which might also distort the results. Hence, other techniques except self-report, such as eye-tracking, physiological measures (Garau,

2003), functional magnetic resonance imaging (fMRI) (Singer et al., 2004), should be considered and employed to measure brain mechanism of trust. Researches based on the usage of new techniques can record the cognitive process and brain mechanism of trust. Another advantage of these techniques is that it provides the possibility to control potential sources of error variance.

CONCLUSION

Human-machine interaction is an important research area. In this chapter, we examined the concept of trust in human-machine interaction. We firstly presented various definitions and analyzed the different dimensions of trust in the literature. Then, we reviewed the main factors influencing trust from three perspectives: human, machine and context with regard to human-machine interaction. Based on our study, we pointed out the main problems (such as under-trusting) in e-commerce, which introduce new challenges into human-machine interaction. Furthermore, we recommended four elements to establish and improve trust in human-machine interaction for e-commerce. Future research is needed to assess the effectiveness of these methods. Although the methods proposed in this chapter might not be comprehensive, we think we provided useful means for achieving successful business in e-commerce by overcoming trust issues in human-machine interaction in order to release the consumers' uncertainty and risk. We believe professional design should consider reliability, security and the consumers' needs. The third party certification could be used to establish emotional trust in e-commerce. Personality and the emotion of consumer, as well as culture play a modulating action in trust establishment and improvement, which should be considered in the design and development of the machine system and e-commerce services.

REFERENCES

Ajzen, I., & Fishbein, M. (1980). *Understanding attitudes and predicting social behavior*. Upper Saddle River, NJ: Prentice Hall.

Ba, S., & Pavlou, P. A. (2002). Evidence of the effects of trust building technology in electronic markets: price premiums and buyer behavior. *MIS Quarterly*, *26*(3), 243–268. doi:10.2307/4132332

Baba, M. L., Falkenburg, D. R., & Hill, D. H. (1996). Technology management and American culture: Implications for business process redesign. *Research Technology Management*, *39*(6), 44–54.

Bagheri, N., & Jamieson, G. A. (2004). The impact of context-related reliability on automation failure detection and scanning behaviour. In *Systems, Man and Cybernetics, 2004 IEEE International Conference*.

Barber, B. (1983). *The logic and limits of trust*. New Brunswick, NJ: Rutgers University Press.

Chellappa, R. K., & Pavlou, P. A. (2002). Perceived information security, financial liability, and consumer trust in electronic commerce transactions. *Journal of Logistics Information Management*, *15*(5/6), 358–368. doi:10.1108/09576050210447046

Cohen, M. S., Parasuraman, R., & Freeman, J. (1999). *Trust in decision aids: A model and its training implications* (Tech. Report USAATCOM TR 97-D-4). Arlington, VA: Cognitive Technologies.

Corritore, C. L., Kracher, B., & Wiedenbeck, S. (2003). On-line trust: concepts, evolving themes, a model. *International Journal of Human-Computer Studies*, *58*(6), 737–758. doi:10.1016/S1071-5819(03)00041-7

Cox, B. (1999). Security, Privacy remain top consumer concerns. *InternetNews.com* [On-line], Retrieved from http://www.internetnews.com/ec-news/article.php/4_95031

Deutsch, M. (1960). Trust, trustworthiness, and the F Scale. *Journal of Abnormal and Social Psychology*, *61*(1), 138–140. doi:10.1037/h0046501

Deutsch, M. (1973). *The resolution of conflict*. New Haven, CT: Yale University Press.

Doney, P. M., Cannon, J. P., & Mullen, M. R. (1998). Understanding the influence of national culture on the development of trust. *Academy of Management Review*, *23*, 601–620. doi:10.2307/259297

Dunn, J. R., & Schweitzer, M. E. (2005). Feeling and believing: the influence of emotion on trust. *Journal of Personality and Social Psychology*, *88*(5), 736–748. doi:10.1037/0022-3514.88.5.736

Dzindolet, M. T., Peterson, S. A., Pomranky, R. A., Pierce, L. G., & Beck, H. P. (2003). The role of trust in automation reliance. *International Journal of Human-Computer Studies*, *58*(6), 697–718. doi:10.1016/S1071-5819(03)00038-7

Egger, F. N. (2000). Towards a Model of Trust for E-Commerce System Design. In *Proceedings of the CHI 2000 Workshop Designing Interactive Systems for 1-to-1 E-commerce*, Zurich.

Ernst & Young. (2001). *E-security and privacy: The role of web seals on the Internet*. Retrieved from http://www.ey.com/global/vault.nsf/international/eSecurityandPrivacy/$file/eSecurity&Privacylowreslocked.pdf

Fogg, B., Marshall, J., Kameda, T., Solomon, J., Rangnekar, A., Boyd, J., et al. (2001). Web credibility research: A method for online experiments and early study results. In *CHI 2001 Conference on Human Factors in Computing Systems* (pp. 293-294). New York: Association for Computing Machinery.

Gaines, S. O., Panter, A. T., Lyde, M. D., Steers, W. N., Rusbult, C. E., Cox, C. L., & Wexler, M. O. (1997). Evaluating the circumplexity of interpersonal traits and the manifestation of interpersonal traits in interpersonal trust. *Journal of Personality and Social Psychology, 73*, 610–623. doi:10.1037/0022-3514.73.3.610

Garau, M. (2003). *The impact of avatar fidelity on social interaction in virtual environments.* Unpublished doctoral dissertation, Department of Computer Science, University College, London.

Gefen, D. (2000). E-Commerce: the role of familiarity and trust. *International Journal of Management Science, 28*, 725–737.

Gefen, D., & Heart, T. (2006). On the need to include national culture as a central issue in e-commerce trust beliefs. *Journal of Global Information Management, 14*(4), 1–30.

Greenspan, R. (2002). *Trust is in the Details*. CyberAtlas. Retrieved from http://cyberatlas.internet.com/markets/retailing/article/0,6061_1369641,00.html

Gurtman, M. B. (1992). Trust, distrust, and interpersonal problems: A circumplex analysis. *Journal of Personality and Social Psychology, 62*, 989–1002. doi:10.1037/0022-3514.62.6.989

Hoffman, D. L., Novak, T. P., & Peralta, M. (1999). Building consumer trust online. *Communications of the ACM, 42*(4), 80–85. doi:10.1145/299157.299175

Huang, H., Keser, C., Leland, J., & Shachat, J. (2002). *Trust, the Internet and the digital divide* (RC22511). Yorktown Heights, NY: IBM Research Division.

Jarvenpaa, S., & Tractinsky, N. (2000). Consumer trust in an Internet store. *Information Technology and Management, 1*(1–2), 45–71. doi:10.1023/A:1019104520776

Jarvenpaa, S., Tractinsky, N., & Vitale, M. (2000). Consumer Trust in an Internet Store. *International Journal of Information Technology and Management, 1*(1-2), 45–71.

Jarvenpaa, S. L., Tractinsky, N., & Saarinen, L. (1999). Consumer Trust in an Internet Store: A Cross-Cultural Validation. *Journal of Computer-Mediated Communication, 5*(2).

Karsh, R., Walrath, J. D., Swoboda, J. C., & Pillalamarri, K. (1995). *Effect of battlefield combat identification system information on target identification time and errors in a simulated tank engagement task* (Technical report ARL-TR-854). Aberdeen Proving Ground, MD, USA: Army Research Lab.

Karvonen, K. (2001). Designing trust for a universal audience: A multicultural study on the formation of trust in the internet in the Nordic countries. In C. Stephanidis (Ed.), *First International Conference on Universal Access in Human-Computer Interaction* (Vol. 3, pp. 1078-1082). Mahwah, NJ: Erlbaum.

Kim, D., Song, Y., Braynov, S., & Rao, H. (2001). A B-to-C Trust Model for On-line Exchange. In *Americas Conference on Information Systems*, Boston (pp. 784-787).

Kim, D. J., Ferrin, D. L., & Rao, H. R. (2003). A Study of the Effect of Consumer Trust in Consumer Expectations and Satisfaction: the Korean Experience. In *Proceedings of the Fifth International Conference on Electronic Commerce (ICEC'2003),* Pittsburgh, USA (pp. 310-315).

Kollock, P. (1999). The production of trust in online markets. In E. J. Lawler, S. R. Thye, MW. Macy, & H. A. Walker (Eds.), *Advances in Group Processes* (pp. 99-123). Greenwich, CT: JAI Press.

Kramer, R. M. (1999). Trust and distrust in organizations: Emerging perspectives, enduring questions. *Annual Review of Psychology, 50*, 569–598. doi:10.1146/annurev.psych.50.1.569

Kramer, R. M., & Tyler, T. R. (1996). *Trust in organizations: Frontiers of theory and research.* Thousand Oaks, CA: Sage.

Lee, J., & Moray, N. (1992). Trust, control strategies, and allocation of functions in human-machine systems. *Ergonomics, 35*, 1243–1270. doi:10.1080/00140139208967392

Lee, J. D., & Moray, N. (1994). Trust, self-confidence, and operators' adaptation to automation. *International Journal of Human-Computer Studies, 40*, 153–184. doi:10.1006/ijhc.1994.1007

Lee, J. D., & See, K. A. (2004). Trust in automation: Designing for appropriate reliance. *Human Factors, 46*(1), 50–80.

Lumsden, J., & Mackay, L. (2006). How does personality affect trust in B2C e-commerce? In *Proceedings of the ACM Conference on Electronic Commerce* (pp. 471-476).

Madsen, M., & Gregor, S. (2000). Measuring human-computer trust. In *Proceedings of Eleventh Australasian Conference on Information Systems*, Brisbane.

Masalonis, A. J. (2000). *Effects of situation-specific reliability on trust and usage of automated decision aids.* Unpublished doctoral dissertation, Catholic University of America, Washington, DC.

Mayer, R. C., Davis, J. H., & Schoorman, F. D. (1995). An integrative model of organizational trust. *Academy of Management Review, 20*, 709–734. doi:10.2307/258792

McCord, M., & Ratnasingam, P. (2004). The Impact of Trust on the Technology Acceptance Model in Business to Consumer e-Commerce. In *Proceedings of the International Conference of the Information Resources Management Association: Innovations Through Information Technology*, New Orleans, USA (pp. 921-924).

McKnight, D. H., Choudhury, V., & Kacmar, C. (2000). Trust in e-commerce vendors: a two stage model. In *Proceedings of Twenty-First Annual International Conference on Information Systems*, Brisbane.

McKnight, D. H., Cummings, L. L., & Chervany, N. L. (1998). Initial trust formation in new organizational relationships. *Academy of Management Review, 23*(3), 473–490. doi:10.2307/259290

Meyer, J. (2001). Effects of warning validity and proximity on responses to warnings. *Human Factors, 43*, 563–572. doi:10.1518/001872001775870395

Mui, L. (2003). *Computational models of trust and reputation: agents, evolutionary games, and social networks.* Unpublished doctoral dissertation, Massachusetts Institute of Technology.

Muir, B. (1994). Trust in automation: Part 1. Theoretical issues in the study and human intervention in automated systems. *Ergonomics, 37*, 1905–1923. doi:10.1080/00140139408964957

Muir, B., & Moray, N. (1996). Trust in automation. Part II. Experimental studies of trust and human intervention in a process control simulation. *Ergonomics, 39*(3), 429–460. doi:10.1080/00140139608964474

Nass, C., & Lee, K. N. (2001). Does computer-synthesized speech manifest personality? Experimental tests of recognition, similarity-attraction, and consistency-attraction. *Journal of Experimental Psychology. Applied, 7*, 171–181. doi:10.1037/1076-898X.7.3.171

Nass, C., Moon, Y., Fogg, B. J., Reeves, B., & Dryer, D. C. (1995). Can computer personalities be human personalities? *International Journal of Human-Computer Studies, 43*, 223–239. doi:10.1006/ijhc.1995.1042

Nielsen, J. (1999). *Trust or bust: communicating trustworthiness in Web design. Jacob Nielsen's Alertbox.* Retrieved from http://www.useit.com/alertbox/990307.html

Norman, D. A., Ortony, A., & Russell, D. M. (2003). Affect and machine design: Lessons for the development of autonomous machines. *IBM Systems Journal, 42*, 38–44.

Parasuraman, R., & Riley, V. (1997). Humans and automation: Use, misuse, disuse, abuse. *Human Factors, 39*, 230–253. doi:10.1518/001872097778543886

Picard, R. W. (1997). *Affective computing.* Cambridge, MA: MIT Press.

Rempel, J. K., Holmes, J. G., & Zanna, M. P. (1985). Trust in close relationships. *Journal of Personality and Social Psychology, 49*(1), 95–112. doi:10.1037/0022-3514.49.1.95

Resnick, P., Zeckhauser, R., Friedman, E., & Kuwabara, K. (2000). Reputation systems. *Communications of the ACM, 43*(12), 45–48. doi:10.1145/355112.355122

Riley, V. (1996). Operator reliance on automation: Theory and data. In R. Parasuraman & M. Mouloua (Eds.), *Automation and human performance: Theory and applications* (pp. 19-35). Hillsdale, NJ: Lawrence Erlbaum Associates, Inc.

Rotter, J. B. (1967). A new scale for the measurement of interpersonal trust. *Journal of Personality, 35*, 651–665. doi:10.1111/j.1467-6494.1967.tb01454.x

Rotter, J. B. (1980). Interpersonal trust, trustworthiness, and gullibility. *The American Psychologist, 35*, 1–7. doi:10.1037/0003-066X.35.1.1

Salam, A. F., Iyer, L., Palvia, P., & Singh, R. (2005). Trust in e-Commerce. *Communications of the ACM, 48*(2), 72–77. doi:10.1145/1042091.1042093

Shaw, M. J. (2000). Electronic commerce: Review of critical research issues. In *Information Systems Frontiers* (pp. 95-106).

Shneiderman, B. (2000). Designing trust into online experiences. *Communications of the ACM, 43*(12), 57–59. doi:10.1145/355112.355124

Siau, K., & Shen, Z. (2003). Building customer trust in mobile commerce. *Communications of the ACM, 46*(4), 91–94. doi:10.1145/641205.641211

Singer, T., Kiebel, S. J., Winston, J. S., Dolan, R. J., & Frith, C. D. (2004). Brain responses to the acquired moral status of faces. *Neuron, 41*, 653–662. doi:10.1016/S0896-6273(04)00014-5

Singh, I. L., Molloy, R., & Parasuraman, R. (1993). Individual differences in monitoring failures of automation. *The Journal of General Psychology, 120*, 357–373.

Sparaco, P. (1995, January 30). Airbus seeks to keep pilot, new technology in harmony. *Aviation Week & Space Technology*, 62–63.

Sutherland, P., & Tan, F. B. (2004) The Nature of Consumer Trust in B2C Electronic Commerce: A Multi-Dimensional Conceptualization. In *Proceedings of the International Conference of the Information Resources Management Association: Innovations Through Information Technology*, New Orleans, USA (pp. 611-614).

Yamagishi, T., & Yamagishi, M. (1994). Trust and commitment in the United States and Japan. *Motivation and Emotion, 18*, 129–166. doi:10.1007/BF02249397

Yan, Z., Liu, C. H., Niemi, V., & Yu, G. L. (in press). *Evaluation of displaying trust information's effects on mobile application usage.*

Zak, P. J., & Knack, S. (2001). Trust and growth. *The Economic Journal, 111*, 295–321. doi:10.1111/1468-0297.00609

Zuboff, S. (1988). *In the age of smart machines: The future of work technology and power*. New York: Basic Books.

Chapter 21
Rethinking Realistic Wireless Network Mobility:
Model and Trust

Lu Yan
University of Hertfordshire, UK

ABSTRACT

With recent advances of wireless ad hoc networking, especially opportunistic forwarding and cognitive radio, there is an increasing concern that existing mobility models are insufficient to represent network mobility in real world settings. In this chapter, the author discusses his proposal for a more realistic mobility model which captures key features of human movements in pervasive markets. His findings lead to a non-traditional mobility model which can be used to reconstruct the statistical patterns commonly observed in the literature, and facilitate the study of mobile communication and software engineering design problems under the context of pervasive computing for markets.

INTRODUCTION

The communication environment surrounding our daily experience is increasingly characterized by mobile devices that can exchange information and provide access to various services of complex nature. The trend is clear that future personal computing experience would be more and more based on pervasive communication devices and services, and the underlying mobile networks are becoming cooperative as mobile devices are increasingly rely on nearby nodes to maintain connectivity or relay messages.

DOI: 10.4018/978-1-61520-682-7.ch021

In the future scenarios of wireless ad hoc networking like above, local connections and user mobility are as important as infrastructure access today for delivering data (Su et al., 2007), but those mobility issues are not well studied in the past. As mobile devices are often attached to users, understanding their mobility patterns would lead to more realistic network simulation and better software and communication system design in general. However, existing mobility models are either too simplistic or do not represent the key characteristics of user mobility (Camp et al., 2002). In the literature, most commonly used mobility models can be categorized into two types: individual mobility model and group mobility model.

Individual mobility models address the movement at individual node level, where each node is assumed to be independent from others: the Random Walk model (Nain et al., 2005) is the de facto mobility model for most mobile network simulations, which is a direct implementation of Brownian motion. The Random Waypoint model (Yoon et al., 2003; Navidi et al., 2004) is also widely used in mobile network simulations, where nodes travel between randomly chosen locations. The Gauss-Markov model (Liang et al., 1999) was designed to adapt to different levels of randomness, where nodes updates their speed and direction at each time step, taking previous values into account.

In a group mobility model, the movement of a node is calculated relatively to the movement of a reference point in the group it belongs to: the Reference Point Group model (Hong et al., 1999) was based on the observation that mobile nodes in real world tend to coordinate their movement (e.g., in battlefield, a number of soldiers may move together in a group or platoon; or during disaster relief, various rescue crews form different groups and work cooperatively), where nodes are assumed to be in groups of one leader and a number of members. The movement of the group leader determines the mobility behavior of the entire group. The Social Network and Community model (Musolesi et al., 2004; Boldrini et al., 2007) is a recent approach to deriving mobility traces based on the analysis of community structure in social networks, which further considers the group dynamics and clustering techniques in the node movement calculations.

Observing that above approaches are all top-down: they try to define the real characteristics that a mobility model should capture and then build the model accordingly, we take a reversed thinking bottom-up that mobility models should be inferred from observations made in real world networks, due to two facts: (1) real characteristics are actually hard to define; (2) node mobility

characteristics in real world are very application specific.

DATA COLLECTION

Camden market was chosen for collecting user mobility traces. Camden market is a large craft and clothing market in Camden town and the fourth most popular visitor attraction in London, attracting approximately 100,000 people each weekend (Wikipedia, n.d.). HP GPS rx5730 handheld receiver is used for data collection, with a position accuracy of better than 3 meters most of the time. Users were supposed to keep the GPS receiver with them for as much of their visiting time as possible, with most carrying the GPS receiver in pockets. Occasionally, tracking information has discontinuity mainly when users move inside the indoor part of Camden market where GPS signals cannot be received.

The GPS receiver takes reading of the user's position every second and records it into a trace log. The trace log contains at least the following data:

Latitude; Longitude; Altitude; Speed; Date; Heading (1)

For the preliminary study, we collected traces of 4 market visitors (2 male and 2 female) over two month period. The assumption we taken here is that every visitor in the Camden market has the same statistical mobility tendency, and we believe it is reasonable to analyze the aggregative statistical patterns instead of individual statistical patterns. This assumption is also found in (Viswanathan et al., 1996; Barabási, 2005; Brockmann et al., 2006; Edwards et al., 2007; Sims et al., 2008). Therefore we believe it is reasonable to use this assumption in our analysis.

From those traces, we extract the following information: movement length, stay time, direction, and speed. Since we are mainly interested in

Figure 1. Sample GPS trace from Camden market

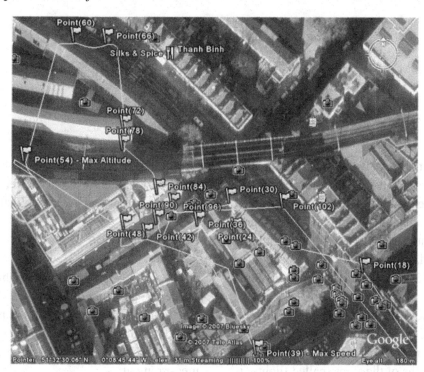

two dimensional mobility models, we map the raw data from GPS reading into two dimensional ones. Other treatments of the raw dataset are similar to (Kim et al., 2006). Figure 1 shows a sample GPS trace visualized in the Google earth.

A LEVY WALK MOBILITY MODEL

Many recent studies (Shlesinger et al., 1993; Viswanathan et al., 1996; Viswanathan et al., 1999; Viswanathan et al., 2000; Barabási, 2005; Brockmann et al., 2006; Edwards et al., 2007; Sims et al., 2008) have found, in various areas of real world mobility ranging from physical particles, biology, human behaviors, to computer networks, some fascinating common features pervade them: the once abstract notions of fractal space and time appear naturally and inevitably in dynamical systems like above (Shlesinger et al., 1993), which are not present in traditional random process models.

More specifically, what all these movements have in common is that their mobility patterns are shown to strongly resemble the Levy walk (Viswanathan et al., 2000) process. A Levy walk is comprised of random sequences of movement-segments, with length l, drawn from a probability distribution function having a power-law tail:

$$p(l) \propto l^{-\gamma} \tag{2}$$

where $\gamma \in (1,3]$. Such a distribution is said to have a heavy-tail (Barabási, 2005) because large-length values are more prevalent than would be present within other random distributions, such as Poisson or Gaussian.

Levy walk was used to model animal foraging patterns (Sims et al., 2008). According to the foraging theory, animals are presumed to search for nutrients and obtain them in a way to maximize the ratio of energy intake over the time spent for foraging. Levy walk is a commonly observed searching strategy in animal foraging,

Figure 2. Abstract graphical model of human shopper

and it is proved that Levy walk strategy minimizes the mean distance traveled and presumably the mean energy expended before encountering a target (Viswanathan et al., 2000). Recent literature demonstrated that the Levy walk system is also very similar to the way that humans shop (Barabási, 2005; Brockmann et al., 2006; Sims et al., 2008).

Figure 2 shows an abstract model of market visitors' traces: (1) a visitor's directions of successive steps are uncorrelated; (2) the distribution of the lengths of the steps (called flights) is characterized by a long tail.

EXPERIMENTAL CONFIRMATION

It is confirmed from our measurement that Camden market visitor's trace also statistically resembles the Levy walk model: the flight distance, which is defined as the longest possible straight line between locations without a directional change or pause, follows a power-law distribution.

Flight Distance

A power-low distribution of flight distances is the defining feature of Levy walk. We first show a statistical result from our measurement in the Camden market, and then use curve-fitting techniques to extract the scale parameter from the measurement.

We used a similar statistical method as (Sims et al., 2008). For market visitors' movements, we first do a spectrum analysis as Figure 3, which already shows some evidences of an intermittent structure of longer flights. Using the frequency counts from the spectrum, we can normalize the distance distribution and derive a distance probability density graph as Figure 4.

Figure 3. Spectrum analysis of market visitors' movements

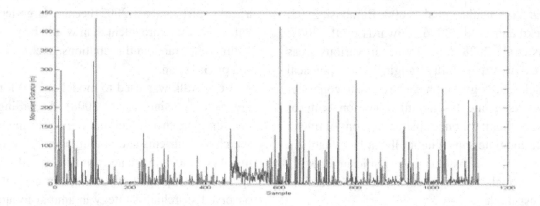

Figure 4. Normalized distance distribution based on frequency

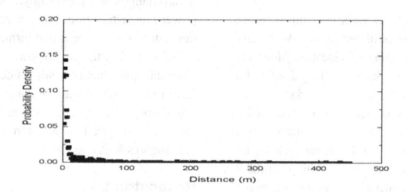

Figure 4 already exhibits the long tail characteristic of the visitor's movements, but we can show it more clearly in a log-log plot refinement as Figure 5, where the levy characteristic is highlighted as a red line. Though the levy tendency is evident in Figure 5, we still need to quantitatively validate the Levy model with a scale parameter.

We used the maximum likelihood estimation (MLE) to estimate the scale parameter:

$$\gamma = 1 + n[\sum_{i=1}^{n} \ln \frac{x_i}{x_{\min}}]^{-1} \qquad (3)$$

where γ is the estimated scale parameter and x_i is the data sample. With this estimated scale param-

eter γ, we are already able to reconstruct a levy distribution curve. But at this point, we are not yet sure if the reconstructed curve is really a good fit of the original dataset. Thus a goodness-of-fit test is needed, and we used Kolmogorov-Smirnov statistic to validate the fitness:

$$f = \max_{x \geq x_{\min}} |S(x) - P(x)| \qquad (4)$$

where f is the goodness-of-fit, $S(x)$ is the cumulative distribution function (CDF) of the data, and $P(x)$ is the CDF from our reconstructed curve.

Figure 6 shows the quantitative analysis result with an estimated scale parameter $\gamma = 1.8790$ and its goodness-of-fit $f = 0.0421$.

Figure 5. Log-log plot refinement of Figure 4

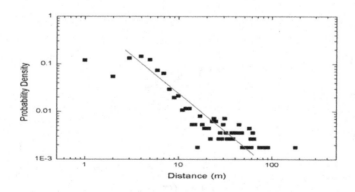

Stay Time and Turning Angle

The definition of Levy walk does not require a power-law distribution of the stay time Δt, which is defined as the pause time in a location. However, surprisingly, we also observed a levy distribution of stay time from the Camden market visitor's traces. Using the same techniques developed in Section 4.1, we can derive a quantitative result with $\gamma = 1.8700$ and $f = 0.0849$ as shown in Figure 7. However, a goodness-of-fit value $f = 0.0849$ implies that Levy tendency in stay time distribution is not as strong as that in distance distribution.

Though power-law distribution of stay time is not necessary in the Levy work definition, it would be interesting to further investigate whether this phenomenon is a pure coincidence or a common feature.

The turning angle θ, which measures the directional changes, not surprisingly, does not follow a power-law distribution. One reasonable assumption can be made here is that turning angles may be influenced by the geographical characteristics since shop placements in the Camden market must follow the geographical and council regulations, a quadrimodal distribution is expected here since urban architecture is dominated by right angles (see Figures 8, 9, and 10).

Reconstruction

Now we are ready to reconstruct the user mobility traces in Camden market with a Levy walk model. The feature of each movement tuple M is captured by three variables:

Figure 6. Quantitative analysis of distance

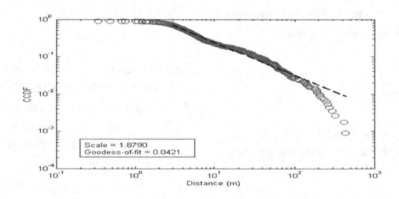

Figure 7. Quantitative analysis of time

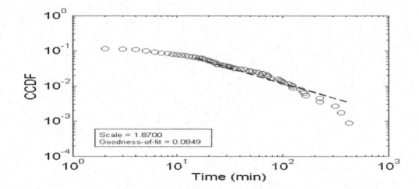

$$M = (l, \Delta t, \theta) \qquad (5)$$

where l, Δt, and θ are flight distance, stay time, and turning angle respectively. When reconstructing the mobility traces, our model would calculate M_t at time t and randomly generate l_t and $(\Delta t)_t$ with the Levy distribution; while θ_t follows a uniform distribution. We use the following probability density function to calculate the Levy walk (Bracewell, 2000):

$$f(x,c) = \sqrt{\frac{c}{2\pi}} \frac{e^{-\frac{c}{2x}}}{x^{\frac{3}{2}}} \qquad (6)$$

where c is the scale parameter and needs fine-tuning in the reconstruction process. Figure 11 shows a comparison of reconstructed sample mobility traces with the random walk model, the random waypoint model, and the Levy walk model respectively.

A Trust-Based Refinement

Though it is shown in Section 4 that the Levy walk model is better in modeling user mobility traces in real world pervasive markets, this model can still be further refined for improvements: the Levy walk model is built on the uniform distribution assumption that the precise location of the targets

Figure 8. Turning angle distribution

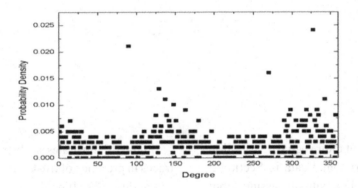

Figure 9. Log-log plot of turning angle distribution

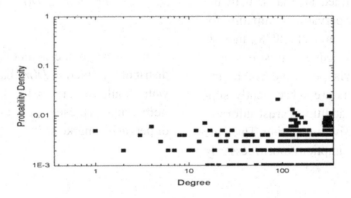

Figure 10. Cumulative distribution of turning angle

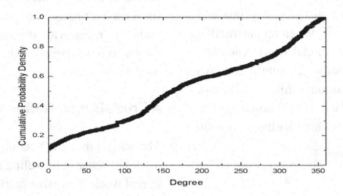

Figure 11. Reconstructed sample mobility traces with a. the random walk model, b. the random waypoint model, and c. the Levy walk model; (from left to right)

is not known a priori but their spatial distribution is uniform. Our experimental data in Section 2 were also collected in line with this assumption: the visitors had no prior information on trust (Sassone et al., 2007; Lathia et al., 2008), defined in the broad sense, of shops in Camden market.

However, for a refined approach, with the vision provided by our pervasive computing for markets project (Robinson et al., 2008), there is often presumptive knowledge of trust on shops available to visitors via pervasive computing technology, and visitors are subsequently supposed to best use this additional trust information provided by pervasive computing. Thus, the uniform distribution assumption is not necessarily true in this case.

Figure 12 illustrates an abstract model of visitor traces in presence of trust, where we label that the trust value $s_1 \geq s_2$. If we denote a trust-biased probability distribution function of movements m as $D(m)$, it should satisfy the following condition:

$$\forall s_1 \geq s_2: \exists D: D(m_1) \geq D(m_2) \text{ and } D \in P(Levy) \tag{7}$$

It is our hypothesis that this new probability distribution function $D(m)$ based trust and Levy walk should capture the key features of user mobility traces in presence of trust under the context of pervasive markets.

Figure 12. Abstract graphical model of trust-biased human shopper

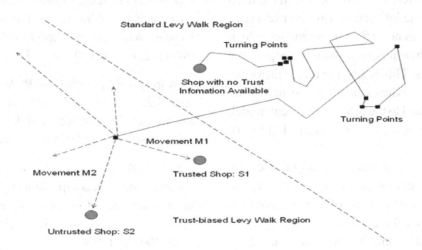

CONCLUSION

Network mobility is an important research area in pervasive computing. Understanding user mobility is critical for simulations of mobile devices in a wireless network, but current mobility models often do not reflect real user movements.

This paper presented a non-traditional phenomenological approach to user mobility modeling in pervasive markets. We introduced the Levy walk model to the user mobility patterns, based on the assumption of no prior trust information. The preliminary study in Camden market confirmed that market visitor's trace statistically resembles the Levy walk model.

We then relaxed the uniform distribution assumption and proposed a trust biased refinement to the Levy walk model. It is our hypothesis that user mobility patterns in presence of trust follow a trust-biased Levy walk distribution as Equation 7. However, we still need real world measurement date in pervasive markets to validate our hypothesis, which can be one of the future works in this research.

Because of resource constraints, the experimental data collected in our preliminary study in the Camden market is relatively limited. Our model presented in this paper mainly captures the features of individual movements at node level. It would be interesting to study both individual and group movements with and without trust information in various types of pervasive markets (Heath et al., 2007).

FUTURE PLAN AND DISCUSSION

In terms of future research, more empirical study should be done to prove the trust-based refinement hypothesis. One future experiment would be to go back to the original data and see whether reliable trust value could be fetched from the participants of the study. However, this will be done carefully without the danger of falling either into "data massage": accepting/providing data that fits into the model or into "temporal bias": trust values are assigned based on the end state of the experiment whereas the movement patterns should be affected by the trust values that exist during the experiment.

Another planned experiment would be on the user's preference analysis. The trust-based refinement, at this stage, does not distinguish the user's preference regard shops/locations with trust. However, the relationship between preference and trust should be further investigated since some preferences are not directly related to trust. Also, the interaction between users (i.e., social trust) does not reflect in our model, which could be another important issue in shaping the mobility traces. This is also the major factor we would consider when extending the individual movement model to the group movement model, which can be done via the empirical study of group dynamics.

Last but not least, the model so far does not include any temporal factor. It is interesting to study the temporal patterns of user behaviors in the market (i.e., the controlled group study of user traces in different timeslots across the day). We plan to apply the time-series technique to the dataset, and incorporate the temporal properties to the original model to build a new space-time model, which will better reflect the reality.

ACKNOWLEDGMENT

This work was partly funded by EPSRC under grant EP/D07696X/1.

REFERENCE

Barabási, A.-L. (2005). The origin of bursts and heavy tails in human dynamics. *Nature, 435,* 207–211. doi:10.1038/nature03459

Boldrini, C., Conti, M., et al. (2007). Impact of Social Mobility on Routing Protocols for Opportunistic Networks. In *IEEE International Symposium on a World of Wireless, Mobile and Multimedia Networks (WoWMoM'07)*, Helsinki, Finland.

Bracewell, R. N. (2000). The *Fourier Transform and Its Applications*. Boston: McGraw Hill.

Brockmann, D., & Hufnagel, L. (2006). The scaling laws of human travel. *Nature, 439,* 462–465. doi:10.1038/nature04292

Camp, T., & Boleng, J. (2002). A survey of mobility models for ad hoc network research. *Wireless Communications and Mobile Computing, 2*(5), 483–502. doi:10.1002/wcm.72

Edwards, A. M., & Phillips, R. A. (2007). Revisiting Lévy flight search patterns of wandering albatrosses, bumblebees and deer. *Nature, 449,* 1044–1048. doi:10.1038/nature06199

Heath, C., & Luff, P. (2007). Ordering competition: the interactional accomplishment of the sale of fine art and antiques at auction. *The British Journal of Sociology, 58,* 63–85. doi:10.1111/j.1468-4446.2007.00139.x

Hong, X., Gerla, M., et al. (1999). A group mobility model for ad hoc wireless networks. In *2nd ACM international workshop on Modeling, analysis and simulation of wireless and mobile systems (MSWiM'99)*, Seattle, WA, USA.

Kim, M., Kotz, D., et al. (2006). Extracting a Mobility Model from Real User Traces. In *25th IEEE International Conference on Computer Communications (INFOCOM'06)*, Barcelona, Spain.

Lathia, N., Hailes, S., et al. (2008). Trust Based Collaborative Filtering. In *Joint iTrust and PST Conferences on Privacy, Trust management and Security (iTrust'08)*, Norway.

Liang, B., & Haas, Z. J. (1999). Predictive distance-based mobility management for PCS networks. In *18th Annual Joint Conference of the IEEE Computer and Communications Societies (INFOCOM'99)*, New York, USA.

Musolesi, M., Hailes, S., et al. (2004). An ad hoc mobility model founded on social network theory. In *7th ACM international symposium on Modeling, analysis and simulation of wireless and mobile systems (MSWiM'04)*, Venice, Italy.

Nain, P., Towsley, D., et al. (2005). Properties of random direction models. In *24th Annual Joint Conference of the IEEE Computer and Communications Societies (INFOCOM'05)*, Miami, FL, USA (pp. 1897- 1907).

Navidi, W., & Camp, T. (2004). Stationary distributions for the random waypoint mobility model. *IEEE Transactions on Mobile Computing, 3*(1), 99–108. doi:10.1109/TMC.2004.1261820

Robinson, J., Wakeman, I., et al. (2008). The North Laine Shopping Guide: A Case Study in Modelling Trust in Applications. In *Joint iTrust and PST Conferences on Privacy, Trust management and Security (iTrust'08)*, Norway.

Sassone, V., Nielsen, M., et al. (2007). Towards a Formal Framework for Computational Trust. In *Formal Methods for Components and Objects* (pp. 175-184).

Shlesinger, M. F., & Zaslavsky, G. M. (1993). Strange kinetics. *Nature, 363*, 31–37. doi:10.1038/363031a0

Sims, D. W., & Southall, E. J. (2008). Scaling laws of marine predator search behaviour. *Nature, 451*, 1098–1102. doi:10.1038/nature06518

Su, J., Scott, J., et al. (2007). Haggle: Seamless Networking for Mobile Applications. In *9th International Conference on Ubiquitous Computing (UbiComp'07)*, Innsbruck, Austria.

Viswanathan, G. M., & Afanasyev, V. (1996). Lévy flight search patterns of wandering albatrosses. *Nature, 381*, 413–415. doi:10.1038/381413a0

Viswanathan, G. M., Afanasyev, V., et al. (2000). Lévy flights in random searches. *Physica A: Statistical Mechanics and its Applications, 282*(1-2), 1-12.

Viswanathan, G. M., & Buldyrev, S. V. (1999). Optimizing the success of random searches. *Nature, 401*, 911–914. doi:10.1038/44831

Wikipedia. (n.d.). *Camden Market*. Retrieved from http://en.wikipedia.org/wiki/Camden_Market

Yoon, J., Liu, M., et al. (2003). Random waypoint considered harmful. In *22nd Annual Joint Conference of the IEEE Computer and Communications Societies (INFOCOM'03)*, San Francisco, CA, USA.

Compilation of References

3GPP SA3. (2008). *3rd Generation Partnership Project; Technical Specification Group Service and System Aspects; Feasibility Study on Remote Management of USIM Application on M2M Equipment; (Release 8), TR 33.812 v1.1.0 (S3-081211).* Retrieved January 12, 2009, from ftp://ftp.3gpp.org/TSG_SA/WG3_Security/TSGS3_53_Kyoto/Docs/S3-081211.zip

3GPP SA3. (2009). *3rd Generation Partnership Project; Technical Specification Group Service and System Aspects; Security of H(e)NB; (Release 8), TR 33.820 V8.0.0 (S3-090482).* Retrieved March 30, 2009, from ftp://ftp.3gpp.org/TSG_SA/WG3_Security/ADHOCs/TSGS3_ADHOC_Mar09_Sophia/Docs/S3-090482.zip

3GPP SA3. (2009). *Web Site of 3GPP SA3: Security.* Retrieved January 19, 2009, from http://www.3gpp.org/SA3/

Abdul-Rahman, A., & Hailes, S. (1997, September). A distributed trust model. In *Proceedings of the ACM New Security Paradigms Workshop* (pp. 48-60).

Abdul-Rahman, A., & Hailes, S. (2000, January). Supporting trust in virtual communities. In *Proceedings of the 33th Hawaii International Conference on System Sciences (HICSS)* (pp. 1769-1777).

Aberer, K., & Despotovic, Z. (2001). Managing Trust in a Peer-to-Peer Information System. In H. Paques, L. Liu, & D. Grossman (Eds.), *Proc. Of the 10th ACM Intl. Conf. on Information and Knowledge Management* (pp. 310-317). New York: ACM.

Aboba, B., & Simon, D. (1999). PPP EAP TLS Authentication Protocol. *IETF Network Working Group. RFC 2716.* Retrieved March 10, 2009, from http://www.ietf.org/rfc/rfc2716.txt

Abrams, L. C., Cross, R., Lesser, E., & Levin, D. Z. (2003). Nurturing interpersonal trust in knowledge-sharing networks. *The Academy of Management Executive, 17,* 64–77.

Adams, C., & Lloyd, S. (2003). *Understanding PKI: concepts, standards, and deployment considerations* (2nd ed.). Reading, MA: Addison-Wesley Press.

Adnane, A., Bidan, C., & De Sousa, R. T., Jr. (2008). Effectiveness of Trust Reasoning for Attack Detection in OLSR. In *Proceedings of the 6th International Workshop on Security in Information Systems (WOSIS-2008),* Barcelona, Spain.

Adnane, A., De Sousa, R. T., Jr., Bidan, C., & Mé, L. (2007). Analysis of the implicit trust within the OLSR protocol. In *Proceedings of the IFIPTM-2007 Joint iTrust and PST Conferences on Privacy, Trust Management and Security,* Moncton, New Brunswick, Canada. Berlin, Germany: Springer.

Adnane, A., De Sousa, R. T., Jr., Bidan, C., & Mé, L. (2008). Autonomic Trust Reasoning Enables Misbehavior Detection in OLSR. In *Proceedings of the 23rd Annual ACM Symposium on Applied Computing (ACM SAC 2008): Trust, Recommendations, Evidence and other Collaboration Know-how (TRECK track),* Fortaleza, Ceará, Brazil. New York: ACM.

Adomavicius, G., & Tuzhilin, A. (2005). Toward the next generation of recommender system: a survey of the state-of-the-art and possible extensions. *IEEE Transactions* on *Knowledge and Data Engineering, 17*(6), 734–749. doi:10.1109/TKDE.2005.99

Aeronautical Radio Inc. (2002). *ARINC Report 665: Loadable software standards, August.*

Aeronautical Radio Inc. (2005). *ARINC Report 811: Commercial aircraft information security concepts of operation and process framework, December.*

Aeronautical Radio Inc. (2008). *ARINC Report 827: Electronic distribution of software by crate (EDS crate), June.*

Aeronautical Radio Inc. (2009). *ARINC Report 664, Part 2: Aircraft Data Network, Part 2 - Ethernet Physical and Data Link Layer Specification, January.*

Agi, I., & Gong, L. (1996). An empirical study of MPEG video transmissions. In *Proceedings of the Internet Society Symposium on Network and Distributed System Security,* San Diego, CA (pp. 137-144).

Ahn, J., Shim, H., Jeon, B., & Choi, I. (2004). Digital Video Scrambling Method Using Intra Prediction Mode. In *Proceedings of the 2004 Pacific-Rim Conference on Multimedia (PCM2004)* (LNCS 3333, pp. 386-393). Berlin, Germany: Springer.

Aiello, W., Kushilevitz, E., Ostrovsky, R., & Rosen, A. (2000). Adaptive packet routing for bursty adversarial traffic. *Journal of Computer and System Sciences, 60*(3), 482–509. doi:10.1006/jcss.1999.1681

Ajayi, O., Sinnott, R., & Stell, A. (2008). Dynamic trust negotiation for flexible e-health collaborations. In D. S. Katz, C. Lee, T. Kosar, S. Jha, & O. Rana (Eds.), *Proc. of the 15th ACM Mardi Gras conference: From lightweight mash-ups to lambda grids: Understanding the spectrum of distributed computing requirements, applications, tools, infrastructures, interoperability, and the incremental adoption of key capabilities* (pp. 1-7). New York: ACM.

Ajzen, I., & Fishbein, M. (1980). *Understanding attitudes and predicting social behavior.* Upper Saddle River, NJ: Prentice Hall.

Akyildiz, I. F., Melodia, T., & Chowdhury, K. R. (2006). A survey on wireless multimedia sensor networks. *Journal of Computer Networks, 51*(4), 921–960. doi:10.1016/j.comnet.2006.10.002

Akyildiz, I. F., Su, W., Sankarasubramaniam, Y., & Cayirci, E. (2002). Wireless sensor networks: a survey. *Journal of Computer Networks, 38*(4), 393–422. doi:10.1016/S1389-1286(01)00302-4

Albers, P., Camp, O., Percher, J., Jouga, B., Mé, L., & Puttini, R. S. (2002). Security in Ad hoc Networks: a General Intrusion Detection Architecture Enhancing Trust Based Approaches. In Q. H. Mahmoud (Ed.), *Wireless Information Systems, Proceedings of the 1st International Workshop on Wireless Information Systems, WIS 2002* (pp. 1-12). Ciudad Real, Spain: ICEIS Press.

Alfieri, R., Cecchini, R., Ciaschini, V., dell'Agnello, L., Frohner, Á., Gianoli, A., et al. (2003). VOMS, an Authorization System for Virtual Organizations. In *Proceedings of the Grid Computing, First European Across Grids Conference* (LNCS 2970, pp. 33-40). Berlin, Germany: Springer.

Alge, B. J., Wiethoff, C., & Klein, H. J. (2003). When does the medium matter? Knowledge-building experiences and opportunities in decision making teams. *Organizational Behavior and Human Decision Processes, 91,* 26–37. doi:10.1016/S0749-5978(02)00524-1

Allen, J. F. (1983). Maintaining knowledge about temporal intervals. *Communications of the ACM, 26*(11), 832–843. doi:10.1145/182.358434

Almenarez, F., Marin, A., Diaz, D., & Sanchez, J. (2006). Developing a Model for Trust Management in Pervasive Devices. In *Proceeding of the fourth Annual IEEE International Conference on Pervasive Computing and Communications Workshops (PERCOM'06),* Italy (pp. 267-271).

Al-Muhtadi, J., Campell, R., Kapadia, A., Mickunas, M., & Yi, S. (2002). Routing Through the Mist: Privacy Preserving Communication In Ubiquitous Computing Environments. In *Proceedings of the International*

Conference of Distributed Computing Systems (ICDCS 2002), Vienna, Austria (pp. 65-74).

Alomair, B., Lazos, L., & Poovendran, R. (2007). Passive attacks on a class of authentication protocols for RFID. In *Proceedings of the International Conference on Information Security and Cryptology* (pp. 102-115). Berlin, Germany: Springer.

Alpcan, T., & Basar, T. (2003). Global stability analysis of an end-to-end congestion control scheme for general topology networks with delay. In *Proceedings of the 42nd IEEE Conference on Decision and Control* (pp. 1092-1097).

Alpcan, T., Singh, J. P., & Basar, T. (2007). A robust flow control framework for heterogenous network access. In *Proceedings of the 5th Intl. Symposium on Modeling and Optimization in Mobile, Ad Hoc, and Wireless Networks* (pp. 1-8).

Alvarez, C., Blesa, M., & Serna, M. (2004). A Characterization of Universal Stability in the Adversarial Queuing Model. *SIAM Journal on Computing, 34,* 41–66. doi:10.1137/S0097539703435522

Alvarez, C., Blesa, M., & Serna, M. (2004). The Impact of Failure Management on the Stability of Communication Networks. In *Proceedings of the 10th International Conference on Parallel and Distributed Systems* (pp. 153-160).

Alvarez, C., Blesa, M., Diaz, J., Fernandez, A., & Serna, M. (2003). Adversarial Models for Priority-Based Networks. In *Proceedings of the 28th International Symposium on Mathematical Foundations of Computer Science Vol. 2747* (pp. 142-151).

AMD. (2003). AMD platform for trustworthy computing. *Microsoft Win-HEC 2003.* Retrieved December 30, 2008, from http://download.microsoft.com/download/5/7/7/577a5684-8a83-43ae-9272-ff260a9c20e2/AMD_WinHEC-2003_whitepaper.doc

AMD. *(2005).* AMD64 Virtualization Codenamed "Pacifica" Technology-Secure Virtual Machine Architecture Reference Manual. *AMD.*

American Psychological Association. (n.d.). *Psychological Abstracts.* Retrieved February 2, 2009, from http://www.apa.org/psycinfo/

Anancha, S., D'souza, P., Perich, F., Joshi, A., & Yesha, Y. (2003, January). P2P M-commerce in pervasive environments. *ACM SIGecom Exchange, 3*(4), 1-9.

Anderson, R. (2001). *Security Engineering: A Guide to Building Dependable Distributed Systems.* New York: John Wiley & Sons Inc.

Anderson, R., & Manifavas, C. (1997). Chameleon - a new kind of stream cipher. In *Fast Software Encryption* (LNCS 1267, pp. 107-113). Berlin, Germany: Srpinger-Verlag.

Andrews, M., Awerbuch, B., Fernandez, A., Kleinberg, J., Leighton, T., & Liu, Z. (2001). Universal Stability Results for Greedy Contention-Resolution Protocols. *Journal of the ACM, 48,* 39–69. doi:10.1145/363647.363677

Apvrille, A., Gordon, D., Hallyn, S., Pourzandi, M., & Roy, V. (2004). *DigSig: Run-time authentication of binaries at kernel level.* Paper presented at the 18th USENIX Large Installation System Administration Conference, LISA'04, Atlanta, USA.

Arbaugh, W. A., Farber, D. J., & Smith, J. M. (1997). A secure and reliable bootstrap architecture. In *Proc. of the 1997 IEEE Symposium on Security and Privacy* (pp. 65-71). Washington, DC: IEEE.

Archer, M., Leonard, E., & Pradella, M. (2003). *Analyzing security-enhanced Linux policy specifications.* Paper presented at IEEE 4th International Workshop on Policies for Distributed Systems and Networks, POLICY 2003.

Ardichvili, A., Page, V., & Wentling, T. (2003). Motivation and barriers to participation in virtual knowledge-sharing communities of practice. *Journal of Knowledge Management, 7,* 64–77. doi:10.1108/13673270310463626

Areal, J. L., Puttini, R. S., & De Sousa, R. T., Jr. (2008). A New Trust-Based Extension to the HELLO Message Improves the Choice of Routes in OLSR Networks. In *Proceedings of the 7th International Information and Telecommunication Technologies Symposium I2TS'2008,* Foz do Iguaçu, Brazil.

Arenas, A., Aziz, B., & Silaghi, G. C. (2008). Reputation Management in Grid-based Virtual Organisations. In *Proceedings of the Third International Conference on Security and Cryptography (SECRYPT 2008)*. INSTICC.

Aringhieri, R., Damiani, E., De, S., Vimercati, C., Paraboschi, S., & Samarati, P. (2006). Fuzzy Techniques for Trust and Reputation Management in Anonymous Peer-to-Peer Systems. *Journal of the American Society for Information Science and Technology, 57*(4), 528–537. doi:10.1002/asi.20307

Arkko, J., & Haverinen, H. (2006). Extensible Authentication Protocol Method for 3rd Generation Authentication and Key Agreement (EAP-AKA). *IETF Network Working Group. RFC 4187*. Retrieved January 21, 2009, from http://www.ietf.org/rfc/rfc4187.txt

ARM. (2008). *ARM 1176 JZFS Technical reference manual*. Retrieved April 27, 2009, from http://infocenter.arm.com/help/topic/com.arm.doc.ddi0301g/DDI0301G_arm1176jzfs_r0p7_trm.pdf

Arnold, E. (2001). *The trouble with Tripwire*. Retrieved April 25, 2009, from http://www.security focus.com/infocus/1398

Artz, D., & Gil, Y. (2007). A Survey of Trust in Computer Science and the Semantic Web. In *Web Semantics: Science, Services and Agents on the World Wide Web*. Retrieved November, 2008, from http://www.isi.edu/~gil/papers/jws-trust-07.pdf

Avizienis, A., Laprie, J.-C., Randell, B., & Landwehr, C. E. (2004). Basic Concepts and Taxonomy of Dependable and Secure Computing. *IEEE Trans. Dependable Sec. Comput., 1*(1), 11–33. doi:10.1109/TDSC.2004.2

Avoine, G. (2007). *Bibliography on Security and Privacy in RFID systems*. Retrieved April 2, 2009, from http://lasecwww.epfl.ch/~gavoine/download/bib/bibliography-rfid.pdf

Axelrod, R. (1984). *The Evolution of Cooperation*. New York: Basic Books.

Ayachi, M. A., Bidan, C., Abbes, T., & Bouhoula, A. (2009). Analyse de la confiance dans AODV. In *Actes de la 4ème Conférence sur la Sécurité des Architectures Réseaux et des Systèmes d'Information*. France: Publibook.

Ayoade, J., Takizawa, O., & Nakao, K. (2005, April). *A prototype System of the RFID Authentication Processing Framework*. Paper presented at the International Workshop in Wireless Security Technologies, London, UK.

Azzedin, F., & Maheswaran, M. (2002). Towards Trust-Aware Resource Management in Grid Computing Systems. In *Proc. of the 2nd IEEE/ACM International Symposium on Cluster Computing and the Grid* (pp. 452-457). Washington, DC: IEEE.

Ba, S., & Pavlou, P. A. (2002). Evidence of the effects of trust building technology in electronic markets: price premiums and buyer behavior. *MIS Quarterly, 26*(3), 243–268. doi:10.2307/4132332

Baba, M. L., Falkenburg, D. R., & Hill, D. H. (1996). Technology management and American culture: Implications for business process redesign. *Research Technology Management, 39*(6), 44–54.

Bacharach, M., & Gambetta, D. (2000). Trust as Type Identification. In C. Castelfranchi & Y. Tan (Eds.), *Trust and Deception in Virtual Societies* (pp. 1-26). Amsterdam: Kluwer Academic Publishers.

Backhouse, J., & Halperin, R. (2007). A Survey on EU Citizen's Trust in ID Systems and Authorities. *FIDIS Journal, 1*(2007). Retrieved from http://journal.fidis.net/fileadmin/journal/issues/1-2007/Survey_on_Citizen_s_Trust.pdf

Bagheri, N., & Jamieson, G. A. (2004). The impact of context-related reliability on automation failure detection and scanning behaviour. In *Systems, Man and Cybernetics, 2004 IEEE International Conference*.

Bai, H., Atiquzzaman, M., & Lilja, D. (2004). Wireless sensor network for aircraft health monitoring. In *Proceedings of 1st International Conference on Broadband Networks (BROADNETS)* (pp. 748-750). Washington, DC: IEEE Press.

Balachander, S. (2001). Warranty signaling and reputation. *Management Science, 47*(9), 1282–1289. doi:10.1287/mnsc.47.9.1282.9783

Balboni, G. P., & Bosco, P. G. (1996). *A TINA Structured Service Gateway.* Paper presented at the Telecommunications Information Networking Architecture Conference.

Balfanz, D., Smetters, D., Stewart, P., & Wong, H. (2002). Talking to Strangers: Authentication in Adhoc Wireless Networks. In *Proceedings of the ISOC Network and Distributed Systems Security Symposium.*

Bandara, A. K., Lupu, E., Moffett, J. D., & Russo, A. (2004). A goal-based approach to policy refinement. In *Proceedings of the Intl. Workshop on Policies for Distributed Systems and Networks* (pp. 229-239). Washington, DC: IEEE.

Banks, T. (2006). *Web Services Resource Framework (WSRF) – Primer v1.2. OASIS Committee Draft 02 - 23 May 2006.* Retrieved March 30, 2009, from http://docs.oasis-open.org/wsrf/wsrf-primer-1.2-primer-cd-02.pdf

Bansal, S., & Baker, M. (2003). *Observation-based cooperation enforcement in ad hoc networks.* Retrieved October 2008, from http://arxiv.org/pdf/cs.NI/0307012

Barabási, A.-L. (2005). The origin of bursts and heavy tails in human dynamics. *Nature, 435,* 207–211. doi:10.1038/nature03459

Barber, B. (1983). *The logic and limits of trust.* New Brunswick, NJ: Rutgers University Press.

Barefoot, J. C., Maynard, K. E., Beckham, J. C., Bramme, B. H., Hooker, K., & Siegler, I. C. (1998). Trust, health and longevity. *Journal of Behavioral Medicine, 21,* 517–526. doi:10.1023/A:1018792528008

BBC News. (2008). *MoD Admits Loss of Secret Files.* Retrieved from http://news.bbc.co.uk/1/hi/uk/7514281.stm

Bearden, W. O., & Shimp, T. A. (1982). The use of extrinsic cues to facilitate product adoption. *JMR, Journal of Marketing Research, 19*(5), 229–239. doi:10.2307/3151623

Beattie, S., Black, A., Cowan, C., Pu, C., & Yang, L. (2000). *CryptoMark: locking the stable door ahead of the trojan horse* [white paper]. WireX Communications Inc.

Becker, E., Buhse, W., Günnewig, D., & Rump, N. (Eds.). (2003). *Digital Rights Management –Technological, Economic, Legal and Political Aspects.* New York: Springer-Verlag.

Becker, L. C. (1996). Trust as Noncognitive Security about Motives. *Ethics, 10,* 743–761.

Becker, M. Y., Fournet, C., & Gordon, A. D. (2007). Design and Semantics of a Decentralized Authorization Language. In *Proceedings of the 20th IEEE Computer Security Foundations Symposium (CSF)* (pp. 3-15). Washington, DC: IEEE.

Bell, D. E. (2005). Looking Back at the Bell-La Padula Model. In *Proceedings of the 21st Annual Computer Security Applications Conference* (pp. 337-351). Washington, DC: IEEE.

Bellotti, V. (1997). Design for Privacy in Multimedia Computing and Communications Environments. In *Technology and Privacy: The New Landscape* (pp. 63-98).

Benassi, P. (1999). TRUSTe: An online privacy seal program. *Communications of the ACM, 42*(2), 56. doi:10.1145/293411.293461

Bender, W., Gruhl, D., Morimoto, N., & Lu, A. (1996). Techniques for data hiding. *IBM Systems Journal, 35*(3-4), 313–316.

Berdie, D. R., Anderson, J. F., & Niebuhr, M. A. (1992) *Questionnaires: Design and use.* Lanham, MD: Scarecrow Press.

Berg, J., Dickhaut, J., & McCabe, K. (1995). Trust, Reciprocity, and Social History. *Games and Economic Behavior, 10,* 122–142. doi:10.1006/game.1995.1027

Bernath, M. S., & Feshbach, N. D. (1995). Children's trust: Theory, assessment, development, and research directions. *Applied & Preventive Psychology, 4,* 1–19. doi:10.1016/S0962-1849(05)80048-4

Berrached, A., & Korvin, A. (2006). Reinforcing Access Control Using Fuzzy Relation Equations. In *Proceedings of the 2006 International Conference on Security and Management (SAM06)* (pp. 489-493).

Berth, M. B. T., & Klein, B. (1994). Valuation of trust in open networks. In *Proceedings of the European Symposium on Computer Security (ESORICS)* (LNCS 875 pp. 3-18). Berlin, Germany: Springer-Verlag.

Bertino, E., Ferrari, E., & Squicciarini, A. (2004). Privacy Preserving Trust Negotiations. In *Proceedings of the fourth International workshop Privacy Enhancing Technologies* (pp. 283-301).

Bertino, E., Ferrari, E., & Squicciarini, A. (2004). Trust-X A Peer to Peer Framework for Trust Establishment. *IEEE Transactions on Knowledge and Data Engineering, 16*(7), 827–842.doi:doi:10.1109/TKDE.2004.1318565

Bertino, E., Ferrari, E., & Squicciarini, A. (2004b). Trust-X: A Peer to Peer Framework for Trust Establishment. *IEEE Transactions on Knowledge and Data Engineering, 16*(7), 827–842. doi:10.1109/TKDE.2004.1318565

Bertino, E., Khan, L., Sandhu, R., & Thuraisingham, B. (2006). Secure Knowledge Management: Confidentiality, Trust, and Privacy. *IEEE Transactions on Systems, Man, and Cybernetics . Systems and Humans, 36*(3), 429–438.

Beth, T., Borcherding, M., & Klein, B. (1994, November). *Valuation of Trust in Open Networks.* Paper presented at the Third European Symposium on Research in Computer Security, Brighton, UK.

Bettini, C., Jajodia, S., Wang, X. S., & Wijesekera, D. (2002). Provisions and obligations in policy management and security applications. In *Proc. of the 28ᵗʰ intl. Conf. on Very Large Data Bases* (pp. 502-513). Hong Kong, China: VLDB Endowment.

Bhargav-Spantzel, A., Squicciarini, A., & Bertino, E. (2007). Trust Negotiation in Identity Management. *IEEE Security and Privacy, 5*(2), 55–63. doi:10.1109/MSP.2007.46

Bhattacherjee, A. (2002). Individual trust in online firms: scale development and initial trust. *Journal of Management Information Systems, 19*(1), 213–243.

Bird, G., Christensen, G., Lutz, D., & Scandura, P. (2005, November). *Use of integrated vehicle health management in the field of commercial aviation.* Paper presented in NASA ISHEM Forum, Napa, CA.

Bishop, M. (2003). *Computer Security: Art and Science.* Reading, MA: Addition-Wesley Press.

Blaze, M., Feigenbaum, F., & Keromytis, A. D. (1998). KeyNote: Trust Management for Public-Key Infrastructures. In *Proceedings of the 1998 International Workshop of Security Protocols* (LNCS 1550, pp. 59-63).

Blaze, M., Feigenbaum, J., & Lacy, J. (1996). Decentralized trust management. In *Proceedings of the 17th Symposium on Security and Privacy* (pp. 164-173). Washington, DC: IEEE Computer Society Press.

Blaze, M., Feigenbaum, J., & Strauss, M. (1998). Compliance Checking in the PolicyMaker Trust Management System. In *Proceedings of the 2nd International Conference of Financial Cryptography* (pp. 254-274).

Blaze, M., Feigenbaum, J., Ioannidis, J., & Keromytis, A. (1999). *The KeyNote Trust Management System (version 2).* Retrieved from http://www.crypto.com/papers/rfc2704.txt

Blaze, M., Ioannidis, J., & Keromytis, A. D. (2003). Experience with the KeyNote Trust Management System: Applications and Future Directions. In *Proc. of the First Int. Conf. on Trust Management iTrust 2003* (LNCS 2692, pp. 284-300). Berlin, Germany: Springer.

Blesa, M., Calzada, D., Fernandez, A., Lopez, A., Martinez, A., Santos, A., & Serna, M. (2005). Adversarial Queueing Model for Continuous Network Dynamics. In *Proceedings of the 30th International Symposium on Mathematical Foundations of Computer Science Vol. 3618* (pp. 144-155).

Blum, M., & Kanna, S. (1989). Designing programs that check their work. In *Proceedings of the twenty-first an-*

nual ACM Symposium on Theory of Computing, Seattle, WA (pp. 86-97).

Bodo, Y., Laurent, N., & Dugelay, J. (2003). Watermarking video, hierarchical embedding in motion vectors. In *Proceedings of IEEE International Conference on Image Processing*, Spain (Vol. 2, pp. 739-742).

Bohmann, K. (1989). About the Sense of Social Compatibility. *AI & Society, 3*(4), 323–331. doi:10.1007/BF01908622

Bojadziev, G., & Bojadziev, M. (1997). *Fuzzy Logic for Business, Finance, and Management*. Singapore: World Scientific.

Boldrini, C., Conti, M., et al. (2007). Impact of Social Mobility on Routing Protocols for Opportunistic Networks. In *IEEE International Symposium on a World of Wireless, Mobile and Multimedia Networks (WoW-MoM'07)*, Helsinki, Finland.

Bollen, K. A., & Long, J. S. (1993). *Testing Structural Equation Models*. Newbury Park, CA: SAGE Publications.

Bonatti, P., & Samarati, P. (2000, November). *Regulating Access Services and Information Release on the Web*. Paper presented at the Seventh ACM Conference on Computer and Communications Security, Athens, Greece.

Boneh, D., & Shaw, J. (1998). Collusion-secure fingerprinting for digital data. *IEEE Transactions on Information Theory, 44*(5), 1897–1905. doi:10.1109/18.705568

Boon, S., & Holmes, J. (1991). The dynamics of interpersonal trust: Resolving uncertainty in the face of risk. In R. Hinde & J. Groebel (Eds.), *Cooperation and Prosocial Behavior* (pp. 190-211). Cambridge, UK: Cambridge University Press.

Borodin, A., Kleinberg, J., Raghavan, P., Sudan, M., & Williamson, D. (2001). Adversarial Queueing Theory. *Journal of the ACM, 48*, 13–38. doi:10.1145/363647.363659

Borodin, A., Ostrovsky, R., & Rabani, Y. (2001). Stability Preserving Transformations: Packet Routing Networks with Edge Capacities and Speeds Adversarial Queueing Theory. In *Proceedings of the 12th Annual ACM-SIAM Symposium on Discrete Algorithms* (pp. 601-610).

Boss, G., Malladi, P., Quan, D., Legregni, L., & Hall, H. (2007). *Cloud Computing* (IBM HiPODS Report). Armonk, NY: IBM.

Botha, R. A., & Eloff, J. H. P. (2001). Separation of duties for access control enforcement in workflow environments. *IBM Systems Journal, 40*, 666–682.

Bounkong, S., Toch, B., Saad, D., & Lowe, D. (2004). ICA for watermarking digital images . *Journal of Machine Learning Research, 4*(7-8), 1471–1498. doi:10.1162/jmlr.2003.4.7-8.1471

Boyd, D. M., & Ellison, N. B. (2007). Social network sites: Definition, history, and scholarship. *Journal of Computer-Mediated Communication, 13*(1), 11.

Boyle, J., Cohen, R., Herzog, S., Rajan, R., & Sastry, A. (2000). The COPS (Common Open Policy Service) Protocol. *IETF Network Working Group. RFC 2748*. Retrieved February 13, 2009, from http://www.ietf.org/rfc/rfc2748.txt

Bracewell, R. N. (2000). The *Fourier Transform and Its Applications*. Boston: McGraw Hill.

Braun, M., Hess, E., & Meyer, B. (2008). Using elliptic curves on RFID tags. *International Journal of Computer Science and Network Security, 8*(2), 1–9.

Braynov, S., & Sandholm, T. (2002). Contracting With Uncertain Level Of Trust. *Computational Intelligence, 18*(4), 501–514. doi:10.1111/1467-8640.00200

Breese, J., Heckerman, D., & Kadie, C. (1998). Empirical analysis of predictive algorithms for collaborative filtering. In *Proceedings of the Fourteenth Conference on Uncertainty in Artificial Intelligence* (pp. 43-52). San Francisco: Morgan Kaufmann Publisher.

Breslau, L., Cao, P., Fan, L., Phillips, G., & Shenker, S. (1999). Web Caching and Zipf-like Distributions: Evidence and Implications. In *Proceedings of INFOCOM '99: Eighteenth Annual Conference of the IEEE Computer and Communications Societies* (pp. 126-134).

Brett, A., & Leicher, A. (2009). *Ethemba Trusted Host Environment Mainly Based on Attestation.* Retrieved January 29, 2009, from http://www.ethemba.info/cms/

Brickell, E., Camenisch, J., & Chen, L. (2004). Direct anonymous attestation. In B. Pfitzmann & P. Liu (Eds.), *Proc. of the 11th ACM Conf. on Computer and Communications Security* (pp. 132-145). New York: ACM.

Bridges, L. J. (2003). Trust, attachment, and relatedness. In M. H. Bornstein & L. Davidson (Eds.), *Well-being: Positive development across the life course. Crosscurrents in contemporary psychology* (pp. 177-189). Mahwah, NJ: Lawrence Erlbaum Associates.

Brockmann, D., & Hufnagel, L. (2006). The scaling laws of human travel. *Nature, 439,* 462–465. doi:10.1038/nature04292

Buchegger, S., & Boudec, J. V. (2004). A Robust Reputation System for Peer-to-Peer and Mobile Ad-hoc Networks. In *Proceedings of P2PEcon 2004.*

Buchegger, S., & Le Boudec, J. (2002). Performance Analysis of the CONFIDANT Protocol: Cooperation of Nodes — Fairness in Dynamic Ad-hoc Networks. In *Proceedings of the IEEE/ACM Symposium on Mobile Ad Hoc Networking and Computing* (pp. 226-236).

Buchegger, S., & Le Boudec, J. Y. (2005). Self-policing mobile ad hoc networks by reputation systems. *Communications Magazine, 43*(7), 101–107. doi:10.1109/MCOM.2005.1470831

Buiati, F., Puttini, R. S., De Sousa, R. T., Jr., Abbas, C. J. B., & Garcia-Villalba, L. J. (2004). Authentication and Autoconfiguration for MANET Nodes. In *Proceedings of Embedded and Ubiquitous Computing EUC 2004,* Aizu-Wakamatsu, Japan (pp. 41-52). Berlin, Germany: Springer.

Bunker, D., Kautz, K., & Nguyen, A. L. T. (2006). The Role of Value Compatibility in Information Technology Adoption. In B. Donnellan, T. J. Larsen, L. Levine, & J. I. DeGross (Eds.), *The Transfer and Diffusion of Information Technology for Organizational Resilience, IFIP vol. 206* (pp. 53-70). Berlin, Germany: Springer.

Burn, M., Marshall, P., & Wild, M. (1999). Managing Changes in the Virtual Organisation. In *Proceedings of the Seventh European Conference on Information Systems* (pp. 40-54).

Burrows, M., Abadi, M., & Needham, R. M. (1990). A Logic of Authentication. *ACM Transactions on Computer Systems, 8*(1), 18–36.doi:doi:10.1145/77648.77649

Buskens, V. (2002). *Social Networks and Trust, Theory and Decision Library, Series C, Game Theory, Mathematical Programming, and Operations Research.* London: Kluwer Academic Publishers.

Buzzelli, C. A. (1988). The development of trust in children's relations with peers. *Child Study Journal, 18,* 33–46.

CA/Browser Forum. (2007). *Guidelines for the Issuance and Management of Extended Validation Certificates* (Technical Report). Retrieved April 25, 2009, from http://cabforum.org/ EV_Certificate_Guidelines.pdf

Cahill, V., Gray, E., Seigneur, J., Jensen, C., Chen, Y., & Shand, B. (2003). Using Trust for Secure Collaboration in Uncertain Environments. *IEEE Pervasive Computing Mobile and Ubiquitous Computing, 2*(3), 52–61.

Calcutt, D. (1990). *British House of Commons, Committee on Privacy and Related Matters* (Report of the Committee on Privacy and Related Matters, Cm 1102). London.

Callas, J., Donnerhacke, L., Finney, H., Shaw, D., & Thayer, R. (2007). *OpenPGP Message Format* (RFC 4880). Retrieved from http://tools.ietf.org/html/rfc4880

Camarihna-Matos, L. M., & Afsarmanesh, H. (2003). Elements of a VE Infrastructure. *Journal of Computers in Industry, 51*(2), 139–163. doi:10.1016/S0166-3615(03)00033-2

Camenisch, J. (2004). Better Privacy for Trusted Computing Platforms. In *Proc. of the 9th European Symposium On Research in Computer Security (ESORICS 2004)* (pp. 73-88). Berlin, Germany: Springer-Verlag.

Camerer, C. (2003). *Behavioral Game Theory: Experiments in Strategic Interaction.* Princeton, NJ: Princeton University Press.

Camp, L. J. (2003). Design for Trust. In R. Falcone (Ed.), *Trust, Reputation and Security: Theories and Practice* (pp. 15-29). Berlin, Germany: Springer-Verlag.

Camp, T., & Boleng, J. (2002). A survey of mobility models for ad hoc network research. *Wireless Communications and Mobile Computing*, 2(5), 483–502. doi:10.1002/wcm.72

Campbell, R., Al-Muhtadi, J., Nadldurg, P., Sampemane, G., & Mickunas, M. (2002). Towards Security and Privacy for Pervasive Computing. In *Proceedings of the ISSS*, Tokyo, Japan (pp. 1-15).

Capkuny, S., Buttyan, L., & Hubaux, J. (2003). Self-organized Public-Key Management for Mobile Ad Hoc Networks. *IEEE Transactions on Mobile Computing*, 2(1).

Capra, L. (2004). Engineering human trust in mobile system collaborations. In *Proceedings of the 12th International Symposium on Foundations of Software Engineering* (pp. 107-116).

Caronni, G. (2000). Walking the Web of Trust. In *Proceedings of the 9th IEEE International Workshops on Enabling Technologies* (pp. 153-158).

Castelfranchi, C., & Falcone, R. (1998). Principles of Trust for MAS: Cognitive Anatomy, Social Importance and Quantification. In Y. Demazeau (Ed.), *Proc. of the 3rd Intl. Conf. on Multi-Agent Systems (ICMAS'98)* (pp. 72-79). Washington, DC: IEEE.

CCRA. (1999). *Common criteria for information technology security evaluation version 2.1* (Technical Report). Retrieved April 25, 2009, from http://www.commoncriteriaportal.org/ thecc.html

Chadwick, D. W., & Otenko, A. (2002). The PERMIS X.509 role based privilege management infrastructure. In *Proceedings of the Seventh ACM Symposium on Access Control Models and Technologies (SACMAT 2002)* (pp. 135-140). New York: ACM Press.

Chandrasekaran, B., Josephson, J., & Benjamins, V. (1999). What are ontologies, and why do we need them? *IEEE Intelligent Systems and Applications*, 14, 20–26. doi:10.1109/5254.747902

Chang, B. E., Crary, K., DeLap, M., Harper, R., Liszka, J., Murphy, T., & Pfenning, F. (2002). Trustless Grid Computing in ConCert. In *Proceedings of the Third International Workshop on Grid Computing* (LNCS 2536, pp. 112-125). Berlin, Germany: Springer.

Chang, H., & Atallah, M. J. (2001). Protecting Software Code by Guards. In . *Proceedings of the Digital Rights Management Workshop*, 2320, 160–175.

Chaum, D. (1985). Security without Identification: Transaction Systems to make Big Brother Obsolete. *Communications of the ACM*, 28(10), 1030–1044. doi:10.1145/4372.4373

Checkland, P. (2000). Soft Systems Methodology: A Thirty Year Retrospective. *Systems Research and Behavioral Science*, 17, 11–58. doi:10.1002/1099-1743(200011)17:1+<::AID-SRES374>3.0.CO;2-O

Checkland, P., & Scholes, J. (1990). *Soft Systems Methodology in Action*. Chichester, UK: John Wiley.

Chellappa, R. K., & Pavlou, P. A. (2002). Perceived information security, financial liability, and consumer trust in electronic commerce transactions. *Journal of Logistics Information Management*, 15(5/6), 358–368. doi:10.1108/09576050210447046

Chen, G., & Kotz, D. (2000). *A Survey of Context-Aware Mobile Computing Research* (Tech. Rep. Dartmouth Computer Science Technical Report TR2000-381).

Chen, L., Landfermann, R., Löhr, H., Rohe, M., Sadeghi, A.-R., Stüble, Ch., & Görtz, H. (2006). A protocol for property-based attestation. In *Proceedings of the first ACM workshop on Scalable trusted computing (STC '06)* (pp. 7-16). New York: ACM.

Chen, M., & Singh, J. (2001). Computing and using reputations for internet ratings. In *EC '01: Proceedings of the 3rd ACM conference on Electronic Commerce* (pp. 154-162). New York: ACM Press.

Chen, P.-M. (2000). A visible watermarking mechanism using a statistic approach. In *Proceedings of 5th International Conference on Signal Processing (WCCC-ICSP 2000)* (Vol. 2, pp. 910-913).

Chen, R., & Yeager, W. (2001). *Poblano – A Distributed Trust Model for Peer to Peer Networks. Sun Microsystems.* Retrieved May, 2008, from http://gnunet.org/papers/jxtatrust.pdf

Chen, Z. (2000). *Java Card Technology for Smart Cards: Architecture and Programmer's Guide.* Reading, MA: Addison-Wesley Longman Publishing Co., Inc.

Cheshire, S., Aboba, B., & Guttman, E. (2004). *IETF Internet Draft – Dynamic Configuration of IPv4 Link-Local Addresses.* Fremont, CA: IETF.

Cho, C. H., Cheon, H. J., & Kang, J. (2006). Online Shopping Hesitation. *Cyberpsychology & Behavior, 9*(3), 261–274. doi:10.1089/cpb.2006.9.261

Chopra, K., & Wallace, W. (2003). Trust in Electronic Environments. In *Proceedings of the 36th Annual Hawaii International Conference on System Sciences* (pp. 331.1). Washington, DC: IEEE Computer Society.

Christensen, E., Curbera, F., Meredith, G., & Weerawarana, S. (2001). *Web Services Description Language (WSDL) 1.1.* Retrieved March 30, 2009, from http://www.w3.org/TR/wsdl

Chu, Y.-H., Feigenbaum, J., LaMacchia, B., Resnick, P., & Strauss, M. (1997). REFEREE: Trust management for Web applications. *Computer Networks and ISDN Systems, 29*(8-13), 953-964.

Chun, B., & Bavier, A. (2004). Decentralized Trust Management and Accountability in Federated Systems. In *Proceedings of the 37th Hawaii International Conference of System Sciences Vol. 9* (90279a).

Chun, Y., Qin, L., Yong, L., & Meilin, S. (2000). Routing Protocols Overview and Design Issues for Self-Organized Network. In *Proceedings of 2000 IEEE International Conference on Communication Technology ICCT 2000* (pp. 1298-1303). Washington, DC: IEEE.

Cimatti, A., Clarke, E., Giunchiglia, E., Giunchiglia, F., Pistore, M., Roveri, M., et al. (2002). NuSMV Version 2: An OpenSource Tool for Symbolic Model Checking. In K. Brinksma & L. Guldstrand (Eds.), *Proc. of the 14th Intl. Conf. on Computer-Aided Verification (CAV 2002)* (pp. 359-364). Berlin, Germany: Springer-Verlag.

Clark, D. (1988). The Design Philosophy of the DARPA Internet Protocols. *ACM Computer Communication Reviews, 18*, 106–114. doi:10.1145/52325.52336

Clausen, T., & Jacquet, P. (2003). *IETF RFC 3626 – Optimized Link State Routing Protocol (OLSR).* Fremont, CA: IETF.

CMU's CERT. (2009). *CERT Statistics.* Retrieved April 25, 2009, from http://www.cert.org/stats/

Cofta, P. (2007). *Trust, Complexity and Control: Confidence in a Convergent World.* Indianapolis, IN: Wiley.

Cofta, P. (2008) Confidence-compensating privacy protection. In *Proc. of PST2008, The Sixth Annual Conference on Privacy, Security and Trust*, Canada.

Cofta, P. (2009). Towards a better citizen identification system. *FIDIS Journal.*

Cohen, M. S., Parasuraman, R., & Freeman, J. (1999). *Trust in decision aids: A model and its training implications* (Tech. Report USA ATCOM TR 97-D-4). Arlington, VA: Cognitive Technologies.

Coleman, J. S. (1990). *Foundations of social theory.* Cambridge, MA: Harvard University Press.

Collberg, C. S., & Thomborson, C. (1999). Software watermarking: models and dynamic embeddings. In *Proceeding of ACM SIGPLAN-SIGACT Symposium on Principles of Programming Languages (POPL99)*, San Antonio, TX (pp. 311-324).

Colombo, M., Martinelli, F., Mori, P., & Vaccarelli, A. (2007). Extending the Globus Architecture with Role-based Trust Management. In *Proceedings of the 11th International conference on Computer Aided Systems Theory (Eurocast'07)* (LNCS 4739, pp. 448-456). Berlin, Germany: Springer.

Colombo, M., Martinelli, F., Mori, P., Petrocchi, M., & Vaccarelli, A. (2007). Fine Grained Access Control with Trust and Reputation Management for Globus. In *Proceedings of the OTM International Conferences* (LNCS 4804, pp. 1050-1515). Berin, Germany: Springer.

Coltue, D., & Bolon, P. (1999). Watermarking by histogram specification. In *Proceeding of SPIE Electronic Imaging'99, Security and Watermarking of Multimedia Contents*, San Jose (pp. 252-263).

Common Criteria. (2007). *Common criteria (CC) for information technology security evaluation, Rev 3.1.* Retrieved April 2, 2009, from http://www.commoncriteriaportal.org/

Common Criteria. (2009). *Official CC/CEM versions - The Common Criteria Portal*. Retrieved February 4, 2009, from http://www.commoncriteriaportal.org/thecc.html

Connected Device Configuration (CDC). *Sun Microsystems*. (n.d.). Retrieved August 2008, from http://java.sun.com/javame/technology/cdc/index.jsp

Consumer Reports. (2008). *Why don't you need an extended warranty.* Retrieved August 20, 2008, from http://www.consumerreports.org/cro/money/news/november-2006/why-you-dont-need-an-extended-warranty-11-06/overview/extended-warranty-11-06.htm

COPP. (2006). *Using Certified Output Protection Protocol*. Retrieved February 28, 2009, from http://msdn2.microsoft.com/en-us/library/Aa468617.aspx

Corbitt, B., Thanasankit, T., & Yi, H. (2003). Trust and e-commerce: a study of consumer perceptions. *Electronic Commerce Research and Applications, 2*, 203–215. doi:10.1016/S1567-4223(03)00024-3

Cornelli, F., Damiani, E., Capitani, S., & Paraboschi, S. (2002). Choosing Reputable Servants in a P2P Network. In *Proceedings of the 11th World Wide Web Conference* (pp. 376-386).

Corritore, C. L., Kracher, B., & Wiedenbeck, S. (2003). On-line trust: concepts, evolving themes, a model. *International Journal of Human-Computer Studies, 58*(6), 737–758. doi:10.1016/S1071-5819(03)00041-7

Corson, S., & Marker, J. (1999). *IETF RFC 2501 – Mobile Ad Hoc Networking (MANET): Routing Protocol Performance Issues and Evaluation Consideration.* Fremont, CA: IETF.

COSoDIS. (2009). *Contract-Oriented Software Development for Internet Services*. Retrieved January 28, 2009, from http://www.ifi.uio.no/cosodis/

Costa, P. T., & McCrae, R. R. (1992). *Revised NEO Personality Inventory and NEW Five-Factor Inventory Professional Manual*. Odessa, FL: Psychological Assessment Resources, Inc.

Couch, L. L., & Warren, H. J. (1997). Measuring levels of trust. *Journal of Research in Personality, 31*, 319–336. doi:10.1006/jrpe.1997.2186

Covington, M., Long, W., Srinivasan, S., Dey, A., Ahamad, M., & Abowd, D. G. (2001). Securing Context-Aware Applications Using Environments Roles. In *Proceedings of the sixth ACM Symposium on Access Controls Models and Technologies* (pp. 10-20).

Cowan, C., Wagle, F., Calton, P., Beattie, S., & Walpole, J. (2000). *Buffer overflows: attacks and defenses for the vulnerability of the decade*. Paper presented at DARPA Information Survivability Conference and Exposition, DISCEX '00.

Cox, B. (1999). Security, Privacy remain top consumer concerns. *InternetNews.com* [On-line], Retrieved from http://www.internetnews.com/ec-news/article.php/4_95031

Cox, I. J., Miller, M. L., & Bloom, J. A. (2002). *Digital Watermarking*. San Francisco: Morgan-Kaufmann.

Cranor, L., & Wenning, R. (2002). *Platform for Privacy Preferences (P3P) Project*. Retrieved March 4, 2009, from http://www.w3.org/P3P/

Cranor, L., Reagle, J., & Ackerman, S. M. (1999). *Beyond Concern: Understanding net USERS' attitudes about online privacy* (Technical report TR 99.4.3). AT&T Labs Research.

Dahill, B., Sanzgiri, K., Levine, B. N., Shields, C., & Royer, E. (2002). A Secure Routing Protocol for Ad Hoc Networks. In *Proceedings of the 2002 IEEE International Conference on Network Protocols INCP 2002*. Washington, DC: IEEE.

Damiani, E., di Vimercati, S. D. C., Paraboschi, S., Samarati, P., & Violante, F. (2002). A reputation based approach for choosing reliable resources in PeertoPeer networks. In *Proceedings of ACM CCS'02* (pp. 207-216).

Danielson, A. J., & Holm, H. J. (2007). Do you trust you brethren? *Journal of Economic Behavior & Organization, 62*, 255–271. doi:10.1016/j.jebo.2004.10.011

Davis, F. D. (1989). Perceived usefulness, perceived ease of use, and user acceptance of information technology. *MIS Quarterly, 13*(3), 319–340. doi:10.2307/249008

Davis, J. H., Schoorman, F. D., Mayer, R. C., & Tan, H. H. (2000). The trusted general manager and business unit performance: Empirical evidence of a competitive advantage. *Strategic Management Journal, 21*, 563–576. doi:10.1002/(SICI)1097-0266(200005)21:5<563::AID-SMJ99>3.0.CO;2-0

de Laat, C., Gross, G., Gommans, L., Vollbrecht, J., & Spence, D. (2000). Generic AAA Architecture. *IETF Network Working Group. RFC 2903*. Retrieved February 20, 2009, from http://tools.ietf.org/html/rfc2903

Deering, S., Estrin, D., Farinacci, D., Jacobson, V., Liu, C.-G., & Wei, L. (1994). An Architecture for Wide Area Multicast Routing. In *Proceedings of the ACM SIGCOMM* (pp. 126-135).

Dell. (2006). Enhancing IT Security with Trusted Computing Group standards. *Dell Power Solutions.* Retrieved from http://www.dell.com/downloads/global/vectors/2007_tcgs.pdf

Dellarocas, C. (2000). Immunizing online reputation reporting systems against unfair ratings and discriminatory behavior. In *Proceedings of the 2nd ACM conference on Electronic commerce* (pp. 150 - 157).

Demchenko, Y., Gommans, L., de Laat, C., & Oudenaarde, B. (2005). Web services and Grid Security Vulnerabilities and Threat Analysis and Model. In *Proc. of the 6th IEEE/ACM Intl. Workshop on Grid Computing* (pp. 262-267). Washington, DC: IEEE.

DeNeve, K., & Cooper, H. (1998). The happy personality: A meta-analysis of 137 personality traits and subjective well-being. *Psychological Bulletin, 124*, 197–229. doi:10.1037/0033-2909.124.2.197

Dennett, D. C. (1989). *The Intentional Stance.* Cambridge, MA: Bradford Books.

Department of Defense. (1985, December 26). *Department of Defense Trusted Computer System Evaluation Criteria* (DoD 5200.28-STD).

Deutsch, M. (1958). Trust and suspicion. *The Journal of Conflict Resolution, 2*, 265–279. doi:10.1177/002200275800200401

Deutsch, M. (1960). Trust, trustworthiness, and the F Scale. *Journal of Abnormal and Social Psychology, 61*(1), 138–140. doi:10.1037/h0046501

Deutsch, M. (1962). Cooperation and trust: Some theoretical notes. In M. R. Jones (Ed.), *Nebraska Symposium on Motivation* (pp. 275-319). Lincoln, NE: University of Nebraska Press.

Deutsch, M. (1973). *The resolution of conflict.* New Haven, CT: Yale University Press.

Dey, A. K. (2001). Understanding and using context. *Personal and Ubiquitous Computing Journal, 5*(1), 4-7. Retrieved February 23, 2009, from http://www.cc.gatech.edu/fce/ctk/pubs/PeTe5-1.pdf

Dey, A. K., & Abowd, G. D. (2000). Towards a better understanding of context and context-awareness. The *Proceedings of the CHI 2000 Workshop on the What, Who, when, and How of Context-Awareness*, The Hague, The Netherlands. Retrieved January 8, 2009, from ftp://ftp.cc.gatech.edu/pub/gvu/tr/1999/92-22.pdf

Dierks, T., & Allen, C. (1999). *RFC 2246 - The TLS Protocol (version 1.0).*

Diffie, W., & Hellman, W. E. (1976). New directions in cryptography. *IEEE Transactions on Information Theory, IT-22*, 644–654. doi:10.1109/TIT.1976.1055638

Dillman, D. A. (1978). *Mail and Telephone Surveys: The Total Design Method.* New York, NY: John Wiley.

Dimitrakos, T. (2001). System Models, e-Risk and e-Trust. In *Proceedings of the First IFIP Conference on*

E-Commerce, E-Business, E-Government: Towards The E-Society: E-Commerce, E-Business, and E-Government (I3E 2001) (pp. 45-58). Amsterdam: Kluwer.

Dimmock, N., Bacon, J., Ingram, D., & Moody, k. (2005). Risk Models for Trust-Based Access Control (TBAC). In *Proceeding of the 3rd Annual Conference on Trust Management,* France (pp. 364-371).

Dimmock, N., Belokosztolszki, A., Eyers, D., Bacon, J., & Moody, K. (2004). Using trust and risk in role-based access control policies. In *Proceedings of the ninth ACM symposium on Access control models and technologies* (pp. 156-162).

Dionysiou, I. (2006). *Dynamic and Composable Trust for Indirect Interactions.* Unpublished doctoral dissertation, Department of Electrical Engineering and Computer Science, Washington State University, Pullman.

Dionysiou, I. (2008). *Hestia++ Conceptual Framework* (Technical Report). University of Nicosia, Nicosia.

Dionysiou, I., Bakken, D., Hauser, D., & Frincke, D. (2008, July). Formalizing end-to-end context-aware trust relation ships in collaborative activities. In *Proceedings of the International Conference on Security and Cryptography (SECRYPT 2008), Special Session on Trust,* Porto, Portugal (pp. 546-553).

Dionysiou, I., Frincke, D., Bakken, D., & Hauser, C. (2007, October). An approach to trust management challenges for critical infrastructures. In *Proceedings of the 2nd International Workshop on Critical Information Infrastructures Security (CRITIS07),* Malaga, Spain (LNCS 5141, pp. 173-184). Berlin, Germany: Springer.

Dirks, K. T. (1999). The effects of interpersonal trust on work group performance. *The Journal of Applied Psychology, 84,* 445–455. doi:10.1037/0021-9010.84.3.445

Dirks, K. T., & Ferrin, D. L. (2001). The role of trust in organizational settings. *Organization Science, 12,* 450–467. doi:10.1287/orsc.12.4.450.10640

Donato, D., Paniccia, M., Selis, M., Castillo, C., Cortese, G., & Leonardi, S. (2007). *New metrics for reputation Management in P2P networks.* Paper presented at the 3rd International Workshop on Adversarial Information retrieval on the web.

Doney, P. M., Cannon, J. P., & Mullen, M. R. (1998). Understanding the influence of national culture on the development of trust. *Academy of Management Review, 23,* 601–620. doi:10.2307/259297

Doorn, L., Ballintijn, G., & Arbaugh, W. (2001). *Signed Executables for Linux* (Technical Report CS-TR-4256). University of Maryland.

Douceur, J. R. (2002). The sybil attack. In P. Druschel, F. Kaashoek, & A. Rowstron (Eds.), *Proc. of the First International Workshop on Peer-to-Peer Systems (IP-TPS 2002)* (pp. 251-260). Berlin, Germany: Springer-Verlag.

DRM. (2009). *Digital Rights Management.* Retrieved February 28, 2009, from http://en.wikipedia.org/wiki/Digital_rights_management

Droms, R. (1997). *IETF RFC 2131 – Dynamic Host Configuration Protocol.* IETF.

Dulay, N., Lupu, E., Sloman, M., & Damianou, N. (2002). A Policy Deployment Model for the Ponder Language. In G. Pavlou, N. Anerousis, & A. Liotta (Eds.), *Proc. of the IEEE/IFIP Intl. Symposium on Integrated Network Management (IM'2001)* (pp. 529-543). Washington, DC: IEEE.

Duma, C., Shahmehri, N., & Caronni, G. (2005). Dynamic Trust Metrics for Peer-to-Peer Systems. In *Proc. of the 2nd IEEE Workshop on P2P Data Management, Security and Trust.*

Dunn, J. R., & Schweitzer, M. E. (2005). Feeling and believing: the influence of emotion on trust. *Journal of Personality and Social Psychology, 88*(5), 736–748. doi:10.1037/0022-3514.88.5.736

Dutton, P. (2000). Trust Issues in E-Commerce. In *Proceedings of the 6th Australasian Women in Computing Workshop,* Griffith University (pp. 15-26).

DVB-CPCM. (2007). *Digital Video Broadcasting Content Protection & Copy Management (DVB-CPCM)* (DVB Document A094 Rev. 1).

Dwyer, N., & Cofta, P. (2008). Understanding the grounds to trust: Game as a cultural probe. In *Proceedings of the First International Workshop on Web 2.0 Trust*, Trondheim, Norway.

Dwyer, N., & Cofta, P. (2008). *Understanding the grounds to trust: game as a cultural probe*. Paper presented at Web 2.0 Trust (W2Trust), Trondheim, Norway in conjunction with IFIPTM 2008.

Dzindolet, M. T., Peterson, S. A., Pomranky, R. A., Pierce, L. G., & Beck, H. P. (2003). The role of trust in automation reliance. *International Journal of Human-Computer Studies, 58*(6), 697–718. doi:10.1016/S1071-5819(03)00038-7

Eastlake, D., & Hansen, T. (2006). *US Secure Hash Algorithms (SHA and HMAC-SHA)* (RFC 4634). Retrieved April 25, 2009, from http://www.ietf.org/rfc/rfc4634.txt

Edwards, A. M., & Phillips, R. A. (2007). Revisiting Lévy flight search patterns of wandering albatrosses, bumblebees and deer. *Nature, 449*, 1044–1048. doi:10.1038/nature06199

EGEE. (2004). The Global Security Architecture: For Web and Legacy Services. In *EU Deliverable DJRA3.1.*

Egger, F. N. (2000). *From Interactions to Transactions: Designing the Trust Experience for Business-to-Consumer Electronic Commerce*. Unpublished, doctoral dissertation, Eindhoven University of Technology, The Netherlands.

Egger, F. N. (2000). Towards a Model of Trust for E-Commerce System Design. In *Proceedings of the CHI 2000 Workshop Designing Interactive Systems for 1-to-1 E-commerce*, Zurich.

Einwiller, S., & Will, M. (2001). The role of reputation to engender trust in electronic markets. In *Proceedings of the Fifth International Conference on Corporate Reputation, Identity, and Competitiveness*, Paris. Retrieved October 31, 2002, from http://www.communicationsmgt.org/modules/pub/view.php/communicationsmgt-11

Einwiller, S., Geissler, U., & Will, M. (2000). Engendering trust in Internet businesses using elements of corporate branding. In H.M. Chung (Ed.), *Proceedings of the 2000 Americas Conference on Information Systems (AMCIS)* (pp. 33-739). Long Beach, CA: AIS.

Ekberg, J.-E. Asokan, N., Kostiainen, K., & Rantala, A. (2008A). *On-Board Credentials Platform Design and Implementation* (Nokia Research Center Technical Report NRC-TR-2008-01). Retrieved April 27, 2009, from http://research.nokia.com/files/NRCTR2008001.pdf

Ekberg, J.-E., & Kylänpää, M. (2007). *Mobile Trusted Module (MTM) - an introduction* (Nokia Research Center, Technical report NRC-2007-015). Retrieved April 27, 2009, from http://research.nokia.com/

Ekberg, J.-E., Asokan, N., Kostiainen, K., & Rantala, A. (2008). Scheduling execution of credentials in constrained secure environments. In *Proceedings of the 3rd ACM workshop on Scalable trusted computing*. Folding@ home. (2007). *The folding@home project*. Retrieved December 30, 2008, from http://folding.stanford.edu/

Ekberg, J.-E., Asokan, N., Kostiainen, K., & Rantala, A. (2008B). Scheduling execution of credentials in constrained secure environments. In *Proceedings of the 3rd ACM Workshop on Scalable Trusted Computing.*

Elmasri, R., & Navathe, S. (2000). *Fundamentals of Database Systems*. Reading, MA: Addison-Wesley Longman, Inc.

eMarketer. (2007). *Canada B2C E-Commerce*. Mindbranch. Retreived December 10, 2008, from http://www.mindbranch.com/Canada-B2C-Commerce-R203-462/

Emerson, E. A. (1996). Model Checking and the Mu-calculus. In N. Immerman & P. G. Kolaitis (Eds.), *Descriptive Complexity and Finite Models* (pp. 185-214). Providence. RI: American Mathematical Society.

English, C., Nixon, P., Terzis, S., McGettrick, A., & Lowe, H. (2002). Dynamic Trust Models for Ubiquitous Computing Environments. In *Proceedings of the UBICOMP2002-Workshop on Security in Ubiquitous Computing*, Goteborg, Sweden.

Erikson, E. H. (1963). *Childhood and society* (2nd ed.). New York: Norton.

Ernst & Young. (2001). *E-security and privacy: The role of web seals on the Internet.* Retrieved from http://www.ey.com/global/vault.nsf/international/eSecurityandPrivacy/$file/eSecurity&Privacylowreslocked.pdf

Escrow. (2009). Retrieved from http://www.escrow.com/

European Comission. (2008). *Communication from the Commission to the European Parliament, the Council, the European Economic and Social Committee and the Committee of the Regions - Communication on future networks and the internet.* Retrieved December 23, 2008, from http://eur-lex.europa.eu/LexUriServ/LexUriServ.do?uri=CELEX:52008DC0594:EN:NOT.

European Commission. (2008). *The Future of the Internet. A Compendium of European Projects on ICT Research Supported by the EU 7th Framework Programme for RTD.* Retrieved January 12, 2009, from http://ec.europa.eu/enterprise/newsroom/cf/document.cfm?doc_id=772

Evers, J. (2005). Microsoft's leaner approach to Vista security. *CNET News.* Retrieved from http://m.news.com/Microsofts+leaner+approach+to+Vista+security/2163-7355_3-5843808.html

FAA. (2007). 14 CFR Part 25, Special Conditions: Boeing model 787-8 airplane; systems and data networks security isolation or protection from unauthorized passenger domain systems access (Docket No. NM364 Special Conditions No. 250701SC). *Federal Register, 72*(71). Retrieved April 2, 2009, from http://edocket.access.gpo.gov/2007/pdf/E7-7065.pdf

FAA. (2007). 14 CFR Part 25, Special Conditions: Boeing model 787-8 airplane; systems and data networks security protection of airplane systems and data networks from unauthorized external access (Docket No. NM365 Special Conditions No. 250702SC). *Federal Register, 72*(72). Retrieved April 2, 2009, from http://edocket.access.gpo.gov/2007/pdf/07-1838.pdf

FAA. (2008). *FAA policy for passive-only RFID devices.* Retrieved April 2, 2009, from http://rgl.faa.gov/Regulatory and Guidance Library/rgPolicy.nsf/0/495367dd1bd773e18625715400718e2e Garfinkel, S., & Rosenberg, B. (2005). *RFID Applications, Security, and Privacy.* Reading, MA: Addison-Wesley.

Faden, G. (2006). *Solaris Trusted Extensions: An architectural overview.* Sun Microsystems. Retrieved April 25, 2009, from http://www.opensolaris.org/os/community/security/projects/tx/ TrustedExtensions-Arch.pdf

Falcone, R. (Ed.). (2006). *Ninth Int. Workshop on Trust in Agent Societies (TRUST), Proc. of Fifth Int. Conf. on Autonomous Agents and Multiagent Systems AAMAS-06,* Hakodate, Japan.

Falk, R., Kohlmayer, F., Koepf, A., & Li, M. (2008). High-assured Avionics multi-domain processing system. In *Proceedings of the IEEE RFID conference* (pp. 43-50). Las Vegas, NV: IEEE Press.

Farid, H. (2006). Exposing digital forgeries in scientific images. In *Proceeding of ACM MM&Sec'06*, Geneva, Switzerland (pp. 29–36).

Federal Trade Commission. (2000). *U.S. Implementation of the OECD E-Commerce Guidelines Remarks on TACD 2000 Meeting.* Retrieved March 28, 2009, from http://www.ftc.gov/speeches/thompson/thomtacdremarks.shtm

Feeney, L., Ahlgren, B., & Westerlund, A. (2001). Spontaneous Networking: an Application-Oriented Approach to Ad Hoc Networking. *IEEE Communications Magazine, 39*(6). doi:10.1109/35.925687

Ferraiolo, D. F., Sandhu, R., Gavrila, S., Kuhn, D. R., & Chandramouli, R. (2001). Proposed NIST Standard for Role-Based Access Control. *ACM Transactions on Information and System Security, 4*(3), 224–274. doi:doi:10.1145/501978.501980

Ferrin, D. L., Dirks, K. T., & Shah, P. P. (2006). Direct and indirect effects of third-party relationships on interpersonal trust. *The Journal of Applied Psychology, 91*, 870–883. doi:10.1037/0021-9010.91.4.870

Feruzan, A. (2007). *Context Modeling and Reasoning using Ontologies*. Retrieved February 15, 2009, from http://www.ponnuki.de/cmaruo/cmaruo.pdf

Fichtinger, B., Herrmann, E., Kuntze, N., & Schmidt, A. U. (2008). Trusted Infrastructures for Identities. In R. Grimm & B. Hass (Eds.), *Proc. of the 5th Intl. Workshop for Technical, Economic and Legal Aspects of Business Models for Virtual Goods*. Hauppauge, NY: Nova Publishers.

Fielding, R. T. (2000). *Architectural Styles and the Design of Network based Software Architectures*. Retrieved July 2008, from http://www.ics.uci.edu/~fielding/pubs/dissertation/fielding_dissertation_2up.pdf orrest, S., Hofmeyr, S., Somaya, A., & Longstaff, T. (1996) A sense of for self UNIX processes. In *Proceedings of the 1996 Symposium on Security and Privacy*.

Fitzgerald, S., Foster, I., Kesselman, C., von Laszewski, G., Smith, W., & Tuecke, S. (1997). A Directory Service for Configuring High-Performance Distributed Computations. In *Proceedings of the Sixth IEEE Symposium on High-Performance Distributed Computing (HPDC 1997)* (pp. 365-375). Washington, DC: IEEE Computer Society.

Floyd, S., & Fal, K. (1999). Promoting the use of end-to-end congestion control in the internet. *IEEE/ACM Transactions on Networking, 7*, 458-472.

Floyd, S., & Paxson, V. (2001). Difficulties in Simulating the Internet. *IEEE/ACM Transactions on Networking, 9*, 392-403.

Floyd, S., Jacobson, V., McCanne, S., Liu, C.-G., & Zhang, L. (1995). A Reliable Multicast Framework for Light-weight Sessions and Application Level Framing. In *Proceedings of the ACM SIGCOMM* (pp. 342-356).

Fogg, B., Marshall, J., Kameda, T., Solomon, J., Rangnekar, A., Boyd, J., et al. (2001). Web credibility research: A method for online experiments and early study results. In *CHI 2001 Conference on Human Factors in Computing Systems* (pp. 293-294). New York: Association for Computing Machinery.

Forrester Research. (2007). *Total Online Sales Expected To Hit $259 Billion In 2007 Washington*. Retreived January 5, 2009, from http://www.forrester.com/ER/Press/Release/0,1769,1145,00.html

Foster, I. (2005). Globus Toolkit version 4: Software for Service Oriented Systems. In *Proceedings of the IFIP International Conference on Network and Parallel Computing* (LNCS 3779, pp. 2-13). Berlin, Germany: Springer.

Foster, I., & Kesselman, C. (2003). *The Grid: Blue Print for a New Computing Infrastructure*. San Francisco, CA: Morgan Kaufmann Publishers.

Foster, I., Kesselman, C., & Tuecke, S. (2001). The Anatomy of the Grid: Enabling Scalable Virtual Organizations. *The International Journal of Supercomputer Applications, 15*(3), 1–4.

Foster, I., Kishimoto, H., Savva, A., Berry, D., Djaoui, A., Grimshaw, A., et al. (2006). *The Open Grid Service Architecture (OGSA), Version 1.5. Open Grid Forum Document Series: GFD-I.080*. Retrieved March 30, 2009, from http://www.ogf.org/documents/GFD.80.pdf

Fowler, H. J., & Murphy, J. W. (1996). Network Management Considerations for Interworking ATM Networks with Non-ATM Services. *IEEE Communications Magazine, 34*(6), 102–106. doi:10.1109/35.506816

Fridrich, J., Soukal, D., & Lukas, J. (2003). Detection of copy-move forgery in digital images. In *Proceedings of 2003 Digital Forensic Research Workshop (2003)*, Cleveland, OH, USA. Retrieved from http://www.ws.binghamton.edu/fridrich/Research/copymove.pdf

Friedman, E. J., & Resnick, P. (2001). The social cost of cheap pseudonyms. *Journal of Economics & Management Strategy, 10*, 173–199. doi:10.1162/105864001300122476

F-Secure. (2007). *F-Secure reports amount of malware grew by 100% during 2007*. Retrieved April 25, 2009, from http://www.f-secure.com/en_EMEA/about-us/pressroom/news/2007/ fs_news_20071204_1_eng.html

Fujihara, Y., Murayama, Y., & Yamaguchi, K. (2008). A user survey on the sense of security, Anshin. In S. Jajodia, P. Samarati, & S. Cimato (Eds.), *Proceedings of The Ifip Tc 11 23rd International Information Security Conference of IFIP International Federation for Information Processing* (pp. 699-703). New York, NY: Springer.

Fujihara, Y., Murayama, Y., & Yamaguchi, K. (2008, October). *User survey on the Anshin with civil servants for a local government* (in Japanese). Paper presented at Computer Security Symposium 2008, Okinawa, Japan.

Fukuyama, F. (1996). *Trust: The Social Virtues and the Creation of Prosperity*. Clearwater, FL: Touchstone Books.

Gaines, S. O., Panter, A. T., Lyde, M. D., Steers, W. N., Rusbult, C. E., Cox, C. L., & Wexler, M. O. (1997). Evaluating the circumplexity of interpersonal traits and the manifestation of interpersonal traits in interpersonal trust. *Journal of Personality and Social Psychology, 73*, 610–623. doi:10.1037/0022-3514.73.3.610

Gambetta, D. (1988). Can we trust trust? In D. Gambetta (Ed.), *Trust: Making and breaking cooperative relationships* (pp. 213-237). Cambridge, UK: Basil Blackwell.

Gamma, E., Helm, R., Johnson, R., & Vlissides, J. (1995). *Design Patterns: Elements of Reusable Object-Oriented Software*. Reading, MA: Addison Wesley.

Gang, L., Akansu, A. N., Ramkumar, M., & Xie, X. (2001). Online Music Protection and MP3 Compression. In *Proceedings Of International Symposium on Intelligent Multimedia, Video and Speech Processing* (pp. 13-16).

Garau, M. (2003). *The impact of avatar fidelity on social interaction in virtual environments*. Unpublished doctoral dissertation, Department of Computer Science, University College, London.

Garfinkel, T., Pfaff, B., Chow, J., Rosenblum, M., & Boneh, D. (2003). Terra A Virtual Machine-Based Platform for Trusted Computing. In *Proceedings of the SOSP'03*, Bolton Landing, NY, USA.

Garg, A., & Battiti, R. (2005). *WikiRep: Digital Reputations in Virtual Communities* (Technical Report). University of Trento, Italy.

Gaubatz, G., Kaps, J. P., Ozturk, E., & Sunar, B. (2005). State of the art in ultra-low power public key cryptography for wireless sensor networks. In *Proceedings of the 3rd International IEEE Pervasive computing and Communications Worskshops (PerCom)* (pp. 146-150). Washington, DC: IEEE Press.

Gefen, D. (2000). E-Commerce: the role of familiarity and trust. *International Journal of Management Science, 28*, 725–737.

Gefen, D., & Heart, T. (2006). On the need to include national culture as a central issue in e-commerce trust beliefs. *Journal of Global Information Management, 14*(4), 1–30.

Gefen, D., Karahanna, E., & Straub, D. W. (2003). Trust and TAM in online shopping: an integrated model. *MIS Quarterly, 27*(1), 51–90.

Gehlen, A. (1980). *Man in the Age of Technology* (P. Lipscomb, Trans.). New York: Columbia University Press.

Gehrmann, C., & Ståhl, P. (2006). *Mobile Platform security* (Ericsson review no 02). Retrieved April 27, 2009, from http://www.ericsson.com/ericsson/corpinfo/publications/review/2006_02/03.shtml

Gerck, E. (1998). Trust Points. In J. Feghhi, J. Feghhi, & P. Williams (Eds.), *Digital Certificates: Applied Internet Security* (pp. 194-195). Reading, MA: Addison-Wesley.

Gerling. (2009). Retrieved from http://www.gerling.de/

Giddens, A. (1984). *The Constitution of Society: Outline of the Theory of Structuration*. Cambridge, UK: Polity Press.

Giddens, A. (1988). *The Consequences of Modernity*. Cambridge, UK: Polity Press.

Gilson, L. (2003). Trust and the development of health care as a social institution. *Social Science & Medicine, 56*, 1453–1468. doi:10.1016/S0277-9536(02)00142-9

GIMPS. (2007). *The great internet mersenne prime search*. Retrieved December 30, 2008, from http://www.mersenne.org/prime.htm

Glanville, J. L., & Paxton, P. (2007). How do we learn to trust? A confirmatory tetrad analysis of the sources of the sources of generalized trust. *Social Psychology Quarterly, 70*, 230–242.

Globus Security Team. (2005). *Globus Toolkit Version 4 Grid Security Infrastructure: A Standards Perspective*.

Goldman, K., Perez, R., & Sailer, R. (2006). Linking Remote Attestation to Secure Tunnel Endpoints. In *Proceedings of the First ACM Workshop on Scalable Trusted Computing* (pp. 21-24).

Google. (2009). *Security and Permissions in Android*. Retrieved April 27, 2009, from http://code.google.com/android/devel/security.html

Goold, S. D. (2001). Trust and the ethics of health care institutions. *The Hastings Center Report, 31*(6), 26–33. doi:10.2307/3527779

Gorrieri, R., Rensink, A., & Zamboni, M. A. (2001). Action refinement. In J.A. Bergstra, P. DiSaia, A. Ponse, & S.A. Smolka (Eds.), *Handbook of Process Algebra* (pp. 1047-1147). Amsterdam: Elsevier.

Goudge, J., & Gilson, L. (2005). How can trust be investigated? Drawing lessons from past experience. *Social Science & Medicine, 61*, 1439–1451. doi:10.1016/j.socscimed.2004.11.071

Goyal, P., Lam, S., & Vin, H. M. (1997). Determining end-to-end delay bounds in heterogeneous networks. *Multimedia Systems, 5*, 157–163. doi:10.1007/s005300050052

Grabner-Krauter, S., & Kaluscha, E. A. (2003). Empirical Research in on-line trust: a review and critical assessment. *Human-Computer Studies, 58*, 783–812. doi:10.1016/S1071-5819(03)00043-0

Grandison, T. (2001). *Trust specification and analysis for internet applications*. Unpublished doctoral dissertation, Imperial College of Science Technology and Medicine, Department of Computing, London.

Grandison, T. (2003). *Trust Management for Internet Application*. Unpublished doctoral dissertation, Imperial College London.

Grandison, T. (2007). Conceptions of trust: Definition, constructs and models. In R. Song (Ed.), *Trust in E-Services: Technologies, Practices and Challenges* (pp. 1-28). Hershey, PA: Idea Group Inc.

Grandison, T., & Sloman, M. (2000). A Survey of Trust in Internet Applications. *IEEE Communications Surveys and Tutorials, 3*(4), 2–16. doi:10.1109/COMST.2000.5340804

Granovetter, M. (1985). Economic Action and Social Structure: The Problem of Embeddedness. *American Journal of Sociology, 91*, 481. doi:10.1086/228311

Greenleaf, E. A., & Lehmann, D. R. (1995). Reasons for substantial delay in consumer decision making. *The Journal of Consumer Research, 22*, 186–199. doi:10.1086/209444

Greenspan, R. (2002). *Trust is in the Details*. CyberAtlas. Retrieved from http://cyberatlas.internet.com/markets/retailing/article/0,6061_1369641,00.html

Grimes, R. (n.d.). *Authenticode*. Microsoft Technet. Retrieved April 25, 2009, from http://technet.microsoft.com/en-us/library/cc750035.aspx

Gruber, T. R. (1993). A translation approach to portable ontology specifications. *Knowledge Acquisition, 5*(2), 199–220. doi:doi:10.1006/knac.1993.1008

Gruhl, D., Lu, A., & Bender, W. (1996). Echo Hiding. In *Pre-Proceedings: Information Hiding*, Cambridge, UK (pp. 295-316).

Gruninger, M., & Lee, J. (2002). Ontology-Applications and Design. *Communications of the ACM, 45*(2), 39–65. doi:10.1145/503124.503146

GSM-03.20. (1997). *European Telecommunications Standards Institute, GSM Technical Specification GSM 03.20 (ETS 300 534): "Digital cellular telecommunication system (Phase 2): Security related network functions"*.

Gu, L., Ding, X., Deng, R. H., Xie, B., & Mei, H. (2008). Remote Attestation on Program Execution. In *Proceedings of the STC '08: the 2008 ACM workshop on Scalable Trusted Computing.*

Gu, L., Ding, X., Deng, R. H., Zou, Y., Xie, B., Shao, W., et al. (2008). Model-Driven Remote Attestation: Attesting Remote System from the Behavioral Aspect. In *Proceedings of the International Symposium on Trusted Computing (TrustCom 08).*

Guerrero, M., & Asokan, N. (2002). Securing Ad Hoc Routing Protocols. In *Proceedings of 2002 ACM Workshop on Wireless Security WiSe'2002.* New York: ACM.

Guha, R., Kumar, R., Raghavan, P., & Tomkins, A. (2004, May). *Propagation of Trust and Distrust.* Paper presented at the Thirteenth International World Wide Web Conference, New York, NY.

Gurses, E., & Akan, O. B. (2005). Multimedia communication in wireless sensor networks. *Annales des Télécommunications, 60*(7-8), 799–827.

Gurtman, M. B. (1992). Trust, distrust, and interpersonal problems: A circumplex analysis. *Journal of Personality and Social Psychology, 62*, 989–1002. doi:10.1037/0022-3514.62.6.989

Gutscher, A., Heesen, J., & Siemoneit, O. (2008). Possibilities and Limitations of Modeling Trust and Reptuation. In *Proceedings of the WSPI 2008.*

Guttman, J., Herzog, A., Millen, J., Monk, L., Ramsdell, J., Sheehy, J., et al. (2008). *Attestation: Evidence and Trust* (MITRE Technical Report, MTR080072). Bedford, MA: MITRE Corporation. Retrieved January 27, 2009, from http://www.mitre-corp.org/work/tech_papers/tech_papers_07/07_0186/07_0186.pdf

Haag, R. (1992). *Local Quantum Physics.* Berlin, Germany: Springer-Verlag.

Hair, J. F., Jr., Black, W. C., Babin, B. J., & Anderson, R. E. (2009). *Multivariate data analysis* (7th ed.). Upper Saddle River, NJ: Prentice Hall.

Haldar, V., & Franz, M. (2004). Symmetric behavior-based trust: a new paradigm for internet computing. In *Proceedings of the New Security Paradigms Workshop 2004,* Nova Scotia, Canada (pp. 79-84).

Haldar, V., Chandra, D., & Franz, M. (2004). Semantic remote attestation: A virtual machine directed approach to trusted computing. In *Proceedings of the USENIX Virtual Machine Research and Technology Symposium (VM '04)* (pp. 29-41). Berkley, CA: USENIX.

Haldar, V., Chandra, D., & Franz, M. (2004). Semantic Remote Attestation —A Virtual Machine directed approach to Trusted Computing. In *Proceedings of the Third virtual Machine Research and Technology Symposium (VM '04). USENIX.*

Halim, F., & Ramnath, R. Sufatrio, Wu, Y., & Yap, R.H.C. (2008). *A lightweight binary authentication system for windows.* Paper presented at Joint iTrust and PST Conferences on Privacy, Trust Management and Security, IFIPTM.

Handley, M., Floyd, S., Pahdye, J., & Widmer, J. (2003). *TCP Friendly Rate Control (TFRC): Protocol Specification* (RFC 3448).

Hardin, R. (2002). *Trust and Trustworthiness.* New York: Russell Sage Foundation.

Harman, H. H. (1976). Modern factor analysis (3rd ed.). Chicago, IL: University of Chicago Press

Hauser, C. H., Bakken, D., Dionysiou, I., Gjermundrod, H., Irava, V., Helkey, J., & Bose, A. (2007). Security, trust and qos in next-generation control and communication for large power systems. *International Journal of Critical Infrastructures, 4*(1/2), 3–16. doi:10.1504/IJCIS.2008.016088

HDCP. (2008). *High-bandwidth Digital Content Protection System Version 2.0.* Retrieved from http://www.digital-cp.com/

He, Q., Wu, L., & Khosla, P. (2004). Quest for Personal Control over Mobile Location Privacy. *IEEE Communications Magazine, 42*(5), 130–136. doi:10.1109/MCOM.2004.1299356

Heath, C. (2006). *Symbian OS Platform Security: Software Development Using the Symbian OS Security Architecture*. Hoboken, NJ: John Wiley & Sons Inc.

Heath, C., & Luff, P. (2007). Ordering competition: the interactional accomplishment of the sale of fine art and antiques at auction. *The British Journal of Sociology, 58*, 63–85. doi:10.1111/j.1468-4446.2007.00139.x

Henderson, R., Rickwood, D., & Roberts, P. (1998). The beta test of an electronic supermarket. *Interacting with Computers, 10*, 385–399. doi:10.1016/S0953-5438(98)00037-X

Hengartner, U., & Steenkiste, P. (2004). Implementing access control to people location information. In *SACMAT '04, Proceedings of the 9th ACM symposium on Access Control Models and Technologies* (pp. 11-20). New York: ACM.

Heretick, D. M. L. (1981). Gender-specific relationships between trust-suspicion, locus of control, and psychological distress. *The Journal of Psychology, 108*, 267–274.

Herlihy, M. P., & Wing, J. (1990). Linearizability: A Correctness Condition for Concurrent Objects. *ACM Transactions on Programming Languages and Systems, 12*(3), 463–492. doi:10.1145/78969.78972

Hermoso, R., Billhardt, H., & Ossowski, S. (2006). Integrating Trust in Virtual Organisations. In *Proceedings of the AAMAS06 Workshop on Coordination, Organization, Institutions and Norms in Agent Systems (COIN 2006)* (LNCS 4386, pp. 19-31). Berlin, Germany: Springer.

Herrigel, A., Oruanaidh, J., Petersen, H., Pereira, S., & Pun, T. (1998). Secure copyright protection techniques for digital images. In *Proceedings of the Second Information Hiding Workshop (IHW)* (LNCS 1525, pp. 169-190). Berlin, Germany: Springer-Verlag.

Herzberg, A., Mass, Y., & Michaeli, J. (2000). Access Control Meets Public Key Infrastructure, or: Assigning Roles to Strangers. In *Proceedings of the 2000 IEEE Symposium on Security and Privacy* (pp. 2-14).

Hikage, N., Hauser, C., & Murayama, Y. (2007). Joho security gijutsu ni taisuru anshinkan no kozo ni kansuru tokeiteki kento [A statistical discussion of the sense of security, Anshin]. *Information Processing Society of Japan Journal, 48*(9). (in Japanese)

Hochreich, D. J. (1973). A children's scale to measure interpersonal trust. *Developmental Psychology, 9*, 141. doi:10.1037/h0035085

Hoffman, D. L., Novak, T. P., & Peralta, M. (1999). Building consumer trust online. *Communications of the ACM, 42*(4), 80–85. doi:10.1145/299157.299175

Hoffman, K., Zage, D., & Nita-Rotaru, C. (2008). A Survey of Attack and Defense Techniques for Reputation Systems. *ACM Computing Surveys*.

Hoffman, L. J., Lawson-Jenkins, K., & Blum, J. (2006). Trust beyond security: an expanded trust model. *Communications of the ACM, 49*(7), 94–101. doi:10.1145/1139922.1139924

Hong, I. J., & Landay, A. L. (2004). An Architecture for Privacy-Sensitive Ubiquitous Computing. In *Proceeding of the Second International Conference on Mobile Systems, Applications and Services (MobiSys 2004)* (pp. 177-189).

Hong, X., Gerla, M., et al. (1999). A group mobility model for ad hoc wireless networks. In *2nd ACM international workshop on Modeling, analysis and simulation of wireless and mobile systems (MSWiM'99)*, Seattle, WA, USA.

Horne, B. G., Matheson, L. R., Sheehan, C., & Tarjan, R. E. (2001). Dynamic Self-Checking Techniques for Improved Tamper Resistance. In . *Proceedings of the Digital Rights Management Workshop, 2320*, 141–159.

Housley, R., Ford, W., Polk, W., & Solo, D. (1999). *RFC 2459 – Internet X.509 Public Key Infrastructure Certificate*.

Hsu, M.H., Ju, T.L., Yen, C.H., & Chang, C.M. (2007). Knowledge sharing behavior in virtual communities: The relationship between trust, self-efficacy, and outcome expectations. *Human-computer studies, 65*, 153-169.

Hu, Y. C., Johnson, D., & Perrig, A. (2002). SEAD: Secure efficient distance vector routing for mobile wireless ad hoc networks. In *Proceedings of the Fourth IEEE Workshop on Mobile Computing Systems and Applications WMCSA '02* (pp. 3-13). Washington, DC: IEEE.

Hu, Y. C., Perrig, A., & Johnson, D. B. (2002). Ariadne: A secure On-demand routing protocol for ad hoc networks. In *Proceedings of ACM MobiCom 2002*. New York: ACM.

Hu, Y., Kwong, S., & Huang, J. (2006). An Algorithm for Removable Visible Watermarking. *IEEE Transactions on Circuits and Systems for Video Technology, 16*(1), 129–133. doi:10.1109/TCSVT.2006.884011

Huang, H., Keser, C., Leland, J., & Shachat, J. (2002). *Trust, the Internet and the digital divide* (RC22511). Yorktown Heights, NY: IBM Research Division.

Huang, L. H., Zhong, Z. J., & Murthy, D. N. P. (2007). Optimal reliability, warranty and price for new products. *IIE Transactions, 39*(8), 819–827. doi:10.1080/07408170601091907

Huang, Y., Fan, W., Lee, W., & Yu, P. (2003). Cross-feature analysis for detecting ad-hoc routing anomalies. In *Proceedings of the 23rd International Conference on Distributed Computing Systems*. Washington, DC: IEEE Computer Society.

Hubaux, J., Buttyan, L., & Capkuny, S. (2001). The quest for security in mobile ad hoc networks. In *Proceedings of ACM MobiHOC*. New York: ACM.

Hudson, A. (2003). *Equity and Trusts* (3rd ed.). London: Cavendish Publishing.

Hull, R., Kumar, B., Lieuwen, D., Patel-Schneider, P. F., Shuguet, A., Varadarajan, S., & Vyas, A. (2004). Enabling Context-Aware and Privacy-Conscious User Data Sharing. In *Proc. of the 2004 IEEE International Conference on Mobile Data Management* (pp.187-198).

Huynh, T., Jennings, N., & Shadbolt, N. (2004). FIRE: An integrated trust and reputation model for open multi-agent systems. In *Proceeding of the 16th European Conference on Artificial Intelligence*, Spain (pp. 18-22).

Ic3. (2008). *Reported Dollar Loss From Internet Crime Reaches All Time High*. Retrieved January 10, 2009, from http://www.ic3.gov/media/annualreport/2007_IC3Report.pdf

IETF. (1999). *IETF Draft 2560: X.509 Internet public key infrastructure online certificate status protocol – OCSP*. Retrieved April 2, 2009, from http://tools.ietf.org/html/rfc2560

Imber, S. C. (1973). Relationship of trust to academic performance. *Journal of Personality and Social Psychology, 28*, 145–150. doi:10.1037/h0035644

Intel. (2006). *LaGrande Technology Preliminary Architecture Specification*. Intel Corporation.

International Telecommunication Union. (1997). *X.509-Information Technology-Open Systems Interconnection-The Directory: Authentication Framework*.

Ioannidis, S., Keromytis, A. D., Bellovin, S. M., & Smith, J. M. (2000). Implementing a Distributed Firewall. In *Proceedings of the SIGSAC: 7th ACM Conference on Computer and Communications Security*.

Isham, J. (2000). *The Effect of Social Capital on Technology Adoption: Evidence from Rural Tanzania. Opportunities in Africa: Micro-evidence on Firms and Households*. Retrieved October 18, 2007, from http://www.csae.ox.ac.uk/conferences/2000-OiA/pdfpapers/isham.PDF

ISMACryp 1.1. (2004). *ISMA Encryption & Authentication Specification 1.1*. Retrieved from http://www.isma.tv/

ISMACryp 2.0. (2007). *ISMA Encryption & Authentication Specification 2.0*. Retrieved from http://www.isma.tv/

Jacob, C., Pfeffer, H., Zhang, L., & Steglich, S. (2008). *Establishing service communities in Peer-to-Peer Networks*. Paper presented at the 1st IEEE Internation Peer-to-Peer for Handheld Devices Workshop CCNC 2008, Las Vegas, NV, USA.

Jaeger, T., Sailer, R., & Shankar, U. (2006). PRIMA: policy-reduced integrity measurement architecture. In *Proceedings of the eleventh ACM symposium on Access control models and technologies*.

Jajodia, S., Samarati, P., & Subrahmanian, V. (1997, May). *A Logical Language for Expressing Authorizations.* Paper presented at the Annual IEEE Symposium on Security and Privacy, Oakland, CA, USA.

Jarvenpaa, S. L., & Todd, P. A. (1996). Consumer reactions to electronic shopping on the World Wide Web. *International Journal of Electronic Commerce, 1*(2), 59–88.

Jarvenpaa, S. L., Tractinsky, N., & Saarinen, L. (1999). Consumer Trust in an Internet Store: A Cross-Cultural Validation. *Journal of Computer-Mediated Communication, 5*(2).

Jarvenpaa, S., & Tractinsky, N. (2000). Consumer trust in an Internet store. *Information Technology and Management, 1*(1–2), 45-71. doi:10.1023/A:1019104520776

Jarvenpaa, S., Tractinsky, N., & Vitale, M. (2000). Consumer Trust in an Internet Store. *International Journal of Information Technology and Management, 1*(1-2), 45–71.

Jendricke, U., Kreutzer, M., & Zugenmair, A. (2002). Pervasive Privacy with Identity Management. In *Proceedings of the 1st Workshop Security, UbiComp.*

Jeong, Y., Shin, J., & Choi, H.-K. (2005). Channel-Adaptive GPS Scheduling for Heterogeneous Multimedia in CDMA Networks. In . *Proceedings of the ICCNMC, 3619,* 93–101.

Jiancheng, N., Zhishu, L., Zhonghe, G., & Jirong, S. (2007). Threat Analysis and Prevention for Grid and Web Service Security. In *Proceedings of the Software Engineering, Artificial Intelligence, Networking, and Parallel/Distributed Computing (SNPD 2007)* (pp. 526-531).

Jiang, T., Zheng, S., & Liu, B. (2004). Key distribution based on hierarchical access control for Conditional Access System in DTV broadcast. *IEEE Transactions on Consumer Electronics, 50*(1), 225–230. doi:10.1109/TCE.2004.1277866

Jiang, X., & Landay, J. A. (2002). Modeling Privacy Control in Context-Aware Systems. *Pervasive Computing, 1*(3), 59–63. doi:10.1109/MPRV.2002.1037723

Johnson, D. B., Maltz, D. A., & Hu, Y. C. (2004). *Autoconf WG Internet-Draft – The Dynamic Source Routing Protocol for Mobile Ad Hoc Networks (DSR).* Fremont, CA: IETF.

Johnson, M. K., & Farid, H. (2005). Exposing digital forgeries by detecting inconsistencies in lighting. In *Proc. of the ACM Multimedia Security Workshop* (pp. 1-10).

Johnson, R. A., & Wichern, D. W. (1998). *Applied Multivariate Statistical Analysis* (4th ed.). Upper Saddle River, NJ: Prentice Hall.

Jones, A. J. I., & Firozabadi, B. S. (2000). On the Characterization of a Trusting Agent -- Aspects of a Formal Approach. In C. Castelfranchi & Y. Tan (Eds.), *Trust and Deception in Virtual Societies* (pp. 163-174). Amsterdam: Kluwer Academic Publishers.

Jones, B. (2008). *Comparative Study: Grids and Clouds, Evolution or Revolution?* (EGEE Document number 925013). EGEE.

Jones, G. R., & George, J. M. (1998). The experience and evolution of trust: Implications for cooperation and teamwork. *Academy of Management Review, 23,* 531–546. doi:10.2307/259293

Jones, K. (1996). Trust as an Affective Attitude. *Ethics, 10,* 74–125.

Jöreskov, K. G. (1969). A general approach to confirmatory maximum likelihood factor analysis. *Psychometrika, 21,* 85–96.

Jøsang, A. (1997, December). *Artificial Reasoning with Subjective Logic.* Paper presented at the Second Australian Workshop on Commonsense Reasoning, Perth, Australia.

Josang, A. (1997, July). Prospectives of modeling trust in information security. In *Proceedings of the 2nd Australasian Conference on Information Security and Privacy,* Sydney, Australia.

Jøsang, A. (1998, September). *A Subjective Metric of Authentication.* Paper presented at the Fifth European Symposium on Research in Computer Security Louvain-la-Neuve, Belgium.

Jøsang, A. (1999, February). *An Algebra for Assessing Trust in Certification Chains.* Paper presented at the Network and Distributed Systems Security Symposium(NDSS'99), San Diego, California.

Jøsang, A. (2001). A Logic for Uncertain Probabilities. *International Journal of Uncertainty, Fuzziness, and Knowledge Based Systems, 9*(3), 279–311.

Josang, A., & Knapskog, S. J. (1998). A Metric for Trusted Systems. In *Proceedings of the 21ˢᵗ NIST-NCSC National Information Systems Security Conference* (pp. 16-29).

Jøsang, A., & LoPresti, S. (2004). Analysing the Relationship between Risk and Trust. In *Trust Management* (pp. 135-145). Berlin, Germany: Springer.

Jøsang, A., Bhuiyan, T., Xu, Y., & Cox, C. (2008). Combining Trust and Reputation Management for Web-Based Services. In . *Proceedings of TrustBus, 2008,* 69–75.

Jøsang, A., Gray, E., & Kinateder, M. (2003). Analysing Topologies of Transitive Trust. In T. Dimitrakos & F. Martinelli (Eds.), *Proc. of the 1ˢᵗ Intl. Workshop of Formal Aspects of Security and Trust (FAST).* Pisa, Italy: CNR.

Josang, A., Gray, E., & Kinateder, M. (2006). Simplification and analysis of transitive trust networks. *Web Intelligence and Agent Systems, 4*(2), 139–161.

Josang, A., Hayward, R., & Pope, S. (2006). Trust network analysis with subjective logic. In *Proc. of the 29th Australasian Computer Science Conference (ACSC '06)* (pp. 85-94).

Josang, A., Hird, S., & Faccer, E. (2003). Simulating the effect of reputation systems on e-markets. In *Proceedings of the Trust Management: First Internationl Conference, iTrust 2003* (LNCS 2692, pp. 179-194). Retrieved May, 2008, from http://sky.fit.qut.edu.au/~josang/papers/JHF2003-iTrust.pdf

Jøsang, A., Ismail, R., & Boyd, C. (2007). A survey of trust and reputation systems for online service provision. *Decision Support Systems, 43*(2), 618–644. doi:10.1016/j.dss.2005.05.019

Joumaa, H., & Davoine, F. (2005). An ICA based algorithm for video watermarking. In *Proc. of the 2005 International Conference on Acoustics, Speech, and Signal Processing (ICASSP 2005)* (Vol. 2, pp. 805-808).

Jules, A. (2006). RFID security and privacy, a research survey. *IEEE Journal on Selected Areas in Communications, 24*(2), 381–395. doi:10.1109/JSAC.2005.861395

Jules, A. (2008). *Four aspirations for RFID security research.* Paper presented at the ACM Conference on Wireless Network Security, Alexandria, VA. Retrieved April 2, 2009, from http://sconce.ics.uci.edu/wisec08-rfid-panel/RFID-Juels.pdf

Jurca, D., & Frossard, P. (2006). Media-specific rate allocation in heterogeneous wireless networks. In *Proceedings of the 15th International Packet Video Workshop Vol. 7* (pp. 713-726).

Jurca, R., & Faltings, B. (2003). An Incentive Compatible Reputation Mechanism. In *Proceedings of the 6th International Workshop on Deception Fraud and Trust in Agent Societies (at AAMAS'03)* (pp. 1026-1027).

Kagal, L., Finin, T., & Joshi, A. (2001). Trusted-based Secuirty in Pervasive Computing Environments. *IEEE Computer Society Press, 34*(12), 154–157.

Kagal, L., Undercoffer, J., Perich, F., Joshi, A., & Finin, T. (2002). Vigil: Enforcing Security in Ubiquitous Environments. In *Proceedings of the Grace Hopper Celebration of Women in Computing 2002.*

Kagal, L., Undercoffer, J., Perich, F., Joshi, A., & Finin, T. (2002). A Security Architecture Based on Trust Management for Pervasive Computing. In *Proceeding of the Grace Hopper Celebration of Women in Computing.*

Kamvar, S. D., Schlosser, M. T., & Garcia-Molina, H. (2003). The Eigentrust Algorithm for Reputation Management in P2P Networks. In *Proceedings of the Twelfth International Conference on World Wide Web (WWW '03)* (pp. 640-651). New York: ACM Press.

Kang, M. H., Park, J. S., & Froscher, J. N. (2001). Access Control Mechanisms for Inter-organisational Workflow. In *Proceedings of the Sixth ACM Symposium on Access*

Control Models and Technologies (pp. 66-74). New York: ACM Press.

Kanji, G. K. (1999). *100 Statistical Tests.* Newbury Park, CA: SAGE Publications.

Kankanhalli, M. S. Rajmohan, & Ramakrishnan, K.R. (1999). Adaptive visible watermarking of images. In *Proceedings of 1999 IEEE International Conference on Multimedia Computing and Systems* (pp. 568-573).

Kapadia, A., Henderson, T., Fielding, J. J., & Kotz, D. (2007). Virtual Walls: Protecting Digital Privacy in Pervasive Environments. In *Proceedings of the Fifth International Conference on Pervasive Computing (Pervasive)* (pp. 162-179). Berlin, Germany: Springer-Verlag.

Karsh, R., Walrath, J. D., Swoboda, J. C., & Pillalamarri, K. (1995). *Effect of battlefield combat identification system information on target identification time and errors in a simulated tank engagement task* (Technical report ARL-TR-854). Aberdeen Proving Ground, MD, USA: Army Research Lab.

Karvonen, K. (2001). Designing trust for a universal audience: A multicultural study on the formation of trust in the internet in the Nordic countries. In C. Stephanidis (Ed.), *First International Conference on Universal Access in Human-Computer Interaction* (Vol. 3, pp. 1078-1082). Mahwah, NJ: Erlbaum.

Katzy, B. R., Zhang, C., & Löh, H. (2000). Reference Models for Virtual Organizations. In L. Camarinha-Matos, H. Afsarmanesh, C. Zhang, V. Stich, I. Karvonen, B. Katzy, & A. Pawlak (Eds.), *Virtual Organizations: Systems and Practices* (pp. 45-58). Berlin, Germany: Springer.

Kaya, S. V., Savas, E., Levi, A., & Ercertin, O. (2009). Public key cryptography based privacy preserving multicontext RFID infrastructure. *Ad Hoc Networks, 7*(1), 136–152. doi:10.1016/j.adhoc.2007.12.004

Kelly, F., Maulloo, A., & Tan, D. (1998). Rate control for communication networks: Shadow prices, proportional fairness and stability. *The Journal of the Operational Research Society, 49*(3), 237–252.

Kelton, K., Fleischmann, K. R., & Wallace, W. A. (2008). Trust in Digital Information. *Journal of the American Society for Information Science and Technology, 59*(3), 363–374. doi:10.1002/asi.20722

Kennell, R., & Jamieson, L. H. (2003). Establishing the Genuinity of Remote Computer Systems. In *Proceedings of the 12th USENIX Security Symposium*, Washington, D.C., USA.

Kerschbaum, F., Haller, J., Karabulut, Y., & Robinson, P. (2006). Pathtrust: A Trust-based Reputation Service for Virtual Organization Formation. In Proceedings of the *Fourth International Conference on Trust Management (iTrust2006)* (LNCS 3986, pp. 193-205). Berlin, Germany: Springer.

Kiesler, S., Soroull, L., & Waters, K. (1996). A prisoner's dilemma experiment on cooperation with people and human-like computers. *Journal of Personality and Social Psychology, 70*, 47–65. doi:10.1037/0022-3514.70.1.47

Kikkawa, T., Shirato, S., Fujii, S., & Takemura, K. (2003). Gijutsuteki anzen to shakaiteki Anshin [The pursuit of informed reassurance ('An-Shin' in Society) and technological safety ('An-Zen')] [in Japanese]. *Journal of SHAKAI-GIJUTSU, 1*, 1–8. doi:10.3392/sociotechnica.1.1

Kim, D. J., Ferrin, D. L., & Rao, H. R. (2003). A Study of the Effect of Consumer Trust in Consumer Expectations and Satisfaction: the Korean Experience. In *Proceedings of the Fifth International Conference on Electronic Commerce (ICEC'2003)*, Pittsburgh, USA (pp. 310-315).

Kim, D. S., Shin, T. H., & Park, J. S. (2007). A security framework in RFID multi-domain system. In *Proceedings of the 2nd International Conference on Availability, Reliability and Security, 2007(ARES 2007)* (pp. 1227-1234). Washington, DC: IEEE Press.

Kim, D., Song, Y., Braynov, S., & Rao, H. (2001). A B-to-C Trust Model for On-line Exchange. In *Americas Conference on Information Systems*, Boston (pp. 784-787).

Kim, G., & Spafford, E. (1993). *The design and implementation of Tripwire: A file system integrity checker.*

Paper presented at ACM Conference on Computer and Communications Security.

Kim, J., Kim, Z., & Kim, K. (2007). A lightweight Privacy Preserving Authentication and Access Control Scheme for Ubiquitous Environment. In *Proceeding of the 10th international Conference on Information Security and Cryptography, ICISC 2007* (pp. 37-48).

Kim, M., Kotz, D., et al. (2006). Extracting a Mobility Model from Real User Traces. In *25th IEEE International Conference on Computer Communications (INFOCOM'06)*, Barcelona, Spain.

Kim, W., & Suh, Y. (2004). Short N-secure fingerprinting code for image. In *Proceeding of 2004 International Conference on Image Processing* (pp. 2167-2170).

Kinateder, M., & Rothermel, K. (2003). Architecture and Algorithms for a Distributed Reputation System. In *Proceedings of the 1st International Conference on Trust Management* (pp. 1-16).

Kini, A., & Choobineh, J. (1998). Trust in Electronic Commerce: Definition and Theoretical Considerations. In *Proceedings of Thirty-First Annual Hawaii International Conference on System Sciences (HICSS)* (Vol. 4, pp. 51).

Kline, R. B. (2005). *Principles and Practice of Structural Equation Modeling.* New York, NY: The Guilford Press, Kuan, H. H., & Bock, G. W. (2005). The collective reality of trust: An investigation of social relations and networks on trust in multi-channel retailers. In *Proceedings of the 13th European Conference on Information Systems.* Retrieved February 9, 2007, from http://is2.lse.ac.uk/asp/aspecis/20050018.pdf

Knight, D. H., & Chervany, N. L. (1966). The meaning of trust (Technical Report WP9604). University of Minnesota, Management Information Systems Research Center.

Kollock, P. (1999). The production of trust in online markets. In. E. J. Lawler, S. R. Thye, MW. Macy, & H. A. Walker (Eds.), *Advances in Group Processes* (pp. 99-123). Greenwich, CT: JAI Press.

Komiak, S. X., & Benbasat, I. (2004). Understanding customer trust in agent-mediated electronic commerce, web-mediated electronic commerce, and traditional commerce. *Information Technology and Management, 5*(1-2), 181–207. doi:10.1023/B:ITEM.0000008081.55563.d4

Konar, A. (2000). *Artificial Intelligence and Soft Computing: Behavioral and Cognitive Modeling of the Human Brain.* Boca Raton, FL: CRC Press.

Kong, J., Zerfos, P., Luo, H., Lu, S., & Zhang, L. (2001). Providing robust and ubiquitous security support for MANET. In *Proceedings of IEEE ICNP 2001.* Washington, DC: IEEE.

Konidala, D. M., & Kim, K. (2006, January). *Mobile RFID Security Issues.* Paper presented at the Symposium on Cryptography and Information Security (SCIS), Hiroshima, Japan.

Konrad, K., Fuchs, G., & Bathel, J. (1999). Trust and Electronic Commerce - More than a Technical Problem. In *Proceedings of the 18th Symp. Reliable Distributed Systems. Lausanne, Switzerland.* Retrieved March 3, 2009, from http://ftp.informatik.rwth-aachen.de/dblp/db/conf/srds/srds99.html

Korpela, E., Werthimer, D., Anderson, D., Cobb, J., & Lebofsky, M. (2001). SETI@home-Massively Distributed Computing for SETI. *Computing in Science & Engineering, 3*(1), 78–83. doi:10.1109/5992.895191

Kostiainen, K., Ekberg, J.-E., Asokan, N., & Rantala, A. (2009). On-board Credentials with Open Provisioning. In *Proceedings of ASIACCS'09, ACM Symposium on Information, Computer & Communication Security.*

Koufaris, M., & Hampton-Sosa, W. (2002). *Customer trust online: examining the role of the experience with the Web-site* (CIS Working Paper Series). Zicklin School of Business, Baruch College, New York, NY. Retrieved October 31, 2002, from http://cisnet.baruch.cuny.edu/papers/cis200205.pdf

Koukopoulos, D. (2005). The Impact of Dynamic Link Slowdowns on Network Stability. In *Proceedings of the 8th International Symposium on Parallel Architectures, Algorithms and Networks* (pp. 340-345).

Koukopoulos, D. (2008). Stability of Heterogeneous Multimedia Networks against Adversarial Attacks. In *Proceedings of the 3rd International Conference on Communications and Networking* (pp. 1259-1263).

Koukopoulos, D., & Nikolopoulos, S. D. (2006). Heterogenous Networks Can Be Unstable at Arbitrarily Low Injection Rates. In *Proceedings of the 6th International Conference on Algorithms and Complexity* (pp. 93-104).

Koukopoulos, D., Mavronicolas, M., Nikoletseas, S., & Spirakis, P. (2002). On the Stability of Compositions of Universally Stable, Greedy, Contention-Resolution Protocols. In *Proceedings of the 16th Int. Symposium on DIStributed Computing Vol. 2508* (pp. 88-102).

Koukopoulos, D., Mavronicolas, M., Nikoletseas, S., & Spirakis, P. (2005). The Impact of Network Structure on the Stability of Greedy Protocols. *Journal Theory of Computing Systems, 38*, 425–460. doi:10.1007/s00224-004-1181-3

Koukopoulos, D., Mavronikolas, M., & Spirakis, P. (2007). The Increase of the Instability of Networks due to Quasi-Static Link Capacities. *Journal Theoretical Computer Science, 381*, 44–56. doi:10.1016/j.tcs.2007.04.008

Kramer, R. M. (1999). Trust and distrust in organizations: Emerging perspectives, enduring questions. *Annual Review of Psychology, 50*, 569–598. doi:10.1146/annurev.psych.50.1.569

Kramer, R. M., & Tyler, T. R. (1996). *Trust in organizations: Frontiers of theory and research*. Thousand Oaks, CA: Sage.

Krawczyk, H., Bellare, M., & Canetti, R. (1997). *HMAC: keyed-hashing for message authentication* (RFC 2104). Retrieved April 25, 2009, from http://www.ietf.org/rfc/rfc2104.txt

Kühn, U., Selhorst, M., & Stüble, C. (2007). Realizing property-based attestation and sealing with commonly available hard- and software. In *Proceedings of the STC '07: the 2007 ACM workshop on Scalable trusted computing* (pp. 50-57).

Kumar, S. (1995). *Classification and detection of computer intrusions*. Unpublished doctoral dissertation, Dept. Computer Science, Purdue University. La, R. J., & Anantharam, V. (2002). Utility-based rate control in the internet for elastic traffic. *IEEE Transactions. on Networking, 10*(2), 272-285.

Kumar, S., & Spafford, E. H. (1994). A Pattern Matching Model for Misuse Intrusion Detection In *Proceedings of the 7th Nation Computer Security Conference,* Baltimore, Maryland (pp. 11-21).

Kundur, D., & Karthik, K. (2004). Video fingerprinting and encryption principles for digital rights management. *Proceedings of the IEEE, 92*(6), 918–932. doi:10.1109/JPROC.2004.827356

Kuntze, N., & Schmidt, A. U. (2006). Transitive trust in mobile scenarios. In G. Müller (Ed.), *Proc. of the Intl. Conf. Emerging Trends in Information and Communication Security (ETRICS 2006)* (pp. 73-85). Berlin, Germany: Springer-Verlag.

Kuntze, N., & Schmidt, A. U. (2006). Trusted Computing in Mobile Action. In H. S. Venter, J. H. P. Eloff, L. Labuschagne, & M. M. Eloff (Eds.), *Proc. of the ISSA 2006 From Insight to Foresight Conference*. Johannesburg, South Africa: Information Security South Africa (ISSA).

Kuntze, N., & Schmidt, A. U. (2007). Trustworthy content push. In *Proc. of the Wireless Communications and Networking Conference WCNC 2007* (pp. 2909-2912). Washington, DC: IEEE.

Kuntze, N., & Schmidt, A. U. (2007) Trusted Ticket Systems and Applications. In H. Venter, M. Eloff, L. Labuschagne, J. Eloff, & R. von Solms (Eds.), *New Approaches for Security, Privacy and Trust in Complex Systems* (pp. 49-60). New York: Springer-Verlag.

Kuntze, N., Mähler, D., & Schmidt, A. U. (2006). Employing Trusted Computing for the forward pricing of pseudonyms in reputation systems. In K. Ng, A. Badii, & P. Bellini (Eds.), *Proc. of the 2nd Intl. Conf. on automated production of cross media content for multi-channel distribution (AXMEDIS). Workshops Tutorials Applications and Industrial Sessions* (pp. 145-149). Florence, Italy: Firenze University Press.

Kuntze, N., Schmidt, A. U., Rudolph, C., & Velikova, Z. (2008). Trust in Business Processes. In *Proc. of the 9th Intl. Conf. for Young Computer Scientists, 2008. ICYCS 2008.* (pp. 1992-1997). Washington, DC: IEEE.

La Padula, L. J., & Bell, D. E. (1973). *Secure Computer Systems: A Mathematical Model* (Technical Report MTR–2547, Vol. I & II). Bedford, MA: MITRE Corporation. Retrieved January 26, 2009, from http://www.albany.edu/acc/courses/ia/classics/belllapadula1.pdf

Lacohée, H., Cofta, P., Phippen, A., & Furnell, S. (2008). *Understanding Public Perceptions: Trust and Engagement in ICT Mediated Services.* International Engineering Consortium.

Lacohée, H., Crane, S., & Phippen, A. (2006). *Trustguide: Final Report.* Retrieved January 5, 2007, from http://www.trustguide.org

Ladebo, O. J. (2006). Perceptions of trust and employees' attitudes: A look at Nigeria's agricultural extension workers. *Journal of Business and Psychology, 20,* 409-427.

Lahlou, S., & Jegou, F. (2004). *European Disappearing Computer Privacy Design Guidelines (version 1.1), Ambient Agoras Programme Report* (IST-2000-25134). Disappearing Computer Initiative.

Lamb, W. E. (1969). An Operational Interpretation of Nonrelativistic Quantum Mechanics. *Physics Today, 22,* 23–28. doi:10.1063/1.3035523

Lamb, W. E. (2001). Super Classical Quantum Mechanics: The best interpretation of nonrelativistic quantum mechanics. *American Journal of Physics, 69,* 413–422. doi:10.1119/1.1349542

Langfred, C. W., & Moye, N. A. (2004). Effects of task autonomy on performance: an extended model considering motivational, informational, and structural mechanisms. *The Journal of Applied Psychology, 89,* 934–945. doi:10.1037/0021-9010.89.6.934

Langheinrich, M. (2001). Privacy by Design-Principles of Privacy-Aware Ubiquitous Systems. In *Proceeding of the 3rd International Conference on Ubiquitous Computing (UbiComp 2001)* (LNCS 2201, pp. 273-291). Berlin, Germany: Springer.

Langheinrich, M. (2002). A Privacy Awareness System for Ubiquitous Computing Environments. In *Proceeding of the 4th International Conference on Ubiquitous Computing (UbiComp2002),*(LNCS 2498, pp. 237-245). Berlin, Germany: Springer.

Lathia, N., Hailes, S., et al. (2008). Trust Based Collaborative Filtering. In *Joint iTrust and PST Conferences on Privacy, Trust management and Security (iTrust'08),* Norway.

Latze, C., & Ultes Nitsche, U. (2008). A proof-of-concept implementation of EAP-TLS with TPM support. In H. S. Venter, J. H. P. Eloff, L. Labuschagne, & M. M. Eloff (Eds.), *Proc. of the Information Security South Africa (ISSA) Innovative Minds Conference.* Johannesburg, South Africa: ISSA.

Lau, D. C., & Liden, R. C. (2008). Antecedents of Coworker Trust: Leaders' Blessings. *The Journal of Applied Psychology, 93,* 1130–1138. doi:10.1037/0021-9010.93.5.1130

Law, K. L. E., & Saxena, A. (2003). Scalable design of a policy-based management system and its performance. *IEEE Communications Magazine, 41*(6), 72–79. doi:10.1109/MCOM.2003.1204750

Lee, J. D., & Moray, N. (1994). Trust, self-confidence, and operators' adaptation to automation. *International Journal of Human-Computer Studies, 40,* 153–184. doi:10.1006/ijhc.1994.1007

Lee, J. D., & See, K. A. (2004). Trust in automation: Designing for appropriate reliance. *Human Factors, 46*(1), 50–80.

Lee, J., & Moray, N. (1992). Trust, control strategies, and allocation of functions in human-machine systems. *Ergonomics, 35,* 1243–1270. doi:10.1080/00140139208967392

Lee, P. M. (2002). Behavioral Model of Online Purchasers in E-Commerce Environment. *Electronic Commerce Research, 2*(1-2), 75–85. doi:10.1023/A:1013340118965

Lee, S., Yoo, C. D., & Kalker, T. (2007). Reversible Image Watermarking Based on Integer-to-Integer Wavelet Transform. *IEEE Transactions on Information Forensics and Security, 2*(3), 321–330. doi:10.1109/TIFS.2007.905146

Leicher, A., Kuntze, N., & Schmidt, A. U. (2009). Implementation of a Trusted Ticket System. In *Proceedings of the IFIP sec2009*. Boston, MA: Springer-Verlag.

Lemos, R. (2000). Mitnick teaches 'social engineering'. *ZDNet News*. Retrieved from http://zdnet.com.com/2100-11-522261.html?legacy=zdnn

Lemos, R. (2006). U.S. Army requires trusted computing. *Security Focus*. Retrieved from http://www.securityfocus.com/brief/265

Levine, D., & Kessler, G. (2002). Denial of Service Attacks. In *Computer Security Handbook* (4th ed.). John Wiley & Sons.

Lewicki, R. J., & Bunker, B. B. (1995). Trust in relationships: A model of development and decline. In B. B. Bunker, J. Z. Rubin, & Associates (Eds.), *Conflict, cooperation and justice: Essays inspired by the work of Morton Deutsch* (pp. 133-173). San Francisco: Jossey-Bass.

Lewicki, R. J., & Bunker, B. B. (1996). Developing and maintaining trust in work relationships. In R. M. Kramer & T. R. Tyler (Eds.), *Trust in organizations: Frontiers of theory and research* (pp. 114-139). Thousand Oaks, CA: Sage Publications, Inc.

Lewicki, R. J., & Stevenson, M. A. (1998). Trust development in negotiation: Proposed actions and a research agenda. *Journal of Business and Professional Ethics, 16*(1-3), 99–132.

Lewicki, R. J., McAllister, D., & Bies, R. (1998). Trust and distrust: New relationships and realities. *Academy of Management Review, 23*, 439–458. doi:10.2307/259288

Lewicki, R. J., Tomlinson, E. C., & Gillespie, N. (2006). Models of Interpersonal Trust Development: Theoretical Approaches. *Empirical Evidence, and Future Directions, 32*, 991–1022.

Lewis, D. J., & Weigert, A. (1985). Trust as a social reality. *Social Forces, 63*(4), 967–985. doi:10.2307/2578601

Li, H., & Singhai, M. (2007). Trust Management in Distributed Systems. *IEEE Computer, 40*(2).

Li, L. X., & Liu, L. (2003, June). *A Reputation-Based Trust Model For Peer-To-Peer Ecommerce Communities.* Paper presented at the IEEE Conference on E-Commerce (CEC'03), Newport Beach, California.

Li, M., Fung, C., Sampigethaya, K., Robinson, R., Poovendran, R., Falk, R., & Koepf, A. (2008). Public-key based authentication for secure integration of RFID and sensor data. In *Proceedings of the 1st ACM workshop on heterogonous sensor and actor networks* (pp. 61-66). New York: ACM Press.

Li, M., Poovendran, R., Falk, R., Koef, A., Braun, M., Sampigethaya, K., et al. (2008, September). *Multi-domain RFID access control using asymmetric key based tag-reader mutual authentication.* Paper presented at the 26th Congress of the International Council of the Aeronautical Sciences (ICAS), Anchorage, AK.

Li, N., & Mitchell, J. C. (2003). Datalog with Constraints: A Foundation for Trust-Management Languages. In *Proc. of the Fifth International Symposium on Practical aspects of Declarative Languages* (pp. 58-73).

Li, N., & Mitchell, J. C. (2003). RT: A Role-based Trust-management Framework. In *Proceedings of the 3rd DARPA Information Survivability Conference and Exposition* (pp. 201-212).

Li, N., Mitchell, J. C., & Winsborough, W. H. (2002). Design of a Role-based Trust Management Framework. In *Proceedings of the Symposium on Security and Privacy* (pp. 114-130). Washington, DC: IEEE Computer Society.

Li, N., Winsborough, W., & Mitchell, J. (2003). Distributed Credential Chain Discovery in Trust Management. *Journal of Computer Security, 11*(1), 35–86.

Li, S., Chen, G., Cheung, A., Bhargava, B., & Lo, K.-T. (2007). On the design of perceptual MPEG-Video encryption algorithms. *IEEE Transactions on Circuits and Systems for Video Technology, 17*(2), 214–223. doi:10.1109/TCSVT.2006.888840

Li, W. (2001). Overview of fine granularity scalability in MPEG-4 video standard. *IEEE Transactions on Circuits and Systems for Video Technology, 11*(3), 301–317. doi:10.1109/76.911157

Li, W., & Chao, X. (2007). Call Admission Control for an Adaptive Heterogeneous Multimedia Mobile Network. *IEEE Transactions on Wireless Communications, 6*(2), 515–525. doi:10.1109/TWC.2006.05192

Li, X., Lyu, M. R., & Liu, J. (2004). A trust model based routing protocol for secure ad hoc networks. In *Proceedings of the Aerospace Conference IEEEAC'04.*

Li, X., Valacich, J. S., & Hess, T. J. (2004). Predicting User Trust in Information Systems: A Comparison of Competing Trust Models. In *Proc. of the 37th Hawaii Int. Conf. on System Sciences HICSS2004.*

Li, X.-Y., Shen, C.-X., & Zuo, X.-D. (2006). An Efficient Attestation for Trustworthiness of Computing Platform. In *Proceedings of the 2006 International Conference on Intelligent Information Hiding and Multimedia Signal Processing (IIH-MSP'06).*

Li, Y., & Liu, H. (2007). Developing Questionnaire for Trust of Students in Teachers. *Psychological Development and Education, 4*, 88-94.

Lian, S. (2008). Digital Rights Management for the Home TV Based on Scalable Video Coding. *IEEE Transactions on Consumer Electronics, 54*(3), 1287–1293. doi:10.1109/TCE.2008.4637619

Lian, S. (2008). *Multimedia Content Encryption: Techniques and Applications.* Boca Raton, FL: Auerbach Publications, Taylor & Francis.

Lian, S. (2009). *Multimedia communication security: recent advances.* Hauppauge, NY: Nova Science Publishers.

Lian, S., & Liu, Z. (2008). Secure Media Content Distribution Based on the Improved Set-Top Box in IPTV. *IEEE Transactions on Consumer Electronics, 54*(2), 560–566. doi:10.1109/TCE.2008.4560130

Lian, S., & Wang, Z. (2008). Collusion-traceable Secure Multimedia Distribution Based on Controllable Modulation. *IEEE Transactions on Circuits and Systems for Video Technology, 18*(10), 1462–1467. doi:10.1109/TCSVT.2008.2002829

Lian, S., & Zhang, Y. (2009). *Handbook of Research on Secure Multimedia Distribution.* Hershey, PA: Information Science Reference.

Lian, S., Liu, Z., Ren, Z., & Wang, H. (2006). Secure advanced video coding based on selective encryption algorithms. *IEEE Transactions on Consumer Electronics, 52*(2), 621–629. doi:10.1109/TCE.2006.1649688

Lian, S., Liu, Z., Ren, Z., & Wang, H. (2006). Secure Distribution Scheme for Compressed Data Streams. In *Proceeding of 2006 IEEE Conference on Image Processing (ICIP 2006)* (pp. 1953-1956).

Lian, S., Liu, Z., Ren, Z., & Wang, Z. (2007). Multimedia data encryption in block based codecs. *International Journal of Computers and Applications, 29*(1), 18–24. doi:10.2316/Journal.202.2007.1.202-1780

Lian, S., Sun, J., & Wang, Z. (2004). Perceptual cryptography on SPIHT compressed images or videos. In *Proceedings of the IEEE International Conference on Multimedia and Expro (I) (ICME2004)* (Vol. 3, pp. 2195-2198).

Lian, S., Sun, J., Zhang, D., & Wang, Z. (2004). A selective image encryption scheme based on JPEG2000 Codec. In *Proceedings of the 2004 Pacific-Rim Conference on Multimedia (PCM2004)* (LNCS 3332, pp. 65-72). Berlin, Germany: Springer.

Lian, S., Wang, X., Sun, J., & Wang, Z. (2004). Perceptual cryptography on wavelet transform encoded videos. In *Proceedings of the 2004 International Symposium on Intelligent Multimedia, Video and Speech Processing (ISIMP'2004)* (pp. 57-60).

Liang, B., & Haas, Z. J. (1999). Predictive distance-based mobility management for PCS networks. In *18th Annual Joint Conference of the IEEE Computer and Communications Societies (INFOCOM'99),* New York, USA.

Libman, R. E., Midani, M. T., & Nguyen, H. T. (1995). The Interactive Video Network: An Overview of the Video Manger and the V Protocol. *AT&T Tech. Journal, 74*(5), 92–105.

Lin, C., Varadharajan, V., Wang, Y., & Pruthi, V. (2004). Enhancing Grid Security with Trust Management. In *Proceedings of the IEEE Intl. Conference on Services Computing* (pp. 303-310).

Lin, K., Lu, H., Yu, T., & Tai, C. (2005). A Reputation and Trust Management Broker Framework for Web Applications. In *Proceedings of the International Conference on e-Technology, e-Commerce, and e-Services* (pp. 262-269). Washington, DC: IEEE Press.

Linden, G., Smith, B., & York, J. (2003). Amazon.Com Recommendations: Item-To-Item Collaborative Filtering. *IEEE Internet Computing, 7*(1), 76–80. doi:10.1109/MIC.2003.1167344

Lintelman, S., Li Robinson, R., von Oheimb, M., & Sampigethaya, D. K., & Poovendran, R. (2006, October). *Security Assurance for IT Infrastructure Supporting Airplane Production, Maintenance, and Operation.* Paper presented at the National Workshop on Aviation Software Systems, Alexandria, VA. Retrieved April 2, 2009, from http://chess.eecs.berkeley.edu/hcssas/papers/Lintelman-HCSS-Boeing-Position_092906_2.pdf

Liu, J., & Issamy, V. (2004, March-April). *Enhanced Reputation Mechanism for Mobile Ad Hoc Networks.* Paper presented at the Second International Conference on Trust Management, Oxford, UK.

Liu, L., & Xiong, L. (2002). Building Trust in Decentralized Peer to Peer Electronic Communities. In *Proceedings of the fifth International Conference on Electronic Commerce Research.*

Liu, Z., Lian, S., Gautier, J., Wang, R., et al. (2007). Secure video multicast based on desynchronized fingerprint and partial encryption. In *Proceeding of 2007 International Workshop on Digital Watermarking (IWDW2007)* (LNCS 5041, pp. 335-349).

Liu, Z., Lian, S., Wang, R., & Ren, Z. (2006). Desynchronization in compression process for collusion resilient video fingerprint. In *Proceedings of the IWDW2006* (LNCS 4283, pp. 308-322). Berlin, Germany: Springer.

London School of Economics. (2005). *The Identity Project. An assessment of the UK Identity Cards Bill & its implications. Interim Report.* Retrieved July 14, 2006, from http://www.lse.ac.uk/collections/pressAndInformationOffice/PDF/IDreport.pdf

Lonkila, M. (1997). Informal exchange relations in post-soviet Russia: a comparative perspective. *Sociological Review Online.* Retrieved from http://www.socresonline.org.uk/socresonlime/2/2/9.html

Lorenzi, F. (2007). A multiagent knowledge-based recommender approach with truth maintenance. In *RecSys07: Proceedings of the ACM conference on Recommender systems* (pp. 195-198).

Loscocco, P., & Smalley, S. (2001). *Integrating flexible support for security policies into the Linux operating system.* Paper presented at the 2001 USENIX Annual Technical Conference (FREENIX '01).

Loscocco, P., & Smalley, S. (2001). *Meeting critical security objectives with Security-Enhanced Linux,* Paper presented at the 2001 Ottawa Linux Symposium.

Love, J. (2001). *Comments to the Australian AG's on the proposed Hague Convention on Jurisdiction and Foreign Judgments* (Issues paper 3). Australian Consumers' Association. Retrieved March 3, 2009, from http://lists.essential.org/pipermail/hague-jur-commercial-law/2001-February/000009.html

Luhmann, N. (1979). *Trust and Power.* New York: John Wiley & Sons.

Luhmann, N. (1989). *Vertrauen. Ein Mechanismus der Reduktion sozialer Komplexit.at* (3rd ed.). Enke, Stuttgart.

Luhmann, N. (Ed.). (1990). *Trust: making and breaking cooperative relations.* Oxford, UK: Blackwell.

Lumsden, J., & Mackay, L. (2006). How does personality affect trust in B2C e-commerce? In *Proceedings of the ACM Conference on Electronic Commerce* (pp. 471-476).

Luo, H., Zerfos, P., Kong, J., Lu, S., & Zhang, L. (2002). Self-securing Ad Hoc Wireless Networks. In *Proceedings of the Seventh IEEE International Symposium on Computers and Communications (ISCC'02)*. Washington, DC: IEEE.

Lynch, N. (1996). *Distributed Algorithms*. San Francisco: Morgan Kaufmann.

Lyon, F. (2000). Trust, networks and norms: the creation of social capital in agricultural economies in Ghana. *World Development, 28*(4), 663–681. doi:10.1016/S0305-750X(99)00146-1

Madsen, M., & Gregor, S. (2000). Measuring human-computer trust. In *Proceedings of Eleventh Australasian Conference on Information Systems*, Brisbane.

Madsen, P., & Maler, E. (2005). *SAML V2.0 Executive Overview* (OASIS SSTC Committee Draft).

Mahmood, O. (2008). Modelling trust recognition and evaluation in an electronic environment . *International Journal of Networking and Virtual Organizations, 5*(3/4), 349–368. doi:10.1504/IJNVO.2008.018827

Malek, B., Miri, A., & Karmouch, A. (2008). A Framework for Context-Aware Authentication. In *Proceedings of the IET 4th International Conference on Intelligent Environments* (pp. 1-8). Washington, DC: IEEE Computer Society Press.

Manchala, D. W. (2000). E-commerce trust metrics and models. *Journal Internet Computing, 4*(2), 36–44. doi:10.1109/4236.832944

Mao, Y., & Mihcak, M. K. (2005). Collusion-resistant international de-synchronization for digital video fingerprinting. In . *Proceedings of the IEEE Conference on Image Processing, 1*, 237–240.

Maresch, O. M. (2005). *Reputationsbasierte Trust Metriken im Kontext des Semantik Web*. Unpublished diploma thesis, Technische Universität Berlin, Germany.

Marsh, S. (1994). *Formalising trust as a computational concept*. Unpublished doctoral dissertation, Department of Computer Science, University of Sterling.

Marti, S., & Garcia-Molina, H. (2004). Limited reputation sharing in p2p systems. In *Proceedings of ACM EC'04* (pp. 91-101).

Marti, S., & Garcia-Molina, H. (2006). Taxonomy of Trust: Categorizing P2P Reputation Systems. *Computer Networks, 50*(4), 472–484. doi:10.1016/j.comnet.2005.07.011

Marti, S., Giuli, T. J., Lai, K., & Baker, M. (2000). Mitigating routing misbehaviour in mobile ad hoc networks. In *Proceedings of the Sixth Annual International Conference on Mobile Computing and Networking*, Boston, MA, USA.

Martinelli, F., & Petrocchi, M. (2007). On relating and integrating two trust management frameworks. In *Proceedings of the Second International Workshop on Views on Designing Complex Architecturs (VODCA'06)* (pp. 191-205). ENTCS 168.

Masalonis, A. J. (2000). *Effects of situation-specific reliability on trust and usage of automated decision aids*. Unpublished doctoral dissertation, Catholic University of America, Washington, DC.

Maxemchuk, N. F., & Low, S. H. (1998). Performance comparison of two text marking methods. *IEEE Journal on Selected Areas in Communications, 16*(4), 561–572. doi:10.1109/49.668978

Mayer, R. C., & Davis, J. H. (1995). An integrative model of organizational trust. *Academy of Management Review, 20*(3), 709–735. doi:10.2307/258792

Mayer, R. C., Davis, J. H., & Schoorman, F. D. (1995). An Integrative Model of Organizational Trust. *Academy of Management Review, 20*(3), 709–734. doi:10.2307/258792

McAllister, D. J. (1995). Affect-and Cognition-Based Trust as Foundations for Interpersonal Cooperation In Organizations. *Academy of Management Journal, 38*, 24–59. doi:10.2307/256727

McCanne, S., Jacobson, V., & Vetterli, M. (1996). Receiver-driven Layered Multicast. In *Proceedings of the ACM SIGCOMM* (pp. 117-130).

McCord, M., & Ratnasingam, P. (2004). The Impact of Trust on the Technology Acceptance Model in Business to Consumer e-Commerce. In *Proceedings of the International Conference of the Information Resources Management Association: Innovations Through Information Technology*, New Orleans, USA (pp. 921-924).

McCune, J. M., Parno, B. J., Perrig, A., Reiter, M. K., & Isozaki, H. (2008). Flicker: an execution infrastructure for tcb minimization. In *Proceedings of the 3rd ACM SIGOPS/EuroSys European Conference on Computer Systems 2008*.

McDonald, R. P., & Ho, M. R. (2002). Principles and practice in reporting structural equation analyses. *Psychological Methods*, 7, 64–82. doi:10.1037/1082-989X.7.1.64

McKnight, D. H., & Chervany, N. L. (1996). *The Meanings of Trust*. Retrieved from http://www.misrc.umn.edu/wpaper/wp96-04.htm

McKnight, D. H., Choudhury, V., & Kacmar, C. (2000). Trust in e-commerce vendors: a two stage model. In *Proceedings of Twenty-First Annual International Conference on Information Systems*, Brisbane.

McKnight, D. H., Choudhury, V., & Kacmar, C. (2002). The impact of initial consumer trust on intentions to transact with a web site: a trust building mode. *The Journal of Strategic Information Systems*, 11(3-4), 297–323. doi:10.1016/S0963-8687(02)00020-3

McKnight, D. H., Cummings, L. L., & Chervany, N. L. (1998). Initial trust formation in new organizational relationships. *Academy of Management Review*, 23(3), 473–490. doi:10.2307/259290

Mechanic, D., & Meyer, S. (2000). Concepts of trust among patients with serious illness. *Social Science & Medicine*, 51(5), 657–668. doi:10.1016/S0277-9536(00)00014-9

Meka, K., Virendra, M., & Upadhyaya, S. (2006). Trust based routing decisions in mobile ad-hoc networks. In *Proceedings of the Workshop on Secure Knowledge Management SKM 2006*.

Melski, A., Thoroe, L., Caus, T., & Schumann, M. (2007). Beyond EPC - insights from multiple RFID case studies on the storage of additional data on tags. In *Proceedings of International Conference on Wireless Algorithms, Systems and Applications* (pp. 281-286). Chicago, IL: IEEE Press.

Meyer, J. (2001). Effects of warning validity and proximity on responses to warnings. *Human Factors*, 43, 563–572. doi:10.1518/001872001775870395

Micali, S. (2002). NOVOMODO - Scalable certificate validation and simplified PKI management, In *Proceedings of 1st Annual PKI Research Workshop* (pp. 15-25). Retrieved April 2, 2009, from http://www.cs.dartmouth.edu/~pki02/Micali/paper.pdf

Michiardi, P., & Molva, R. (2002). Core: A collaborative reputation mechanism to enforce node cooperation in mobile ad hoc networks. In *Proceedings of IFIP TC6/TC11 6th Joint Working Conference on Communications and Multimedia Security CMS'02* (pp. 107-121). Berlin, Germany; Springer.

Microsoft Developer Network. (2008). *SignTool*. Retrieved April 25, 2009, from http://msdn.microsoft.com/en-us/library/aa387764.aspx

Microsoft. (2001). *Microsoft Security Bulletin MS01-017 (March 22, 2001): Erroneous VeriSign-Issued Digital Certificates Pose Spoofing Hazard*. Retrieved from http://www.microsoft.com/technet/security/bulletin/MS01-017.asp

Microsystems, S. (n.d.). *JAVA*. Retrieved August 2008, from http://java.sun.com/

Miller, A. S., & Mitamura, T. (2003). Are surveys on trust trustworthy? *Social Psychology Quarterly*, 66, 62–70. doi:10.2307/3090141

Miller, C., Honoroff, J., & Mason, J. (2007). *Security evaluation of Apple's IPhone*. Retrieved April 27, 2009, from http://content.securityevaluators.com/iphone/exploitingiphone.pdf

Miller, N., Resnick, P., & Zeckhauser, R. (2003). *Eliciting Honest Feedback in Electronic Markets in Kennedy*

School of Government Working paper originally prepared for the SITE'02 workshop. Retrieved January 5, 2009, from http://ksgnotes1.harvard.edu/Research/wpaper.ns f/46ad8749e613af608525693c0014d6cc/d997a59b1cb90 7cb85256c39004c241c/$FILE/elicit.pdf

Minami, K., & Kotz, D. (2002). *Controlling Access to Pervasive Information in the "Solar" system* (Dartmouth Computer Science Technical Report TR2002-422).

Mishra, A. K. (Ed.). (1996). *Trust in Organizational responses to crisis: The centrality of trust.* Thousand Oaks, CA: Sage Publications.

Misra, A., Das, S., McAuley, A., & Das, S. K. (2001). Autoconfiguration, Registration and Mobility Management for Pervasive Computing. *IEEE Personal Communications, 8*(4).

Misztal, B. (1996). *Trust in Modern Societies: The Search for the Bases of Social Order,* Polity Press, ISBN 0-7456-1634-8.

Mitchell, C. J. (Ed.). (2005). *Trusted Computing.* London, UK: IET.

Mittal, V., & Vigna, G. (2002). Sensor-based intrusion detection for intra-domain distance-vector routing. In R. Sandhu (Ed.), *Proceedings of the ACM Conference on Computer and Communication Security (CCS'02).* Washington, DC, USA: ACM Press.

Mohan, A., & Blough, M. (2008). Attribute Trust-a Framework for Evaluating Trust in Aggregated Attributes via a Reputation System. In *Proceeding of the 6th Annual Conference on Privacy, Security and Trust* (pp. 201-212). Washington, DC: IEEE Computer Society Press.

Mohsin, M., & Prakash, R. (2002). IP Address Assignment in a Mobile Ad Hoc Network. In *Proceedings of IEEE Milcom.* Washington, DC: IEEE.

Molnar, D. (2000). *The SETI@Home Problem.* Retrieved December 30, 2008, from http://www.acm.org/cross-roads/columns/onpatrol/september2000.html

Moore, D., Shannon, C., Brown, D. J., Voelker, G. M., & Savage, S. (2006). Inferring Internet Denial-of-Service

Activity. *ACM Transactions on Computer Systems, 24*(2), 115–139. doi:10.1145/1132026.1132027

Morgan, R. M., & Hunt, S. D. (1994). The commitment - trust theory of relationship marketing. *Journal of Marketing, 58*(3), 20–38. doi:10.2307/1252308

Mui, L. (2003). *Computational models of trust and reputation: agents, evolutionary games, and social networks.* Unpublished doctoral dissertation, Massachusetts Institute of Technology.

Mui, L., Mohatashemi, M., & Halberstadt, A. (2002). A computational model of trust and reputation. In *proceedings of the 35th International Conference on System Science* (pp. 280-287).

Mui, L., Mohtashemi, M., & Halberstadt, A. (2002). A computational model of trust and reputation. In *Proceedings of the 35th Hawaii International Conference on System Sciences* (pp. 2431-2439).

Muir, B. (1994). Trust in automation: Part 1. Theoretical issues in the study and human intervention in automated systems. *Ergonomics, 37,* 1905–1923. doi:10.1080/00140139408964957

Muir, B., & Moray, N. (1996). Trust in automation. Part II. Experimental studies of trust and human intervention in a process control simulation. *Ergonomics, 39*(3), 429–460. doi:10.1080/00140139608964474

Murayama, Y., Hauser, C., Hikage, N., & Chakraborty, B. (2008). The Sense of Security and Trust. In M. Gupta & R. Sharman (Eds.), *Handbook of Research on Social and Organizational Liabilities in Information Security.* Hershey, PA: IGI Global.

Murthy, D. N. P., & Blischke, W. R. (Eds.). (2005). *Warranty Management and Product Manufacture.* London: Springer Verlag.

Musolesi, M., Hailes, S., et al. (2004). An ad hoc mobility model founded on social network theory. In *7th ACM international symposium on Modeling, analysis and simulation of wireless and mobile systems (MSWiM'04),* Venice, Italy.

Muthukumaran, D., Sawani, A., Schiffman, J., Jung, B. M., & Jaeger, T. (2008). Measuring integrity on mobile phone systems. In *Proc. of the 13ᵗʰ ACM Symposium on Access Control Models and Technologies*. New York: ACM.

Myles, G., Friday, A., & Davies, N. (2003). Preserving Privacy in Environments with Location-Based Applications. *IEEE Pervasive Computing / IEEE Computer Society [and] IEEE Communications Society, 2*(1), 56–64. doi:10.1109/MPRV.2003.1186726

Nagaratnam, N., Janson, P., Dayka, J., Nadalin, A., Siebenlist, F., Welch, V., et al. (2002). *Security Architecture for Open Grid Services*. Retrieved November 11, 2008, from http://www.cs.virginia.edu/~humphrey/ogsa-sec-wg/OGSA-SecArch-v1-07192002.pdf

Nain, P., Towsley, D., et al. (2005). Properties of random direction models. In *24th Annual Joint Conference of the IEEE Computer and Communications Societies (INFOCOM'05)*, Miami, FL, USA (pp. 1897- 1907).

Nakajima, Y., Yoneyama, A., & Hatori, Y. (2003). A Fast Logo Insertion Algorithm for MPEG Compressed Video. In *Proceeding of IEEE International Conference on Consumer Electronics (ICCE 2003)* (pp. 38-39).

Naquin, C. E., & Paulson, G. D. (2003). Online Bargaining and Interpersonal Trust. *The Journal of Applied Psychology, 88*, 113–120. doi:10.1037/0021-9010.88.1.113

Nass, C., & Lee, K. N. (2001). Does computer-synthesized speech manifest personality? Experimental tests of recognition, similarity-attraction, and consistency-attraction. *Journal of Experimental Psychology. Applied, 7*, 171–181. doi:10.1037/1076-898X.7.3.171

Nass, C., Moon, Y., Fogg, B. J., Reeves, B., & Dryer, D. C. (1995). Can computer personalities be human personalities? *International Journal of Human-Computer Studies, 43*, 223–239. doi:10.1006/ijhc.1995.1042

National Identity Scheme Delivery Plan. (2008). *Home Office*. Retrieved from http://www.ips.gov.uk/identity/downloads/national-identity-scheme-delivery-2008.pdf

National Institute of Standards and Technology. (2009). *Tentative Timeline of the Development of New Hash Functions*. Retrieved April 27, 2009, from http://csrc.nist.gov/groups/ST/hash/timeline.html

Navidi, W., & Camp, T. (2004). Stationary distributions for the random waypoint mobility model. *IEEE Transactions on Mobile Computing, 3*(1), 99–108. doi:10.1109/TMC.2004.1261820

Navqi, S., & Riguidel, M. (2005). Threat Model for Grid Security Services. In *Proceedings of the Advances in Grid Computing (EGC 2005)* (LNCS 3470, pp. 1048-1055). Berlin, Germany: Springer.

Nebbett, G. (2000). *Windows NT/2000 native API reference*. Sam Publishing.

Necula, G. C. (1997). Proof-Carrying Code. In *Proceedings of the Twenty-fourth ACM SIGPLANSIGACT Symposium on Principles of Programming Languages (POPL 1997)* (pp. 106-119). New York: ACM Press.

Neisse, R., Wegdam, M., van Sinderen, M., & Lenzini, G. (2007). *Trust Management Model and Architecture for Context-Aware Service Platforms*. Paper presented at the On the Move to Meaningful Internet Systems 2007: CoopIS, DOA, ODBASE, GADA, and IS.

Nesargi, S., & Prakash, R. (2002). MANETconf: Configuration of hosts in a mobile ad hoc network. In *Proceedings of INFOCOM 2002 Assurance Workshop* (pp. 60-65).

Neumann, C., Yu, T., Hartman, S., & Raeburn, K. (2005). The Kerberos Network Authentication Service (V5). *IETF Network Working Group. RFC 4120*. Retrieved January 27, 2009, from http://www.ietf.org/rfc/rfc4120.txt

Newell, S., & Swan, J. (2000). Trust and inter-organizational networking. *Human Relations, 53*, 1287–1328.

Nguyen, P. Q. (2004). Can We Trust Cryptographic Software? Cryptographic Flaws in GNU Privacy Guard v1.2.3. In *Proceedings of the Advances in cryptology - EUROCRYPT 2004* (LNCS 3027, pp. 555-570). Berlin, Germany: Springer.

Nielsen, J. (1999). *Trust or bust: communicating trustworthiness in Web design. Jacob Nielsen's Alertbox*. Retrieved from http://www.useit.com/alertbox/990307.html

Nissenbaum, H. (2004). Privacy as Contextual Integrity. *Washington Law Review, 17*, 101-139. Retrieved June 10, 2006, from http://crypto.stanford.edu/portia/papers/RevnissenbaumDTP31.pdf

NIST. (2001). *National Institute of Standards and Technologies, About Pervasive Computing*. Retrieved December 13, 2008, from http://www.nist.gov/pc2001/about-pervasive.html

Noack, P., Kerr, M., & Olah, A. (1999). Family Relations in Adolescence. *Journal of Adolescence, 22*, 713–717. doi:10.1006/jado.1999.0265

Nooteboom, B. (2002). *Trust: Foundations, Functions, Failure and Figures*. Cheltenham, UK: Edward Elgar Publishing Inc. *P2PBazaar*. (n.d.). Retrieved from http://www.p2pbazaar.com/index.html/

Nooteboom, B. (2005). Framing, attribution and scripts in the development of trust. In *Proc. of symposium on 'Risk, trust and civility'*, Victoria College, University of Toronto.

Norman, D. A., Ortony, A., & Russell, D. M. (2003). Affect and machine design: Lessons for the development of autonomous machines. *IBM Systems Journal, 42*, 38–44.

NSA. (1998). National Security Agency. *NSA Glossary of Terms Used in Security and Intrusion Detection*. Retrieved October 23, 2008, from http://www.sans.org/newlook/resources/glossary.html

OECD. (1980). *Organization for Economic Co-operation and Development, Recommendation of the council concerning guidelines on the Protection of Privacy and Transborder Flows of Personal Data*. Retrieved December 14, 2008, from http://www.oecd.org/document

Ogier, R., Templin, F., & Lewis, M. (2004). *IETF RFC 3684 – Topology Dissemination Based on Reverse-Path Forwarding (TBRPF)*. Fremont, CA: IETF.

Oh, J.-T., Park, S. K., Jang, J.-S., & Jeon, Y.-H. (2005). Detection of DDoS and IDS Evasion Attacks in a High-Speed Networks Environment. *International Journal of Computer Science and Network Security, 7*(6), 124–131.

Olive, M., Oishi, R., & Arentz, S. (2006). Commercial aircraft information security – an overview of ARINC report 811. In *Proceedings of 25th IEEE/AIAA Digital Avionics Systems Conference* (pp. 1-12). Portland, OR: IEEE Press.

OMA DRM 2.0. (2006). *Open Mobile Alliance, Digital Rights Management 2.0*.

Omodei, M. M., & Mclennan, J. (2000). Conceptualizing and Measuring Global Interpersonal Mistrust-Trust. *The Journal of Social Psychology, 140*(3), 279–294. doi:10.1080/00224540009600471

OMTP. (2009). *Open Mobile Terminal Platform. Advanced Trusted Environment, OMTP TR1 v1.03*.

Organisation for Economic Co-operation and Development [OECD]. (2008). *Malicious software (malware): A security threat to Internet economy, Ministerial Background Report, DISTI/ICCP/Reg(2007)5/Final*. Retrieved April 25, 2009, from http://www.oecd.org/dataoecd/ 53/34/40724457.pdf

OWL. (2004). *Web Ontology Language Overview* (W3C Recommendation 10 February 2004). Retrieved January 28, 2009, from http://www.w3.org/TR/owl-features/

Padmanabhan, V. (1997). Manufacturers Returns Policies and Retail. *Competition Marketing Science, 16*(1), 81–94.

Pagnia, H., Vogt, H., & Gärtner, F. C. (2003). Fair Exchange. *The Computer Journal, 46*(1), 55–75. doi:10.1093/comjnl/46.1.55

Papadimitratos, P., & Haas, Z. J. (2002). Secure routing for mobile ad hoc networks. In *Proceedings of SCS Communication Networks and Distributed Systems Modeling and Simulation Conference (CNDS 2002)*.

Papaioannou, T. G., & Stamoulis, G. D. (2004). Effective Use of Reputation in Peer-to-Peer Environments.

In *Proceedings of the Fourth International Scientific Workshop on Global and Peer-to-Peer Computing* (pp. 259-268).

Parasuraman, R., & Riley, V. (1997). Humans and automation: Use, misuse, disuse, abuse. *Human Factors, 39*, 230–253. doi:10.1518/001872097778543886

Park, J., & Sandhu, R. (2004). The UCON Usage Control Model. *ACM Transactions on Information and System Security, 7*(1), 128–174. doi:10.1145/984334.984339

Park, K. A., & Waters, E. (1989). Security of attachment and preschool friendships. *Child Development, 60*, 1076–1081. doi:10.2307/1130781

Park, K. A., Lay, K., & Ramsay, L. (1993). Individual differences and developmental changes in preschooler's friendships. *Developmental Psychology, 29*, 264–270. doi:10.1037/0012-1649.29.2.264

Park, S., Jeong, J., & Kwon, T. (2006). Contents Distribution System Based on MPEG-4 ISMACryp in IP Set-top Box Environments. *IEEE Transactions on Consumer Electronics, 52*(2), 660–668. doi:10.1109/TCE.2006.1649694

Pashalidis, A., & Mitchell, C. J. (2003). Single sign-on using trusted platforms. In *Proc. of the 6ᵗʰ Intl. Conf. Information Security (ISC 2003)* (pp. 54-68). Berlin, Germany: Springer-Verlag.

Patel, J. (2007). *A Trust and Reputation Model for Agent-Based Virtual Organizations.* Unpublished doctoral dissertation, University of Southampton, School of Electronics and Computer Science, Faculty of Engineering and Applied Science, Southampton, UK.

Patel, J., Teacy, W. T. L., Jennings, N. R., & Luck, M. (2005). A Probabilistic Trust Model for Handling Inaccurate Reputation Sources. In P. Herrmann, V. Issarny, & S. Shiu (Eds.), *Proceedings of Third International Conference on Trust Management,* Rocquencourt, France (pp. 193-209). Berlin, Germany: Springer.

Paul, D. L., & McDaniel, R. R. Jr. (2004). A field study of the effect of interpersonal trust on virtual collaborative relationship performance. *MIS Quarterly, 28*, 183–227.

Pavlou, P. A., & Fygenson, M. (2006). Understanding and predicting electronic commerce adoption: an extension of the theory of planned behavior. *MIS Quarterly, 30*, 115–143.

Pavlou, P. A., & Gefen, D. (2004). Building effective online marketplaces with institution-based trust. *Information Systems Research, 15*, 35–62. doi:10.1287/isre.1040.0015

Paxton, P. (1999). "Is Social Capital Declining in the United States?" A Multiple Indicator Assessment. *American Journal of Sociology, 105*, 88–127. doi:10.1086/210268

Pearlman, L., Welch, V., Foster, I., Kesselman, C., & Tuecke., S. (2002). A Community Authorization Service for Group Collaboration. In *Proceedings of the Third International Workshop on Policies for Distributed Systems and Networks (POLICY 2002)* (pp. 50-59). Washington, DC: IEEE Computer Society.

Pearson, S. (2002). *Trusted Computing Platforms, the Next Security Solution.* (Tech. Rep. HPL-2002-221). Trusted E-Services Laboratory. HP Laboratories Bristol. Retrieved January 23, 2009, from http://www.hpl.hp.com/techreports/2002/HPL-2002-221.pdf

Pearson, S. (2002). *How Can You Trust the Computer in Front of You?* (Tech. Rep. HPL-2002-221). Trusted E-Services Laboratory. HP Laboratories Bristol. Retrieved January 23, 2009, from http://www.hpl.hp.com/techreports/2002/HPL-2002-222.pdf

Pearson, S., et al. (2002). *Trusted Computing Platforms: TCPA Technology In Context.* Upper Saddle River, NJ: Prentice-Hall.

Pennington, A., Strunk, J., Griffin, J., Soules, C., Goodson, G., & Ganger, G. (2003). *Storage-based intrusion detection: watching storage activity for suspicious behavior.* Paper presented at 12th USENIX Security Symposium.

Percher, J. M., Puttini, R. S., Mé, L., Camp, O., Jouga, B., & Albers, P. (2004). *Un système de détection d'intrusion distribué pour réseaux ad hoc.* France: TSI.

Perkins, C. E., & Royer, E. M. (2003). *IETF RFC 3561 – Ad hoc on-demand distance vector (AODV) Routing*. Fremont, CA: IETF.

Perkins, C. E., Malinen, J., Wakikawa, R., Royer, E. M., & Sun, Y. (2001). *MANET WG Internet-Draft – IP Address Autoconfiguration for Ad hoc Networks*. Fremont, CA: IETF.

Pescador, F., Sanz, C., Garrido, M. J., Santos, C., & Antoniello, R. (2006). A DSP Based IP Set-Top Box for Home Entertainment. *IEEE Transactions on Consumer Electronics, 52*(1), 254–262. doi:10.1109/TCE.2006.1605055

Petroni, N. L., Jr., Fraser, T., Molina, J., & Arbaugh, W. A. (2004). Copilot - a coprocessor-based kernel runtime integrity monitor. In *Proceedings of the 13th conference on USENIX Security Symposium - Volume 13*.

Pfarrhofer, R., & Uhl, A. (2005). Selective image encryption using JBIG. In *Proceeding of 2005 IFIP Conference on Communications and Multimedia Security* (pp. 98-107).

Pfeffer, H., Krüssel, S., & Steglich, S. (2008). *A Fuzzy Logic based Model for Representing and Evaluating Service Composition Properties*. Paper presented at the International Conference on Advances in Human-oriented and Personalized Mechanisms, Technologies, and Services (I-CENTRIC 2008), Sliema, Malta.

Pfleeger, C. P., & Pfleeger, S. L. (2006). *Security in computing* (4th ed.). Upper Saddle River, NJ: Prentice Hall.

Picard, R. W. (1997). *Affective computing*. Cambridge, MA: MIT Press.

Pichler, R. (2000). *Trust and Reliance - Enforcement and Compliance: Enhancing Consumer Confidence in the Electronic Marketplace*. Stanford Law School. Retrieved from http://www.oecd.org/dsti/sti/it/secur/act/online trust/Consumer Confidence.pdf

Pinch, T., & Bijker, W. (1987). The Social Construction of Facts and Artifacts: Or How the Sociology of Science and the Sociology of Technology Might Benefit Each Other. *Social Studies of Science, 14*(3).

Pirzada, A. A., & Mcdonald, C. (2004). Establishing trust in pure ad-hoc networks. *Proceedings of the 27th conference on Australasian computer science (ACSC'04), 26*(1), 47-54.

Podesser, M., Schmidt, H. P., & Uhl, A. (2002). Selective bitplane encryption for secure transmission of image data in mobile environments. In *Proceedings of the 5th IEEE Nordic Signal Processing Symposium (NORSIG 2002)*, Tromso-Trondheim, Norway.

Podilchuk, C. I., & Zeng, W. (1998). Image-adaptive watermarking using visual models. *IEEE Journal on Selected Areas in Communications, 16*(4), 525–539. doi:10.1109/49.668975

Popescu, A. C., & Farid, H. (2005). Exposing digital forgeries by detecting traces of re-sampling. *IEEE Transactions on Signal Processing, 53*(2), 758–767. doi:10.1109/TSP.2004.839932

Popescu, A. C., & Farid, H. (2005). Exposing digital forgeries in color filter array interpolated images. *IEEE Transactions on Signal Processing, 53*(10), 3948–3959. doi:10.1109/TSP.2005.855406

Porad, K. (2005). RFID in commercial aviation. *Aircraft technology engineering & maintenance, 75*, 92-99.

Poritz, J. A. (2006). Trust[ed | in] computing, signed code and the heat death of the internet. In *Proceedings of the 2006 ACM symposium on Applied computing*, Dijon, France.

Poritz, J., Schunter, M., Herreweghen, E. V., & Waidner, M. (2004). *Property attestation—scalable and privacy-friendly security assessment of peer computers* (IBM Research Report RZ 3548).

Presti, S. L., Cusack, M., Booth, C., Allsopp, D., Kirton, M., Exon, N., et al. (2003). *Trust issues in pervasive environments* (Technical report wp2-01). University of Southampton and QinetiQ.

Prigent, N., Bidan, C., Andreaux, J. P., & Heen, O. (2003). Secure Long Term Communities in Ad Hoc Networks. In *Proceedings of ACM SASN*. New York: ACM.

Protected critical infrastructure information (PCII) program. (2006). Retrieved January 19, 2009, from http://www.dhs.gov

Protégé. (2009). *The Protégé Ontology Editor and Knowledge Acquisition System.* Retrieved January 28, 2009, from http://protege.stanford.edu/

Pu, P., & Chen, L. (2006). Trust building with explanation interfaces. In *Proceedings of the 11th international conference on Intelligent user interfaces (IUI'06)* (pp. 93-100).

Purser, S. (2001). A Simple Graphical Tool For Modelling Trust. *Computers & Security, 20*(6), 479–484. doi:doi:10.1016/S0167-4048(01)00605-8

Puttini, R. S. (2004). *Um Modelo de Segurança para Redes Móveis Ad Hoc.* Unpublished, doctoral dissertation, University of Brasília, Brazil.

Puttini, R. S., Mé, L., & De Sousa, R. T., Jr. (2004). On the Vulnerabilities and Protection of Mobile Ad Hoc Network Routing Protocols. In *Proceedings of the 3rd International Conference on Networking ICN2004* (pp. 676-684). New Jersey, USA: IEEE.

Puttini, R. S., Mé, L., & De Sousa, R. T., Jr. (2004). Preventive and Corrective Protection for Mobile Ad Hoc Network Routing Protocols. In *Proceedings of the 1st International Conference on Wireless On-demand Network Systems.* Berlin, Germany: Springer.

Puttini, R. S., Percher, J. M., Mé, L., & De Sousa, R. T., Jr. (2004). A Fully Distributed IDS for MANET. In *Proceedings of 9th IEEE International Symposium on Computers Communications.* Washington, DC: IEEE.

Puttini, R. S., Percher, J. M., Mé, L., Camp, O., & De Sousa, R. T., Jr. (2003). A Modular Architecture for a Distributed IDS for Mobile Ad Hoc Networks. In *Proceedings of the International Conference on Computer Science and Applications* (pp. 105-113). Berlin, Germany: Springer.

Quercia, D., & Hailes, S. (2007). MATE: Mobility and Adaptation with Trust and Expected-utility. *International Journal Internet Technology and Secured Transactions, 1.*

Quercia, D., Hailes, S., & Capra, L. (2006, May). *B-trust: Bayesian Trust Framework for Pervasive Computing.* Paper presented at the Fourth International Conference on Trust Management, Pisa, Italy.

Quercia, D., Lad, M., Hailes, S., Capra, L., & Bhatti, S. (2006). STRUDEL: Supporting Trust in the Dynamic Establishment of peering coalitions. In *Proceedings of the 21st ACM Symposium on Applied Computing* (pp. 1870-1874).

Quisquater, J.-J., & Samyde, D. (2002). Side channel cryptanalysis. In *Proceedings of the SECI□02, Securité des Communications sur Internet.*

Radio Technical Commission for Aeronautics (RTCA). (1992). *DO-178B: Software considerations in airborne systems and equipment certification.*

Radio Technical Commission for Aeronautics (RTCA). (2008). *DO-294B: Civil operators' training guidelines for integrated night vision imaging system equipment, December.*

Raffo, D. (2005). *Security Schemes for the OLSR Protocol for Ad Hoc Networks.* Unpublished doctoral dissertation, University of Paris 6 Pierre et Marie Curie, Paris, France.

Rahman, A. A. (1997). The PGP trust model. *The Journal of Electronic Commerce.* Retrieved from http://www.wim.uni-koeln.de/uploads/media/The_PGP_Trust_Model.pdf

Ramnath, R. Sufatrio, Yap, R.H.C., & Yongzheng, W. (2006). *WinResMon: A Tool for Discovering Software Dependencies, Configuration and Requirements in Microsoft Windows.* Paper presented at 20th Large Installation System Administration Conference, LISA'06.

Rand Corporation. (1970). *Security Controls for Computer Systems. Report of Defense Science Board Task Force on Computer Security.* Retrieved December 23, 2007, from http://seclab.cs.ucdavis.edu/projects/history/papers/ware70.pdf

Rangan, P. V. (1988, April). *An Axiomatic Basis of Trust in Distributed Systems.* Paper presented at the Annual

IEEE Symposium on Security and Privacy, Oakland, California.

Ratnasingam, P. (2005). Trust in inter-organizational exchanges: a case study in business to business electronic commerce. *Decision Support Systems, 39*(3), 525–544. doi:10.1016/j.dss.2003.12.005

Ray, I., & Chakraborty, S. (2004, September). *A Vector Model of Trust for Developing Trustworthy Systems.* Paper presented at the Ninth European Symposium on Research in Computer Security, Sophia Antipolis, Frech Riviera, France.

Ray, I., Bertino, E., Squicciarini, A., & Ferrari, E. (2005). Anonymity Preserving Techniques in Trust Negotiations. In *Proceedings of the 5th International Workshop on Privacy Enhancing Technologies (PET)*, Cavtat, Croatia (pp. 93-109).

Ray, I., Ray, I., & Chakraborty, S. (2009). An Interoperable Context-Sensitive Model of Trust. *Journal of Intelligent Information Systems, 32*(1).doi:doi:10.1007/s10844-007-0049-9

Rehak, M., Foltyn, M., Pechoucek, M., & Benda, P. (2005). Trust Model for Open Ubiquitous agent systems. In *Proceedings of the IEEE/WIC/ACM/ International Conference on Intelligent Agent Technology (IAT),* Compiegne University of Technology, France (pp. 536-542).

Rempel, J. K., Holmes, J. G., & Zanna, M. P. (1985). Trust in close relationships. *Journal of Personality and Social Psychology, 49*(1), 95–112. doi:10.1037/0022-3514.49.1.95

Ren, K., & Lou, W. (2005). Privacy Enhanced Access Control in Ubiquitous Computing Environments. In *Proceedings of the 2nd International Conference of Broadband Networks* 2005 (Vol. 1, pp. 356-365).

Ren, K., & Lou, W. (2007). Privacy-Enhanced, Attack-Resilient Access Control in Pervasive Computing Environments with Optional Context Authentication Capability. *Mobile Networks and Applications, 12*(1), 79–92. doi:10.1007/s11036-006-0008-7

Ren, K., Lou, W., & Zhang, Y. (2007). Multi-user broadcast authentication in wireless sensor networks. In *Proceedings of IEEE Conference on Sensor and Ad Hoc Communications and Networks* (pp. 223-232). San Diego, CA: IEEE Press.

Ren, K., Lou, W., Kim, K., & Deng, R. (2006). A Novel Privacy Preserving Authentication and Access Control Scheme for Pervasive Computing Environments. *IEEE Transactions on Vehicular Technology, 55*(4), 1373–1384. doi:10.1109/TVT.2006.877704

Resnick, P., & Zeckhauser, R. (2001). Trust Among Strangers in Internet Transactions: Empirical Analysis of eBay's Reputation System [working paper]. In *Proceedings of the NBER Workshop on Empirical Studies of Electronic Commerce.*

Resnick, P., & Zeckhauser, R. (Eds.). (2002). *Trust among strangers in internet transactions: empirical analysis of eBay's reputation system* (Vol. 11).

Resnick, P., Kuwabara, K., Zeckhauser, R., & Friedman, E. (2000). Reputation systems. *Communications of the ACM, 43*(12), 45–48. doi:10.1145/355112.355122

RESTAC. *a Java REST framework for Rest-style interactions.* (n.d.). Retrieved August 2008, from https://developer.berlios.de/projects/restac/

RFC 2401. (1998). *Security Architecture for the Internet Protocol (IPSec).* Retrieved from http://www.ietf.org/rfc/rfc2401.txt

RFC 3711. (2004). *Secure Real-time Transport Protocol (SRTP) Security profile for Real-time Transport Protocol. IETF Request for Comments document.* Retrieved from http://tools.ietf.org/html/rfc3711

Richardson, M., Agrawal, R., & Domingos, P. (2003). Trust Management for the Semantic Web. In *Proceedings of the 2nd International Semantic Web Conference* (pp. 351-368).

Riebak, M. R., Crispo, B., & Tanenbaum, A. S. (2006). Is your Cat Infected with a Computer Virus. In *Proceedings of 4th Annual IEEE International Conference on Pervasive Computing and Communications (IEEE PerCom)* (pp. 170-179). Washington, DC: IEEE Press.

Riegelsberger, J., Sasse, M. A., & McCarthy, J. D. (2003). Privacy and trust: Shiny happy people building trust? Photos on e-commerce websites and consumer trust. *Proceedings of CHI, 5*(1), 121–128.

Riegelsberger, J., Sasse, M. A., & McCarthy, J. D. (2005). The Mechanics of Trust: A Framework for Research and Design. *International Journal of Human-Computer Studies, 62*(3), 381–422. doi:10.1016/j.ijhcs.2005.01.001

Ries, S. (2007). Certain Trust: A Trust Model for Users and Agents. In *Proceeding of the 22nd Annual ACM Symposium on Applied Computing* (pp. 1599-1604). New York: ACM Press.

Riley, V. (1996). Operator reliance on automation: Theory and data. In R. Parasuraman & M. Mouloua (Eds.), *Automation and human performance: Theory and applications* (pp. 19-35). Hillsdale, NJ: Lawrence Erlbaum Associates, Inc.

Robinson, J., Wakeman, I., et al. (2008). The North Laine Shopping Guide: A Case Study in Modelling Trust in Applications. In *Joint iTrust and PST Conferences on Privacy, Trust management and Security (iTrust'08)*, Norway.

Robinson, R., Li, M., Lintelman, S., Sampigethaya, K., Poovendran, R., & von Oheimb, D. (2007). Challenges for IT Infrastructure Supporting Secure Network-Enabled Commercial Airplane Operations. In *Proceedings of the AIAA Infotech@Aerospace Conference.*

Robinson, R., Li, M., Lintelman, S., Sampigethaya, K., Poovendran, R., von Oheimb, D., et al. (2007). Electronic distribution of airplane software and the impact of information security on airplane safety. In *Proceedings of 26th International Conference on Computer Safety, Reliability and Security (SAFECOMP)* (pp. 28-39). Nuremberg, Germany: Springer Press.

Robinson, R., Li, M., Lintelman, S., Sampigethaya, K., Poovendran, R., von Oheimb, D., & Bußer, J.-U. (2007, September). *Impact of public key enabled application on the operation and maintenance of commercial airplanes.* Paper presented at the AIAA ATIO Conference, Belfast, Northern Ireland.

Rong, L., & Burnett, I. (2006). Facilitating Universal Multimedia Adaptation (UMA) in a heterogeneous Peer-to-Peer Network. In *Proceedings of the Second International Conference on Automated Production of Cross Media Content for Multi-Channel Distribution* (pp. 105-109).

Rongen, P. M., Macs, M. B., & Overveld, C. (1999). Digital image watermarking by salient point modification, In *Proc. of the SPIE Electronic Imaging'99, Security and Watermarking of Multimedia Content*, San Jose (Vol. 3657, pp. 273-282).

Rotenberg, K. J. (1984). Sex differences in children's trust in peers. *Sex Roles, 11*, 953–957. doi:10.1007/BF00287822

Rotenberg, K. J. (1986). Same-sex partners and same-sex differences in the trust-value basis of children's friendships. *Sex Roles, 15*, 613–626. doi:10.1007/BF00288218

Rotenberg, K. J. (1991). Children's cue use and strategies for detecting deception. In K. J. Rotenberg (Ed.), *Children's interpersonal trust: Sensitivity to lying, deception, and promise violations.* New York: Springer-Verlag.

Rotenberg, K. J. (1991). The trust-value basis of children's friendship. In K. J. Rotenberg (Ed.), *Children's interpersonal trust: Sensitivity to lying, deception, and promise violations.* New York: Springer-Verlag.

Rotenberg, K. J. (1994). Loneliness and interpersonal trust. *Journal of Social and Clinical Psychology, 13*, 152–173.

Rotenberg, K. J. (1995). The socialisation of trust: Parents' and children's interpersonal trust. *International Journal of Behavioral Development, 18*, 713–726. doi:10.1177/016502549501800408

Rotenberg, K. J. (2001). Trust across the life-span. In N. J. Smelser & P. B. Baltes (Eds.), *International encyclopedia of the social and behavioural sciences* (pp. 7866-7868). New York: Pergamon.

Rotenberg, K. J., & Cerda, C. (1995). Racially based trust expectancies of Native American and Caucasian children. *The Journal of Social Psychology, 134*, 621–631.

Rotenberg, K. J., & Pilipenko, T. A. (1983-1984). Mutuality, temporal consistency, and helpfulness in children's trust in peers. *Social Cognition, 2,* 235–255.

Rotenberg, K. J., & Sliz, D. (1988). Children's restrictive disclosure to friends. *Merrill-Palmer Quarterly, 34,* 203–215.

Rotenberg, K. J., Boulton, M. J., & Fox, C. L. (2005). Cross-Sectional and Longitudinal Relations Among Children's Trust Beliefs, Psychological Maladjustment and Social Relationships: Are Very High as Well as Very Low Trusting Children at Risk? *Journal of Abnormal Child Psychology, 33,* 595–610. doi:10.1007/s10802-005-6740-9

Rotenberg, K. J., Fox, C., & Green, S. (2005). Construction and validation of a children's interpersonal trust belief scale. *The British Journal of Developmental Psychology, 23,* 271–292. doi:10.1348/026151005X26192

Rotter, J. B. (1967). A new scale for the measurement of interpersonal trust. *Journal of Personality, 35,* 651–665. doi:10.1111/j.1467-6494.1967.tb01454.x

Rotter, J. B. (1971). Generalized expectancies for interpersonal trust. *The American Psychologist, 26,* 443–452. doi:10.1037/h0031464

Rotter, J. B. (1980). Interpersonal trust, trustworthiness, and gullibility. *The American Psychologist, 35,* 1–7. doi:10.1037/0003-066X.35.1.1

Royer, E., & Toh, C. (1999). A review of current routing protocols for ad hoc mobile wireless networks. *IEEE Personal Communications Magazine,* 46-55.

Ruohomaa, S., & Kutvonen, L. (2005). Trust Management Survey. In P. Herrmann, et al. (Eds.), *Proceedings of the iTrust 2005* (pp. 77-92). Berlin, Germany: Springer.

Russinovich, M. E. (2009). *Sigcheck v1.6.* Retrieved April 25, 2009, from http://technet.microsoft.com/en-us/sysinternals/bb897441.aspx

Russinovich, M. E., & Solomon, D. A. (2005). *Microsoft Windows internals: Microsoft Windows Server 2003, Windows XP, and Windows 2000* (4th ed.). Redmond, WA: Microsoft Press.

Ryotov, T., Neuman, C., Zhou, L., & Foukia, N. (2007). Initial trust formation in virtual organizations. *International Journal of Internet Technology and Secured Transactions, 1,* 81–94. doi:10.1504/IJITST.2007.014835

Sabater, J., & Sierra, C. (2005). Review on Computational Trust and Reputation Models. *Artificial Intelligence Review, 24,* 33–60. doi:10.1007/s10462-004-0041-5

Sadeghi, A.-R., & Stüble, Ch. (2004). Property-based attestation for computing platforms: caring about properties, not mechanisms. In C. F. Hampelmann & V. Raskin (Eds.), *Proceedings of the 2004 workshop on new security paradigms NSPW '04* (pp. 67-77). New York: ACM.

SAE International. (2008). *SAE standard AS5678 - Passive RFID tags intended for aircraft use.*

Safford, D., Kravitz, J., & Doorn, L. V. (2003). Take Control of TCPA. *Linux Journal.* Retrieved from http://www.linuxjournal.com/article/6633

Sailer, R., Jaeger, T., Zhang, X., & van Doorn, L. (2004). Attestation-based policy enforcement for remote access. In B. Pfitzmann & P. Liu (Eds.), *Proc. of the 11th ACM Conf. on Computer and Communications Security* (pp. 308-317). New York: ACM.

Sailer, R., Zhang, X., Jaeger, T., & van Doorn, L. (2004). Design and implementation of a TCG-based integrity measurement architecture. In *Proceedings of the 13th USENIX Security Symposium* (pp. 223-238). Berkley, CA: USENIX.

Salam, A. F., Iyer, L., Palvia, P., & Singh, R. (2005). Trust in e-Commerce. *Communications of the ACM, 48*(2), 72–77. doi:10.1145/1042091.1042093

Saltzer, J., & Schroeder, M. (1975). The protection of information in computer systems. *Proceedings of the IEEE Computer Society Press, 63*(9).

Sampigethaya, K., Li, M., Poovendran, R., Robinson, R., Bushnell, L., & Lintelman, S. (2007). Secure wireless collection and distribution of commercial airplane health data. In *Proceedings of 26th IEEE/AIAA Digital Avionics Systems Conference* (pp. 4.E.6-1-4.E.6-8). Washington, DC: IEEE Press.

Sampigethaya, K., Poovendran, R., & Bushnell, L. (2008). Secure operation, control and maintenance of future e-enabled airplanes. *Proceedings of the IEEE, 96*(12), 1992–2007. doi:10.1109/JPROC.2008.2006123

Samuelson, K., Valovage, E., & Hall, D. (2006). Enhanced ADS-B research. In *Proceedings of IEEE Aerospace Conference* (IEEEAC paper #1282). Washington, DC: IEEE Press.

Samyde, D., Skorobogatov, S., Anderson, R., & Quisquater, J.-J. (2002). On a new way to read data from memory. In *Proceedings of the First International IEEE Security in Storage Workshop.*

Sandhu, R. S., Coyne, E. J., Feinstein, H. L., & Youman, C. E. (1996). Role-based Access Control Models. *IEEE Computer, 29*, 38–47.

Sandhu, R., Zhang, X., Ranganathan, K., & Covington, M. J. (2006). Client-side access control enforcement using trusted computing and PEI models. *Journ. High Speed Networks, 15*, 229–245.

Sankur, B., Bayram, S., Avcibas, I., & Memon, N. (2006). Image manipulation detection. *Journal of Electronic Imaging, 15*(4), 041102. doi:10.1117/1.2401138

Sarmenta, L. F. G. (2002). Sabotage-tolerance mechanisms for volunteer computing systems. *Future Generation Computer Systems, 18*(4), 561–572. doi:10.1016/S0167-739X(01)00077-2

Saroiu, S., Gummadi, P. K., & Gribble, S. D. (2002). A Measurement Study of Peer-to-Peer File Sharing Systems. In *Proceedings of Multimedia Computing and Networking.*

Sassone, V., Nielsen, M., et al. (2007). Towards a Formal Framework for Computational Trust. In *Formal Methods for Components and Objects* (pp. 175-184).

Schilit, B., Adams, N., & Want, R. (1994). Context-Aware Computer Applications. In *Proceedings of the Workshop on Mobile Computing Systems and Applications* (pp. 85-90).

Schindler, P. L., & Thomas, C. C. (1993). The structure of interpersonal trust. *Journal of Personality, 35*, 651–665.

Schlosser, M. T., Condie, T. E., & Kamvar, S. D. (2003). Simulating a File-Sharing P2P Network. In *Proceedings of the Workshop on Semantics in Peer-to-Peer and Grid Computing.*

Schmid, M., Hill, F., Ghosh, A., & Bloch, J. (2001). *Preventing the execution of unauthorized Win32 applications.* Paper presented at DARPA Information Survivability Conf. & Exposition II.

Schmidt, A. U. (2008). On the Superdistribution of Digital Goods. In *Proc. of the 3rd Intl. Conf. on Communications and Networking in China (CHINACOM'08)* (pp. 1236-1243). Washington, DC: IEEE.

Schmidt, A. U., & Kuntze, N. (2009). Trust in the Value-Creation Chain of Multimedia Goods. In S. Lian & Y. Zhang (Eds.), *Handbook of Research on Secure Multimedia Distribution* (pp. 405-426). Hershey, PA: IGI Global.

Schmidt, A. U., & Loebl, Z. (2005). Legal Security for Transformations of Signed Documents: Fundamental Concepts. In D. Chadwick & Z. Gansen (Eds.), *Proceedings of the Second European PKI Workshop: Research and Applications, EuroPKI 2005* (pp. 255-270). Berlin, Germany: Springer-Verlag.

Schmidt, A. U., Kreutzer, M., & Accorsi, R. (Eds.). (2007). *Long-Term and Dynamical Aspects of Information Security: Emerging Trends in Information and Communication Security.* Hauppauge, NY: Nova.

Schmidt, A. U., Kuntze, N., & Abendroth, J. (2008). Trust for Location-based Authorisation. In *Proc. of the Wireless Communications and Networking Conf. (WCNC 2008)* (pp. 3169-3174). Washington, DC: IEEE.

Schmidt, A. U., Kuntze, N., & Kasper, M. (2008). Subscriber Authentication in Cellular Networks with Trusted Virtual SIMs. In *Proceedings of the 10th International Conference on Advanced Communication Technology (ICACT2008)* (pp. 903-908). Washington, DC: IEEE.

Schneider, G. P. (2003). *Electronic Commerce- Fourth Annual Edition.* Boston, MA.

Schneier, B. (2002). Palladium and the TCPA. *Crypto-Gram Newsletter.* Retrieved from http://www.schneier.com/crypto-gram-0208.html

Schreckenbach, F., Schnell, M., Scalise, S., & Platt, P. (2007). NEWSKY -Networking the sky for aeronautical communications. In *Proceedings of the 1st International CEAS European Air and Space Conference. Council of the European Aerospace Societies.*

Schyndel, R. G., Tirkel, A. Z., & Osborne, C. F. (1994). A digital watermark. In *Proc. of the IEEE Int. Conf. on Image Processing,* Austin, TX (Vol. 2, pp. 86-90).

Scut. (2001). *Exploiting format string vulnerabilities.* Team teso. Retrieved April 25, 2009, from http://julianor.tripod.com/bc/formatstring-1.2.pdf

Seamons, K. E., Winslett, M., & Yu, T. (2001). Limiting the Disclosure of Access Control Policies During Automated Trust Negotiation. In *Proceedings of the Network and Distributed System Security Symposium,* San Diego, CA.

Seidenman, P., & Spanovich, D. J. (2007). Predicting the future: eEnabled maintenance. *Overhaul and Maintenance, 23*(9), 32–36.

Seigneur, J., & Jensen, C. (2004). Trading Privacy for Trust. In *Proceedings of the 2ⁿᵈ International Conference on Trust Management* (pp. 93-107).

Seshadri, A., Luk, M., Perrig, A., van Doorn, L., & Khosla, P. (2006). SCUBA: Secure Code Update By Attestation in Sensor Networks. In *Proceedings of the ACM Workshop on Wireless Security (WiSe 2006).*

Seshadri, A., Luk, M., Shi, E., Perrig, A., Doorn, L. v., & Khosla, P. (2005, October 23-26). Pioneer: Verifying Code Integrity and Enforcing Untampered Code Execution on Legacy Systems. In *Proceedings of the SOSP '05,* Brighton, United Kingdom.

Seshadri, A., Perrig, A., Doorn, L. v., & Khosla, P. (2004). SWATT: softWare-based attestation for embedded devices. In *Proceedings of the IEEE Symposium on Security and Privacy.* SETI@Home. (2007). *The search for extraterrestrial intelligence project.* Retrieved December 30, 2008, from http://setiathome.berkeley.edu

Shacham, H., Page, M., Pfaff, B., Goh, E. J., Modadugu, N., & Boneh, D. (2004). *On the effectiveness of address-space randomization.* Paper presented at the 11th ACM Conference on Computer and Communications Security.

Shafer, G. (1976). *A Mathematical Theory of Evidence.* Princeton, NJ: Princeton University Press.

Shaha, N., Desai, A., & Parashar, M. (2001). Multimedia Content Adapatation for QoS Mnagement over Heterogeneous Networks. In *Proceedings of the International Conference on Internet Computing* (pp. 642-648).

Shamir, A. (1999). How to Share a Secret. *Communications of the ACM, 22*(11), 612–613. doi:10.1145/359168.359176

Shaneck, M., Mahadevan, K., Kher, B., & Kim, Y. (2005). Remote Software-Based Attestation for Wireless Sensors. In R. Molva, G. Tsudik, & D. Westhoff (Eds.), *Security and Privacy in Ad-hoc and Sensor Networks* (pp. 27-41). Berlin, Germany: Springer-Verlag.

Shankar, G. (1994). Detweminants of long-term orientation in buyer-service provider relationships. *Journal of Marketing, 58*(1), 1–19. doi:10.2307/1252247

Shankar, U., Jaeger, T., & Sailer, R. (2006). Toward Automated Information-Flow Integrity Verification for Security-Critical Applications. In *Proceedings of the Network and Distributed System Security Symposium (NDSS).*

Shapiro, D., Sheppard, B. H., & Cheraskin, L. (1992). Business on a handshake. *Negotiation Journal, 8,* 365–377. doi:10.1111/j.1571-9979.1992.tb00679.x

Shaw, M. J. (2000). Electronic commerce: Review of critical research issues. In *Information Systems Frontiers* (pp. 95-106).

Shek, D. T. L. (2005). Perceived Parental Control Processes, Parent-Child Relational Qualities, and Psychological Well-Being in Chinese Adolescents With and Without Economic Disadvantage. *The Journal of Genetic Psychology, 166,* 171–188. doi:10.3200/GNTP.166.2.171-188

Shi, C., & Bhargava, B. (1998). A fast MPEG video encryption algorithm. In *Proceedings of the 6th ACM*

International Multimedia Conference, Bristol, UK (pp. 81-88).

Shi, E., Perrig, A., & van Doorn, L. (2005). BIND: A fine-grained attestation service for secure distributed systems. In *Proc. of the 2005 IEEE Symposium on Security and Privacy* (pp. 154-168). Washington, DC: IEEE.

Shlesinger, M. F., & Zaslavsky, G. M. (1993). Strange kinetics. *Nature*, *363*, 31–37. doi:10.1038/363031a0

Shmatikov, V., & Talcott, C. (2005). Reputation-Based Trust Management. *Journal of Computer Security*, *13*(1), 167–190.

Shneiderman, B. (2000). Designing trust into online experiences. *Communications of the ACM*, *43*(12), 57–59. doi:10.1145/355112.355124

Siau, K., & Shen, Z. (2003). Building consumer trust in mobile commerce. *Communications of the ACM*, *46*(4), 91–93. doi:10.1145/641205.641211

Siebenlist, F., Nagaratnam, N., Welch, V., & Neuman, C. (2003). Security for Virtual Organizations: Federating Trust and Policy Domains. In I. Foster & C. Kesselman (Eds.), *The Grid: Blue Print for a New Computing Infrastructure*. San Francisco, CA: Morgan Kaufmann Publishers.

Silaghi, G. C., Arenas, A., & Silva, L. (2007). *Reputation-based Trust Management Systems and their Applicability to Grids* (Technical Report TR-0064). Institutes on Knowledge and Data Management and System Architecture, CoreGrid – Network of Excellence.

Silicon.com. (2008). *Home Office Loses Data on 84,000 Prisoners*. Retrieved from http://www.silicon.com/publicsector/0,3800010403,39274254,00.htm

Siljeee, B. I. J., & Bosloper, I. E. (2004). A classification framework for storage and retrieved of context. In *Proceedings of the First International Workshop on Modeling and Retrieval of Context (MRC2004)*.

Silverman, D. (2006). *Qualitative Research. Theory, Method and Practice*. San Francisco: Sage Publications.

Sims, D. W., & Southall, E. J. (2008). Scaling laws of marine predator search behaviour. *Nature*, *451*, 1098–1102. doi:10.1038/nature06518

Singer, T., Kiebel, S. J., Winston, J. S., Dolan, R. J., & Frith, C. D. (2004). Brain responses to the acquired moral status of faces. *Neuron*, *41*, 653–662. doi:10.1016/S0896-6273(04)00014-5

Singh, A., & Liu, L. (2003). TrustMe: Anonymous Management of Trust Relationships in Decentralized P2P Systems. In . *Proceedings of the Peer-to-Peer Computing, 2003*, 142–149.

Singh, I. L., Molloy, R., & Parasuraman, R. (1993). Individual differences in monitoring failures of automation. *The Journal of General Psychology*, *120*, 357–373.

Slaviero, M., Kroon, J., & Olivier, M. (2005). *Attacking signed binaries*. Paper presented at 5th Annual Information Security South Africa Conference.

Solomon, R. C., & Flores, F. (2001). *Building Trust in Business, Politics, Relationships and Life*. Oxford, UK: Oxford University Press.

Song, D., Berezin, S., & Perrig, A. (2001). Athena: A novel approach to efficient automatic security protocol analysis. *JCS*, *9*(1,2), 47-74.

Sparaco, P. (1995, January 30). Airbus seeks to keep pilot, new technology in harmony. *Aviation Week & Space Technology*, 62–63.

Sparks, E. (2007). *A Security Assessment of Trusted Platform Modules* (Dartmouth College, Computer Science Technical Report TR2007-597). Retrieved April 27, 2009, from http://www.ists.dartmouth.edu/library/341.pdf

Spearman, C. (1904). General intelligence objectively determined and measured. *The American Journal of Psychology*, *15*, 201–293. doi:10.2307/1412107

Spenser, J. (2005). Technology Pollination. *Boeing Frontiers*. Retrieved April 2, 2009, from http://www.boeing.com/news/frontiers/archive/2005/december/ts_sf10.html

Squicciarini, A., Bertino, E., Ferrari, E., & Ray, I. (2006). Achieving Privacy in Trust Negotiations with an Ontology-Based Approach. *IEEE Transactions on Dependable and Secure Computing, 3*(1), 13–30. doi:10.1109/TDSC.2006.3

Squicciarini, A., Bertino, E., Ferrari, E., Paci, F., & Thuraisinghm, B. (2007). PP-Trust-X: A system for Privacy Preserving Trust Negotiations. [TISSEC]. *ACM Transactions on Information and System Security, 10*(3). doi:10.1145/1266977.1266981

Squicciarini, A., Spantzel, A., Bertino, E., Ferrari, E., & Ray, I. (2006). Trust Negotiations with Customizable Anonymity. In *Proceedings of the IEEE/WIC/ACM International Conference on Web Intelligence and Intelligent Agent Technology (WI-ATW06)* (pp. 69-72).

Srage, J., & Azema, J. (2005). *M-Shield mobile security technology* [white paper]. Texas Instruments. Retrieved April 27, 2009, from http://focus.ti.com/pdfs/wtbu/ti_mshield_whitepaper.pdf

Sridharan, S., Dawson, E., & Goldburg, B. (1991). Fast Fourier transform based speech encryption system. *IEEE Proceedings of Communications . Speech and Vision, 138*(3), 215–223.

Srivatsa, M., Xiong, L., & Liu, L. (2005). TrustGuard: Countering Vulnerabilities in Reputation Management for Decentralized Overlay Networks. In *Proceedings of the International World Wide Web Conference.*

Stajano, F. (2002). *Security for Ubiquitous Computing.* New York: Halsted Press.

Standifera, R. L., & James, A. W. Jr. (2003). Managing conflict in B2B e-commerce. *Business Horizons, 46*(2), 65–70. doi:10.1016/S0007-6813(03)00011-9

Steiner, J. G., Neuman, C., & Schiller, J. I. (1988) Kerberos: An Authentication Service for Open Network Systems. In R. Isaacs & Y. Zhou (Eds.), *Proc. of the 2008 USENIX Annual Technical Conference* (pp. 191-102). Berkley, CA: USENIX.

Stephens, R. T. (2004). A framework for the identification of electronic commerce design elements that enable

trust within the small hotel industry. In *Proceedings of ACMSE* (pp. 309-314).

Stevens, J. (2001). *Applied Multivariate Statistics for the Social Sciences* (4th ed.). Mahwah, NJ: Lawrence Erlbaum Assoc Inc.

Stevens, M., & Williams, P. D. (2007, April). *Use of Trust Vectors for CyberCraft and the Limits of Usable Data History for Trust Vectors.* Paper presented at the IEEE Conference on Computational Intelligence for Security and Defense Applications, Honululu, Hawaii.

Stojanovic, N., Maedche, A., Staab, S., Studer, R., & Sure, Y. (2001, October). *SEAL - A Framework for Developing Semantic Portals.* Paper presented at the First International Conference on Knowledge Capture, Victoria, Canada.

Strader, T. J., Lin, F., & Shaw, M. J. (1998). Information Structure for Electronic Virtual Organization Management. *Decision Support Systems, 23,* 75–94. doi:10.1016/S0167-9236(98)00037-2

Su, J., Scott, J., et al. (2007). Haggle: Seamless Networking for Mobile Applications. In *9th International Conference on Ubiquitous Computing (UbiComp'07),* Innsbruck, Austria.

Sufatrio, Y. R.H.C., & Zhong, L. (2004). *A machine-oriented integrated vulnerability database for automated vulnerability detection and processing.* Paper presented at 18th Large Installation System Administration Conference, LISA'04.

Sundaresan, H. (2003). *OMAP platform security features, July 2003* [white paper]. Texas Instruments. Retrieved April 27, 2009, from http://focus.ti.com/pdfs/vf/wireless/platformsecuritywp.pdf

Sutherland, P., & Tan, F. B. (2004) The Nature of Consumer Trust in B2C Electronic Commerce: A Multi-Dimensional Conceptualization. In *Proceedings of the International Conference of the Information Resources Management Association: Innovations Through Information Technology,* New Orleans, USA (pp. 611-614).

Swanson, M. D., Zhu, B., Tewfik, A. H., & Boney, L. (1998). Robust audio watermarking using perceptual masking. *Signal Processing, 66*(3), 337–355. doi:10.1016/S0165-1684(98)00014-0

Symbian. (2007). *Symbian Signed Whitepaper.* Retrieved April 27, 2009, from https://www.symbiansigned.com/Symbian_Signed_White_Paper.pdf

Szwabe, A., Schorr, A., Hauck, F. J., & Kassler, A. J. (2006). Dynamic multimedia stream adaptation and rate control for heterogeneous networks. In *Proceedings of the 15th International Packet Video Workshop Vol. 7* (pp. 63-69).

Taipale, K. A. (2005). The Trusted Systems Problem: Security Envelopes, Statistical Threat Analysis, and the Presumption of Innocence, Homeland Security - Trends and Controversies. *IEEE Intelligent Systems, 20*(5), 80–83.

Takabi, H., Amini, M., & Jalili, R. (2006). Enhancing Role-Based Access Control Model through Fuzzy Relations. In *Proceedings of the third International Conference on Information Assurance and Security (IAS07)* (pp. 131-136). Washington, DC: IEEE Computer Society Press.

TalebiFard. P., & Leung, V. C. M. (2008). Efficient Multimedia Call Delivery over IP-Based Heterogeneous Wireless Access Networks. In *Proceedings of the MobiWac* (pp. 85-92).

Tang, L. (1996). Methods for encrypting and decrypting MPEG video data efficiently. In *Proceedings of the Fourth ACM International Multimedia Conference (ACM Multimedia'96)*, Boston, MA (pp. 219-230).

TCG. (2003). *Trusted Computing Group.* Retrieved December 30, 2008, from http://www.trustedcomputinggroup.org

TCG. (2006). *TCG Infrastructure Working Group. Architecture Part II - Integrity Management. Specification Version 1.0 Revision 1.0.*

TCG. (2007). *TPM Specification Version 1.2 Revision 103.*

TCG. (2008). *Mobile Trusted Module Specification Version 1.0. Revision 6.*

TCG. (2008). *TCG Mobile Reference Architecture Specification Version 1.0. Revision 5.*

TCG. (2008). *TNC Architecture for Interoperability. Specification Version 1.3. Revision 6.*

TCG. (2009). *Trusted Computing Group: FAQs.* Retrieved from https://www.trustedcomputinggroup.org/faq/

Tchepnda, C., & Riguidel, M. (2006). Distributed Trust Infrastructure and Trust-Security Articulation: Application to Heterogeneous Networks. In *Proceedings of the 20th International Conference on Advanced Information Networking and Applications* (pp. 33-38).

Telegraph News. (2008). *Is Our Data Safe in the Government's Hands?* Retrieved from http://www.telegraph.co.uk/news/newstopics/politics/liberaldemocrats/1569947/Is-our-data-safe-in-the-Government's-hands.html

Teng, H. S., Chen, K., & Lu, S. C. Y. (1990). Adaptive real-time anomaly detection using inductively generated sequential patterns. In *Proceedings of the 1990 IEEE Symposium on Research in Security and Privacy* (pp. 278-284). Washington, DC: IEEE Computer Society.

Tentori, M., Favela, J., Gonzalez, V., & Rodriguez, M. (2005). Supporting Quality of Privacy (QOP) in Pervasive Computing. In *Proceeding of the Sixth Mexican International Conference on Computer Science* (pp. 58-67). New York: ACM Press.

Toivonen, S., Lenzini, G., & Uusitalo, I. (2006). *Context-aware Trust Evaluation Functions for Dynamic Reconfigurable Systems.* Paper presented at the Annual World Wide Web Conference.

Toone, B., Gertz, M., & Devanbu, P. (2003). Trust Mediation for Distributed Information Systems. In D. Gritzalis, S. De Capitani di Vimercati, P. Samarati, & S. K. Katsikas (Eds.), *Security and Privacy in the Age of Uncertainty, Proc. of the IFIP TC11 18th Intl. Conf. on Information Security (SEC2003)* (pp. 1-12). Dordrecht, The Netherlands: Kluwer.

Torrubia, A., & Mora, F. (2002). Perceptual cryptography on MPEG Layer III bitstreams. *IEEE Transactions on Consumer Electronics, 48*(4), 1046–1050. doi:10.1109/TCE.2003.1196437

TPM. (2008). *Trusted Platform Module (TPM) Specifications*. Retrieved from https://www.trustedcomputinggroup.org/specs/TPM/

Trust. (2009). Retrieved from http://en.wikipedia.org/wiki/Trust

Trusted Computing Group TCG. (2004). *TCG Specification Architecture Overview*. Retrieved January 19, 2009, from https://www.trustedcomputinggroup.org

Trusted Computing Group. (2006). *Trusted Platform Module (TPM) Main Specification. Version 1.2, Revision 103*. Retrieved December 30, 2008, from http://www.trustedcomputinggroup.org

Trusted Computing Group. (2008). *TPM Specification, version 1.2 Revision 103*. Retrieved April 27, 2009, from https://www.trustedcomputinggroup.org/specs/TPM/

Trusted Computing Group. (2008). *Mobile Trusted Module Specification, Version 1.0 Revision 1*. Retrieved April 27, 2009, from https://www.trustedcomputinggroup.org/specs/mobilephone

Trusted Computing Group. (2008). *Mobile Trusted Module Reference Architecture, Version 1. 0*. Retrieved April 27, 2009, from https://www.trustedcomputinggroup.org/specs/mobilephone

Trusted Computing Group. (2009). *Mobile Phone Work Group Selected Use Case Analysis, v 1.0*. Retrieved April 27, 2009, from https://www.trustedcomputinggroup.org/specs/mobilephone

Tsai, M. J., Yu, K. Y., & Chen, Y. Z. (2000). Joint wavelet and spatial transformation for digital watermarking. *IEEE Transactions on Consumer Electronics, 46*(1), 241–245.

Tsai, Y.-R., & Chang, C.-J. (2006). SIM-based subscriber authentication mechanism for wireless local area networks. *Computer Communications, 29*, 1744–1753. doi:10.1016/j.comcom.2005.09.016

Tseng, C. Y., Balasubramanyam, P., Ko, C., Limprasittiporn, R., Rowe, J., & Levitt, K. (2003). A specification-based intrusion detection system for AODV. In *Proceedings of the ACM Workshop on Security of Ad Hoc and Sensor Networks (SASN'03)*. New York: ACM.

Tyler, T. R. (Ed.). (1996). *Trust in organizations: Frontiers of theory and research*. Thousand Oaks, CA: Sage.

U.S. Canada Power System Outage Task Force. (2004). *Final report on the August 14, 2003 Blackout in the United States and Canada: Causes and Recommendations, March 2004*. Retrieved January 19, 2009, from https://reports.energy.gov/BlackoutFinal-Web.pdf

U.S. Census Bureau. (2007). *Annual Retail Trade Survey – 2007*. Retrieved December 10, 2008, from http://www.census.gov/svsd/www/artstbl.html

U.S. Department of Defense. (1985). *Department of Defense Trusted Computer System Evaluation Criteria*. Retrieved April 25, 2009, from http://nsi.org/Library/Compsec/orangebo.txt

Ultes-Nitsche, U., Latze, C., & Baumgartner, F. (2007) Strong Mutual Authentication in a User-Friendly Way in EAP-TLS. In *Proc. of the 15th Intl. Conf. on Software, Telecommunications and Computer Networks (SoftCOM 2007)*. Washington, DC: IEEE.

Uschold, M., & Gruninger, M. (1996). Ontologies: Principles, Methods, and Applications. *The Knowledge Engineering Review, 11*(2), 93–155.doi:doi:10.1017/S0269888900007797

Vacca, J. (2004). *Public Key Infrastructure: Building Trusted Applications and Web Services*. London: Auerbach Publications.

Valdes, J., Tarjan, R. E., & Lawler, E. L. (1979). The Recognition of Series Parallel Digraphs. In *Proceedings of the 11ᵗʰ Annual ACM Symposium on Theory of Computing* (pp. 1-12).

Venkatesh, V., Morris, M. G., Davis, G. B., & Davis, F. D. (2003). User acceptance of information technology: Toward a unified view. *MIS Quarterly, 27*(3), 425–478.

Vigna, G., Gwalani, S., Srinivasan, K., Belding-Royer, E. M., & Kemmerer, R. A. (2004). An intrusion detection tool for AODV-based ad hoc wireless networks. In [Washington, DC: IEEE.]. *Proceedings of the IEEE ACSAC, 04*, 16–27.

Vijayakumar, V., & Wahida Banu, R. S. D. (2008). Security for Resource Selection in Grid Computing Based On Trust and Reputation Responsiveness. *International Journal of Computer Science and Network Security, 8*(11), 107–115.

Vishik, C., Johnson, S., & Hoffman, D. (2007). *Infrastructure for trusted environment: In search of a solution*. Paper presented at ISSE/SECURE 2007 Securing Electronic Business Processes, Vieweg.

Viswanathan, G. M., & Afanasyev, V. (1996). Lévy flight search patterns of wandering albatrosses. *Nature, 381*, 413–415. doi:10.1038/381413a0

Viswanathan, G. M., & Buldyrev, S. V. (1999). Optimizing the success of random searches. *Nature, 401*, 911–914. doi:10.1038/44831

Viswanathan, G. M., Afanasyev, V., et al. (2000). Lévy flights in random searches. *Physica A: Statistical Mechanics and its Applications, 282*(1-2), 1-12.

von Laszewski, G., Alunkal, B. E., & Veljkovic, I. (2005). Towards Reputable Grids. *Scalable Computing: Practice and Experience, 6*(3), 95–106.

Vu, L. H., Hauswirth, M., & Aberer, K. (2005). QoS-Based Service Selection and Ranking with Trust and Reputation Management. In *Proceedings of the OTM Confederated International Conferences 2005* (pp. 446-483).

Vu, T., Smith, P., & Bennett, T. (1999). *BizRate.com, NPD Joint Survey Reveals 75 percent of Online Customers are Abandoning Shopping Cart*. Retrieved March 5, 2009, from http://www.highbeam.com/doc/1G1-56901280.html

Wander, A., Gura, N., Eberle, H., Gupta, V., & Shantz, S. (2005). Energy analysis of public-key cryptography on small wireless devices. In *Proceedings of 3rd International IEEE Pervasive computing and Communications Worskshops (PerCom)* (pp. 324-328). Washington, DC: IEEE Press.

Wang, M., Lamont, L., Mason, P., & Gorlatova, M. (2005). An Effective Intrusion Detection Approach for OLSR MANET Protocol. In *Proceedings of the First Workshop on Secure Network Protocols (NPSec)*, Boston, Massachusetts, USA.

Wang, W., & Farid, H. (2006). Exposing digital forgeries in video by detecting double MPEG compression, *Proceedings of the 9th workshop on Multimedia & security (MM&Sec'06)*, September 26–27, 2006, Geneva, Switzerland, pp. 35-42.

Wang, X., & Yu, H. (2005). *How to break MD5 and other hash functions*. Paper presented at 24th Annual International Conference on the Theory and Applications of Cryptographic Techniques.

Wang, Y., & Singh, M. (2007). Formal Trust Model for Multiagent Systems. In *Proceeding of the 20th International Joint Conference on Artificial Intelligence*, Boston (pp. 1-6).

Wang, Y., & Varadharajan, V. (2004a). Interaction trust evaluation in decentralized environments. In *Proceedings of 5th International Conference on Electronic Commerce and Web Technologies (EC-Web04)* (LNCS 3182, pp. 144-153).

Wang, Y., & Varadharajan, V. (2004b). A time-based peer trust evaluation in p2p e-commerce environments. In *Proceedings of 5th International Conference on Web Information Systems Engineering (WISE'04)* (LNCS 3306, pp. 730-735). Berlin, Germany: Springer-Verlag.

Wang, Y., & Varadharajan, V. (2005). Trust²: Developing trust in peer-to-peer environments. In *Proceedings of 2005 IEEE International Conference on Services Computing (SCC 2005)* (pp. 24-31).

Wang, Y., Li, M., Dillon, E., Cui, L., Hu, J., & Liao, L. (2008, April). *A Context-aware Computational Trust Model for Multi-agent Systems*. Paper presented at the IEEE International Conference on Network, Sensing and Control, Sanya, China.

Wang, Y., Lin, K.-J., Wong, D. S., & Varadharajan, V. (2007). The design of a rule-based and event-driven trust management framework. In *Proceedings of The IEEE International Conference on e-Business Engineering (ICEBE 2007)* (pp. 97-104).

Wang, Z. J., Wu, M., Trappe, W., & Liu, K. J. R. (2004). Group-oriented fingerprinting for multimedia forensics. *EURASIP Journal on Applied Signal Processing*, (4): 2153–2173. doi:10.1155/S1110865704312151

Wargo, C., & Dhas, C. (2003). Security considerations for the eEnabled aircraft. In *Proceedings of IEEE Aerospace Conference* (pp. 4_1533-4_1550). Washington, DC: IEEE Press.

Wasserman, H., & Blum, M. (1997). Software Reliability via Run-Time Result-Checking. *JACM . Journal of the ACM*, 44.

Watson, R. (2001). *TrustedBSD: Adding trusted operating system features to FreeBSD*, Paper presented at 2001 USENIX Annual Technical Conference.

Web Transitions, Inc. (2004). *Advantages of an e-commerce website*. Virginia: Boons Mill. Retrieved March 5, 2009, from http://www.letmeshop.com/ecommerce-design-info/advantages-of-ecommerce.asp

Weinard, M. (2006). Deciding the FIFO Stability of Networks in Polynomial Time. In *Proceedings of the 8ᵗʰ International Conference on Algorithms and Complexity Vol. 3998* (pp. 81-92).

Welch, V., Siebenlist, F., Foster, I., Bresnahan, J., Czajkowski, K., Gawor, J., et al. (2003). Security for Grid Services. In *Proceedings of the Twelfth IEEE International Symposium on High Performance Distributed Computing* (pp. 48-57). Washington, DC: IEEE Computer Society Press.

Weniger, K. (2003). Passive Duplicate Address Detection in Mobile Ad Hoc Networks. In *Proceedings of the IEEE WCNC 2003*. Washington, DC: IEEE.

Wentzel, K. R. (1991). Relations between social competence and academic achievement in early adolescence. *Child Development*, *62*, 1066–1078. doi:10.2307/1131152

Wesner, S., Shubert, L., & Dimitrakos, Th. (2006). Dynamic Virtual Organizations in Engineering. In R. Dienstbier (Ed.), *Proceedings of the Computational Science and High Performance Computing II: The 2nd Russian-German Advanced Research Workshop* (pp. 289-302). Berlin, Germany: Springer.

West, A. G., Aviv, A. J., Chang, J., Prabhu, V. S., Blaze, M., Kannan, S., et al. (2009). QuanTM: A Quantified Trust Management System. In *EUROSEC 2009*, Nuremberg, Germany (pp. 28-35).

Westin, F. A. (1967). *Privacy and Freedom*. New York: Atheneum.

Whitby, A., Jøsang, A., & Indulska, J. (2004). Filtering out unfair ratings in bayesian reputation systems. In *Proceedings of the 7th International Workshop on Trust in Agent Societies*.

Whitten, A., & Tygar, D. (1999). Why Johnny can't encrypt: A usability evaluation of PGP 5.0. In *Proceedings of the 9th USENIX Security Symposium* (pp. 169-184).

Wikipedia. (n.d.). *Camden Market*. Retrieved from http://en.wikipedia.org/wiki/Camden_Market

Williams, M. (2002). *Anti-trojan and trojan detection with in-kernel digital signature testing of executables*. Retrieved April 25, 2009, from http://www.netxsecure.net/downloads/sigexec.pdf

Wilson, B. (2001). *Soft Systems Methodology*. New York: John Wiley & Sons Ltd.

Windley, P. (2005). *Digital Identity*. Sebastopol, CA: O'Reilly Media Inc.

Winsborough, W. H., & Li, N. (2006). Safety in Automated Trust Negotiation. *ACM Transactions on Information and System Security*, *9*(3), 352–390. doi:doi:10.1145/1178618.1178623

Winsborough, W. H., & Mitchell, J. C. (2003). Distributed Credential Chain Discovery in Trust Management. *Journal of Computer Security*, *11*(1), 36–86.

Winsborough, W., & Li, N. (2002). Towards Practical Automated Trust Negotiation. In *Proceedings of the*

3rd International Workshop on Policies for Distributed Systems and Networks (pp. 92-103). Washington, DC: IEEE Computer Society Press.

Winslett, M., Yu, T., Seamons, K. E., Hess, A., Jacobson, J., & Jarvis, R. (2002). Negotiating Trust on the Web. *IEEE Internet Computing, 6*(6), 30–37. doi:10.1109/MIC.2002.1067734

Winslett, M., Yu, T., Seamons, K. E., Hess, A., Jacobson, J., & Jarvis, R. (2002). The Trustbuilder architecture for trust negotiation. *IEEE Internet Computing, 6*(6), 30–37. doi:10.1109/MIC.2002.1067734

Winter, J. (2008): Trusted computing building blocks for embedded Linux-based ARM TrustZone platforms. In *Proceedings of the 3rd ACM Workshop on Scalable Trusted Computing.*

Wobber, E., Abadi, M., Burrows, M., & Lampson, B. (1994). Authentication in the Taos operating system. *ACM Transactions on Computer Systems, 12*(1), 3–32. doi:10.1145/174613.174614

Wood, M., & Erlinger, M. (2003). *IETF Internet Draft – Intrusion Detection Message Exchange Requirements.* Fremont, CA: IETF.

Workflow Patterns. (2007). *Workflow Patterns initiative home page.* Retrieved January 28, 2009, from http://www.workflowpatterns.com/

Worna, K., & Gomez, L. (2005). Context-Aware Security and Secure Context-Awareness in Ubiquitous Computing Environments. In *SAP research, XXI Autumn Meeting of Polish Information Processing Society Conference Proceedings* (pp. 255-265).

Wright, T. L., & Kirmani, A. (1977). Interpersonal trust, trustworthiness, and shopliing? in highschool. *Psychological Reports, 41*, 1165–1166.

Wrightsman, L. S. (1964). Measurement of philosophies of human nature. *Psychological Reports, 14*, 743–751.

Wrightsman, L. S. (1974). *Assumptions about human nature: A social psychological approach.* Monterey, CA: Brooks/Cole.

Wrightsman, L. S. (1991). *Interpersonal trust and attitudes toward human mature, and measures of personality and psychological attitudes.* San Diego, CA: Academic.

Wrightsman, L. S. (1992). *Assumptions about Human Nature: Implications for Researchers and Practitioners.* Newbury Park, CA: Sage.

Wu, M., Tang, E., & Liu, B. (2000). Data hiding in digital binary images, In *Proc. of the IEEE Int'l Conf. on Multimedia and Expo*, New York, NY (pp. 393-396).

Wu, M., Trappe, W., Wang, Z. J., & Liu, R. (2004). Collusion-resistant fingerprinting for multimedia. *IEEE Signal Processing Magazine, 21*(2), 15–27. doi:10.1109/MSP.2004.1276103

Wu, Z., & Weaver, A. (2006). Application of Fuzzy Logic in Federated Trust Management for Pervasive Computing. In *Proceeding of the 30th Annual International Computer Software and Applications Conferences (COMPSAC06)* (pp. 215-222). Washington, DC: IEEE Computer Society Press.

Wurster, G., & van Oorschot, P. C. (2007). *Self-signed executables: restricting replacement of program binaries by malware.* Paper presented at 2nd USENIX workshop on Hot topics in security.

Wurster, G., van Oorschot, P. C., & Somayaji, A. (2005). A Generic Attack on Checksumming-Based Software Tamper Resistance. In *Proceedings of the IEEE Symposium on Security and Privacy* (pp. 127-138).

Xia, H., Malcolm, J., Christianson, B., & Zhang, Y. (2007). Hierarchical Trustworthy Authentication for Pervasive Computing. In Proceedings 4th Annual International Conference on Mobile and Ubiquitous Systems: Networking and Services (pp. 1-3). Washington, DC: IEEE Society Press.

Xiao, S., & Benbasat, I. (2003). The formation of trust and distrust in recommendation agents in repeated interactions: A process-tracing analysis. In *Proceedings of the 5th International Conference on Electronic Commerce* (pp. 287-293).

Xiong, L., & Liu, L. (2002). *PeerTrust: A trust mechanism for an open peer-to-peer information system* (Technical Report GIT-CC-02-29). Georgia Institute of Technology.

Xiong, L., & Liu, L. (2004). PeerTrust: Supporting reputation-based trust for peer-to-peer electronic communities. *IEEE Transactions on Knowledge and Data Engineering, 16*(7), 843–857. doi:10.1109/TKDE.2004.1318566

Xiu, D., & Liu, Z. (2004). *A Dynamic Trust Model for Pervasive Computing Environments. A Research Paper. Research Supported by the NSF Grant0406325*. Retrieved from http://coitweb.uncc.edu/~zhliu/Research/Papers/asc.pdf

Xu, W., Xin, Y., & Lu, G. (2007). A Trust Framework for Pervasive Computing Environments. In Proceeding of the International Conference on Wireless Communications, Networking and Mobile Computing (WiCom 07) (pp. 2222-2225). Washington, DC: IEEE Society Press.

Yahalom, R., & Klein, B. (1994). Trust-based Navigation in Distributed Systems. *Computing Systems, 7*(1), 45–73.

Yahalom, R., Klein, B., & Beth, T. (1993). Trust Relationships in Secure Systems – A Distributed Authentication Perspective. In *Proc. of the 1993 IEEE Symposium on Security and Privacy* (pp. 150-164). Washington, DC: IEEE.

Yamagishi, T. (1998). *The structure of trust: The evolutionary games of mind and society* (in Japanese). Tokyo: Tokyo University Press. Retrieved April 2007, from http://lynx.let.hokudai.ac.jp/members/yamagishi/english.htm

Yamagishi, T., & Yamagishi, M. (1994). Trust and commitment in the United States and Japan. *Motivation and Emotion, 18*, 129–166. doi:10.1007/BF02249397

Yamazaki, M., & Kikkawa, T. (2006). The Structure of Anxiety Associated with Avian Influenza and Pandemic Influenza. In *Proceedings of the 47th annual conference of the Japanese Society of Social Psychology* (in Japanese) (pp. 676-677).

Yan, Z. (2006). A conceptual architecture of a trusted mobile environment. In *Proceedings of IEEE SecPerU'06*, France (pp. 75-81).

Yan, Z., & Holtmanns, S. (2007). Trust modeling and management: From social trust to digital trust. In R. Subramanian (Ed.), *Computer Security, Privacy and Politics: Current Issues, Challenges and Solutions* (pp. 1-28). Hershey, PA: IGI Global.

Yan, Z., Liu, C. H., Niemi, V., & Yu, G. L. (in press). *Evaluation of displaying trust information's effects on mobile application usage.*

Yan, Z., Zhang, P., & Virtanen, T. (2003). Trust evaluation based security solution in ad hoc networks. In *Proceedings of the seventh Nordic Workshop on Secure IT Systems (NordSec03)*, Norway.

Yang, B., Kamvar, S. D., & Garcia-molina, H. (2003). *Secure Score Management for P2P Systems* (Technical report). Stanford University.

Yang, H., Meng, X., & Lu, S. (2002). Self-Organized Network Layer Security in Mobile Ad Hoc Networks. In *Proceedings of ACM Workshop on Wireless Security 2002 (WiSe'2002)*. New York: ACM Press.

Yau, D. K. Y., Lui, J.C.S., Liang, F., & Yam, Y. (2005). Defending against Distributed Denial-of-Service Attacks with Max-Min Fair Server-Centric Router Throttles. *IEEE/ACM Transactions on Networking, 13*(1), 29-42.

Ye, D., Mao, Y., Dai, Y., & Wang, Z. (2004). A multi-feature based invertible authentication watermarking for JPEG Images. In *Proceedings of the 3rd International Workshop on Digital Watermarking (IWDW2004)*, Seoul, Korea (pp. 152-162).

Yoon, J., Liu, M., et al. (2003). Random waypoint considered harmful. In *22nd Annual Joint Conference of the IEEE Computer and Communications Societies (INFOCOM'03)*, San Francisco, CA, USA.

Yosano, A., & Nahoko, H. (2005). Social Stratifications, Intermediary Groups, and Creation of Trustfulness. *Sociological Theory and Methods, 20*, 27–44.

Yu, B., & Singh, M. P. (2002). An evidential model of distributed reputation management. In *Proceedings of First International Joint Conference on Autonomous Agents and Multiagent Systems* (pp. 294-301).

Yu, B., & Singh, M. P. (2003). Detecting deception in reputation management. In *Proceedings of Second International Joint Conference on Autonomous Agents and Multiagent Systems* (pp. 73-80).

Yu, B., Singh, M. P., & Sycara, K. (2004). Developing trust in large-scale peer-to-peer systems. In *Proceedings of 2004 IEEE First Symposium on Multi-Agent Security and Survivability* (pp. 1-10).

Yu, T. (2003). *Automated Trust Establishment In Open Systems*. Unpublished doctoral dissertation, University of Illinois at Urbana-Champaign.

Yu, T., & Winslett, M. (2003, May). *A Unified Scheme for Resource Protection in Automated Trust Negotiation.* Paper presented at the Annual IEEE Symposium on Security and Privacy, Oakland, CA.

Yu, T., Winslett, M., & Seamons, K. E. (2001). Interoperable strategies in automated trust negotiation. In *Proceedings of ACM Conference on Computer and Communications Security 2001* (pp. 146-155).

Yu, T., Winslett, M., & Seamons, K. E. (2003). Supporting Structured Credentials and Sensitive Policies through Interoperable Strategies for Automated Trust Negotiation. *ACM Transactions on Information and System Security, 6*(1).

Yuan, W., Guan, D., Lee, S., Lee, Y., & Gavrilov, A. (2006). Finding Reliable Recommendations for trust model. In *Proceeding of the 7ᵗʰ International Conference on Web Information Systems Engineering (WISE06)* (pp. 375-386).

Yuan, W., Guan, D., Lee, S., Lee, Y., & Lee, H. (2006). Filtering out unfair recommendations Finding for trust model in ubiquitous environments. In *Proceeding of the second International Conference on Information Systems Security (ICISS '06)* (pp. 258-263).

Zadeh, L. A. (1973). Outline of a new Approach to the Analysis of Complex Systems and Decision Processes. *IEEE Transactions on Systems, Man, and Cybernetics, 3*(1), 28–44.

Zak, P. J., & Knack, S. (2001). Trust and growth. *The Economic Journal, 111*, 295–321. doi:10.1111/1468-0297.00609

Zeng, W., & Lei, S. (2003). Efficient frequency domain selective scrambling of digital video. *IEEE Transactions on Multimedia, 5*(1), 118–129. doi:10.1109/TMM.2003.808817

Zhang, N., Ryan, M., & Guelev, D. P. (2005). Evaluating access control policies through model checking. In J. Zhou, J. Lopez, R. H. Deng, & F. Bao (Eds.), *Proc. 8th Intl. Conf. on Information Security (ISC 2005)* (pp. 446-460). Berlin, Germany: Springer-Verlag.

Zhang, Q., Yu, T., & Irwin, K. (2004). A Classification Scheme for Trust Functions in Reputation-Based Trust Management. In *Proceedings of the ISWC Workshop on Trust, Security, and Reputation on the Semantic Web.*

Zhang, X., Seifert, J.-P., & Aciicmez, O. (2009). Building Efficient Integrity Measurement and Attestation for Mobile Phone Platforms. In A. U. Schmidt & S. Lian (Eds.), *Proc. of the 1ˢᵗ International ICST Conference on Security and Privacy in Mobile Information and Communication Systems (MobiSec 2009)*. Berlin, Germany: Springer.

Zhang, Y., & Lee, W. (2000). Intrusion detection in wireless ad hoc networks. In *Proceedings of 6th ACM Annual International Conference on Mobile Computing and Networking (MOBICOM 2000)*. New York: ACM Press.

Zhang, Y., Lin, K. J., & Klefstad, R. (2006). DIRECT: A Robust Distributed Broker Framework for Trust and Reputation Management. In *Proceedings of the 8ᵗʰ IEEE Conference on E-Commerce Technology.*

Zhou, H., Ni, L., & Mutka, M. (2003). Prophet Address Allocation for Large Scale MANETs. In *Proceedings of IEEE INFOCOM 2003*. Washington, DC: IEEE.

Zhou, L., & Haas, Z. J. (1999). Securing ad hoc networks. *IEEE Network Magazine, 13*(6), 22–30.

Zhu, X., Singh, J. P., & Girod, B. (2006). Joint routing and rate allocation for multiple video streams in ad hoc wireless networks. In *Proceedings of the 15th International Packet Video Workshop Vol. 7* (pp. 727-736).

Zimmer, T. (2004). Toward a better understanding of Context attributes. In *Proceedings of the second IEEE Annual Conference on Pervasive Computing and Communications Workshops (PERCOMMW04)* (pp. 23). Washington, DC: IEEE Computer Society.

Zimmermann, P. (1995). *PGP Source Code and Internals*. Cambridge, MA: MIT Press.

Zimmermann, P. (1995). *The official PGP User's Guide*. Cambridge, MA: MIT Press.

Zipf, G. K. (1949). *Human Behavior and the Principle of Least Effort*. Reading, MA: Addison-Wesley Press.

Zouridaki, C., Mark, B. L., Hejmo, M., & Thomas, R. K. (2006). Robust cooperative trust establishment for MANETs. In *Proceedings of the fourth ACM workshop on Security of ad hoc and sensor networks SASN '06*. New York: ACM.

Zuboff, S. (1988). *In the age of smart machines: The future of work technology and power*. New York: Basic Books.

Zuidweg, M. (2003). Using P3P in a Web Services-Based context-aware Application Platform. In *Proc. of 9th Open European Summer School and IFIP Workshop on Next Generation Networks (EUNICE 2003)*, Hungary.

About the Contributors

Zheng Yan received the B. Eng in electrical engineering and the M. Eng in computer science and engineering from the Xi'an Jiaotong University in 1994 and 1997, respectively. She received the second M. Eng in information security from the National University of Singapore in 2000. She received the Licentiate of Science and the Doctor of Science in Technology in electrical engineering from the Helsinki University of Technology in 2005 and 2007, respectively. She is currently a member of research staff at the Nokia Research Center, Helsinki. Before joining in the Nokia in 2000 as a research engineer and later on a senior research scientist, she worked as a research scholar at the Institute for Information Research from 1997 to 1999 and a software engineer at the IBM partner SingaLab from 1999 to 2000, Singapore. She sole-authored and first-authored about thirty articles and three book chapters. She is the inventor and co-inventor of eight patents and patent applications. Her research interests are in trust modeling and management; trusted computing; mobile applications and services; reputation systems, usable security/trust, distributed systems and digital rights management. Dr. Yan is a member of the IEEE. She also serves as an organization committee member and a program committee member for a number of international conferences and workshops.

* * *

Jemal H. Abawajy is a faculty member in the School of School of Engineering and Information Technology, Deakin University, Australia. Dr. Abawajy has guest edited several journals and served as a chair and program committee of numerous international and national conference. His research interests are in the areas of high-performance distributed computing, pervasive computing, performance modelling and evaluation security. He has published extensively in refereed journals and conference proceedings in these areas. He has given invited talks and chaired several conferences and organized special sessions. He is the director of Pervasive Computing and Network research group at Deakin University.

Pierre E. Abi-Char received a Master Diploma in Physics from the faculty of Sciences at Lebanese University, Beirut Lebanon. He received an M.S. degree in Computer and Communications Engineering from University of Balamand (UOB) in 2000. Moreover, he received a DEA (Diplome D'etudes Approfondies) degree in Network Security in 2004 from University Pierre & Marie Curie (UPMC)-France in collaboration with France telecom (ENST), Lebanese University Lebanese, Faculty of Engineering (Lebanon), and Institut National de la Recherche Scientifique (INRS-Telecommunication, Canada). Currently, he is PHD researcher at UPMC & Telecom-SUPPARIS (ex. INT), Paris, France. In 2001, he joined Balamand University as an instructor and IT Security Officer. His research interests are wireless security, context-aware security technologies, cryptography protocols, access control, information theory, privacy, trust management and risk assessment.

Alvaro Arenas is a principal scientist at STFC Rutherford Appleton Laboratory in the UK. His research interests include information security, large scale distributed systems such as Grids and multi-agent systems, and the application of formal methods to safety and security critical systems. Dr. Arenas holds a D.Phil in Computation from Oxford University. He is member of the board of the ERCIM WG on formal methods for industrial critical systems, leading the topic on "trust and security in large-scale distributed systems" in the ERCIM WG on Grids, P2P and services, a senior member of the ACM, and a member of the BCS.

Benjamin Aziz holds a M.Sc. in Networks and Distributed Systems from Trinity College Dublin and a Ph.D. in the formal verification of security properties in mobile and cryptographic systems from Dublin City University and is currently a senior research scientist in e-Science Centre, STFC Rutherford Appleton Laboratory. Benjamin is the author of over 40 publications in areas related to security and trust management, formal methods, requirements engineering and distributed systems. He is a member of the ERCOM working groups on Security and Trust Management, Formal Methods for Industrial Critical Systems and the CoreGrid group on Grids, P2P and Service computing.

David E. Bakken is an associate professor of computer science in the School of Electrical Engineering and Computer Science (EECS) at Washington State University (WSU). His research interests include middleware, distributed computing systems, fault tolerance, and quality of service frameworks. Prior to joining WSU, he was a scientist at BBN Technologies where he was an original co-inventor of the Quality Objects (QuO) framework. He has consulted for Amazon.com, Network Associates Labs, and others, and he has also worked as a software developer for Boeing.

Inhyok Cha has graduated from Seoul National University with a B.S ('88). and an M.S. ('90), and from the University of Pennsylvania ('95) with a Ph.D. in EE. Dr. Cha has worked as a R&D researcher and then as a technical group manager at Lucent Technologies between 1996 and 2003, during which period he made contributions in such as areas as advanced speech codec development, wireless system engineering, UMTS radio access network standards development, baseband and radio resource management algorithm development, and DSP system integration testing. Since 2004, Dr. Cha has been with InterDigital Communications Corporation, first as an engineering group manager and then as a staff in the CTO department of the company. His current research interest includes topics such as machine-to-machine communications, wireless and cellular communication security and trusted computing. Dr. Cha is an author of several journal papers, 20+ conference papers, and an inventor with 8 U.S. patents awarded and more than 30 pending patents.

Sudip Chakraborty is an Assistant Professor in the Mathematics and Computer Science Department at Valdosta State University. He joined the faculty of Computer Science at Valdosta State in August 2008. He received his Ph.D in Computer Science from Colorado State University, USA in 2008. He received his M.Tech in Computer Science from Indian Statistical Institute, India in 2001 and his M.Sc and B.Sc in Mathematics from University of Calcutta, India, in 1999 and 1997 respectively. Dr. Chakraborty's teaching at Valdosta State includes various courses, from different levels, in Computer Science. His research interest is in Computer Security, specifically in the areas of trust in security including trust modeling and application of trust in security, access control mechanisms, security in ubiquitous computing, and privacy. He is a member of ACM since 2005.

Soon-keow Chong received her BSc degree with honours in computer science from Deakin University, Geelong, Australia in 2006. She is currently working toward her Ph.D. with a focus on trust management in e-commerce at the School of Engineering and Information Technology, Deakin University, Australia. Her research interests include trust management, e-Commerce, business Intelligence and security. She is a member of the IEEE.

Piotr Cofta is with British Telecom (UK) as a Chief Researcher, Identity and Trust. He is responsible for strategic research in trust, identity and privacy. Previously he has been working for many years for Nokia and more recently for Media Lab Europe, concentrating on the relationship between technology and society. Dr Cofta's has published his book "Trust, Complexity and Control: Confidence in a Convergent World" and has co-authored other books on trust and technology. He is an author of several patents and publications, from areas such as trust management, digital rights management and electronic commerce. Dr Cofta is a contributor to several international standards; he publishes and speaks frequently. Piotr Cofta received his PhD in computer science from the University of Gdansk, Poland. He is a CISSP and CEng and a member of BCS and IEEE. You can contact him at piotr.cofta@bt.com or at http://piotr.cofta.eu

Rafael Timóteo De Sousa Júnior was born in Campina Grande – PB, Brazil, on June 24, 1961. He graduated in Electrical Engineering, Federal University of Paraíba – UFPB, Campina Grande – PB, Brazil, 1984, and got his Doctorate Degree in Telecommunications, University of Rennes 1, Rennes, France, 1988. He worked as a software engineer in the company AQL (Rennes, 1988-1989) and as a network engineer in the company SGA (Brasília, Brazil, 1989-1996). Since 1996, He is a Network-Engineering Professor in the Electrical Engineering Department, at the University of Brasília, Brazil, and, from 2006 to 2007, sponsored by CNPq – Brazil, He took a sabbatical year in the Group for the Security of Information Systems and Networks, at Ecole Superiéure d´Electricité, Rennes, France, on leave from the University of Brasília. His field of study is network management and security and his current research interest is trust management for spontaneous self-organized networks.

Robert H. Deng received his B.Eng from National University of Defense Technology, China, his MSc and PhD from the Illinois Institute of Technology, USA. He has been with the Singapore Management University since 2004, and is currently Professor, Associate Dean for Faculty & Research, and Director of SIS Research Center, School of Information Systems. Prior to this, he was Principal Scientist and Manager of Infocomm Security Department, Institute for Infocomm Research, Singapore. He has 26 patents and more than 200 technical publications in international conferences and journals in the areas of computer networks, network security and information security. He served as general chair, program committee chair and member of numerous international conferences. He received the University Outstanding Researcher Award from the National University of Singapore in 1999 and the Lee Kuan Yew Fellow for Research Excellence from the Singapore Management University in 2006.

Xuhua Ding received his Ph.D. in Computer Science from the University of Southern California in 2003. Before that, he received his B.Eng and M.Sc in Computer Science from the Shanghai JiaoTong University in 1995 and 1999, respectively. He is currently an Assistant Professor of the School of Information Systems at the Singapore Management University. His research areas include trusted computing, applied cryptography, and distributed system security.

Ioanna Dionysiou is an assistant professor of computer science in the School of Sciences at the University of Nicosia. Dionysiou received her PhD, MS, and BS degrees in computer science from Washington State University in 2006, 2000, 1997 respectively and Diploma degree from Higher Technical Institute in 1994. During her PhD work, Dionysiou has worked on projects funded by the National Institute of Technology and the National Science Foundation and served as a reviewer for several scientific conferences and journals. Dionysiou's research focuses on trust modeling and management in collaborative environments.

Yan Dong, born in 1976, received her Bachelor Degree in 1999 and Master Degree in 2003 from department of psychology, Northeast Normal University. She received the Ph.D. in 2006 from the Institute of Psychology, Chinese Academic of Science; major in educational and developmental psychology. From 2006, she is a lecture in the Institute of Psychology, Renmin University of China. Her teaching covers the areas of emotion psychology, health psychology, psychometrics, and psychological statistics. She has published more than 20 papers in journals. Her current research interests are academic emotions, mental health and interpersonal trust, etc.

Jan-Erik Ekberg, M.Sc., got his degree in Computer Science from Helsinki University of technology in 1995. His current affiliation is with Nokia Research Center, Finland as a Principal Member of the Engineering Staff. His recent research interests are in the field of platform security including trusted computing and MTM.

Yasuhiro Fujihara is a lecturer in the Department of Software and Information Science, at Iwate Prefectural University, Japan. His main research fields are educational technology (educational measurement, collaborative learning, and e-learning) and "Anshin" (an emotional part of trust) in information security. He graduated the Faculty of Education of Kobe University in 1993. He received his master's degree in education in 1995 from Kobe University, and Ph.D. in 2007 from the Graduate University for Advanced Studies (SOKEN-DAI). He is a member of IEEE, ACM, IPSJ and IEICE.

Liang Gu received his B.S. in Computer Science and Technology (Software Technology) from University of Electronic Science and Technology of China in 2005. He is now a Ph.D. candidate in School of Electronic Engineering and Computer Science, Peking University, P.R.China. His research interests include: System Security, Trusted Computing, Software Reuse and Software Component Technology.

Felix Halim holds a B.Comp. in computer science from Bina Nusantara University. He is currently a Ph.D. candidate in the School of Computing at National University of Singapore. His interests include analysis of data structure and algorithm designs, web application development, and self-management in distributed systems. He has published several papers in the area constraint programming, self-adaptive and self-organizing systems, and peer-to-peer systems security. He has been very actively participating in programming contests/competitions like TopCoder and Google Code Jam. He can be reached electronically at halim@comp.nus.edu.sg.

Bachar EL Hassan got his engineering Diploma in 1991 from the faculty of engineering of the Lebanese university, Tripoli Lebanon, his MS in signal and image processing in 1992 for the National polytechnic institute (INPG) of Grenoble, France and his PHD in electronics in 1995 from the INPG-France in collaboration with France telecom. Since 1995 till now he is working at the faculty of engineering of the Lebanese university Tripoli Lebanon. He is now an associate professor and chairman of the electrical department since January 2004. His research interests concern digital communications and wireless networks. In 2009 he participated to the implementation of the electronic systems, telecommunications and networking laboratory "LaSTRe" that is associated to the PHD school of the Lebanese university. He is since January 2009 the director of telecommunications and networking research team at "LaSTRe".

Carsten Jacob studied Computer Science at the Humboldt-Universität zu Berlin and the Swiss Federal Institute of Technology Zurich (ETH Zurich). After graduation from the Humboldt-Universität zu Berlin in 2006 he started working as a research associate and project manager at the Fraunhofer Institute for Open Communication Systems (FOKUS). In the area of intelligent content and services his main research activities and publications pertain to context-aware applications, content-centric networking, and Semantic Web technologies. He has been involved in several national and international projects addressing decentralized software architectures, semantics, and future Web applications.

Sampath Kannan is a Professor in Computer and Information Science at the University of Pennsylvania. He is currently on leave and serving as the Director of the Computing and Communications Foundations Division at NSF. His research interests are in algorithms, program reliability, and security. Dr. Kannan received a PhD from the University of California, Berkeley. Contact him at kannan@cis.upenn.edu.

Dimitrios Koukopoulos, born in 1975, obtained his Engineering Diploma from the Department of Computer Engineering and Informatics of the University of Patras, Greece, in 1998. M.Sc. in Communications and Signal Processing from Imperial College, University of London, UK (1999). Ph.D. in Computer Engineering and Informatics from University of Patras, Greece (2003). Currently, he is a Lecturer at the Department of Cultural Heritage Management and New Technologies of the University of Ioannina, Greece. He worked as a researcher at the Computer Technology Institute, Greece (1999-2003). He taught at the Department of Information Technology Applications in Management and Economics of the Technological Education Institute of Ionian Islands, Greece, as an Assistant Professor (2006-08), and at the Department of Cultural Heritage Management and New Technologies of the University of Ioannina, Greece, as Visiting Lecturer (2004-08). His research interests cover Algorithms, Networks, Cultural Technology and Security in Multimedia Networking.

Hazel Lacohée is a Principal Researcher at British Telecom (UK) undertaking qualitative social research for BT Innovate. She is responsible for investigation of the commercial, socio-economic and customer impact of ICT applications and systems and providing thought leadership on social and market implications. She is currently focused on issues concerning privacy, security and trust, and is lead author of the Trustguide report. Prior to joining BT in 1998 she spent two years with Hewlett Packard Laboratories undertaking user needs research in the UK, USA and Denmark followed by appointment as Senior Research Fellow at the University of the West of England for a BT funded project concerning the social aspects of software systems. Hazel Lacohée obtained an ESRC funded PhD in Psychology from the University of Bristol in 1996. She is author of a diverse range of publications and has contributed to a number of patents at BT.

Insup Lee is the Cecilia Filter Moore Professor of Computer and Information Science at the University of Pennsylvania. His research interests include embedded and real-time systems, cyber-physical systems, medical device systems, model-based development, and quantitative trust management. Dr. Lee received a PhD in computer science from the University of Wisconsin, Madison. Contact him at lee@cis.upenn.edu.

Andreas Leicher received his diploma in computer science at Frankfurt University in 2009. Having his main focus on IT security, he developed a framework for Trusted Computing applications, implementing a Trusted Ticket System by enhancing the Kerberos authentication protocol. He is working as a consultant with novalyst IT, in the areas of Trusted Computing, IT security, privacy, Identity Management, mobile systems and 3GPP.

Mingyan Li is an advanced computing technologist at Boeing Research & Technology (BR&T) and an affiliated assistant professor in the department of Electrical Engineering (EE) at University of Washington (UW). She received her Doctor of Philosophy degree from Network Security Laboratory (NSL) at UW in 2006. Her research interests are in the area of network security and user privacy, with applications to sensor networks, RFID systems, software distribution systems, eEnabled airplane systems, digital healthcare systems, vehicular ad hoc networks (VANET), distributed storage, and secure multicast. She led Boeing-Siemens collaborative projects on wireless and RFID security. She is a recipient of BR&T silver teamwork award 2008, the second author of an IEEE PIMRC best student paper award 2007, a recipient of the UW EE departmental Chair's Award 2006, and the outstanding Society of Women Engineer (SWE) Graduate award 2003.

Shiguo Lian got his Ph.D. from Nanjing University of Science and Technology in 2005. He was a research assistant in City University of Hong Kong in 2004. He has been a research scientist with France Telecom R&D (Orange Labs) Beijing since July 2005. He is the author or co-author of more than 70 refereed international journal and conference papers, and book chapters. He has held 16 patents, authored and co-edited 5 books, e.g., "Multimedia Content Encryption: Techniques and Applications" (CRC Press, 2008), "Handbook of Research on Secure Multimedia Distribution" (IGI Global, 2009), "Intelligent Multimedia Transmission: Techniques and Applications" (Springer, 2009), and "Intelligent Multimedia Analysis for Security Applications" (Springer, 2009), etc. He got the Nomination Prize of "Innovation Prize in France Telecom" in 2006, and "Top 100 Doctorate Dissertation in Jiangsu Province" in 2005. He has co-edited several special issues for international journals. He is the organization member of some conferences, e.g., MINES2009, MobiSec2009 and MUSIC'08. He is the TPC member of refereed conferences, e.g., IEEE ICC2008/2009, IEEE GLOBECOM2008/2009/2010, IEEE CCNC2009, IWDW2008, etc., and invited reviewers of refereed magazines and journals, e.g., IEEE Communications Magazine, IEEE Transactions on Image Processing, Computer Communications, etc.

His research interests include multimedia communication and security, intelligent computing, ubiquitous communication and services.

Conghui Liu, PhD of psychology, was born in Shijiazhuang city of Hebei province in august, 1977. He graduated from department of psychology in Hebei Normal University in 1999, after graduation, he had been engaged in teaching in second normal school for one year. He received a PhD degree in basic psychology from school of psychology in Beijing Normal University, Beijing, China, in 2006. Now, he is a psychological researcher in the Institute of Psychology, Renmin University of China. His main research interests include trust in human-human interaction and human-machine interaction, communication. He has published several papers and research reports in domestic and international public academic journals.

Fabio Martinelli (M.Sc. 1994, Ph.D. 1999) is a senior researcher of IIT-CNR, Pisa, where He is the scientific coordinator of the security group. His main research interests involve security and privacy in distributed and mobile systems and foundations of security and trust. He serves as PC-chair/organizer in several international conferences/workshops. He is the co-initiator of the International Workshop series on Formal Aspects in Security and Trust (FAST). He is serving as scientific co-director of the international research school on Foundations of Security Analysis and Design (FOSAD) since 2004 edition. He chairs the WG on security and trust management (STM) of the European Research Consortium in Informatics and Mathematics (ERCIM). He usually manages R&D projects on information and communication security and he is involved in several FP6/7 EU projects.

Hong Mei received the Ph.D. degree in Computer Science from Shanghai Jiao Tong University in 1992. Then he joined in Peking University as a post-doctoral research fellow. From 1999 to 2000, he worked at Software Production Research in Bell Labs at Naperville, IL as a visiting Scientist. Currently he is a professor in School of Electronics Engineering and Computer Science, Peking University, P.R.China. His current research interests include: Software Engineering and Software Engineering Environment, Software Reuse and Software Component Technology, Distributed Object Technology, Software Production Technology, and Programming Language. He also served at various Program Committees of international conferences.

Abdallah M'hamed, Associate professor in Network security and dependability, received his Doctor degree in dependability studies from the Technological University of Compiègne, France. In 1990 he joined the National Institute of Telecommunications, in Evry, France, where he was involved in developing security and dependability courses for engineers. His current teaching activities, are dealing with network security services, cryptographic protocols and access controls. As a member of the Handicom laboratory, his recent research activities are focused on authentication protocols and architectures, security and user privacy in pervasive environments dedicated to dependant people.

Mounir Mokhtari is an Associate Professor at Institut TELECOM (TELECOM SudParis) in France. He recently joined IPAL CNRS Lab (joint lab with Infocomm Institute of Research and National University of Singapore) as a full time research member. Mounir Mokhtari collaborated with University Pierre and Marie Curie and INSERM laboratory to obtain his Ph.D in Computer Science in 1997. Mounir Mokhtari's research activity focuses mainly on Human-Machine interaction, Ambient Assistive living, rehabilitation robotics and health telematics. He obtained his Research Habilitation from the University Pierre and Marie Curie, in Computer Sciences, in 2002. Mounir Mokhtari, who got his first European project in 1996 (FP4), is leading several European and national projects involving research organizations and industrials partners. He contributed actively, since 1994, in the creation of the first technological platform dedicated to people with disabilities (pilot site) within the rehabilitation hospital of Garches (Paris). Mounir Mokhtari is the head and founder of Handicom Lab (Handicap Engineering and Communication Lab) created in 1999. Mounir Mokhtari is the founder of ICOST conference (International Conference on Smart homes and health Telematics - www.icost-conference.org).

Paolo Mori received his M.Sc. in Computer Science from the University of Pisa in 1998, and his Ph.D. in Computer Science from the same University in 2003. He is currently a researcher of the Information Security Group of the Istituto di Informatica e Telematica of the Consiglio Nazionale delle Ricerche. His main research interests involve high performance computing, and security in distributed systems, such as the Grid, and in mobile devices, such as smart phones or PDAs. He is co-author of several papers on international journals and conference/workshop proceedings. He is involved in some european projects on information and communication security.

Yuko Murayama is a Professor in the Department of Software and Information Science at Iwate Prefectural University, Japan. Her research interests include internet, network security and human aspects of security and trust. She has been leading a project on Anshin and Trust funded by Japan Science and Technology Agency (JST) since 2005. She had M.Sc. and Ph.D. both from University of London (attended University College London) in 1984 and 1992 respectively. She had been a visiting lecturer from 1992 to 1994 at Keio University, a lecturer at Hiroshima City University from 1994 to 1998. She has been with Iwate Prefectural University since April 1998. Her interests include internetworking and its applications as well as network security. She is a member of IEEE, ACM, IPSJ, IEICE, and ITE.

Valtteri Niemi received a PhD degree from the University of Turku, Finland, Mathematics Department, in 1989. After serving in various positions in the University of Turku, he was an Associate Professor in the Mathematics and Statistics Department of the University of Vaasa, Finland, during 1993-97. He joined Nokia Research Center (NRC), Helsinki in 1997 and in 1999 he was nominated as a Research Fellow. During 2004-2006, he was responsible for Nokia research in wireless security area as a Senior Research Manager. During 2007-2008, Dr. Niemi led the Trustworthy Communications and Identities team in the Internet laboratory of NRC, Helsinki. He recently moved to the new NRC laboratory in Lausanne, Switzerland, where his main focus is on privacy-enhancing technologies. He was also nominated as a Nokia Fellow in 2009. Dr. Niemi's work has been on security issues of future mobile networks and terminals, the main emphasis being on cryptological aspects. He has participated 3GPP SA3 (security) standardization group from the beginning. Starting from 2003, he has been the chairman of the group. Before 3GPP, Niemi took part in ETSI SMG 10 for GSM security work. In addition to cryptology and security, Dr. Niemi has done research on the area of formal languages. He has published more than 40 scientific articles and he is a co-author of three books.

André Paul studied Computer Science at the Technische Universität Berlin. After graduation in 2008, he started to work as research associate at the Fraunhofer Institute for Open Communication Systems (FOKUS). His main research areas comprise the design and modeling of middleware interaction frameworks for mobile networks as well as the realization of future community applications focused on privacy and recommendation dependencies between users. Also, he is involved in ongoing internet standardization activities and industry projects that especially focusing on the evolution of fields of applications for mobile devices and Web platforms.

Marinella Petrocchi received her M.Sc. in Telecommunication Engineering from the University of Pisa in 1999, and her Ph.D. in Information Engineering from the same University in 2005. She is currently a researcher of the Information Security Group of the Istituto di Informatica e Telematica of the Consiglio Nazionale delle Ricerche. Her main research interests involve formal models and analysis of security and trust, particularly focused on bio-inspired and distributed systems, and on techniques for context-awareness information sharing. She is co-author of several papers on international journals and conference/workshop proceedings. She is involved in both FP6 and FP7 European projects on information and communication security. She also serves as PC-chair/organizer in several international conferences/workshops.

Heiko Pfeffer studied Computer Science at the Rheinische-Friedrich-Wilhelms-Universität Bonn and the Université Claude Bernard Lyon I. After graduation, he started to work as scientific researcher at the group of Open Communication Systems (OKS) at the Technische Universität Berlin and the Fraunhofer Institut FOKUS. He is now project manager and group leader at the Competence Center for Future Applications and Media at Fraunhofer FOKUS. His main research areas comprise the modeling of service collaboration and interaction within service oriented computing environments and the mobile Web. He has been involved in and led multiple national and international projects within the area of service oriented architectures, mobile computing, and technologies for future Web applications.

Radha Poovendran received the Ph.D. degree in Electrical Engineering from the University of Maryland, College Park, in 1999. He is an Associate Professor and founding Director of the Network Security Lab (NSL), Electrical Engineering Department, University of Washington, Seattle. His research interests are in the areas of applied cryptography for multiuser environment, wireless networking, and applications of information theory to security. He is a coeditor of the book Secure Localization and Time Synchronization in Wireless Ad Hoc and Sensor Networks (Springer-Verlag, 2007). Dr. Poovendran was a recipient of the NSA Rising Star Award and Faculty Early Career Awards, including the National Science Foundation CAREER Award in 2001, the Army Research Office YIP Award in 2002, the Office of Naval Research YIP Award in 2004, PECASE in 2005 for his research contributions to multiuser security, and a Graduate Mentor Recognition Award from the University of California San Diego in 2006. He co-chaired the first ACM Conference on Wireless Network Security (WiSec) in 2008.

Ricardo Staciarini Puttini was born in Brasilia – DF, Brazil, on April 05, 1974. He graduated in Electrical Engineering, Federal University of Brasília - UnB, Brazil, 1995, and got his Master of Science and Doctorate Degrees in Electrical Engineering from University of Brasília, 1997 and 2004. He developed part of his doctorate studies in Ecole Superiéure d´Electricité, Rennes - France, where he worked from 2001 to 2002. Since 1997, he is a Network-Engineering Professor at University of Brasília. He was responsible for the development of the Unique Identification System, which defines the new smartcard based document for Brazilian Citizens. Prof. Puttini is member of the Brasília Institute for Technological Innovation's Council and coordinates the deployment of the research infrastructure for the Digital

Capital Technological Park in Brasília. His field of study is network management and security and his current research interest is security for spontaneous self-organized networks.

Rajiv Ramnath is currently an Associate Scientist in Temasek Laboratories, National University of Singapore. He joined Temasek Laboratories in 2007 after completing his bachelor's degree in Computer Engineering at the National University of Singapore. His interests are in computer security, operating systems and biometrics. He can be reached electronically at tslrr@nus.edu.sg.

Indrakshi Ray is an Associate Professor in the Computer Science Department at Colorado State University, which she joined in August 2001. Prior to that she was an Assistant Professor of Computer and Information Science at the University of Michigan-Dearborn. She received her Ph.D. in Information Technology from George Mason University in Fairfax, VA in 1997. Indrakshi's main research interests are in the areas of access control policy and modeling, formal methods, trust models, database systems, and privacy. She has published over 70 peer-reviewed technical articles in internationally renowned journals and conferences. She has been the advisor to several master's and doctoral students. She is on the editorial board of 2 journals – Computer Standards and Interfaces and Journal of Autonomic and Trusted Computing. She has served as the guest editor of several special issues of journals, as program co-chairs of several conferences, on program committees, and on several grant review panels. She is a member of IEEE-CS, ACM, ACM SACMAT and IFIP WG 11.3.

Indrajit Ray is an Associate Professor in the Computer Science Department at Colorado State University, which he joined in August 2001. Prior to that he was an Assistant Professor of Computer and Information Science at the University of Michigan-Dearborn. He received his Ph.D. in Information Technology from George Mason University in Fairfax, VA in 1997. Indrajit's main research is in the areas of computer and network security, trust modeling, privacy, database systems, and digital forensics. He has published over 60 peer-reviewed technical articles in internationally renowned journals and conferences. He has supervised a number of master's and doctoral students. He is currently on the editorial board of 3 journals - the International Journal of Security and Networks, the Digital Investigations Journal and the International Journal of Digital Crime and Forensics. He has served and is currently serving on several conference program committees. He has served as external reviewers for faculty at other institutions and also as reviewer for different research projects. He was one of the founding members and the first chair of the IFIP TC-11 WG 11.9 group on Digital Forensics. He is a member of the IEEE, IEEE-CS, ACM, ACM SACMAT, IFIP WG 11.3 and IFIP WG 11.9.

Krishna Sampigethaya received the Ph.D. degree in electrical engineering from the University of Washington, Seattle, in 2007. He is currently an Advanced Computing Technologist with Boeing Research & Technology, Bellevue, WA. He is also an Affiliate Assistant Professor in the Department of Electrical Engineering and co-director of the Network Security Lab (NSL) at the University of Washington. He is serving as the technical chair for aviation cyber-physical security area at the 2009 SAE AeroTech conference and as a technical co-chair for trustworthy aviation systems area at the 2010 AIAA Infotech@Aerospace conference. His research interests include e-enabled airplane security, high confidence cyber-physical systems, vehicular networks, privacy, and electronic voting.

Andreas U. Schmidt received his doctorate in mathematics at the University of Frankfurt/Main in 1999. After research stays in Durban South Africa and Pisa, he worked as a senior researcher in the Fraunhofer Institute for Secure Information Technology SIT, Darmstadt, Germany. He was a team leader in the FP5/FP6 European research project, and led the security workpackage in the FP7 STREP NanoDataCenters. He further worked in numerous industry-funded research projects. He now is the head of the security area of CREATE-NET, and leads a private research consultancy, novalyst IT AG. Andreas is the coordinator of the Trusted Computing activities of CREATE-NET. His current research foci are: Applications of Trusted Computing with focus on mobile domain, Identity management, privacy, Security and electronic signatures for Voice-over-IP, Theoretical questions in information economy, Long-term security of, and secure transactions with, digital data. Andreas has produced over 50 publications in his various fields of research, works as reviewer for renowned journals in security and served as a program committee member for numerous conferences. He actively participates in the Trust, Security, and Dependability working group of the NESSI technology platform. He organizes as general chair the conference MobiSec on mobile security.

Oleg Sokolsky is a Research Associate Professor of Computer and Information Science at the University of Pennsylvania. His research interests include application of formal methods to model-based development and real-time systems, quantitative trust management, and runtime verification. Dr. Sokolsky received a PhD in computer science from Stony Brook University. Contact him at sokolsky@cis.upenn.edu.

Stephan Steglich is director of Competence Center Future Applications and Media (FAME) at Fraunhofer FOKUS. He received his M.Sc. in computer science (1998) and PhD (2003) in Computer Science from the TU Berlin. His fields of interest include, e.g., context-awareness, user-interaction, and adaptive systems. In 1998 and 1999 he has worked intensively in the research area of Intelligent Mobile Agents. Since 1999 he has started research activities in the area of user-centric communication. He has been involved in many international projects that were related to Service Front-ends. Stephan is managing international and national level research activities and has been an organizer and a member of program committees of several international conferences. He has actively participated in standardization activities in these research areas and gives lectures in 'Mobile Telecommunication Systems', 'Advanced Communication Systems' at the TU Berlin.

Sufatrio holds a B.Sc. from University of Indonesia and a M.Sc. from National University of Singapore, both in computer science. He is currently a Ph.D. candidate in the School of Computing and an Associate Scientist in Temasek Laboratories at National University of Singapore. His interests include Intrusion Detection System (IDS), infrastructure for secure program execution, Public-Key Infrastructure, and formal methods. He has published several papers in the area of IDS, vulnerability management, resource monitoring infrastructure, authentication logic, and network security. He can be reached electronically at tslsufat@nus.edu.sg.

Yan Wang is currently a Senior Lecturer in the Department of Computing at Macquarie University, Australia. He received his B. Eng, M. Eng and Doctorate Degree of Engineering in computer science and technology in 1988, 1991 and 1996 respectively from Harbin Institute of Technology (HIT), P.R.

China. He was a visiting scholar at the City University of Hong Kong in 1997, 1999 and 2007 respectively. Prior to joining Macquarie University, he was a Research Fellow at the Department of Computing Science, the National University of Singapore from 1999 to 2003. He has served as a PC member of 30 international conferences. He is on the editorial board of the International Journal of Web Engineering and Technology (IJWET), Inderscience Publisher, and the guest co-editor of the special track on e-commerce of IEEE Internet Computing in 2008. His research interests include trust computing, e-commerce, software agent and security.

Andrew G. West is a second-year PhD student in the Department of Computer and Information Science at the University of Pennsylvania (Philadelphia, PA). Mr. West did his undergraduate study at Washington & Lee University (Lexington, VA) where he received a B.S. in computer science in 2007. His research interests include reputation management, quantitative trust management, and computational number theory. Contact him at westand@cis.upenn.edu.

Michael Wilson is a principal scientist at the Rutherford Appleton Laboratory which provides UK researchers with access to large scientific facilities including satellites, synchrotrons, telescopes, and lasers. Michael holds a PhD in psycholinguistics from Cambridge University and held a visiting professorship in computer science at Queen Mary, University of London. Michael's research has produced over 100 academic publications in HCI, knowledge engineering and distributed systems, and has influenced several technical standards and product designs. Since 2001 he has been manager of the UK and Ireland Office of the World Wide Web Consortium (W3C) as a result of which Internet Magazine included him in its 2002 list of the 50 "movers and shakers" in the UK Internet industry.

Yongzheng Wu holds a B.Comp. in computer science from National University of Singapore. He is currently a Ph.D. candidate in the School of Computing at National University of Singapore. His interests include systems security and operating system. He has published several papers in the area of software security auditing, program confinement, resource monitoring infrastructure on Microsoft Windows, and peer-to-peer systems security. He can be reached electronically at wuyongzh@comp.nus.edu.sg.

Bing Xie received his Ph.D. degree from National University of Defense Technology (NUDT) in 1998. He then worked in PKU as postdoctoral researcher, Associate Professor and Professor, in School of Electronic Engineering and Computer Science (EECS), Peking University (PKU), P.R.China. Currently he is a Professor and Vice-director of the Software Institute in EECS, PKU. His main research interests include Software Engineering, Distributed Systems and Computer Theory. He also served at various Program Committees of international conferences.

Lu Yan is a senior lecturer at the School of Computer Science in University of Hertfordshire, UK. Dr. Yan previously worked at the Department of Computer Science in University College London, UK, the Computer Laboratory in University of Cambridge, UK, the Department of Information Technologies in Åbo Akademi, Finland and the Turku Centre for Computer Science, Finland. He also held adjunct faculty positions in École Supérieure d'Ingénieurs généralistes, France and École Supérieure de Commerce de Rouen, France.

Roland H.C. Yap obtained his Ph.D. from Monash University. He is currently an associate professor in the School of Computing at National University of Singapore. His interests include programming languages, artificial intelligence, systems security, operating systems, and distributed systems. He can be reached electronically at ryap@comp.nus.edu.sg.

Index